Import Practice

Customs and International Trade Law

Second Edition

Import Practice

Customs and International Trade Law

Second Edition

David Serko

B1-1327
Practising Law Institute
New York City

"This publication is designed to provide accurate and authoritative information in regard to the subject matter covered. It is sold with the understanding that the publisher is not engaged in rendering legal, accounting or other professional service. If legal advice or other expert assistance is required, the services of a competent professional person should be sought."

—from Declaration of Principles jointly adopted by Committee of American Bar Association and Committee of Publishers and Associations

ISBN: 0-87224-026-6

Library of Congress Catalog Card Number: 91-066871

To my beloved family—

my wife, Joan;
my son Richard and his wife Terri;
my son Jonathan and his wife Tracey;
my daughter, Wendy Jo, and
her husband Peter C. Lewis;
and my grandchildren, Ronald David
and Jessica Ann

About the Author

DAVID SERKO is the senior partner of the law firm of Serko & Simon, which specializes in customs and international trade law and is based in New York.

Born in Havana, Cuba, Mr. Serko spent his childhood in Panama. He came to the United States in 1948 to attend Syracuse University, where he received his B.A. degree in psychology in 1952. He was graduated from New York University Law School in 1956. While attending law school as an evening student, he worked for an attorney who specialized in customs and trade law, and he became fascinated with the field.

Mr. Serko is admitted to the New York bar, Supreme Court of the United States, United States Court of International Trade, United States Court of Appeals for the Federal Circuit, United States District Court for the Southern District of New York, and United States District Court for the Eastern District of New York. He is a member of the New York State Bar Association, American Bar Association, New York County Lawyers Association and Customs and International Trade Bar Association.

In addition to his law practice, Mr. Serko has been a member or director of, or chaired, customs, import, and export committees for the American Association of Exporters and Importers. He is currently a director of the organization. He has been active in other organizations in the international trade field.

David Serko has lectured and spoken widely in the United States, and he has lectured abroad. He has addressed professional groups, trade associations, college and law school groups, and conferences sponsored by government agencies such as the Customs Service and Commerce Department. He presently serves as Legal Editor to *Global Trade Executive* magazine and Contributing Editor to *World Wide Shipping* magazine.

Mr. Serko's thirty-five years of practice have been devoted to the practice of customs and international trade.

Summary of Contents

Table of Contents

Part II: Importation

Part III: Special Services and Facilities

Part IV: Incentives to Import or Export

Part VI: Administration and Enforcement

Preface to the Second Edition

Since the publication in 1985 of the first edition of *Import Practice: Customs and International Trade Law*, monumental changes have taken place in the area. Indeed, throughout the approximately two years of work on this revised volume, changes—some major, some minor—have been constant.

Among the major changes was the adoption, in January, 1989, of a new system of classification: the Harmonized Tariff Schedule of the United States (HTSUS) replaced the Tariff Schedules of the United States (TSUS), which had been in place since August, 1963. The simple addition of an *H* in front of *TSUS* is not indicative of the reality that the new system is vastly different and much more complex in its structure.

The period from 1985 to 1991 has seen new trade agreements (most significantly the United States–Canada Free Trade Agreement), duty-free and duty-reduction programs, new regulations, countless Customs directives and rulings, and numerous court cases.

However, some of the most significant changes did not necessarily come as the consequence of momentous legislation or legal decision. Rather, they were a result of a decided shift in philosophy within the foremost agency having responsibilities in the field of international trade, the United States Customs Service.

Preface to the Second Edition

With the establishment of the National Drug Policy Board in 1987, the Customs Service began to take an active role as a leader in the nation's fight against drugs. About the same time, with a new infusion of funds and personnel into its enforcement divisions, Customs was becoming more interested in commercial fraud and related activities involving country of origin marking, quota, trademark, and copyright violations. As a consequence, many in the importing community found themselves drawn into the Customs Service's widening enforcement net. The resulting strain of contending with harsh penalties, administrative delays, and the Customs Service's apparent movement away from the facilitation of international trade made many importers feel that Customs had become an unsympathetic adversary.

To its credit, the Customs Service realized that it may have neglected its commercial administrative functions and, with a change in leadership, made a renewed commitment to serving the needs of the trading community. That commitment is clearly demonstrated by recent emphasis on programs such as Automated Broker Interface (ABI), which provides for the exchange of electronic entry data with brokers and importers; Automated Manifest System (AMS), which allows for the exchange of electronic manifest data with carriers; the administrative rulings program, which greatly improved the efficiency of the Customs Service's procedure for processing ruling requests; and implementation by Customs of a new "paperless" release system.

Therefore, in this new edition I have attempted to reflect the philosophical changes that have taken place within the Customs Service since the first edition, as well as the many changes in law that have occurred in the field itself. Consequently, I have added six new chapters, completely rewritten chapter 3, which deals with the classification of merchandise, and expanded and updated all of the remaining chapters.

However, I caution the reader to be aware that, as the extent of this revised edition indicates, the field of international trade law is constantly changing. Therefore, while I have attempted to provide the most recent information available, by the time the reader consults this volume, some of the cited authorities may have been revised, reversed, repudiated, or replaced. In addition, principles of law are usually open to different interpretations, and I have presented variant views on a variety of subjects, along with discussions concerning the present state of the law, to demonstrate how even traditional legal principles can be reexamined and applied in new ways.

Accordingly, the reader should not view all of the material in the volume as immutable. The intent of this new edition is not merely to present the results of particular rulings or court decisions but, rather, to remain faithful to the goal set in the original volume: to inform, alert, and instruct those wishing to import foreign merchandise into the United States. In this way, I hope to continue to assist those wishing to learn about this increasingly important area of international trade law.

The statement in my preface to the original edition—"International trade has emerged as one of the major political and economic issues of the 1980s"—is even more applicable to the 1990s. Witness the appearance of the E.E.C. 1992, which will make for an enormous unified trading and market area; the impasse of the negotiations of the Uruguay Round over agricultural issues; the proposal for a North American Free Trade Agreement to include the United States, Mexico, and Canada and the polarization of views of proponents and opponents about the desirability of such an agreement, particularly with respect to environmental and labor issues; the continuation of Most Favored Nation (MFN) tariff treatment for China, made most controversial after the Tiananmen Square incident in June, 1989; and the granting of MFN treatment to the Soviet Union.

It is my hope that this book will assist those individuals who will participate in the evolutionary process of world trade in this last decade of the twentieth century.

Preface to the First Edition

This volume is intended to inform, alert, and instruct those wishing to import foreign merchandise into the United States. It is addressed to the importer, his attorney, accountant, and customs broker, the student of foreign trade, and that portion of the general business public interested in the practical and legal aspects of dealing with the numerous government officials, in various departments and agencies, having responsibilities in the field of international trade. Foremost among these agencies is one of the oldest and most professionally staffed bureaus in our government: the United States Customs Service. Others include the International Trade Commission, the Treasury Department, the State Department, the Commerce Department, the Food and Drug Administration, and the Office of the United States Trade Representative.

The emphasis of this treatise is on understanding the administrative process, for the issues and problems that arise in connection with foreign trade are resolved in many instances at the administrative level of government. Examples of some specific approaches to government officials will be cited and analyzed. Although appeal to the courts is provided in most circumstances when administrative remedies have been exhausted, this book does not analyze court decisions extensively; they would only be useful in the context of a specific set of facts and legal problems. Selected decisions of major impact are examined, however. Rulings of the United States Customs Court and the Court of Customs and Patent Appeals, recently superseded by the Court of International Trade and the United States Court of Appeals for the Federal Circuit, respectively, are published by the Government Printing Office and, in some cases, private companies like West Publishing. Chapter 20 is devoted to the process of judicial review of issues relating to international trade.

Some of the material in this book is based upon actual importing case histories, in order to illustrate in practical terms the nuts and bolts of a customs transaction. We hope to impart an understanding of the many variables faced by importers and their professional representatives in their day-to-day dealings with the Customs Service.

We also discuss many of the major current issues in world trade, such as the effect of quotas, countervailing duties, dumping, the generalized system of preferences for underdeveloped countries, and the extensive changes wrought by the Trade Acts of 1974 and 1979.

Having stated what is included, we believe it important also to indicate what is not covered. This volume does not address such related subjects as banking procedures, letters of credit, terms of sale, contracts, claims against shippers and insurance companies, shipping documents, and other material of that nature. Nor do we intend this to be a comprehensive reference text on tariff laws, customs regulations, and trade laws. Compilations of these are available from many public and private sources. Nevertheless, we have included certain significant source material in the appendixes, while the text cites statutory and case law where relevant.

International trade has emerged as one of the major political and economic issues of the 1980s. Accompanying this development has been the growth and increased complexity of government regulation of imports. A thorough knowledge of customs law is crucial to the prudent person in business and his or her counsel. This book should assist those wishing to learn about this fascinating area of the law.

Acknowledgments

The revised edition is about to be published nearly seven years after the first edition of February 13, 1985.

The original was six years in the making; this revised edition, approximately two.

Again, my special thanks to the Practising Law Institute and its staff for its support and encouragement and in particular to Bill Cubberley and Keith Voelker.

My thanks to my colleagues Leibert L. Greenberg and Christopher M. Kane at Serko & Simon for their support and effort and my special appreciation to my associate Daniel J. Gluck for his extraordinary assistance.

Again, special thanks to my partner, Joel K. Simon, for his encouragement and understanding throughout this process.

Finally, thanks to the many individuals in the public and private sectors who have encouraged me to produce this sequel.

David Serko
New York City
September, 1991

Part I: The Tariff System

1. An Overview of Customs and International Trade Law

Introduction

The Congress shall have Power To lay and collect Taxes, Duties, Imposts and Excises . . . ; To regulate Commerce with foreign Nations. . . .[1]

Congress has exercised its constitutional power. Anyone considering engaging in an import transaction within the United States should start by examining our foreign trade laws, particularly those administered by the United States Customs Service.[2] Customs duties and restrictions on imported goods (e.g., safety requirements) may make importation uneconomic, quotas may limit the quantity that can be imported, and public policy may prohibit importation entirely (e.g., articles of ivory, pelts of endangered species, switchblade knives).

The law is not, however, composed solely of restrictions. Provisions of the customs laws waive duties on imports in

1. U.S. CONST. art. I, § 8.
2. The Service is a separate agency under the Department of the Treasury, successor (as of Aug. 1, 1973) to the Bureau of Customs. For a brief survey of its composition and functions, consult the current *United States Government Manual*. For a more detailed history of the Customs Service, we suggest C.E. PRINCE & M. KELLER, THE U.S. CUSTOMS SERVICE: A BICENTENNIAL HISTORY (1989).

certain circumstances (e.g., from the least developed developing countries), and there is a structure of trade regulation laws to protect domestic producers from unfair competition. Further, the Customs Service supervises facilities (bonded warehouses and foreign trade zones) that importers may use to their advantage.

Having identified the costs, risks, and opportunities of controls on imports, the United States importer is prepared to estimate the costs of compliance, to avoid the risks of noncompliance, to take advantage of the incentives, and even to shift some of the burdens of compliance to others[3] (for example, by securing the services of a United States–licensed broker to handle the formalities of making proper entry). Even more generally, familiarity with customs laws and regulations is essential to importers, businesses facing potential competition from imports, businesses contesting or injured by foreign-trade-related matters,[4] and their counsel.

The purpose of this chapter is to survey (1) the legal framework within which United States import practice operates; (2) the administrative framework by which the customs, tariff, and trade laws of the United States are executed; and (3) the realities of the execution of those laws (i.e., the specific importation controls). Because chapters 2–26 deal with discrete aspects of law and administration in some detail, the survey of importation controls has been keyed to them.

The Legal Framework

Foreign trade policy is determined by general national policy. If the national policy favors low prices and a wide

3. 1 W. Streng & J. Salacuse, International Business Planning: Law & Taxation (United States) 18-1–18-5 (1982).
4. See, e.g., *id.* at 3-28–3-29; chapter 20 *infra*.

selection of goods for consumers, tariffs and nontariff measures will place few restrictions on imports, i.e., a free trade policy will be followed. If tariffs are the major source of government revenue, as was the case with the United States from 1789 to the ratification of the sixteenth amendment in 1913 (income tax provision), an attempt will be made to maximize returns.[5] Finally, if the national policy is to protect domestic industries and especially their workers from foreign competition, tariffs and nontariff measures will restrict imports, i.e., a protectionist policy will be followed.

Protectionist sentiment in the United States was very strong in the late nineteenth and early twentieth centuries, peaking in 1930 with passage of the Smoot-Hawley Tariff Act,[6] which set some of the highest general tariff rates ever. The rest of the industrialized world responded with equally stiff barriers, and international trade collapsed.[7]

To reverse the collapse of international trade, Smoot-Hawley was amended in 1934 by the Trade Agreements Act,[8] which gave the President of the United States authority to enter into trade agreements with foreign countries for the reciprocal reduction of tariff barriers. Trade agreements under this Act produced a gradual, but discernible, decline in tariffs.[9]

Current United States import practice is governed by (1)

---

5. In practice, of course, the nineteenth century was a more protectionist period; often cited were Alexander Hamilton's arguments for infant industries.
6. Tariff Act of 1930, ch. 361, 46 Stat. 590 (1930) (codified at 19 U.S.C. § 1202). Section 1202 is also referred to as the Tariff Schedules of the United States (TSUS) (1962).
7. Some economists attribute the Crash of 1929 to anticipation of passage of Smoot-Hawley. European inability to earn dollars by exporting to the United States has also been viewed as a reason for severe monetary problems in this era.
8. Trade Agreements Act, ch. 474, 48 Stat. 943 (1934) (codified at 19 U.S.C. §§ 1351–1366).
9. J. Dobson, Two Centuries of Tariffs 1–3, 31–38 (1976).

customs and trade statutes, (2) bilateral trade treaties negotiated by the President, and (3) United States participation in the General Agreement on Tariffs and Trade (GATT).[10]

Customs Statutes

The Smoot-Hawley Tariff Act, commonly referred to as the Tariff Act of 1930, is the basis for all present-day customs statutes. Indeed, the vast majority of customs law provisions in effect today represent the Act and its amendments.

Under the reciprocal Trade Agreements Act,[11] Congress first delegated authority to the President to negotiate tariff reductions. The Trade Act of 1974[12] authorized the President to negotiate with other countries the reciprocal reduction of nontariff barriers.

Not only does the Trade Act of 1974 define the scope of United States participation in the current session of GATT negotiations,[13] but it expands the trend initiated in 1962[14] of providing such nontariff relief as the "escape clause" and "unfair trade practices" provisions for United States industries and workers injured by foreign trade.

The Customs Procedural Reform and Simplification Act of 1978,[15] a major piece of customs legislation, was designed

---

10. General Agreement on Tariffs and Trade, *opened for signature*, Oct. 30, 1947, 61 Stat. A3, T.I.A.S. No. 1700, 55 U.N.T.S. 187 (effective Jan. 1, 1948). The current version of GATT appears in 4 GENERAL AGREEMENT ON TARIFFS & TRADE, BASIC INSTRUMENTS & SELECTED DOCUMENTS (1969). See also discussion below.
11. Trade Agreements Act, *supra* note 8.
12. Trade Act of 1974, Pub. L. No. 93-618, 88 Stat. 1978 (1974) (codified at 19 U.S.C. §§ 2101–2487).
13. Discussed below.
14. Tariff Classification Act of 1962, Pub. L. No. 87-456, 76 Stat. 72, *as amended by* Pub. L. No. 87-794, 76 Stat. 882 (1962).
15. Customs Procedural Reform and Simplification Act of 1978, Pub. L. No. 95-410, 92 Stat. 888 (1978).

to streamline significant customs practices (e.g., by establishing new entry and duty-collection processes and by imposing new record-keeping requirements on importers) and to add new safeguards in the basic penalty and fraud provisions of the customs laws.[16]

The Trade Agreements Act of 1979[17] was passed to implement the trade agreements signed by the United States on an ad referendum basis[18] during the Tokyo Round of trade negotiations under GATT. The Act deals mainly with such nontariff measures as subsidies, countervailing duties, antidumping duties, customs valuation, government procurement, and technical barriers to trade.[19]

Recent legislative acts, implemented between January 1985 and January 1990, have also had direct and significant bearing on customs and international trade law. In 1985 the Trade and Tariff Act of 1984 (TTA)[20] amended various provisions of the Trade Act of 1974 and the Tariff Act of 1930, as well as adding other provisions. The Trade Act of 1974 was amended with respect to the General System of Preferences (GSP),[21] relief provisions under the "escape clause,"[22] and executive powers to respond to foreign international trade and investment barriers.[23] The Tariff Act of 1930 was amended with respect to customs broker regulations,[24] pay-

16. By amending Tariff Act of 1930, ch. 497, § 592, 46 Stat. 750 (1930) (codified at 19 U.S.C. § 1592). *See also* chapter 22.
17. Pub. L. No. 96-39, 93 Stat. 144 (1979).
18. Ad referendum agreements are subject to the approval of the home government; in this case, they required congressional enactment and repeal of conflicting provisions.
19. These topics are discussed throughout the book, particularly in chapters 18–21.
20. Pub. L. No. 98-573, 98 Stat. 2948 (1984).
21. *See* chapter 11.
22. *See* chapter 21.
23. *See* chapter 21.
24. *See* chapter 7.

ment of interest on increased duties,[25] and regulations protecting industry from unfair foreign competition in the U.S. market—including provisions concerning countervailing and antidumping duties.[26] The TTA also addresses drawback,[27] foreign trade zones,[28] duty-free shops,[29] Caribbean products entered into Puerto Rico,[30] restraints on steel, barriers to U.S. wine trade,[31] and the unlawful export or import of certain vehicles.[32]

The Anti-Drug Abuse Act of 1986 (19 U.S.C. § 1595a(c))[33] substantially augmented the seizure powers available to the U.S. Customs Service with respect to commercial shipments having nothing to do with drugs.

The third important legislative act during this period was the Omnibus Trade and Competitiveness Act of 1988.[34] That Act replaced the Tariff Schedule of the U.S. (TSUS) with the Harmonized Tariff Schedules of the U.S. (HTSUS).[35] Accordingly, the implementation of the HTSUS in 1989 was a transition of utmost significance to the trade community. The development of the new tariff schedule was, in part, necessitated by vast changes in technology since the implementation of the TSUS in 1962. But more importantly, the efficiencies in trade created by the growing international adoption of the Brussels Nomenclature[36] prompted a

25. *See* chapter 24.
26. *See* chapters 20 and 21.
27. *See* chapter 17.
28. *See* chapter 10.
29. *See* chapter 9.
30. *See* chapter 12.
31. *See* chapter 22.
32. *See* chapter 22.
33. Pub. L. No. 99-570, 100 Stat. 3207 (1986) (seizure provision codified at 19 U.S.C. § 1595a(c)). *See* chapter 23.
34. Pub. L. No. 100-418, 102 Stat. 1107 (1988).
35. *See* chapter 3.
36. The "Brussels Nomenclature" is a systematic classification drawn up by the Customs Cooperation Counsel, an international organization,

sixteen-year effort that brought forth the Harmonized System which includes a Harmonized Tariff Schedule. Our government's participation in this effort and its system was motivated by the desire of the United States and its major trading partners to bring about greater efficiencies in the flow of international trade. The HTSUS was implemented on January 1, 1989, pursuant to section 1217(b) of the Omnibus Trade and Competitiveness Act of 1988.

Beyond implementing the HTSUS, the Omnibus Trade and Competitiveness Act of 1988 has had an impact on a number of important trade issues. Among the issues the Act addresses are certain types of trade sanctions, such as retaliatory measures invoked by the President, antidumping and countervailing duties,[37] the negotiation and/or implementation of various trade agreements, intellectual property protection, certain trade agency procedures, tariffs on particular goods, import control, export enhancement, and international financial policy.

Other legislation during this period also having a significant bearing on customs and international trade law includes the following:

The Consolidated Omnibus Budget Reconciliation Act of 1985[38] establishes various user fees, including the Customs user fee.[39]

---

for use by member nations to facilitate international trade by making laws more uniform in phraseology.

37. *See* chapters 20 and 21.

38. Pub. L. No. 99-272, 100 Stat. 82 (1986).

39. The GATT has recently found that the U.S. Customs practice of charging a user fee by percentage of value (formerly 0.17 percent) did not reflect true administrative costs in processing shipments—significantly overcharging importers of high value merchandise. As a result the user fee was contrary to accepted international user fee rules. A press release dated March 1, 1990, from the Senate Committee on Finance stated that the Finance Committee had approved legislation that would reduce the current user fee from 0.17 percent ad valorem to 0.15 percent ad valorem with a $403 cap on manual entries and a

The Omnibus Budget Reconciliation Act of 1986[40] amends the user fee provisions established in the prior Act as well as sets forth certain regulations on excise tax deposits for imports of tobacco, distilled spirits, wine and beer.

Two free trade agreements were negotiated and signed between 1984 and 1989. Both the United States–Israel Free Trade Area Agreement[41] and the United States–Canada Free Trade Agreement[42] seek to promote trade between the United States and the respective signatories by eliminating tariff and nontariff trade barriers. The structure and provisions of the two agreements, however, differ in some respects. Congress enacted the United States–Israel Free Trade Area Agreement into law on June 11, 1985, and enacted the United States–Canada Free Trade Agreement into law on September 28, 1988.

The Export Administration Act of 1985[43] in the most part amends the Export Administration Act of 1979. An autono-

---

$400 cap on automated entries. There would also be a minimum fee of $23 on manual entries and $20 on automated entries. The committee set a $14 fee on informal manual entries and a $11 fee on informal automated entries, but urged the administration to correct inequities in the fees on informal entries. These user fees would expire on September 30, 1991.

As of this writing Customs has requested that the user fee be charged as a percentage of the value of goods entered on each entry release form (CF 3461) up to the specified dollar ceiling. Currently, the user fee can be charged as a percentage of the value of goods listed on an entry summary (CF 7501). Because several releases could be consolidated on an entry summary (e.g., several air shipments being held to enable consolidation on one entry summary), Customs anticipates that importers could attempt to consolidate as many releases as possible onto a single entry summary thus avoiding paying a user fee on each separate entry.

40. Pub. L. No. 99-509, 100 Stat. 1874 (1986).

41. Pub. L. No. 99-47, 99 Stat. 82 (1985). For further discussion *see* chapter 1, p. 33 *infra*, and chapter 13.

42. Pub. L. No. 100-449, 102 Stat. 1851 (1988). For further discussion *see* chapter 1, p. 33 *infra*, and chapter 14.

43. Pub. L. No. 99-64, 99 Stat. 120 (1985).

mous office is created under the Secretary of Commerce. An Undersecretary of Commerce for export administration is appointed by the President after consulting with and obtaining the consent of the Senate. The Act affects export control laws and licensing procedures. It addresses search and seizure regulations as well as the penalties available to punish violators. Sanctions for violating export controls can include a denial of certain import privileges. The Act also addresses export promotion activities, regulations on the use of international barter by the federal government, and certain administrative procedures within the agency.

The Anti-Drug Abuse Act of 1988[44] affects importers principally by calling upon the Secretary of the Treasury to prescribe regulations and establish procedures that will ensure the uniform classification of merchandise at all ports of entry. Furthermore, Customs is required to take steps that ostensibly will ensure greater uniformity in deciding upon ruling requests.[45] The 1988 Act also covers certain matters relating to seizure of goods as well as the disposition of seized property and proceeds thereof.

Under the Comprehensive Anti-Apartheid Act of 1986[46] a host of export and import restrictions, among other restrictions, were established in light of the South African government's continued racist policies and activities. The list of goods prohibited for export includes primarily products and technology having potential military application. The list of goods banned from import is more extensive and includes any products sold by parastatal (i.e., government-funded) enterprises. Violators of this Act are subject to criminal prosecution.

---

44. Pub. L. No. 100-690, 102 Stat. 4181 (1988).
45. See chapter 24.
46. Pub. L. No. 99-440, 100 Stat. 1086 (1986); see discussion in chapter 22.

It should be noted that title IX of the Technical Corrections and Miscellaneous Revenue Act of 1988[47] provides certain amendments to the Omnibus Trade and Competitiveness Act of 1988 as well as technical and substantive amendments to various other trade legislation. When applying a statute, regulation, or tariff schedule, it is, of course, necessary to compare it with the most current amendments in the appropriate supplement.

The new trade reciprocity provisions were enacted in 1984 as the International Trade and Investment Act.[48] The Act seeks to foster United States economic growth and employment by expanding competitive United States exports in foreign markets and by improving the ability of the President to achieve the elimination of barriers to (1) international trade in services,[49] (2) foreign direct investment, and (3) high technology industries.[50] The trade reciprocity provisions of the Tariff and Trade Act of 1984[51] follow the Trade Act of 1974 in amending the reciprocal Trade Agreements Act of 1934.[52]

Specific provisions of the 1984 Act deal with the negotiating objectives and the negotiating authority given to the President for the first time in these areas. In order to carry out the objectives of any high-technology agreement negotiated by the President, he is given authority to eliminate or modify duty or continue existing duty or duty-free treat-

---

47. Pub. L. No. 100-647, 102 Stat. 3342 (1988).
48. 19 U.S.C.A. §§ 2114a–2242, 2411–2441 & 3101–3104 (West Supp. 1989).
49. "Services" are economic activities whose outputs are other than tangible goods. The term includes, but is not limited to, "banking, insurance, transportation, communications and data processing, retail and wholesale trade, advertising, accounting, construction. . . ." 19 U.S.C.A. § 2114b(5) (West Supp. 1990).
50. 19 U.S.C.A. §§ 2102 note, 2114a, 2114b (West Supp. 1989).
51. Trade Agreements Act, *supra* note 8.
52. Trade Act of 1974, *supra* note 12.

ment for a five-year period on certain listed products, e.g., transistors, semiconductors.[53]

A new provision directs the Secretary of Commerce to establish a service industries development program in order to devise policies to increase the competitiveness of United States service industries abroad. The Secretary is directed to collect and analyze information on both foreign and domestic matters in this area that affect the international competitiveness of United States service industries and to report his findings to Congress and the President every two years beginning in 1986.[54]

Among the negotiating objectives, in the area of foreign direct investment, is the direction to develop rules for dispute resolution that ensure a free flow of foreign direct investment.[55]

If the President determines that a foreign country is denying the United States benefits under a trade agreement or burdening or restricting United States commerce, he has the power to modify the trade agreements and impose duties on the products of that country.[56] This authority to retaliate against unfair practices extends to investments as well as goods and services.

The President's retaliatory authority was modified under title III of the Omnibus Trade and Competitiveness Act of 1988. The Act provides the United States Trade Representative (USTR) with the ability to determine unfair trade practices and retaliatory measures, subject to the President's approval. A determination by the USTR that foreign trade practices are unjustified would require the USTR to seek mandated retaliatory measures. Where the USTR determines

53. 19 U.S.C.A. §§ 2114e, 2138 (West Supp. 1989).

54. Trade & Tariff Act of 1984 § 306(a), 98 Stat. 3008–09 (codified at 19 U.S.C.A. § 2114b (West Supp. 1989)).

55. 19 U.S.C.A. § 2112(a) (West Supp. 1989).

56. Trade Act of 1974 § 301, 88 Stat. 2041–2043, TA 88, 1301(a), 102 Stat. 1164–1165 (codified at 19 U.S.C.A. § 2411 (West Supp. 1985)).

that a foreign trade practice is unreasonable or discriminatory, the USTR has discretion whether to seek retaliatory measures. Additionally under the 1988 Act, the USTR makes annual reports to Congress on trade liberalization priorities.[57]

The onset of the executive branch's investigation into a foreign country's unfair trade practices frequently leads to an exchange of accusations that the other party is hindering free trade and violating the GATT.[58] The United States has in certain instances imposed retaliatory trade sanctions, but the imposition of sanctions has in some cases escalated into limited trade wars.[59] Such trade wars can result in economic and political loss to both sides. More often, therefore, the United States and its trade partners endeavor to resolve disputes without resorting to trade sanctions.[60]

---

57. 49 I.T.R.D. (BNA) 102–03 (1990). For further discussion see chapter 21.
58. E.g., U.S.–E.C. dispute over E.C. ban on meat from animals injected with growth hormones. After a series of threats and counterthreats on the imposition of stiff sanctions, the E.C. and the United States seem to have resolved the matter. More recently the USTR named Japan, India, and Brazil as countries whose trade practices would be investigated for trade discrimination. Japan is being investigated for unfair import policies concerning telecommunications, supercomputers, satellites, and forest products. (The United States and Japan reached a tentative accord on the supercomputer dispute on Mar. 23, 1990.) India's trade practices are being investigated regarding investment and insurance, and Brazil's trade practices are being investigated regarding import restriction including import licensing. All three countries have responded by stating that any retaliatory measures taken by the United States would be in violation of the GATT. 6 I.T.R.D. (BNA) 684–89 (1989).
59. A clear example of this occurred in 1976 when the United States retaliated against "preferential tariffs" provided by the E.C. on certain citrus products imported from certain Mediterranean countries by imposing prohibitive duties on pasta imports from the E.C. The E.C. counter-retaliated by imposing excessive duties on E.C. imports of U.S. lemons and walnuts. The limited trade war was not resolved until August 1986.
60. E.g., in 1986 President Reagan directed an investigation of Taiwan's

Preferential Trade Programs and Bilateral Trade Treaties

Since the reciprocal Trade Agreements Act of 1934,[61] the President's delegated authority to negotiate and enter into trade agreements with other countries has been constantly extended. A milestone in that extension is the Trade Act of 1974,[62] in which the President is authorized not only to enter into agreements for mutual reduction of both tariff and nontariff barriers, but also to extend duty-free treatment to less developed countries on certain eligible goods for a ten-year period (the Generalized System of Preferences (GSP)).[63]

The GSP is part of a worldwide effort by the industrialized nations to benefit the "beneficiary developing countries" (BDCs). The President has designated over 140 BDCs

---

export performance requirements in the automotive sector. The investigation was in response to Taiwan's agreement with Japan's Toyota automotive company that makes Toyota's operating a manufacturing facility in Taiwan conditional on Toyota's exporting at least 12.5 percent of the facility's output. The Reagan administration anticipated that the required exports would largely be targeted to the United States. The administration also reasoned that it should challenge Taiwan's agreement with Toyota in order to discourage Taiwan and other countries from further engaging in the implementation of export requirements. 3 I.T.R.D. (BNA) 427,524 (1986). Without resorting to sanctions, the United States and Taiwan reached an agreement that called for Taiwan to lift automatic export performance requirements and that eased restrictions on expanding existing investments in their automotive industry. ITR 49:08041 (1988). More recently the United States and South Korea resolved a USTR investigation begun in March 1988 concerning barriers to South Korea's beef imports. The matter was resolved on March 21, 1990, just five weeks before the USTR was required to decide on whether to apply sanctions. 7 I.T.R.D. (B.N.A.) 428–29 (Mar. 28, 1990).

61. Trade Agreements Act, *supra* note 8.
62. Trade Act of 1974, *supra* note 12.
63. See chapter 14. The ten-year period, which ended January 3, 1985, has been extended through July 4, 1993. 19 U.S.C.A. § 2465(a) (West 1980 and Supp. 1989).

and issued extensive lists of eligible articles for duty-free treatment on importation from BDCs.

In addition to granting preferences to BDCs, the United States has undertaken trade incentives to expedite the economic development of the Caribbean Basin.[64] The Caribbean Basin Economic Recovery Act, or the Caribbean Basin Initiative (CBI) as it is commonly called, provided twenty-two countries in the region with somewhat better access to the U.S. market than would be available under the GSP as well as providing a greater degree of permanence in respect to their preferred status.

The United States, in following its agenda to further reduce trade barriers, and in response to initiatives taken by the European Community, has steered its trade policy toward engaging in free trade (area) agreements (FTAs) with, at least, those countries to which the United States already has close ties. In 1985, the United States entered into an FTA with Israel.[65] Subsequently, an FTA was signed with Canada in 1989.[66] On the congressional agenda are deliberations on whether to authorize President George Bush to engage in FTA negotiations with Mexico and Taiwan (recently removed from GSP status) and other Pacific Rim countries. Unlike the GSP and CBI programs, FTAs are mutually beneficial and, on the whole, offer the United States opportunities to compete more effectively. Several more specialized agreements have also been implemented. Among them, the agreement known as "Super 807" provides more liberal quotas to Mexican and Caribbean textile products incorporating fabric components formed and cut in the United States.[67] The Automotive Products Trade Act allows duty-

64. See Pub. L. No. 98-67, 97 Stat. 369 (1983). For further discussion, see chapter 12.

65. U.S.–Israel Free Trade Area Agreement, *supra* note 41.

66. U.S.–Canada Free Trade Agreement, *supra* note 42.

67. HTSUS 9802.00.80.10. For further discussion, see chapter 15.

free imports of Canadian-manufactured motor-vehicle parts sold to U.S. motor-vehicle manufacturers.[68] Also significant is the Agreement on Trade in Civil Aircraft, allowing duty-free trade of civil aircraft and components thereof among signatory countries.[69]

In addition to the programs and agreement mentioned in this section, the United States is a party to a complex network of bilateral trade agreements.[70] Beyond a general commitment to furthering trade between the two countries, the usual focus of these agreements is a mutual grant of most-favored-nation status, that is, each agrees to treat the products of the other no less favorably than those of any other country.

United States Participation in GATT

To foster international trade, the nations of the world, including the United States, have entered into a variety of multilateral agreements to curb the imposition of tariffs and nontariff barriers by individual nations. The most important multilateral trade agreement is the General Agreement on Tariffs and Trade (GATT), which seeks to extend the principle of most-favored-nation treatment from bilateral treaties to all members of GATT.

---

68. Pub. L. No. 89-283, 79 Stat. 1016 (1965) (codified at 19 U.S.C. §§ 2001 *et seq.*) implements the Agreement.
69. Pub. L. No. 96-39 § 303, *amended by* Pub. L. No. 98-573 § 234. *See* 19 U.S.C. § 2513.
70. Other countries with which the United States currently has bilateral trade agreements include: Japan, Hong Kong, Mexico, People's Republic of China, South Korea, and Taiwan; e.g., U.S.–Mexican Bilateral Framework Agreement on Trade and Investment, November 6, 1987, 27 I.L.M. 438 (1988). Additionally the United States has obtained Voluntary Restraint Agreements (VRAs) for a variety of products and commodities. For example the United States has already completed negotiations on new two-and-one-half year VRAs for steel with sixteen countries and the twelve members of the EEC (Broker Power News, Feb. 9, 1990, at 5).

Since 1948, the members of GATT[71] have engaged in several distinct rounds of trade negotiations. The seventh round ("Tokyo Round") sought the elimination, reduction, or harmonization of certain nontariff barriers. Twelve areas in international trade were addressed by agreements prepared at the Tokyo Round. The main impact of the Tokyo Round on United States customs law was the reduction in rates in the Tariff Schedules of the United States[72] and a new approach to appraising imported goods.[73]

The eighth and current round ("Uruguay Round") is aimed at strengthening the institutionalization of the GATT as well as tackling new issues of concern to industrialized and lesser developed countries. For those engaging in international trade, the most important issue at this time is whether the United States will prevail in obtaining a product-by-product reduction in duties as opposed to a flat percentage reduction in rates on all products. The United States has argued that such across-the-board reductions favor countries that have in place exorbitant tariffs on certain sensitive products. For example, a 20 percentage-point across-the-board reduction will reduce a 55 percent tariff on automobiles to 35 percent, but the resulting tariff will still preclude foreign manufacturers from market access. Other pressing issues include whether, or to what degree, the GATT will govern the following matters: trade in services, protection of intellectual property rights, rules of origin, multifiber agreements, and trade distorting investment practices. Also at issue are protective trade measures on certain sensitive products such as agriculture and textiles as well

---

71. See *supra* note 10.
72. See *supra* note 6.
73. The customs valuation code agreed upon at the Tokyo Round adopts transaction value as the primary standard for appraising imported goods, and attempts to harmonize United States valuation practices with those of other countries. See chapter 4.

as options to exercise such protective trade measures for other industries in the event they are imperiled by imports.

Of these latter issues, the divergent national policies concerning agriculture have engendered the severest discord,[74] the resolution of which is critical to the successful completion of the Uruguay Round.[75] The Uruguay Round was "concluded" at a meeting of the foreign ministers of the ninety-six contracting parties in Brussels in December, 1990. However, a final agreement was not reached. There has been movement toward reviving the round, but it is unlikely that an agreement will be reached in time to meet the original January 1, 1992, target date for U.S. implementation.

The Administrative Framework[76]

United States Customs Service

The United States Customs Service, a separate agency under the Treasury Department, is the principal government agency vested with the authority to administer and enforce the customs, tariff, and trade laws of the United States.

---

74. For insights on agricultural issues that divide the contracting parties, *see* Hanrahan, *Agriculture in the Uruguay Round*, 11 FLETCHER F. 33–41 (1987).

75. United States Trade Representative Carla Hills recently commented that the negotiations concerning treatment of agriculture in the GATT "are 'the key' to a successful completion of the . . . Uruguay Round." *See Logjam in Farm Trade Negotiations Tops the Agenda for US–EC Talks*, J. of Com. & Commercial, Sept. 8, 1989, 1A, Col. 1. The coverage of agriculture trade concerns under the GATT has remained the most critical issue throughout most of the Uruguay Round. *See also* Aho, *The Uruguay Round: Will It Revitalize the Trading System*, 11 FLETCHER F. 1–12 (1987).

76. Some of this material derives from Office of the Federal Register, *United States Government Manual 1983/84*, 439–40, 133–35, 634–37 (1983).

The Service is charged with assessing and collecting customs duties, excise taxes, fees, and penalties due on imported merchandise; interdicting and seizing contraband; processing persons, carriers, cargo, and mail into and out of the United States; administering certain navigation laws; detecting and apprehending persons engaged in fraudulent practices designed to circumvent customs and related laws; and enforcing copyright, patent, and trademark provisions, quotas, and marking requirements for imported merchandise.

The Customs Service also cooperates with and assists numerous government agencies in the enforcement of federal laws and regulations. For example, it ensures that imported chemicals and pesticides meet the Environmental Protection Agency's requirements; that foodstuffs, drugs, and medical devices comply with regulations of the Food and Drug Administration; and that the fiber and care labeling requirements administered by the Federal Trade Commission are strictly adhered to. All of these laws are enforced by the Customs Service in the first instance and referred, if necessary, to the proper agencies.

Headquartered in Washington, D.C., the United States Customs Service is headed by the Commissioner of Customs, who is appointed by the Secretary of the Treasury. The customs territory of the United States includes only the states, the District of Columbia, and Puerto Rico. The territory is divided into seven customs regions[77] (each headed by a regional commissioner). The regions are further divided into subordinate districts or area offices (each headed by a district director or area director). The Customs Service oversees more than three hundred ports of entry, which are

77. The most important of which is region II (New York). See chapter 24 and 19 C.F.R. § 101.3 (1988). See also appendix 29 for a list of Customs Service regions and the regional headquarters locations.

not necessarily at border points, but may be inland for cargo shipped by air, truck, or vessel in bond.

U.S. International Trade Commission

The International Trade Commission (ITC) is an independent agency originally created by an act of Congress in 1916 as the United States Tariff Commission. The name was changed to the ITC by the Trade Act of 1974.[78] The ITC is given broad powers of investigation related to the customs laws.

Among its many functions, the ITC:

1. Advises the President in the area of trade negotiations (for example, on the probable economic effect on domestic industry and consumers of the modification of duties and other trade barriers or of the preferential removal of the duty on imports from designated developing countries);
2. Conducts investigations as provided under the antidumping laws;[79]
3. Conducts investigations as provided under the countervailing duties laws;[80]
4. Conducts investigations to determine whether unfair methods of competition or unfair acts are being committed in the importation of articles into the United States or in their domestic sale, the effect of which is to injure, destroy, or prevent the establishment of such an industry in the United States;[81] and
5. Conducts investigations upon petition on behalf of an industry, a firm, a group of workers, or other

78. Trade Act of 1974, *supra* note 12.
79. *See* chapter 20.
80. *Id.*
81. *See* chapter 21.

entity representing an industry to determine whether an article is being imported in such increased quantities as to be a cause or threat of serious injury to that particular domestic industry.

In order to carry out its responsibilities, the ITC is required to engage in extensive research, conduct specialized studies, and maintain a high degree of expertise in all matters relating to the commercial and international trade policies of the United States.

Department of Commerce

Among its numerous responsibilities to serve, encourage, and promote the nation's international trade, economic growth, and technological advancement, the Commerce Department administers (1) the antidumping and countervailing duty laws; (2) the quotas on the importation of wearing apparel, textiles, footwear, etc.; (3) the authorization of duty-free importation of scientific and technical equipment (in cooperation with the departments of the Treasury and Health and Human Services); and (4) tasks concerning the establishment and operation of foreign trade zones and importation for use in trade fairs.

International Trade Administration

The International Trade Administration (ITA) of the Commerce Department was established to promote world trade and strengthen the international trade and investment position of the United States. The ITA is also responsible for developing and implementing departmental programs on issues of the administration of imports and exports (e.g., the antidumping and countervailing duty laws, industrial resource administration, foreign boycotts, and foreign trade zones). The ITA determines the sufficiency of petitions filed before initiating investigations regarding penalties for dumping or foreign export subsidies.[82]

Federal Maritime Commission

The Federal Maritime Commission (FMC) is an independent federal government regulatory agency formed in 1961. The FMC has regulatory responsibility over the inbound and outbound ocean-borne commerce of the United States. The agency is governed by a regulatory philosophy designed to encourage the maintenance of ocean carrier services sufficient to meet the transportation and national security needs of the United States with a minimum of government intervention. The regulatory scheme under which the agency operates limits cutthroat competition by allowing joint action by carriers, which would otherwise be prohibited under the antitrust laws. FMC authority includes the overseeing of the practices of liner steamship carriers, of shippers and consignees, and of transportation "middlemen," such as ocean freight forwarders and non-vessel-operating common carriers (NVOCCs). Among the practices under its scrutiny are the enforcement of rates published by common carriers and filed with the agency in the form of freight tariffs, which are the schedules of ocean transportation charges of general application, and service contracts, which represent transportation arrangements agreed to individually between carriers and shippers. The FMC also monitors the interactions among ocean common carriers under the qualified statutory antitrust immunity that allows them to act in concert, provided they publish and file with the FMC the terms of their agreements. The FMC has the power to levy penalties against carriers, shippers, consignees, and others who deviate from or otherwise unfairly circumvent

82. 19 C.F.R. §§ 353.37 & 355.27 (1988).

the proper charges for the ocean transportation of goods found in the tariffs and service contracts filed with the agency, or who act without prior approval under agreements required to be filed.

Import Controls

Import controls fall into two broad classes: tariffs and nontariff barriers (e.g., quotas, restrictions, and the like). With the demise of the political issue of "a tariff for revenue only" and the eclipse of extreme protectionism, the classes are not so clearly defined as they once were (for example, as will be discussed in chapter 11, the GSP both encourages imports from developing nations by admitting them duty-free and imposes de facto quotas with its competitive-need limitations).

For purposes of this book, import controls will be discussed in six groupings:

1. The tariff system (how rates are kept uniform, to what they are applied, how they are calculated);
2. Importation (what an importer or traveler should know);
3. Special services and facilities (deferral of duties in warehouses and zones);
4. Incentives to import or export (the treatment of goods from developing countries; assembly abroad, goods not really in the country; and goods for export with imported components);
5. Nontariff measures and trade regulation (marking, quotas, antidumping laws, countervailing duties, and unfair trade practices); and
6. Administration and enforcement (what the Customs Service can do, how it does it, how an aggrieved party can protest, what judicial review is available).

The remainder of this book will examine the specifics of these groupings, as will be more fully explained in the remainder of this chapter.

The Tariff System (Chapters 2–4)

Broadly, tariff assessment is the application to each product of one of three types of rates: (1) ad valorem, (2) specific, and (3) compound (a combination of 1 and 2). The rate is set by Congress, taking into account the agreements discussed above. Chapter 2 discusses the practicalities of application, particularly maintaining uniformity at more than three hundred ports of entry. Chapter 3 discusses the classification of goods. Chapter 4 discusses the valuation of goods to which the ad valorem rate applies.

Uniformity of Customs Procedures Throughout the United States (Chapter 2)

Chapter 2 discusses in detail the United States Customs Service's efforts to establish and maintain uniformity in the administration and enforcement of customs regulations as seen through the responsibilities and functions of the Import Specialists and National Import Specialists.

The chapter also explores the concept and implications of "uniform and established practice"; that is, the importing community's dependence upon the classification of, or the levying of duties at consistent rates for, identical merchandise imported over a long period of time at the various ports of entry. Finally, the chapter analyzes the impact of the Freedom of Information Act on Customs Headquarters in its responsibilities to make available or give wide publicity to past rulings and decisions that may have a bearing on a current legal problem experienced by an importer. (The new procedures for customs officers' decisions, implemented to achieve uniformity in rulings, are discussed in chapter 24.)

Classification (Chapter 3)

Under the Harmonized Tariff Schedule of the United States (HTSUS), products are classified into thousands of categories and subcategories tagged with identifying numbers and applicable rates of duty. The exact amount of duty, therefore, depends on the exact category into which a product is placed. Given the vast variety of products, an item of merchandise may be similarly described in two or more product descriptions, which requires detailed analysis as to which is more appropriate.

The Harmonized System Committee of the Customs Cooperative Council (an international organization) has prepared the harmonized code, a new system of classification of products for international use. The United States has participated in the development of the harmonized system in accordance with section 608(c) of the Trade Act of 1974. It has been adopted by the United States and more than forty other nations, including the European Economic Community (EEC). Its purpose is to implement a policy whereby all countries will use the same basic descriptions and classification numbers, so that not only will merchandise be more uniformly classified among the signatory nations, but more accurate statistics for world trade balances will be available. The ITC has prepared new tariff schedules which convert the TSUS into the harmonized system.

Rates of duty are affected by the many bilateral and multilateral agreements to which the United States is a party. For example, mutual grant of most-favored-nation status provides for reciprocal nondiscriminatory treatment of each treaty party's exports and imports. Statutory provisions like the Trade Act of 1974 also extend duty-free treatment to products of developing countries under the Generalized System of Preferences.[83]

83. Discussed below and in chapter 11.

Under the HTSUS, the rates of duty may be stated as a percentage of the value of the product ("ad valorem rate"), as an amount charged per unit of measure ("specific rate"), or as a combination of those two measures ("compound rate").

Valuation (Chapter 4)

Where the duty on a product is levied based on a percentage of the value of the import (ad valorem rate), then the value placed on the import must be determined before the pertinent rate of duty can be applied. The United States has traditionally employed a valuation system that determines the value of the goods at the point of shipment from the exporting country (f.o.b.). Under the uniform system of valuation (title II of the Trade Agreements Act of 1979),[84] which implements the customs valuation agreement under GATT's Tokyo Round, most merchandise will be appraised on its "transaction value." Transaction value is defined as "the price actually paid or payable for the merchandise when sold for exportation to the United States" plus the addition of other costs (e.g., packing costs, commission) where appropriate.[85]

Importation (Chapters 5–8)

How the customs laws and regulations are administered can be a subtle form of control and limitation on imports. Chapters 5 through 8 provide discussion on how customs laws and regulations can be brought to bear on private individuals, on merchants, and on the customs broker. Chapter 5 discusses the most visible part of the Customs Service's work: its treatment of persons arriving in the United States.

---

84. Pub. L. No. 96-39, 93 Stat. 144 (1979).
85. 19 U.S.C.A. §1401a(b) (West Supp. 1991).

Chapter 6 discusses the practicalities of importing goods while focusing on the interplay of the customs broker and the customs attorney. Chapter 7 highlights the role of the customs broker in the importation of goods and the regulations under which the customs broker operates. Chapter 8 discusses the role of the Federal Maritime Commission.

Customs Treatment of Persons Arriving in the United States (Chapter 5)

Aside from Customs Service activities related to commercial transactions, an important part of the Service's mission is to ensure that persons arriving in the United States do not enter contraband, that the proper duties are paid on the articles they do import, and that all other applicable federal laws are complied with.

Chapter 5 outlines and explains the regulations that pertain to the noncommercial importation of personal articles by United States residents and nonresident travelers.

Processing a Shipment Through Customs: The Customs Broker and the Customs Attorney (Chapter 6)

In an effort to give a concrete example of the process through which imported merchandise moves through the United States Customs Service, and to relate how an importer can effectively safeguard its interests and avoid pitfalls in this area, chapter 6 presents a scenario in which a company imports merchandise whose classification under a heading subject to a higher rate of duty is contested by the importer. The focus is on the importing process, from the planning stages through the final procedure of receiving a refund of duties from the Customs Service. Illustrated are the roles of the customs attorney, the customshouse broker (who will expedite the processing of the entry), and the

Customs Service officials who are involved in the entry, classification, valuation, and liquidation of the shipment and the subsequent review of documents.

Licensing and Regulation of Customs Brokers (Chapter 7)

The customs broker is the average importer's contact with the Customs Service. The broker's job is complex and exacting, and it carries with it heavy responsibilities both to the importer and to Customs, which closely monitors the brokerage industry through tightly enforced laws and regulations covering licensing and discipline. Every aspect of customs broker's activities, from granting of licenses to the daily transaction of customs business, is subject to exacting requirements and tight scrutiny.

As international trade becomes increasingly automated with the approach of the twenty-first century, the customs broker's importance remains undiminished: pilot programs developed by customs for "paperless" transactions hinge on an "Automated Broker Interface." Broker licensing and discipline are now intimately linked with the Customs Service's drive to automate.

The Federal Maritime Commission's Role in Import/Export Trade (Chapter 8)

Besides feeling the impact of the Customs Service, importers and exporters, brokers and freight forwarders are affected by the transportation statutes and regulations administered by the Federal Maritime Commission (FMC). The FMC's regulatory philosophy, economic philosophy, and regulatory scheme are described in chapter 8. The chapter enumerates FMC requirements most likely to affect those involved in ocean shipping either as buyers or sellers of goods or as entities involved in providing the services necessary to secure the delivery or receipt of ocean-borne cargo.

Among the areas discussed are freight tariffs, which are the published schedules of freight charges and related accommodations offered by steamship lines. Freight tariffs are required to be filed with the FMC and to be open to public inspection in the offices of the ocean carriers. Attention is also directed in this chapter to the importance of the description of the cargo and rebates, and the problems that can result from the misdescription of cargo or the receipt of accommodations outside the carrier's published freight tariffs. Service contracts, which represent a legal means of securing unique terms for particular shippers, are discussed, along with the prescribed contents of these arrangements. Included is an analysis of the pitfalls of service contract negotiations and execution of the terms whereby shippers promise to ship and carriers promise to supply space aboard their vessels during an agreed time period for agreed transportation charges.

The chapter addresses the licensing of ocean freight forwarders, i.e., the transportation intermediaries who act as "free-lance export departments" to dispatch ocean shipments on behalf of the actual owners of the goods. The transportation role of "quasi-carriers" known as non-vessel-operating common carriers (NVOCCs) is described, along with the 1991 bonding regulations that were imposed to provide protection for those shippers utilizing NVOCCs as middlemen between the owners of the cargo and the actual steamship vessel operators.

The final portion of the chapter is concerned with the qualified antitrust exemption applied to ocean common carriers through the publication and filing of their agreements to fix rates, allocate ports or revenues, or otherwise act in concert to affect ocean transportation services.

Special Services and Facilities (Chapters 9 and 10)

Among other topics, the next section discusses the tariff reductions available for exporters that use imported components (chapter 17) and the duty-free importation of goods in transit to another country or for destruction (chapter 16). Integral to those substantive provisions are the facilities discussed in this section.

Customs-Bonded Warehouses (Chapter 9)

One special facility authorized by the Customs Service as a part of the temporary import system is the bonded warehouse, which provides for the free entry under bond of otherwise dutiable merchandise. Chapter 9 covers the different classes of bonded warehouse, and the ways an importer can use them to advantage for the storage and manipulation of merchandise.

Foreign Trade Zones (Chapter 10)

Compared to other elements of the temporary import system, foreign trade zones (FTZs) offer the most flexibility and greatest advantages to the importer. FTZs are considered outside the customs territory of the United States, and such activities as manufacturing, processing, manipulation, assembly, storage, or exhibition can be carried out within them. Payment of duties is required upon entry of goods from an FTZ into United States customs territory.

Incentives to Import or Export (Chapters 11–17)

Preferential Programs and Trade Agreements (Chapters 11–14)

During recent years, the United States has entered into several agreements with other countries that unilaterally or mutually reduce or eliminate tariffs. Duty-free treatment for a wide variety of imports is provided to a large number of developing countries under a Generalized System of Preferences (GSP) program. The United States has agreed to unilaterally reduce or eliminate tariffs on goods imported from those countries in order to facilitate the economic development of each beneficiary country. A similar yet more beneficial system was implemented for Caribbean countries under the Caribbean Basin Economic Recovery Act (CBERA). The preferences extended to designated Caribbean countries under this Act are more beneficial than preferences extended to designated countries under GSP, which face greater restrictions in country of origin and direct shipping regulations and for which fewer items are eligible for reduced tariffs. Additionally, goods imported from the Virgin Islands and other U.S. insular possessions are duty free if they meet certain rules of origin requirements. More recently, the United States has entered into mutual free trade agreements. The first such agreement was concluded with Israel in 1985 and was followed by a pact with Canada in 1989. Other free trade arrangements are on the horizon.[86] Under the FTAs with Israel and Canada, tariffs and most other barriers to trade are removed by each party according to the terms and over the period of time agreed to by the parties and thereafter implemented by each party under its respective laws.

Generalized System of Preferences (Chapter 11): In addition to explaining the inner workings of the GSP, chapter 11 features practical pointers and examples for the importer. For instance, an importer should know when a particular article retains, loses, regains, or newly acquires GSP eligi-

86. Discussions concerning the possible negotiation of FTAs with Mexico, certain South American countries, and Taiwan and other Pacific Rim countries have been held.

bility and that great care is required to qualify for GSP benefits if one's imports are either about to go off or be added to the list.[87]

Caribbean Basin Initiative (Chapter 12): The Caribbean Basin Initiative (CBI), ushered in under the CBERA, extends enhanced preferential trade treatment to twenty-two countries in that region until September 30, 1995, unless reviewed. With the growth of Caribbean export industries in response to the CBI, rules governing imports from Caribbean countries will be frequently encountered by U.S. importers. Chapter 12 explores the rules governing the eligibility of goods, how CBI differs from GSP, and certain procedural aspects of importing under the CBI.

United States–Israel Free Trade Agreement (Chapter 13): Unlike the CBI and the GSP, a free trade agreement requires mutual elimination of import barriers. Israel is the first country to have entered into a free trade agreement with the United States. The agreement provides for the elimination or, depending on the item, staged elimination of duties on goods meeting the rules of origin requirement. The rules of origin are essentially the same as those under the CBI legislation. The treaty addresses the elimination of certain nontariff trade barriers as well. Chapter 13 will serve to introduce the reader to the essential scope of free trade agreements and how they affect trade between the signatories countries.

United States–Canada Free Trade Agreement (Chapter 14): The chapter begins by discussing the planned timetable for reducing tariffs under the United States–Canada free trade agreement. Those items which are not duty free as of

87. Chapter 11 also discusses documenting the claim to GSP treatment and form A.

the implementation of the agreement are to have their duties eliminated in one or three stages. The staged elimination extends for three-year, five-year, or ten-year periods resulting in the removal of tariffs between the parties. The chapter then explains at some length how this agreement departs from the basic rules of determining origin applied, with some variations, under the prior tariff reduction agreements. Three basic categories of origin requirements are present in the agreement. The first concerns goods wholly produced or obtained in either country; the second concerns foreign goods which are processed in either country, thereby altering the goods so as to change the HTSUS subheadings under which they are classified, and the third category concerns two very limited situations in which certain goods must also meet a value-added content requirement.

Examples are provided to demonstrate how determinations regarding the status of goods under the agreement are rendered. The chapter concludes by delineating the documentary procedures.

Special Classification Provisions and Other Provisions for Tariff Reduction, Remission, and Refund (Chapters 15–17)

Several circumstances exist under which dutiable goods are brought into the United States and are not placed in, or removed from, the stream of commerce. In circumstances where the United States has determined that it would be categorically inappropriate or counterproductive to levy duties on such goods, exceptions have been provided. Imports that are American products returning from abroad or that further a socially sanctioned purpose within the United States are also duty free. Re-exportation is encouraged by the provision for temporary importation under bond. Exportation of goods manufactured or assembled in the United States with foreign components is encouraged by the drawback provision.

American Goods Returned and Special Provisions (Chapter 15): Some categories of products are duty free in whole or in part because they are entered under particular circumstances or intended for specific uses. Chapter 15 focuses on American articles exported and returned and articles entered under certain conditions or dedicated for certain exclusive uses.

Temporary Importation Under Bond (Chapter 16): Articles that are not imported for sale or for sale on approval may enter the United States temporarily free of duty under bond, provided they are exported or destroyed under Customs Service supervision within a year of importation. Chapter 16 sets forth the major items in this classification of merchandise and the procedures for temporary importation under bond.

Drawback of Customs Duties (Chapter 17): Drawback represents refund of duties or taxes paid upon goods previously imported and incorporated into domestically produced articles or kept in its original condition that are subsequently exported. The legislative intent behind the provision is to stimulate and encourage American commerce, manufacture, or both; that is, it permits the American manufacturer to compete more effectively in foreign markets by overcoming the disadvantage of including in its costs (and hence its selling price) the duty imposed on the imported components of its finished product.

Chapter 17 discusses the various categories of drawback available and the conditions and requirements for eligibility (direct-identification drawback, merchandise not conforming to sample or specification or shipped without consent of consignee, and same-condition drawback). The chapter also specifies the procedures for acquiring the different classes of drawback.

Nontariff Measures and Trade Regulation (Chapters 18–21)

Imported merchandise must show the country of origin to enable consumers to make informed choices. The most basic nontariff control on imports is, of course, the quota. When imports harm or threaten domestic industries, the antidumping statutes and countervailing duties may be invoked. Similarly, there are remedies for market disruption and unfair trade practices like patent, copyright, and trademark infringement.

Marking of Imported Merchandise (Chapter 18)

Country of origin marking carries out the principle of United States trade policy that all imported merchandise be clearly marked to ensure that domestic purchasers can make an informed choice in their selection of merchandise. However, the Customs Service's requirement of marking serves more than the mere function of indicating the merchandise's origin. Among other purposes, depending upon the country of origin or manufacture, that designation signifies the correct rate of duty to be applied, free allowance under GSP, CBI, IFTA, and CFTA, or the meeting of quota requirements.

Chapter 18 gives a detailed treatment of the practical implications of the marking requirements from the importer's standpoint—the complex legal technicalities related to the method and location of marking, merchandise exempted from the requirements, the procedure for compliance, and the procedural consequences of noncompliance apart from the sanctions and penalties imposed.

Quotas and Voluntary Restraint Agreements (Chapter 19)

One of the basic mechanisms through which specific limitations (or quantitative restrictions) are imposed is the quota system. A quota is a limitation on the amount of a designated item that may be imported into the United States. Such controls are placed on imported merchandise by Congress or the executive branch or agencies pursuant to authority delegated by Congress.

Chapter 19 discusses the general categories of quotas, their functions, and their effect. Considerable attention is devoted to the procedural aspects of quotas as administered by the Customs Service or administered by other agencies and enforced by the Service.

Antidumping Duties and Countervailing Duties (Chapter 20)

Chapter 20 details the two most important import relief measures offered to American industries beleaguered by competition from imported merchandise: antidumping duties and countervailing duties. The chapter attempts to guide both American industries seeking to initiate proceedings and foreign industries preparing their defenses.

Unfair Trade Practices, the "Escape Clause," and Other Protection (Chapter 21)

In addition to the protection against unfair trade practices discussed in chapter 20, section 337 of the Tariff Act of 1930, as amended,[88] grants relief for patent infringement and other practices found to be unfair by the International Trade Commission. Section 337 was drafted to provide pro-

88. 19 U.S.C.A. § 1337 (West 1980 & Supp. 1983).

tection additional to that under the antidumping and countervailing duty laws or under such antitrust statutes as section 5 of the Federal Trade Commission Act.[89] Furthermore, section 301 of the Trade Act of 1974, as amended through the Omnibus Trade and Competitiveness Act of 1988, enables the President to impose unilateral trade sanctions against foreign countries engaging in trade practices unfair to legitimate United States trade interests.

Relief under the escape clause in sections 201 to 203 of the Trade Act of 1974[90] is available to a domestic industry when an "article is being imported into the United States in such quantities as to be a substantial cause of serious injury, or the threat thereof, to the domestic industry producing an article like or directly competitive with the imported article."[91] Relief is not dependent upon a finding of unfair trade practices, but rather is granted whenever market disruptions are caused by rapidly increasing imports that are injurious to domestic industries. Chapter 21 focuses on the prerequisites for eligibility for the relief and the procedural requirements for attaining such relief. Finally, considerable protection is afforded the owners of copyrights, trademarks, and trade names. Chapter 21 covers this protection, including relief from pirates and importers of gray market goods.

Administration and Enforcement (Chapters 22–26)

Chapter 22 emphasizes the entry of goods under false pretenses (section 592 penalties), but it also discusses the broad enforcement powers of the Customs Service. Chapter 23 explores the enhanced seizure powers of the Customs Service under the Anti-Drug Abuse Act of 1986 and the

89. 15 U.S.C.A. § 45 (West 1973 & Supp. 1983).
90. Pub. L. No. 93-618, title II, §§ 201–203, 88 Stat. 2011–15 (1975) (codified at 19 U.S.C.A. §§ 2251–2253).
91. 19 U.S.C.A. § 2251(b)(1) (West 1980).

Act's ramifications for importers. Chapter 24 describes rulings by the Service; chapter 25, their administrative appeal; and chapter 26, their judicial review.

Penalties, Searches, Customs Fraud (Chapter 22)

When customs and related laws are violated, the Customs Service generally exercises its enforcement authority by assessing civil penalties, criminal penalties, or both. Also available to the Service is seizure and forfeiture of the imported merchandise.

Although covering all those topics, chapter 22 emphasizes the penalties for fraud, gross negligence, or negligence arising from the entry or introduction of merchandise into the United States by means of material false statements or documents or the omission of material information (section 592 of the Tariff Act of 1930).[92] The procedural aspects of section 592 cases, particularly petitions for remission or mitigation of penalties, are also discussed. The chapter concludes with illustrative case histories of commercial violations and frauds.

Seizure and Forfeiture of Commercial Importations (Chapter 23)

After being largely restricted to contraband or prohibited merchandise, or used as security for penalty payments by absent or insolvent importers, the Customs Service's power to seize imported merchandise and subject it to forfeiture proceedings was greatly expanded under the provisions of an anti-drug law. We explore the background and practical ramifications of this controversial measure, codified at 19 U.S.C. § 1595a(c).

92. 19 U.S.C.A. § 1592 (West 1980 & Supp. 1983).

Administrative Rulings by the Customs Service (Chapter 24)

Administrative rulings on classifications and appraisement prior to an actual importation are available to the importing community upon request. Chapter 24 gives an in-depth exposition of the various categories of Customs Service rulings available to the importing community covering prospective, current, or completed transactions; the effect (binding or otherwise) of the rulings from the different administrative levels (headquarters in Washington, regional commissioners, and selected rulings by the New York region, district directors, or local Customs Service officers); and the procedures for obtaining reviews of the rulings. Significant changes occurred in this area in legislation and regulations in 1988 and 1989.

Protests (Chapter 25)

An interested party (importer, authorized agent, or customshouse broker) dissatisfied with the assessed duties, appraised value of merchandise, classification, exclusion of merchandise from entry, liquidation, or reliquidation of an entry can file a formal protest with the district director whose decision is being contested.

Since the procedural requirements for exercising the right to object to government action are strictly construed, chapter 25 is devoted to the practical considerations of the filing of a protest, such as the time of filing, specificity of content of a protest, procedures for, and availability of, an amendment to claims under a protest, review and disposition of a protest, and availability of further review of a protest.

Mention is also made of procedures whereby an American manufacturer, producer, or wholesaler may contest the appraised value as being too low, or the classification or rate of duty as being incorrect.

Judicial Review of Issues Relating to International Trade (Chapter 26)

Judicial review of administrative decisions (by the Customs Service, the Department of Commerce, and the International Trade Commission), as well as the history of the Court of International Trade, are discussed in chapter 26. The substance and practice of civil actions arising from customs transactions, including the review of protests involving the classification, valuation, or exclusion of merchandise, are discussed.

Conclusion

This chapter has surveyed the legal and administrative framework of United States customs and international trade law more fully developed in the chapters to follow.

2. Uniformity of Customs Procedures Throughout the United States

The Constitution guarantees each person, including every corporation, equal treatment under the laws of the land.[1] Although these basic rights historically have been assumed to apply to importers of foreign merchandise, the Customs Procedural Reform and Simplification Act of 1978[2] specifically includes the following language:

> The Secretary [of the Treasury] shall also provide, to the maximum extent practicable, for the protection of the revenue, the facilitation of the commerce of the United States, and the equal treatment of all consignees of imported merchandise.[3]

The United States Customs Service takes very seriously its obligation under the Constitution to achieve the goal of uniformity of treatment for all importers.

For example, in the complex field of tariffs, the two basic factors upon which duties are calculated are (1) the classifi-

---

1. *See* United States v. Supreme Merchandise Co., 48 Cust. Ct. 714 (1962).
2. Pub. L. No. 95-410, 92 Stat. 888 (1978).
3. *Id.* § 102(a)(1), codified at 19 U.S.C.A. § 1484(a)(2)(D) (West Supp. 1983). The Tariff Schedule Revisions of 1983, Pub. L. No. 97-446, § 201(d)(1)(C), 96 Stat. 2329, 2350 (1983), changed "consignees" to "importers of record."

cation or proper description of the goods under the tariff schedules, which determines the rate of duty, and (2) the appraisement or valuation, which determines the amount of money to which the rate is applied. A large part of this book is devoted to the legal complexities in arriving at those two figures under specific conditions. How does the Customs Service ensure that one importer who enters merchandise at one port of entry in the United States or Puerto Rico pays the same amount of duty as another importer who enters identical merchandise on the same date at a different port? The conscientious importer who pays duty at the nearby port of entry should not have to face a competitor who made trial shipments of foreign merchandise to various ports of entry until it found an idiosyncratically low rate or appraisement, which it then used as a loophole.

In November 1988, Congress mandated the Secretary of the Treasury to effect uniformity in customs determinations.[4] In August 1989, the Customs Service established new regulations aimed at achieving greater uniformity in its responses to ruling requests.[5] These new regulations are addressed in chapter 24.

The requirement of uniformity of treatment extends, of course, to all regulatory aspects, including quotas, restricted and prohibited merchandise, etc. Despite the excellence of the Service's system for achieving this difficult goal—and its considerable success—there do exist instances where the system has failed, primarily because of the human factor of disparate individual judgments and the perennial problem within governmental agencies of budgetary cuts or limitations.

---

4. Anti-Drug Abuse Act of 1988, Pub. L. No. 100-690, 102 Stat. 4181 § 7361 (1988).
5. 19 C.F.R. pt. 177 (1990).

The Customs Information Exchange System

Import specialists have front-line responsibility (1) to ensure uniform assessment of duties under the tariff schedules and (2) to enforce compliance with requirements of legal marking, quota restrictions, antidumping provisions, and prohibitions on the importation of certain articles. In addition, import specialists report violations of laws other than tariff statutes to the administering agencies, including the Drug Enforcement Administration, Federal Trade Commission, Environmental Protection Agency, Consumer Protection Agency, and Food and Drug Administration.

The system for interchange of information among all the import specialists throughout the United States and Puerto Rico is the Customs Information Exchange (CIE), located in the Customshouse, 6 World Trade Center, New York, NY 10048. Most CIE functions are now performed in the office of the national import specialists in New York. There are kept such records as reports of shipments made by import specialists around the country, price lists, catalogs, brochures, reports by customs representatives in foreign countries, currency exchange reports from the Federal Reserve Bank, State Department reports of economic conditions in foreign countries, and other material of that nature. Decisions and rulings by Headquarters, United States Customs Service, are received there and disseminated to the various ports.

When an import specialist at any port outside New York processes a shipment of merchandise for which he has no prior record or only a noncurrent record, he sends a report of the shipment to New York, giving certain basic information. In the report, he also expresses an opinion as to classification, appraisement, any applicable restrictions, etc. A national import specialist at New York then reviews the report, furnishes the sending port any available information, and states an opinion as to the legal questions raised by the report. In the event there is a disagreement between import specialists at different ports that cannot be reconciled after reviews by supervisors, the report is forwarded to Headquarters in Washington for a decision. That ruling, when issued, is disseminated to all ports, or at least to interested ports, for their guidance, and it must be followed, unless changed by Headquarters itself or by a court decision.[6] Because the national import specialist is usually highly specialized in the types of merchandise with which he or she deals, has access to the information from CIE records, and has great experience in and knowledge of trade practices and importations processed, his or her opinion carries much authority and is often followed by other ports and by Headquarters in Washington.

The CIE system makes uniform treatment of all importations an ever-present ideal. Failures to reach the ideal do, however, occur from time to time, causing grief to individual importers. One real problem—which is not truly an exception to the system itself—is that a backlog of work frequently exists both in the port of entry and in New York: it may take many months for information to filter back from New York to the port of entry. An importer may be informed by its local customshouse, orally or even in a "nonbinding" written opinion, that a certain rate of duty applies to certain merchandise. Acting on this information, the importer prices and sells its merchandise. Months later, the import specialist who made the original decision learns from the national specialist at New York that another, higher rate is correct. The entry has not been liquidated,[7] and now the importer is informed of its liability for addi-

6. *See* chapter 26.

7. "Liquidation" is the completion of the transaction of entry of the goods, and may include increasing or decreasing the actual duty. *See* chapter 5.

tional duties. This situation occurs all too often. In ensuing sections of this chapter, we shall see how the importer can protect itself to a great degree from this kind of problem and how Customs has begun to implement new programs to speed up the process.

A "Uniform and Established Practice"

One can imagine the confusion that would result within the American importing community if importers could not depend upon rules that allow them to discover with some degree of certainty the amount of duty that would be levied against entry of specific foreign merchandise. Importers realize that innovations may be hard to price. For repetitive shipments of identical merchandise over long periods of time, however, how can the importer price its merchandise for sale if it is constantly subjected to changed interpretations giving rise to different rates of duty or different appraised values? In view of the complexities in tariff classification and valuation, there is always the danger that new interpretations of existing laws and regulations can have a devastating effect upon the importer's business.

One concept that has been developed to protect the importer against capricious and harmful decisions is the "uniform and established practice." An "established practice" results, in theory, when a specific item of merchandise imported over a long period of time at ports of entry throughout the country has continuously been classified under a uniform rate of duty. Such an "established practice" may be based upon a "binding ruling" issued and published by Headquarters, United States Customs Service and the National Import Specialist's Office.[8]

As a practical matter, it is extremely difficult to obtain

8. See chapter 24.

approval for the position that certain merchandise should not be assessed at a higher rate of duty than before, on the basis that the earlier assessment is a "uniform and established practice." There is no rule of thumb regarding the length of time, frequency, and number of different ports at which entries must be liquidated consistently to create a "uniform and established practice."

The following extracts from a letter sent to an attorney in 1973 by the Director, Classification and Value Division, Headquarters, United States Customs Service, both illustrate the problem and cite leading decisions of the courts that have a bearing on it:

> You further state that before further importations of this merchandise can be classified under item . . . , TSUS, . . . a notice of a change of practice must be published in conformance with sections 16.10 and 16.10(a) of the Customs Regulations.
>
> As support for your position you have submitted a list of 40 entries covering the merchandise imported through the port of . . . during the years 1965 to 1971 which have been classified under item . . . as . . . The dates of liquidations shown for these entries extend from the year 1967 to 1971.
>
> As to the question of what constitutes an established and uniform practice your attention is invited to a decision of the Court of Customs and Patent Appeals in the case of *Washington Handle Co. v. United States*, 34 C.C.P.A. 80 (1946), which held that as many as 28 entries liquidated at two different ports over a period of two years did not create an established and uniform practice. In addition the rule has been laid down by the Supreme Court that for an administrative practice to be even persuasive in a case it must be proved to have been long continued, uniform and general.
>
> Your attention is also invited to the case of . . . decided in 1967, wherein the Customs Court laid down certain salient characteristics of . . . articles which appear to have been ignored at the port of . . . during the years when this merchan-

dise was entered by . . . which throw considerable doubt on the accuracy of the classifications involved.

We do not believe that the liquidations of the entries covering the . . . at the port of . . . constitute an established and uniform practice for the following reasons:

(a) The criteria for what constitutes [named classification of] article set forth in C.D. . . . were not followed.

(b) The administrative practice at [port] to liquidate entries of the subject merchandise under item . . . TSUS, was long continued but cannot be considered uniform and general because only one port was involved.

Although the letter illustrates how difficult it is to obtain a change-of-practice ruling, we must recognize that in the particular case the port of entry failed to follow a court decision when classifying the merchandise and, further, was the only port involved. There is reason to believe that, if the classification had been based upon a new interpretation rather than on an error, and if more than one port had been involved, the forty entries from 1965 to 1971 would have been sufficient to constitute an "established and uniform practice."

A case of interest in this regard is *Siemens America, Inc. v. United States.*[9] This involved approximately 100 entries of certain surge voltage protectors, which were imported over a period of two years at the port of New York. These were assessed under one classification and later changed to a higher rate of duty. The Federal Circuit sustained the Court of International Trade and held that this record was insufficient to create a uniform and established practice, stating:

[T]he record, at best, shows only that for two years, appellants' imported SVPs were uniformly classified at the Port of

9. Siemens Am., Inc. v. United States, 692 F.2d 1382 (Fed. Cir. 1982).

> New York and that, thereafter, they were classified under TSUS item 685.90. Further, as noted by the trial court, appellants failed to prove that they were the sole importer of SVPs and that SVPs were imported solely at the Port of New York.[10]

Thus we see that each situation must stand on its own merits. If an importer is subject to an increase in rate based on a new administrative interpretation after having imported identical merchandise for a reasonably long period of time at a lower rate, and even if its importations have been at only one port, its attorney should raise the question of change of practice. Customs Headquarters would usually determine then which other ports in the United States have received such merchandise, and at what rate or rates the merchandise has been passed. A decision will then be made as to whether the importer is entitled to relief and to the protection of the statute.[11]

With the implementation of the Hamonized Tariff Schedule of the United States (HTSUS), another significant issue is raised. Will published classification rulings and court decisions regarding the classification of specifically defined articles under the older Tariff Schedules of the United States (TSUS) create established and uniform practices for similar treatment under the HTSUS? For example, if an importer had been importing articles termed "shovels" in accordance with a published ruling of Customs specifically describing the importer's articles as "shovels," could Customs now classify these same articles as "spades" for HTSUS purposes, when the HTSUS provides for "shovels" in the same way as the TSUS provision did? Could it do so without at least giving the importer notice that it was intending to do so?

Chances are this question will ultimately have to be de-

10. *Id.* at 1384 (footnote omitted).
11. 19 C.F.R. § 177.10(c) (1990).

cided by the courts. However, importers should be aware that articles which they may feel confident will be defined and treated under the HTSUS as they were under the TSUS may not be so treated. Accordingly, a rose may not be a rose any longer, and an importer may not be so informed until after its entry has been rejected.

The Freedom of Information Act

The Freedom of Information Act (FOIA)[12] is designed to make most government documents easily accessible to the public. Government agencies are required to publish current indexes of final opinions and orders, statements of policy and interpretation, administrative staff manuals and instructions, and the like. They are further required to respond to inquiries for information within ten working days[13] after receiving the request. If the request is denied, and the inquirer appeals, a determination on the appeal must be made by the agency within twenty working days after receiving the notice of appeal.

One of the most important effects of the FOIA has been the pressure on Customs Headquarters to give wide publicity to rulings and decisions that were previously considered purely internal matters. Further, each importer now has a legal basis for demanding copies of existing rulings that may bear on a particular problem the importer may have. The FOIA has significantly advanced the goal of uniformity of treatment on the part of the Service.

We shall not discuss the details of this statute, found in 5 U.S.C. § 552, but shall focus on the type of material ex-

12. As amended, 5 U.S.C.A. § 552 (West 1977 & Supp. 1989).
13. It is the current practice of Customs to respond to FOIA requests initially by letter (within the ten-day limit) indicating receipt of the request and stating that the request will be attended to as quickly as possible.

empted from disclosure, since the exemptions go to the heart of any problem an importer or its representative may encounter in seeking information from the Service, the Department of Commerce, the International Trade Commission, or other governmental departments dealing with any aspect of foreign trade. We have included at the end of this chapter the pertinent customs regulations enumerating the exemptions to disclosure under FOIA. In brief, these regulations enumerate which documents will be found to be exempt from disclosure. Included in these exemptions are those documents which the president has designated as "secret" based on a specific national interest. For example, certain information deemed vital to the nation's defense or foreign policy will be exempt from disclosure. Documents deemed to release information regarding the internal rules and procedures of the Customs Service are also excluded from being disclosed. In addition, documents pertaining to trade secrets, or information which would expose to public view a business's operation or confidential commercial or financial information would likewise be exempt from disclosure. Information contained in Customs import or export documentation (e.g., invoices, entry summaries, etc.) which contain information claimed to be of a privileged or confidential nature, or which contain interagency material are exempt from disclosure as well as material which if released would invade a person's privacy. Finally, information which relates to a Customs investigation will also generally be withheld.

Although there is a history of case law on various aspects of the FOIA, the exemptions pertaining to the availability of interagency or intra-agency memoranda or letters and the exemptions regarding records or information compiled for law enforcement purposes are issues which are often the most relevant to cases involving customs regulations. In addition, parties in a customs dispute at times face the vexing predicament of obtaining or releasing confidential or privileged information involving trade secrets as well as commercial or financial information. Parties to such an action would need to examine the pertinent provisions covering the exemptions regarding interagency and intra-agency information as well as the provisions covering information compiled for law enforcement purposes in light of other FOIA provisions and the Privacy Act.[14]

Interagency or Intra-Agency Memoranda or Letters

An agency claiming a privilege based on the claim that the requested information involves interagency or intra-agency memoranda or letters must show that such information would not be given to a party involved in civil litigation. In short, if a court would order such information turned over to a party involved in a court case, an agency could not claim this material is exempt from disclosure.

The exemption only protects an agency's "predecisional opinions" and opinions which would reveal the agency's "deliberative process."[15] "Predecisional materials" are those generated before the adoption of an agency's policy, and "deliberative materials" are those reflective of the give and take of the consultative process. Thus where the disclosure of factual segments would result in an impairment of the deliberative-decisional process, these segments would be privileged,[16] as are segments which are inextricably intertwined with the policy-making process of an agency.[17]

Regardless of the above exceptions, "exemptions from dis-

---

14. 5 U.S.C.A. § 552a (West 1977 & Supp. 1991). More information might be obtainable via discovery if the dispute reaches the court.
15. Wolfe v. Department of Health & Human Servs., 839 F.2d 768 (D.C. Cir. 1988).
16. Ryan v. Department of Justice, 617 F.2d 781 (D.C. Cir. 1980).
17. Soucie v. David, 448 F.2d 1067, 1078 (D.C. Cir. 1971).

closure are to be construed narrowly and in such a way as to provide the maximum access consonant with the overall purpose of the act."[18] The purpose is "to establish a general philosophy of full agency disclosure unless information is exempted under clearly delineated statutory language."[19]

Therefore, in order for the government to prevail on an exemption concerning the predecisional and deliberative process privilege, it must show that the material in question played a part in the consultative process which determined the resulting decision or policy,[20] and the court must be able to pinpoint the agency decision or policy to which the material contributed.[21]

Records of Information Compiled for Law Enforcement Purposes

The amendment of 1974[22] limited the specific exemption of "investigatory records compiled for law enforcement purposes" and curtailed existing restrictions on disclosure previously upheld by the courts.[23] In addition, the 1974 amendment made it insufficient for an agency to claim an exemption merely by showing that the information requested is in an investigatory file. Therefore, after the 1974 amendment, a record, in order to be exempt, had to be compiled for investigatory and law enforcement purposes. The agency also needed to convince the court that the disclosure of a document will have caused specific harm to

---

18. Vaughn v. Rosen, 484 F.2d 820, 823 (D.C. Cir. 1973), *cert. denied*, 415 U.S. 977 (1974).
19. EPA v. Mink, 410 U.S. 73, 80 (1973) (quoting S. REP. NO. 813, 89th Cong., 1st Sess. 3).
20. Vaughn v. Rosen, 523 F.2d 1136, 1144 (D.C. Cir. 1975).
21. Paisely v. CIA, 712 F.2d 686, 698 (D.C. Cir. 1983).
22. Pub. L. No. 93-502, 88 Stat. 1561 (1974).
23. *See* Center for Nat'l Policy Review on Race & Urban Issues v. Weinberger, 502 F.2d 370 (D.C. Cir. 1974).

the government or an individual before the courts would have upheld an exemption to disclosure. Further, pursuant to the 1974 amendment, even if a document is withheld, any reasonably segregable portions must be provided (after deletion of the confidential material).

The 1986 amendment[24] to subsections pertaining to records or information compiled for law enforcement purposes had the effect of lowering the standards required of an agency to prevail under this exemption. The burden of sustaining the privilege remained on the Customs Service. However, pursuant to the 1986 amendment, Customs need only group the documents in a functional manner so as to permit the reviewing court "to trace a rational link between the nature of the document and the alleged likely interference."[25] Accordingly, Customs would not have to supply a detailed explanation as to how the release of the subject material would interfere with its law enforcement activity. Nonetheless, courts will reject such a privileged claim by Customs if it lacks a factual basis supporting the claimed exception.[26]

Most significantly, the amendment discarded the "investigatory" component formerly required, and extended "records" to include "records or information" compiled for law enforcement purposes. The effect of this change in language was to expand the coverage of the exemption of material deemed to have been compiled for law enforcement purposes to include not only that information compiled for and included in official investigatory records, but also any

24. Anti-Drug Abuse Act of 1986, Pub. L. No. 99-570, §§ 1801–1804, 100 Stat. 3207, 3207-48 to 3207-50 (1986) (Freedom of Information Reform Act of 1986).

25. Gould Inc. v. General Servs. Admin., 688 F. Supp. 689, 703 (D.D.C. 1988) (quoting Bevis v. Department of State, 801 F.2d 1386, 1389 (D.C. Cir. 1986)).

26. Lamont v. Department of Justice, 475 F. Supp. 761, 768 (S.D.N.Y. 1979).

information or documentation gathered in informal or preliminary settings. In addition, Customs may claim the exemption merely by offering proof that such release of information "could" interfere with its enforcement efforts rather than that it "would" so interfere.

As a result of this change in statutory language, more information can be withheld from a requesting party.

The courts have in recent years held the following arguments as valid reasons for withholding information under the claim that such information was compiled for law enforcement purposes:

First, if the information were to be released, it would allow the requesting party to withhold or destroy vital information or enable him to "doctor" his records to shield himself from possible prosecution.

Second, if the information were to be released, it would reveal the source of the information and perhaps inhibit further communications with this source. For example, Customs may have received such information from an informant it may wish to call upon again in the future.

Third, if the source were identified through the released information, harassment or intimidation of this source might result, and thus have "a chilling effect on potential witnesses."[27] In *Alyeska Pipeline Service Co. v. United States Environmental Protection Agency*, the court held that danger of witness intimidation is enough; it need not be shown that it is certain to result.[28] Accordingly, Customs need merely show that the release of the requested information would allow the person requesting the information to threaten the informant or the one giving Customs the information.

---

27. Gould Inc. v., General Servs. Admin., 688 F. Supp. 689, 704 (D.D.C. 1988).
28. Alyeska Pipeline Serv. Co. v. United States Envtl. Protection Agency, 856 F.2d 309, 311 (D.C. Cir. 1988).

Last, if the information were to be disclosed, the size, scope, and direction of the investigation would prematurely be revealed.

A recent Supreme Court case, *John Doe Agency v. John Doe Corp.*,[29] considered whether documents which were not originally created for, but were later "compiled" for, law enforcement purposes are exempt from disclosure. The Court's decision will result in less information being released to a requesting party.

In this case, John Doe Corporation, a defense contractor, had corresponded with the Defense Contract Auditing Agency (DCAA) concerning the corporation's accounting treatment of certain costs. Eight years after this exchange of correspondence, a federal grand jury subpoenaed all of the corporation's documents relating to the cost allocation question raised by the DCAA. The corporation thereupon made an FOIA request of the DCAA for the correspondence. The DCAA denied the request stating that the information was compiled for law enforcement purposes. Thereafter the requested documents were sent to the FBI. The corporation renewed its FOIA request this time to the FBI and was again denied the documents pursuant to the claim that the information was compiled for law enforcement purposes.

The Supreme Court failed to accept the corporation's argument that since the information was originally gathered for a nonlaw enforcement purpose it should not later be exempt from disclosure when it is recompiled for a law enforcement purpose. The Court interpreted the language of the statute to cover documents which are already collected by the government but which were collected for nonlaw enforcement purposes. The Supreme Court held that "documents need only to have been compiled when the response to the FOIA request must be made."[30]

---

29. John Doe Agency v. John Doe Corp., 110 S. Ct. 471 (1989).
30. *Id.* at 477.

Accordingly, the government may invoke the exemption of "records compiled for law enforcement purposes" to prevent the disclosure of documents which were originally gathered by the government for some purpose other than for a law enforcement purpose (at which time the documents would be accessible pursuant to the FOIA) but which are later compiled for a law enforcement purpose.

Trade Secrets and Commercial or Financial Information

"Trade secrets and commercial or financial information obtained from a person and privileged or confidential" are also exempt from disclosure.[31] Individuals have a right to privacy and protection against unwarranted disclosure of confidential or privileged information. Corporations, of course, are not entitled to the same protection as individuals. However, certain information furnished by corporations to the government is protected against disclosure. If confidentiality is desired with respect to information furnished to a government agency, the accompanying cover letter should make a claim for exemption under the FOIA, coupled with a request for notification if the exemption is denied.

Along with the amendments to the FOIA, Congress passed the Privacy Act[32] in 1974. Pursuant to this Act, all records maintained by an agency on an individual are private and may not be disclosed to a third party without the express written consent of the individual. An individual may request access to his or her own records and may also request amendment of any record he or she believes is not accurate, timely, or complete. There are several exceptions

31. 5 U.S.C. § 552(b)(4).
32. 5 U.S.C.A. § 552a (West 1977 & Supp. 1991).

to nondisclosure, the most important being disclosure for a routine use compatible with the purpose for which the records were collected and disclosure for use by another agency for law enforcement purposes. The access provisions of the Privacy Act must also be read in conjunction with the FOIA.

The case of *National Parks & Conservation Association v. Morton*[33] holds that the exemption is valid if disclosure would likely cause substantial harm to the competitive position of the person who submitted the information or is likely to impair the government's ability to obtain necessary information in the future.

Obtaining Information in Practice

Against this broad survey of the essentials of the FOIA and Privacy Act, let us turn to some problems encountered in practice. One of the great difficulties in customs practice was the tremendous work load thrust upon Customs Headquarters for a considerable time following the enactment of the 1974 amendments. Inability of the Service to meet the ten-day deadline forced it to request extended delays, permitted under exceptional circumstances when the agency is exercising due diligence. Although the crisis is over, delays in responding to requests for information still seem to be the rule rather than the exception.

One noted frustration results when incomplete responses are received to requests for information on certain general subjects. For example, a requesting party may have heard that a particular ruling on "assists" exists, which may have a bearing on the party's proposed transaction. However, the requesting party does not know the ruling number or any

33. National Parks & Conservation Ass'n v. Morton, 498 F.2d 765 (D.C. Cir. 1974).

salient particulars about the circumstances described in the ruling. In an effort to secure such a ruling, a requesting party actually confronted with this problem made a request "for all currently effective Headquarters rulings dealing with 'assists.' " (See chapter 4 for a discussion of the meaning of "assists.") The response (after the Service requested the usual delays) consisted of a selected group of "ruling" letters on the subject. How the group was selected is not known, but it is known that it was far from complete. However, in such situations Customs will usually claim that such broad requests lack the specificity necessary for compliance. Customs regulations state that requests must describe records in reasonably sufficient detail so as not to place an unreasonable burden on the Customs Service in locating the requested records. While a specific ruling dealing with "assists" may be easily located if Customs is supplied with a ruling number or is given a detailed description of the nature of the ruling, the wide range of documents included under such a broad subject may be burdensome to locate and the request therefore may be denied.[34]

Even in situations where Customs is responsive to a broad request for documents, as when a party asks for all "assists" rulings, the requesting party cannot be confident that the particular ruling he or she was looking for is among those contained in the response. The ruling in question might have been omitted by Customs, and the requesting party would have no reason to be aware of its absence.

Recently, Customs has taken steps to improve the public's access to rulings. In addition to making rulings available on microfiche, either by subscription or at Customs reading rooms located at Headquarters (and at some ports), Customs has made available computer diskettes that include certain rulings of Customs Headquarters and the National Import

34. 19 C.F.R. § 103.5 (1990).

Specialists Office. It is hoped that, in the future, all manner of Customs rulings and directives will be made available in this or some equally accessible form.

The case of Mr. Crassby (the name is fictitious), an importer of certain food products, illustrates the use of the Freedom of Information Act to protect a client's interests. Mr. Crassby was penalized by the Customs Service for importing merchandise on the basis of an invoice that was false on a technicality.[35] In addition to the technical inaccuracy, the Service asserted that the merchandise was statutorily undervalued, but it did not make a charge of fraud. Prior to writing a petition for mitigation of the penalty, Mr. Crassby's counsel made a request under the Freedom of Information Act for the information that was used as the basis for the contemplated statutory advance in value. The regional commissioner denied the request in the following language:

> By letters dated July 8 and 12, 1977 you requested, pursuant to the Freedom of Information Act, materials in the Investigative Report concerning penalty No. . . . which bears on value advances proposed by Import Specialist. . . . You further requested any documents which show how the appraised value of the merchandise involved in the penalty case was arrived at and evidence of entries by other importers during the period . . . through . . . which concern the importation of . . . into the United States.
>
> Your request is denied for the reason that the subject information is contained in investigatory files compiled for law enforcement purposes and the production of such records would interfere with enforcement proceedings and that furthermore, the information requested, is commercial and financial information obtained from a person and privileged or confidential, and as such is exempt from disclosure pursuant

35. See chapter 22.

> to 5 U.S.C. §§ 552(b)(5) and (7)(A) and 31 C.F.R. 1.2(c)(v) and (vii)(A).
>
> You may appeal in writing within thirty-five (35) days after the date of this notification to the Commissioner of Customs, U.S. Customs Service, 1301 Constitution Avenue, N.W., Washington, D.C. 20229. In the event the Commissioner of Customs should 1) fail to issue a determination of your appeal within twenty (20) working days of its receipt (plus ten (10) additional working days if you are notified in writing that an extension of time is required and applicable) or 2) deny your appeal, you may obtain judicial review pursuant to 5 U.S.C. § 552(a)(4)(B) in the United States District Court for the district in which you reside, or have a principal place of business, or in which the agency records are situated, or in the United States District Court for the District of Columbia.

Following receipt of this letter, a strategy was devised to obtain information desired by (1) appealing the decision, (2) divorcing the request from the entries that were the subject of the penalty and relating it to later entries of identical merchandise that were threatened with the same statutory value advances on the basis of the same information, and (3) restating questions to make a refusal to provide the answers more difficult to defend, as follows:

> Commissioner of Customs
> U.S. Customs Service
> 1301 Constitution Avenue N.W.
> Washington, D.C. 20229
>
> Re: . . .
>
> Dear Commissioner:
>
> Reference is made to subject letter, denying our two requests for information under the Freedom of Information Act. We are hereby appealing this decision in accordance with directions in the letter.

First, we desire to limit our appeal to the entries subsequent to those involved in the penalty case, so that we seek only information bearing on the proposed appraisement of those entries made after. . . . Next, we want to focus in on certain specific information which we feel is not proprietary and which is necessary for us in order to understand the reasons for the higher values.

. . .

The information is as follows:

. . .

We have attempted in this appeal to phrase these questions so nothing proprietary need be revealed, and have purposely kept the information we seek to a minimum so that there should be the least difficulty in your furnishing it.

The points of information sought are not exempt because they are purely factual and not in any way deliberative or advisory; they are not inter-agency or intra-agency memorandums or letters; they are not trade secrets, within the meaning of 5 U.S.C. § 552(b)(5). Nor are these matters as now requested within the exception of (7)(A) for investigatory records as . . . therein.

Pursuant to the above letter, the Commissioner of Customs granted the appeal in the following response:

Dear . . .

This is in reply to letter dated . . . in which you appeal the decision of the Regional Commissioner of Customs . . . denying your two requests for information under the Freedom of Information Act.

It appears that your letter has reformulated and limited the scope of your initial request and the information that you now desire does not include the information denied by the Regional Commissioner. As we understand it, you request the following information:

. . .

Accordingly, we are referring your request for this infor-

> mation to the Regional Commissioner of Customs . . . and instructing him to furnish you with the. . . .
>
> . . .

After the successful appeal and the receipt of the information, the penalty case against Mr. Crassby, despite the technical invoicing violation committed, was cancelled. It became apparent that the penalty was linked to both the contemplated statutory advance in value and the technical violation. Later when counsel was able to add sufficient facts to the information obtained through the appeal and to present legal arguments to the import specialist and his supervisors, the advance in value itself was also abrogated.

This is a good example of the value of legal advice in dealing with government agencies. Mr. Crassby would have been devastated, and quite possibly forced out of business, if he had not taken steps to defend the rights granted to him under the law, and if counsel had not used every legal means to enforce those rights. Further, we must stress that this was all accomplished at administrative levels. Although it is conceivable that the matter would have been ultimately resolved in Mr. Crassby's favor by the courts, the expenses of depositing the additional duties and penalties required, the legal fees attendant upon litigation, and the delays and difficulties of trial would probably have been too much for a small-business man like Mr. Crassby. Justice by way of the courts in these matters is often too time-consuming and expensive for small and medium-sized businesses. If not attainable through administrative action, justice can be denied.

Another example which demonstrates that a tenacious approach must be taken when attempting to obtain vital information from Customs involves an actual attempt to secure a license to operate a bonded warehouse. In this case the application of "Mr. Jones" for a bonded warehouse license was denied by Customs. Pursuant to the FOIA, counsel for

Mr. Jones requested the entire file pertaining to Mr. Jones's license application. When the file was ultimately received certain information was withheld (i.e., various portions of the background investigation report were redacted). Rather than accepting the Customs Service's claimed exemption that the release of the subject information would "constitute an unwarranted invasion of personal privacy," counsel for Mr. Jones wanted to submit to Customs signed releases from Mr. Jones and all of his prospective employees allowing the dissemination of any and all references to them individually in the file in question. As a result Mr. Jones might have learned that one of his prospective employees had a criminal record and that this would have been one of the primary reasons why Mr. Jones had been denied a license to operate a bonded warehouse. Unfortunately, Mr. Jones had decided for reasons of his own simply to abandon his attempts at gaining a license.

For those more determined individuals, it is important to remember that an initial denial by Customs to release requested information need not be accepted as a final disposition of the matter. Furthermore, abandoning one's request prematurely may result in the unwarranted denial of the requesting party's entitlement.

Freedom of Information Act Exemptions 31 C.F.R. § 1.2(c) (1988)

Exemptions. 1. *In general.* Under 5 U.S.C. § 552(b), the disclosure requirements of section 552(c) do not apply to certain matters which are:

(i) (A) Specifically authorized under criteria established by an Executive order to be kept secret in the interest of the national defense or foreign policy and (B) are in fact properly classified pursuant to such Executive order (See 31 CFR, Part 2);

(ii) Related solely to the internal personnel rules and practices of an agency;

(iii) Specifically exempted from disclosure by statute;

(iv) Trade secrets and commercial or financial information, obtained from a person and privileged or confidential;

(v) Inter-agency or intra-agency memorandums or letters which would not be available by law to a party other than an agency in litigation with the agency;

(vi) Personnel and medical files and similar files the disclosure of which would constitute a clearly unwarranted invasion of personal privacy;

(vii) Records or information compiled for law enforcement purposes, but only to the extent that the production of such law enforcement records or information (A) could reasonably be expected to interfere with enforcement proceedings, (B) would deprive a person of a right to a fair trial or an impartial adjudication, (C) could reasonably be expected to constitute an unwarranted invasion of personal privacy, (D) could reasonably be expected to disclose the identity of a confidential source, including a state, local, or foreign agency or authority or any private institution which furnished information on a confidential basis, and, in the case of a record or information compiled by a criminal law enforcement authority in the course of a criminal investigation or by an agency conducting a lawful national security intelligence investigation, information furnished by a confidential source, (E) would disclose techniques and procedures for law enforcement investigations or prosecutions, or would disclose guidelines for law enforcement investigations or prosecutions if such disclosure could reasonably be expected to risk circumvention of the law, or (F) could reasonably be expected to endanger the life or physical safety of any individual;

(viii) Contained in or related to examination, operating or condition reports prepared by, on behalf of, or for the use of an agency responsible for the regulation or supervision of financial institutions; or

(ix) Geological and geophysical information and data, including maps, concerning wells.

2. (i) Whenever a request is made which involves access to records described in § 1.2(c)(1)(vii)(A), and—

(A) The investigation or proceeding involves a possible violation of criminal law; and

(B) There is a reason to believe that the subject of the investigation or proceeding is not aware of its pendency, and disclosure of the existence of the records could reasonably be expected to interfere with enforcement proceedings, the agency may, during only such time as circumstance continues, treat the records as not subject to the requirements of this section.

(ii) Whenever informant records maintained by a criminal law enforcement agency under an informant's name or personal identifier are requested by a third party according to the informant's name or personal identifier, the agency may treat the records as not subject to the requirements of this section unless the informant's status as an informant has been officially confirmed.

(iii) Whenever a request is made which involves access to records maintained by the Federal Bureau of Investigation pertaining to foreign intelligence or counterintelligence, or international terrorism, and the existence of the records is classified information as provided in paragraph (b)(1) of this section, the Bureau may, as long as the existence of the records remains classified information, treat the records as not subject to the requirements of this section.

3. The exemptions set forth in paragraph (c)(1) of this section apply to each of the three categories of information set forth in paragraph (a) of this section.

4. *Segregable portions of records.* Portions of some records may be denied leaving the remaining reasonably segregable portions which must be released to the requester. These portions are released only when the meaning is not distorted by deletion of the denied portions and when it reasonably can be assumed that a skillful and knowledgeable person could not reconstruct the deleted information. When a record is denied in whole, the response advising the requester of that determination shall specifically state that it is not reasonable to segregate portions of the record for release.

5. *Application of exemptions.* Even though an exemption described in paragraph (c)(1) of this section may be fully applicable to a matter in a particular case, a component of the Department of the Treasury may, if not precluded by law, elect under the circumstances of that case not to apply the exemption. The fact that the exemption is not applied by a component in that particular case will have no precedent significance in other cases, but is merely an indication that, in the particular case involved, the component finds no compelling necessity for applying the exemption.

3. Classification Under the Harmonized System

On January 1, 1989, the Harmonized Tariff Schedules of the United States (HTSUS) replaced the previous Tariff Schedules of the United States (TSUS), which went into effect in 1963. Made necessary by the increasing interdependence of the world's trading nations and the creation of new products based upon emerging technologies, the HTSUS is intended to standardize existing commodity classifications, create new categories where needed, and resolve tariff classification differences among countries.

This new system, however, represents only the latest in a number of tariff classification frameworks in the history of the United States.

Historical Basis for the Harmonized System in the United States

Prior to this nation's founding in 1776, several attempts were made by Parliament to impose taxes on trade to the colonies in British North America. The colonists, however, resisted and generally avoided these levies by avoiding the use of the taxed products.

During the Revolutionary War and the postwar confederation period, the individual states imposed discriminatory and arbitrary duties upon each other's products. This practice resulted in tariff anarchy, interstate hostility, and confusion among foreign traders.[1] The founding fathers, therefore, in drawing up the Constitution in 1787, gave primary and ultimate power to the federal government, through the Congress, to regulate interstate commerce and to set tariff rates for goods imported into the United States.

The first Congress in its very first session in 1789 acted upon the powers given it by passing an "Act for Laying a Duty on Goods, Wares, and Merchandise Imported into the United States." The Act listed specific duties on certain enumerated articles, which duties were necessary for the support of the government, for the discharge of the nation's debts, and for the encouragement and protection of manufacturers. The purpose of this tariff was dual, in that it provided the federal government with income to finance its operations and also restricted the importation of specific merchandise from abroad, to protect industry in the United States.

The following century saw depressions and recessions as various tariff acts were implemented, although the beginning of the twentieth century saw an era of relative prosperity. Nevertheless, an economic turn for the worse had begun by the 1920s due largely to the depressed state of agriculture. As a result, Representative Willis C. Hawley of Oregon and Senator Reed Smoot of Utah traded support of higher tariffs on imported industrial goods for increases in agricultural duties.

The Tariff Act of 1930, known as the Smoot-Hawley Tariff, set up the highest tariffs the country had ever experienced. It is considered by many as a regressive step in the history of United States trade relations and is generally

---

1. J. M. Dobson, Two Centuries of Tariffs: The Background and Emergence of the U.S. International Trade Commission, 6 (1976).

viewed by economists as one of the prime causes of the Great Depression of the 1930s.

In addition to the fact that the duty rates imposed by the Tariff Act of 1930 were so high that they greatly reduced U.S. imports, the classification system was extremely cumbersome. The Act divided merchandise into sixteen schedules, and within each schedule were hundreds of long paragraphs listing and grouping merchandise in ways that made it extremely difficult to classify imports. This Act was in effect until 1963, although amendments and treaties had by then modified many of the high duty rates which had stifled trade in the early 1930s.

Near the end of the 1950s, the U.S. Tariff Commission (now the International Trade Commission (ITC)) undertook the restructuring of our classification system by preparing and offering to Congress a new tariff proposal. Known as the Tariff Schedules of the United States (TSUS), the proposal was enacted as the Tariff Classification Act of 1962 and became effective in 1963. The TSUS attempted to simplify tariff classification by dividing the tariff into nine tariff schedules. Within each schedule was a description of every item stated as clearly as possible in order to avoid the difficulties presented by the 1930 Act.

By 1970, it had become apparent that the classification system of the United States was not in conformity with that of its major trading partners. This was creating problems for American exporters with regard to uniform classification of merchandise. As a result, President Nixon in July 1972 asked the Tariff Commission to prepare a draft of the TSUS that would conform to the Brussels Tariff Nomenclature,[2] which ultimately became the Harmonized System. The in-

---

2. The Brussels Nomenclature was the system of Tariff schedules created at the Brussels Convention of Nomenclature of 1950 and used by certain European countries in their classification systems. The HTSUS actually is a combination of the Brussels Nomenclature, the TSUS, and other tariff schedules used by other countries.

tent was to create a new tariff classification system without changing the rates of duty as set out in the TSUS.

The resulting Harmonized Tariff Schedules of the United States (HTSUS) is a truly international system for the uniform classification of goods, conforming to the tariff classification systems of all the major trading countries of the world. Its goal is to simplify the classification of merchandise among increasingly interdependent nations, provide international uniformity of trade data, thereby aiding in formulating marketing strategies, and finally, save importers and exporters both time and money.

By design, the HTSUS was intended to simplify the classification of goods by providing coverage, by name, of new products created since the implementation of the TSUS, by eliminating many of the catchall "basket" provisions[3] found in the TSUS, and by facilitating its easy use by members of the trading community.

To a certain extent this aim has been accomplished. However, there are situations that arise in the context of classifying articles that involve complicated issues, both legal and practical, and that demand superior familiarity and expertise with the workings of the HTSUS.

In addition, it will take some time for the total impact of the new tariff schedules to be felt. After twenty-five years of operating under the TSUS, the trade community must master the intricacies of a new tariff schedule. It remains to be seen how smoothly the transition will be made. As new rulings from Customs are issued and new court decisions are rendered, we will begin to get a clearer picture of how much things have changed and how much they have stayed the same.

---

3. The term "basket provisions" means those classification provisions in the tariff schedules which provide for merchandise using very broad descriptive language rather than language which describes merchandise with great particularity.

It is important to remember that when the TSUS replaced the previous tariff schedules established under the Tariff Act of 1930, it was also the intention of the drafters of the TSUS to eliminate and restrict, where possible, the basket provisions provided for in the old schedules, by adding a significant number of new item categories. Twenty-five years later this leading objective remains a primary reason for the creation and implementation of the HTSUS, and just as the TSUS superseded the prior schedules in an effort to meet this goal of simplification and comprehensive coverage of new articles, so does the HTSUS effectively supersede the TSUS. However, as with the conversion to the TSUS, the conversion to the HTSUS does not mean that every principle of interpretation applicable to the prior tariff scheduled must be abandoned. To the contrary, many of the conceptual principles present in the TSUS will still apply to the HTSUS. For example, the primary rule of construction of tariff acts is to interpret their terms in keeping with the intent of Congress.[4] In determining such intent, courts will look to the statutory language, which is presumed to be used in its ordinary and normal sense.[5] Thus, if there exists a HTSUS subheading specifically covering a particular article such as a table fork, which was similarly provided for in the TSUS and which had been defined by a Customs ruling or court decision to mean a "two, three or four pronged instrument used in eating at table," it appears that an importer may rely upon these interpretations applicable under the TSUS in classifying the same item under the HTSUS. Such consistency in defining terms is also in keeping with the guidelines the President set for the International Trade Commission in its attempts to convert the TSUS into the HTSUS: to avoid changes in the rate of duty on individual products.

4. S&T Imports, Inc. v. United States, 78 Cust. Ct. 45 (1977).
5. B&E Sales Co. v. United States, 9 Ct. Int'l Trade 69 (1985).

In addition to prior rulings and court decisions that set forth various principles of classification and tariff construction under the TSUS, certain other general principles applied under the TSUS will no doubt be applicable under the HTSUS. For example, court decisions and Customs rulings interpreting the "substantial transformation" concept in determining the origin of goods should continue to have precedential effect under the HTSUS. Rulings and court determinations whether goods have been "repaired or altered" for purposes of item 806.20, TSUS should remain applicable for such determinations under the new HTSUS subheading covering these goods (9802.00.40, HTSUS). Likewise, terms such as "further processing" and "assembly" defined for purposes of item 806.30, TSUS, and item 807.00, TSUS should remain applicable for the new HTSUS subheadings covering such goods (9802.00.60, HTSUS and 9802.00.80, HTSUS). Again, as new Customs rulings and court decisions begin to address the proper classification of items under the HTSUS, we will learn exactly which principles will remain from the TSUS and which will be superseded by the HTSUS.

Structure of the New Harmonized Tariff Schedules

The HTSUS is divided into twenty-two sections. Unlike the eight schedules found in the TSUS, the HTSUS is divided into sections that are identified by roman numerals in sequential order. These sections are further subdivided into ninety-nine chapters, identified by arabic numerals in sequential order. For example, Section I is subdivided into chapters 1 through 6. In the United States version of the HTSUS, chapter 77 is blank because the United States has reserved it for "possible future use."

Section XXII is subdivided into chapter 98 (roughly corresponding to schedule 8 of the TSUS) and chapter 99 (roughly corresponding to schedule 9 of the TSUS). Chapter 98 contains special classifications provisions that often deal with duty-free merchandise or merchandise partially exempted from duty: importers should carefully study these provisions. Chapter 99 contains temporary provisions that result from temporary legislation and modifications proclaimed pursuant to trade agreements. Additional import restrictions (such as cheese quotas) also appear in chapter 99. Thus, importers must be familiar with section XXII of the HTSUS.

As in the TSUS, the HTSUS begins with agricultural products and concludes with industrial and high-technology products. In general, the sections of the HTSUS group together articles from similar branches of industry and commerce. For example, section I is Live Animals and Animal Products; section II, Vegetable Products; section V, Mineral Products; section XI, Textiles and Textile Articles. Nevertheless, in about the last third of the HTSUS, commodities are grouped according to their function or use. For example, section XII is Footwear, Headgear, etc.; section XIX, Arms and Ammunition. These groupings are not absolute but rather serve as a guide to the proper classification provision.

The HTSUS utilizes a ten-digit number. The first eight digits are the subheading numbers, and they represent the item; there is also two-digit statistical suffix. Thus, the subheading number for beet sugar is 1701.12.00; if it is not to be further refined or improved in quality, the statistical suffix is added so as to read 1701.12.00.25.

Classification—First Steps

Most writing on the classification of merchandise under the tariff schedules starts with the principles and rules of tariff classification, defining the rules and giving examples of their application. Importers, however, start not with a rule but with an actual article, which must then be classified under a provision of the HTSUS.

Therefore, in an effort to demonstrate the full array of principles involved in classifying articles, we shall proceed in this chapter to classify an article, actually ruled on by Customs, in a way that will involve numerous principles of classification and rules of interpretation under the HTSUS in order to arrive at the appropriate classification.[6]

The importer in this case wished to import a combination tool chest–roller cabinet item purchased in country X.

The article combines a steel cabinet on casters with a steel tool chest, situated on top of the cabinet and connected to it by means of latches; when the latches are released, the tool chest can be removed from the cabinet. In effect, it is two products in one. The cabinet portion opens by way of a hinged door. Its interior contains removable shelves. The tool chest is a box-like container without a handle, also made of steel, designed to hold a variety of tools (e.g., hammer, screwdriver, wrench).

The HTSUS takes a systematic approach to the classification of articles. This necessitates the logical and progressive application of the sections (the groupings of specific chapters), the chapters (the groupings of various materials, products, or articles), the headings corresponding to four-digit numbers (which were referred to in the TSUS as main or superior headings), the subheadings which fall under the headings, the legal notes appearing in the sections and

---

6. This example is similar to an item that was the subject of a ruling request and subsequent decision by Customs Headquarters. *See* HQ 082064, Mar. 16, 1989. A significant difference between our tool chest–cabinet and the one described in HQ 082064 is that the tool chest portion of our article is *latched* to the cabinet portion and thus would not normally be sold separately.

chapters (which define, include, limit, exclude, etc., goods in a section, chapter, heading, or subheading), simultaneously with the General Rules of Interpretation (GRIs).

The GRIs provide the basic principles upon which the uniform classification of goods under the HTSUS is based, and they also provide the necessary direction for the resolution of classification questions whose answers are not apparent from the application of the headings and the legal notes. The first four GRIs are applied in sequential order.

The first step to be taken in arriving at the proper HTSUS classification of our tool chest–cabinet article is to apply the principles of GRI 1. GRI 1 states:

> The table of contents, alphabetical index, and titles of Sections, Chapters and Sub-chapters *are provided for ease of reference only;* for legal purposes, classification shall be determined according to the terms of the Headings and any relative Section or Chapter Notes and, provided such Headings or Notes do not otherwise require, according to the following provisions. . . . (emphasis added)

Our importer, in this case, may have decided that a quick look at the alphabetical index of the HTSUS might prove a good starting point in the effort to classify the tool chest–cabinet article. The importer would remember, of course, that GRI 1 states that the index, as well as the table of contents, titles of sections, etc., is provided for ease of reference only. They may not be looked upon as the final word in classifying items in the HTSUS. In this instance, the importer would have found no mention of "tool chest" in the index. The terms "tool bags" and "tool cases . . . of wood" do appear, but our item is neither a bag nor made of wood. While the term "cabinets" appears, it refers to "refrigerating" or "freezing" cabinets.

The next step would be to check the table of contents in an effort to find a chapter or chapters that provide for items that are used in similar fashion or function in the same way as the tool chest–cabinet. For example, chapter 94 provides for, among other things, "furniture." Although this does not specifically provide for our tool chest–cabinet item, one could say that the cabinet portion of the item functions in the same way as a piece of furniture. Next, the importer would check the section (legal) notes and the chapter (legal) notes to make sure that the item's function is represented and that the tool chest–cabinet is not specifically excluded from the chapter. Examining the notes, the importer would discover that the chapter does provide for items similar to the cabinet portion of the tool chest–cabinet item and that the item is not specifically excluded from coverage. The importer must then search for a chapter heading that is most descriptive of the tool chest–cabinet item. Examining the chapter headings, the importer would discover heading 9403, which covers "other furniture and parts thereof."

Further, at the subheading level, the importer would come upon subheading 9403.20.00, which covers "other metal furniture," which would include the cabinet portion of our tool chest–item, at a duty rate of 4 percent.

If an item cannot be found among the various HTSUS chapters based upon its function, as is the case with the tool chest portion[7] in our example, then an importer must search for a chapter which covers items that consist of the same material as the one he wishes to classify. In this case, the importer would be directed to HTSUS chapter 73, which covers "articles of iron or steel." Again, the importer must verify that the section and chapter notes do not expressly exclude the item and ensure that the chapter covers items made of the same material as the subject item.

7. If the tool chest portion had a handle and was portable, it could be classified in HTSUS subheading 4202.19, which covers trunks, suitcases, and similar containers. *See* HQ 074639 (Feb. 15, 1985) and HQ 087115 (Aug. 31, 1990).

Searching for the Most Specific Heading

In searching the headings for the most specific description of the tool chest portion of the example item, the importer would find only one general heading which applies. Heading 7326 covers "other articles of iron or steel." Further, the search for the most appropriate subheading would lead the importer to subheading 7326.90.90 covering "articles of iron or steel . . . other . . . other," at a duty rate of 2.4 percent. Such generally described headings and subheadings are often encountered when classifying items under the HTSUS. Other examples of items classified by general description include such detailed descriptions as "other made up articles, . . . other . . . other" in subheading 6307.90.95, HTSUS, and such broad descriptions as "Electrical articles, and electrical parts of articles, not specifically provided for" in heading 8543, HTSUS. Such broad provisions as heading 8543 are among the "basket provisions" that apply generally to items which are not specifically provided for elsewhere in the tariff schedules. If, on the other hand, we were attempting to classify an item such as a billiard table, we would find in the alphabetical index a listing for "tables for billiards" and a designation to subheading 9504.20, HTSUS. An examination of this subheading (and the superior heading) will reveal that "billiard tables" are provided for by name. Such provisions which specifically provide for an item by name are called *eo nomine* provisions. When encountering such provisions, importers should note that, unless otherwise specified, names used in *eo nomine* descriptions and all other words of description in the HTSUS are to be given their common or commercial meaning. Sometimes the HTSUS will use scientific names for such things as chemicals or species of wood. Commercial or scientific dictionaries and technical lexicons may be consulted when necessary. As can be seen by our attempts to classify the tool chest and cabinet portions of the example item, not all items are covered so specifically in the HTSUS.

Returning to the attempted classification of our example item, we see that the tool chest, if imported by itself, would be classified under subheading 7326.90.9090, HTSUS,[8] which provides for "articles of iron or steel." The cabinet would be classified under subheading 9403.20.0029, HTSUS, which provides for "other furniture and parts thereof, other metal furniture." However, even though the two components could be imported separately, our importer wished to import these items together as a unit. That is how he intended to sell them and that is how they were designed to be used. Therefore, our importer must examine GRI 1 for further assistance.

Applying GRI 1, the importer would note, from an examination of the language in the pertinent subheadings, that the two distinct components of this item cannot be classified as a unit according to any of the subheadings or relevant section or chapter notes. That is, no single subheading provides for a tool chest–cabinet unit. In fact, there are two separate subheadings which apply to each of the unit's two components and neither of these subheadings is by its terms comprehensive enough to cover both features of this article. Moreover, the notes to each of the chapters covering the two components do not provide any assistance in classifying the unit as a whole. Therefore, as directed by GRI 1, our importer would have to proceed to an examination of the principles in GRI 2.

Classification of Incomplete and Unassembled Articles

GRI 2 contains two clauses, which state:

(a) Any reference in a Heading to an article shall be taken to

8. HQ 082064, *supra* note 6.

include a reference to that article incomplete or unfinished, provided that, as entered, the incomplete or unfinished article has the essential character of the complete or finished article. It shall also include a reference to that article complete or finished (or failing to be classified as complete or finished by virtue of this rule), entered unassembled or disassembled.

(b) Any reference in a Heading to a material or substance shall be taken to include a reference to mixtures or combinations of that material or substance with other materials or substances. Any reference to goods of a given material or substance shall be taken to include a reference to goods consisting wholly or partly of such material or substance. The classification of goods consisting of more than one material or substance shall be according to the principles of Rule 3.

Clearly, the provisions of GRI 2 do not apply to our tool chest–cabinet article.

GRI 2(a) governs the classification of articles that are either incomplete or unfinished. For example, if we were importing a motor vehicle without its wheels, such item would be classified under heading 8703, HTSUS, which would provide for such vehicles as if they were complete with wheels. Likewise, if the motor vehicle were shipped unassembled with all its parts, it would still be classified as if it were assembled, in this same heading.

If, however, the various parts of an item cannot be identified as capable of making an identifiable article, i.e., it no longer has the essential character of a motor vehicle, they cannot be classified as the complete or finished articles (e.g., a motor vehicle without its engine, transmission, wheels, and chassis). In any case, the articles in our example were complete and finished. Therefore, GRI 2(a) was not relevant.

GRI 2(b) was also inapplicable to our example because no question was presented in regard to mixtures and combinations of materials or substances. Accordingly, our importer would have to consult GRI 3 for further directions.

GRI 3 contains three clauses, which state:

> When, by application of Rule 2(b) or for any other reason, goods are, *prima facie*, classifiable under two or more Headings, classification shall be effected as follows:
> (a) The Heading which provides the most specific description shall be preferred to Headings providing a more general description. However, when two or more Headings each refer to part only of the materials or substances contained in mixed or composite goods or to part only of the items in a set put up for retail sale, those Headings are to be regarded as equally specific in relation to those goods, even if one of them gives a more complete or precise description of the goods.
> (b) *Mixtures, composite goods consisting of different materials or made up of different components*, and goods put up in sets for retail sale, which cannot be classified by reference to 3(a), shall be classified as if they consisted of the material or component which gives them their essential character, insofar as this criterion is applicable. [our emphasis]
> (c) When goods cannot be classified by reference to 3(a) or 3(b), they shall be classified under the Heading which occurs last in numerical order among those which equally merit consideration.

Finding the Most Specific Description

GRI 3(a) is designed to cover an item which may appear to consist of two distinct components or materials but which is, in fact, a single item made from one piece of material which nevertheless can be described in more than one HTSUS heading. For example, Customs was presented with a reversible toy item. The item consisted of a single piece of material which could be converted into either a birdlike creature or a ball merely by reversing the body of the item. When in the ball form, the birdlike creature was completely hidden from sight. Likewise, when the bird was displayed, the ball was removed from sight. Accordingly, Customs found this item not to be a composite good consisting of two or more components or materials and thus determined that this single item was classifiable, in accordance with GRI 3(a), in the heading which provided the most specific description. The two provisions applicable to the product were subheading 9503.30.80, HTSUS, providing for "toys representing animals or non-human creatures . . ." at 6.8 percent (which covers the bird) and subheading 9503.49.00, HTSUS, providing for "other toys" also at 6.8 percent (which covers the ball). The first provision being more specific, Customs classified the reversible item under the provision for "toys representing animals."[9]

Accordingly, we see that GRI 3(a) does not apply to composite goods, such as that presented in our example item, because there are two HTSUS headings or subheadings that actually provide for the specific type of composite good we are attempting to classify. It is not a situation in which "two or more Headings each refer to part only of the materials or substances contained in mixed or composite goods. . . ." For example, if the HTSUS included two subheadings, one that provided for "tool chests with cabinets" and another that provided for "articles of steel with furniture," by application of GRI 3(a), the first provision would control since it more specifically describes the item.

Classifying Composite Goods

In our example, the tool chest–cabinet article would be considered composite goods, i.e., an article made of two or

9. In effect, there is little likelihood that the application of GRI 3(a) will be substantially different from the application of General Headnote 10(c) of TSUS, which held that

    1. A description by name is more specific than a description by class (e.g., "steel forks" as opposed to "table articles");
    2. A description that more clearly identifies a product is more specific than one which is less complete (e.g., in classifying a carpet for an automobile, the provision for carpets and other textile floor coverings is more specific than parts and accessories of motor vehicles).

more different components, as provided for in GRI 3(b): "Composite goods consisting of different components . . . which cannot be classified by reference to 3(a) shall be classified as if they consisted of the material or component which gives them their essential character. . . ." It is clear that when items are made up of different components that are physically attached, such items are included in the term composite goods. However, in our example, the tool chest component may be separated from the cabinet component. The question then arises, does the term composite goods include articles made up of physically separable different components? The answer can be found in the explanatory notes to the HTSUS. The explanatory notes generally provide further guidance as to how goods should be classified under the HTSUS. Although not legally binding, Customs refers to the explanatory notes for assistance in classification and has stated that such notes will be consulted in interpreting HTSUS tariff provisions.[10]

An examination of the explanatory notes pertinent to our example indicates that composite goods consisting of different components will include items whose components may

10. In addition to the consideration given to the explanatory notes, Customs, when determining tariff classification, will give "considerable weight" to the compendium of classification opinions which "officially interpret" the tariff schedules. The Customs Cooperation Council (CCC) published the compendium. These opinions are issued by the Harmonized System Committee (HSC) (the committee charged with the administration of harmonized system nomenclature) regarding the proper classification of various products that were presented to the HSC. When such a decision is considered particularly instructive it is published in the compendium. Further, Customs will refer to the Harmonized System Committee Reports in determining the intent behind the various HTSUS provisions. See T.D. 89-80, 23 Cust. B. & Dec. 36 (1989) for a more complete analysis of the weight accorded by Customs to the various types of documents generated by the CCC to interpret the HTSUS.

be physically separated but which are adapted to one another and are mutually complementary.[11]

Accordingly, as stated in GRI 3(a), "when two or more Headings each refer to part only of the materials or substances contained in mixed or composite goods," those headings are to be regarded as equally specific in relation to those goods, even if one of them gives a more complete or precise description of the goods. In a case like our tool chest–cabinet article, where each of two headings does refer to only one of the constituent elements of the composite goods, the competing headings are thus regarded as equally specific in relation to the goods. Therefore, our importer would have to proceed to GRI 3(b) and a determination of which component of the subject article gives the entire unit its "essential character," if such a determination is possible.

Essential Character

By application of GRI 3(b), the goods become classifiable as if they consisted wholly of the component which gives them their essential character. The concept of essential character is not new. However, this concept is subjective and not easily defined, and the factors that determine essential character will vary between different kinds of goods.

Application of the essential character concept in the HTSUS is perhaps the most significant change from the way goods were classified under the TSUS. Under the TSUS, articles like the tool chest–cabinet item in our example were often classified by applying the "more than" concept.

11. Explanatory notes to GRI 3 state that "composite goods made up of different components shall be taken to mean not only those in which the components are attached to each other to form a practically inseparable whole but also those with separable components, provided these components are adapted to one another and are mutually complimentary and that together they form a whole which would not normally be offered for sale in separate parts."

For example, under the TSUS, a device for controlling the heat in an electric oven, consisting of a combination of a mechanical switch and a thermostat, was held to be properly classifiable as a part of a cooking stove or range. The device was not adequately described as either a "switch" or a "thermostat," because both of these parts are important in its operation. A third, more general TSUS provision therefore becomes applicable.[12]

Generally, under the TSUS, when an item was made up of two or more components, it would be regarded as "more than" any of those components, and most likely would be classified in a basket provision rather than in one of the provisions specifically covering any of the item's components. The "more than" concept does not have application under the HTSUS. Therefore, when an importer is presented with an item made up of various materials or components and that item *as a unit* cannot be classified with reference to the HTSUS notes or headings, the importer must seek to determine which component or material gives the entire item its essential character.

Explanatory note 3(b)(VIII) to GRI 3(b) enumerates the factors for establishing essential character. They include bulk, weight, value, quantity, and the role of a constituent material or component.

Most important among these factors is the determination of which component or material is most vital to the realization of the item's use or functions.[13] In regard to textiles consisting of more than one material, Customs will usually classify the item according to the material which predominates by weight over any other single material. However,

---

12. Harper-Wyman Co. v. United States, 1 Ct. Int'l Trade 108 (1981).
13. The U.S. Customs publication entitled *Harmonized System Handbook* states in pertinent part that "the essential character of a product has generally been construed to mean the attribute which strongly marks or serves to distinguish what an article is; that which is indispensable [sic] to the structure, care or condition of the article."

there is no general rule that such goods must be classified according to chief weight.

If no single component or material gives an item its essential character, then GRI 3(c) applies, and the items will be classified "under the Heading which occurs last in numerical order among those which equally merit consideration."

Classifying Composite Goods When Essential Character Cannot Be Determined

In our example, neither the tool chest nor the cabinet can be said to impart the "essential character" of the unit.[14] No one component dominates the other in terms of the factors listed in explanatory note 3(b) (VIII) to GRI 3(b). While the cabinet provides the unit with more bulk and weight, the tool chest probably has the greater role in the unit's function as a storage compartment and transporter of tools. Accordingly, the goods in question cannot be classified by reference to either GRI 3(a) or GRI 3(b), since the applicable HTSUS heading covering each of the article's two components equally merits consideration, and neither component can be said to impart the "essential character" of the combined unit. Therefore, our importer would proceed to a consideration of GRI 3(c).

By virtue of GRI 3(c), the goods are classified under the heading which occurs last in numerical order among those which equally merit consideration; that is, the heading identified by the highest number.

Consequently, the tool chest–cabinet article in our example would be classified pursuant to subheading 9403.20.00, HTSUS, at a duty rate of 4 percent, rather than pursuant to subheading 7326.90.90, HTSUS, which provides for a duty rate of 2.4 percent.

---

14. See HQ 082064, *supra* note 6.

Classifying Articles with Articles to Which They Are Most Akin

If, in our example, the tool chest–cabinet article could not be classified according to the principles enunciated in GRIs 1 through 3, we would then be required to classify this article according to the principles in GRI 4. GRI 4 states: "Goods which cannot be classified in accordance with the above Rules [GRI 1 through 3] shall be classified under the Heading appropriate to the goods to which they are most akin."

This rule provides for the classification of goods that are similar to the goods to which they are most akin. It is the last resort in classification and applies only where all other rules have failed. It is anticipated that this rule will see little application. However, when it is applied, the determination should be made on the basis of a comparison of factors such as materials, intended use, designation, production process, and the nature of the goods.

For example, the Customs Cooperation Counsel (CCC) was faced with the problem of classifying "wine coolers." Keeping in mind that certain wine-producing member countries of the HTSUS were reluctant to have such items classified as wine, the CCC went about the task of classifying this mixture of spirits and fruit juices. It could not be classified according to GRI 1 because no HTSUS heading specifically covered the item. Chapter 22 contains headings which apply to wine, but no heading specifically covers the wine-juice mixture. While chapter 20 contains headings which apply to juice, it does not specifically provide for the juice-wine mixture. GRI 2(a) did not apply, since the item was finished and complete. GRI 2(b) directed that the mixture be classified according to GRI 3, since GRI 2(b) states "the classification of goods consisting of more than one material or substance shall be according to the principles of Rule 3." GRI 3(a) (stated previously on page 82) was not applicable, since the HTSUS headings covering each ingredient were equally specific. GRI 3(b) (stated previously on page 82) was not applicable, because it was impossible to determine which ingredient gave the item its essential character. However, when it came to application of GRI 3(c) (stated previously on page 82), the CCC determined that none of the headings in chapter 22 (covering beer, wine, etc.) merited consideration. The reason for such a determination, we can only surmise, was to prevent the classification of the item as wine in deference to the concerns of the wine-producing members of the HTSUS. Accordingly, the CCC went to GRI 4 and classified the item in what is now heading 2207, covering "other fermented beverages" (e.g., cider), as being the item most akin to the wine cooler.

Additional General Rules of Interpretation

In addition to the four GRIs discussed above, the HTSUS enumerates two more GRIs (the last of the international rules). The latter are not to be applied sequentially as are GRI 1 through 4.

Containers

GRI 5[15] provides in pertinent part that cases, boxes, and similar containers imported with the articles for which they

15. GRI 5 states:

> In addition to the foregoing provisions [GRI 1 through 4], the following Rules shall apply in respect of the goods referred to therein:
>
> (a) Camera cases, musical instrument cases, gun cases, drawing instrument cases, necklace cases and similar containers, specially shaped or fitted to contain a specific article or set of articles, suitable for long-term use and entered with the articles for which they are intended, shall be classified with such articles when of a kind normally sold therewith. The Rule does not, however, apply to containers which give the whole its essential character;

are intended should be classified with such articles if they are of a kind normally sold with them (for example, gun cases, musical instrument cases, camera cases, etc.). The rule does not apply to containers which give the whole its essential character or to packing materials and containers suitable for repetitive use. For example, a Tiffany glass bowl filled with popcorn and a Baccarat crystal wine decanter filled with cheap wine would not normally be considered the usual containers for such items. The disparity between the cost of the containers and their contents and the likelihood that the containers in these examples would be reused would indicate that the containers give the units their essential character. Therefore, the Tiffany bowl and the Baccarat decanter would be classified separately from the popcorn and the wine, respectively.

Uniformity

GRI 6[16] is the last general rule of interpretation and it is intended to ensure uniformity at the subheading level. GRI 6 provides that the classification of articles described in the subheadings shall be based on the terms of the subheading and any relevant legal notes and that the GRIs apply as well. This rule further provides that only subheadings at

---

(b) Subject to the provisions of Rule 5(a) above, packing materials and packing containers entered with the goods therein shall be classified with the goods if they are of a kind normally used for packing such goods. However, this provision does not apply when such packing materials or packing containers are clearly suitable for repetitive use.

16. GRI 6 states:

For legal purposes, the classification of goods in the Subheadings of a Heading shall be determined according to the terms of the Subheadings and any related Subheading Notes and, *mutatis mutandis*, to the above Rules, on the understanding that only Subheadings at the same level are comparable. For the purposes of this Rule, the relative section, Chapter and subchapter Notes also apply, unless the context otherwise requires.

the same level (appearing equally indented from the same superior heading in the schedules) are comparable.[17]

Use Descriptions

Under the HTSUS, the classification of items based upon how they are used is a rarity. However, there are instances when use becomes a critical factor in the classification of an item under HTSUS. When such an occurrence presents itself importers must look to the additional U.S. rules of interpretation. These rules are applicable only in the United

---

17. The explanatory notes to GRI 6 state the following:

I. Rules 1 to 5 above govern, *mutatis mutandis*, (meaning "with the necessary changes having been made," e.g. when applying GRI 1 at the Subheading level the "necessary change" to be made is the substitution of the term "Subheading" for the term "heading" thereby making GRI 1 at the *Subheading* level read, " . . . classification shall be determined according to the terms of the Subheadings . . .") classification at Subheading levels within the same Heading.

II. For the purposes of Rule 6, the following expressions have the meanings hereby assigned to them:

a. "Subheadings at the same level": one-dash Subheadings (level 1) or two-dash Subheadings (level 2).

Thus, when considering the relative merits of two or more one-dash Subheadings within a single Heading in the context of Rule 3(a), their specificity or kinship in relation to a given article is to be assessed solely on the basis of the texts of the competing one-dash Subheadings. When the one-dash Subheading that is most specific has been chosen and when that Subheading is itself subdivided, then, and only then, shall the texts of the two-dash Subheadings be taken into consideration for determining which two-dash Subheading should be selected.

b. "unless the context otherwise requires": except where Section or Chapter Notes are incompatible with Subheading texts or Subheading Notes.

This occurs, for example, in Chapter 71 where the scope assigned to the term "platinum" in Chapter Note 4(b) differs from that assigned to "platinum" in Subheading Note 2. For the purpose of interpreting Subheadings 7110.11 and 7110.19, therefore, Subheading Note 2 applies and Chapter Note 4(b) is to be disregarded.

III. The scope of a two-dash Subheading shall not extend beyond that of the one-dash Subheading to which the two-dash Subheading belongs; and the scope of a one-dash Subheading shall not extend beyond that of the Heading to which the one-dash Subheading belongs.

States and as such are not binding internationally. U.S. Rule 1(a) states:

> In the absence of special language or context which otherwise requires—
> (a) a tariff classification controlled by use (other than actual use) is to be determined in accordance with the use in the United States at, or immediately prior to, the date of importation, of goods of that class or kind to which the imported goods belong, and the controlling use is the principal use. . . .

Actual Use

There are only four subheadings in the HTSUS that apply the actual use concept. Subheadings 5101.11.10 and 5101.19.10, HTSUS, both employ the words "wool for special uses." Such words require that the merchandise described shall be directly used for the purpose specified in the description. If that and other conditions are met, the entry is usually duty-free, without regard to the principal use of the entire class of goods.

The other HTSUS provisions which apply the actual use concept are subheadings 9817.00.50 and 9817.00.60, HTSUS, covering machinery, equipment, and implements to be used for agricultural or horticultural purposes and parts to be used in such articles.

If an importer wishes to take advantage of one of these actual use provisions, the following requirements must be met:

1. The described use must be intended at the time of importation and a declaration to that effect must be filed with the Customs Service at the time the merchandise is entered.
2. The merchandise must, in fact, be used for the intended purpose.
3. The importer must furnish the Customs Service with proof that the merchandise was so used within three

years of the date of entry. Entry will not be liquidated until that proof is provided.[18]

If the conditions are not met, the goods will be liquidated under a dutiable provision (for the specific heading or subheading covering such goods) usually carrying a rate of duty as against the free provision. Such "actual use" provisions represent one of the infrequently encountered special conditions in which identical merchandise can be rated in two different ways under the tariff schedules.

Principal Use

The concept of principal use replaces the "chief use" concept of the TSUS. Chief use under the TSUS was determined to mean the predominant normal use of the article (or articles of its class and kind) throughout the United States at the time of the article's importation. Chief use therefore required that an item's use *exceed all other uses combined*. For example, if an article has three uses, the chief use would be that use which predominates over all the other uses combined, so that if use 1 exceeds uses 2 and 3 combined it will be considered the article's chief use. Under the principal use concept, principal use is that use which *exceeds any other individual use*. For example, if an article has three uses, the principal use would be that use which predominates over any one of the other uses, so that if use 1 exceeds uses 2 and 3 individually it will be considered the article's principal use.

Since the language describing principal use is similar to the TSUS definition of chief use, determinations of such

18. U.S. Rule 1(b) states: "a tariff classification controlled by the actual use to which the imported goods are put in the United States is satisfied only if such use is intended at the time of importation, the goods are so used and proof thereof is furnished within 3 years after the date the goods are entered."

use may prove to be as difficult as the determination of chief use under the TSUS.

An example of a principal use provision in the HTSUS is found in additional U.S. Note 3 to chapter 27's definition for motor fuel as "any product derived primarily from petroleum, shale or natural gas, whether or not containing additives, which is principally used as a fuel in internal combustion or other engines."

Parts

U.S. Rule 1(c) provides that the term "parts" encompasses products solely or principally used as parts but shall not prevail over a specific provision for such part.[19]

There are special pointers to observe on the importation of parts of merchandise. Unless a tariff description specifically includes a provision for parts of the described article, parts of the article cannot be classified under the provision. Usually when parts are included, the statutory text will contain such language as "and parts thereof" following the main description. In the absence of "parts" language, the part may be specifically provided for elsewhere (e.g., switches), or a basket provision may apply (e.g., articles of plastic not specially provided for).

Customs has also enumerated, in its seminars on the HTSUS, the following criteria for determining whether an item is a part:

1. Generally, an article is a part if it cannot be used on its own.
2. A part must be combined with other articles to be used.

---

19. U.S. Rule 1(c) states: "a provision for parts of an article covers products solely or principally used as a part of such articles but a provision for "parts" or "parts and accessories" shall not prevail over a specific provision for such part or accessory."

3. A part must be identifiable by shape or other characteristics as an article solely or principally used as a part.
4. A part must be an integral, constituent, or component part, without which the article to which it is joined could not function.
5. A part lends to the safe and efficient operation of the article.

Definitions

The HTSUS contains both qualified definitions (applicable only in the context in which they appear)[20] and unqualified definitions (applicable throughout the HTSUS). It is important to note that an HTSUS unqualified definition can appear in any chapter or section note, and its coverage need not be limited to that chapter or section. For example, in legal note 1 to chapter 39, the following unqualified definition appears:

> Throughout the tariff schedule the expression "*plastics*" means those materials of Headings 3901 to 3914 which are or have been capable, either at the moment of polymerization or at some subsequent stage, of being formed under external influence (usually heat and pressure, if necessary with a solvent or plasticizer) by molding, casting, extruding, rolling or other process into shapes which are retained on the removal of the external influence.
>
> Throughout the tariff schedules, any reference to "*plastics*" also includes vulcanized fiber. The expression, however, does

20. For example, note 3 to chapter 42 states: "For the purposes of Heading 4203, the expression 'articles of apparel and clothing accessories' applies, inter alia, to gloves (including sports gloves), aprons and other protective clothing, braces, belts, bandoliers and wrist straps, but excluding watch straps (Heading 9113)."

not apply to materials regarded as textile materials of section XI.[21]

---

21. Other examples of unqualified definitions include:

Legal Note 1, Chapter 54:
Throughout the Tariff Schedule:
a. "Wool" means the natural fiber grown by sheep or lambs;
b. "Fine animal hair" means the hair of alpaca, llama, vicuna, camel, yak, Angora, Tibetan, Kasmir or similar goats (but not common goats), rabbit (including Angora rabbit), hare, beaver, nutria or muskrat;
c. "Coarse animal hair" means the hair of animals not mentioned above, excluding brush making hair and bristles (heading 0502) and horsehair (heading 0503).

Legal Note 1, Chapter 54:
Throughout the Tariff Schedule, the term "man-made fibers" means staple fibers and filaments of organic polymers produced by manufacturing processes, either:
a. By polymerization of organic monomers, such as polymerism, polyesters, polyurethanes or polyvinyl derivatives; or
b. By chemical transformation of natural organic polymers (for example, cellulose, casein, proteins or algae), such as viscose rayon, cellulose acetate, cupro or alginate.

Legal Note 3, Chapter 60:
Throughout the Tariff Schedule, any reference to "knitted" goods includes reference to stitch-bonded goods in which the chain stitches are formed of textile yarn.

Legal Note 5, Chapter 70:
Throughout the Tariff Schedule, the expression "glass" includes fused quartz and other fused silicia.

Legal Note 7, Chapter 71:
Throughout the Tariff Schedule, the expression "metal clad with precious metal" means material made up with a base of metal upon one or more surfaces of which there is affixed, by soldering, brazing, welding, hot-rolled or similar mechanical means, a covering of precious metal. Except where the context otherwise requires, the expression also covers base metal inlaid with precious metal.

Legal Note 2, Chapter 41:
Throughout the Tariff Schedule, the expression "composition leather" means only substances of the kind referred to in Heading 4111.

Accordingly, a careful reading of all the relevant sections and chapter notes must be made before attempting to classify a particular article. It would be easy to overlook a legal note containing a definition that has applicability elsewhere in the schedules. However, the consequence may well be the misclassification of that article.

Textile Mixtures

When classifying items made up of a mixture of textile materials, importers must apply U.S. Rule 1(d), which states that "the principles of Section XI regarding mixtures of two or more textile materials shall apply to the classification of goods in any provision in which a textile material is named."

U.S. Rule 1(d) further provides that articles of named textile materials which are classified as "of textile materials" will be classified in accordance with the provision of note 2 to section XI.

This note states that articles composed "of a mixture of two or more textile materials are to be classified as if consisting wholly of the textile material which predominates by weight over each other single textile material." For example, a textile suitcase with an outer surface composed of textile material which is *by weight* 60 percent man-made fiber and 40 percent cotton fiber would be considered a

---

Legal Note 1, Chapter 40:
Except where the context otherwise requires, throughout the Tariff Schedule, the expression "rubber" means the following products, whether or not vulcanized or hard: natural rubber, blatta, gutta-percha, quayle, chicle and similar natural gums, synthetic rubber, factice derived from oils, and such substances reclaimed.

suitcase of man-made fiber. Thus, the *value* of the respective component materials is irrelevant.

Problems with Classifying Sets

In our discussion earlier in this chapter of the classification of the tool chest–cabinet item, we touched upon some of the classification principles that arise when an importer is faced with the problem of classifying composite goods. Our example led us through the application of GRIs 1, 2, and 3, until we were able ultimately to resolve our classification problem pursuant to the principles of GRI 3.[22]

GRI 3 also comes into play when faced with the problem of classifying "goods put up in sets for retail sale." The

---

22. The tool chest–cabinet article used in our classification example was based upon an article that Customs had, in HQ 087115, classified as a cabinet ("other furniture and parts thereof . . .," 9403.20.00, HTSUS).

In another ruling, HQ 082064, Customs classified a similar tool chest–cabinet article as a cabinet, also applying the principles of GRI 3(c) (classifying items "under the Heading which occurs last in numerical order among those which equally merit consideration"). However, in that case, the limited analysis of GRI 3(b) by Customs resulted in a finding that the particular article under consideration was a set, not a composite good. Although that analysis made no practical difference in the ultimate classification of the article (i.e., the article was classified as a cabinet pursuant to GRI 3(c)), we imparted certain physical characteristics to the article in our example that were not present in the articles described in HQ 087115 and HQ 082064 in order to provide a better illustration of the application of GRI 3(b) to the classification of goods.

In still another case, Customs ruled in HQ 084717 that a toolbox-cabinet article was classified in HTSUS subheading 4202.99, which provides for "trunks, suitcases, . . . and similar containers," because the toolbox portion of the article had a handle and was found to impart to the toolbox-cabinet unit its essential character.

explanatory notes to GRI 3 set forth the following criteria to be used in defining sets:

(a) a set must consist of at least two different articles
(b) which are prima facie classifiable in different headings;
(c) a set must also consist of products or articles put up together to meet a particular need or to carry out a specific activity; and
(d) sets must be put up for sale directly to users without repacking.

Thus, to be regarded as a set under the HTSUS, a product must meet all of the above conditions. Merely packaging various items together for retail sale does not mean that the product will be considered to be a set. For example, Customs has ruled that a five-piece luggage product consisting of two suitcases, two shoulder tote bags, and a small travel bag all packaged together for retail sale would be considered a set,[23] while a "golfer's kit" consisting of a towel, brush, nylon cloth, cleaning solution used for treating and cleaning golf clubs, and a can of powder used to enhance a golfer's grip, packaged together for retail sale, would not be a set.[24] It was the conclusion of Customs that neither of these example sets would be classifiable according to GRI 1, since no subheading would specifically provide for classification of these items contained in such combination. GRI 2(a) would not apply, since both products are complete and finished; GRI 2(b) would also be inapplicable, because no question arises, in either case, of headings referring to materials on substances. Customs further found that the provisions of GRI 3(a) would apply to both products, since in each situation two or more headings each refer to only part of the items in each group of items put up for re-

---

23. HQ 082171 (Oct. 17, 1988).
24. See J. BUNIN, LIVING IN HARMONY: "ADVENTURES IN GRI (3)" (1989) (unpublished Customs paper).

tail sale. As discussed previously in this chapter, GRI 3(a) states that

> when two or more Headings each refer to part only of the materials or substance contained in mixed or composite goods or to part only of the items in a set put up for retail sale, those Headings are to be regarded as equally specific in relation to those goods, even if one of them gives a more complete or precise description of the goods.

Accordingly, each subheading would be regarded as equally specific. However, the "golf kit" would not be considered to be a set under GRI 3, since the explanatory note 3 to GRI 3 requires that a set consist of products put up together to "meet a particular need or carry out a specific activity." While the towel, brush, cloth and cleaning solution would all be used to carry out the specific activity of cleaning golf clubs, the powder, Customs points out, is dedicated to a different function, i.e., to enhance a golfer's grip on the club handle. The suitcase product would be considered a set because each item fulfills the particular activity of holding personal articles when someone is traveling. In addition, these items were intended to be sold together (i.e., they were made of the same material, were the same color, and were styled alike). Customs has also decided that even if some of the items within a grouping are dedicated to a single function (e.g., the cleaning items in the golf kit), an importer may not, in effect, break out the smaller group of items from within the larger grouping and treat the smaller group as a set.

By having several items classified as a set, an importer may reap certain economic advantages. For example, if an importer packages items *X*, *Y*, and *Z* together as a set and item *X* is determined to impart the unit's essential character (or if the set's essential character cannot be determined and item *X* is classified last in the HTSUS), then the entire set will be classified under the subheading covering item *X* and the duty rate covering item *X* will be used notwithstanding the fact that the duty rates for items *Y* and *Z* are greater.

Special Programs Relating to Classification

While the HTSUS attempts to describe merchandise as precisely as possible under several thousands of provisions, and provides numerous guiding principles such as the GRIs and interpretive aids such as the explanatory notes to ensure the proper classification of items, conflicts and problems still arise. The proper classification of merchandise may involve questions of law, questions of fact, and mixed questions of law and fact. The interpretation and application of the tariff statutes today is the result of interpretations by many bodies of many pieces of legislation since the founding of the republic.

In an effort to afford the trading community greater security in the classification of its products, Customs has instituted two programs—the pre-entry classification program and the binding ruling program—so that importers and other interested parties (such as foreign vendors) can obtain written binding tariff classifications on their line of merchandise.[25]

The pre-entry classification program is administered by the National Import Specialists (NIS) in New York or by the Deputy National Import Specialists (DNIS) who may be located at various ports of entry throughout the country. The program involves the review and examination of the importer's line of merchandise by the NIS or DNIS and the issuing of written tariff classifications. By participating in the pre-entry classification program, Customs agrees to be bound by its written tariff classifications at all ports of entry. These classifications are binding unless reviewed and

25. For a more detailed discussion on the pre-entry and ruling program see chapter 24.

revoked by the Office of Regulations and Rulings at Customs Headquarters, Washington, D.C. Even then Customs will not apply the new detrimental classification for ninety days if an importer can prove he has relied on the ruling when placing orders.[26]

By participating in the pre-entry classification program, the importer agrees to enter all shipments according to Customs pre-entry classification; to notify the broker(s) of the classifications; and to advise Customs on any changes or modification that are subsequently made to articles that have already been classified under the pre-entry program.

Customs has indicated that importers do not give up their protest rights on tariff classifications by participating in the pre-entry classification program. However, importers are required to enter their merchandise at the higher rate of duty until the protest has been reviewed at higher levels in Washington, D.C. The Customs Service's form letter to importers that outlines its position on the pre-entry classification program is reprinted at the end of this chapter.

The binding tariff classification ruling program provides an importer with the Customs Service's written *binding positions* on the imported articles' classification. The rulings are issued by the NIS in New York or by attorneys at the Office of Regulations and Rulings in Customs Headquarters. The ruling program is limited to prospective transactions (that is, transactions which are not already pending before a Customs Service office by reason of arrival, entry, or otherwise).

In order to obtain a binding tariff classification ruling from Customs, an importer can make written application at any district where the importer has reason to do business. A full description of the merchandise and a sample (if possible) is provided to Customs. Then Customs will issue its

---

26. See discussion on procedures involved when Customs revokes prior rulings in chapter 24.

ruling. The target turn-around time for a binding ruling is 30 days, or 120 days if Headquarters is involved. Customs limits ruling requests to five items of the same class or kind of merchandise. The rulings are binding on all Customs officials unless reviewed and revoked by Headquarters in Washington, D.C. Again, an importer does not give up his right to file a protest by participating in the binding tariff classification ruling program.[27]

Although it is prudent for an importer to resolve ambiguities or conflicts administratively through pre-entry classification or binding rulings from Customs before importation, that is not always feasible. If administrative remedies have been exhausted and the ambiguity or conflict remains, the courts may be the final arbiters.

Finally, a provision of the tariff schedules that harms the interests of a substantial part of the economy may be attacked at its source. An interested domestic group, association of importers, or individual party may petition Congress through the International Trade Commission to change or delete the provision. If the provision does not or should not reflect the intent of Congress, and if the petition is pressed with adequate support, the petition may be successful.

27. See discussion on obtaining binding rulings from Customs in chapter 24.

DEPARTMENT OF THE TREASURY
U.S. CUSTOMS SERVICE
NEW YORK, N.Y.

Dear _______________:

Thank you for your interest in the pre-entry classification project. In an effort to avoid confusion, the following outline will clarify the obligations placed on both you and on the U.S. Customs Service.

The U.S. Customs Service agrees to the following: all pre-entry classifications given by the National Import Specialist (NIS) or Deputy National Import Specialists (DNIS) will be binding on both the U.S. Customs Service and the importer. Entry of merchandise will be accepted at all ports of entry at the classification provided by the NIS/DNIS. U.S. Customs will notify all expected ports of entry of the pre-entry classification decision. All Customs rulings will be binding unless revoked by the Office of Regulations and Rulings. If the revocation is detrimental to the importer and the importer can prove he relied on the ruling, Customs will not apply the new classification for ninety (90) days.

By agreeing to participate in this program, you have also agreed to the following: notifying U.S. Customs of any changes, alterations, or modifications made to the items which were pre-entry classified; enter all shipments according to pre-entry classification advice; notifying your brokers of the pre-entry classification and requiring them to use these classifications; and assuring that all your employees involved in Customs transactions are aware of the correct pre-entry classifications. The pre-entry classification you have received is binding only for your company; the pre-entry classification will apply to shipments of merchandise identical to merchandise which has been pre-entry classified.

In the event you disagree with a pre-entry classification for merchandise which is currently being imported, you may protest entries which cover pre-entry classified merchandise. If no importations have been made, you may request a review from the NIS or the Office of Regulations and Rulings according to section 177, Customs Regulations.

Your signature on this document by an Officer of the company, indicated that you understand and agree to the terms of the pre-entry classification program. It in no way abrogates your right to protest the liquidated classification or to request a review at a high level.

Thank you for your cooperation and participation in this program. If you have any questions, please contact Mr./Ms. ______________ at ______________ .

Sincerely,

____

District Director

IMPORTER: ________________

TITLE: ______________________

4. Valuation for Customs Duty

In 1979, as a result of the Tokyo Round of the Multilateral Trade Negotiations (MTN) under the auspices of the General Agreement on Tariffs and Trade (GATT), the United States adopted customs valuation provisions as part of the uniform international customs valuation system.[1] The valuation of imported merchandise is a crucial component of the entry system for at least two reasons:

1. Most duty rates are assessed as a percentage of the value of the import (the ad valorem rate).
2. National governments find it necessary to keep accurate records of their nations' international trade balances.

The international goal of the MTN customs valuation agreement was to establish a uniform, fair, and neutral system by which the value, for customs purposes, of imported merchandise would be based on the actual value of the import on which duty was assessed or on like merchandise.

1. The agreement was designated the Agreement on Implementation of Article VII of the General Agreement on Tariffs and Trade. It is also known as the valuation code.

Title II of the Trade Agreements Act of 1979[2] implements the MTN customs valuation agreement by providing a customs valuation system applicable to merchandise exported to the United States on or after July 1, 1980. Title II repealed preexisting valuation law (sections 402 and 402a of the Tariff Act of 1930).[3]

This chapter focuses on the current customs valuation law (revised section 402[4]), which applies to all imports that were exported on or after July 1, 1980, and no mention will be made of the valuation standards under the old sections 402 and 402a (final list) with respect to merchandise exported to the United States prior to that date.

Revised Section 402[5]

Consistent with the MTN valuation code, revised section 402 endorsed and adopted a standard of valuation that is based upon the transaction value (the price actually paid or payable by the buyer to the seller). Only when the transaction value is impossible to determine or when a relationship between the buyer and seller affects the price paid do alternative bases of valuation take effect.

Title II provides the following five bases for appraising imported merchandise, in descending order of preference:[6]

1. Transaction value of imported merchandise
2. Transaction value of identical merchandise
3. Transaction value of similar merchandise
4. Deductive value
5. Computed value

---

2. Pub. L. No. 96-39, 93 Stat. 144 (1979), as amended by Pub. L. No. 96-490, 94 Stat. 2556 (1980) (codified at scattered sections of 19 U.S.C.).
3. 19 U.S.C.A. §§ 1401 & 1402 (West 1980 & Supp. 1989).
4. Codified at 19 U.S.C.A. § 1401a (West Supp. 1983).
5. *Id.*
6. 19 U.S.C.A. § 1401(a) (West Supp. 1989).

Transaction Value of Imported Merchandise

Transaction Value[7]

The transaction value of imported merchandise is the price actually paid or payable for the merchandise when sold for exportation to the United States plus amounts equal to

1. The packing costs incurred by the buyer;
2. Any selling commission incurred by the buyer;
3. The value of any "assist";[8]
4. Any royalty or license fee that the buyer is required to pay as a condition of the sale; and
5. The proceeds accruing to the seller of any subsequent resale, disposal, or use of the imported merchandise.

The above amounts are added only when they are not included as part of the purchase price[9] and only if they can be determined accurately. Insufficient information as to any item precludes the use of the standard of transaction value.

International freight and insurance charges are always excluded from transaction value, even when they are included in the purchase price, as under a C.I.F. term of sale.

The price may be expressed in the currency of any nation. It will be converted to United States dollars at the certified Federal Reserve Bank exchange rate published by the Customs Service that is in effect on the date of exporta-

7. 19 U.S.C.A. § 1401a(b) (West Supp. 1989).
8. An "assist" is property supplied by the buyer for use in connection with the seller's production or sale of the goods, as discussed below.
9. For example, where the value of an assist is not deducted from the sales price, it would be redundant to add that value as an assist. Although this is conceptually simple, errors of this nature are not infrequent.

tion. That rate may not, of course, be the same as that used for actual payment, because the time and method of actual payment are governed by the contract of sale.

Adjustments: Additions to Price

Packing Costs Incurred by Buyer[10]

If the costs of packing for international shipment are not included in the purchase price (e.g., when the goods are purchased "ex-works"), the packing costs separately incurred by the buyer will be added to the invoice price. In all instances, a packing list must be provided to the Customs Service in addition to the invoice and other documentation.

Selling Commissions Incurred by Buyer[11]

Under transaction value, a commission paid to the seller or the seller's agent as well as other commissions "inuring to the benefit of the seller"[12] are dutiable. Other commissions paid are not dutiable. Commonly, disputes arise as to whether an agent who is paid a commission is the agent of the seller or is the agent of the buyer. If the agent is a buying agent then the commission paid is not dutiable. The following tests help determine whether a payment is a buying or selling commission.

Selling Commission

1. Party is exclusive intermediary between seller and buyer.
2. Party acts on behalf of and subject to control of seller, or acts itself as a reseller.

---

10. 19 U.S.C.A. § 1401a(b)(1)(A) (West Supp. 1989).
11. 19 U.S.C.A. § 1401a(b)(1)(B) (West Supp. 1989).
12. Moss Mfg. Co. v. United States, 714 F. Supp. 1223 (Ct. Int'l Trade 1989).

Buying Commission

1. Party acts on behalf of and subject to control of buyer.
2. Party is reimbursed by buyer for expenses incurred.
3. Party has no power to change terms or conditions of order without approval of buyer.
4. Party is not related financially to seller.[13]

Recent case law establishes the following additional factors that the courts will consider in deciding whether the commission in question was paid to a bona fide buying agency:[14]

5. The existence of a buying agency agreement and whether it was carried out;
6. Whether the importer (principal) could have purchased directly from the manufacturer without the agent;
7. Whether the agent purchased more merchandise than was specified by the importer, apparently for purposes other than those consistent with the buying agency (essentially warehousing the merchandise); and
8. Whether the agent assumed the risk of loss of the merchandise.

While these are factors upon which the courts will base a determination of whether a true agency relationship exists, no one factor is determinative and, in combination, they are merely indicators of the courts' primary consideration,

---

13. *Id.*
14. See, e.g., J.C. Penney Purchasing Corp. v. United States, 80 Cust. Ct. 84, 451 F. Supp. 973 (1978); Rosenthal-Netter Inc. v. United States, 679 F. Supp. 21 (Ct. Int'l Trade 1988), *aff'd*, 861 F.2d 261 (Fed. Cir. 1988); Jay-Arr Slimwear Inc. v. United States, 681 F. Supp. 875 (Ct. Int'l Trade 1988).

which is whether the agent is actually under the control of the principal.[15]

When considering whether or not to claim a commission as nondutiable, importers should remember that the party making such a claim bears the burden of proof in establishing the existence of a bona fide agency relationship and that the payments were in fact bona fide buying commissions.[16]

Assists[17]

An assist is defined in the regulations as follows:[18]

(1) "Assist" means any of the following if supplied directly or indirectly, and free of charge or at reduced cost, by the buyer of imported merchandise for use in connection with the production or the sale for export to the United States of the merchandise:

(i) Materials, components, parts, and similar items incorporated in the imported merchandise.[19]

---

15. "[W]hether the relationship is one of buyer-seller or agent-principal is to be determined by the substance of the transaction—not the labels the parties attached to it." Pier 1 Imports, Inc. v. United States, 13 Ct. Int'l Trade, slip op. 89-25 at 13 (quoting Dorf Int'l, Inc. v. United States, 61 Cust. Ct. 604, 245 F. Supp. 690 (1968)). Nevertheless, language indicating a sales commission may create a presumption that is difficult to surmount. At least where such language is found in Customs invoices, it must be overcome by clear and convincing proof that the statement at the time of entry was erroneous. Globemaster Midwest Inc. v. United States, 67 Cust. Ct. 539, 337 F. Supp. 465 (1971), *citing* United States v. Manhattan Novelty Corp., 63 Cust. Ct. 699, 704 (1969); Morris Friedman v. United States, 52 Cust. Ct. 660 (1964).
16. *See* Monarch Luggage Co. v. United States, 715 F. Supp. 1115, 1116 (Ct. Int'l Trade 1989), *citing* New Trends Inc. v. United States, 10 Ct. Int'l Trade 637, 640, 645 F. Supp. 957, 960 (1986).
17. 19 U.S.C.A. § 1401a(h) (West Supp. 1989).
18. 19 C.F.R. § 152.102(a) (1988).
19. Note that components which are destroyed, scrapped, or lost and which are not physically incorporated into the imported article are not assists under the TAA. HQ 543093 (Apr. 30, 1984), cited in Cust. Serv. Dec. 88-35 (1988).

(ii) Tools, dies, molds, and similar items used in the production of the imported merchandise.

(iii) Merchandise consumed in the production of the imported merchandise.

(iv) Engineering, development, art work, design work, and plans and sketches that are undertaken elsewhere than in the United States and are necessary for the production of the imported merchandise.

(2) No service or work to which (a)(1)(iv) of this section applies will be treated as an assist if the service or work: (i) is performed by an individual domiciled within the United States; (ii) is performed by that individual while acting as an employee or agent of the buyer of the imported merchandise; and (iii) is incidental to other engineering, development, art work, design work, or plans or sketches that are undertaken within the United States.

(3) The following apply in determining the value of assists described in (a)(1)(iv) of this section:

(i) The value of an assist that is available in the public domain is the cost of obtaining copies of the assist.

(ii) If the production of an assist occurred in the United States and one or more foreign countries, the value of this assist is the value added outside the United States.

(iii) If the assist was purchased or leased by the buyer from an unrelated person, the value of the assist is the cost of the purchase or of the lease.

Actual materials supplied free to the manufacturer in the form of parts and components (e.g., cloth to be cut and sewn into suits) were dutiable under old law, and they continue to be dutiable as assists under the current law no matter where the source.

The significant change in valuation law with regard to assists is that engineering, designs, artwork, plans, blueprints, sketches, and production work performed in the United States or by a United States resident are no longer regarded as assists. Under the old law any United States design or engineering work necessary for the production of the merchandise was considered an assist and its cost or value was dutiable. However, design or art work that was in the nature of mere specifications was not considered to be an assist. It was often difficult to determine whether design work was in the nature of production assistance or mere specifications. An example of specifications not considered to be an assist is furnishing various basic sizes and configurations for special purpose lenses, these being selected from known standards. Under the current valuation law, however, as long as the design or engineering work originates in the United States, it makes no difference whether the work is necessary for production or simply in the nature of specifications; the costs will not be included in the dutiable value. The distinction will still be necessary, however, when the design or art work is furnished from outside the United States and done by a nonresident.

There still exists potential for confusion when assists that are used in the manufacturing process are provided by the United States company and the question arises whether the tools, dies, molds, or similar items are in the nature of manufacturing equipment or are design or art work.

Assume, for example, that an importer purchases mechanisms for generating sounds from Japan, each using a miniature phonograph disc. The recordings are messages of a type specified by the importer's customers. A reel of magnetic tape of the messages was made in a sound studio in the United States by the importer or its domestic customer. The Japanese manufacturer then produced a master record from the tape furnished by the importer, which master record was used to stamp out the individual miniature phonograph discs. The discs were imported into the United States either separately or as part of the sound devices. The sound devices were then delivered to the importer's customer in the United States, which incorporated them into the many items it manufactured.

The Customs Service has held that the sound tapes are in the nature of design work or product development necessary for the production of imported merchandise and, therefore, since produced in the United States, are not dutiable assists.[20]

On the other hand, consider the following example.[21] The importer produces stereo records. It contracts with a recording artist and hires musicians, a recording studio, and the various technicians necessary to produce a digital recording of the artist's sessions. From the tape is produced a lacquer master, which is plated to make the metal master, from which is made the "mother," from which is made the stamper. Stampers are then used, one for each side of the record, to stamp out the vinyl records that are the products imported and sold at the retail level. The whole process described above is done in the United States up to and including the production of the stampers. The stampers are exported to the manufacturer in Japan for making records to be sent to the importer in dust covers.

The invoice price of the records represents only the charge for the materials, labor, and profit of the manufacturer. The Customs Service held that the metal stampers were in the nature of molds or similar items used in the production of the imported merchandise and were therefore a dutiable assist.

The interesting part is the value put on the stamper by the Service. The importer advised that the following costs were incurred to produce the metal stampers:

1. Musicians and arrangements	$8,100
2. Rehearsal pay	1,000
3. Rehearsal hall rent	450
4. Agency fee	350
5. Studio costs	3,500
6. Digital recorder	4,000
7. Engineer	1,000
8. Cartridge	100
9. Mastering	800
10. Plating	1,500
11. Producer	8,000
Total costs	$28,800

20. *See* TAA No. 37, HQ 542446 (July 23, 1981).

21. *See* TAA No. 54, HQ 542936 (Nov. 12, 1982); *see also* TAA No. 21, HQ 542355 (Apr. 3, 1981).

Because the stamper could not have been brought to its completed condition without the particular music contained on it, the Customs Service determined that the dutiable value of the stampers was $28,800.

If the producer had taken the record production in the United States only to the recording level, however, and had sent the tape to Japan to be mastered and made into stampers, the artist's recording cost of producing the stamper would not have been dutiable (as design work or product development). Of course, the cost of making the lacquer master, metal master, and "mother" would have been included in the Japanese dutiable cost.

Finally, consider a company that imports greeting cards manufactured in England. The importer furnishes the foreign manufacturer with photographic negatives, which are converted by the manufacturer into positives. The images on the positives are etched onto printing plates, which, in turn, are used to print the acetate-faced greeting cards by offset lithography. The Customs Service determined that the photographic negative produced in the United States was in the nature of design work or product development and, therefore, was not included in the transaction value of the imported greeting card. Presumably, if the importer had taken the process through production of the printing plates and sent those to the English manufacturer, the costs of the plates, including the cost of the negative, would have been dutiable.

As noted above, molds, dies, and other manufacturing equipment supplied by the importer to the exporter are assists whatever the source, and their cost or value will be included in the dutiable value.[22] The duty on the cost of such molds or dies may be paid totally on the first entry of the merchandise produced from them, amortized over the

22. 19 U.S.C.A. § 1401a(h) (West Supp. 1989).

total produced worldwide to the date of exportation, or divided among the total number of items of merchandise contracted for. Note, however, that the value of the assist must be included in a dutiable shipment.

Assume, for example, that a United States importer imports automotive parts from Canada. Parts may be entered free of duty[23] under "actual use" provisions if, among other requirements, they are intended for use in the United States in the manufacture of motor vehicles as defined in the Automotive Products Trade Act of 1965.[24] Parts not so intended are dutiable. It is, therefore, common for particular vehicle parts to be duty-free on one entry and dutiable on the next. The importer wishes to include all assists for a given part on a duty-free entry. Then, on subsequent dutiable entries, the value of the assist would not be included in the dutiable value. The Customs Service's interpretation of the law, however, is that the value of an assist might be apportioned over the "first shipment if the importer wished to pay duty on the entire value at one time," but that there is no authority under the Trade Agreements Act to apportion the value of an assist on the first duty-free entry.

Royalty or License Fees

Any royalty or license fee related to the merchandise that the buyer is required to pay directly or indirectly, as a condition of the sale of the imported merchandise for exportation to the United States, is included in transaction value.[25]

The royalty or license fee need not be payable to the seller. If a fee is payable to a third party holding a patent or

---

23. See chapter 10 for discussion on Automotive Products Trade Act.
24. Pub. L. No. 89-283, 79 Stat. 1016 (1965) (codified at 19 U.S.C. §§ 2001 *et seq.*).
25. 19 U.S.C.A. § 1401a(b)(1)(D) (West Supp. 1989).

copyright as a condition of sale, the payment is dutiable as an addition to the transaction value. The key words in this section, however, are "as a condition of the sale of the imported merchandise for exportation to the United States."

For example, assume an importer entered into an agreement with another United States company (licensor), which held patent rights to a computerized game. All research and development were performed in the United States. Under the terms of the agreement, the licensor would grant the importer the "non-exclusive right to make, have made, use and/or sell" the game throughout the world. The licensor would also furnish molds to the foreign manufacturer for use in production. In return, the importer would pay the licensor a royalty in the amount of $2.50 for each licensed product received from the foreign manufacturer. One dollar of each payment, up to a cumulative $38,160, would be the charge for the tooling furnished by the licensor to the manufacturer. None of the parties is related to another party.

The tooling charge is dutiable as an assist. The remaining royalty payment is not dutiable, however, because it is not "a condition of sale of the imported merchandise for exportation to the United States," but is for the right to obtain and use the United States patent and for other related rights.

If, however, the royalty was included in the purchase price (for example, the manufacturer held the patent or made the royalty payment to a third-party holder of the patent), the full amount would be dutiable as part of the price paid or payable.

Proceeds of Resale

The proceeds of any subsequent resale, disposal, or use of the imported merchandise that accrued directly or indirectly to the seller will be dutiable as an addition to the transaction value. Transaction value will not be eliminated in instances where the proceeds of a subsequent resale are unknown at the time of importation.

For example, assume a United States company imports chemicals, which it further processes in the United States into pharmaceutical tablets that are resold in the domestic market. The original product is sold to the importer for a specific base price. Under the contract, however, if the importer increases its resale price in the United States by a certain percentage above the base amount, the exporter's sale price for all of the imported chemicals in the importer's inventory will be retroactively increased by the same percentage. Conversely, if the importer's resale price falls below a certain level, the price for the chemical already imported and in inventory will be comparably reduced by means of a rebate from the foreign exporter.

The Customs Service has ruled that the price increases will be dutiable on the basis of transaction value even though the final price is not known at the time of importation. When the price paid or payable is determined by a formula, a firm price need not be known or even ascertainable at the time of importation, as long as the formula fixing the final price is known.[26]

An inequity in the law allows for the dutiability of postimportation increases but disregards any postimportation decrease in the sales price. Section 402(b)(4)(B) states:

> Any rebate of, or other decrease in, the price actually paid or payable that is made or otherwise effected between the buyer and seller after the date of the importation of the merchandise into the United States *shall be disregarded* in determining the transaction value. . . . [27]

Thus, in the above example, if the importer resold the product at a price less than the established base resale price, the rebate received from the exporter would be disregarded for purposes of the Customs Service's appraised

26. Cust. Serv. Dec. 82-117, 16 Cust. B. & Dec. 27 (1982).
27. (Emphasis supplied) 19 U.S.C.A. § 1401a(b)(4)(B) (West Supp. 1989).

value. The law was written so that the government need be concerned only with those postimportation price adjustments that result in increased duties and not those that would lessen the duty liability.

Financing Charges

Financing charges usually take the form of interest payments, but they occasionally take the form of flat fees or commissions. Financing charges are generally included neither in the determination of transaction value nor in the determination of value under any other method, provided certain criteria are met.

Originally, the focus of the ruling on financing fees under transaction value concerned whether a financing fee, in the form of interest, was paid to the seller or a party related to the seller or otherwise accrued to the seller's benefit. If the answer to that question was yes, then the outcome of the case had generally depended on whether the financing arrangement was intended to benefit the particular transaction, i.e., to obtain an extension of credit (which was included as value, whereas a general financing arrangement may not have been). Where it was clear that the financing fee was paid to an unrelated entity such as a bank which issued a letter of credit, the fee was normally excluded from transaction value. The focus of finance fee rulings changed after the inclusion of interest payments in the appraisement of valuation was found to be violative of the General Agreement on Tariffs and Trade (GATT).[28]

In response to the GATT position, Customs issued a memorandum to its field personnel on April 25, 1985, which stated that interest payments would not be dutiable under any method of valuation if [29]

28. Adapted on April 26, 1984, by the Committee on Customs Valuation of the GATT with respect to article VII of the GATT.
29. Originally published on July 8, 1985, 50 Fed. Reg. 27,886, and republished on July 17, 1989, 54 Fed. Reg. 29,973. For further background see T.D. 85-111.

1. Such payment is separately identifiable from the price of the goods;
2. The financing agreement is in writing;
3. Upon request by Customs, the buyer will prove
   a. that the goods under appraisement are actually sold at the price declared, and/or
   b. that the amount charged does not exceed the interest fees prevailing at the time for the given transaction in the country where the financing was provided.

Although there are various ways of meeting the proof requirements for requests 3(a) and (b), Customs has stated that it will be satisfied "if the claimed charges for interest and principal are consistent with those usually reflected in sales of identical or similar merchandise."

The Customs Service has also been reasonable in appraising merchandise where interest rates exceed the rates that Customs finds acceptable. A notice from Customs states:[30]

> If the claimed amount of interest is inconsistent with that usually reflected in sales of identical or similar merchandise, or is inconsistent when compared to the level for such transactions prevailing in the country where, and at the time when, the financing was provided, only that amount which is consistent shall be allowed as nondutiable, the excess being disallowed.

In practice, the GATT criteria for excluding interest fees from value, as essentially adopted by the Customs Service, principally serve to enable finance fees to be excluded from value even in such instances where the seller provides financing to a purchaser for the particular transaction or where the financing fee otherwise accrues to the benefit of the seller. The new criteria are also applicable to financing fees paid to unrelated financiers. Although by design the

30. New York Regional Informational Pipeline No. 1073 (May 16, 1985), published by the Dep't of Treasury, U.S. Customs Service (New York).

criteria ostensibly should have little impact on the exclusion of those fees, they are rules of which the importer should be mindful.

It should also be noted that the new criteria specifically address "interest charges"[31] as the applicable finance charge. Are other types of finance charges also treated under these criteria? Customs has generally treated flat fees and other types of finance charges as acceptable substitutes. To meet criterion 3b (as cited above), Customs will likely convert those charges to equivalent interest fees.[32]

The Customs Service is mindful of the fact that fees reported as finance fees may actually be other fees which are included in value. For this reason, Customs will often carefully investigate whether the sum an importer claims to be a financing fee is not actually another type of fee, dutiable under the particular method of valuation.

Misunderstandings are more likely to arise where an alternative style of financier or financing fee arrangement is employed. Misunderstandings of this nature can generally be avoided through clear wording of financing agreements and careful documentation of pertinent transactions. If the arrangement is highly unconventional, an advance ruling can be sought. For example, in a case where a financier was precluded from charging interest on a loan under the laws of Islam, as promulgated in the financier's country, the financier found that he was permitted to lend the money under a scenario where the lender purchased the goods and resold them to the actual purchaser for a price that was equivalent to principal and interest charges. Because the

31. Customs has noted that "interest" does "not simply refer to interest charges arising out of delayed payment," but that "bona fide interest charges are those payments that are carried on the importer's books as interest expenses in conformance with generally accepted accounting principles." *See* 23 Cust. B. & Dec. 16 (1989).

32. This was the prior practice of Customs. See for example Customs ruling HQ 543118 (July 29, 1983).

purchase price from a reseller is generally included in the appraisement of merchandise under transaction value, the financier sought an advance ruling from Customs on whether the interest charge included in the resale price would be excluded from transaction value. Customs agreed that this would be a financing arrangement and thus excluded the increase in price under the arrangement from valuation.[33]

Reductions in Transaction Value

Under the statutory definition of transaction value, adjustments must be made to exclude the following items if they have been included in the price of the import. However, such exclusions must be identifiable separately.[34] The excluded items include

1. Any reasonable cost or charge incurred for
   a. constructing, erecting, assembling, maintaining, or providing technical assistance with respect to the goods after importation into the United States, or
   b. transporting the goods inland after importation; and
2. The customs duties and other federal taxes, including any federal excise tax for which sellers in the United States are ordinarily liable.

Restrictions on Applicability of Transaction Value

Transaction value is applicable in appraising the value of the merchandise only if certain limitations do not exist. The prescribed limitations can be grouped into four categories:[35]

33. *Id.*
34. 19 U.S.C.A. § 1401a(b)(3) (West Supp. 1989).
35. 19 U.S.C.A. § 1401a(b)(2)(A) (West Supp. 1989).

1. The seller restricts the buyer's disposition or use of the imported merchandise, except when that restriction
   a. is imposed by law,
   b. limits the geographical area of resale, or
   c. does not substantially affect the value of the merchandise.
2. The sale of, or the price actually paid or payable for, the merchandise is subject to a condition or consideration for which a value cannot be determined.
3. Part or all of the proceeds of any subsequent resale, disposal, or use of the imported merchandise accrue directly or indirectly to the seller.
4. The buyer and seller are related (*see* immediately below) and the transaction value is not otherwise acceptable (*see* below).

For appraisement purposes, the following persons are considered related:[36]

1. Members of the same family, including brothers and sisters (whether by whole or half blood), spouse, ancestors, and lineal descendants.
2. An officer or director of an organization and the organization.
3. An officer or director of an organization and an officer or director of another organization, if each such individual is also an officer or director in the other organization.
4. Partners.
5. Employer and employee.
6. A person directly or indirectly owning, controlling, or holding with power to vote, 5 percent or more of

36. 19 U.S.C.A. § 1401a(g)(1) (West Supp. 1989).

the outstanding voting stock or shares of an organization and that organization.

7. Two or more persons directly or indirectly controlling, controlled by, or under common control with any person.

The Trade Agreements Act of 1979 provides that a price paid between a related buyer and seller is acceptable under transaction value (1) if the circumstances indicate that the relationship did not affect the price actually paid or (2) if the transaction value closely approximates (a) the transaction value of identical or similar merchandise in sales to unrelated buyers in the United States or (b) the deductive value or (c) the computed value for identical or similar merchandise.[37]

Transaction Value of Identical or Similar Merchandise[38]

If the imported merchandise is disqualified for appraisement under transaction value by any of the above restrictions, then the other bases of value must be considered in order of preference.

The additions, exclusions, and limitations that apply in determining the transaction value of the imported merchandise (discussed above) also apply in determining the transaction value of identical or similar merchandise. The following additional factors apply to the selection of identical or similar merchandise as the basis for appraisement under transaction value.[39]

Identical merchandise is defined as merchandise that is identical in all respects to, produced in the same country as, and produced by the same person as the merchandise

37. 19 U.S.C.A. § 1401a(b)(2)(B) (West Supp. 1989).
38. 19 U.S.C.A. § 1401a(c) (West Supp. 1989).
39. 19 U.S.C.A. §§ 1401a(c)(1) & 1401a(c)(2) (West Supp. 1989).

being appraised.[40] If no merchandise produced by the same person can be found, the first two criteria are sufficient.

Similar merchandise is defined as merchandise that was produced in the same country and by the same person as the merchandise being appraised, is like the merchandise being appraised in characteristics and component materials, and is commercially interchangeable with the merchandise being appraised.[41] If no merchandise produced by the same person can be found, the remaining criteria are sufficient. Trade reputation, quality of goods, and existence of a trademark are among the tests of similarity.

The transaction value of either identical or similar merchandise must be taken at or about the time the merchandise being appraised was exported, and adjustment must be made when necessary for any difference in commercial level or quantity from the merchandise being appraised.[42] If two or more transaction values for identical or similar merchandise are found, the imported merchandise should be appraised on the basis of the lower or lowest value.[43]

If the transaction value of the actual merchandise, identical merchandise, or similar merchandise cannot be used, either deductive or computed value (described below) will be used. The deductive value method is given preference over the computed value method. If the deductive value cannot be determined, the computed value method would be the next alternative. The importer, however, is able to request that the computed value method be applied instead of the deductive value method. The request to have the computed value method applied should be made at the time the entry summary is filed with the appropriate cus-

---

40. 19 U.S.C.A. § 1401a(h)(2) (West Supp. 1989). Merchandise can be considered identical to the merchandise being appraised even with minor differences in appearance.
41. 19 U.S.C.A. § 1401a(h)(4)(A) (West Supp. 1989).
42. 19 U.S.C.A. § 1401a(c)(2) (West Supp. 1989).
43. *Id.*

toms district director. Where the importer exercises this option and computed value cannot be determined, the deductive value method will be employed.[44] Where neither transaction value, deductive value, nor computed value can be determined, a value derived from one of those methods will be used.[45]

Deductive Value[46]

Deductive value is determined by taking the sales price at which the merchandise being appraised, identical merchandise, or similar merchandise is being sold in the United States and making certain deductions. That price depends on the condition of the merchandise and the time of sale.

Price Standards When Merchandise Is Sold in the Condition as Imported

The price used as a starting point in deductive value is the unit price at which the merchandise concerned[47] is sold between unrelated parties in the condition as imported in the greatest aggregate quantity. In determining deductive value, the imported, identical, or similar merchandise may be used as defined and in the same order of preference as discussed above. The sales used in determining the price will be chosen in the following order of preference: first, sales at or about the date of importation; second, sales taking place within ninety days after importation.[48]

44. 19 C.F.R. § 152.101(b) & (c) (1988).
45. See p. 132 *infra*.
46. 19 U.S.C.A. § 1401a(d) (West Supp. 1989).
47. "Merchandise concerned" is defined for this purpose as the merchandise being appraised, identical merchandise, or similar merchandise. 19 U.S.C.A. § 1401a(d)(1) (West Supp. 1989).
48. 19 U.S.C. § 1401(a)(d)(2).

Price Standards When Merchandise Is Not Sold in the Condition as Imported

When the condition of the merchandise has been changed, there have been no sales within ninety days, and the importer has made the appropriate election requesting appraisement under deductive value at the time of filing the entry summary, the price of the imported, identical, or similar merchandise sold in the United States after further processing within 180 days of importation may be used to fix the price, based on the unit price of the greatest aggregate quantity of goods sold.[49] Assume, for example, that the importer sells processed merchandise to unrelated parties from a price list offering quantity discounts. The following sales were made within the 180 days at the prices indicated:

Sale Quantity	Unit Price	No. of Sales	Total Quantity Sold at Each Price
1–10 units	$100	10 sales of 5 units and 5 sales of 3 units	65
11–25 units	$ 95	5 sales of 11 units	55
Over 25 units	$ 90	1 sale of 30 units and 1 sale of 50 units	80

The unit price at the greatest aggregate quantity is $90, established after a sufficient number of sales have been made to unrelated persons.

Deductions from Price

After a unit price has been determined, amounts equal to the following will be deducted:[50]

49. 19 U.S.C. § 1401(a)(d)(2)(A)(iii).
50. *See* 19 U.S.C.A. § 1401a(d) (West Supp. 1989).

1. Any commission usually paid or agreed to be paid, or the addition usually made for profit and general expenses in connection with sales in the United States of imported merchandise that is of the same class or kind, regardless of the country of exportation of the merchandise concerned, will be deducted.[51] The deduction made for profit and general expenses (taken as a whole) will be based upon the importer's profit and general expenses, unless its profit and general expenses are inconsistent with those reflected in sales in the United States of imported merchandise of the same class or kind from all countries, in which case the deduction will be based on the usual profit and general expenses reflected in those sales, as determined from sufficient information. Any state or local tax imposed on the importer with respect to the sale of imported merchandise will be treated as a general expense. To determine deductions for commissions and usual profit and general expenses, it is necessary to examine sales in the United States of the narrowest group or range of imported merchandise of the same class or kind, including the merchandise being appraised, for which sufficient information can be provided. It is unclear how the Customs Service will determine the importer's profit and general expenses if they are computed in a manner inconsistent with those of other merchandise of the same class or kind. The importer would be well advised to have the merchandise of the same class or kind defined so narrowly as to include only the merchandise being appraised or merchandise identical to it.

2. The actual costs and associated costs of transportation and insurance incurred with respect to international shipments of the merchandise concerned from the country of exportation to the United States will also be deducted. These costs would include not only those items deducted

51. 19 U.S.C.A. § 1401(a)(d)(3)(A)(i).

under transaction value but also any fees paid to customs-house brokers by the importer.[52]

3. The usual costs and associated costs of transportation and insurance incurred with respect to shipments of the merchandise concerned from the place of importation to the place of delivery in the United States will be deducted if those costs have not been included as a general expense.[53]

4. Customs duties and other federal taxes currently payable on the merchandise concerned by reason of its importation, and any federal excise tax on, or measured by the value of, the merchandise for which vendors in the United States ordinarily are liable will be deducted.[54]

"Super Deductive Value"

When merchandise is to be further processed in the United States before sale, the importer has the option of asking that deductive value be based on the further-processed price. This is, for convenience, referred to as "super deductive value." In cases where the price determined reflects further processing of the imported merchandise, the value added by the processing of the merchandise will be deducted if there is sufficient information relating to the cost of that processing.[55]

Deductions for further processing will be based on objective and quantifiable data relating to the cost of the work performed. Accepted industry formulas, recipes, methods of construction, and other industry practices would form the basis for the deduction. The deduction also will take into consideration amounts for spoilage, waste, or scrap derived from the further process.

If the imported merchandise loses its identity in the further processing, deductive value will not be available un-

52. 19 U.S.C.A. § 1401a(d)(3)(A)(ii).
53. 19 U.S.C.A. § 1401a(d)(3)(A)(iii).
54. 19 U.S.C.A. § 1401a(d)(3)(A)(iv).
55. 19 U.S.C.A. § 1401a(d)(3)(A)(v).

less the value added can be determined accurately without "unreasonable" difficulty for either importers or the Service. If the imported merchandise maintains its identity, but in the processing forms a minor element of the merchandise sold in the United States, deductive value will be unjustified.

Computed Value[56]

The final statutory method of valuation, and the method that may be used before deductive value at the importer's option, is computed value. This basis of valuation is the sum of the following items.

Materials, Fabrication, and Other Processing Used in Producing the Imported Merchandise

The cost or value of materials and production of the merchandise is based upon information provided by or on behalf of the producer and on the commercial accounts of the producer, which accounts must be consistent with generally accepted accounting principles (GAAP) applied in the country of production.[57]

Note that the GAAP relating to costs of materials and production are those of the country of origin rather than the United States. In determining deductive value, a GAAP in use in the United States is used. If the foreign seller cannot or will not furnish cost data, computed value may not be used.

Profits and General Expenses

The producer's profits and general expenses are used if these are consistent with those usual in the country of ex-

56. *See* 19 U.S.C.A. § 1401a(e) (West Supp. 1989).
57. *Id.*

portation for producers of merchandise of the same class or kind. As with costs of materials and production, the figures for profit and general expenses must be supplied by the foreign producer and must be calculated in a manner consistent with GAAP of the exporting country. They must also be consistent with those for sales of merchandise of like class and kind from the country of exportation. If they are inconsistent, then the usual profit and expenses of those other producers will be used in place of the profit and expenses of the producer in question.[58]

Assists Not Included in Other Items

The rules governing assists discussed under transaction value[59] apply equally in computed value. Be sure that values for assists are not entered more than once, using prorating methods previously discussed.

Packing Costs

Include all costs of containers and wrappings, as well as labor and materials used in placing the merchandise in a packed condition ready for shipment to the United States.[60]

Derived Value[61]

If none of the preceding bases of valuation can be legally determined to apply to the imported merchandise, then the Customs Service must reach a value using a method derived from one of the five bases of valuation, reasonably adjusted as necessary. Adjustments may take the form of waiving time-of-sale requirements or the requirement that identical

58. 19 U.S.C.A. § 1401a(e)(1)(B).
59. See pp. 110–120 *supra*.
60. 19 U.S.C.A. § 1401a(e)(1)(D).
61. 19 U.S.C.A. § 1401a(f) (West Supp. 1989); 19 C.F.R. § 152.107 (1990).

or similar merchandise be produced in the same country as the imported merchandise.

Prohibited Bases of Valuation[62]

The law forbids the use of any of the following methods of appraisal for customs valuation:

1. The selling price in the United States of merchandise produced in the United States.
2. A system that provides for the appraisement of imported merchandise at the higher of two alternative values.
3. The price of merchandise in the domestic market of the country of exportation.
4. A cost of production, other than a value determined under computed value, for merchandise identical or similar to the merchandise being appraised.
5. The price of merchandise for export to a country other than the United States.
6. Minimum values for appraisement.
7. Arbitrary or fictitious values.

62. 19 U.S.C.A. § 1401a(f)(2) (West Supp. 1989). These prohibited bases parallel article 7.2 of the MTN valuation code: unfair or arbitrary handicaps to trade.

Part II: Importation

5. Customs Treatment of Persons Arriving in the United States

Although most customs activities relate to commercial transactions, the customs laws also apply to international travelers and to the articles they bring into the country. Accordingly, an important part of the Customs Service's mission is to see to it that persons arriving in the United States do not enter contraband, that proper duties are paid on the articles they import, and that all other applicable customs and general laws are obeyed. The authority of Customs to search and seize at the borders is absolute. Congress has granted it the right to conduct warrantless boardings and searches of vessels, even on the high seas.[1] Vehicles may be stopped and searched without a warrant well inland of the border if Customs has "reasonable cause to suspect" that they are carrying contraband.[2]

At each port of entry, be it an airport, seaport, or border crossing, travelers entering the United States from foreign countries must undergo the familiar customs inspection. The meteoric rise in the number of such travelers has led to a great deal of confusion and apprehension on the part of the general public when facing the Customs Service. This is

1. 19 U.S.C. §§ 1581 & 1587.
2. 19 U.S.C. § 482.

due largely to ignorance or misunderstanding of the customs laws that govern international travelers.

It is the goal of this chapter to eliminate that confusion by explaining the regulations that pertain to the noncommercial importation of personal articles by residents and nonresidents.

Customs regulations[3] and the Harmonized Tariff Schedule of the United States[4] deal with personal exemptions from duty and federal tax for the international traveler, detailing the articles covered and the conditions under which they may be imported, and defining relevant terms.

Residents and Nonresidents

Since different regulations apply to residents and nonresidents, it is beneficial to establish at the outset working definitions of these key terms. A returning resident is (1) a citizen of the United States or (2) someone who formerly resided in the United States and is resuming residence after a period of travel, work, or study abroad and who has not established a home elsewhere. Returning American citizens who had resided in the insular possessions of American Samoa, Guam, or the American Virgin islands are also considered United States residents upon their return.[5] The residence of a wife is considered to be that of her husband unless it can be shown that she had established a separate residence elsewhere. Minor children are presumed to have the same residence as their parents. However, children who were born abroad but have never lived in the United States, although they are citizens of the United States, are considered nonresidents for customs purposes.

Any person arriving in the United States who, by defini-

3. 19 C.F.R. pt. 148 (1987).
4. HTSUS chapter 98, subchapters IV–VII.
5. 19 C.F.R. § 148.2(b) (1987).

tion, is not a resident, or who, though a resident of the United States, is not returning from abroad, is considered a nonresident.[6] This category includes persons emigrating from a foreign country to the United States, visitors from foreign countries, and individuals in transit to a place outside United States customs territory. Additionally, residents who are visiting from abroad for a short period of time and who expect to return abroad after the visit have the option of claiming nonresident status if it is to their advantage to do so.[7]

The great majority of travelers entering the United States are returning residents who may be classified in four categories:

1. Persons who have been out of the country for forty-eight hours or more and who have not claimed exemption from duty within thirty days.
2. Persons who do not meet the forty-eight-hour or thirty-day requirement.
3. Persons arriving while on duty as employees of a vessel, vehicle, or aircraft engaged in international traffic or from a trip during which they were so employed (crewmembers).
4. Government and military personnel returning from extended foreign assignments.

Precautionary Notes

Before embarking on the subject of personal duty exemptions for purchases made while the individual was abroad, it would be wise to consider the problem of how to avoid having to pay duties on foreign-made articles that were

6. 19 C.F.R. § 148.2(c) (1987).
7. 19 C.F.R. § 148.2(d) (1987).

owned prior to departure, were carried abroad, and are returning with the traveler. Need he or she prove to the Customs Service that the articles were not obtained during the trip? Sometimes the necessity to prove that does arise.

Normally clothing, furs, cameras, watches, and other personal articles that have obviously been used for a prolonged period of time present no problem on reentry. Problems may arise, however, when a diligent Customs Service inspector assumes, sometimes correctly, that the camera, watch, or fur is not one that left the country with the traveler, but was purchased abroad during the trip. To prevent an incorrect assumption of purchase, there are several methods by which an individual can prove that ownership predates departure. The best course to follow is to register articles having distinctive markings (e.g., serial numbers) with a Customs Service office before departure and to present the registration form, Customs Form 4457, to the inspecting Customs Service officer upon return.[8] Unfortunately, registration must be in person and cannot be conducted through the mails. If it is not feasible to obtain Form 4457, proof of prior ownership can be established by presenting alternative documentation (e.g., a bill of sale, store receipt, insurance policy, jeweler's appraisal, etc.) to Customs Service officials at the appropriate time. In the case of automobiles, aircraft, and pleasure boats, preregistration is unnecessary, because certificates of registration with state or federal agencies are acceptable as identification of the articles that were taken abroad.[9]

Another potential problem for many travelers is money—not too little, but too much. Most people are unaware of the fact that, although there is no limit to the amount of money they may carry out of or into the country, failure to declare an amount exceeding $10,000 in any form (e.g., American

8. CF 4457.
9. 19 C.F.R. § 148.32 (1987).

or foreign currency, traveler's cheques, money orders, negotiable securities, etc.) is illegal.[10]

A traveler's cheque which has been signed once by its purchaser is not a "bearer instrument" as that term is defined under the Uniform Commercial Code, and it cannot be negotiated unless it has been countersigned.[11] Customs nonetheless takes the position that such nonnegotiable traveler's cheques are indeed "monetary instruments," and it includes them among the types of instruments which must be declared.

A traveler with very little understanding of English carrying over $10,000 in cash and a large sum in traveler's cheques recently arrived in the United States. The cheques were signed but neither countersigned nor endorsed. On the airplane, an English-speaking flight attendant helped him fill out his Customs declaration. He was told that "money" had to be declared if it was over $10,000. He therefore checked the box indicating that he had over $10,000. The Customs inspector at the terminal asked him how much "money" he had, and the traveler replied with the full amount of the cash. However, he did not mention the traveler's cheques. When his bag was searched, the traveler's cheques were found alongside the cash. After an interpreter was brought to him, he explained that he did not realize that the definition of "money" included traveler's cheques. The Customs officials present showed little sympathy for his failure of understanding. The traveler spent six hours in custody, undergoing searches of his person and luggage (the linings of his suitcases were ripped out) and interrogation. Although the declaration of the cash was not in question, Customs seized over half of it along with the cheques.

---

10. 31 U.S.C.A. § 5316 (West 1983). Persons transporting currency or monetary instruments in an amount exceeding $10,000 must execute a Customs Form 4790 (reprinted in appendix 2).
11. For a complete discussion of the differences between traveler's cheques and other kinds of negotiable instruments, see Xanthopoulos v. Thomas Cook, Inc., 629 F. Supp. 164 (S.D.N.Y. 1985).

Customs Service officials may search any vessel, vehicle, or individual merely to determine whether over $10,000 in undeclared monetary instruments are being carried.[12] Most violations of the reporting requirement are detected during routine customs inspections. If, upon arrival, no indication is made on the Customs Service declaration[13] that one is carrying over $10,000 and a Customs Service official finds the money in the course of baggage inspection, the official will, in all likelihood, confiscate the money on the spot.

The Customs Service enforces this provision strictly. In one instance, a husband and wife traveling together were carrying less than $20,000. But the wife had more than $10,000 in her purse and the Service seized it. There would have been no violation and no seizure had each person carried half of the money.

It is possible, in most cases, to recover a substantial portion of the money seized by the Customs Service, although the process can be extremely time-consuming. Before returning the money, the Customs Service must investigate the violation and issue a report of the circumstances—a process that can take months. In some instances, it may be necessary to sue the government to get the money back. In the meantime, the owner of confiscated funds can suffer considerable inconvenience and financial hardship.

Not only can one's money be seized, but one may also be faced with severe criminal and civil penalties for failure to report the excess money. If one willfully violates this law, one may be fined $1,000 or imprisoned for a year or both fined and imprisoned. An additional criminal penalty can be assessed if a reporting violation occurred in the furtherance or commission of any other violation of federal law or was a part of a pattern of illegal activity involving transactions exceeding $100,000 in any twelve-month period. If

12. 31 U.S.C. § 5317.
13. CF 6059B, reprinted in appendix 3.

either of these conditions is found, an individual may be fined up to $500,000 or imprisoned for up to five years or both fined and imprisoned. Although this law is clearly aimed at participants in organized crime, it is applicable to anyone.[14] The civil penalty can also be quite harsh. The amount that should be reported can be forfeited.[15]

Exemptions

Anyone, resident or nonresident, may import, free of duty, books, libraries, usual and reasonable furniture, and similar household effects if they had been used abroad by the person or the person's family for more than one year and were not intended for any other person or for sale. The year of use need not have been continuous or even immediately preceding the time of importation for the exemption to be applicable. Also permitted are professional books, implements, and tools of a trade, occupation, or employment that had been taken abroad by the individual or, if the person is emigrating, that were owned or used by the person abroad.[16] In order to obtain free entry of articles under the year-of-use requirement, the use of these effects abroad for the required year must be proven to the satisfaction of the district director of the Customs Service with the submission of a declaration at the time of entry.[17] On some occasions, other evidence of use may be required in addition to the declaration. If it is impracticable to submit the declaration at the time of entry of the importation, the importer may post a bond for the production of the owner's declaration within

14. 31 U.S.C.A. § 5322 (West 1983).
15. 31 U.S.C.A. § 5317 (West 1983); *see also* United States v. $359,500 in United States Currency, 828 F.2d 930 (2d Cir. 1987).
16. 19 C.F.R. § 148.52 (1987).
17. CF 3299, reprinted in appendix 4.

six months.[18] Generally, household effects arriving more than ten years after the last arrival of the importer from the country of use are not admitted duty-free. However, if the district director is satisfied with the importer's explanation as to why the goods were unavoidably detained beyond the ten-year limit, the time may be extended to a maximum of twenty-five years.[19]

Residents

Residents are entitled to bring in, free of duty and internal revenue tax, all personal and household effects they took abroad. These effects should be registered with the Customs Service prior to departure to ensure their duty-free return. If any of these articles have been advanced in value by repairs or alterations while abroad (except those made incidental to use), the expenses of the repairs or alterations are dutiable. If the repairs or alterations changed the article into a different one, the whole article is dutiable as a different product.[20]

Articles that were the personal and household effects of a citizen of the United States who died abroad are admitted free of duty upon proper identification to the district director of the Customs Service by a person having proper knowledge of the deceased.[21]

The statutory limits for personal exemptions for residents have been subject to change by Congress at various times in recent history; however, at this writing, each returning resident (regardless of age) who meets the forty-eight-hour and thirty-day requirements may claim, as exempt from duty, $400 in retail value (in the country of acquisition) of merchandise that was acquired abroad for his or her personal

18. CF 7551 or CF 7553.
19. 19 C.F.R. § 148.52 (1987).
20. 19 C.F.R. § 148.31 (1987).
21. 19 C.F.R. § 148.54 (1987).

or household use. The goods in question must not have been imported for the account of others (except as bona fide gifts) or intended for sale. The returnee is also permitted to enter a maximum of 200 cigarettes and 100 cigars. Cuban cigars (or, for that matter, any Cuban products) are, at this time, not to be brought into the country. Any attempt by the traveler to bring them into the United States will result in their confiscation and may subject the individual to civil or criminal penalties. Adults over the age of twenty-one are permitted to bring in up to one liter of alcoholic beverages.[22]

If the trip abroad included a visit to American Samoa, Guam, or the United States Virgin Islands, the maximum duty-free exemptions for the returning resident are as follows:

1. Goods having a value of $800, with not more than $400 worth acquired elsewhere than the insular possessions.
2. One thousand cigarettes, with not more than 200 acquired elsewhere.
3. Four liters of alcoholic beverages per adult, with not more than one liter acquired elsewhere.[23]

These exemptions can be consolidated and jointly applied toward a family's total exemptions; for example, a family of four may import goods having an aggregate value of $1,600 regardless of individual ownership.

It is important to be aware that all articles free of duty in the HTSUS are permitted free entry aside from the duty-free allowances (e.g., antiques and certain works of art).[24] In order to be classified as antiques, ethnographic objects

22. 19 C.F.R. § 148.33 (1987).
23. *Id.*
24. HTSUS 9701.00.00–9706.00.00.

made in traditional aboriginal styles must have been made at least 50 years before importation; other objects must be at least 100 years old. It must be proven to the satisfaction of the Customs Service that the antiques are for the traveler's personal use and not for sale and that they meet the age requirements. Sometimes the article in question speaks for itself, but an antique coin dated "B.C." might be difficult to authenticate. It is best to purchase antiques from a reputable dealer and to obtain a certificate of age in order to avoid such problems as fakes or pieces that are insufficiently old. In such cases, the buyer, in addition to being cheated, is liable for duty on the merchandise.

"Works of art" that are free of duty include paintings, pastels, drawings, and sketches, whether or not originals, executed wholly by hand; engravings, etchings, lithographs, and woodcuts, unbound and printed by hand; sculptures and statuary (including the first ten castings or reproductions) wrought by hand or cast; original mosaics; and other original works of the free fine arts, including works that are productions of American artists residing temporarily abroad.

Also admitted free of duty to returning residents are such metal articles as trophies, medals, and other prizes that were bestowed upon him or her abroad, along with hunting trophies. Endangered species trophies are not, however, permitted.

Residents carrying goods whose aggregate value exceeds the allowed exemption must pay a flat-rate duty on the next $1,000 worth of merchandise. The flat rate of duty is 10 percent (5 percent on $2,000 worth of goods acquired in a United States insular possession). After the exempt and flat-rate limits have been met, the remainder of the goods are dutiable as provided for under the appropriate item number in the HTSUS.[25]

---

25. 19 C.F.R. §§ 148.01 *et seq.* (1987).

For example, assume that a returning resident buys a car overseas for $10,000. After the $400 exemption has been applied, the next $1,000 of the cost is dutiable at a rate of 10 percent (or 5 percent), with the remainder dutiable under item number 8703 of the HTSUS at the specified rate.

Where the traveler brings in a variety of articles whose aggregate value exceeds the $400 (or $800 from insular possessions) exemption, the exemption must be applied to those articles that would normally be subject to the highest rates of duty. The 10 percent (or 5 percent) flat rate of duty applicable to the next $1,000 (or $2,000) in merchandise must be similarly applied to goods normally having the highest rate of duty. The same rule applies to the determination of applicable internal revenue taxes.

Also exempt from duty are automobiles that were rented by a resident while abroad and brought in to be used here for personal transportation (including of family and guests) for no longer than thirty days. If the automobile in question is used for commercial purposes or not returned abroad within the thirty-day period, it or its value is subject to forfeiture. The penalty may be avoided if the resident notifies the Customs Service within the thirty days and pays the duty that would have been payable at the time of entry if the automobile had been entered without the benefit of the exemption.[26]

While on the subject of exemptions from duty, it would be appropriate to consider duty-free shops. Duty-free shops, which are found in airports throughout the world, are actually customs-bonded warehouses that operate subject to the customs laws of the country in which they are located.[27]

---

26. 19 C.F.R. § 148.39 (1987).

27. A duty-free sales enterprise is "a person that sells, for use outside the customs territory, duty-free merchandise that is delivered from a bonded warehouse to an airport or other exit point for exportation by, or on behalf of, individuals departing from the customs territory." 19 U.S.C.A. § 1555(b)(8)(D) (West Supp. 1990). State or local govern-

That is, goods are imported free of duty by the shop's proprietor under the condition that they be sold only to departing travelers and not allowed to enter into the commerce of the country. Thus, the international traveler avoids payment of the foreign country's duty on the merchandise. However, goods purchased in duty-free shops abroad are subject to United States duties upon return. If, for instance, an expensive camera is purchased in the Shannon Airport free of Irish duty, it is not free of duty when it enters the United States with the purchaser unless it can be included within the allowable personal exemption.

In many duty-free shops, goods are sold that were made in the country in which the shop is located. In such cases, there is no advantage to be gained by the shopper, because no duty is avoided (inasmuch as the item was not imported into that country) and because the merchandise is usually equally available in many other shops (frequently at lower prices). It is, therefore, advisable for the traveler to restrict his purchases in such locations to articles made in other countries.

There are several other considerations to be taken into account with regard to duty-free stores, the most important of which is that the prices, even exclusive of duty, may be higher than the cost of the same or a comparable item purchased at home. Another consideration is that the merchandise may prove to be defective, with no U.S. agency immediately available to the returnee for recourse. These factors should be taken into consideration when deciding to make an expensive purchase overseas.

---

mental authorities having jurisdiction over any airport, seaport, or other facility that operates a duty-free sales enterprise may now require that a concession or some form of approval be obtained before the enterprise begins operation. *Id.* § 1555 (b)(4).

Nonresidents

Each nonresident, regardless of age, is entitled to duty-free entry for wearing apparel, articles of personal adornment, toilet articles, and similar personal effects. "Similar personal effects" includes all articles intended and appropriate for the personal use of the nonresident while traveling, such as hunting and fishing equipment, pets and hunting dogs, etc. Any jewelry or similar articles having an aggregate value of $300 or more that were part of the personal exemption may not be sold for a period of three years after the date of importation unless duty is paid to a district director of the Customs Service before the sale is completed.[28] Adult nonresidents may bring in one liter of alcoholic beverages and not more than two hundred cigarettes, fifty cigars, or two kilograms of smoking tobacco, or a proportionate amount of a combination of forms of tobacco. The nonresident may claim, as free of duty and internal revenue tax, articles up to $100 in value for use as gifts for other persons, provided the traveler remains in the United States for more than seventy-two hours and has not claimed this exemption for at least six months. This exemption may include one hundred cigars in addition to those allowed as part of the personal exemption.[29]

If the traveler meets the requirement for the $100 gift exemption, he or she may bring in articles up to $25 in value, free of duty for personal or household use. This can include fifty cigarettes, ten cigars, 150 milliliters of alcoholic beverages, or 150 milliliters of alcoholic perfume. If these limitations are exceeded or if the total value of the dutiable articles exceeds $25, no exemption can be applied.

As previously noted, the nonresident may import furniture and other household effects that had been used by him

---

28. 19 C.F.R. § 148.46(a)(1) (1987).
29. 19 C.F.R. § 148.44 (1987).

or her or in a household in which he or she was a resident member. Professional equipment permitted free of duty does not include theatrical apparel, scenery, or properties or any articles for use in any manufacturing establishment.

Personal and household effects entitled to free entry need not accompany the arrival. These may be shipped at a later, more convenient time. When they arrive, they must be cleared by the Customs Service at the first port of arrival unless arrangements have been made to have them sent, in bond, to another port of entry for Customs Service clearance. A customs declaration for free entry of the goods must be presented in order for them to clear.

Nonresidents may import, exempt from duty, an automobile, trailer, airplane, motorcycle, boat, or similar vehicle for personal use, whether the stay is temporary or indefinite. If the vehicle is sold within one year of its importation, the appropriate duty must be paid to the nearest Customs Service office before the sale is completed.[30]

Vehicles belonging to temporary visitors who intend to export them within one year of importation need not meet the safety and air pollution control standards in effect in the United States. However, emigrants from a foreign country are bound by the standards, and their vehicles must conform at the time of entry, or they must import them under bond with the proviso that they be brought into conformity within 120 days.[31]

Nonresidents in Transit

A nonresident who is in transit to a place outside United States Customs territory may take along, free of duty and internal revenue tax, dutiable articles not exceeding $200 in value, including not more than four liters of alcoholic bev-

30. 19 C.F.R. § 148.45 (1983).
31. This period may be extended to 180 days upon request.

erages. It is suggested that nonresidents in transit leave any baggage that is not required during their stay in the United States in the custody of the arriving airline, which will then forward it directly to the port of departure to accompany the travelers to their ultimate destination. This procedure, in addition to relieving the travelers of the need to care for the luggage during their transit, also eliminates unnecessary Customs Service inspection. Necessity dictates that such arrangements should be made in advance of arrival.

Generalized System of Preferences for Travelers

The generalized system of preferences (GSP) provides for the duty-free importation of otherwise dutiable products from certain developing nations (beneficiary developing countries, or BDCs) in order to improve the economic or financial condition of those countries.[32] The United States Customs Service is responsible for determining eligibility for duty-free entry under GSP. GSP, unless extended by Congress, will expire July 4, 1993.[33]

The international traveler should be aware of the duty-free benefits under GSP and their requirements:

1. The article must be a product of a BDC and imported directly from that country. If the item is acquired in a duty-free shop, it is not eligible for GSP unless it was produced in the country in which the duty-free shop is located. Articles may accompany the traveler or may be shipped directly from the developing country to the United States.
2. For goods valued at more than $250, a certificate of

32. See chapter 10.
33. 19 U.S.C.A. § 2465 (West 1980).

origin (form A)[34] may be required by the Customs Service. This form would normally be obtained from the seller of the eligible article.
3. Applicable internal revenue tax must be paid when required; only the customs duty is suspended.

Travelers who have questions concerning GSP are best advised to contact their nearest Customs Service office for complete information.[35]

GSP articles, like all duty-free items, should not be included within the allowable personal exemptions, which should be applied to dutiable items only.

In addition to the GSP, travelers also should be aware of the duty-free benefits available under the Caribbean Basin Initiative (CBI)—which extends duty-free treatment to certain items from several designated Caribbean countries—and the duty-free and duty-reduction benefits provided for pursuant to the United States–Israel Free Trade Agreement and the United States–Canada Free Trade Agreement, all of which are discussed in greater detail in chapters 12, 13, and 14.

Special Cases

The definitions of and exemptions for crewmembers of commercial carriers, military and civilian employees of the United States, evacuees, and personnel of foreign governments and international organizations are spelled out in the customs regulations.[36]

The regulation pertaining to the clearance of military personnel returning on carriers operated by or for the Department of Defense requires that the people being transported,

34. Reprinted in appendix 5.
35. See chapter 11.
36. 19 C.F.R. §§ 148.61–.90 (1988).

including crewmembers, execute written baggage declarations, thereby relieving the commanding officer of that obligation, as had been the case under prior regulations.[37]

Restricted or Prohibited Articles

The government prohibits or restricts the importation of a number of articles into the United States. The entry of some of these articles may contravene customs laws; others are prohibited or restricted by such federal agencies as the Department of Justice, Department of Agriculture, United States Fish and Wildlife Service, and United States Public Health Service. The Customs Service cooperates with these agencies to ensure compliance with the import regulations.

Most people are aware of the prohibition against narcotics and dangerous drugs. Small amounts of controlled substances are subject to mandatory administrative penalties of up to $1,350 for maximum amounts provided on a table prepared by Customs[38] (e.g., thirty-two ounces of marijuana; fourteen grams of cocaine), plus additional sums per unit over the maximum if the case does not result in prosecution (e.g., $100 per ounce of marijuana, $200 per gram of cocaine).

However, the general public is unaware of the large number of other products that either are totally prohibited or are restricted to importation under very tightly controlled circumstances. Some of these items are immoral materials, merchandise produced by convict or forced labor, endangered animals and their byproducts, cultural treasures or artifacts (especially pre-Columbian), certain foodstuffs and seeds, counterfeit coins and currency, and merchandise originating in Iran, North Korea, Vietnam, Cambodia, or

---

37. 19 C.F.R. § 148.73 (1988).
38. U.S. Customs, *Fines, Penalties and Forfeitures Handbook*, DEC–8 (1986).

Cuba. There are several government publications available from Customs Service offices that cover this subject in greater detail.[39] An interesting example of a little-known prohibited article is Jequerity beans and their products. The beans are decorative tropical seeds used in making necklaces. They are, however, highly poisonous; until they were prohibited, they were the cause of many poisonings, especially of children.

The well-publicized outcry for enforcement of the ban on further elephant ivory production led to almost universal action in the importing nations to halt the trade. After the Fish and Wildlife Service amended its regulations to ban all further importation of ivory (except a limited amount of "trophy" ivory allowed under strict quotas),[40] United States Customs enforced the prohibition vigorously. A traveler who was abroad with ivory bangles that she had owned for years was astonished when Customs seized them upon her return. Customs returned them only after she obtained affidavits from acquaintances, attesting to her prior ownership of the pieces.

The ban on importation of semiautomatic assault rifles announced by "drug czar" Bennett on March 14, 1989, similarly caught returning hunters by surprise.

---

39. Useful publications include Harmonized Tariff Schedule of the United States, Annotated Code of Federal Regulations title 19 (ch. I) United States Customs publications:

No. 503: *Currency Reporting*
No. 511: *U.S. Customs Hints for Travelers*
No. 512: *Know Before You Go*
No. 515: *GSP and the Traveler*
No. 520: *Importing a Car*
No. 527: *Temporary Importation Under Bond*

United States Department of Agriculture publication:

Animal and Plant Health Inspection Service Program Aid No. 1083

40. *See* 16 U.S.C. §§ 4201–4225; 54 Fed. Reg. 24,758 (June 9, 1989).

Another prohibition, the ban on gold coins minted in the Soviet Union introduced as part of the Anti-Apartheid Act of 1986,[41] gave rise to a case of failure to declare that illustrates the Customs Service's vigilance in inspecting incoming passengers. Soviet coins were included in the Act because the Senate would not accept a bill sanctioning South African human rights violations without a condemnation of the same kinds of abuses in the U.S.S.R.[42]

A father and son, naturalized residents from the U.S.S.R., were returning to the United States with cash (dollars and deutsche marks), jewelry, and Tsarist (pre-Soviet) gold coins that represented their extended family's pooled life savings—wealth accumulated with great difficulty in, and exported at great risk from, the Soviet economy of the Brezhnev era.

They knew they had to make a declaration of the merchandise on their arrival, but they also knew that the value of the jewelry in rubles at the official rate of exchange would inflate their dollar value by a factor of up to fifteen. The Customs Form 6059B (reprinted in appendix 3) on which the declaration is made asks only for the dollar value of goods acquired abroad at the price payable in the country of origin. The travelers decided to ask the Customs Service to advise them on the valuation of the goods at the airport, and so left the value space blank.

The inspector at the gate noted that the cash was declared, and he prepared the separate declaration for monetary instruments. He then asked the value of any goods the travelers might have, to which he received the response that the travelers did not know the value. Taking their hesitancy to signify a negative reply, the inspector called them aside for further questioning.

---

41. 22 U.S.C.A. § 5100 (West 1990).
42. Some sources indicate that South African and Soviet gold were being commingled in third-country markets. *See* FORBES 8 (Dec. 1, 1986); *but see* Associated Press Aug. 15, 1986.

The travelers left the interrogation room believing that an import specialist would assess the merchandise and that they could pay duty and obtain its release. Two weeks later they received a notice from Customs informing them that the goods were seized and subject to forfeiture for failure to declare them, under section 497 of the Tariff Act of 1930.

The gold coins are free of duty. However, they came into this seizure case, and were claimed subject to forfeiture separately from the jewelry, as "prohibited merchandise." The coins in question were minted before 1917, and thus before there was a Soviet Union. The Customs officials preparing the case made no distinction between post-1917 Soviet coins (banned) and Tsarist coins (allowable). The inspector's report (and all other Customs documents in the case based on it) read: "Importation of gold coins minted in Russia is prohibited." Thirteen months after the seizure, the admissibility issue was still pending before the Treasury Department's Office of Foreign Assets Control, which administers the South African sanctions and which will be required to approve release of the Tsarist coins.

Violations

Unfortunately, many travelers feel that undergoing Customs Service inspection is more a game of wits than a legal obligation. They "overlook" or underestimate the value of expensive purchases when completing the declaration, or they try to bring in prohibited materials. This constitutes fraud or smuggling (as the case may be), and the law may impose severe penalties on the violator. The lighter penalties include payment of full duty and applicable internal revenue tax due on the article, payment of the article's domestic value, and seizure of the article. The penalties may be mitigated or remitted if the undeclared or improperly declared articles are free of duty or if the failure to declare was not due to willful negligence or fraudulent intent. Most passengers are not aware of the rewards offered to informers who notify the Customs Service of an intended fraudulent action on the part of a passenger. On occasion, employees of foreign establishments report expensive purchases made by travelers to the Customs Service in the expectation that the travelers will fail to declare the items properly. In those cases, the informer may be paid 25 percent of any duties, fine, or penalty imposed, up to $50,000.

The entering passenger submitting an improperly written declaration can avert this unpleasantness by making an oral declaration to a Customs Service officer prior to baggage examination that, in effect, amends the written one.

The Customs Service has been using a computerized enforcement aid known as the Treasury Enforcement Communications System (TECS), with terminals at each international airport and border crossing. TECS communicates with similar systems used by other law enforcement agencies, both domestic and international (e.g., the Internal Revenue Service, the Drug Enforcement Administration, and Interpol). The system is used by Customs Service officers to alert themselves to individuals having a record of customs law violations here or elsewhere by calling up a complete profile of the person, including physical description, detailed history of previous customs violations, and the like. The inclusion of a person's name in TECS will likely precipitate a very thorough search of his or her baggage and may even result in a body search.

Because the names of offenders remain in the system for several years, many individuals, once so labeled, are suspect each time they enter the country during that period. If, as occasionally happens, a person's name is listed by error, the name can be purged from TECS by contacting the Director of the Passenger Enforcement and Facilitation Office, Office of Inspection and Control, United States Customs Service, 1301 Constitution Avenue N.W., Washington, D.C. 20229, and informing the director of all the facts.

There are occasions, however, when incidents involving smuggling take an unexpected turn. A case in point is an incident where a returning traveler attempted to smuggle unset diamonds into the country and was apprehended. The diamonds were seized and the traveler, much to his dismay, was forced to pay a penalty of only a few dollars, rather than the large sum he had anticipated. Upon examination by the Customs Service laboratory, the "diamonds" proved to be glass.

Yachts

A yacht is defined as a vessel that is used exclusively for pleasure; it may not transport merchandise or carry passengers for pay. Yachts are subject to all the customs laws and may be boarded by the Coast Guard to ensure compliance with those laws. A United States–documented yacht is permitted to proceed from port to port in the United States or to foreign ports without clearing and is not subject to entry upon arrival in a port of the United States, provided it has not visited a hovering vessel.

Visiting yachtsmen from certain countries[43] may obtain a cruising license from the Customs Service, which permits them to arrive and depart from the United States for a period of one year without entering and clearing customs and without filing manifests.

43. 19 C.F.R. § 4.94 (1990).

6. Processing a Shipment Through Customs: The Customs Broker and the Customs Attorney

In this chapter we shall follow the fictional Novelties Unlimited, a company that imports gift items. Although identities have been masked, most of the material is based upon an actual case history taken from the files of the author's office. This example is not that of a typical, routinely processed shipment, but is intended to illustrate the more complex procedures involved when legal issues affect the rates of duty. The basic mechanics of entry, normal processing, and liquidation, however, are equally applicable to all entries. We shall therefore focus on the entire importing process, from planning, through the actual formalities of entry, to the final receipt of a refund of duties from the United States Customs Service.

The statutory principles for determining the duty rate at which goods may be entered were changed by the Omnibus Trade Act of 1988. All imported merchandise entered since January 1, 1989, has been classified under a new law, the Harmonized Tariff Schedule of the United States (HTSUS). Not only did details of nomenclature and commodity groupings change, but the legal bases for resolving classification issues also changed. The practical result for both the Customs Service and the importing community has been that twenty-six years of legal precedent for tariff classification under the former statute, the Tariff Schedules of the

United States (TSUS), must be reexamined in light of the new law. It remains to be seen how much precedential value the older decisions will retain.

The hypothetical case presented here can therefore only parallel our experience under the new statute up to a point. In particular, the United States Court of International Trade has ruled on only a few HTSUS issues at trial. The portions of the case study presented here following liquidation of the entries are thus based on experience under the former statute.

We shall examine the roles of the customs attorneys representing Novelties Unlimited in the planning and protest stages of the shipment, the customs broker who will expedite the processing of the actual entries, and the government officials involved in the entry, classification, valuation, liquidation, and subsequent documentary review.

The description of this process will present a very general view of how imported merchandise is moved through the United States Customs Service and how an importer can most effectively safeguard its interests.

Planning to Import

Novelties Unlimited imports gift and houseware items from Taiwan, Hong Kong, South Korea, Malaysia, and the Philippines. Novelties Unlimited retains the customs and international trade law firm of Serko & Simon to furnish advice on obtaining maximum tariff benefits for these importations. Serko & Simon, based in New York City, is close to the United States Customshouse, New York Region. The New York ports still lead the nation in import volume, and Novelties Unlimited's merchandise usually arrives in that region.

Serko & Simon employs a staff of attorneys as well as other experts in customs matters, including former United

States Customs Service employees and paralegal personnel engaged in the day-to-day collection of vital documentary information.

Novelties Unlimited normally provides samples of its line of goods to Serko & Simon for advice on the most economical ways to bring them into the country. As a high-volume importer, Novelties Unlimited has qualified for "pre-entry" classification, a process in which a National Import Specialist (NIS) from New York seaport or a deputy named by the NIS will actually visit the importer's premises to review items proposed for importation. Serko & Simon will have an opportunity then to advocate that certain classifications be adopted.[1]

Mr. Novel, principal owner of Novelties Unlimited, has come to confer with the firm regarding shipments of flat magnets contained in ceramic holders shaped like Christmas trees, used for hanging notes and Christmas shopping lists on refrigerators.

The area director of customs at the New York seaport had classified these articles as "ceramic household articles" under heading 6912 of the Harmonized Tariff Schedule, with duty at 7 percent of the invoice value. Serko & Simon had applied to the NIS in New York for a ruling on Novelties Unlimited's behalf that the magnets were entitled to entry at a 5.8 percent duty rate, on the theory that they qualified as "festive articles" under heading 9505 because of their holiday theme. The NIS, however, ruled that refrigerator magnets were not a "traditional" holiday item, thus upholding the area director's classification.

Serko & Simon appealed to Customs Headquarters, arguing that the NIS's use of the term "traditional" was a misreading of the nonstatutory interpretative language of the HTSUS explanatory note for "festive articles," which uses

1. See chapter 24.

the word "traditional" to refer to the articles' symbolic content (e.g., Santa Claus for Christmas, turkeys for Thanksgiving) rather than to the articles themselves. Certainly, the language of the HTSUS, which is a Congressional enactment and thus controlling, does not raise such doubts. The word "traditional" is not mentioned either in the tariff heading or in its legal notes.

The Headquarters attorneys in the Office of Regulations and Rulings concurred in Serko & Simon's suggested classification. They overruled the NIS's finding and returned the classification to "festive articles" because of the magnets' undeniably festive nature. Novelties Unlimited was thus allowed to enter the magnets at the lower rate.

Entry of the Goods

Let us turn to the formalities of processing the shipment through customs. Novelties Unlimited uses the services of Bright Customs Brokers, Inc. to execute the paperwork necessary to enter the merchandise in a lawful and efficient manner, to aid in expediting delivery of the merchandise to the importer, and to assist in complying with the various requirements of all the other governmental agencies involved in the administration of trade.

The entry process involves filing forms containing sufficient information for the Customs Service to determine (1) that the merchandise is admissible, (2) that it is eligible for release, (3) the duties to be assessed, and (4) that all legal requirements have been or will be met.

After the filing of entry documents, the process goes through payment of duties as a result of the release of the goods from the Customs Service, examination, classification,[2] liquidation, final assessment of duty, and any additional payment or refund determined by the liquidation.

2. See chapters 2 and 3. The Trade and Tariff Act of 1984 (TTA) requires payment of "increased or additional duties" fifteen days after the date

Advances in Customs procedure are overtaking the standard description of the entry process presented below. Although importation still involves the creation and retention of large volumes of paper, Customs has launched a concerted drive to automate the process. Since 1982, therefore, Customs has been building a data processing environment for its operations, called the Automated Commercial System (ACS).

Much legislative drafting and enactment and sweeping regulatory changes remain necessary before "paperless entry summary" becomes a reality, but Bright Brokers has already acquired the necessary hardware and software to participate in the "Automated Broker Interface" (ABI), the communication link between ACS and importers and customs brokers, who will be filing "paperless" entry summaries in the future.

The forms described in this chapter are still physically produced. Importers and brokers are still required by law to retain them for five years as evidence of the transactions.[3] The Customs Service has access under the same recordkeeping statute to importation records and other documents pertaining to compliance with the customs laws, and it can request the testimony of importers and other persons with relevant information regarding customs transactions.[4]

---

the date of liquidation or reliquidation, and it provides for interest if payments are delinquent. Duties are considered delinquent if not received within thirty days after liquidation or reliquidation and interest will accrue from the fifteenth day after liquidation or reliquidation. The TTA also requires the payment of interest by the Customs Service on increased or additional duties refunded as a result of a successful protest or court action. The rules governing increase or additional payments are governed by 19 C.F.R. § 24.3(a) (1988). Note that "increased or additional duties" would appear to be used interchangeably and distinguished from "excess deposits of estimated duty" even when the deposit results from a government demand at the time of entry.

3. 19 U.S.C. § 1508.

4. 19 U.S.C. §§ 1509 & 1510.

Notwithstanding that enabling statutes and the regulations needed to enforce them were still in the drafting stage, the actual entry filing process took place over the wire in over 80 percent of Customs transactions as of early 1990.

Bright Brokers will handle most routine matters of the entry process. Under Customs Service regulations, all merchandise imported into the country is considered the property of the person to whom it is consigned. The regulations[5] define the importer as the one who is "primarily liable for the payment of duties on the merchandise, or an authorized agent acting on his behalf." Thus, Bright Brokers can, as an agent under the law, properly enter the goods for Novelties Unlimited, but with some qualifications.

The entry may be made by the consignee (person who will normally receive delivery of imported goods), by an agent of the consignee authorized by a proper power of attorney, by an agent who does not have power of attorney but who makes a separate special declaration, or by a nominal consignee who makes entry in its own name.[6] If the broker acts as the nominal consignee (as opposed to the ultimate or actual owner-importer), it is liable for the payment of duties as the importer of record. For tariff purposes, any of the foregoing parties may be the "importer of record." Whoever is the importer of record is, in the first instance, responsible for the duty. If it desires to be relieved of the statutory liability, it must file a declaration of the actual owner, through which the owner acknowledges that it will pay any increased duties.

Alternatively, if Novelties Unlimited is not the importer of record and does not furnish the necessary documentation and superseding bond, then Novelties Unlimited has no right to file a protest questioning the original action by the

5. 19 C.F.R. § 101.1(1) (1988).

6. *See* 19 C.F.R. §§ 141.19 & 141.20 (1988).

Service. That right would reside with the broker as the importer of record.

The documents enabling Bright Brokers as authorized agent to enter Novelties Unlimited's goods generally consist of the following:

1. Customs Form 3461 (the entry) (reprinted in appendix 6).
2. Evidence of the right to make entry where required.[7]
3. A commercial invoice or pro forma invoice with indication alongside each item or group of items to show the importer's assertion as to the applicable HTSUS item numbers and rates of duty.[8]
4. Packing lists, detailing the specific contents, item by item, of each package or case in the shipment.
5. A proper bond, usually supplied by a surety bonding company licensed by the Treasury Department to underwrite entry bonds. The basic entry bond assures that estimated duties will be deposited on entries released under immediate delivery and that any additional duty will be paid on all entries. The bond conditions also allow the government to claim liquidated damages for a variety of defaults under the customs laws, including failure to supply missing documents timely and failure to redeliver goods recalled for not conforming to the marking statute or other legal requirements.

Once Bright Brokers furnishes these documents, the "entry summary" must be assembled, containing the following:

1. The entry summary on CF 7501 (reprinted in appen-

7. A bill of lading or carrier's certificate.
8. A pro forma invoice is one prepared by the importer when the commercial invoice is unavailable at the time entry is to be made.

dix 7), showing the value, the charges, and whether the shipper and importer are "related" or "not related."
2. Copies of the commercial invoice, packing list, and bill of lading (or other document of title).
3. CF 5101 (the entry record).[9]
4. Other documents necessary and required to determine the admissibility of the particular merchandise.[10]
5. A copy of any ruling bearing on the classification or valuation of the merchandise.

If an entry is made (i.e., a CF 3461 is filed), the entry summary, duties, and the other documents required by the regulations must be submitted within ten days.

Essentially, CF 7501 summarizes all the data relating to the importer of record, appraisement, and HTSUS classification of the merchandise. In addition, the consumption entry form contains other information, such as statistical data, the name of the carrier bringing in the shipment, and the country (or countries) of exportation and origin of the goods.

The commercial invoice must be prepared in a manner customary in the trade, must be in English or have the English translation, and must contain the information required by the regulations, i.e., port of entry, buyer and seller, time and place of sale, a detailed description of the merchandise, quantities, purchase price (or value if not shipped pursuant to purchase), currency, charges, rebates, drawbacks, bounties, and discounts.[11] Additional information is required for certain classes of merchandise to aid the Customs Service's import specialists in ascertaining the classification or quota status of the goods.[12]

---

9. See appendix 8.
10. See chapter 22 for liability and penalties for false documentation.
11. 19 C.F.R. §§ 141.81 *et seq.*
12. See 19 C.F.R. § 141.86 (1988).

In addition, the Customs Service may under certain circumstances require substantiation of production costs of the shipment by the manufacturer of the goods (e.g., if the importer is a party related to the seller and a question has been raised as to the applicability of transaction value). Bright Brokers must indicate all the deductions involving charges that may be considered nondutiable (e.g., insurance and freight costs and buying commissions) and must provide specific information relating to the total entered value, the unit value, and how the invoiced unit value differs, if it does, from the stated unit value multiplied by the quantity.

Under ABI procedures in place at the beginning of 1990, Bright Brokers inputs into the ABI system the information contained in the CF 3461. The system will respond to this information by indicating "paperless" or "entry documents required."

If the "paperless" release is granted, and the steamship line is on the automated manifest system (AMS), the line is notified electronically to release the magnets. If the steamship line is not on the AMS, the information is transmitted electronically to the Documents Analysis Unit (DAU) at the port. After the DAU has the information, a stamped release is given to Bright Brokers for presentation to the steamship line and the magnets are released.

If, after import of the CF 3461 information, entry documents are required, Bright Brokers must present the CF 3461 and other required documents to the DAU by hand. Then the DAU will either allow release of the magnets or order an inspection. (If release is granted, the steamship line, if it is on AMS, will be notified electronically; if it is not on AMS, Bright Brokers must present the stamped release documents.)

The combination of importer, exporter, and merchandise is electronically checked against the Customs Service's "selectivity" criteria, which are combinations of variables including the importer's record with Customs, violations involving the exporter, and classification or other types of problems with the kinds of goods involved.

If the selectivity test shows little risk of a violation, the magnets will be released to Novelties Unlimited. Suspect goods are retained in the Customs Service's custody for examination. Once they have passed inspection, they proceed under the "delivery authorized document" (DAD).

If the entry is in order, the date of entry (determined by the release date of the CF 3461) is then confirmed, the entry is approved. If the ACS selectivity criteria so indicate, the customs inspector at the port has discretion to examine Novelties Unlimited's shipment before releasing the goods (assuming the examination finds everything to be in order). In some instances, the import specialist may order a sample from the shipment (even an entire case or package) to be sent to the commodity specialist team for more detailed scrutiny.

The entry summary filing procedure under ABI is virtually the same as described, except that the data required on the CF 7501, invoice, and other documents are electronically transmitted to Customs. Brokers participating in one automated clearinghouse pilot program can actually make wire transfers of estimated duty deposits to Customs at the time of filing of the CF 7501 entry summary, "batching" the funds for multiple entries together.

Once Bright Brokers has filed all the necessary information in a timely and proper fashion, the Customs Service begins processing of the documents, now referred to as the "entry/entry summary package." If the entry is singled out by the ACS as likely or possibly involving irregularities, based on the performance records of the importer and exporter in the database, and the kind of goods involved, the import specialist responsible for items classified in HTSUS chapter 95 will review all filings for correctness. If the proposed duty deposit accompanying the entry is not correct, or if any of the necessary information has not been filed in conformity with the customs regulations, the entire entry package will be rejected, indicating the correct estimated duties to be deposited or the correct information to be filed or both.

It should be noted that the overwhelming majority of nonquota import shipments are released under CF 3461 (entry) release procedure regulations without examination or sampling.

Customs has the option subsequently to review the entry summary and either to accept all its claims (as to classification, value, admissibility) or to change them to conform to the Service's assessment of them. In that process, called liquidation (the finalization of the entry procedure),[13] the duties may be increased or decreased by the import specialist. Presently, however, most liquidations are computer-generated, occurring on a schedule set by the selectivity criteria within the Automated Commercial System (pursuant to the "bypass" system). The liquidated duties become the actual duties assessed against Novelties Unlimited's shipment. According to statute, the Customs Service has an obligation to liquidate Novelties Unlimited's entry within one year of the date of entry. Otherwise, the entry is deemed automatically liquidated at the entered rate and value. However, the Customs Service may postpone liquidation by notice to the importer of record for further yearly periods up to four years from the date of entry. This may be done only when there are specific grounds to do so as provided in the pertinent customs regulations.[14] The importer may also re-

---

13. *See* chapter 25.
14. An importer may request that liquidation be extended by showing "good cause" that warrants such an extension. For example, an importer may need time to supply information concerning the proper valuation of the merchandise being imported. Likewise, Customs may extend liquidation if it needs more information concerning an entry. *See* 19 C.F.R. § 159.12; *see also* 19 C.F.R. § 159.51 (suspension of liquidation).

quest extensions of the time before automatic liquidation by writing to the district director and giving reasons for its request.[15]

The official and crucial date of liquidation is the date that the liquidated entry is posted on a "bulletin," a printout showing the entry number, the filer number (usually the unique three digit identifying number assigned to importers and brokers by Customs), the entry date, and the liquidation date. Notices of liquidation sent to the importer of record are deemed to be "courtesy notices."

The customs regulations require that bulletin notices of liquidated entries be posted in a conspicuous place in the customhouse. If the bulletins for any given liquidation cycle (entries are liquidated on a weekly basis) are improperly placed so as to be inconspicuous, or if the Customs Service fails to post proper notice of the place where the bulletin notices are located, or if there is any discrepancy in the listing of the importer of record or the entry number, the liquidation can be deemed illegal, null, and void. Mistakes in the "courtesy notice," or even the failure of Customs to provide it, do not affect the validity of the notice of liquidation, if the bulletin notice is correct.

The first draft regulations covering automated entry filing propose eliminating the bulletin notice of liquidation in favor of electronic notification to the filer via ABI.[16]

Protest and Litigation

We now return to the classification of the ceramic magnets. We left the issue of "ceramic household goods" versus

---

15. *See* 19 C.F.R. § 159.12 (1988). Penalties may be assessed on delinquent duties.
16. 19 C.F.R. part 143, subparts A and D, 55 Fed. Reg. 2535 (Jan. 25, 1990).

"festive articles" where it rested in reality, with a favorable ruling for the importer.

Because the HTSUS is a new statute (effective in January, 1989), and no case has yet been decided by the courts, the author has chosen to illustrate, using the ceramic magnet controversy, what would ensue had the Customs Service ruled against the importer rather than in its favor.

Had the ruling been adverse, the import specialist would continue to liquidate the entries of magnets at the higher rates for ceramic household goods. The staff of Serko & Simon would review Novelties Unlimited's entries for protestable liquidations of the magnets. They would fill out "liquidation memoranda," recording all the information regarding potentially protestable points about the liquidation of the entry, including appraisement and appropriate HTSUS numbers on the entered shipment. Calculations would be made to show any increases or decreases of duty.

The staff members formerly prepared their memos working in the customhouse from the Customs entry files themselves. Now, however, as paperless entries increasingly prevail, it is usually necessary to work from the importers' or customs brokers' copies of the documents.

Serko & Simon would thus obtain the information necessary to file CF 19, a protest against the Customs Service's classification decision.[17] The responsible attorney would see to the preparation of this document, which must be filed with the district director (area director, in the New York region) of the port where entry is made. The protest with accompanying entry documents would, after some time, be assembled by the protest section and returned to the import specialist for action on the protest.

Since Customs Headquarters has already ruled on the issue, the importer's protests would be denied, and the rem-

17. *See* chapter 25 and appendix 9.

edy would be to sue the government in the United States Court of International Trade (CIT).[18]

We now assume that the importer wins in the CIT and the government appeals to the United States Court of Appeals for the Federal Circuit (CAFC). During the pendency of the appeal, further protests would be denied, and summonses would have to be filed within 180 days of the denial dates. We further assume that the CAFC affirms the decision of the CIT in the importer's favor.

The importer's protests would be processed as follows:

1. Those protests acted on before the CAFC decision became final would be denied, and summonses would be filed in the CIT. (A summons must be filed within 180 days after the denial of a protest.)[19]
2. The protests acted on after the CAFC decision became final (there are generally many, because of the ninety-day period for filing and the time taken to assemble documents) would be approved and reliquidated for refunds.

Summonses would be processed by stipulations through the court, citing the CAFC case as authority and attesting for each entry that the merchandise was the same as that in the case that was tried. After much paperwork, the documents would be returned to the residual liquidation section

---

18. The importer would be able to file a summons and complaint with the CIT contesting the protest denial. For a more detailed discussion of the procedures involved in bringing such an action, see chapter 26.
19. See generally chapter 24, Protests. 19 U.S.C. § 1515(a) requires that the notice of denial of a § 1514(a) protest include notice of the protestant's right to judicial review of the decision. Customs has construed this language to deprive it of jurisdiction to review any protest once the denial notice is mailed. The Court of International Trade has agreed with Customs. San Francisco Newspaper Printing Co. v. United States, 620 F. Supp. 738 (Ct. Int'l Trade 1985).

of the customhouse for reliquidation in harmony with the court decision. Finally, after reliquidation, a refund, with interest, would be issued.

Every importation creates its own set of facts in the diverse fabric of customs law and regulation. The case we have presented is meant to illustrate some of the themes common to all imports and, above all, to stress that importers must carefully heed the options open to them within the law in order properly to protect their economic interests.

7. Licensing and Regulation of Customs Brokers

In 1910, the United States Congress passed the first legislation requiring customs brokers (then known as "customhouse brokers") to be licensed.[1] The government recognized the key role the broker played as intermediary between the importer and Customs, and the law focused on the brokers' responsibilities to both parties. Applicants were to be investigated for good character and their knowledge of the customs laws. Under the early licensing laws, brokers' licenses could be revoked for cause, but for many years the only stated ground for revocation of a license in the regulations was failure to pay income tax.[2]

The Customs Broker Today

Businesses worldwide are able to effect the movement of goods today with more ease than similar transactions between domestic parties involved a generation ago. Unlike trade in an era when the details of transactions had to be sent by ship or even by aircraft, electronic communication has become so widespread and simple that a price list or

1. Act of June 10, 1910.
2. Customs Regulations, Art. 1272 (1922).

inquiry sent by facsimile or computer can result, within hours, in a sale in which the goods can be moving to an overseas delivery point.

Buyers, sellers, carriers, and banks are becoming more and more accustomed to paperless transactions. The customs brokerage community, always at a key juncture in international transactions, increasingly finds itself challenged to adapt its practices to the automated climate.

For American brokers, the challenge has been laid down directly by Customs in a pilot automation program for entry transactions. Using the "Automated Broker Interface" (ABI), brokers or importers communicating electronically with Customs Service's computers send entry information directly to the Service's database, the Automated Commercial System (ACS).

As noted in chapter 6, the transaction of a broker's business with the Customs Service requires that a large amount of information be passed to Customs and that records thereof be retained by the broker. To date, the Customs documentation and record-keeping requirements for brokers have entailed the production and retention of large amounts of paper. What follows is a brief reminder of the kinds of records generated in connection with virtually every importation.

No broker may transact customs business on behalf of another person without a written power of attorney from that person authorizing the broker to do so.[3] Powers of attorney must be kept current in the broker's place of business and retained for five years after the client ceases to be active.[4] Brokers must also keep, for five years, records of all information required to make entry: invoices, packing lists, and various certifications.

3. 19 U.S.C.A. § 1484 (West 1980 & Supp. 1991). A sample power of attorney form is reprinted in appendix 10.
4. 19 C.F.R. § 111.23(a)(2) (1990).

Ordinarily, in a process known as "live entry," the entry declaration must be filed (usually on Customs Form [CF] 7501, reprinted in appendix 7) and estimated duties paid no later than five days after the shipment arrives. Otherwise, the goods are placed in "general order" warehouses[5] to await clearance. However, importers with large volumes or need for speedy delivery of their goods may obtain "immediate release" of merchandise under the terms of their importation bond.[6] The broker prepares a CF 3461 (reprinted in appendix 6) giving key particulars of the shipment including the carrier's name and bill of lading or airway bill number, the kind of merchandise involved, its quantity and invoice value, and its location. If Customs decides to release the goods without inspection, the Form 3461 is stamped for immediate delivery, and the goods may proceed. Customs may decide to inspect the merchandise and release it later. In either case, the completed entry summary on CF 7501 and the estimated duty payment are due ten days after release.

The storage of such voluminous documentation often constitutes a significant portion of a broker's overhead.

The Customs Service's experimental automation programs are well under way, with many importers and brokers trans-

5. Where storage charges will be incurred.

6. Liabilities for possible charges arising from entry of merchandise, including additional duty, are secured for the United States by the posting of surety bonds. These can be in the form of 100 percent collateral deposited by the importer, but in fact are almost universally underwritten by large commercial insurers under the general requirements of 19 C.F.R. part 113.

The basic entry bond assures that estimated duties will be deposited on entries benefiting from immediate delivery, and that any additional duty will be paid on all entries. The bond conditions also allow the government to claim liquidated damages for a variety of defaults under the customs laws, including failure to supply missing documents timely and failure to redeliver goods recalled for not conforming to the marking statute or other legal requirements.

mitting immediate delivery and entry information directly to Customs since 1986. Filing of the forms with Customs for such transactions is still required, but merely for backup and verification purposes. The actual entry transaction is recorded in the Customs Service's electronic database, the ACS. By 1990, over 80 percent of all consumption entries were filed through ABI.

Although full implementation of entry automation is still some time away, Customs has put the brokerage community on notice that brokers' participation in the "paperless" Customs environment is conditioned upon their good behavior. As explained below, Customs tries to assure that the broker licensing process eliminates persons likely to conduct themselves improperly, and it bases its disciplinary program on those aspects of the brokers' business with which it has immediate contact.

Licensing of Customs Brokers

Brokers' Responsibilities

Congress ended years of attempts to regulate all aspects of the customs brokerage industry when it passed the Customs Brokers Act of 1984 (the Act).[7] The Act limited the Customs Service's oversight of broker conduct to scrutiny of the "customs business" they transact, leaving ancillary cargo management activities such as forwarding and insurance brokerage to the broker's own business judgment. The statute defines "customs business" as "those activities involving transactions with the Customs Service concerning the entry and admissibility of merchandise, its classification and valuation, the payment of duties, taxes, or other charges assessed or collected by the Customs Service upon

7. Pub. Law No. 98-573, 98 Stat. 2978 (1986) (codified at 19 U.S.C. § 1641).

merchandise by reason of its importation, or the refund, rebate, or drawback thereof."[8]

The Act prescribes a penalty of $10,000 per transaction against persons transacting customs business without a broker's license.

The Act also provides the first statutory definition of a broker's duties: "to exercise responsible supervision and control over" its customs business.[9] Pursuant to the Act's delegation of powers to the Secretary of the Treasury,[10] regulations written under it allow Customs officials in the field to recommend monetary penalties against brokers in lieu of the license suspensions and revocations which had previously been the only significant disciplinary sanction.

Customs Headquarters has read the statute to authorize the setting of standards of responsible supervision and control, but to date only the disciplinary guidelines for infractions deemed to show the absence of supervision and control allow a glimpse of the standards that may finally emerge.[11] Since an understanding of this concept is crucial to the brokerage industry in its relations with both Customs and the importing public, we shall explore it at greater length below.

The Customs Broker's License

In order to transact customs business for the account of anyone other than oneself, one must hold a valid customs broker's license, either as an individual or as a corporation, association, or partnership.[12] No corporation or association may be licensed unless at least one of its officers holds an

8. 19 U.S.C.A. § 1641(a)(2) (West Supp. 1991).
9. 19 U.S.C.A. § 1641(a)(4) (West Supp. 1991).
10. 19 U.S.C.A § 1641(f) (West Supp. 1991).
11. 19 C.F.R. pt. 177, app. C (1990).
12. 19 U.S.C.A. § 1641(b)(1) (West Supp. 1991).

individual license, and no partnership may obtain its license unless one member is a licensed customs broker.[13]

A corporation, association, or partnership loses its license by operation of law if it fails to have the qualifying licensed individual for 120 consecutive days.[14] If a licensee is the sole proprietor of an unincorporated brokerage business, the business must stop if the licensee dies or otherwise loses the license. All that the heirs or employees are permitted to do is to wind up the business.[15]

In a major departure from earlier law, brokerage firms no longer need a separate license for each customs district in which they do business. Instead, a permit will be granted for each such district if the company employs at least one licensed individual in the particular district. A company may also be granted a permit, subject to Customs approval, for a district where no licensed individual is employed, if it employs a licensed individual within the same region as that district and can assure Customs that its procedures allow it "to exercise responsible supervision and control" over its transactions within that district. Permits will be revoked by operation of law if no licensed individual is employed in the district for 180 consecutive days, unless a waiver is obtained from the regional commissioner of the district.[16]

The individual customs broker's license is available to any United States citizen at least twenty-one years old and of good moral character.[17] Notice of application is posted for two weeks in the customshouse of the district where the application is submitted, and comments concerning the applicant's reputation and background are invited from the

13. 19 U.S.C.A. § 1641(b)(3) (West Supp. 1991).
14. 19 U.S.C.A. § 1641(b)(5) (West Supp. 1991).
15. 19 U.S.C.A. § 1641(b)(6) (West Supp. 1991).
16. 19 U.S.C.A. § 1641(c) (West Supp. 1991).
17. 19 U.S.C.A. § 1641(b)(2) (West Supp. 1991); 19 C.F.R. § 111.11 (1990).

public.[18] In order to obtain a license, a person must pass an examination (renowned among the candidates for its difficulty) in "customs and related laws, regulations and procedures, bookkeeping, accounting, and all other appropriate matters."[19]

Denial of Broker's Licenses

While "good moral character" is not defined, the list of grounds for denial of a license includes:

- A failure to establish the business integrity and good character of the applicant;
- Any willful misstatement of pertinent facts in the application;
- Any conduct which would be deemed unfair in commercial transactions by accepted standards; and
- A reputation imputing to the applicant criminal, dishonest, or unethical conduct, or a record of such conduct.[20]

In addition, applications will be denied for any infraction, listed in 19 C.F.R. § 111.53, which would be grounds for revocation or suspension of an existing license, or assessment of a monetary penalty. These include any material false statement or omission of a material fact in any filing with Customs; knowing participation in a violation of the customs laws; and knowingly defrauding, misleading, or threatening a client in the course of customs business. Conviction of any crime involving importation or the conduct of customs business, can also be grounds for license denial.[21]

18. 19 C.F.R. § 111.12 (1990).
19. 19 C.F.R. § 111.13 (1990).
20. 19 C.F.R. § 111.16(b) (1990).
21. 19 C.F.R. § 111.16 (1990).

Finally, no one may receive a license without scoring at least 75 points on the licensing examination.[22]

Appealing the Denial of a License

Applicants denied a license may apply in writing for review of the denial by the commissioner of customs. The appeal must be received at Customs Headquarters within sixty days of the denial. The appeal may be by written statement or personal appearance.[23]

If the commissioner upholds the decision not to grant the license, a further request for review may be filed with the Secretary of the Treasury, to be received by the Treasury Department within sixty days of the Customs decision.[24] The regulations allow an appeal of the Secretary's affirmation of denial to the Court of International Trade if filed with the court within sixty days of the date of denial.[25]

However, the review in the court proceeding will be an examination of the administrative agency's records with the provision that "[t]he findings of the Secretary [of the Treasury] as to the facts, if supported by substantial evidence, shall be conclusive."[26]

As in other areas of administrative law, the record certified to the court will function as the statement of facts on which the decision will be based. On application by the claimant, the court may hold additional evidence to be required to be presented to an administrative law judge for an additional certification of fact. Generally, the final administrative decision will be upheld if it is not "arbitrary, capricious, an abuse of discretion, or otherwise not in accordance with law."[27] No case has decided an appeal of a

22. *Id.*
23. 19 C.F.R. § 111.17(a) (1990).
24. 19 C.F.R. § 111.17(b) (1990).
25. 19 C.F.R. § 111.17(c) (1990).
26. 19 U.S.C.A. § 1641(e)(3) (West Supp. 1991).
27. 5 U.S.C.A. § 706 (West 1977).

license denial since the Customs Brokers Act of 1984 became law.

Disciplinary Actions Against Brokers

Revocation or Suspension of License as Sole Sanction

The only sanction in certain cases is suspension or revocation of the broker's license. This penalty *must* be assessed against a licensed broker for a conviction of any crime of financial dishonesty (larceny, theft, robbery, extortion, forgery, counterfeiting, fraudulent concealment, embezzlement, fraudulent conversion, or misappropriation of funds).[28] The consequences of such actions can be devastating: a license revocation "with prejudice" will absolutely prevent the former licensee from working for (or even "assisting") any customs broker for five years, and thereafter only with permission of the Commissioner of Customs.[29]

A broker may request a license cancellation "without prejudice" or "with prejudice."[30] Although neither the statute nor the regulations explicitly states so, there is an implication in section 111.51(b) of the regulations that the revocation or cancellation of a broker's license as a result of a disciplinary action taken against the broker will only be "with prejudice": "The effect of a [voluntary] cancellation 'with prejudice' is in all respects the same as if the license or permit had been revoked for cause by the Secretary."

It may thus be presumed that a revocation with the full due process proceeding can only be "with prejudice." The same section of the regulations strengthens the inference: An attempt to have one's license cancelled "without prejudice" in the face of disciplinary proceedings can only be approved by the Secretary of the Treasury.[31]

28. 19 U.S.C.A. § 1641(d)(1) (West Supp. 1991).
29. 19 C.F.R. § 111.51(b) (1990); 19 C.F.R. § 111.79 (1990).
30. 19 C.F.R. § 111.51 (1990).
31. 19 C.F.R. § 111.51(a) (1990).

General Grounds for Monetary Sanctions Under the Statute

As mentioned above, one of the novel aspects of the 1984 legislation was the authorization of administrative monetary penalties for brokers committing infractions. The statute empowers the secretary of the treasury to impose the penalties under regulations.[32] In practice, guidelines promulgated under the regulations allow district directors to set proposed penalties up to $10,000 and to recommend monetary sanctions up to the statutory maximum of $30,000 to Customs Headquarters.[33]

The Act lists six grounds for sanctions short of revocation or suspension of a license (although Customs may seek license suspension or revocation as well):

1. False statements on license applications or reports to Customs;
2. Conviction of a crime involving the importation or exportation of goods or arising out of the conduct of customs business;
3. Violation of the customs laws or regulations;
4. Counseling or knowingly aiding or abetting any violation of the customs laws or regulations;
5. Knowingly employing a convicted felon without written permission; and
6. Willfully deceiving, misleading, or threatening a client with intent to defraud.[34]

The maximum aggregate penalty authorized under the statute is $30,000. Such penalties may not be levied in cases where the broker is convicted of a crime involving dishon-

32. 19 U.S.C.A. § 1641(f) (West Supp. 1991).
33. 19 C.F.R. pt. 171, app. C, & § 111.94 (1990).
34. 19 U.S.C.A. § 1641(d)(1) (West Supp. 1991).

esty. As noted above, such convictions lead only to revocation or suspension of the broker's license.

Specific Grounds for Monetary Penalties Under the Regulations

The customs regulations list numerous "Duties and Responsibilities of Customs Brokers" in 19 C.F.R. Part 111, Subpart C. Failure to comply with these prescriptions can result in monetary penalties.

Record Keeping

The record-keeping requirements for brokers are stringent. The "current, orderly, and itemized" records required by the regulations must be in proper form and accessible to Customs auditors.[35] Records of individual transactions must be kept for five years, and powers of attorney from former clients must be kept for five years after the date the client revokes the power or ceases to do business with the broker.[36]

Brokers with permits to do business in more than one district may keep centralized records if authorized to do so, subject to supervision by Customs of their retention.[37] Although the regulations do not specifically allow it yet, according to recent rulings records of current and expired powers of attorney may be electronically accessible from branch offices,[38]

Brokers must keep Customs apprised of changes of address or of the location of their records and of changes in the name or organization of their business.[39] In addition,

35. 19 C.F.R. § 111.21 (1990).
36. 19 C.F.R. § 111.23(a)(2) (1990).
37. 19 C.F.R. § 111.23(e) (1990).
38. Customs Telex 00684, 04101 (May 22, 1989).
39. 19 C.F.R. § 111.30 (1990).

every three years, every licensed broker must file a status report stating whether it is engaged in business.[40] If so, the business address and, if applicable, the name of the broker's employer should be reported.

Employee Lists

Brokers are required to file lists of their employees at Customs and keep them current. For any employee working for the broker less than three years, the record must include that person's employment history for the three years before he or she was hired. New employees must be reported to Customs within ten days after the end of their first thirty days on the job, and terminations must be reported within thirty days. Customs must be notified "immediately" in writing of the termination of a licensed individual broker whose license qualifies the firm to hold a license as an association, partnership, or corporation.[41]

The section of the regulations governing these requirements is entitled "responsible supervision." The title is an indication of an important aspect of the broker's statutorily defined duty to exercise responsible supervision and control over the customs business it transacts.

Prohibitions

The regulations expressly forbid customs brokers to do certain acts in the course of their business. While some of the acts are repeated from the statute, such as making false statements or employing a former felon without the permission of Customs, others elaborate on the theme of responsible supervision and control of customs business.

Conflicts of interest are prohibited. No former government employee may represent anyone before Customs on matters

40. 19 U.S.C.A. § 1641(g) (West Supp. 1991).
41. 19 C.F.R. § 111.28(b) (1990).

which that person handled in government service, nor may a broker assist a former government employee in such a transaction or share fees with that person. If a brokerage firm imports goods on its own behalf, it may not accept work from an importer of competing merchandise without his or her knowledge. The same restriction applies if a broker's employee is a competing importer.[42]

Brokers may not gain unauthorized access to government information.[43] Attempted influence on government employees, whether by extortion or bribery, is expressly prohibited.[44] Brokers may not split fees with attorneys who handle cases before Customs or the courts. If a broker assists an attorney in the handling of a case, he may be paid the value of his time and skills for those services.[45]

Brokers may not "lend" their licenses to or split fees with unlicensed persons.[46] They may, however, pay commissions to freight forwarders for obtaining brokerage business as long as the importer knows in advance who the broker will be, and the importer is not forbidden to contact the broker directly.[47] The regulation specifically requires a broker to transmit to the importer in such cases

> (i) A true copy of his brokerage charges if the fees and charges are to be collected by or through the freight forwarder, or
> (ii) A statement of his brokerage charges and an itemized list of any charges to be collected for the account of the freight forwarder if the fees and charges are to be collected by or through the broker.[48]

---

42. 19 C.F.R. § 111.31 (1990).
43. 19 C.F.R. § 111.33 (1990).
44. 19 C.F.R. § 111.34 (1990).
45. 19 C.F.R. § 111.35 (1990).
46. 19 C.F.R. § 111.36(a) (1990).
47. 19 U.S.C.A. § 1641(i) (West Supp. 1991); 19 C.F.R. § 111.36(b)(3) (1990).
48. 19 C.F.R. § 111.36(b)(2) (1990).

It is not clear whether the "statement of brokerage charges" the regulation refers to means a schedule of the charges and fees for each individual entry, or whether the broker may satisfy the requirement by furnishing importers with schedules of fees and keeping them up to date.

No broker may allow its license or permit to be used by an unlicensed party (other than its own employees) or by a party whose own broker's license or permit is suspended.[49] A further regulation prohibits brokers from doing business as "associate, correspondent, officer, employee, agent, or subagent [for] any person who is notoriously disreputable or whose license as broker shall have been revoked for any cause, or whose license is under suspension, or who has had his license canceled 'with prejudice.' "[50] However, licensed brokers may do customs business for persons within the forbidden class if the latter are bona fide importers or exporters.

Finally, brokers are required to exercise "due diligence in making financial settlements, in answering correspondence, and in preparing or assisting in the preparation and filing of records" pertaining to their customs business.[51] Information from Customs indicates that this section is the most frequently invoked cause for penalties against brokers. The chief forms in which such Customs claims against brokers occur is for late submission of duty checks or for tendering checks with insufficient funds.

The Court of Appeals for the Federal Circuit has held that an importer's advancing of the proper amount of duty on an entry to its broker for transmittal to Customs does not relieve it of the responsibility to pay duties if the broker fails to tender the funds to Customs.[52] As a direct result of that

49. 19 C.F.R. § 111.37 (1990).
50. 19 C.F.R. § 111.42(a) (1990).
51. 19 C.F.R. § 111.29 (1990).
52. United States v. Federal Ins. Co., 805 F.2d 1012 (Fed. Cir. 1986), *cert. denied*, 107 S. Ct. 2179 (1987).

case, the regulations were amended to require brokers to remind their clients at least once a year of the importer's right to submit a separate check for duties and taxes to the broker along with payment of the broker's bill for fees and other charges.[53]

Disciplinary Procedures

Much of the licensing statute and the supporting regulations is concerned with procedural safeguards for applicants or licensees appealing denials, revocations, or suspensions of licenses. We have already touched briefly on the regulations covering administrative appeals of license denials and the statutory standard for judicial review.

Disciplinary proceedings must be begun within five years of the time the infraction is alleged to have occurred, unless fraud is claimed, in which case the statute of limitations runs for five years from the date the fraud is discovered.[54] In cases of contemplated sanctions against licensed brokers, the Act requires that written notice be given to them and that they be given the opportunity to show cause why they should not be penalized.[55] The time to respond is thirty days from the date of the notice, after which the Service's decision must be sent to them in writing.[56]

Monetary Penalties

Brokers facing monetary penalties may petition for mitigation under 19 U.S.C. § 1618, and they may submit supplementary petitions if dissatisfied with the first decision in their case.[57]

53. 19 C.F.R. § 111.29(b) (1990).
54. 19 U.S.C.A. § 1641(d)(4) (West Supp. 1991).
55. 19 U.S.C.A. § 1641(d)(2)(A) (West Supp. 1991).
56. *Id.*
57. *Id.*

A customs brokers supplement to the Customs Service's *Fines, Penalties & Forfeitures Handbook* went into effect on March 19, 1990.[58] It constituted a substantial revision of the guidelines for penalty cases contained in appendix C to Part 171 of the Customs Regulations. After stating that "assessment of a monetary penalty is an alternative sanction to revocation or suspension of the broker's license or permit," the guideline outlines the circumstances under which brokers will *ordinarily* face license suspension or revocation:

1. False statements on license applications if a license would not have been issued had the truth been known.
2. Conviction of a crime involving importation or customs business subsequent to filing license application.
3. Knowingly employing a person with a felony conviction, and continuing to do so after Headquarters refuses permission.

For offenses 2 and 3, Customs *may* elect to impose a monetary penalty. As to criminal convictions, however, it should be recalled that conviction of a crime involving fiscal dishonesty (larceny, theft, robbery, extortion, forgery, counterfeiting, fraudulent concealment, embezzlement, fraudulent conversion, or misappropriation of funds) *requires* the sanction of license suspension or revocation under the statute, with no penalty proceeding allowed.[59]

Although the regulations have given district directors the authority to assess broker penalties up to $10,000 since the 1986 revision, the practice until publication of the new guideline was for Headquarters to review all proposed broker discipline cases. The new guideline specifically returns

58. 19 C.F.R. pt. 171, app. C (1990).
59. 19 U.S.C.A. § 1641(d)(1) (West Supp. 1991).

to district directors the authority to levy penalties up to $10,000.

The power to penalize is not to be used routinely, however. Customs foresees a liberal use of admonition or counseling for infractions: "Penalties should be imposed to punish *patterns* of prohibited behavior, and are *not intended to be assessed automatically* in the case of individual isolated infractions." (emphasis added)

Suspension or Revocation Proceedings

Brokers facing suspension or revocation of their licenses are entitled to a hearing within fifteen days (later if good reason is given in a request for extension) if Customs rejects their written response to the notice of intent to invoke the sanction, or if they fail to respond within the thirty days allowed.[60] If the broker waives the hearing or fails to appear, the recommendation of Customs will be based on the written record to that time.

If a hearing is held, the Administrative Procedure Act will govern it, and an administrative law judge will be appointed as hearing officer. The broker may be represented by counsel, and all testimony will be given under oath, with both parties having the right of cross-examination. A transcript will be provided to the broker, who has the right to file a posthearing brief. The hearing officer's findings and recommendations are reviewed by the Secretary of the Treasury, who issues the final decision. The Secretary may settle a case or impose a sanction less than that sought, including monetary penalties not exceeding $30,000 in cases of threatened suspension or revocation of a broker's license.[61]

The procedure and standards for judicial appeal are the

60. 19 U.S.C.A. § 1641(d)(2)(B) (West Supp. 1991).
61. 19 U.S.C.A. § 1641(d)(3) (West Supp. 1991).

same as those for denial of a license. Court proceedings stay the denial or suspension as long as they are pending.[62]

If a hearing was held, no objection to the administrative record not raised before the hearing officer may be raised in court unless there were reasonable grounds for the failure to do so at the hearing. If additional evidence is sought to be introduced, the court may allow it to be taken before the hearing officer. The Secretary of the Treasury may then issue a new recommendation in the case, if it is warranted.[63]

"Responsible Supervision and Control"

The phrase "responsible supervision and control" is not defined in the statute, and the legislative history does not shed any light on the usage of the terms. Moreover, although Customs Headquarters has been promising a definition of the phrase for many years,[64] the only concrete guidelines to have emerged concern the supervision and control of a licensed broker's employees.

However, "responsible supervision and control" is a concept with a long history in the regulation of customs brokers. It appears to stand for two related, but separate, ideas: the particular idea of monitoring of unlicensed employees' transaction of customs business on behalf of the licensee and the more general idea that a licensed person actually attends to and knows the quality of its customs transactions according to a standard of due diligence and care.

Its initial context is akin to the definition of "responsible supervision and control" currently found at 19 C.F.R. § 111.11 (d):

> The term "responsible supervision and control" means that degree of supervision and control necessary to ensure that

62. 19 U.S.C.A. § 1641(e)(5) (West Supp. 1991).
63. 19 U.S.C.A. § 1641(e)(4) (West Supp. 1991).
64. Headquarters Ruling 710700 (Sept. 4, 1979).

the employee provides substantially the same quality of service in handling customs transactions that the licensed broker is required to provide.

The appendix to the regulations covering assessment and mitigation of penalties against brokers requires Customs to create a standard defining "responsible supervision and control."[65] However, the clearest definition to date is the listing of what Customs will consider as signs of its *absence*, in the same appendix, which authorizes monetary penalties for various breaches of the customs laws, all of which are presumably related to supervision and control.

It begins by noting that the statutory provision for violation of laws enforced by Customs should be cited alongside the one for failure to exercise responsible supervision and control in all penalty notices under that part.

The penalty levels are clearly defined, beginning with a class of $1,000 penalties. These are for brokers who:

1. Continuously make the same errors on a particular type of entry;
2. Fail to properly instruct employees about Customs business, resulting in incorrect entry filings or mishandling of transactions relating to customs business;
3. Knowingly allow their bond to be used to release goods in districts where they do not have a permit; and
4. A catch-all clause for violations not warranting higher penalties.

Penalties of $5,000 are authorized against brokers who cannot produce, on request, documents relating to a specific transaction (except for documents which brokers are not

65. 19 C.F.R. pt. 171, app. C (1990).

required to keep). Five-thousand-dollar penalties are also authorized for failure to show a working knowledge of "any operation material to his or her ability to render valuable service to others in the conduct of customs business": automated operations, cash flow procedures, surety bond retention and sufficiency, district filing systems and document storage, and "continuous monitoring to ensure timely payment of all obligations."

Ten-thousand-dollar penalties are authorized against brokers who fail to maintain satisfactory accounting records or records of filings with Customs. This penalty appears to be based on findings on an audit, as opposed to the $5,000 penalty for inability to produce a specific document on demand.

Finally, $5,000 penalties are authorized against brokers "who fail to exercise responsible supervision and control over the customs business that [they] conduct" as defined in the list of factors following. The list is virtually identical to the list found in the prior guideline, but the specific penalty is a new feature:

1. "High" rate of entry rejections (compared to other brokers in the district);
2. "High" rate of liquidated damages claims for late filing (compared to other brokers in the district);
3. "High" number of missing document cases (compared to other brokers in the district);
4. "Inordinate" (not defined) number of duty-free entry claims without supporting documentation;
5. Inability to assist or failure to cooperate in an audit (includes failure to provide necessary records);
6. Failure to settle or petition liquidated damages claims timely;
7. Evidence that clients do not receive timely duty refunds or that they are not accounted for (this item overlaps the specific penalties in an earlier section

for failing to exercise diligence in remittances); and
8. Employing a licensed individual in the district for a minimal period to keep a company's corporation, partnership, or association license active.

Mitigation

The penalty guideline includes mitigation guidelines as well. They begin, however, by denying relief against $1,000 penalties unless "extraordinary" mitigating factors are present. These are not defined in the guideline.

The $5,000 penalty for failure to produce documents will drop to the $2,000–$3,500 range if they are produced late. If they are never produced, the penalty will not be mitigated unless the broker can show that the failure was beyond his control (for example relations with the party responsible for generating them were broken off). Theft or accidental destruction of documents will be grounds for remission.

Remedial steps taken immediately to prevent recurrence will allow mitigation of penalties for failure to exercise responsible supervision and control and failure to have a working knowledge of operations. These remedial steps include improving employee training and supervision.

A $10,000 penalty for failing to keep adequate accounting records will apparently be cancelled ("mitigated in full") if the broker shows that the accounting system is in fact satisfactory. Such penalties will be reduced if the broker made a bona fide effort to improve accounting systems but was unsuccessful in fully doing so.

Finally, the mitigation guidelines allow reduction of assessments for failure to pay or account for obligations. The basic penalty is the value of the nonpayment or the sum not accounted for. Such penalties are not included in the section on responsible supervision and control but are allowed (up to $30,000) in an earlier section on "violation of any law enforced by Customs." If monies were paid or accounted for in thirty days or less, the penalty will be mitigated to 25 percent of the value of the payment or $250, whichever is more. The penalty rises to 50 percent of the value, but not less than $1,000, if payment or accounting is made more than thirty days after the due date.

It is noteworthy that under the former mitigation guideline, failure to remit or account for client funds was not mentioned by name. Penalties were assessed under section 1641 (d)(1)(C): violation of "any law enforced by the Customs Service or the rules or regulations issued under any such provision." The suggested penalty was the same—the value of the omitted payment, up to $30,000. However, the mitigation guideline was milder: to be based on "negligence."

Since negligence was not defined in the former broker discipline guideline, the Customs Service presumed that the negligence definition included in the penalty mitigation guideline under section 592, for mitigation of penalties based on false statements upon entry, was intended. If the 592 guideline was what was intended, Customs might have reduced broker penalties to as little as 5 percent or as high as 20 percent of the claim.[66] Thus, brokers still facing such claims which arose while the old guideline was in effect might do well to ask for it to be applied.

In recent years, Customs has invoked the phrase "responsible supervision and control" in one form or another in most of the rulings, public notices, and guidelines it has produced in the context of the discipline of customs brokers. For example, recent Headquarters rulings recommending disciplinary sanctions against brokers have suggested the following penalties for failure to exercise responsible discipline and control over customs business:

---

66. 19 C.F.R. pt. 171, app. B(D)(3) (1990).

1. For failing to pay duty bills promptly and keeping inadequate records of financial transactions—$15,000;
2. For failing to furnish an accounting to clients for monies received—equal to amounts not accounted for—up to the $30,000 maximum;
3. For failing to properly declare invoices underlying entry transactions—$5,000;
4. For failing to notify clients of their debts to the government—$5,000;
5. For persisting in erroneous classifications despite warnings from Customs—$5,000;
6. For errors in counting cartons of merchandise—$1,000; and
7. For filing follow-up consumption entries under different entry numbers from those indicated on the early release documents—$5,000.[67]

Further, Customs Headquarters routinely recommended broker penalties of $1,000 under the 1984 Act for each of the following violations: failing to maintain valid powers of attorney ($1,000 for each defective or missing power of attorney), conducting customs business without a permit in the district, and misuse of license (entering goods for another broker without power of attorney). The full $30,000 assessment has been levied against brokers knowingly assisting importers in transshipment schemes to avoid trade embargoes, brokers acting as the undisclosed "import departments" of freight-forwarding firms, and brokers whose record keeping allegedly failed to reflect a large portion of the business they conducted.

In addition, a recent notice from Headquarters has signalled brokers that it is a sign of failure to exercise respon-

67. Unpublished Headquarters rulings obtained by the author under the Freedom of Information Act.

sible supervision and control if entry documents are withheld from timely filing while the broker awaits the importer's tender of the monies payable as estimated duties. Brokers were reminded that they are required to file whatever they have available as of the due date and to notify Customs that the entry is incomplete.[68] In that regard, we should also note that if an importer remits a late duty payment to the broker, the broker must pay Customs the money within five days of receipt of funds.[69]

Anticipating the format of "paperless" land entries, Customs introduced a new immediate release form, the Customs Form 3461-ALT for use at the land borders. It is perforated into two parts: one part to serve as a control sticker to be placed on the shipment, and the other, containing the manifest information needed for immediate release, to be kept with the entry documentation.

Brokers at ports along the land border had developed various ways for one broker to clear a shipment before the importer's actual broker received the invoice and other documents needed to make entry. This was necessary at some of the urban ports of entry, where facilities were lacking for all brokers to maintain full-time staff at the crossings. It incidentally allowed smaller brokers to forgo the expense of keeping employees at the actual crossing on a twenty-four-hour basis when their volume would not justify the expense.

The practice of allowing one broker to file a release form for another broker's shipment was widespread when the Form 3461-ALT was introduced. The new form required no more input from the brokerage community than the previous immediate delivery systems had, with one exception: it was specific to the broker of record, and it was to be signed by that broker.

Customs takes the position that it would demonstrate a

68. T.D. 89-49, 23 Cust. B. & Dec. 23 (1989).
69. 19 C.F.R. § 111.29(a) (1990).

lack of responsible supervision and control over customs business for a broker who is not an employee of the broker of record to perform *any* part of the entry process, including the completion of another broker's Form 3461-ALT. Customs rejected the argument that having a licensed broker perform the essentially clerical task of completing the Form 3461-ALT and filing it with Customs allowed greater control over customs business.[70]

In the dispute over the new form, Customs may have overemphasized the aspect of supervision and control of employees in arriving at a definition of "responsible supervision and control of customs business." It can be argued that traditional agency principles allow a principal to employ independent contractors to perform part of its task, if the work is properly supervised and reviewed.

Responsible Supervision in the Age of Automation

The Customs Service's drive to automate its operations has not proceeded without problems, as can be expected in a change of the size and scope it entails. Apart from the usual technological difficulties such as "bugs" in the programming and growth exceeding capacity, the paperless Customs Service cannot exist without revisions to the regulations and, in some cases, even the underlying statutes.

For example, after a promising pilot program (referred to as "National Entry Processing," "Triangle Processing," or "Free Market Processing") ran its course, a plan to allow importers who make entries at many ports nationwide to file all the necessary data at a single port close to their place of business was delayed to await legislation allowing it to continue.[71] The laws governing entry and examination

70. Position Statement on Relations Between Customs Brokers, 54 Fed. Reg. 13136 (1989).

71. United States Customs Serv., N.Y. Region Informational Pipeline No. 1811 (Apr. 3, 1989).

of merchandise do not presently allow one district director to examine goods while another clears the entry.

In another example, a Customs ruling allows brokers with permits to operate in more than one district to maintain electronic records of their clients' powers of attorney at remote locations as long as a "central" office maintains the physical files.[72] However, the regulations pertaining to record keeping make no mention of computer storage of accounting and transaction records, although they do allow microfilming of such files.

The Customs Service's vision of the role of the broker in the automated future was plainly stated in an internal Headquarters memorandum discussing establishment of the Service's broker evaluation program:

> Customs is rapidly moving toward electronic filing of entries and entry summaries. More reliance than ever before will be placed on brokers in a "paperless environment," and we must be confident in them.

The program's goals are defined as resulting from a "dual approach":

> The bad broker—We will get tough with incompetence. We will identify objective indicators and set guidelines to counsel, fine, or otherwise penalize poor broker performance.
> The good broker—We will permit good brokers to participate in paperless processing and use them in "good" relationships. To do that, we will develop universal standards for electronic filing certification and for selectivity criteria development and updating.[73]

Finally, we find the following item required of licensed customs brokers at the *top* of the list of elements in the disciplinary guideline to be considered as evidence of the exercise of responsible supervision and control: "A working

72. Customs Telex 00684, 04101 (May 22, 1989).

73. Internal Memorandum from Acting Director, Customs Office of Commercial Compliance, Ref. BRO-3-CO:C:F:B BD (Oct. 2, 1987).

knowledge of all automated systems in use in the district including ABI, where applicable."

It is thus clear that in the Customs Service's thinking, broker discipline and an operational automation program are being considered as complementary aspects of the way merchandise is entered into the United States.

The coming years will be exciting and challenging times for the customs brokerage industry. Brokers who can meet the challenges of maintaining their dual responsibilities to Customs and importers while adapting to changed ways of performing transactions will always be needed to aid businesses in the growth of the global marketplace.

8. The Federal Maritime Commission's Role in Import/Export Trade

In addition to the requirements of United States Customs, importers, exporters, brokers, and forwarders are impacted by other government agencies. For those engaged in the movement of goods by ocean, familiarity with the jurisdiction of the Federal Maritime Commission (FMC) is indispensable. The FMC is a regulatory agency operating under a statutory mandate:

1. To establish a nondiscriminatory regulatory process for the common carriage of goods by water in the commerce of the United States with a minimum of government intervention and regulatory costs;
2. To provide an efficient and economic transportation system in the ocean commerce of the United States that is, insofar as possible, in harmony with, and responsive to, international shipping practices; and
3. To encourage the development of an economically sound and efficient United States–flag liner fleet capable of meeting national security needs.[1]

The agency is governed by a regulatory philosophy designed to encourage the maintenance of ocean carrier serv-

1. 46 U.S.C.A. app. § 1701 (West Supp. 1991).

ices sufficient to meet the transportation and national security needs of the United States. The regulatory philosophy is derived from an economic philosophy that considers the steamship industry to be one that needs regulation to protect it from itself and its tendencies toward cutthroat competition. The regulatory scheme limits such competition by allowing joint action by carriers. It establishes a milieu in which they may coexist, earning reasonable profits yet providing choices for their patrons with comparably priced, regularly scheduled services to and from the trading partners of the United States.

Commercially, importers and exporters must be cognizant of the costs of transporting their goods and the most economical means of delivery either as part of the landed cost on which their resale profit in the United States will be measured, or as part of the sale made as exporters to overseas customers. The rates, charges, and practices of the ocean carriers that ply the trades between the United States and foreign countries, both inbound and outbound, in what is termed "regular liner service," are regulated by the FMC. This includes all the scheduled ocean carriers of general cargo but excludes both the unscheduled services of "tramp" operators[2] and the bulk tanker operators. The regulated rates must be published in tariffs or service contracts, and they must be charged to any shipper meeting the terms and conditions filed by the carriers with the FMC.

Special services and facilities such as Customs-bonded warehouses (chapter 9) and foreign trade zones (chapter 10) and incentives to import or export, such as temporary importation under bond (chapter 16) and drawback of customs

2. In Rates of General Atlantic S.S. Corp., 2 U.S.M.C. 681 (1943), "tramp" service was defined as follows:

> A "tramp" is a "free-lance (vessel)" and has earned its name from its gypsy-like existence . . . in addition to having no regular time of sailing has . . . no fixed route and is ever seeking those ports where profitable cargo is most likely to be found.

duties (chapter 17), are affected by the regulation of ocean shipping. Steamship lines will charge in accordance with rates filed with the FMC on the nature and description of the goods. They may recognize the status of "returned shipments," by filing rates in their tariffs covering goods which they previously transported into the United States and which are later subsequently exported after staying in bonded warehouses or foreign trade zones or are otherwise qualified for drawback. That can mean a savings over the regular rates that might apply for the same goods tendered for shipment without this kind of history. Negotiation of special rates is lawful as long as the parties comply with the administrative filing and actual cargo-shipping requirements imposed by law and regulation. Importers and exporters would do well to be aware not only of the regulations imposed on ocean shipping lines but also of those that govern the transportation middlemen who can become involved in the transaction. Brokers, licensed by Customs as described in the preceding chapter, should know that they can dispatch goods via ocean on behalf of their import accounts as forwarders only if they simultaneously hold a license as an ocean freight forwarder.

The regulatory framework under the FMC in these and other areas is set out in detail in the discussion that follows.

Composition

The FMC is an independent regulatory agency of the United States government. Unlike Customs, which is an executive branch agency, the FMC is considered a congressional agency, annually reporting to Congress on its activities in regulating the ocean-borne commerce of the United States. It is headed by a group of five commissioners. The chairperson is appointed by the President, as are the other commissioners, subject to confirmation by the Senate, but the position is not a presidential cabinet post.[3]

Of the five members of the commission, no more than three are members of the same political party. In our two-party system, this means in practice that three members are of the same party as the President, with the remaining two seats being held by the opposition party.

A three-commissioner quorum is required to vote on any matter. In recent years, absences, resignations, and reassignments, have occasionally caused the FMC to lack a quorum to conduct business requiring a vote.

The commission has a staff of approximately two hundred and fifty civil service employees, who carry on the day-to-day functions of the agency. The FMC operates from its headquarters in Washington, D.C. and its field offices in New York, Miami, Houston, New Orleans, Los Angeles, San Francisco, and Puerto Rico.

The staff is assigned to various bureaus and offices, which are under bureau direction in most instances. What follows is a description of some of the bureaus and offices with which the shipping public is likely to have contact.

There are two bureaus that are made up of attorneys and supporting staff. General Counsel, among other responsibilities, articulates the legal positions of the agency. Hearing Counsel prosecutes claims in formal proceedings. It also enters into settlement agreements on behalf of the agency involving suspected violations of the laws and regulations administered by the FMC. It performs a "public counsel" role in ensuring that the public interest is protected in FMC proceedings.

3. The FMC is often confused with the Maritime Administration (MarAd), a separate agency within the Department of Transportation. The FMC's role is regulatory, while MarAd's role is promotional, especially of shipping via U.S.-flag ocean carriers. MarAd is within an executive agency, under the authority of the Secretary of Transportation, which is a cabinet level post.

The Bureau of Tariffs, Certification and Licensing is more than domestic in its scope. It includes the following offices:

- Office of Carrier Tariff and Service Contract Operations
- Office of Terminal Operations
- Office of Freight Forwarder and Passenger Vessel Operations
- Tariff Control Center
- Information Support Unit

The Bureau of Trade Monitoring, responsible for oversight of agreements required to be filed with the FMC, is made up of the following offices:

- Office of Agreements and Information
- Office of Monitoring—Trade Group I
- Office of Monitoring—Trade Group II

The Bureau of Administration handles most of the internal administration of the agency, but it is also involved in the development of computerization, which will affect the public in its dealings with the FMC. It comprises these offices:

- Office of Personnel
- Office of Budget and Financial Management
- Office of Administrative Services
- Office of Information Resources Management

The investigative activity of the agency is conducted in a variety of ways through the bureaus and offices alone and in conjunction with one another; it especially involves the field offices within the Bureau of Investigations.

The Office of the Secretary handles the publication of agency actions in the *Federal Register* and maintains the record in all FMC proceedings.

The Office of Informal Inquiries and Complaints is a focal point of industry contact with the agency. That office is frequently called upon to mediate disputes between the public and FMC-regulated entities.

Laws and Regulations Administered by the FMC

The FMC regulates liner cargo vessel operators, shippers, consignees, marine terminals, cruise operators, and middlemen including ocean freight forwarders and the quasi carriers known as non-vessel-operating common carriers. The primary statutory authority of the FMC is found in the Shipping Act of 1984.[4] Many of the features of the 1984 Act were found in the Shipping Act of 1916.[5] Carrier tariff filing, agreement filing, qualified antitrust exemptions, and the licensing of ocean freight forwarders were all found in the original 1916 Act and its amendments. The earlier Act covered the inbound and outbound trades to and from the United States, both foreign and domestic. It remains in effect as amended with the passage of the 1984 Act, but its scope is limited to the domestic all-water trades of the United States. The 1984 Act addresses the ocean-borne trade with foreign countries, both inbound and outbound.

The regulations administered by the FMC are found in title 46 of the *Code of Federal Regulations*, part 500 to the end.[6] The regulations specify the requirements for compliance with the shipping acts and other statutes under FMC authority, including the laws regarding financial responsibility for passenger vessels[7] and the Foreign Shipping Practices Act.[8]

4. 46 U.S.C.A. app. §§ 1701 *et seq.* (West Supp. 1991).
5. 46 U.S.C.A. §§ 801 *et seq.* (West 1975 & Supp. 1991).
6. 46 C.F.R. 500 *et seq.*
7. 46 U.S.C.A. app. §§ 817d, 817e (West 1975).
8. 46 U.S.C.A. app. § 1710a (West Supp. 1991).

The FMC is a quasi-legislative agency in its power to promulgate regulations affecting the regulated industry. It is quasi-administrative in its policing of statutory and regulatory requirements. It is also quasi-judicial in the hearings it is empowered to conduct.

Those hearings are subject to the Administrative Procedures Act and are designed to secure "a just, speedy and inexpensive determination" in every proceeding according to the FMC's Rules of Practice and Procedure (46 C.F.R. § 502.1). Parties enjoy the right to counsel in all FMC proceedings. In what are termed "nonadjudicatory" fact-finding investigations under subpart R of the agency's Rules of Practice and Procedure, the right to counsel is restricted. There, the person compelled under subpoena to testify or to produce evidence may be accompanied by counsel, which may offer advice; but counsel may not otherwise as a matter of right participate in the investigation.

Fact-finding investigations are often used as an enforcement tool, with parties compelled to testify before an investigative officer, under oath and on the record. The information provided in the fact-finding hearing has been used as the basis for settlement of penalty enforcement claims by the FMC against alleged violators. This tool has been used in the North Atlantic and Trans Pacific Fact Finding Investigations, which have been ongoing for several years. In these proceedings, trial attorneys from the Bureau of Hearing Counsel have served as the investigative officers.

FMC hearings are usually heard by an administrative law judge assigned to the agency, whose initial decision is subject to review by the commissioners. After the agency decision becomes administratively final, appeal may be brought to the federal court of appeals, which can affirm the agency decision, remand the case to the FMC, or order a trial de novo in the federal district court. The court of appeals decision may also be the basis for an appeal to the Supreme

Court, which has the option of denying hearing in addition to the options available to the court of appeals.

FMC Requirements Affecting Importers, Exporters, Brokers, and Forwarders

Among the most important statutory and regulatory requirements to be kept in mind by importers, exporters, brokers, and forwarders are those that relate to the following areas, discussed below:

- Freight tariffs
- Description of the cargo and rebates
- Service contracts
- Licensing of ocean freight forwarders
- NVOCC bonding
- Agreement filing by carriers

Freight Tariffs

Steamship vessel operators and the quasi carriers known as non-vessel-operating common carriers (NVOCCs) engaged in the common carriage of goods subject to mark and count are required to publish the rates they charge for ocean transportation to or from a U.S. port. The rate-filing requirements on ocean common carriers and NVOCCs also apply to such goods shipped *through* a U.S. port to or from a point in the United States.

Under the 1984 Act, steamship operators are called "ocean common carriers."[9] An NVOCC is a legal fiction first created by FMC case law in docket number 815, *Determination of Common Carrier Status*.[10] In that 1961 proceeding, it was held that trucking companies, express compan-

9. 46 U.S.C.A. app. § 1702(18) (West Supp. 1991).
10. Determination of Common Carrier Status, 6 F.M.B. 245 (1961).

ies, and others were as part of their business providing the service of moving household goods and other personal property using trucks and vans which they did own, and ocean ships which they did not own and operate. Because of the advertising of the through movement of the goods, the companies' role in packing and transporting them, and their handling the claims for loss or damage, these "non-vessel operators" were nonetheless found to be "common carriers" subject to the 1916 Act. Thereafter, NVOCCs were compelled to file rates not only for personal effects but for all commercial cargo for which ocean common carriers filed rates. The notion of NVOCC status was sanctioned by its inclusion in the 1984 Act. There, NVOCC is defined as "a common carrier that does not operate the vessels by which ocean transportation is provided, and a shipper in its relationship with an ocean common carrier."[11]

In addition to publishing their rates, carriers and NVOCCs must file freight tariffs in the form and manner prescribed by the FMC. Freight tariffs must contain the rates, charges, services, and accommodations offered on the routes served by the filing party.

In 1990, the FMC began the process of implementing an Automated Tariff Filing Information system (ATFI), which promises to revolutionize the filing and retrieval of tariff information.

Regardless of the mode of filing, the rates and charges set forth in the applicable tariff are the legal rates that carriers and NVOCCs must charge. It is a violation of law for the charge to be greater than, less than, or different from what has been published in the tariffs filed with the FMC.[12]

Under the 1984 Act, shippers are required to pay and carriers are required to collect proper ocean freight charges. For the most part, what is proper is what is published in

11. 46 U.S.C.A. app. § 1702(17) (West Supp. 1991).
12. 46 U.S.C.A. app. § 1709(b) (West Supp. 1991).

the pertinent carrier or conference tariff or service contract on file at the FMC. However, shippers and carriers are not necessarily bound by mistakes or failure to file rates as negotiated.

Suppose a quotation on ocean freight charges has been made, supported by written communications reflecting the shipper-carrier negotiations. The shipper and carrier come to agreement and the shipment is made. Later, the freight bill shows charges that differ from the negotiated rate. If the negotiated rate was not filed, as a result of a clerical or administrative error or inadvertence in failing to file a new tariff, the carrier may be able to waive collection of any increase in cost above the negotiated rate. The waiver can be achieved through the Special Docket procedures of the FMC, under the 1984 Act, provided the Special Docket application is filed within 180 days of the shipment.[13] The Special Docket application can be filed by either the carrier or the shipper/consignee to correct the mistake that resulted in the failure to file the rate as negotiated.

If the shipment moved under a service contract, the error can be corrected, but the proposed correction must be submitted within forty-five days of the filing of the contract under the service contract regulations in 46 C.F.R. 581.

Even after the relatively short time periods for Special Dockets and service contract corrections have elapsed, shippers who believe they have been overcharged and carriers who believe they have been underpaid may still be able to use the auspices of the FMC. They may be able to bring before the FMC a reparation action against a party for an alleged violation of the Shipping Act. The time for filing such an action is three years from the date the cause of action accrues.[14] Shippers have used reparation actions to

13. 46 C.F.R. § 502.92.
14. 46 U.S.C.A. app. § 1710(g) prescribes a three-year statute of limitations for violations of the Act.

protest alleged tariff violations, unfair practices, or discrimination that has resulted in overcharges or other financial losses. Carriers have brought actions against shippers for failure to pay tariff ocean freight charges, alleging the refusal to pay proper charges as an unfair practice by the shippers.

It should be noted that a deliberate agreement between a carrier or carriers and a shipper to circumvent the tariff filing requirements would constitute a violation of the law by the shipper and whoever entered into such an agreement with it. The parties would be subject to the agency's penalty assessment authority.[15] Each party might face a civil penalty up to $25,000 per bill of lading within the context of an FMC assessment proceeding. Alternatively, the parties might be offered the opportunity to settle the agency's potential claim under the provisions for compromising the collection of civil penalties.[16] Thereunder, the parties individually or together might agree to a settlement with the FMC in lieu of contesting the allegation of violations of FMC-administered statutes or regulations. Settlement agreements often involve not only the payment of money but also an agreement to take remedial steps to avoid repetition of the alleged misconduct and/or a promise to cooperate with the FMC in eliminating the misconduct involving others.

Description of the Cargo and Rebates

Accurate description of goods is essential for customs classification and duty purposes, as well as for compliance with Bureau of Census regulations and hazardous substance regulations. It is also essential for the proper assessment of charges by carriers and NVOCCs both into and out of the United States.

---

15. 46 U.S.C.A. app. § 1712 (West Supp. 1991).
16. 46 C.F.R. 505.

If the goods are misdescribed or in other ways misdeclared (such as through misweighing or false report of weight), lower than otherwise applicable ocean freight charges may be achieved. However, arrangements of these types, or untariffed kickback schemes known as rebates, can result in the invocation of penalties by the FMC against shippers, consignees, carriers, NVOCCs, and their agents, to the extent they participate in unfair means[17] to deviate from published and filed tariff rates.

It should be pointed out that ambiguities can occur in freight tariffs. The FMC has held that neither a carrier nor a shipper can rely on an unnatural construction of a freight tariff. However, it has recognized that two commodity descriptions may adequately describe the cargo. In the case of a tariff containing items for both Marble and Tile, without specific delineation of the differences, the FMC has held that a shipment of Travertine Tile is entitled to the lower of the two rates.[18] Ambiguities are construed against the carrier in other FMC decisions, such as *Misclassification of Diatomaceous Earth as Silica.*[19] There and elsewhere, the FMC has said that the shipper is entitled to the lower of the two rates involved in the ambiguity but "the construction must be fair and reasonable."[20]

As the existence of an ambiguity is often a question of perspective, it is one that might not be easily resolved between a carrier or NVOCC and a shipper account without the filing of an action at the FMC. At the FMC, a determi-

17. The notion of "unfair means" generally involves subterfuge, partiality, and denial of similar arrangements to others while allowing one or more entities to enjoy an advantage.
18. Bratti v. Prudential, 8 F.M.C. 375, 379 (1961).
19. Misclassification of Diatomaceous Earth as Silica, 6 F.M.C. 289, 298 (1961).
20. Dow Chem. Int'l, Inc. v. American President Lines, Ltd., 19 F.M.C. 531.

nation may be made concerning the possibility of an ambiguity and the correct interpretation of the freight tariff. If there is a specific commodity listed in the tariff, for example, Wooden Chairs, that item will apply even if there is a separate nonspecific listing for Furniture, which would cover a variety of items not otherwise specified.

Prohibited rebates may take a variety of forms and need not be so obvious as the traditional cash payment. "Deferred" rebates involve the refunding of a portion of the freight paid during a carrier-established period of time, with the payment being deferred until after the period has elapsed, on the condition that the shipper continue to ship with the same carrier. Deferred rebates have been prohibited as a kind of unfair tying device repugnant to United States antitrust law. Other prohibited rebates include the direct or indirect enjoyment of lower than otherwise applicable charges, which may involve a payment to a third party (e.g., a trucking company, warehouse, creditor of the shipper, or other designated recipient). Another form of prohibited rebate, not involving a cash payment, is a waiver of the collection of a payment due and owing to the carrier. The bottom line, when it comes to rebates, is that if a privilege is not extended under tariff authority, it must be paid for in full, without an under-the-table refund or other means to reduce the cost of shipping.

Service Contracts

Since the passage of the 1984 Act, shippers have had the option of moving their cargo under the regular liner tariffs of steamship carriers or negotiating service contracts to cover goods shipped on the same carriers during specifically stated time periods under agreed terms. Service contracts are often, but not necessarily, a discount arrangement between carriers and shippers. A service contract may simply freeze present tariff rates on shipments by the contract shipper for the contract duration. If the regular tariff has not changed during the duration of the contract, there has been no discount. Service contracts may also include amenities not available outside the contract format. Recently, when several carriers tried to extend credit privileges to a specific description of cargo, only to be ordered by the FMC to remove the provision from their regular tariffs, a competitor circumvented the prohibition by putting the credit provision in a service contract.[21] The service contract provision was not contested by the FMC, since service contracts are intended to be the result of individualized terms agreed to by the parties.

Like liner tariffs, service contracts are filed with the FMC. Differing from regular tariffs, however, is the confidentiality accorded service contracts. The *names* of shipper signators of service contracts are kept confidential. The *terms* agreed to by the carrier or conference not only are public, as part of a published service contract tariff, but may be requested by other shippers. There is a minimum thirty-day period after a service contract is filed wherein other shippers may opt in for a similar arrangement. The period can be extended either in the original filed service contract tariff or by amendment to that tariff, at the option of the carrier. If the shipper delays and does not take the opportunity to "me-too" a contract, or if negotiations cannot be successfully concluded during the time set by the carrier or conference, the opportunity may be lost. (The shipper might still bring an action at the FMC, alleging that the carrier or conference refused to negotiate in good faith. This possibility is discussed later in this section.)

Since the 1984 Act first made service contracts an option,

21. Credit Practices of Sea-Land, Inc. & Nedlloyd, F.M.C. No. 90-07 (order entered Dec. 20, 1990).

some pitfalls have become apparent. The following discussion is meant to help the parties avoid some of the difficulties that may arise.

Terms of Service Contracts

Service contracts require the shipper to commit a specified volume of cargo to be shipped with the contracting carrier or conference. The "shipper" may be the traditional shipper from the country of origin, the consignee, an NVOCC, a shippers' association, or an agent of one of these entities. The carrier or conference that is party to the contract commits to a stated level of service (e.g., monthly sailings, sailings between named ports) for an agreed price.

All service contracts contain certain essential terms. Each contract must state the following:

- Duration: specific effective dates.
- Origin and destination: including port ranges, intermodal features, actual locations involved as agreed.
- Contract rates: including rate schedules for various types of service, cargo, or other variables.
- Commodities: description of type(s) of cargo covered by the contract.
- Minimum quantities: volume of cargo required to be shipped.
- Service commitments: carrier's obligation for space, delivery, sailings or other service assurances.

Shortfall Penalties

A failure by the shipper to meet its minimum quantity can be treated in two ways. The contract may provide for liquidated damages, which are pre-established sums agreed to be paid in the event there is nonperformance under the contract. The FMC has ordered that liquidated damages be meaningful. The agency has threatened to reject proposed agreements where liquidated damages are de minimis and thereby give a shipper an unfair advantage where it has not met its obligations under a contract.[22] In the absence of a liquidated damages provision, regulations prescribe that a shipper that does not meet its minimum quantity commitment will have all the cargo originally given the service contract rates rerated at the regular tariff rates of the same carrier or conference.[23]

The FMC scrutinizes performance under service contracts by conducting service contract audits, most frequently through its field offices. If full performance has not been achieved, the agency expects to see the payment of shortfall penalties. There may be an explanation of the failure to pay shortfall penalties, possibly that the carrier failed to meet its service commitments or another legitimate excuse. If no plausible explanation is provided, the FMC not only will expect to see the belated payment of shortfall penalties but also might seek its own penalties from the parties. To date, the collection of penalties for service contract violations has been pursued under the settlement procedures of the agency, rather than in the context of a formal assessment proceeding. Since the statute[24] provides that the exclusive remedy for a service contract breach is an action between the parties in an appropriate *court*, it is not certain that the FMC's authority to hold its own proceeding to correct a breach would be sustained. If the agency were to use an assessment proceeding to levy a penalty against a shipper that had breached a service contract, the agency action could be appealed to the federal court of appeals and from there to the Supreme Court; the agency could be upheld in

22. *See* F.M.C. Circular Letter 1-89.
23. 46 C.F.R. § 581.7(c).
24. 46 U.S.C.A. app. § 1707(c) (West Supp. 1991).

its action or reversed for having abused its discretion and exceeded its statutory authority. To date, however, neither the agency nor the parties with which it has entered into settlement agreements have seen fit to follow the path that leads to judicial review of the agency's actions on service contracts.

Escape Clauses

"Escape clauses" should be part of every contract, allowing a way out of terms that become onerous. Where the contract provides for nonperformance to be excused or for the rates to fluctuate, the conditions that trigger either situation must be set forth. This represents an exception to the general rule that a service contract's terms may not be altered during the life of the contract. Escape clauses include force majeure, a clause that releases contract obligations in case of an intervening "superior force," such as acts of God and government embargoes, but generally not in case of faulty business decisions.

Escape clauses include the so-called "Crazy Eddie" and "most favored shipper" provisions, which allow a shipper to maintain the benefit of a lower than regular tariff service contract rate, when regular tariff rates fall to or below the negotiated service contract rate. Since the passage of the 1984 Act, space availability in ocean transportation has been a buyer's market. Shippers have frequently been able to negotiate, in addition to the Crazy Eddie clause,[25] carrier or conference acquiescence to contract inclusion of a most favored shipper clause, which assures the shipper that the carrier will give no other shipper better rates without extending the same benefit to the contract signator. The two clauses are different in that the Crazy Eddie clause looks to

25. So called because of similarities to deals offered in television advertising by an appliance chain called "Crazy Eddie," which guaranteed to "beat anybody's price" for the same merchandise sold in their stores and in their competitors' stores.

other carriers for any difference from the originally negotiated rate, while the most favored shipper clause guarantees that the contracting carrier or conference itself will not undercut the negotiated price.

Every one of the clauses in a service contract may contain pitfalls that can lead to disputes between the parties or bring penalty actions from the FMC.[26] A contract may also be the basis of an action brought by a third party, as in the case of a shipper that has been denied access to a contract available to others.[27]

Who Is Included?

As incongruous as it might sound, the identity of parties to the contract may not be clearly defined or may exclude persons taken for granted as being covered by the agreement.

If the contract identifies the shipper and adds "and its affiliates as named below," the affiliates must be specified. Even if all the world knows that an affiliation exists between two or more companies, the failure to state the affiliation in a service contract may act to exclude the affiliate from enjoying the contract. "Sharing" a contract with unaffiliated shippers or shippers not named in the original contract is prohibited. Yet the FMC does allow shippers' associations to add members during the life of a contract, and it allows the new members to enjoy the benefits of contracts that predated their joining.

Again, however, the lack of hard precedent at the FMC in interpreting service contracts, the questions concerning the appropriateness of FMC intervention in service contract

---

26. As discussed in the previous section, there is some uncertainty about the validity of the agency's intervention in what essentially is a private contractual arrangement.
27. This raises the question of "similarly situated" shippers discussed later in this section.

matters, and the absence of judicial precedents make this, like other areas of service contracts, a subject of conjecture.

What is clear, however, is that shipping on the vessels of the contracting carrier may not be enough to satisfy a contract. With the proliferation of joint service agreements between and among ocean carriers, Carrier *A* may issue bills of lading on the vessels of Carrier *B*. If your contract is with Carrier *B*, Carrier *B*'s bills of lading would have to cover your shipment in order to count toward your contract.

When Does It Take Effect?

Problems can arise with the effective dates of a contract. The FMC has established a rule that rates must be in effect as of the date the cargo is *received* by the carrier. This is not necessarily the date the cargo is loaded on the vessel. Cargo may be received at the pier days before the vessel arrives. On intermodal movements, the rate must be in effect when the cargo is received at the location at which the ocean carrier assumes responsibility on its bill of lading. Service contracts become effective upon receipt by the FMC. The parties may have no argument about the terms of a contract signed by them on a certain date, but the contract is not effective in the eyes of the FMC until the date it has received the filed contract.[28]

As with all other essential terms, the parties must know what they are agreeing to, including the date the first shipment is expected to move. In addition, the final date of shipment under the contract should be clear, so that the shipper will not try to satisfy a minimum quantity provision *after* the contract has expired.

What Are the Origins and Destinations?

Origins and destinations must be clear, but they should not be overspecific, unless there is no possibility that the

28. 46 C.F.R. § 581.8(c).

cargo can be delivered to any but the specified destinations. For example, naming Charleston as the exclusive port of loading or discharge may be fine if you have a facility in or close to the port. Such specificity may help create a contract no other shipper will opt into, assuming no one has a similar facility in Charleston. If conditions later emerge to make another port more desirable, however, unless the contract permitted an alternate port, the contract is not transferable. If the more desirable port is used anyway, a shortfall may be created under the contract that could trigger either the liquidated damages clause or the rerating of the cargo. In either case, the benefits of using the more desirable port might be offset.

Rates and Rate Schedules

In terms of the rates under the contract, the parties would be well advised to decide how the cargo will be charged, i.e., per container, per weight ton, or per measurement ton. While most liner cargo is containerizable, per-container rates become less than attractive if there are instances when containers are underutilized. To illustrate, a shipper may have slightly more than a twenty-foot container load. A forty-foot container is too large, but after filling a twenty-foot container, the slight overage would also be less than a full load for a twenty. Under these circumstances, a per-ton rate might be in order to pay for the less than containerload and to avoid paying for a second container.

Commodities

As with the origin and destination, shippers should not be overly specific in describing the commodities covered by the contract. For instance, a contract covering trucks does not include truck parts unless it specifically lists truck parts. The category of goods shipped should be broad enough to include all the goods intended to be shipped.

Minimum Quantities

Minimum quantities can also pose difficulties. If a shipper has orders for 200 containers of its goods, should it commit to a service contract with a minimum quantity of 200 containers? What happens if orders are cancelled? Shipping all 200 containers would pressure the shipper to deliver all of the orders for shipment to the same carrier, which might preclude the enjoyment of lower rates from a competitor. It also would put the shipper in an awkward position if, for some reason, a supplier could not provide the goods to fill 200 containers. The shipper would have to fill the shortfall from other sources or risk shortfall penalties. Committing to a lesser amount, such as 100 to 150 containers, would provide some flexibility. If the shipper then could and wanted to ship all 200 containers with the contract carrier, it could do so, so long as all other provisions were met, including the fact that the cargo would be moving during the duration of the contract.

Carrier Service Commitments

The carrier's service commitments cannot be ignored. The carrier has to have the frequency of sailings and availability of space to allow the shipper to meet its obligations. Because a carrier may originally have weekly sailings and later reduce its sailings to monthly, the contract should provide for a commensurate reduction in the shipper's obligation, at the shipper's option. The same optional reduction should be made available to a shipper whose bookings are rejected by an overbooked carrier. A shipper also may be able to negotiate a liquidated damages clause to work against the carrier. For example, if the carrier cannot provide the space, the carrier may be required to pay part of the freight charges of the substitute carrier used by the shipper. This might allow the shipper to pay no more than its original contract rate even if the substitute's charge is higher.

Contract Vigilance

The terms that might change performance or excuse performance, such as force majeure circumstances beyond the control of the parties or changes in the regular tariffs of the same carrier or conference, should be monitored by both parties. Failure to assert rights under these provisions may result in their being lost, especially if the contract has expired and the FMC might be examining performance by the parties. Again, even though the 1984 Act states that the exclusive remedy for breach by one of the parties is in the courts, the FMC has entered into settlement agreements with shippers, carriers, and conferences with respect to their failures to meet service contract provisions.

Similarly Situated Shippers

The terms of any service contract are required to be available to "similarly situated shippers" for a period of not less than thirty days after the filing of a contract. As was seen in the case of *California Shipping v. Yang Ming Line,*[29] qualifying as similarly situated is not always easy. In that case, which could be the subject of a treatise in itself, a carrier was charged by a shipper with unfairly denying the shipper the right to "me-too" a contract. The shipper under the original contract with Yang Ming, as indicated in the agency decision, was General Electric Corporation, a proprietary shipper which owned and/or produced the goods that made up its anticipated cargo for the contract. Within the thirty-day period to opt in to the contract, California Shipping, an

29. California Shipping v. Yang Ming Line, F.M.C. No. 88-15 (decided 1990).

NVOCC,[30] requested the same terms from Yang Ming. The day after the request was made, Yang Ming asked for the record of California Shipping relative to its movement of cargo, completion of prior service contract obligations including payment of shortfall penalties, and a financial statement. In the final FMC decision, it was held that the status of being similarly situated must be determined on a case-by-case basis. A carrier or conference cannot deny a contract solely on the status of the prospective contract party, but it can examine the potential ability of the party to perform under the contract. California Shipping could not be denied solely because it was an NVOCC and General Electric was a proprietary shipper. This does not make a carrier's refusal to offer similar terms to an existing contract any easier, even though in the particular case refusal was upheld.

Conclusion

In the final analysis, some of the pitfalls in service contracts may be unavoidable. As a shipper, you can try to negotiate the "perfect" contract only to have a similarly situated competitor take advantage of your hard-fought negotiations by requesting and getting the same terms from the carrier or conference. Or you can negotiate a contract so nearly unique to you that it might preclude the competition from seeking to "me-too" its provisions, but in so doing, you may set conditions that impede your own ability or desire to meet your contract obligations.

From the carrier or conference point of view, any contract negotiation carries the potential for charges of discrimination. Any successfully negotiated contract carries the poten-

30. As an NVOCC, California Shipping was a transportation middleman, not the owner or producer of the goods, but one that would rely on the goods of others to make up the volume it proposed to ship via Yang Ming.

tial for other shippers to contend that they are similarly situated, raising the specter of the *California Shipping* case. If a shipper enters into a contract and later cannot or will not perform, the carrier or conference is expected to enforce rerating, to invoke a liquidated damages clause, or to excuse nonperformance in accordance with the contract. If a carrier or conference fails to carry out these "unpleasant" aspects of the contract, it risks penalties from the FMC. Questions might even be raised concerning the entry into a contract with a shipper that had no prior shipping or service contract record on which the carrier or conference could have reasonably expected performance by the shipper. In any case, the carrier or conference is expected to act in good faith, and its adherence to nondiscriminatory standards in the negotiation and administration of service contracts may be held up to FMC scrutiny either through an audit of contract records or through formal complaint investigations and hearings.

Service contracts have allowed shippers and carriers to plan expenses and revenues related to transportation services for periods ranging up to five years. Many have been of mutual benefit to shippers and carriers, and have been completed without disputes between the parties or intervention by the FMC. Others have posed problems that might have been reduced or avoided by proper planning. Service contracts can be beneficial, but the obligations they create should be taken seriously. Even though the FMC has not instituted a formal proceeding against parties to a service contract for nonperformance, FMC investigators routinely audit contract records. The FMC has used the penalty provisions of the Shipping Act, which authorize assessment of fines of up to $25,000 per bill of lading, to settle possible service contract violations by shippers, carriers, and conferences. In lieu of the institution of formal assessment proceedings, the FMC and the alleged violators have agreed to adhere to the agency's settlement procedures,[31] wherein the gravity of the alleged violation, policies for future deterrence, and future compliance are considered, along with culpability, history of prior offenses, the ability to pay, and such other matters as justice requires.[32]

Because they have differing interests, all parties to the contract should consider the desirability of maintaining accurate records of activity under and correspondence relating to their service contracts, even if the contracts themselves require only the carrier or conference to keep the records. It may also be advantageous to have qualified outside auditors examine the documentation and recommend remedial action *before* the FMC might become involved.

As in most instances, the advice of counsel at the negotiation stage might head off subsequent problems. But often what was originally contemplated by the parties becomes detoured when an agreement is carried out, so the performance of the contract might also bear scrutiny by counsel. Thus, enlisting counsel early in the process and auditing the service contract during its life might be the most prudent course to follow for shippers, carriers, and conferences that participate in service contracts.

Licensing of Ocean Freight Forwarders

The FMC licenses individuals, partnerships, and corporations to act as ocean freight forwarders. Customs brokers, in addition to handling imports, are often licensed by the FMC to handle ocean export shipments. There is no requirement by either Customs or the FMC that persons licensed by one agency hold the other agency's license as well. However, in order to act as an ocean freight forwarder, including the dispatching of duty drawback shipments via ocean common

31. 46 C.F.R. 505.
32. 46 C.F.R. § 505.3(b).

carriers, an entity must be licensed in the name it conducts ocean freight forwarding business.

Possibly the best description of ocean freight forwarders is that they act as free-lance export departments. Ocean freight forwarders specialize in the handling of the procedures incidental to moving cargo from one place to another, utilizing ocean common carriers for at least a portion of the transportation. They enable exporting companies to have access to qualified professionals on an as-needed basis without maintaining the overhead of their own export personnel. A list of functions performed by ocean freight forwarders appears at the end of this chapter.[33]

The fact that a forwarder might not perform all the listed functions on a particular shipment makes it no less an ocean freight forwarder. The possibility that others, such as banks, typing services, or the shippers themselves, perform some of the functions does not make them ocean freight forwarders.

Definition

An "ocean freight forwarder," as defined in the 1984 Act, is an individual, corporation, partnership, or association in the United States that

> (A) dispatches shipments from the United States via common carriers and books or otherwise arranges for space for those shipments on behalf of shippers; and
>
> (B) processes the documentation or performs related activities incident to those shipments.[34]

Before acting as an ocean freight forwarder in the United States, an entity must apply for a license.

---

33. *See* page 245.
34. 46 U.S.C.A. app. § 1702(19) (West Supp. 1991).

Qualifications for Licensing

Under section 19 of the Act,[35] in considering an application for a license, the FMC must first determine that an individual or organization wishing to act as an ocean freight forwarder has the appropriate experience and character to render forwarding services. Even if an application is approved, a license will not be issued unless the applicant can furnish a bond in the form and amount prescribed by the FMC to establish financial responsibility. Currently, the level of bond coverage is $30,000 for each applicant, subject to an additional $10,000 for each unincorporated branch office from which it would conduct ocean freight forwarding.[36]

Bond coverage continues to be important after the applicant receives its license. By regulation, the FMC can revoke a license *automatically* when a surety bond lapses.[37] Revocation for any other reason can occur only after notice and opportunities for a hearing.[38] In addition to the lapse of surety bond coverage, FMC regulations list five other grounds for revocation:

1. Violation of any provision of the Act, violation of any other statute or regulation related to carrying on the business of forwarding;
2. Failure to respond to any lawful orders or inquiry from the Commission;

35. 46 U.S.C.A. app. § 1718 (West Supp. 1991).
36. 46 C.F.R. § 510.14 (1984).
37. 46 C.F.R. § 510.16 (1984).
38. As indicated earlier, these hearings are subject to the Administrative Procedures Act. Parties enjoy the right to counsel. Revocation proceedings are not brought under the guise of a "nonadjudicatory" fact-finding investigation. However, the possibility exists that information gathered in a fact finding could later be the basis of a revocation hearing.

3. Making a willfully false or misleading statement to the Commission in connection with an application for a license or its continuance in effect;
4. Where the Commission determines that the licensee is not qualified to render freight forwarding services; or
5. Failure to honor the licensee's financial obligations to the Commission, such as for civil penalties assessed or agreed to in a settlement agreement.[39]

The ocean freight forwarder is a fiduciary, a person in a position of trust acting on behalf of others. The Federal Maritime Board, which was the predecessor agency to the FMC, in its *Freight Forwarder Investigation*[40] examined the industry and found abuses such as preferences, indirect rebates, and a general failure to establish and enforce just and reasonable practices. Congress responded by enacting the freight forwarder licensing statute amending the Shipping Act of 1916 as then in effect and empowering the newly created FMC to develop regulations to clarify the application of the law to the industry.[41] The law and regulations were designed to fortify the fiduciary responsibilities of ocean freight forwarders and to ensure their independence from any "shipper connection" that might compromise the forwarder's duty to act in the best interests of the shipper accounts.

Independent Ocean Freight Forwarders

The "independent ocean freight forwarder" could not be a shipper, nor were shipper connections allowed. A shipper connection was found where the forwarder or related per-

39. 46 C.F.R. § 510.16 (1984).
40. Freight Forwarder Investigation, 6 F.M.B. 327 (1961).
41. 46 U.S.C. § 843 (1961).

son had a beneficial interest[42] in goods being shipped via ocean common carrier from the United States to a foreign destination. The shipper connection need not necessarily have occurred on a shipment handled by the forwarder. In the *Cleto Hernandez* case,[43] an employee of an export shipper was denied a license even though it was his stated intention to perform ocean freight forwarding for shippers other than his employer. The standard was so absolute that it prevented even the *possibility* of a forwarder's independence being compromised.

The prohibition against shipper connections continued until 1981, when the law was amended to permit actual shippers to be licensed as ocean freight forwarders, provided that they did not seek or receive the brokerage commissions ordinarily paid by ocean common carriers on shipments where the licensee had a beneficial interest. The removal of the prohibition against shipper connections came at a time when Universal Transcontinental Corporation (UTC) was being examined under a docket at the FMC.[44] Under an order of investigation and hearing published in the *Federal Register* setting out the cause of FMC concern and the possible impact on the licensee, UTC was being taken to task for its affiliation with a shipper of liquid tank containers, which was a subsidiary of UTC's parent company and whose shipments were not being handled

42. "Beneficial interest" includes a lien or interest in or right to use, enjoy, profit, benefit or receive any advantage, either proprietary or financial, from the whole or any part of a shipment of cargo where such interest arises from the financing of the shipment or by operation of law, or by any agreement, express or implied. The term "beneficial interest" shall not include any obligation in favor of a freight forwarder arising solely by reason of the advance of out-of-pocket expenses incurred in dispatching a shipment. 46 C.F.R. § 510.2 (1984).

43. Cleto Hernandez, 19 F.M.C. 104 (1976).

44. Universal Transcontinental Corp., F.M.C. No. 84-29 (dismissed Nov. 16, 1984).

by UTC as a forwarder. The ensuing change in the law not only made the issue in the UTC case moot, but created the possibility for virtually any export shipper to get a license as an ocean freight forwarder.

Although any qualified export shipper can be licensed, regulations require disclosure of the existence of shipper connections.[45] The regulations are designed to prevent improper use of information from an unrelated shipper. Without knowing of the licensee's status, an uninformed shipper might unwittingly reveal proprietary information to a forwarder that is itself (or is related to) an export shipper. An unscrupulous forwarder might then use the information to its own advantage to the detriment of the shipper. The FMC, in its routine field office compliance checks of ocean freight forwarders, pays particular attention to shipper-related forwarders. Examination is made of documents covering shipments made by related export shippers to determine whether ocean freight forwarder compensation (commonly called brokerage) has been received. Failure to disclose the shipper relationship resulting in damage to an unrelated shipper account would also be considered, with possible penalties including revocation of the license for either breach of the pertinent regulations.

Forwarding Fees

Ocean freight forwarders must charge for their services. They cannot rely solely on the brokerage paid by the ocean common carrier as a "finder's commission." However, the ways in which a forwarder can charge for its work are given some latitude under FMC regulations. In the past, the forwarder was required to state on its invoice exactly what it was charged by the suppliers of the various services performed in connection with each shipment. The forwarder's own fee was stated separately, unless included with a ser-

45. 46 C.F.R. § 510.21 (1984).

vice as, for example, "Insurance and Handling." Many ocean freight forwarders continue that type of billing, although they are not required to do so. Present regulations allow the forwarder to aggregate charges and to submit an invoice along these lines:

Invoice

Ocean freight; inland freight;
drayage; wharfage;
heavy lift; oncarriage;
forwarding & handling

Total $15,000

Whether the forwarder continues to itemize in the traditional manner or uses the "lump sum" method shown above, it must still include on its invoice to the shipper the following clause:

> Upon request, we shall provide a detailed breakout of the components of all charges assessed and a true copy of each pertinent document relating to these charges.[46]

In addition, the forwarder is prohibited from withholding information concerning a forwarding transaction from its principal and must exercise due diligence to ascertain the accuracy of any information it imparts to its principal.[47]

The question may arise, Who is the principal? As indicated on the list of functions performed by ocean freight forwarders, the forwarder may be the agent of the shipper or the consignee. Its primary duty is toward the party that has retained its services. That party's identity may not be altogether clear, especially when the forwarder may, on separate occasions, have been enlisted to act by the same shipper and consignee with different consignee and shipper counterparts.

---

46. 46 C.F.R. § 510.22 (1984).
47. *Id.*

Why all the concern? It may be that the consignee is purchasing for consolidation from a variety of United States sources and would not want the sources to know the contents of the consolidated shipment. Conversely, a single shipper could be sending a consolidated shipment destined to be deconsolidated and divided among several foreign consignees. The forwarder, as agent, would owe different degrees of confidentiality in each instance to the participants in the shipments. A simple solution would be for the forwarder to be able to convey information to any participant about that participant's shipment only to the extent it might do so without compromising the rights of other participants. In sum, it should be kept in mind that (1) the forwarder's duties to disclose information vary with its relationship to the party requesting it; and (2) the "principal" in any transaction must be determined by the particular facts at hand.

Compensation from Carriers

Supplementing its forwarding fees, the licensed ocean freight forwarder may be entitled to payment from the ocean common carrier. Referred to earlier as a kind of "finder's fee," it is more than that. The forwarder must certify accurately to the ocean common carrier that it has

> (1) Engaged, booked, secured, reserved or contracted directly with the carrier or its agent for space aboard a vessel or confirmed the availability of that space; and
>
> (2) Prepared and processed the ocean bill of lading, dock receipt, or other similar document with respect to the shipment.[48]

The form of certification is prescribed by regulation.[49] It includes an indication that the necessary work has been

48. 46 C.F.R. § 510.23 (1984).
49. *Id.*

done by the forwarder and that there exists no taint of "beneficial interest" that would disqualify the licensee from payment by the ocean carrier.

The extent of payment by the carrier is governed by the applicable ocean freight tariff. The rate must be published in the carrier or conference tariff. Typically, the commission paid might be 1¼ percent, 2½ percent or 4 percent of the basic ocean freight charge. It may be as high as the carrier will pay and the shipper will bear, provided the tariff reflects the amount to be paid.

It is possible for a forwarder to be paid less than the going rate in a particular trade, but only in the instance of a tariff or service contract item reflecting an exception from the usual rate of compensation specifically identified to the commodity being shipped. A forwarder may not volunteer nor may it be compelled to take less than the amount of compensation authorized by the tariff.

An amendment to the Tax Reform Act of 1986 affected the rate of ocean freight forwarder commissions paid by conferences or groups of two or more ocean common carriers acting in concert to set the level of freight forwarder compensation.[50] If the FMC-licensed ocean freight forwarder is also a licensed customs broker, the amount of compensation paid by the ocean carriers under a common tariff cannot be less than 1¼ percent of the "aggregate tariff assessed against the cargo." Since most tariffs have provided for forwarder commissions to be calculated on the *base* ocean freight, qualified freight forwarders now are entitled to the higher of the regular rate of compensation or the 1¼ percent of the aggregate. Given the proliferation of add-on charges (e.g., bunker surcharges, currency adjustment factors, terminal handling charges), what initially might appear as a meager 1¼ percent payment might well exceed pay-

50. 19 U.S.C.A. § 1641(i) (West Supp. 1991); F.M.C. Circular Letter 86-1.

ment under the "higher" rates premised on ocean freight alone.

Important qualifications should be pointed out in this regard. The amendment does *not* entitle FMC-licensed forwarders/customs brokers to the basic rate of compensation higher than 1¼ percent to be calculated on the aggregated charges, unless the tariff so provides. It also does not entitle extra consideration for dually licensed forwarders on shipments moving via independent (i.e., "non-conference") carriers unless their tariffs so provide.

Relationships Between Forwarders and NVOCCs

In addition to the disqualification of forwarders that have a discernible beneficial interest on a particular shipment from the receipt of freight forwarder compensation, forwarders related to NVOCCs may also be disqualified. Whenever a forwarder that is itself an NVOCC or is related to an NVOCC seeks a commission from the ocean common carrier, it must provide an additional certification before being paid. The required language is as follows:

> The undersigned certifies that neither it nor any related person has issued a bill of lading or otherwise undertaken common carrier responsibility as an NVO for the ocean transportation of the shipment covered by this bill of lading.[51]

The prohibition against the receipt of monies directly or indirectly by an NVOCC on shipments where it has issued its own bill of lading is grounded in the definition of NVOCC and the policy against the receipt of any unfair advantage by a shipper. The NVOCC is a shipper in its relationship with the ocean common carrier. Payment to the NVOCC or its related forwarder is tantamount to a "kickback" to a shipper, which is prohibited under section

51. 46 C.F.R. § 510.23 (1984).

10(a)(1) of the 1984 Act,[52] which has its roots in original section 16 of the 1916 Act.[53] Both sections prohibited direct or indirect use of unfair means to enjoy lower than "otherwise applicable" ocean freight charges. The payment of a forwarder's commission on a shipment where the NVOCC is shipper effectively gives the NVOCC freight charges "lower than otherwise applicable" to any other shipper of the same commodity.

Because the forwarder must affirmatively certify that it is qualified for compensation from the ocean common carrier, it is viewed harshly by the FMC if it *falsely* certifies. Sections of statute and regulation line up against the improper receipt of compensation. Under the 1984 Act, violations that are "knowing and willful" carry penalties of up to $25,000 for each violation.[54] Who would know better than the forwarder whether it had performed the necessary work and was otherwise qualified for the payment? False certification exposes the forwarder to possible invocation by the FMC of penalties for "knowing and willful" violations of pertinent sections of the Act and regulations for *each* bill of lading involved.

Anti-Rebate Policy Requirements

The FMC policy against illegal rebating requires strict adherence by licensed forwarders. An annual Anti-Rebate Certification must be submitted on or before December 31 effective for the next following year by each licensee.[55] A form Anti-Rebate Certification has in recent years been sent to all licensees by the FMC. Failure to return the required certification in a timely manner may result in penalties, as was the case with two common carriers subject to the same

52. 46 U.S.C. app. § 1709.
53. 46 U.S.C. § 815.
54. 46 U.S.C. app. § 1712.
55. 46 C.F.R. § 510.25 (1986).

annual certification requirements which affect forwarders. In October, 1990, they paid $15,000 and $19,500, respectively, for their failure to comply with the filing requirements.[56] The filing obligation obviously is a serious one. In the certification, the licensee is required to set forth efforts in place to avoid participation in illegal rebating, in receiving or arranging such payments. As pointed out earlier, the failure to comply with the filing requirements and the substantive prohibition against participation in illegal schemes carries the potential for penalties up to and including license revocation.

Conclusion

The role of ocean freight forwarders is complex in both a practical and a legal sense. Once qualified for licensing, the sole proprietor, partner, or single corporate qualifying officer is required to oversee the activity under the license whether it is performed by an individual or by a staff of hundreds. The FMC routinely conducts compliance checks of such activity, and it may institute an audit to investigate specific allegations as it sees fit. If a licensed forwarder is not in compliance with pertinent regulations, it may face penalties for even lesser infractions than the illegal rebating and improper compensation problems discussed here. With the assistance of counsel or on its own, each forwarder should periodically review its practices and policies to avoid jeopardy for "knowing and willful" or inadvertent deviations from the law and regulations.

NVOCC Bonding

Effective in April, 1991, the FMC implemented regulations[57] under the Non-Vessel-Operating Common Carrier

56. F.M.C. News Release 90-35 (Oct. 22, 1990).
57. 46 C.F.R. 580, 581, 583.

Amendments of 1990. The law and regulations, postponed from their original effective date in February, 1991, were designed to bring about tariff filing compliance and the establishment of evidence of financial responsibility by NVOCCs domiciled in the United States or abroad, covering NVOCC activity in liner trades to and from the United States.

The regulations have an impact not only on NVOCCs but also on liner operators (VOCCs) in U.S. trades. Ocean freight forwarders and proprietary shippers that use NVOCCs will also be affected.

For NVOCCs, the law and regulations mean filing tariffs and posting of bonds. Tariff filing has been an obligation of NVOCCs since 1961, in both the export and import trades, although the FMC has felt that compliance in the import trades has been substantially less than 100 percent by overseas companies. The bond is a new requirement. It must be established in the amount of $50,000, in the FMC-prescribed form. For some, this may entail the posting of $50,000 collateral or meeting other preconditions set by a bonding company independent of FMC involvement.

The NVOCC that does not comply with the FMC tariff and bonding requirements risks the refusal of its cargo as well as penalties of up to $25,000 per bill of lading under penalty provisions of the 1984 Act.

Co-loading by NVOCCs

In addition to satisfying the tariff and bonding requirements, NVOCCs must be cautious in co-loading cargo with other NVOCCs or accepting cargo from other NVOCCs as shippers. Since the NVOCC is a carrier in its relationship with those tendering cargo to it, it must satisfy the same requirements imposed on VOCCs, where applicable.

Under the original formulation of the rules, liner operator VOCCs, NVOCCs, or their agents were required to ascertain the status of every shipper seeking to have its goods transported to or from the United States under the carrier's regular tariffs. This provision was placed under a stay in the rules that were implemented in April, 1991. Where the shipper is seeking to negotiate a service contract with a VOCC, the carrier must still ascertain the shipper's status.

If the shipper identifies itself as an NVOCC or the carrier knows it is an NVOCC, the carrier must obtain documentation that the NVOCC has a tariff and bond in the prescribed form. If the carrier is not satisfied that the NVOCC has met the regulatory requirements, the carrier faces risks. If the carrier does not reject the cargo, the carrier may subject itself to FMC penalties of up to $25,000 per bill of lading covering cargo transported if the shipper is a noncomplying NVOCC, i.e., one without the requisite tariff and bond.

The FMC has indicated that carriers should not fear invocation of the penalty provisions. The FMC says that carriers may rely on the status representation of the shipper, unless they have reason to know the representation is false. Presently, however, there are no standard indications by which carriers can discern the shipper's status. What does a carrier have to know to dispute a shipper's own declaration of its status?

European "Freight Forwarders"

This may pose serious problems for shippers and carriers. The term "freight forwarder" in the United States is given a different interpretation in Europe. In the United States, the name of the freight forwarder is rarely shown in the shipper identification box of the ocean bill of lading. In Europe, the name of the freight forwarder typically is shown in the shipper box, with no disclosure of the name of the actual shipper/owner of the cargo. Often, the European "forwarder" has issued its own bill of lading, established its own rates, which differ from the underlying ocean carrier, and undertaken common carrier responsibility for the delivery of the cargo. These have historically been considered NVOCC functions by the FMC. If the European "forwarder" wishes to maintain its "forwarder" status, even though it has done what the FMC considers NVOCC activities, what is the ocean carrier to do? The carrier risks a possible $25,000 penalty for dealing with a noncomplying NVOCC, if the carrier does not reject the cargo.

In the case of a shipper claiming "forwarder" status, the VOCC that rejects cargo may be in no better shape than if it accepted a possibly noncomplying shipper's cargo. If the "forwarder" status, rather than NVOCC status, is later upheld by the FMC, the carrier may face charges of discrimination from the shipper and be compelled by the FMC to pay reparations to the shipper.

The carrier can seek to minimize its exposure by complying with the letter of the regulations by obtaining the necessary documents to establish that the NVOCC shipper has a tariff and bond and by making bona fide efforts to ascertain the true status of the shippers that utilize its services.

Under such circumstances, perils may be present regardless of the course of action selected, but their potential should be minimized. The NVOCC bonding law and regulations place a new regulatory tool in the hands of the FMC: industry self-regulation of NVOCCs. Those who would avoid their role in the regulatory scheme by aiding and abetting a noncomplying NVOCC by transporting its goods risk sanctions themselves. These are regulations that should not be taken lightly.

For ocean freight forwarders and proprietary shippers, the amendments and new regulations could present problems from a practical business perspective if they tender cargo to a noncomplying NVOCC. Their shipments could be held up when VOCCs reject the goods offered for shipment by the noncomplying NVOCC. Accordingly, it is imperative for the ocean freight forwarder and proprietary shipper to know if the NVOCC soliciting their cargo has complied with the law and regulations.

Agreement Filing by Carriers

Although importers, exporters, brokers, and forwarders are not subject to the agreement filing requirements of the FMC, they may be substantially affected by agreements entered into by carriers and terminal operators subject to those requirements.

At this writing, the FMC is considering the removal of certain filing requirements previously imposed on marine terminal operators in their relationships with ocean common carriers.[58] If made final, the proposed changes would also affect the tariff filing requirements imposed on marine terminal operators.

As for the agreements between and among ocean common carriers, the ability of the public to intervene and possibly prevent the implementation of carrier agreements has been reduced under the 1984 Act. Continuing the qualified exemption from the antitrust laws, the 1984 Act removed the burden of showing the benefits of a proposed agreement which had been placed on the prospective parties by the 1916 Act. In short, there is a bias in favor of those seeking to enter into an agreement filed with the FMC. Public comment may affect the agency's approval of a proposed agreement, but if the agency does not act within strict time limits to prevent the approval of an agreement, it will automatically take effect. Should the FMC fail or refuse to act to prevent an agreement from taking effect, the public has no standing on its own to contest it. As for the carriers, they are exempt from suit under the antitrust laws to the extent their conduct can be attributed to an agreement filed with the FMC.

---

58. *See* 56 Fed. Reg. 22,384 (May 15, 1991).

Under the circumstances, those who might be most adversely affected by a substantially anticompetitive agreement can only bring their objections to the attention of the FMC and hope that the agency will act to disapprove it or will seek injunctive relief in the United States District Court for the District of Columbia to prevent its taking effect.[59]

Issues for the Future

There have long been rumors about dissolving the FMC, eliminating its functions, or transferring these functions to another agency. At this writing, the Advisory Commission on Ocean Shipping Conferences, mandated under section 18 of the Shipping Act,[60] has begun its review of the conference system which allows steamship lines to concertedly set rates and practices under a qualified exemption from the antitrust laws. Although some sentiment exists to do away with the conference system, replacing it with "free and open competition," those most directly involved in the present structure, the carriers themselves and the shipping public, are largely in favor of maintaining the status quo including the continued existence of the FMC. The Advisory Commission is required to issue a report and recommendations to Congress and the President within one year of its initial meeting in April, 1991.

An early consensus is that the Advisory Commission will not substantially affect the industry as it has existed since the passage of the 1916 Act. Conferences of steamship lines will likely continue to enjoy qualified exemption from the antitrust laws, with new entrants into the ocean shipping trades of the United States being allowed the choice of entering conferences or operating as nonconference lines.

The FMC continues in its plans to implement the Auto-

59. 46 U.S.C.A. app. § 1705 (West Supp. 1991).
60. 46 U.S.C. § 1717(d).

mated Tariff Filing Information system to modernize the filing and retrieval of tariff rate data.

Other areas of concern are the assessment of surcharges by ocean carriers and NVOCCs[61] (which is the subject of an inquiry under which public comments have been solicited) and the ongoing regulation of marine terminal operators.[62] The latter issue is not expected to materially impact the cost of shipping as much as it may reduce what is seen as unnecessary regulation of carrier/terminal contractual relationships. The surcharge issue, however, is considered to be one where FMC action or inaction may substantially affect the predictability of ocean transportation costs. Surcharges have often been added to basic ocean freight charges on ad hoc emergency bases only to become a permanent add-on charge. They have been seen by shippers as a means of obscuring total charges for transportation. Because some surcharges are required to be paid either at port of loading or port of discharge, they have become a cause for confusion and discord between buyers and sellers whose terms of sale do not take them into account. Under the present surcharge system, an F.O.B. or F.A.S.[63] shipment may involve Terminal Handling Charges which will be billed to the shipper. Similarly, release of a C&F[64] shipment may not be accomplished without payment of "collect" Destination Delivery Charges.

In speeches made by FMC Chairman Christopher Koch

---

61. F.M.C. Docket No. 91-14.
62. F.M.C. Docket Nos. 90-6, 91-20.
63. "F.O.B" and "F.A.S." are terms of sale relating to the passage of title at the port of loading, either "free on board" at the time of loading on board the vessel of the ocean carrier or "free along side" at the time the goods are at place of rest alongside the vessel, respectively.
64. "C&F" is a term of sale indicating that the price includes the cost of the goods plus freight, giving rise to the expectation on the part of the receiver of the goods that it will have to pay no freight charges to the carrier.

and by other FMC officials, enforcement of provisions of the Foreign Shipping Practices Act[65] is seen as a major area of concentration. Investigation of the practices of foreign governments affecting U.S. shipping interests has been initiated in the Far East and Latin America, with particular attention to China, Korea, Japan, Chile, Peru, and Ecuador.

Summary of Services Performed by Freight Forwarders and Brokers[66]

General Operations

- Act as agents for American exporters
- Act as agents for foreign importers
- Act as agents for government agencies
- Keep abreast of worldwide developments
- Render needed assistance and advice
- Transmit all necessary correspondence
- Supervise and direct export movements through all United States and Canadian ports
- Maintain and store complete records

U.S. Government Operations

- Negotiate export licenses
- Prepare, co-ordinate and clear Export Declarations
- Prepare and obtain in-transit entries
- Apply for certificates
- Comply with drawback formalities
- Procure all necessary government permits, priorities or allotments
- Represent clients before government bureaus
- Prepare, file and follow up transportation tax forms

---

65. 46 U.S.C. § 1710a.
66. Prepared by Professor William Sembler, SUNY Maritime College, Fort Schuyler, Bronx, N.Y.

Inland Operations

- Procure embargo permits
- Route shipments to seaports
- Trace inland shipments by rail, express, motor truck, barge, or airline
- Arrange government bills of lading
- Arrange in-transit storage

Port Operations

- Arrange rail lighterage to steamer
- Arrange private lighterage to steamer
- Arrange truck delivery to steamer
- Arrange shippers' or suppliers' delivery to steamer
- Arrange car-float delivery to steamer
- Arrange marginal track delivery to steamer
- Follow-up deliveries
- Arrange railroad storage
- Arrange warehouse storage
- Arrange Foreign Trade Zone storage and manipulation
- Arrange representation at all United States and Canadian ports

Steamship Operations

- Negotiate service contracts
- Quote ocean freight rates
- Compile and circularize ocean freight rates
- Issue sailing schedules
- Arrange ocean shipping space, including deep tank space
- Obtain steamer delivery permits
- Compile dock receipts
- Convert weights and measurements to metric system
- Compile ocean bills of lading
- Arrange bill of lading consolidations
- Check ocean freight rates
- Check shippers' packing lists

- Check ocean freight charges
- Reconcile any over- or undercharges
- Secure on-board bills of lading
- Arrange through bills of lading to foreign destinations

Consular Operations

- Have knowledge of worldwide customs requirements
- Convert weights and measurements to metric system
- Compile Consular Invoices in foreign languages and in English
- Compile Certificates of Origin in foreign languages and in English
- Arrange for visa of these consular documents
- Obtain visaed Health or Sanitation Certificates
- Obtain visaed Food and Drug Certificates
- Assist in procurement of Import Permits
- Keep stock of worldwide consular documents
- Maintain library of foreign customs tariffs

Insurance Operations

- Negotiate open marine policies
- Obtain marine insurance rates
- Quote marine insurance rates
- Arrange marine insurance binders
- Issue marine insurance policies
- Secure marine insurance cover notes
- Procure fire and related insurance policies
- Arrange foreign insurance coverages

Banking Operations

- Complete shippers' invoice by adding charges, if required
- Prepare drafts and documents for presentation
- Issue banking instructions
- Negotiate against letters of credit
- Arrange foreign collections and discounts

- Assist in buying and selling foreign exchange
- Follow-up foreign collections and result proceeds to clients

Documentary Operations

- Dispose of ocean documents to shippers
- Dispose of ocean documents to consignee
- Dispose of ocean documents to others at interest

Accessorial Operations

- Present and collect claims against inland carriers
- Present and collect claims against ocean carriers
- Present and collect claims against insurance companies
- Present and collect claims against warehousemen
- Present and collect claims against other parties in interest
- Arrange cable, telegraph, or mail clearances
- Provide messenger service as required
- Arrange for recoopering
- Arrange for export boxing
- Arrange for weighing, railroad or otherwise
- Arrange for inspection
- Arrange for sampling

Financial Operations

- Advance railroad freight charges
- Advance storage or demurrage charges
- Advance lighterage charges
- Advance other accessorial charges
- Advance ocean freight charges
- Advance consular fees
- Pay insurance premiums
- Render invoices for disbursements and service charges

In general foreign freight forwarders may perform every necessary service, from time of placement of order until shipment is delivered at foreign destination.

Part III: Special Services and Facilities

9. Customs-Bonded Warehouses

One of the oldest and more significant features of the United States temporary import system provides for the free entry under bond of otherwise dutiable merchandise into warehouses bonded by the Customs Service (Customs-bonded warehouses). Depending upon the type of warehouse, goods may be stored, cleaned, sorted, repacked, manufactured, or otherwise manipulated. Upon the entry of goods into a bonded warehouse, the importer and warehouse proprietor become subject to a bond liability as security for payment of duties. This liability under bond is cancelled when the goods are (1) exported, (2) withdrawn as supplies for vessels or aircraft in international traffic, (3) destroyed under Customs Service supervision, or (4) withdrawn for consumption in the United States after payment of duty. Customs regulations[1] provide for eight different types of bonded warehouses:

Class one: premises owned or leased by the government and used for the storage of merchandise undergoing Customs Service examination, under seizure, or pending final release from the Service's custody. Unclaimed merchandise stored in class one premises is held under "general order." Goods seized or unclaimed could alternatively be stored in a ware-

1. 19 C.F.R. § 19.1 (1988).

house of class three, four, or five, should space become insufficient or unavailable in class one warehouses.

Class two: importers' private bonded warehouses used exclusively for the storage of merchandise belonging or consigned to the proprietor thereof. A warehouse of class four or five may be bonded exclusively for the storage of goods imported by the proprietor thereof, in which case it is also known as a private bonded warehouse.

Class three: public bonded warehouses used exclusively for storage of imported merchandise.

Class four: bonded yards or sheds for the storage of heavy and bulky imported merchandise; stables, feeding pens, corrals, or other similar buildings or limited enclosures for the storage of imported animals; and tanks for the storage of imported liquid merchandise in bulk.

Class five: bonded bins or parts of buildings or of elevators for the storage of grain.

Class six: warehouses for the manufacture in bond, solely for exportation, of articles made in whole or in part of imported materials or of materials subject to internal revenue tax; and for the manufacture for home consumption or exportation of cigars made in whole of tobacco imported from one country. Cigars may be withdrawn for home consumption upon payment of duties on such tobacco in its condition as imported, and the internal revenue tax will accrue on such cigars in their condition as withdrawn. Articles manufactured in a class six warehouse must be exported under Customs Service supervision. Waste or byproducts from the warehouse may be withdrawn for consumption upon payment of applicable duties.

Class seven: warehouses bonded for smelting and refining imported metal-bearing materials. The end product must be exported or withdrawn for domestic consumption.

Class eight: bonded warehouses established for the purpose of cleaning, sorting, repacking, or otherwise changing in condition, but not manufacturing, imported merchandise under Customs Service supervision, and at the expense of the proprietor. Such imported merchandise may be withdrawn for exportation without the payment of duties or for consumption upon payment of the duties accruing in its condition and quantity and weight at the time of withdrawal from the warehouse even if the authorized manipulation resulted in a change in classification to a lower duty rate.

Uses of Bonded Warehouses

Storage

Imported articles may be stored for up to five years in a Customs-bonded warehouse without the payment of duties.[2] When the merchandise is withdrawn from the warehouse, duty is paid according to the applicable rate and condition prevailing on the date of withdrawal. The appraised values, however, are determined as of the date of exportation from the foreign country to the United States. Where there has been any change in condition of merchandise, other than a manufacture, while in the warehouse, the appraised value may be increased or reduced depending upon the effect the change in condition had on the article prior to its entering consumption. Because of these rules, several advantages may accrue from storage in a Customs-bonded warehouse.

1. Goods subject to quota may be stored in a bonded warehouse until the quota for the applicable category is reopened. Then the merchandise may be "entered" immediately by filing a warehouse withdrawal entry.
2. Storing imported parts, components, or materials for manufacture in a bonded warehouse allows deferring payment of duties until the need arises to withdraw the articles from the warehouse for actual use.
3. Inventory for sale may be stored until a sale is made, at which time the importer has the proceeds out of which to pay the duty, thereby lowering its costs of

2. 19 C.F.R. § 144.5 (1988).

acquiring the inventory. Any number of complete cases or packages out of a shipment may be withdrawn as needed.

4. Pursuant to the Tokyo Round of the Multilateral Tariff Negotiations, dutiable items under the tariff schedules of the United States were made subject to annual rate decreases. Merchandise stored in a warehouse while one or more reductions took effect resulted in the payment of lower duties upon withdrawal. Whether this concept will be continued under the Uruguay Round, which is planned to take effect in 1992, remains to be seen. In addition, merchandise stored in a warehouse while one or more of the staged duty rate reductions covered by the United States–Canada Free Trade Agreement and the United States–Israel Free Trade Agreement takes effect may be withdrawn for consumption at the lower rate. Merchandise that is expected to attain or reattain generalized system of preference (GSP) eligibility at the start of a new GSP year may be imported before the start of that year and stored in a warehouse until GSP status is attained, at which time the merchandise, now a GSP-eligible article, may be withdrawn duty-free.[3]
5. Inventory that is sold to foreign buyers may be exported directly from the warehouse without incurring any duty liability if it is timely exported (i.e., within five years).

Manipulation

Goods may be transferred to a class eight (storage-manipulation) warehouse to be cleaned, repacked, tested, or otherwise manipulated, as long as the process does not

3. *See* chapter 11 on the generalized system of preferences.

amount to manufacturing.[4] A manipulation that results in a change in classification to a lower duty rate is not prohibited by the law. It is advantageous, for example, for the importer to import merchandise whose tariff rate is based on gross weight when the weight can be substantially reduced by extracting unwanted materials before withdrawing the merchandise for consumption.

Manufacture for customs purposes has been defined as requiring a substantial transformation of the material into a "new and different article having a different name, character, or use."[5] For example, the conversion of concentrated orange juice to potable orange juice by addition of water results in a new and different article of commerce and, hence, is not a permissible manipulation in a class eight warehouse.[6] Another example is a ruling[7] holding that the assembly of artificial flowers into floral sprays, designs, or bouquets in a Customs-bonded warehouse is a manufacture prohibited by section 562 of the Tariff Act of 1930.[8] On the other hand, cutting woolen neckwear in a bonded warehouse into scrap or rags is allowed as a manipulation.[9]

The Customs Service has consistently held that a manufacturing process results when the operation involves cutting according to specification and for a definite purpose,[10] as distinguished from cutting solely to facilitate handling or shipping.

---

4. 19 C.F.R. § 19.1(b) (1988).
5. Anheuser-Busch Brewing Ass'n v. United States, 207 U.S. 556, 562 (1907).
6. Cust. Serv. Dec. 82-24, 16 Cust. B. & Dec. 696 (1982).
7. Cust. Serv. Dec. 83-80, 17 Cust. B. & Dec. 45 (1983).
8. 19 U.S.C.A. § 1562 (West Supp. 1990).
9. Cust. Serv. Dec. 80-84, 14 Cust. B. & Dec. 860 (1980).
10. Cutting and rewinding material into smaller rolls to the customer's specifications inside a Customs-bonded warehouse constitutes manufacturing rather than permissible manipulation. Cust. Serv. Dec. 82-25, 16 Cust. B. & Dec. 14 (1982).

The assembly of watch heads (cased movements) by combining imported watch movements into United States- and foreign-made watch cases is a "manufacture" rather than a "manipulation." However, the repackaging of spare watch parts constitutes a manipulation permitted in a bonded manipulation warehouse.[11]

The cutting of large rolls of capacitor tissue into specific sized individual rolls for direct sale to consumers was held to be a manufacture. However, the mere cutting of such capacitor tissue rolls into unspecified smaller rolls to facilitate transport would probably be a permissible manipulation.[12] The above examples underscore the fact that allowable "manipulation" versus "manufacture" is a highly technical issue. Before proceeding with any commercial venture, a written opinion should be secured from the Customs Service.

State and Local Taxes

The United States Supreme Court, in *Xerox Corp. v. County of Harris*,[13] held that merchandise stored in Customs-bonded warehouses and destined for transshipment is exempt from paying state and local ad valorem personal property taxes on inventory, because of Congress's pervasive regulation of customs duties.

In an earlier case,[14] the Court held that imported goods stored in a *general* warehouse awaiting shipment to distribution were not exempt from nondiscriminatory state personal property taxes. Now, however, in light of *Xerox*, imported goods awaiting domestic distribution may be

---

11. Cust. Serv. Dec. 81-118, 15 Cust. B. & Dec. 967 (1981).
12. Cust. Serv. Dec. 82-25, 16 Cust. B. & Dec. 14 (1982).
13. Xerox Corp. v. County of Harris, 459 U.S. 145 (1982). *See also* R.J. Reynolds Tobacco Co. v. Durham County, North Carolina, 479 U.S. 130 (1986).
14. Michelin Tire Corp. v. Wages, 423 U.S. 276 (1976).

stored in a Customs-bonded warehouse, thus avoiding any liability for state or local taxes.

Establishing a Bonded Warehouse[15]

An owner or lessee desiring to establish a bonded warehouse must make written application to the district director of the customs district in which the facility is located. Except for a class two or class seven warehouse, the applicant should state whether the warehouse is to be operated as a private or public bonded warehouse. The applicant should furnish a blueprint of the premises (including measurements and details of material or construction) and state the general type of merchandise that will be stored there, with an estimate of the maximum duties and taxes due on the merchandise at any one time. The applicant must also show evidence of fire insurance coverage. The Customs Service will investigate the qualifications, character, and experience of the applicant and the security, suitability, and fitness of the facility.

On approval of the application, a bond will be executed on Customs Service Form 301 (reprinted in appendix 11) to protect the duty liability on the warehouse goods. The actual amount of the bond is determined by the potential duty that the stored goods would incur upon importation. For those importers who wish to have a bonded warehouse on their own premises, it is recommended that more area be approved than is presently required, to allow for possible expansion. After the premises are approved, a portion of the approved area can be suspended. If the importer decides to expand the warehouse to include the suspended area, the suspension can be lifted upon written application, and thus a repetition of the application, examinations of the premises

15. 19 C.F.R. §§ 19.2 *et seq.* (1988).

and applicant, and payment of additional fees can be avoided.

Record-keeping Requirements

All warehouse entries, withdrawals, and manipulations must be recorded in the warehouse proprietor's inventory records by bond lot number. It is no longer a requirement that the customs warehouse officer be present for, and record, all transactions.[16]

There are no set methods of inventory control required; the only requirement is that the records be maintained "as a prudent businessman in the same type of business can be expected to maintain." Thus, the need for duplicate record keeping is eliminated and the bonded warehouse transactions can be integrated, though separately identified, with the firm's total inventory control system. Records of the merchandise entered or withdrawn from the warehouse, formerly kept by the Customs warehouse officer whose salary was paid by the proprietor, must be maintained by the proprietor.

The system of controlling merchandise was changed to one of annual reporting by the warehouse proprietor,[17] with periodic spot checks of inventory and audits by the Customs Service.[18]

The elimination of the presence of a Customs warehouse officer, while allowing the warehouse proprietor more flexi-

16. 19 C.F.R. § 19.12 (1988).
17. Within forty-five days of the end of his business year, the warehouse proprietor must file a submission with the regional director, regulatory audit. 19 C.F.R. § 19.12(a)(5) (1988).
18. According to a report of the General Accounting Office, the existing procedures for centrally controlling bonded goods at the customshouse, together with the protection of bonds for the customs duties and periodic physical inventories, are adequate to protect government revenues without the additional step of having a warehouse officer present. 49 Fed. Reg. 49,355, 49,357 (1982).

bility in the administration of the bonded facility, has meant that the warehouse proprietor assumes all the rigors and complexities of the record-keeping function. Customs takes this requirement very seriously. Accordingly, if the warehouse proprietor fails to adhere scrupulously to the many record-keeping requirements enunciated in the regulations, severe penalties will be assessed. For example, if a warehouse proprietor fails to properly maintain permit file folders (containing all receipts, damages/shortage reports, manipulation requests, specific removals, etc.) he will be subject to a claim for liquidated damages of $1,000 *per day* for each item that is incorrectly recorded or filed, or not recorded on file, or for each instance of refusal to allow Customs inspection of a permit file folder. Similar penalty assessments will be made for failure to file a warehouse proprietor submission (describing the events occurring in the warehouse during the year, including a complete accounting of the beginning and ending inventories of merchandise) when required. In this instance, a liquidated damage claim for $1,000 per day, for each day following the time such report was due, will be made.[19]

Merchandise can be withdrawn from a bonded warehouse and entered into a foreign trade zone[20] for manufacturing purposes. However, imported merchandise exported to obtain payment of duty drawback or to cancel a temporary importation bond cannot be considered to be exported when it is sent to a foreign trade zone in the United States for manufacturing.

Merchandise in a bonded warehouse may be withdrawn and entered under a temporary bond for subsequent exportation.[21] However, regular temporary importations may be

19. T.D. 82-204 (setting a $100 liquidated damage amount later raised to $1,000).
20. See chapter 10 on foreign trade zones.
21. See chapter 16 on temporary importation under bond.

extended for a maximum of three years, in one-year increments, from the date of *importation*. Therefore, a warehouse withdrawal for temporary importation under bond cannot be accepted if more than two years have elapsed from the date of importation of the merchandise.

10. Foreign Trade Zones

Of all the elements in the temporary import system—Customs-bonded warehouses,[1] drawbacks,[2] temporary importation under bond,[3] and foreign trade zones—the foreign trade zone (FTZ) offers the most flexibility, as well as many other advantages to the importer.[4] An FTZ is a restricted access site, in or adjacent to a customs port of entry, operated pursuant to public utility principles under the sponsorship of a corporation granted authority by the Foreign Trade Zone Board.[5] Proposed amendments have revised the definitions of zone to incorporate the concept that "approved" zone space remains a part of Customs territory until "activation."[6] "Activation" means approval by the grantee[7] and the district director of Customs at the port for

1. See chapter 9.
2. See chapter 17.
3. See chapter 16.
4. In 1988 there were 156 general purpose FTZs and 165 subzones in all but three states. The dollar value in business generated by trade into and out of U.S. FTZs amounted to over $125 billion. J. of Com. & Commercial, Aug. 15, 1989, at 4A.
5. 15 C.F.R. § 400.101 (1983). This regulation will be replaced by 15 C.F.R. § 400.2(g) (proposed) if adopted.
6. 15 C.F.R. §§ 400.100 to 400.110 (1983). These sections will be consolidated and replaced by 15 C.F.R. § 400.2 (proposed) if adopted.
7. A grantee is a public or private corporation to which the privilege of

the FTZ to begin operations and for the admission and handling of merchandise in zone status.[8] It is when "activated" that a zone is legally considered outside the customs territory of the United States. Hence, foreign merchandise may be brought into an FTZ without being subject to the usual Customs Service entry procedures and payment of duty. Within an FTZ, foreign and domestic merchandise can be manipulated, manufactured, assembled, processed, stored, or exhibited, provided these operations are not otherwise prohibited by law. Foreign or domestic merchandise may be exported or entered into customs territory from an FTZ with the payment of the appropriate duties.

Foreign trade zones are the United States equivalent of the free trade zones found in other countries of the world. The United States does not have "free trade zones"; the name "foreign trade zone" reflects the protectionist sentiments of Congress when the FTZ Board was created in 1934.[9]

The FTZ Board issues governing regulations pertaining to the establishment and operation of zones. The United States

---

establishing, operating, and maintaining an FTZ has been granted by the FTZ Board.

8. 19 C.F.R. § 146.1(b)(2) (1990).
9. Foreign Trade Zones Act of 1934, ch. 590, 48 Stat. 998 (1934) (codified at 19 U.S.C. §§ 81a–81u); *see also* 48 Fed. Reg. 7,191 (1983) (codified at 15 C.F.R. § 400.101 (1983)). This regulation will be replaced by 15 C.F.R. § 400.31(b) (proposed) if adopted. Under the new proposed regulations, before authorizing proposed manufacturing activity or in its review of ongoing manufacturing, the Board shall determine that there is no significant evidence that

   1. The activity is not consistent with United States trade and tariff policy;
   2. The use of zone procedures would likely diminish the effectiveness of a United States international trade program; and
   3. If the activity involves items subject to inverted tariffs, that there is or will be a net increase of imports of items on which the duty rate would be reduced under zone procedures as a result of such a reduction.

Customs Service issues regulations regarding the Customs requirements for entry handling and removal of merchandise into, out of, and within the zone areas. The FTZ Board issued proposed amendments to the regulations in January of 1990. These comprehensive amendments include further revisions to earlier regulations as well as changes based upon legislative enactments. The major new proposals will be discussed throughout this chapter.[10]

In 1952, the FTZ Board provided for the creation of subzones to be established in areas separate from existing zones for the specialized purposes of manipulating or manufacturing goods, if the existing zone could not accommodate the desired activity.[11] Zones occupied by single tenants with special needs are becoming increasingly popular for such heavy industrial uses as oil refining, shipbuilding, and assembling automobiles. The former Volkswagen assembly plant in Pennsylvania, for example, was one of the first major subzones.[12]

As a further incentive to zone manufacturing, the Customs Service ruled in 1980 that goods manufactured or processed entirely or in part from nonprivileged foreign or domestic merchandise[13] will not include in their valuation, when entering United States markets for consumption, the cost of United States labor, overhead, assists, and profits.[14]

The legislative intent behind the Foreign Trade Zone Act of 1934 was twofold: (1) to facilitate exports from the United States of goods originating in foreign ports by not treating them as imports subject to United States taxes and

---

10. 55 Fed. Reg. 2760 (Jan. 26, 1990).
11. 15 C.F.R. § 400.304 (1983). This regulation will be replaced by 15 C.F.R. § 400.2(g) (proposed) if approved.
12. *See also* Miller, *Foreign Trade Zones Will Come of Age in the 80s*, AM. IMPORT EXPORT BULL., Mar. 1981 at 22.
13. 19 C.F.R. § 146.65 (1988).
14. 19 C.F.R. § 146.65(b)(2) (1988).

(2) to stimulate the United States economy by involving American production and labor in the manufacturing, processing, repacking, or relabeling of foreign goods admitted into the United States.[15]

FTZs are usually established in or near officially designated customs ports of entry (including air terminals and overland entry sites), at industrial ports of entry, at industrial parks, or at terminal warehouse facilities. In addition to locating a zone in a port, the proposed regulations state that the "adjacency" requirement is met if a zone or subzone is located within thirty-five statute miles from the outer limits of a port of entry or if the zone or subzone can be reached within one hour's driving time from the nearest customs office. They are operated as public utilities by a state or political subdivision, or by a corporation, public or private, chartered for the purpose of operating a foreign trade zone.[16] Subzones are located at a zone user's private facility.

All merchandise in an FTZ is assigned a zone status: privileged foreign (PF), nonprivileged foreign (NF), domestic (D), or zone-restricted (ZR). The status of merchandise determines its customs treatment when it enters the customs territory of the United States (except ZR merchandise, which is prohibited entry into the customs territory).[17]

Privileged foreign status is granted upon application of the importer[18] when the merchandise is brought into the zone and before any manipulation or manufacturing has been performed. The determined duty rate (appraisement and classification) and taxes are fixed at the time of appli-

---

15. *See* 19 U.S.C.A. § 81a (West 1989); A.T. Cross Co. v. Sunil Trading Corp., 467 F. Supp. 47, 50 (S.D.N.Y. 1979).
16. 19 U.S.C.A. § 81n (West 1989); 15 C.F.R. § 400.101 (1983). This regulation will be replaced by 15 C.F.R. § 400.2 (proposed) if approved.
17. *See* 19 C.F.R. §§ 146.41–.44 (1988).
18. On CF 214; *see* appendix 12.

cation and are not subject to future fluctuation. Once established, PF status cannot be changed. Payment of duties and taxes is due when the merchandise is transferred to customs territory.[19]

Domestic status is available for (1) merchandise that is the growth, product, or manufacture of the United States on which all internal revenue taxes, if applicable, have been paid; (2) previously imported merchandise on which duty and taxes have been paid; or (3) merchandise previously admitted duty-free. D merchandise may be returned to the customs territory free of duty and taxes.[20]

Zone-restricted merchandise is entered into the zone for the purpose of exportation or destruction. ZR merchandise may not be returned to the customs territory for domestic consumption except as approved by the FTZ Board. When placed in a zone under ZR status, previously imported merchandise upon which duty has been paid becomes eligible for drawback once it has been exported or destroyed. ZR merchandise may not be manipulated (except to destroy it) or manufactured in a zone.[21]

Nonprivileged status, foreign (NF) and domestic (D), is a residual category for merchandise that does not have PF or ZR status. In the case of NF merchandise,[22] the duty and applicable taxes are determined at the time the merchandise enters into the customs territory of the United States for consumption. Certain domestic merchandise which cannot be positively identified as domestic merchandise will be treated as foreign merchandise.[23]

Merchandise may be transferred to the customs territory, at which time it is considered imported into the customs

---

19. 19 C.F.R. § 146.41 (1988).
20. 19 C.F.R. § 146.43 (1988).
21. 19 C.F.R. § 146.44 (1988).
22. 19 C.F.R. § 146.42 (1988).
23. 19 C.F.R. § 146.42 (1988).

territory and, therefore, subject to entry procedures. The merchandise must be physically removed from the zone as soon as practicable after a permit for transfer has been issued.[24]

To be entitled to duty-free treatment under the generalized system of preferences (GSP),[25] goods must have been imported and entered. Therefore, PF merchandise is not entitled to GSP status, because the goods are not considered entered at the time the privilege is requested. If the merchandise is transferred to the customs territory and entered for consumption, it qualifies for GSP, and any duties paid may be refunded upon the filing of a timely protest. If no privilege is requested, GSP status will be determined at the time of entry into the customs territory for consumption. To avoid losing GSP status, the goods can be first entered into the customs territory and then admitted into the zone under D status.

Nonprivileged merchandise is subject to antidumping and countervailing duties at the time of entry into the customs territory, whereas PF and D merchandise is subject to antidumping and countervailing duties at the time it enters the FTZ.

Uses of a Foreign Trade Zone

An FTZ, like a Customs-bonded warehouse, is primarily used as a place for storing goods[26] or as a site for their manipulation or manufacture. Optimum benefits may be derived by taking advantage of both options. Generally, any firm contemplating using imported materials or exporting merchandise should scrutinize the facilities and benefits afforded by using an FTZ.

24. 19 C.F.R. § 146.71 (1988).
25. *See* chapter 11.
26. *See* chapter 9.

Storage

As noted previously, an FTZ is outside the customs territory of the United States. Therefore, goods located in the FTZ are, for customs purposes, considered in international trade outside the United States. Among the resulting advantages are these:

1. Storing a quantity of merchandise that exceeds the quota limitation for a regulation-specified period is permitted.[27]
2. A manufacturer can wait for a market to develop without paying taxes on its products.
3. The importer can conserve capital because it does not have to pay duty until the goods leave the FTZ and enter the customs territory.
4. Small lots of merchandise may be released from the FTZ for importation with reduced Customs Service formalities.
5. Unlimited storage facilitates exportation to many locations, and exhibition to potential buyers is permitted.
6. Components subject to high duty may be assembled in the zone, which may result in a lower rate of duty for the finished product than if the components had been entered individually or unassembled. For example, an automobile importer could benefit. An auto radio if entered in its condition as a radio is subject to a rate of 8.0 percent. However, if the radio is installed in an auto in the zone it would only be subject to a 2.5 percent rate when imported with the auto.

27. Merchandise may be admitted to an FTZ whether or not its quota is open at that time; quota status is determined at the time of entry into the customs territory for consumption.

Because the goods will be subject to duty only upon entry into the customs territory of the United States from the FTZ, a zone may be used like a Customs-bonded warehouse.[28] The FTZ, however, has definite advantages over the warehouse. For example, there is a five-year limit on storage in a warehouse,[29] but no limit on storage in an FTZ. The proprietor of a warehouse must furnish a single-entry or term bond for each entry,[30] but no bond is required for merchandise stored in an FTZ.[31] Merchandise stored in an FTZ may be exhibited,[32] but not in the case of a bonded warehouse.[33]

The amount of duty payable upon merchandise on withdrawal from a zone into the customs territory may be fixed by requesting privileged status in the zone.[34] Generally, the eventual duty to be paid is fixed as of the time of entry into the zone. This is not permissible for goods in a bonded warehouse, since the statute provides that merchandise shall be dutiable only at the rate in effect upon its withdrawal for consumption.[35]

Manipulation of merchandise (cleaning, sorting, repacking, or otherwise changing its condition, but not manufacturing) may be conducted in a zone as well as in a bonded warehouse.[36]

---

28. 15 C.F.R. § 400.101 (1983). This regulation would be replaced by 15 C.F.R. § 400.2(g) (proposed) if approved. See chapter 9 for a discussion of Customs-bonded warehouses.
29. 19 U.S.C.A. § 1557(a) (West Supp. 1989).
30. 19 C.F.R. § 142.4 (1988).
31. 19 C.F.R. § 146.41 (1988).
32. 15 C.F.R. § 400.101 (1983). This regulation would be replaced by 15 C.F.R. § 400.2(g) (proposed) if approved.
33. *See* 19 C.F.R. § 19.1 (1988); 15 C.F.R. § 400.101 (1983). The latter regulation would be replaced by 15 C.F.R. § 400.2(g) (proposed) if approved.
34. 19 C.F.R. § 146.65 (1988); see also discussion above.
35. 19 U.S.C.A. § 1315 (West 1980).
36. 15 C.F.R. § 400.803 (1983). This regulation would be eliminated as covered by 19 C.F.R. § 146 (proposed) if approved; 19 U.S.C.A. §§ 1555–1556 (West 1980 & Supp. 1989); 19 C.F.R. § 19.11 (1988).

However, if the manipulation in the FTZ would place the goods under a higher duty classification, but the goods had been placed in PF status, the manipulated goods can be taken into the customs territory with payment at the earlier fixed lower rate of duty.[37] On the other hand, if the same manipulation had occurred in a manipulation warehouse, the withdrawal must be at the higher rate.

Counterbalancing the advantages noted above are several disadvantages. Because of the added services of an FTZ, storage rates tend to be higher than in a bonded warehouse. Regulations allow firms to set aside a portion of their premises for the establishment of a bonded warehouse.[38] In the early 1980s, changes in customs regulations greatly reduced the amount of Customs Service supervision of bonded warehouses, rendering operation of an in-house bonded warehouse more convenient and inexpensive than use of the facilities of an FTZ under certain circumstances.[39] Even if the importer plans to subject the imported merchandise to manufacturing processes (for example, smelting and refining imported metal-bearing materials in class 7), an in-house bonded warehouse may still be more cost-effective than an FTZ or a subzone.

In addition, the proposed regulations contain a new provision that states the factors that will be considered by the Board in its public interest evaluation of applications for zone status or ongoing activity in a zone.[40]

A threshold provision would bar zone activity that is not consistent with public policy and U.S. trade programs. It is the policy of the Board to authorize zone activity only when it is consistent with public policy and does not encourage imports.[41]

37. 19 C.F.R. § 146.65 (1988).
38. 19 C.F.R. § 19.1 (1988).
39. 47 Fed. Reg. 49,355 (1982) (codified at various sections of 19 C.F.R. pts. 10, 18, 19, 22, 24, 113, 125, 127, 132, 142 & 144).
40. 19 C.F.R. § 400.31 (proposed).
41. *Id.*

For example, zone operators are permitted to import foreign automotive parts, mix them with domestic components to build a finished automobile, and then ship that finished automobile into the United States for sale at the local car dealership. When the foreign components are about to be utilized in the manufacture of finished automobiles, the importer has the option to select either the 2.5 percent rate usually reserved for finished automobiles or the higher rate usually reserved for automotive parts—averaging from 4 to 11 percent. While the importer invariably chooses the lower rate, even after the costs of operation in the zone are taken into account, the importer has the option under the FTZ program of selecting the rate which applies to the condition of the foreign goods at the time they first enter the FTZ or the rate which applies to the condition of the goods at the time they enter United States customs territory.

Accordingly, although an FTZ may be used as a storage facility in a similar fashion as a Customs-bonded warehouse, the better course is to make storage secondary to the primary objective of using the FTZ for manipulation and manufacturing, which holds considerably more benefits if consistent with public policy and U.S. trade program objectives.

Manufacturing

Reductions or avoidance of otherwise payable duty depends on the nature of the completed manufacture and the status of the merchandise that went into it.[42] The manufacture that is wholly NF, D, or PF is rare.

Assume, for example, that *A* operates a manufacturing facility in an FTZ to build widgets. Widgets are dutiable at 8 percent ad valorem. *A* uses domestic and foreign compo-

42. As discussed above, merchandise can be nonprivileged foreign (NF), domestic (D), or privileged foreign (PF).

nents in its widgets. Some of the foreign components are dutiable at 8 percent or less, some are dutiable at higher rates, and some come from beneficiary developing countries under the generalized system of preferences (GSP)[43] and are, therefore, duty-free. Given these facts, *A* should structure its applications for FTZ status as follows:

1. Domestic components should be admitted to the FTZ under D status.
2. Any foreign components already entered into the customs territory after payment of duty should be admitted to the FTZ under D status.
3. GSP components should be entered directly into the customs territory duty free[44] and then admitted to the FTZ under D status.
4. Foreign components dutiable at 8 percent or less should be admitted to the FTZ under PF status.
5. Foreign components dutiable at more than 8 percent should be admitted to the FTZ under NF status.

The effect of this is that the D merchandise (items 1–3) may be returned to the customs territory free of duty. The PF merchandise enters the customs territory at the low rate fixed when it was admitted to the FTZ with privileged status. The NF merchandise enters the customs territory at the widgets' 8 percent rate. Finally, American labor, overhead, assists, and profit are not included in the appraised value.[45]

When manufacturing[46] is complete, the finished product

---

43. See chapter 11.
44. Goods potentially qualified for GSP treatment must enter the customs territory to avoid duty.
45. See chapter 4.
46. Manufacturing is defined in 15 C.F.R. § 400.2(i) (proposed) as any activity involving foreign merchandise admitted into a zone which results in a change in its customs classification or in its eligibility for entry for consumption.

is a product of the United States and may bear the "Made in U.S.A." legend.[47] Furthermore, if it is exported directly from the zone without passing through the customs territory of the United States, no duty liability will accrue.

Other benefits of manufacturing in an FTZ include:

1. *Transforming dutiable materials into duty-free goods.* For example, a company could use a New Orleans subzone to manufacture barges of imported steel. Barges are commercial vessels, which are not subject to duty. There is no duty liability when the barges enter the customs territory of the United States.[48]
2. *Removing the taint of Communism.* For example, goods from the Soviet Union[49] are subject to a rate of duty well above that for goods from countries with most-favored-nation status.[50] If, however, they are admitted to an FTZ as NF merchandise and substantially transformed, they will be treated as most-favored-nation goods when they come out.[51]
3. *Avoiding quota delays or worse.* Textiles and electronic products, for example, are quota-sensitive—they may be fabricated into nonquota goods in an FTZ.
4. *Culling the shipment.* Rather than pay full duty on excess, waste, damaged, or substandard materials, the user of an FTZ can process or sort them out before they enter the customs territory.

Using a zone can also lower insurance rates and facilitate the recovery of drawbacks.[52] However, imported merchan-

47. 19 U.S.C. § 81(c).
48. Armco Steel Corp. v. Stans, 431 F.2d 779 (2d Cir. 1970).
49. HTSUS General Note 3(b) omits some countries.
50. *Id.*; 19 U.S.C.A. § 1202 (West 1978 & Supp. 1989).
51. Cust. Serv. Dec. 79-41, 13 Cust. B. & Dec. 1056 (1979).
52. See chapter 17.

dise exported to obtain the payment of duty drawback or to cancel a temporary importation bond cannot be considered to be exported when it is sent to an FTZ in the United States for manufacturing.[53]

There is no duty liability for imported merchandise that is consumed in the course of manufacturing in the FTZ, e.g., imported fuel.[54]

An importer, Nissan, seeking to apply this principle to cover production machinery imported from Japan into an FTZ subzone for use there in producing automobiles was denied duty-free treatment for the machinery by the Court of International Trade (CIT) and the Court of Appeals for the Federal Circuit.[55] Nissan entered the machinery, which consisted of an automated integrated system of industrial robots, conveyor and stamping systems, claiming that the use of the production machinery resulted in its "consumption" during the course of production of the completed automobiles. The court of appeals agreed with the CIT and rejected Nissan's contention that such machinery entered into a zone becomes subject to duty only if the machinery is sent into customs territory.

The court held that Nissan's reading of the Foreign Trade Zones Act, 19 U.S.C. §§ 81a–81u (1982), was overbroad. It noted that the CIT was correct in deciding that Congress signaled its intention to make the imposition of immediate duties dependent on the operations that occur in one zone

---

53. TD 89-4 Feb. 27, 1989. *See also* Chrysler Motors Corp. v. United States, 755 F. Supp. 388 (Ct. Int'l Trade 1990), which upholds the Customs Service's ruling; since the merchandise was entered into an FTZ in the United States for manufacture rather than exportation or destruction, no drawback claims were authorized. At the time of this writing, the case was being appealed. *See also* chapter 17.

54. Hawaiian Indep. Refinery v. United States, 460 F. Supp. 1249 (Cust. Ct. 1978).

55. Nissan Motor Mfg. Corp. v. United States, 693 F. Supp. 1183 (Ct. Int'l Trade 1988), *aff'd*, 884 F.2d 1375 (Fed. Cir. 1989).

when it listed the activities that could be performed on the merchandise brought into the zone. The list of permissible activities demonstrated that Congress did not intend a blanket exclusion from customs duties in an FTZ. Accordingly, while material consumed in the course of production would be exempt from duty, the machinery used in the production is not.

In addition, any waste generated, whether from privileged or nonprivileged material, during manufacturing is given NF status.[56] Waste from goods destroyed in an FTZ is likewise nonprivileged.[57]

Mixtures in the Zone

The Customs Service noted that jet fuels, foreign and domestic, are considered to be finished products and that the mixing of the finished products to arrive at a certain specification or to complete customer orders would not involve further processing of the jet fuels through the refinery. Accordingly a Customs Service Decision (CSD)[58] was issued that held that a known volume of domestic jet fuel in an FTZ may be mixed with a known volume of foreign jet fuel and retain its identity as domestic jet fuel, when the proportions of the domestic and foreign components in the mixture have been determined by independent volume measurement prior to mixing.

The statute provides that domestic, duty-paid, or free-of-duty articles may be taken into a zone from customs territory, combined with or made part of other articles while in the zone and returned to customs territory free of duty so long as their identity has not been lost.[59] Essential to the

56. 19 C.F.R. § 146.42 (1988).
57. *Id.*
58. Cust. Serv. Dec. 82-152, 16 Cust. B. & Dec. 989 (1982).
59. 19 U.S.C.A. § 81c(a) (West Supp. 1990).

determination is whether the identity of the domestic jet fuel, privileged foreign jet fuel, and nonprivileged foreign jet fuel can be ascertained after mixing, in order that the portion of the combined product attributable to the domestic jet fuel may be returned to customs territory free of duty. For example, if ten barrels of finished specification domestic jet fuel are mixed with ten barrels of finished specification foreign jet fuel and that blend consistently results in a mixture totalling twenty barrels, and if proof is submitted establishing that the twenty-barrel mixture removed from the zone was the result of mixing ten barrels of domestic jet fuel with ten barrels of foreign jet fuel, the domestic jet fuel does not lose its status as domestic for the purposes of the statute and regulations.

Destruction of Goods

Except for alcohol, merchandise may be entered into an FTZ for destruction. The destruction of merchandise in a zone may be performed in any manner, and it may yield a high amount and quality of waste products, as long as it is a continuous act of destruction.[60] For example, defective electronic semiconductors coated with precious metals may be brought into a zone as zone-restricted (ZR) merchandise. They may be placed in a cyanide bath to remove the metal overlay before being crushed. Although the merchandise brought into the zone for destruction had ZR status (i.e., it could not enter or reenter the customs territory), waste produced by its destruction is nonprivileged and may be entered into the customs territory of the United States upon payment of the applicable duties.

60. 19 C.F.R. § 146.52 (1988).

Procedures for the Foreign Trade Zone

The Customs Service is responsible for the transfer of merchandise into and out of a zone and for matters involving the collection of revenue.[61] The district director of the district in which a zone is located is in charge of the zone as the local representative of the FTZ Board.[62] He or she controls the admission of merchandise into the zone, the handling and disposition of merchandise within the zone, and the removal of merchandise from the zone. Zones are supervised by United States Customs Service officers, whose salaries are reimbursed by the zone grantees to the Service.[63]

Each port of entry in the United States is entitled to have at least one FTZ.[64] A zone may be established when a corporation, public or private, applies to the FTZ Board.[65] The Board, which consists of the Secretary of Commerce, Secretary of the Treasury, and Secretary of the Army, will grant the privilege of establishing an FTZ if it finds that the proposed plans and location will expedite and encourage commerce and that the proposed facilities and appurtenances are sufficient.[66] As part of the process, the applicant must provide information on the economic and environmental impact of the proposed zone, describe the proposed facilities, and demonstrate that it has the ability to finance

61. 19 U.S.C.A. § 81d (West 1989); 19 C.F.R. § 146.3 (1988).
62. 19 C.F.R. § 146.2 (1988).
63. 19 C.F.R. § 146.5 (1988); proposed regulations have eliminated 15 C.F.R. § 400.814 (1983) because it is covered in 19 C.F.R. § 146.
64. 19 U.S.C.A. § 81b (West 1989); 15 C.F.R. § 400.300 (1983). The latter regulation will be replaced by 15 C.F.R. § 400.21 (proposed) if adopted.
65. 19 U.S.C.A. §81b (West 1989); 15 C.F.R. §§ 400.105–.200 (1983).
66. 15 C.F.R. §§ 400.103 & 400.200 (1983). This regulation will be replaced by 15 C.F.R. §§ 400.2 & 400.11 (proposed) if adopted.

and conduct zone operations.[67] A successful applicant is required to operate its FTZ as a public utility,[68] i.e., all the services and facilities must be open to all who apply.

Three forms (CF 214, CF 7501, and CF 216, reprinted in appendixes 12, 7, and 13) are pivotal to FTZ procedure. CF 214 is an application for zone status and to admit merchandise into the zone. CF 7501 is an application for the entry of merchandise into the customs territory of the United States. CF 216 is an application for manipulation, manufacture, exhibition, or destruction of FTZ merchandise. Prior concurrence of the FTZ Board is required when a new manufacturing activity is involved.[69]

---

67. 19 U.S.C.A. § 81f (West 1989); 15 C.F.R. §§ 400.400–.401 (1983). This regulation will be revised by 15 C.F.R. § 400.31(b)(2) which outlines the criteria for approving zones in addition to the threshold provisions set forth in 15 C.F.R. § 400.31(b) (proposed) if approved (note 9, *supra*). The criteria are as follows:
    1. The need for zone services in a port;
    2. The adequacy of operational and financial plans;
    3. Local government support and community goals;
    4. The views of persons and firms affected by the proposed zone activity; and
    5. Certain threshold factors for manufacturing in the zone.
68. 15 C.F.R. § 400.1003 (1983). This regulation will be replaced by 19 C.F.R. § 400.42 (proposed) if approved.
69. 19 C.F.R. § 146.52 (1988).

Part IV: Incentives to Import or Export

11. Generalized System of Preferences

The United States Generalized System of Preferences (GSP) allows duty-free entry for certain eligible articles imported directly from less developed countries designated as beneficiary developing countries (BDCs).[1] The most current listing of BDCs can be found in General Note 3(c)(ii), HTSUS. In addition, we have included a list of BDCs, current at the time of this writing, at the end of the chapter. It is important to note at the outset that the right to have goods imported duty-free under GSP must be claimed. In the absence of a claim for GSP treatment, the Customs Service will levy and collect the full rate of duty.

Most of the trading world's industrialized countries have a system of tariff preferences in favor of the less developed

1. Another preferential system similar to the GSP programs covers the United States insular possessions, e.g., the United States Virgin Islands. Established under HTSUS General Note 3(a), this system gives duty-free treatment to goods from the insular possessions if the following rules of origin are satisfied:

    1. The product is imported directly into the United States;
    2. The product is the growth, product, or manufacture of the insular possession; and
    3. The content of foreign material in the product is valued at no more than 70 percent (50 percent for certain products like textiles and articles of apparel) of the product's appraised value.

countries. Beginning in the mid-1960s, the developing countries of the world, through the forums provided by the United Nations Commission on Trade and Development and the General Agreement on Tariffs and Trade, began to express the need for assistance from the industrialized nations in developing their economies. One of the keys to industrial development in less developed countries has been the adoption by the developed nations of systems of tariff preferences for imports from the developing countries, particularly for manufactured and semimanufactured goods. The tariff schedules of most industrialized nations generally provide graduated rates keyed to the degree of processing or manufacturing performed on the raw material. However, there are many exceptions to this general rule.

Examples illustrating the rule are: bauxite ore is duty-free; unwrought aluminum in uniform cross section in coils has a duty rate of 3 percent ad valorem; angles, shapes, and sections of wrought aluminum are dutiable at 7.8 percent ad valorem; and articles of aluminum not coated or plated with precious metal not specially provided for are dutiable at 8.1 percent ad valorem.

Beginning in 1967 with Australia, the industrialized nations began enacting generalized systems of preferences. The preference systems vary from country to country, but generally they are designed to reduce or eliminate tariffs for a broad range of goods from less developed countries, seeking particularly to eliminate the tariff rate distinction between processed and unprocessed goods.

With the passage of the Trade Act of 1974, the United States became the nineteenth and last industrialized nation to adopt a generalized system of preferences. The United States GSP was established for a ten-year period beginning January 1, 1976, and was amended by the Trade Agreements Act of 1979 to provide termination of the program on January 3, 1985. This provision has been extended for an additional ten years to July 4, 1995.

The Trade Act of 1974 does not designate any GSP-eligible articles nor does it designate any BDCs. Rather, it gives the President authority to make those designations in compliance with certain guidelines and limitations set by Congress.

GSP has not benefited all BDCs equally. Those BDCs with the greatest industrial and capital bases have obtained the largest share of GSP benefits. Taiwan, Hong Kong, and South Korea accounted for 50 percent of all imports under GSP, and Brazil and Mexico for another 20 percent. Critics of the GSP program were quick to point out that the incentives provided by GSP went to those who needed it least, while those at the very bottom of the economic scale have reaped little benefit. In response to such criticism, Congress has caused the removal from GSP eligibility of Taiwan, Hong Kong, South Korea, and Singapore (which countries were removed as BDCs on January 1, 1989), and it has tightened requirements for the more developed BDCs' taking advantage of GSP opportunities in an effort to encourage the development of the least developed developing countries (LDDCs). The United States Trade Representative (USTR) is aggressively removing eligible articles on her own initiative from GSP benefits when imported from the most developed BDCs, and there is also pressure to remove more BDCs from the program entirely.

As previously indicated, the United States GSP program, initiated in 1976, was to expire on January 3, 1985. However, the program was extended by the Trade and Tariff Act of 1984 (TTA). Among the trade measures of the new act, one of the most significant was the authorization of a renewal of the program through July 4, 1995.[2] Certain changes

2. 19 U.S.C.A. § 2465 (West Supp. 1990).

have been made, however, in the operation of the program. These modifications include the following:

1. The President is now required to conduct periodic reviews of all GSP-eligible products.[3] The first review was completed on January 4, 1987, and its findings became effective July 1, 1987.

The purpose of the review is to determine which products have attained a sufficient degree of competitiveness to remove the necessity of duty-free status for such products, resulting in subsequent removal of GSP benefits for those specific products.[4] Where the President, following such periodic review, determines that a specific country is competitive with respect to any eligible product, a lower "competitive-need limit" equal to 25 percent of total United States imports of that product or a certain dollar amount ($25 million in 1985), which has been and will continue to be adjusted annually to reflect the growth in the United States gross national product (GNP), will become applicable. Accordingly, should a particular GSP-eligible product be imported to the United States in amounts equal to or exceeding the applicable competitive-need limit (any eligible article equal to or exceeding 50 percent of the appraised value of the total imports of such article into the United States during the calendar year), the President may lower the limit and eventually remove the product from the GSP-eligible list. Otherwise, the current limits, also adjusted annually, will continue to apply.[5]

Under the 1979 amendments to the program, the 50 percent competitive-need ceiling was waived for products for which total United States imports are de minimis, i.e., not more than $1 million plus annual adjustments for changes in the GNP during the preceding calendar year. The Interna-

3. 19 U.S.C.A. § 2464 (West Supp. 1990).
4. 19 U.S.C.A. § 2464(a) (West Supp. 1990).
5. 19 U.S.C.A. § 2464(d) (West Supp. 1990).

tional Trade Administration (ITA) raised the $1 million maximum to $5 million, retroactive to 1979.[6]

2. The President is now authorized to waive competitive-need limits based on the national economic interest. However, prior to exercising this authority, the President must seek the advice of the International Trade Commission regarding possible adverse effects on United States industries.[7]

3. An amendment provides for the graduation (phasing out from the GSP program) of the more advanced beneficiary countries. A beneficiary country reaching a designated per capita income level will be graduated from GSP privileges by the end of the two-year period following that determination.[8]

4. Handbags, luggage, flat goods, work gloves, and leather wearing apparel were historically not eligible for GSP treatment by virtue of the fact that these articles were simply not designated as GSP-eligible in the tariff schedules. However these import-sensitive articles now have been statutorily designated ineligible for future duty-free treatment.[9]

5. The following factors have been added to those that the President must consider when making a determination concerning designation of a country as a BDC:[10]

- Amount of protection afforded by a beneficiary country to foreign nationals with regard to rights in intellectual property (patents, copyrights, and trademarks);
- Extent to which a country has or is initiating procedures to grant certain "internationally recognized worker rights," i.e., right to organize and bargain collectively, protection against forced labor; and
- Extent to which the country has taken action to reduce unfair trade practices with regard to investment and trade in services.

6. *Id.*
7. 19 U.S.C.A. § 2464(d) (West Supp. 1990).
8. 19 U.S.C.A. § 2463(d), (f) (West Supp. 1990).
9. 19 U.S.C.A. § 2462 (West Supp. 1990).
10. 19 U.S.C.A. § 2462(c) (West 1990).

Designation of Eligible Articles

An "eligible article" must conform to the HTSUS classification number. This number determines the applicable rate of duty, with variables depending upon country of origin and GSP status. Eligible articles are designated by the President and indicated in the tariff schedules by an "A" placed in the GSP column in front of the HTSUS number. The list is subject to change at any time with notice from the office of the USTR.

The President may not designate any article as eligible if it is within one of the following categories of import-sensitive articles:

1. Textile and apparel articles which are subject to textile agreements;
2. Watches;
3. Import-sensitive electronic articles;
4. Import-sensitive steel articles;
5. Footwear articles, handbags, luggage, flat goods, work gloves, and leather wearing apparel;
6. Import-sensitive semimanufactured and manufactured glass products; and
7. Any other articles which the President determines to be import-sensitive in the context of the Generalized System of Preferences.[11]

The term "import-sensitive" is not defined in the statute and has not been defined by the courts. The term, however, may be said to include "merchandise imported under such conditions as to cause or to threaten serious economic injury to domestic producers."

11. 19 U.S.C.A. § 2463(c) (West Supp. 1990).

Ineligibility of Articles from Certain Countries

In cases where the President has determined that an industry in a particular BDC has reached a stage at which it no longer requires preferential treatment, the GSP-eligible articles in question produced from one or more BDCs may be eliminated from duty-free treatment; thereafter, normal duty rates will apply. Those articles from certain BDCs that are ineligible for GSP treatment are specified in the tariff schedule by an asterisk placed after the "A" in the special column. One can then look up the HTSUS number in General Note 3(c)(ii)(D) and find the specific country or countries among all the BDCs for which duty-free treatment is not available for that tariff item.

For example, HTSUS 8512.40.40, etc., indicates special treatment by having an "A*" in the special column as is shown in the following table.

HTSUS General Note 3(c)(ii) shows that special treatment is not available for this item when imported from Brazil and Mexico. Windshield wipers and parts imported from all other BDCs are entitled to duty-free treatment, but if imported from Brazil or Mexico, they are subject to the column 1 duty rate. (The column 2 rate is applicable to countries not enjoying "most favored nation" status, i.e., communist countries.) For merchandise covered by the Automotive Products Act and motor vehicle equipment imported from Canada, the "B" in the special column is indicative of special treatment. The letters E, EI, and CA in the special column indicate special treatment for merchandise imported from the Caribbean Basin countries, Israel, and Canada.

Competitive-Need Limitations

To retain GSP eligibility, each eligible article imported from any given BDC must not have exceeded the competi-

Heading/ Subheading	Stat. Suf. & cd		Article Description	Units of Quantity	Rates of Duty 1 General	Rates of Duty 1 Special	Rates of Duty 2
8512			Electrical lighting or signaling equipment (excluding articles of heading 8539), windshield wipers, defrosters and demisters, of a kind used for cycles or motor vehicles; parts thereof:				
8512.10			Lighting or visual signaling equipment of a kind used on bicycles:				
8512.10.20	00	8	Lighting equipment	X	7.6%	Free (A,E,IL) 6% (CA)	45%
8512.10.40	00	4	Visual signaling equipment	X	2.7%	Free (A,E,IL) 2.1% (CA)	35%
8512.20			Other lighting or visual signaling equipment:				
8512.20.20	00	6	Lighting equipment	X	Free		25%
8512.20.40	00	2	Visual signaling equipment	X	2.7%	Free (A,B,E,IL) 2.1% (CA)	35%
8512.30.00			Sound signaling equipment		2.7%	Free (A,B,E,IL) 2.1% (CA)	35%
	20	4	Horns	X			
	40	0	Other	X			
8512.40			Windshield wipers, defrosters and demisters:				
8512.40.20	00	2	Defrosters and demisters	X	3.9%	Free (A,E,IL) 3.1% (CA)	35%
8512.40.40	00	8	Windshield wipers	X	3.1%	Free (A*,B,E,IL) 2.4% (CA)	25%

tive-need limitation during the previous year. Imports in excess of the competitive-need limitation during one GSP year will result in that article's being taken off the approved list for that BDC in the following year. Two basic limitations apply: (1) any eligible article from any BDC imported into the United States with an appraised value in excess of $25 million in 1974 dollars during a calendar year will be ineligible during the following year; and (2) any country that exported any quantity of an eligible article equal to or in excess of 50 percent of the appraised value of the total imports of that article into the United States during any calendar year shall be ineligible during the following GSP year. There are two exceptions to the 50 percent limitation: (1) a de minimis provision for imports that total an amount not in excess of $5 million; and (2) an exception for goods that are not like, or directly competitive with, goods produced in the United States on or before January 3, 1975.

The recent policy of the administration has been to "permanently graduate" articles that have exceeded the competitive-need limitation. That is, the product will probably become dutiable when imported from that BDC unless there is a substantial drop in imports or a strong case made to the USTR showing why eligibility should be restored for that article.

Whether a particular article retains, loses, regains, or newly acquires GSP eligibility is crucial to importers. The importer has an obligation, in order to protect its own interests, to review import statistics issued by the Department of Commerce on a regular basis. Often the presidential proclamation with respect to eligibility for the coming GSP year is made only a few days before the start of the GSP year, usually April 1. The American Importers and Exporters Association publishes unofficial but very helpful *GSP ALERTS* to warn its members of imports that are nearing either of the two competitive-need limits. Manipulation of the entry date may be advisable to qualify for GSP benefits if one's imports are about to be taken off or added to the list. There are various techniques available to speed up or delay entry that the importer may find helpful. If goods are presently duty-free and about to come off GSP, it is advisable to file an entry/entry summary[12] with a deposit of estimated duties before the effective date. The merchandise, however, must have arrived within the limits of the ports. If goods presently dutiable are about to become duty-free, they can be stored in a bonded warehouse until the effective date passes. Careful coordination with customs brokers and overseas exporters can save entries from being trapped in the GSP year-end changes.

The GSP Annual Review

The annual product review provides an opportunity for GSP friend and foe alike to present petitions to add, delete, or modify the list of eligible articles. As a result of prior reviews, significant modifications have been made. Many products have been added to the list of GSP-eligible articles; others have been deleted. In some instances special tariff classifications have been carved out of existing provisions. Classification breakouts can be very helpful if the imported product is classified under a rather large basket classification provision, whose competitive-need limitations have been met by the country manufacturing a particular product.

The use of "statistical breakouts" under the TSUS was quite useful in this regard. For example, under the TSUS, *X* invents a device that uses preprogrammed integrated circuits to play melodies. The device is incorporated into an article designed to be hung on a Christmas tree and automatically to play a series of Christmas carols. The inventor

12. CF 7501, reprinted in appendix 7 and CF 3461, reprinted in appendix 6.

has the device manufactured in Hong Kong (which at the time was still a BDC) whence it will be exported to the United States. The "Noel Lights," as *X* calls the device, are classified a GSP-eligible article (A), but because of the large number of Hong Kong exports under this basket provision, the competitive-need limitations are regularly exceeded and the importer would not be able to take advantage of the GSP provision for its "Noel Lights." *X* filed a petition before the annual GSP review and persuaded the USTR to grant a classification breakout and a new TSUS item number 688.44, carved out from the basket provision as "Electrical articles using preprogrammed digital integrated circuits to produce sound." The importer now has a classification item virtually for its own use, and because this product was not produced in the United States prior to January 3, 1975, it would not have been subject to the competitive-need limitation unless others begin importing it in large quantities.

This type of classification breakout provision may also be useful under the HTSUS in achieving similar relief from the current competitive-need limitation. If importers encounter deletion of GSP-eligibility of a product they plan to import, they are advised to pursue petitions for favorable item breakouts with the USTR.

Direct Shipment

The 1974 Trade Act requires that in order for an eligible article to enter free of duty, it must be exported directly to the United States from the BDC. If the goods are being transshipped through another country, the bill of lading must show the United States as the ultimate destination. The goods may not enter the commerce of another country en route to the United States.

For example, graduated laboratory beakers are manufactured in the Philippines. The beakers could not be shipped first to another country for testing and packing prior to importation to the United States and still qualify for GSP treatment.

The goods may, however, be shipped from the BDC of origin to a free trade area in another BDC for packing, testing, or other manipulation before shipping to the United States. In addition to the required Form A[13] from the BDC of origin, an additional Form A from the BDC in which the free trade area is located must accompany the goods, recording the work performed on the eligible articles while in the free-trade zone.

Specifically, the laboratory beakers in the example above could be shipped to a free trade area in Malaysia, where they could be tested and packaged and then shipped to the United States for GSP entry accompanied by copies of Form As from Malaysia and the Philippines.

If the eligible articles have entered the commerce of another country, GSP treatment will not be denied as long as the articles are returned to the original BDC and then reshipped to the United States.

For example, assume the laboratory beakers manufactured in the Philippines were shipped to a wholesaler in Thailand. The Thailand importer's purchaser is unable to complete the purchase and the only other buyer the Thailand importer is able to find is an American company. If the beakers are shipped directly to the United States from Thailand, they will not be eligible for GSP treatment. However, the goods may be returned to the Philippines for credit and then exported directly to the buyer in the United States, thereby taking advantage of GSP benefits.

An exception to the direct shipment requirement involves the treatment, for GSP purposes, of eligible articles imported from members of the following associations of countries: the Cartagena Agreement (Andean Group); the

13. Reprinted in appendix 5.

Association of South East Asian Nations (ASEAN), and the Caribbean Common Market (CARICOM).[14]

A GSP-eligible article grown, produced, or manufactured in a member country which is shipped to the United States from *another* member country of the same association will nevertheless meet the GSP direct shipment requirement even if it entered the commerce of the other member country before being exported. For example, furniture assembled in Malaysia (an ASEAN member) from lumber grown in Canada which is then sent to Thailand (an ASEAN member) for finishing and quality testing and then shipped to the United States, would be considered to be imported directly for GSP purposes.

14. General Note 3(c)(ii)(A) contains the following list:

Associations of Countries (Treated as One Country)

Member Countries of the Cartagena Agreement (Andean Group)	Association of South East Asian Nations (ASEAN)	Member Countries of the Caribbean Common Market (CARICOM)
Consisting of:	Consisting of:	Consisting of:
Bolivia	Indonesia	Antigua and Barbuda
Colombia	Malaysia	Bahamas, The
Ecuador	Philippines	Barbados
Peru	Thailand	Belize
Venezuela		Dominica
		Grenada
		Guyana
		Jamaica
		Montserrat
		Saint Kitts and Nevis
		Saint Lucia
		Saint Vincent and the Grenadines
		Trinidad and Tobago

Rules of Origin

The GSP Rules of Origin contained in title 5 of the Trade Act[15] and section 10.176 of the customs regulations required that an appropriately designated article (where "A" appears in the HTSUS special column following the appropriate subheading covering the article) would be eligible for GSP duty-free treatment only if it meets the "product of" requirement established by customs regulations. The regulations provide that an article would be considered produced in, or the "product of" the BDC if (1) the article was wholly the growth, product, or manufacture of the BDC, or (2) the article was substantially transformed into a new and different article of commerce in the BDC. In addition to meeting this "product of" requirement, the article has to meet a value-content requirement which provides that the cost or value of the materials produced in the beneficiary developing country (or any two or more countries which are members of the same association of countries which is treated as one country under section 502(a)(3) of the Trade Act of 1974), plus the direct costs of processing operations performed in such beneficiary developing country (or such member countries) is not less than 35 percent of the appraised value of such article at the time of its entry into the customs territory of the United States.

Thus, for an article to be eligible for GSP treatment, it must first meet the "product of" requirement and then the "35 percent value-content" requirement. For example, unpainted furniture is made in Japan and is imported into Mexico for final painting. Costs of processing and of the materials used in the painting of the furniture amount to more than 35 percent of the appraised value of the article. The original furniture would remain the "product of" Japan rather than Mexico, since the furniture was neither wholly

15. As modified by Pub. L. No. 101-382 § 226, 104 Stat. 629 (1990). *See* 19 U.S.C.A. § 2463 (West Supp. 1991).

the growth, product, or manufacture of Mexico nor was it sufficiently "transformed" into a different article by the painting operation.[16] Accordingly, the painted furniture would not be eligible for GSP treatment, notwithstanding the fact that the "35 percent value-content" requirement was met.

A Window of Opportunity

A recent court decision reversed, for a time, the way Customs had always applied the GSP rules of origin and by so doing it temporarily established an avenue by which nonbeneficiary country material could receive duty-free treatment based solely upon the cost incurred in processing such material in a GSP beneficiary country.[17]

The court of appeals in *Madison Galleries, Ltd. v. United States*[18] affirmed the Court of International Trade's decision,[19] which held that the Customs Service's application of a "product of" requirement, that is, that foreign components (those components not wholly the growth, product, or manufacture of a BDC) must first be substantially transformed in a BDC before the value-added test could be applied, was in error.

The case dealt with the duty-free eligibility under the GSP of certain blank porcelainware (vases, jars, pots, etc.)

---

16. Customs has consistently ruled that minor painting alone does not constitute a substantial transformation. *See* HQ 071362, June 23, 1983 (painting of toy figures is not a substantial transformation); HQ 071363, Aug. 25, 1983 (painting of plastic figures is not a substantial transformation).
17. This decision (Madison Galleries v. United States, 870 F.2d 627 (Fed. Cir. 1989)) was effectively reversed by the Customs and Trade Act of 1990, Pub. L. No. 101-382, § 222, 104 Stat. 659 (1990).
18. Madison Galleries, Ltd. v. United States, 870 F.2d 627 (Fed. Cir. 1989).
19. Madison Galleries, Ltd. v. United States, 688 F. Supp. 1544 (1988).

produced in Taiwan and then shipped to Hong Kong for the addition of designs and scenes as decoration. Simply stated, the issue before the *Madison* court was whether goods imported directly from a BDC, where over 35 percent of its value was added in the BDC, were eligible for GSP duty-free treatment where the goods are assumed to be the "product of" a non-BDC. The government claimed that the porcelainware, like the unpainted furniture in our previous example, while meeting the 35 percent value content requirement, by virtue of the sum of the cost of processing and cost of materials used in the decorating operation, which included painting and firing the blank porcelainware, nevertheless failed to meet the "product of" requirement, since such operation did not substantially transform the porcelainware into a new and different article of commerce. However, the court held that since the decoration process added at least 35 percent to the appraised value of the imported article, the merchandise qualified for GSP duty-free treatment, notwithstanding the failure to meet the "product of" requirement as required by the customs regulations.

If we re-examine the example of the unpainted Japanese furniture painted in Mexico, applying the principles set forth in *Madison Galleries*, the finished painted furniture would receive GSP duty-free treatment notwithstanding the fact that it remained the "product of" Japan, a non-BDC, because the costly painting operation performed in Mexico, a BDC, amounted to more than 35 percent of the appraised value of the unpainted furniture.

Thus, *Madison Galleries* provided a temporary window of opportunity for enterprising importers who were aware of the impact that the court's decision had on GSP eligibility and wisely took advantage of the relaxed rules of origin by entering articles free of duty that would not otherwise have been allowed to be so entered.

Content Requirement

In order for the value of materials that are not wholly the growth, product, or manufacture of the BDC to be included in the 35 percent value-added test, a two-step "substantial transformation" test must be applied to any imported materials to be incorporated into the eligible article in the BDC.

If the eligible article is not wholly the growth, product, or manufacture of the BDC, or if the combination of natively produced material plus the cost of processing is insufficient to meet the 35 percent test, then this two-step process is required:

1. Materials are imported into the BDC and substantially transformed into a new and different article of commerce; and
2. The new article of commerce is then used to manufacture the GSP-eligible article, being substantially transformed in the process.

It is the second substantial transformation that allows the value of the materials used to be included in the 35 percent value-added test.

For example, assume a Philippine chemical firm manufactures di-(2)-ethyl-hexyl phthalate (DOP) from raw materials imported from other countries. The raw materials chemically react to produce a monoester, finally resulting in DOP and water. The Customs Service has ruled that the intermediate monoester cannot be included in the 35 percent value-added requirement because it is not a "product" of the Philippines. Although it is a defined compound, the monoester is simply a transitional state in the manufacture of the DOP and is never traded commercially. Therefore, the Customs Service ruled that it is not a "substantially transformed constituent material," and the value of the monoester could not be used in reaching the 35 percent value-added requirement.[20]

For another example, logs are imported into Mexico, where they are trimmed and sliced into veneer sheets. The veneer sheets are then glued together and cut to size, making plywood. Because the wood veneer is a new and different article of commerce from the log, it could be considered a substantially transformed constituent material of the plywood, and its value can be included in the 35 percent value-added test.[21]

For another example, scrap bronze is imported into Mexico, where it is melted down and cast into yacht fittings. The following two possible conditions may be distinguished: (1) the yacht fittings are incorporated into a sailboat built in a Mexican boatyard (the fittings have been substantially transformed from scrap bronze; their entire value is therefore includable as a constituent material of the finished yacht when the yacht is imported as a GSP-eligible article); and (2) the yacht fittings are exported directly to the United States (in this case the value of the bronze cannot be included in the 35 percent test because there has been only a one-step transformation, from scrap bronze to cast bronze, rather than from scrap-bronze fittings to a completed boat). In order for the fittings alone to be eligible for GSP treatment, the 35 percent value-added test would have to be met solely by the direct costs of processing.

The court of appeals expanded the definition of "substantial transformation" for GSP purposes. In *Torrington Co. v. United States*,[22] the question was whether non-BDC wire processed into BDC sewing-machine needles met the double substantial transformation test. The non-BDC wire was processed in a "swaging" machine. At this stage the wire

---

20. CSD 80-4, 14 Cust. B. & Dec. 729, HQ 055652 (May 18, 1979).
21. 12 Cust. B. & Dec. 1219, HQ 055616 (Oct. 20, 1978).
22. Torrington Co. v. United States, 8 Ct. Int'l Trade 150, 596 F. Supp. 1083 (1984), *aff'd*, 764 F.2d 1563 (Fed. Cir. 1985).

was straightened, cut to length, drawn and beveled at one end. The resulting article called a "swage" was further processed by putting an "eye" in one end, grooming, sharpening, hardening, polishing, and plating the swage to form a completed sewing needle.

Both the Court of International Trade and the appellate court concurred in the finding that the swage was an independent article of commerce and a constituent material further transformed into a second and distinct article of commerce: a finished sewing needle. The appeals court broadly defined the term "article of commerce":

> an "article of commerce"—for the purposes of the pertinent Customs regulation—is one that is ready to be put into a stream of commerce, but need not have actually been bought-and-sold, or actually traded, in the past. Indeed, by requiring proof of actual arms-length transactions by unrelated parties, the Government implies that a new article (never before produced) can never be an article of commerce entitled to GSP treatment—a result not envisaged by Congress.

The import of this decision is twofold. First, by finding that a double substantial transformation occurred in what arguably is a continuous processing operation, the court softened the Customs Service's prior position that clearly defined separate processing must be demonstrated for successful double substantial transformation claims. Secondly, by defining "article of commerce" to include articles that have not been bought and sold, the court broadened the potential GSP coverage of articles to include those only arguably ready "to be put into a stream of commerce."

The *Madison Galleries* court also expanded the substantial transformation concept. Beyond its elimination of the "product of" requirement,[23] the court of appeals recognized

23. The court's elimination of the "product of" requirement was later reversed by legislation. *See* note 15.

the lower court's finding that decorating blank porcelain with designs and scenes through painting and firing, providing surface relief and a multi-dimensional effect, created an article with a new name, character, or use.

Such a liberal interpretation of what constitutes a substantial transformation may now be applied to other relatively minor processing operations, which, prior to this decision, would certainly have come under serious Customs scrutiny.[24]

GSP Direct Cost of Processing

If the second substantial transformation is absent, the value of the materials may not be considered in the 35 percent value-added test, but the cost of processing and any other native materials entering into the product would be counted.

However, if the imported article itself had not been transformed from being the basic product of the nation of origin into a product of the BDC, then the article would not qualify for GSP treatment no matter how high the cost of processing.

For example, metal doors are made in Japan and imported into the Philippines, where they are polished. Costs of processing incurred in polishing the metal doors amount to more than 35 percent of the appraised value of the article. The doors will not be entitled to GSP treatment.

As another example, dental prosthetic devices are manufactured in the Dominican Republic. The devices are connectors that hold dentures in place. They are cast from

24. Prior to the decision of the court of appeals, Customs had issued a limiting decision of the lower court's finding on the substantial transformation issue. However, in view of the appellate court's reference to the Customs Service's concession on appeal concerning this issue, the limiting decision will no longer carry any weight.

imported chrome-cobalt, using stone models of the patients' mouths made in the United States. The chrome-cobalt when cast is substantially transformed, thus meeting the "product of" requirement. However, there has been no second substantial transformation of the prosthetic devices into new and different articles of commerce, so the value of the materials in the devices (imported chrome-cobalt) cannot be used to meet the value-added requirement. Only the direct cost of processing may be used to meet the value-added requirement; if those costs equal or exceed 35 percent of the appraised value of the prosthetic devices, then the article is entitled to GSP treatment.

In the above example, the direct costs of processing would include labor costs (including costs of supervisory personnel), packing costs, and costs of dies, molds, designs, etc., as long as they are allocatable to the specific merchandise. Other includable costs would be rent or depreciation on the portion of the manufacturing facility that was actually used for making the eligible article and utilities supplied to the facility prorated to account only for the manufacturing process. Costs that may not be included are (1) profits; (2) salaries of accounting and payroll personnel; (3) shipping expenses, which may be considered cost of constituent materials; (4) telephone expenses; (5) janitorial supplies; (6) computerized payroll services; (7) fire and liability insurance; (8) taxes; (9) marketing or advertising expenses; and (10) legal fees.

In any given case, it is difficult to determine with any accuracy or certainty which costs the Customs Service will consider "direct." When the value of the materials is not high enough to exceed the 35 percent mark comfortably, and direct costs are crucial in meeting the value-added requirement, extreme care must be taken in arriving at the figures. A foreign exporter may not be thoroughly familiar with which particular costs may be included in the value-added computations.

The United States importer has to attest to the accuracy of all import documentation and may be held liable for any errors in the Form A. If the value added shown on the Form A is close to 35 percent (for safety's sake, say under 50 percent) the direct costs of the operation should be gone over thoroughly with the exporter, preferably with the assistance of a knowledgeable accountant.

It is also important to point out that the value of the article shown on Form A will not necessarily be the same as the "appraised value" of the article. Thus, an article might have direct cost of processing plus BDC-origin materials of $40 and an invoice value of $100. Should the Customs Service appraise the value under the valuation law at $130, the "35 percent of the appraised value" requirement will not be met. Customs generally administers the GSP program in a liberal manner, but there is still a need for caution in close cases, particularly when the value added in the BDC is in the nature of a manipulation of the BDC products.

Documentation

Before discussing the current GSP documentation requirements we should mention that Customs is in the initial stages of its planned conversion to a "paperless" environment.[25] With the advent of the Automated Broker Interface program (ABI), present Customs documentation requirements are changing and will continue to change. However, at the time of this writing we must still contend with the following documentary requirements.

A claim for GSP treatment is made by placing the letter

25. For a more detailed discussion of the ABI program and the Customs Service's efforts toward computerization, see chapter 6 on processing shipments.

"A" before the HTSUS classification number on the entry summary and, for eligible articles that are valued in excess of $1,250, by filing a Form A certificate of origin with the entry papers.[26] The Form A is an international document prepared by the United Nations Conference on Trade and Development and is issued by an authorized governmental agency within the originating BDC.[27]

The Customs Service may not initially scrutinize a Form A very carefully. However, if a Form A appears to be incorrect for any reason, the document is rejected and the merchandise covered by the incorrect document is not permitted free entry. Each item must be shown separately on the form, with the percentage for each item of material and processing originating in the BDC. If a single imported item consists of a commercial entity of different units (e.g., a Christmas decoration composed of a tree, candycanes, balls, etc.), each unit must be separately shown with its own percentage of native materials and processing.

If the eligible article is *wholly the growth, product, or manufacture* of the BDC, the letter "P" is placed in box 8 on Form A. No percentage of value added need be shown.

If the article is *not wholly the growth, product, or manu-*

26. A Form A is not required for eligible articles having a value of under $1,250, but the Customs Service may require the importer to submit proof of origin in the BDC. If the eligible article has a value of less than $1,250 but is part of an entry that has a value greater than $1,250, Form A is not required. It is the total value of each particular type of eligible article in a varied shipment rather than the value of the complete shipment that determines whether or not a Form A is necessary.
27. Form A is reprinted in appendix 5. Pursuant to the Caribbean Basin Economic Recovery Act, Pub. L. No. 98-120, Form A no longer requires certification by the country of origin. The importer merely states that the goods meet the origin requirement. However, if the BDC enters into a separate agreement with the United States, the BDC may still require governmental certification. As of this writing, no such agreement has been entered into.

facture of the BDC, the letter "Y" is placed in box 8 on Form A and the percentage of value added to the article in the BDC is given.

If the original Form A is lost, stolen, or destroyed, the importer may submit a duplicate original Form A certified by the issuing country. In those circumstances a photocopy will not be acceptable.

If, on the other hand, Form A exists, but the importer is unable to present the original because of factors beyond its control, a valid copy is acceptable for purposes of establishing country of origin.

Assume, for example, that *X* has imported a shipment of tractor parts from Brazil. Because of a payment dispute, the Brazilian seller has refused to release the original Form A. *X* makes a claim for GSP treatment of the tractor parts and submits a photocopy of Form A. If *X* can prove to the satisfaction of the Customs Service that the original Form A is in existence, but is unavailable due to circumstances beyond its control, the valid copy will be acceptable for purposes of establishing country of origin for GSP purposes.

If GSP treatment is to be claimed, but the Form A is not available at the time of entry, the importer has two available options. It may claim GSP treatment at the time of entry, and furnish a bond for the production of Form A within sixty days. If the Form A is produced within the sixty days, the goods will be liquidated as entered. If, however, the Form A is not submitted within sixty days or such additional time as the district director may allow, the bond will be cancelled and the goods will be liquidated as dutiable. There is even the possibility that the Customs Service will levy liquidated damages for failure to produce Form A.

A customs regulation states:

> Whenever a free entry or reduced duty document, form, or statement required to be filed in connection with the entry is not filed at the time of the entry or within the period for which a bond was filed for its production, but failure to file

> it was not due to willful negligence, or fraudulent intent, such document, form or statement may be filed at any time prior to liquidation of the entry or, if the entry was liquidated, before the liquidation becomes final.[28]

Therefore, if the Form A is not available at the time of entry, the importer may claim GSP treatment, stating the Form A will be submitted when available. If the Customs Service refuses to accept duty-free entry under GSP in those circumstances, the importer may deposit the duties with the Service and enter the goods as directed. If the importer receives the Form A before the entry is liquidated, it need only submit the Form A to the Customs Service and the entry will be liquidated according to the claim for GSP treatment. If the importer receives the Form A after liquidation, but before liquidation becomes final (i.e., ninety days after liquidation), the importer may file a protest claiming GSP treatment and include the Form A with the protest. Such protests will generally be allowed, and the entry reliquidated free of duty.

If the Form A is unavailable before liquidation and it appears likely that it will not arrive before the liquidation becomes final, the importer may protect its right to duty-free entry by filing a protest after liquidation claiming GSP treatment with a statement that the Form A is not presently available and requesting that a decision on the protest be suspended for ninety days in order to allow the importer to acquire it. In addition, if the shipment is simply the latest of a number of shipments of the same eligible articles from the same foreign manufacturer or supplier and the previous entries have been accompanied by the Form A, the importer may wish to request "further review" in a protest and ask for a waiver of the requirement of a Form A based upon prior compliance on identical merchandise.

28. 19 C.F.R. § 10.112 (1988).

When the percentage shown in column 8 of Form A does not meet the minimum 35 percent of the appraised value, the Customs Service will reject the Form A and require entry under the normal duty rate. The importer may wish to seek a new Form A from the originating BDC, in which case the importer may request return of the original rejected Form A from the Customs Service. In such situations, the Customs Service will retain a copy of the Form A after voiding the original by writing "REJECTED" across its face, and it will return the original to the person making the request. The party involved should be allowed an additional sixty days under appropriate bond or extension for subsequent production of the Form A if it so requests. This procedure is resorted to when it appears that the shipper or manufacturer abroad did not correctly understand the requirements of the Form A.

Least Developed Developing Countries

Another tariff preference available to importers is that afforded to products of the "least developed developing countries" (LDDCs). The United States has granted the full final tariff reductions negotiated at the Tokyo Round of the Multilateral Trade Negotiations (MTN) (without staged reductions) to the products of those countries designated as the least developed developing countries. The LDDCs are listed in HTSUS General Note 3(c)(ii)(B),[29] and include the least industrialized and poorest countries. Reduced tariff rates are available on products that have a rate listed in the LDDC column of the tariff schedule found between the column 1 and column 2 rates. LDDC rates are available for some items that are not GSP-eligible articles.

Even if the imported merchandise is a GSP-eligible ar-

29. Reprinted at the end of this chapter.

ticle, LDDC treatment may be used to advantage when the merchandise fails to meet the direct-shipment or value-added tests.

For example, HTSUS 3707.90.30 ("Chemical preparation for photographic use") is a GSP-eligible article. Its column 1 rate is 8.5 percent ad valorem and its LDDC rate is 6.8 percent ad valorem. Suppose a small plant in Haiti mixes imported materials to make photographic chemicals. The imported chemicals may have been transformed into a new and different product (i.e., photographic chemicals). However, neither the costs of production (i.e., the costs incurred in the mixing operation) nor costs of materials used satisfied the 35 percent value-content requirement (there was no second substantial transformation of constituent material so as to enable the costs of any of the imported chemicals to be counted toward meeting that requirement), so the finished photographic chemicals fail to meet the 35 percent value-added test for free entry. For normal "country of origin" purposes, however, the photographic chemicals are products of Haiti, an LDDC, and upon importation to the United States are entitled to the lower LDDC duty rate.

As the column 1 rates are reduced to the "most favored nation" final rates, the advantage offered by the LDDC rates are gradually disappearing, but in the meantime the LDDC rates can still offer substantial duty savings. It can be expected that Congress will continue to give some form of favored treatment to the poorest nations. More particularly, this is so in view of the dissatisfaction of many with the situation in the past whereby a handful of BDCs were reaping the lion's share of GSP benefits. The advantages to the LDDCs may take the form of "graduating" the more advanced BDCs from the GSP program or by easing the requirements for GSP treatment for products imported from the LDDCs.

Beneficiary Developing Countries and Least Developed Developing Countries (from HTSUS General Note 3(c)(ii))

(ii) Products of Countries Designated Beneficiary Developing Countries for Purposes of the Generalized System of Preferences (GSP)

(A) The following countries, territories, and associations of countries eligible for treatment as one country pursuant to section 502(a)(3) of the Trade Act of 1974 (19 USC § 2462(a)(3)) are designated beneficiary developing countries for the purposes of the Generalized System of Preferences, provided for in Title V of the Trade Act of 1974, as amended (19 USC § 2461 *et seq.*):

Independent Countries

Angola
Antigua and Barbuda
Argentina
Bahamas
Bahrain
Bangladesh
Barbados
Belize
Benin
Bhutan
Bolivia
Botswana
Brazil
Burkina Faso
Burundi
Cameroon
Cape Verde
Central African Republic
Chad
Chile
Colombia
Comoros
Congo
Costa Rica
Cote d'Iboire
Cyprus
Czechoslovakia
Djibouti
Dominica
Dominican Republic
Ecuador
Egypt
El Salvador
Equatorial Guinea
Fiji
Gambia
Ghana
Grenada
Guatemala
Guinea
Guinea Bissau
Guyana
Haiti
Honduras
Hungary
India
Indonesia
Israel
Jamaica
Jordan
Kenya
Kiribati
Lebanon
Lesotho
Madagascar
Malawi
Malaysia
Maldives
Mali
Malta
Mauritania
Mauritius
Mexico
Morocco
Mozambique
Namibia
Nepal
Niger
Oman
Pakistan
Panama
Papua New Guinea
Paraguay
Peru
Philippines
Poland
Rwanda

Saint Kitts
Saint Lucia
Saint Vincent and the Grenadines
Sao Tome and Principe
Senegal
Seychelles
Sierra Leone
Solomon Islands
Somalia
Sri Lanka
Sudan
Surinam
Swaziland
Syria
Tanzania
Thailand
Togo
Tonga
Trinidad and Tobago
Tunisia
Turkey
Tuvalu
Uganda
Uruguay
Vanuatu
Venezuela
Western Samoa
Yemen Arab Republic (Sanaa)
Yugoslavia
Zaire
Zambia
Zimbabwe

(B) The following countries are designated least developed developing countries (LDDCs) pursuant to section 504(c)(6) of the Trade Act of 1974, as amended:

Bangladesh
Benin
Bhutan
Botswana
Burkina Faso
Burundi
Cape Verde
Central African Republic
Chad
Comoros
Djibouti
Equatorial Guinea
Gambia
Guinea
Guinea Bissau
Haiti
Kiribati
Lesotho
Malawi
Maldives
Mali
Mauritania
Mozambique
Nepal
Niger
Rwanda
Sao Tome and Principe
Sierra Leone
Somalia
Tanzania
Togo
Tuvalu
Uganda
Vanuatu
Western Samoa
Yemen Arab Republic (Sanaa)

Whenever an eligible article is imported into the customs territory of the United States directly from one of the countries designated as a least-developed beneficiary developing country, it shall be entitled to receive the duty-free treatment provided for in subdivision (c)(ii)(C) of this note without regard to the limitations (i.e., exporting to the U.S. a quantity of eligible articles having an appraised value in excess of the amount allowed) on preferential treatment of eligible articles in section 504(c) of the Trade Act, as amended. (19 USC § 2464(c)).

12. Caribbean Basin Initiative

On August 5, 1983, President Ronald Reagan signed the Caribbean Basin Economic Recovery Act (CBERA) "[t]o promote economic revitalization and facilitate expansion of economic opportunities in the Caribbean Basin region. . . ." Thus the Caribbean Basin Initiative (CBI) was born.[1] It will remain in effect until September 30, 1995.[2]

The CBERA authorizes the President to grant duty-free treatment for designated eligible articles from any so-called beneficiary country.[3] The term "beneficiary country" will include any country so designated by the President.[4] But the President may choose only from a list of twenty-seven countries and territories for designation as beneficiaries of duty-free treatment. The President may also remove the designation of beneficiary country by issuing a proclamation.

1. Pub. L. No. 98-67, 97 Stat. 369 (1983) (codified as amended at 19 U.S.C. §§ 2701–2706).
2. 19 U.S.C. § 2706. The Custom and Trade Act of 1990, Pub. L. No. 101-382, 104 Stat. 629 (1990) extended the program and expanded its scope. In section 222 of the Act, Congress expanded the "Super 807" (9802.00.80.10, HTSUS) provision to allow for the inclusion of foreign materials in assembly operations and granted the finished articles special quota access (see discussion on Super 807 in chapter 15).
3. 19 U.S.C.A. § 2702(a)(1)(A) (West Supp. 1990).
4. *Id.*

However, the President must notify Congress and the subject country sixty days in advance of such action, enumerating the reasons for such decision.[5] In addition, there are mandatory and waivable conditions under which a country may or may not be designated as a beneficiary.[6]

The President is also required to withdraw or suspend the beneficiary country designation if he determines that circumstances dictate (e.g., a country has violated a mandatory condition for exclusion as a beneficiary).[7]

The CBERA also provides that goods imported from insular possessions of the United States[8] shall receive duty treatment no less favorable than the treatment granted such articles imported from a CBI beneficiary country.[9] As with the GSP, this provision allows an importer of goods from a United States insular possession to choose between CBI or General Note 3(a)(iv) treatment.[10]

---

5. 19 U.S.C.A. § 2702(a)(2).
6. 19 U.S.C.A. § 2702(b).
7. 19 U.S.C.A. § 2702(e). For example, countries that do not cooperate with the United States to prevent the importation of controlled substances into the United States are mandatorily prevented from being designated as beneficiary countries. The exclusion of communist countries is waivable.
8. U.S. insular possessions include the U.S. Virgin Islands, American Samoa, Kingman Reef, Johnston Island, the Midway Islands, and Wake Island.
9. 19 U.S.C.A. § 2702(d) (West Supp. 1990).
10. General Note 3(a)(iv), HTSUS, provides for another preferential system similar to the GSP and CBI programs covering the United States insular possessions. Established under TSUS general headnote 3(a), the system gives duty-free treatment to goods from the insular possessions if the following rules of origin are satisfied:
    1. The product is imported directly into the United States;
    2. The product is the growth, product, or manufacture of the insular possession; and
    3. The content of foreign material in the product is valued at no more than 70 percent (50 percent for certain products like textiles and articles of apparel) of the product's appraised value.

Designation of Eligible Articles

A CBI "eligible article" must be classified in an HTSUS subheading in which a rate of duty of "free" appears in the "Special" column followed by the CBI designating symbol ("E").[11]

The symbol "E" indicates that all articles provided for in the designated subheading are eligible for preferential treatment except for five categories of products specifically excluded from CBI duty-free treatment:

1. Textile and apparel articles that are subject to textile agreements.
2. Footwear, handbags, luggage, flat goods, work gloves, and leather wearing apparel (not designated as CBI-eligible articles at the time of the effective date of CBERA).[12]
3. Tuna, prepared or preserved in any manner, in air-tight containers.
4. Petroleum or any product derived from petroleum provided for in chapter 27 of the HTSUS.
5. Watches and watch parts (including cases, bracelets, and straps) of whatever type, including, but not limited to, mechanical quartz digital or quartz analog, if

---

11. General Note 3(c)(V)(B)(1), HTSUS.
12. The Customs and Trade Act of 1990, Pub. L. No. 101-382, § 212, 104 Stat. 655 (1990), provides for a five-year staged reduction of duties for handbags, flat goods, work gloves, and leather wearing apparel beginning January 1, 1992. These leather-related goods must be the product of a beneficiary country and must not have been designated on August 5, 1983, as eligible articles for purposes of GSP under title V of the Trade Act of 1974.

    The reduction is to result in a rate that is 80 percent of the rate of duty that applies to that article on December 31, 1991. However, the reduction is to be implemented in five equal stages with the first one-fifth reduction on entries or withdrawals from warehouse for consumption on or after January 1, 1992.

> such watches or watch parts contain any material that is the product of any country with respect to which HTSUS column 2 duty rates apply.[13]

The symbol "E*" designation indicates that some articles (e.g., certain beef, veal, sugars, syrups, textiles and apparel, etc.) provided for in the designated subheading are not eligible for preferential treatment.[14]

Direct Shipment

The direct shipment requirement for duty-free treatment set forth in section 213(a)(1)(A) of the CBERA is essentially the same as the GSP statutory provision.[15] However, some differences exist. For example, under the GSP, the article must be produced in, have the "value-added" requirement satisfied in, and be directly shipped from the same beneficiary country.[16] Under the CBI, the article may be the prod-

13. General Note 3(c)(V)(E), HTSUS; 19 U.S.C.A. § 2703(b).
14. General Note 3(c)(V)(C), (c)(V)(D), and (c)(V)(E), HTSUS.
15. 19 U.S.C.A. § 3(a)(1)(A) and the Trade Act of 1974, (b)(1), as amended, 19 U.S.C.A § 3(b)(1) (1982).
16. There is an exception to this general rule. Articles produced in several members of one of the associations of countries listed in HTSUS General Note 3(c)(ii)(A) (e.g., ASEAN, CARICOM, and the Andean Group) may be shipped from any member of the particular group and may meet the value-content requirement through cumulative operations. For example, material from Japan processed in Indonesia (an ASEAN member) may be further processed in Malaysia (an ASEAN member), and the resulting article may then be finished and quality tested in Thailand (an ASEAN member); the cumulative cost of processing and any materials indigenous to any ASEAN member used in the creation of the finished article may be counted toward meeting the 35 percent value-content requirement for GSP purposes. Furthermore, the finished article may be shipped from any one of the ASEAN member countries to the United States and still meet the GSP direct shipment requirement. See discussion on countries' associations in the GSP, chapter 11.

uct of a single beneficiary country or any combination of beneficiary countries. Likewise, the "value-added" requirement may be met by applying the combined processing and/or material costs incurred in several beneficiary countries. Consistent with this approach, a CBI eligible article may be imported directly from any beneficiary country.[17]

Rules of Origin

The rules of origin[18] are of paramount importance in the effective administration of any free trade agreement. They ensure that only goods with sufficient beneficiary country content will receive duty-free treatment, and they prevent the transshipping of nonbeneficiary goods through beneficiary countries in an effort to take advantage of the preferences afforded under such agreements. This becomes a significant concern in the context of the CBI, since the beneficiary countries depend primarily on imported raw materials to support their manufacturing operations.

The criteria for establishing the origin of eligible articles are set forth in section 213 of the CBERA. They provide in pertinent part that any article which is either (1) wholly the growth, product, or manufacture of a beneficiary country or (2) a new or different article of commerce which has been grown, produced, or manufactured in a beneficiary country may qualify for duty-free treatment if

1. The article is imported directly from a beneficiary country into the customs territory of the United States; and

17. A "beneficiary country" for purposes of the direct shipment requirement would not include the U.S. Virgin Islands.
18. The Customs and Trade Act of 1990, Pub. L. No. 101-382, § 223, 104 Stat. 659 (1990), calls on the ITC to make recommendations to the President and Congress regarding changes to the current CBI rules of origin. At the time of this writing, no changes have been effected. However, interested parties should remain alert to that eventuality.

2. At least 35 percent of the appraised value of the article when entered is attributable to the sum of:
   - The cost or value of the materials produced in a beneficiary country or two or more beneficiary countries; and
   - The direct costs of processing operations performed in a beneficiary country or countries.[19]

For purposes of determining the 35 percent value content requirement, any amount added in the U.S. Virgin Islands or the Commonwealth of Puerto Rico may be included.[20] In addition, materials produced in the customs territory of the United States (other than Puerto Rico), not to exceed 15 percent of the appraised value of the article, may also be included in determining the 35 percent figure.

"Product of" Criterion

From the "growth, product, or manufacture" language and the "new or different article of commerce which has been grown, produced, or manufactured" language is derived the first principle upon which country of origin must be established under the CBI.[21]

Simply stated, for an article to be considered an article of a CBI beneficiary country it must either be grown, produced, or manufactured in the beneficiary country or be made from foreign materials or components (materials or components from a nonbeneficiary country) that have been substantially transformed into new and different articles of

19. *See* 19 U.S.C.A. § 2703(a)(1).
20. Puerto Rico and the U.S. Virgin Islands will be considered beneficiary countries for this purpose.
21. CBERA, § 213(a)(1) and (a)(2).

commerce.[22] For example, trees grown in a CBI beneficiary country, used in the making of lumber, would be considered wholly the growth of the CBI beneficiary country. Trees grown outside of a CBI beneficiary country would obviously not be considered wholly the growth of the CBI beneficiary country. However, if those "foreign trees" were imported into the CBI beneficiary country and there processed into lumber, such processing would result in a change of the character, name, or use of the imported trees, thus transforming them into the new completed article (lumber). The lumber would then be considered a product of the CBI beneficiary country, subject to meeting the value-added requirements set forth in section 213(a)(1)(B) of the CBERA.[23]

CBERA section 213(a)(2) expressly provides that a substantial transformation would not be considered to result from an article undergoing

> *(A) simple combining or packaging operations, or*
> *(B) mere dilution with water or mere dilution with another substance that does not materially alter the characteristics of the article.*

Examples of operations limited by these subsections are the simple joining of components by gluing, bolting, or soldering; repackaging or packing components; diluting finished substances with water; adding preservatives; etc.[24]

---

22. For a more detailed analysis of the substantial transformation concept, see the discussion in chapter 18. The application of the concept under the GSP is analogous to the application under the CBI. Consequently, for component material to be considered substantially transformed, it must, as a result of significant processing, be changed in name, character, or use.
23. General Note 3(c)(iii)(B)(v)(B)(1), HTSUS.
24. *See also* Customs Implementing Regulations, 19 C.F.R. § 10.195 (1990).

"Value-Added" Criterion

The second principle for establishing country of origin under the CBI is the "value-added" criterion set forth in section 213(a)(1)(B) of the CBERA.

Accordingly, once the "product of" criterion is met, to comply fully with the CBI rules of origin the second criterion must also be met. That is, at least 35 percent of the appraised value of the finished article when entered must be attributable to the sum of the cost or value of the materials produced in a beneficiary country or two or more beneficiary countries and the direct costs of processing operations performed in a beneficiary country or countries.

As noted above, lumber made from imported trees would meet the "product of" requirement of the CBI, if as a result of processing, the trees were substantially transformed into lumber. The resulting lumber would be considered a product of the CBI beneficiary country in which the processing took place. However, since the trees were of foreign origin, their cost or value may not be included in determining the value-added requirement. Therefore, if the direct cost of processing the trees into lumber was less than 35 percent of the appraised value of the lumber at the time it was entered, the second part of the two-pronged CBI rules of origin test would not be met and the lumber could not enter duty free.

The inclusion of the cost or value of foreign materials may nevertheless be obtained through processing by applying the "double substantial transformation" concept.[25] For example, if the imported trees were transformed into lumber and then transformed a second time into furniture, the total value or cost of the trees may be included in determining the 35 percent criterion.

---

25. The United States "value-added" figure is restricted to cost or value of materials produced in the United States and does not include costs of processing operations performed in the United States.

Differences Between the GSP and the CBI Rules of Origin

Although similar to the rules established under the GSP, the CBI rules of origin contain some significant differences. These differences appear most prominently in the value-added criterion. For example, unlike the GSP,[26] the CBI allows the inclusion of the cost or value of materials plus the direct costs of processing to be cumulative among all CBI beneficiary countries. Thus, the cost or value of material from one CBI beneficiary country or the direct costs of processing therein may be added to the cost of goods manufactured in another CBI beneficiary country and together such costs may be counted toward meeting the 35 percent value-added criterion.

A second difference in the rules of origin under the CBI is the provision in section 213(a)(1) of the CBERA which defines "beneficiary country" for purposes of computing the 35 percent value-added requirement. Under the CBI, the term "beneficiary country" would include the Commonwealth of Puerto Rico and the U.S. Virgin Islands. Thus, the cost or value of materials produced in Puerto Rico and the Virgin Islands, as well as the direct costs of processing operations performed therein, may be applied toward meeting the 35 percent value-added figure.[27]

---

26. See exception described in note 16 *supra*.
27. Pursuant to the Customs and Trade Act of 1990, Pub. L. No. 101-382, § 215, 104 Stat. 657 (1990), in addition to its application toward meeting the 35 percent value-added requirement, CBI duty-free treatment has been extended to articles that are the growth, product, or manufacture of Puerto Rico, if

    1. The articles are imported directly from the beneficiary into the United States;
    2. The articles were by *any* means advanced in value *or* improved in condition in a beneficiary country; and
    3. Any materials were added to such articles in a beneficiary country, such added materials are a product of the beneficiary country or the United States.

Finally, under the CBI rules of origin, up to 15 percent of the appraised value of the finished article may include the cost of *materials* produced in the customs territory of the United States (other than Puerto Rico).[28]

Direct Cost of Processing

Section 213(a)(3) of the CBERA defines the phrase "direct costs of processing operations." The definition generally encompasses the same costs laid out in the comparable GSP provision,[29] including all actual labor costs involved in the growth, production, manufacture, or assembly of the specific merchandise.[30] The regulations also provide for the inclusion of research, development, design, and blueprint costs and the costs of inspecting and testing the merchandise as "direct costs of processing operations" for both CBI and GSP.[31]

Documentation

As with the GSP, the importer or consignee of a shipment of merchandise covered by a formal entry for which duty-free treatment is claimed under the CBI shall file with the

28. Trade Act of 1974, § 503(b)(1), as amended, 19 U.S.C. § 2463(b)(1) (1982). *See also* note 27 for the CBERA amendment regarding the treatment of articles from Puerto Rico.
29. See discussion concerning GSP "direct cost of processing" in chapter 11.
30. The GSP regulations 10.178(a)(3) and 10.178(a)(4) make provision for the inclusion of these items in the direct cost of processing figure. While it was not included in the CBERA, Customs also provided for these costs in regulations designed to express congressional intent and in an effort to apply these terms consistently with the GSP regulations.
31. 19 C.F.R. § 10.197 (1990).

district director together with the entry summary, a certificate of origin, Form A (reprinted in appendix 5), as evidence of the country of origin.[32]

Customs regulations require that a declaration of origin by the exporter in the beneficiary country where the article was produced be submitted to the district director, upon request, containing supporting information regarding the production of the article that formed the basis of the Form A.[33]

If duty-free treatment is claimed after the entry summary is filed, but before liquidation becomes final, the entry summary will be accepted upon the posting of a bond by the importer or consignee and the subsequent delivery of the certificate of origin within sixty days of the date of filing the entry summary or such additional period as the district director shall allow. Failure to submit the declaration within the time prescribed will result in the denial of duty-free benefits. In addition, such records must be retained for a period of five years.[34]

---

32. 19 C.F.R. § 10.198(a)(1) (1985). Form A is reprinted in appendix 5.
33. 19 C.F.R. § 10.198(c)(1). Note also that this requirement is applicable only in cases involving articles that are not wholly the growth, product, or manufacture of a beneficiary country.
34. 19 C.F.R. § 10.198(c)(2) (1988).

13. United States–Israel Free Trade Agreement

Background of Agreement

Under the Trade and Tariff Act of 1984 (TTA), the President was authorized to enter bilateral negotiations with Israel's government toward establishing a free trade area arrangement.[1] The concluded agreement (hereinafter cited as US–IFTA) was implemented on September 1, 1985, incorporating the elimination of tariffs on most items and a staged tariff elimination through 1995 on certain import-sensitive products. The agreement also contains provisions regarding certain nontariff issues which will also be addressed in this chapter.

The treaty provides the United States exporter with access to a small but nevertheless substantial market (nearing twelve billion dollars in annual imports worldwide).[2] Prior

1. The Trade and Tariff Act of 1984, 401-06 Stat. 3013–18. The United States and Israel formally agreed to enter free trade negotiations on November 29, 1983. The concluded agreement was signed on April 22, 1985, and the President was authorized to take steps to implement the agreement under the United States–Israel Free Trade Area Implementation Act of 1985 (99 Pub. L. No. 42, 99 Stat. 82). For a survey of the agreement, see THE ECONOMIC OFFICE, EMBASSY OF ISRAEL. GUIDE TO THE ISRAEL–UNITED STATES FREE TRADE AGREEMENT (1985).
2. U.S. Dep't of Commerce, "Foreign Economic Trends and Their Implications for the United States," *Int'l Mktg. Information Series*, 2 (1988).

to the US–IFTA, Israel's import market was less accessible as a result of high tariff barriers. Additionally, U.S. exporters were significantly disadvantaged in relation to their European counterparts, who took advantage of a somewhat narrower free trade zone established between Israel and the European Community in 1975. The US–IFTA agreement removes prohibitive tariff barriers, thus enabling the United States exporter to compete equally with, and often on better terms than, European exporters. The U.S. Commerce Department noted that "Israel is second only to Canada in per capita imports of U.S. goods" and that "Israelis have a favorable orientation toward the United States."[3] Exports from the United States to Israel climbed 18 percent between 1986 and 1987 and by an additional 17 percent in the following year. This increase, however, was aided by Israel's attempt to keep its unit of currency (the shekel) at a rate equal in relation to the U.S. dollar.

The United States importer is in a prime position to capitalize on duty-free quality goods produced in Israel that were previously undermarketed in the United States. Israel's industries are receiving considerable investment in light of increased U.S. demand for Israel's products.[4] Although, during the first three years of the treaty, United States exporters were more active than importers, this trend has been changing partially because of Israel's need to devalue its currency relative to the dollar.[5] Thus, the attractiveness of importing Israeli products under the US–IFTA is further enhanced by the prevalent strength of the purchasing power of the U.S. dollar in Israel.

---

3. *Id.* at 12, 3.
4. Other reasons for the increasing investment in Israeli industries include the fact that Israel enjoys Free Trade Agreements with both the U.S. and the European Community and the revitalized Israeli–East European trade that followed the recent political transformation of Eastern Europe.
5. The shekel was devalued by 13.4 percent between December 29, 1988, and January 1, 1989, following Israel's elections. U.S. Dep't of

In addition to providing mutual trade advantages, it was intended that the agreement would further solidify ties between the two countries.[6] It was also intended that the US–IFTA agreement complement each state's existing obligations. Under Article 3 of the US–IFTA, the United States and Israel affirm their respective obligations under existing bilateral and multilateral agreements, including the Treaty of Friendship, Commerce and Navigation between the United States and Israel and the General Agreements on Tariffs and Trade (GATT). The US–IFTA provisions, however, take precedence in respect to prior obligations between the parties.

In accordance with the GATT requirements for international free trade agreement arrangements, the US–IFTA will not result in either party's issuing stronger protectionist measures against third countries.[7] Additionally, the US–IFTA removes duty on most goods immediately, while phasing out duties on the remaining sensitive goods in stages over a ten-year period.

The US–IFTA differs significantly from the generalized system of preferences (GSP) and the Caribbean Basin Initiative (CBI) in that the US–IFTA is intended as a reciprocal agreement. Thus, in contrast to the GSP, the trade preferences under the US–IFTA are not phased out according to increased levels of import penetration. Additionally, each

---

Commerce, *Overseas Business Report* 88-11, Errata Mar. 1989. The shekel was further devalued by 10.8 percent between January 1, 1989, and June 25, 1989, and is continuing to face periodic devaluations as of this writing. J. Com. & Com. 26 (June 1989).

6. Free Trade Area Agreement, April 22, 1985, United States–Israel (hereinafter US–IFTA), Preamble (*reprinted in* 24 INT'L LEGAL MATERIALS 65 (1985)).
7. General Agreement on Tariffs and Trade (GATT), 1947 as amended. Article XXIV paragraph 4, reprinted in INT'L TRADE & INVESTMENT: SELECTED DOCUMENTS 56 (J. Barton & B. Fisher ed. 1986).

party can take measures to protect various indigenous interests, which are described later in the chapter.

Rules of Origin

In order for a product exported by one of the parties to the other to be granted the benefits of the free trade agreement, the product must satisfy the rules of origin requirement. The criteria for establishing the origin of eligible articles under the US–IFTA are very similar to those established under the CBI program, except that the US–IFTA origin requirements are reciprocal.[8]

Under the US–IFTA, any article which is either (1) wholly the growth, product, or manufacture of the exporting country or (2) a new or different article of commerce that has been grown, produced, or manufactured in the exporting country may qualify for US–IFTA preferential treatment if

1. The article is imported directly from either country into the customs territory of the other country; and
2. At least 35 percent of the appraised value of the article when entered is attributable to the sum of
   - The cost or value of the materials produced in the exporting country, and
   - The direct costs of processing operations performed in the exporting country.

For purposes of determining the 35 percent value content requirement, the cost or value of materials produced in the other country (Israel or the United States) may also be included in determining the 35 percent figure. However, it

8. The rules of origin under the US–IFTA are derived from and generally follow the rules of origin under the Caribbean Basin Initiative (CBI).
9. For an analysis of how to apply these rules, see chapter 12 on the CBI.

may not exceed 15 percent of the appraised value of the article.[9]

The certificate of origin completed by those who export goods under the US–IFTA is provided in appendix 14. For purposes of the US–IFTA, the party completing this form, generally the manufacturer, indicates if the goods are wholly the growth, product, or manufacture of the exporting party with a symbol "P." If the goods contain foreign components, the symbol "Y" is indicated on Form A, followed by the percentage of the value of the goods that is produced in the exporting country.

Timetable for Tariff Elimination

Under the agreement, tariffs are to be eliminated within one of four timetables. About 50 percent of each country's exportable goods became tariff free on September 1, 1985, concurrent with the effective date of the US–IFTA. The three timetables under which tariffs are not immediately eliminated indicate those goods on lists A through C provided by each respective party. The goods are arranged by their tariff classification number. Both the United States and Israel have adopted the Harmonized Tariff Schedule, with only few variations.

List A contains moderately import-sensitive goods comprising about 30 percent of each party's exportable goods. The tariffs on these goods have been reduced in stages since the agreement went into force and have become totally duty-free as of January 1, 1989.

List B contains goods that are more import-sensitive. Both the United States and Israel have primarily selected list B as a timetable for the elimination of duties on various textile products import-sensitive to the respective party.[10]

List C includes goods that are the most import-sensitive to the party listing the item. The United States has included many agricultural products on this list as well as various goods containing bromine and certain categories of jewelry among others. Israel lists a greater variety of goods, including various prepared foods, paper, certain chemicals, and certain industrial goods, among others. Although Israel has more goods in list C, the value of U.S. and Israeli goods on list C traded between the two countries is about equivalent. All goods contained in list C will become duty-free as of 1995. The United States and Israel met in July 1990 to determine which goods on each party's respective list C can have tariff reductions between 1990 and 1995.[11]

Importers of Israeli goods should become aware of those items imported into the United States from Israel that are duty-free or duty-reduced as a result of Israel's status under the General System of Preferences and their most-favored-nation status. Thus some articles contained on U.S. lists A through C are already duty-free.

---

10. The reduction of duties on list B is to proceed according to the following timetable.

    From Sept. 1, 1985: levied at 80 percent of 1985 rate*
    From Jan. 1, 1986: levied at 70 percent of 1986 rate
    From Jan. 1, 1987: levied at 60 percent of 1987 rate
    From Jan. 1, 1988: levied at 50 percent of 1988 rate
    From Jan. 1, 1989: levied at 40 percent of 1989 rate
    From Jan. 1, 1990: levied at 30 percent of 1990 rate
    From Jan. 1, 1991: levied at 20 percent of 1991 rate
    From Jan. 1, 1992: levied at 10 percent of 1992 rate

    All products will be duty free as of January 1, 1995. The subheading for Israeli products included in list B and the stages of reduction in their rate of duty can be found in 53 Fed. Reg. 47,423 (1988).

    ---

    *Annual rate reflects the general rate of duty applied to a particular imported good.

11. The U.S. position on accelerating the elimination of duties on list C items was preceded by a public comment period. 54 Fed. Reg. 19,273 (1989).

Applying the HTSUS

To determine the current rate of duty applicable to goods imported from Israel, prior to the final stage of tariff elimination, the importer should refer to the rates of duty subcolumn in the HTSUS that is titled "special." Under the rates of duty column titled "special," the symbol "IL" refers to the rate applicable to imports from Israel that meet rules of origin requirements set forth in the agreement. Those requirements are set forth in General Note 3(c)(vi), located at the beginning of the HTSUS.

Most items will already be duty-free under the "IL" notation. For those items to which a rate of duty is listed, the importer should take steps to ascertain whether the duty listed is still applicable, or will be applicable at the time of entry, under the staged elimination. The reader should review the timetables for staged elimination found in section 4(a) of the United States–Israel Free Trade Area Implementation Act of 1985. The importer should be aware that a printing of the timetable that is not current may not reflect the acceleration of the tariff eliminations now under negotiation. A customs broker can most readily obtain information concerning a change in duty reduction from a national import specialist or from published updates.

Rules Governing IFTA Exceptions

The US–IFTA contains provisions regulating the instances where, and the items as to which, a party can suspend the US–IFTA. These provisions buttress the reliability of the agreement by permitting the minimum flexibility needed by the parties coupled with a procedure to work through difficulties in an environment of communication and cooperation.

Neither party may introduce new duties or quotas in

trade between the United States and Israel other than in these few circumstances provided for in the US–IFTA or the GATT.[12] These few circumstances may entail compliance with a narrow standard for import relief or exceptions within certain specified categories. Article 5 enables either party to exclude its products from a general import relief program established by the other party, unless that party's goods are determined to be a substantial cause of the serious injury. This provision provides yet another substantial benefit to trade between the United States and Israel in comparison to exporters from third countries. Because Israel's goods are generally a small percentage of U.S. imports, Israeli goods are even less likely to be subject to import relief.

Furthermore, import relief that solely suspends a US–IFTA duty reduction for a type of goods is only permitted where that duty reduction is itself the cause of the serious injury. Whether the establishment of import relief, which bears negatively on US–IFTA commerce, is applied by a party to all foreign trade or specifically to transactions under the US–IFTA, the party proposing the regulation must notify the other party in writing[13] and withhold action until the parties have consulted[14] (consultations will be expedited and the written notice requirement waived where perishable goods are at issue).

As noted in the above paragraph, the US–IFTA provides for the maintenance, or temporary implementation of, import restrictions regarding certain types of goods to the extent agreed upon between the parties. First, the US–IFTA adopts the national security exceptions under articles XX and XXI of the GATT.[15]

12. US–IFTA article 4, *supra* note 6, at 658.
13. US–IFTA article 18, *supra* note 6, at 664.
14. US–IFTA article 5, *supra* note 6, at 658–659.
15. US–IFTA article 7, *supra* note 6, at 659. See Article XX, "General

Additionally, the US–IFTA protects legislation benefiting religion or ritual. Article 8 of the US–IFTA states: "This Agreement shall not preclude the adoption or enforcement by either Party of measures relating to prohibitions on religious or ritual grounds provided that they are applied in accordance with the principle of national treatment."

The provision addresses a concern of Israeli society. Although secular law prevails in Israel, except in family law where the laws of each family's religion prevails, the Israeli legislature will at times draw from Jewish heritage as a guide to legislation or evoke statutes to foster national heritage. A statute designed to foster national heritage within Israel is the prohibition on importing certain intrinsically unkosher[16] products such as shellfish and pork among others. Exporters to Israel should also be aware that items certified as kosher in the United States will not be accepted as kosher in Israel, unless accord on the standard of supervision is reached with Israel's Chief Rabbinate, the agency responsible for setting those standards.

Agriculture

Of concern to both Israel and the United States is maintaining certain restrictions on the import of agricultural products.[17] The US–IFTA allows the United States and Israel to maintain their nontariff import restrictions, such as quotas and fees. The parties are exempt from any nontariff

---

Exceptions" and Article XXI "Security Exceptions" of the GATT, *supra* note 7, at 53–54.

16. Kosher products adhere to restrictions that primarily center around regulations concerning the consumption of animal flesh, and products thereof, as established under the corpus of Jewish law (e.g., forbidden species, improper slaughter, and meat/poultry—dairy combinations).
17. US–IFTA article 6, *supra* note 6, at 659.

restrictions established after the date of this treaty. Any tariff on agricultural goods still retained must be phased out by 1995.

Additionally, the US–IFTA seeks to provide guidelines for resolving conflicts arising from nonparallel health standards with respect to agricultural, meat, fish, and poultry products that lead to import restrictions. The countries have differing standards concerning the appropriate type and level of pesticides in agricultural products as well as differing health standards governing animal, poultry, and fish products. For that reason, the US–IFTA calls for joint establishment of a working group[18] which will strive to overcome conflicts arising from differing standards, the objective being the optimal facilitation of trade while respecting measures necessary to protect each party's legitimate concerns. The working group approach brings representatives of the United States and Israel together to work on avoiding or defusing trade conflicts. The 1989 trade conflict between the European Community and the United States over the ban on hormone-inoculated beef, highlights the prudence in forming the type of trouble-shooting committee envisioned in the agreement.

Correcting Economic Imbalances

Temporary implementation of import barriers for the purpose of correcting certain economic imbalances are provided for, such as enabling Israel partially to protect certain infant industries and enabling either party to restrict imports for the purpose of correcting a serious negative balance of payments.

Under article 10, Israel may temporarily increase ad va-

18. To be selected by the joint committee established under US–IFTA article 17.

lorem customs duties on goods by an amount not to exceed twenty percentage points, and on no more than 10 percent of the total value of Israel's 1984 level of imports from the United States. Article 10 protection can only be applied to industries which process certain goods, and those industries must not have been in existence prior to the onset of the US–IFTA in 1985. After two years of implementation there must be an annual 5 percent phase-out of those duties. Furthermore, all duties introduced under this provision must terminate by January 1, 1995. Hence, although article 10 appears to be the one provision recognizing the industrial disparity of the two parties, it provides far narrower leeway for Israel to take action in fostering industrial development than would otherwise be provided for countries in its economic situation under article XVIII of the GATT.

In response to a serious balance of payment situation, article 11 provides for the temporary imposition of certain trade restrictive measures. The measures can be combined if inadequate by themselves. The articles call for ongoing review of the propriety of these import restrictions and for cooperation in finding alternative means to ameliorate the serious trade imbalance.

Adjustments are provided to maintain the value of *specific* duties, but not for ad valorem duties. An adjustment in specific duties can be provided if either party experiences a 20 percent depreciation in value of currency[19] since

---

19. US–IFTA article 20, *supra* note 6, at 665–666. For purposes of the adjustment, the U.S. dollar is measured against the basket of currency known as special drawing rights and the Israeli shekel is measured against the U.S. dollar.

A special drawing right (SDR) is a unit of reserve asset the value of which is based on a weighted basket of five currencies (U.S. dollar, Japanese yen, British pound, French franc, and German mark). The International Monetary Fund (IMF) makes SDRs available to participating countries in proportion to their fund quotas. SDRs are a common reserve asset for bookkeeping purposes that are used to facilitate

the prior adjustment. This is an interim provision for items still subject to duty until 1992 or 1995. No such action has been taken to date and to the best information of the author, Israel does not intend to exercise this right.

If the U.S. dollar decreases by 25 percent in value against special drawing rights over the period of time since the last increase in specific duty, the United States can impose a 25 percent increase on the specific duty of items subject to specific duty. The adjustment in specific duty would be significant where goods are imported in large volume. For example, assume Israel has a specific duty on steel rods of $80 per 1,000 kg (this rate is not accurate). A 25 percent decrease in value of the Israeli shekel against the U.S. dollar would cause the specific duty rate to increase by 25 percent to $100 per 1,000 kg.

Other Impediments to Trade Addressed by the Agreement

In addition to requiring the removal of tariffs and the more noticeable nontariff barriers (i.e., quotas, import surcharges, import deposits, etc.) the US–IFTA endeavors to curtail licensing restrictions, bias in government incentives, purchase performance requirements, government procurement restrictions, possible intellectual property right discrepancies, and restrictions on trade in services.

Licensing

The licensing provision[20] requires automatic approval of licenses unless they are "necessary to administer a quantita-

---

greater efficiency in international balance of payment adjustments among IMF participants. *See* F. Root, Int'l Trade & Investment 180–81, 186 (5th ed., 1984).

20. US–IFTA article 13, *supra* note 6, at 662.

tive ceiling on imports or restrictions" justified under the US–IFTA or under GATT provisions that are not inconsistent with the US–IFTA. Each party must respond to inquiries from the other party concerning its respective licensing criteria and should preferably publish its criteria. The parties must publish a list of items subject to license that is timely updated (justifications must be provided for additions to the list).

Purchase Performance Requirements

In respect to purchase performance requirements and government restrictions, the US–IFTA provides as follows:[21]

> Neither Party shall impose, as a condition of establishment, expansion or maintenance of investments by nationals or companies of the other Party, requirements to export any amount of production resulting from such investments or to purchase locally-produced goods and services. Moreover, neither Party shall impose requirements on investors to purchase locally-produced goods and services as a condition for receiving any type of governmental incentives.

Government Procurement

Article 15 requires that the parties limit and endeavor to eliminate their government procurement restrictions. Under the US–IFTA the parties are required to waive all buy national restrictions with respect to government agency purchases of a contract value equal to or above fifty thousand U.S. dollars.[22]

Additionally, the government of Israel agreed to proceed two steps further: they are to include under this provision nonmilitary purchase by their Defense Ministry, and to re-

21. 19 U.S.C.A. § 2518(4)(c) (West Supp. 1989). *See also* Federal Acquisition Regulation § 25.402(2).
22. US–IFTA article 14, *supra* note 6, at 662.

lax offset requirements on all civilian agency procurement.[23] The Joint Committee will consider amending the US–IFTA to apply to this expanded agreement should it proceed.

Intellectual Property

The agreement provides political accord on two key issues of trade policy. It reaffirms each party's "obligation under bilateral and multilateral agreements relating to intellectual property rights"[24] and affirms the parties' commitment to pave the way to an open system of trade in services. Upon signing the US–IFTA, the parties signed a nonbinding declaration of trade in services. The parties set down certain principles and agreed to work together to promote open trade in services. Open trade in services is an integral objective in United States foreign trade policy.

Elimination of Subsidies

An important aspect of the US–IFTA addresses the elimination in phases of certain subsidies utilized in Israel to help foster domestic industrialization.[25] The subsidies to be

23. These "offset requirements" entail a commitment by a foreign seller to use a percentage of the sales price paid by the Israeli government to purchase Israeli-made goods. Thus the loss of capital incurred by Israel in its government's purchase of imports is partially "offset" by the purchase of Israeli-made goods by the foreign exporter. Israel did not require offsets for military procurements, but often did require offsets for government procurement of civilian goods. Israel's government stated in a side letter to the free trade agreement that offsets would be reduced from approximately 40 percent of the value of the procured merchandise "to a level not to exceed 20 percent." The letter also provides that U.S. firms would not be required to purchase goods that are not on competitive terms or take any action that is not commercially justifiable. No offset requirements will be placed on purchases under $500,000. (Letter from Dan Halperin, Minister—[Israel's] Economic Affairs, to Doral Cooper, Ass't United States Trade Representative (USTR), Apr. 22, 1985.)
24. US–IFTA article 16, *supra* note 6, at 663.
25. US–IFTA article 17, *supra* note 6, at 663–664.

eliminated, or refrained from, concern certain export financing programs.

Israel has agreed to continue its policy of not providing loans at preferred interest rates for purposes of export shipment funds or for purposes of export production funds. Israel does not make loans at preferential interest rates for purposes of export production funds and has agreed to continue to refrain from doing so. Israel has provided local currency financing for export production funds, but it has agreed to a freeze on this subsidy and to a timetable for its elimination. Similarly, Israel has agreed to freeze the export subsidies within the import for export fund and to a timetable for its elimination. Israel will also bring certain other export financing programs into conformity with the provisions of the Organization for Economic Cooperation and Development (OECD).

The parties agreed that the elimination of subsidies does not include subsidies for primary products, such as "any product of farm, forest or fishing in its natural form or which has undergone such processing as is customarily required to prepare it for marketing in substantial volume in international trade."

Under this annex, Israel agreed to sign the subsidies code of the GATT. A benefit of signing the subsidies code of the GATT is that the United States will apply to Israeli goods the injury test used in assessing countervailing duties on subsidized exports of signatory states. Israel also agreed to refrain from implementing new export subsidy programs. Nor will Israel increase the level of subsidization on any program beyond the level in place on July 11, 1984. Lastly, neither party will condition investment incentives on export requirements. Annex 4 required significant sacrifices on Israel's part, but in forming stronger trade relations with her major trading partner, the Israeli government realized the necessity of conforming to these standards, albeit stricter than those placed on developing states.

United States–Israel Consultations

The US–IFTA is governed by a joint committee whose objective is to "supervise the proper implementation of this agreement and to review the trade relationship between the parties."[26] Among other functions the joint committee holds "consultations with respect to any matter affecting the operation and the interpretation of this agreement" and considers ways to improve trade relations between the parties.

Also important to the administration of the agreement are the notice and consultation requirements and procedure.[27] Notice and consultation is required whenever either party takes any trade measure with respect to products traded between the parties. Notice is also required by either party committing itself to "reduce barriers to trade applicable to foreign countries" as such action dilutes the other party's trade advantages gained through the US–IFTA. Notice and consultation may be provided after the fact "[i]n special circumstances, where delay or prior notice would cause damage which would be difficult to remedy."

When a dispute arises under the US–IFTA, the first step is to attempt to resolve the dispute through consultations. If consultations fail to produce accord, then either party can take the matter before the joint committee. If the joint committee cannot resolve the dispute within sixty days, or the extended deadline determined by the joint committee, the dispute is sent to a three-member conciliation panel.

Recent examples indicate that the parties are able to work constructively on solving important issues. In 1988 the United States Department of Commerce challenged an established Israeli tax procedure called the TAMA (Hebrew acronym for additional rate of increase). The TAMA is a

26. US–IFTA article 18, *supra* note 6, at 664.
27. *Id.*

coefficient that raises the base price of goods for calculating the purchase tax.[28] The intent is to assume a wholesale price, for purposes of assessing the purchase tax, that is more consistent with the wholesale price of comparable goods manufactured in Israel. In October of 1988, the joint committee met to resolve the issue. After three weeks of intensive negotiations, the members of the joint committee agreed that Israel would legislate the elimination of the TAMA. Through 1995, all but some very low volume importers would be removed from TAMA assessment, by substituting the wholesale value of the imports determined according to the importers' prior year imports. Israel also agreed to remove certain taxes favoring domestic producers.

In February, 1990, the USTR requested public comment on whether U.S. importers are affected by a similar procedure called the "harama." The harama is Israel's near equivalent of a former U.S. customs law valuation provision called the "American selling price."[29] Similar to the TAMA, the harama artificially raises an invoice price to make it more consistent with the wholesale price of comparable goods produced in Israel. The artificial price is then applied as value for purposes of assessing customs duty. Under the harama, the artificial increase is between 2 and 5 percent of goods imported by an exclusive agent and up to 10 percent for other imports. The United States is consider-

---

28. The purchase tax is an ad valorem tax levied on the purchase of foreign or domestic goods by merchants (i.e., importers, manufacturers, wholesalers, and retailers).
29. The American selling price (ASP) artificially raised the base price of an import to an actual or theoretical domestic selling price for purposes of customs valuation. ASP was used where a domestic party demonstrated injury to industry or successfully argued that the imports in question hindered the establishment of United States industry in that area of production. The ASP was found to be contrary to the 1979 GATT Agreement. Subsequently, the U.S. was allowed to convert ASP tariffs to ad valorem or compound rates.

ing requesting Israel to withdraw the harama, pursuant to articles 3 and 19 of the US–IFTA.[30]

The US–IFTA remains an ongoing incentive to enhance trade between Israel and the United States. The success of this agreement has furthered the free trade agenda of the United States.

30. 55 Fed. Reg. 6852-3 (1990).

14. United States–Canada Free Trade Agreement

Introduction

On January 2, 1988, Prime Minister Brian Mulroney and President Ronald Reagan signed the United States–Canada Free Trade Agreement (US–CFTA). Its objectives are

1. To eliminate barriers to trade in goods and services between Canada and the United States;
2. To facilitate conditions of fair competition within the free trade area;
3. To liberalize conditions for investment within North America;
4. To establish effective procedures for the joint administration of the US–CFTA and the resolution of bilateral trade disputes; and
5. To lay the foundation for future bilateral and multilateral cooperation.[1]

To fulfill these objectives the US–CFTA provides for the elimination of tariffs and nontariff barriers to trade in

1. Free Trade Agreement, Jan. 2, 1988, United States–Canada (hereinafter cited as US–CFTA), article 105, *reprinted in* DEP'T OF EXTERNAL AFFAIRS OF CANADA, THE CANADA–U.S. FREE TRADE AGREEMENT 9 (1988).

goods. It also provides for the liberalization of trade in other areas by reducing restrictions on trade in services, finance, and investment and entry of executives, professionals, and other persons for the purpose of conducting business in each other's country.

Principle of National Treatment

At the heart of the agreement lies the principle of national treatment. As in the General Agreement on Tariffs and Trade (GATT), the US–CFTA provides that goods imported into either country must receive the same treatment under the policies, laws, and regulations of the importing country as accorded competitive goods which are produced domestically.[2]

Structure of the Agreement

The agreement is made up of eight parts organized by general topic; each part is divided into chapters, twenty-one in all. Chapters are further divided into articles, which are subdivided into paragraphs and subparagraphs.

Several articles are followed by annexes, located at the end of the chapter. Generally, the annexes limit the scope of the covered articles and establish how articles will be implemented.

Also, definitions are found throughout the US–CFTA. They are located in the last article of a chapter and interpret words used in that chapter. In addition, article 201 contains unqualified definitions for words that are used in the same way throughout the US–CFTA.[3]

2. US–CFTA article 105, *supra* note 1, at 10.
3. Overview of US–CFTA, *supra* note 1, at 1.3.

Implementation of the Agreement

Congress has enacted legislation implementing the agreement.[4] The President has also issued proclamation 5923, implementing the US–CFTA. The presidential proclamation modifies General Note 3(c) to the HTSUS to provide for the US–CFTA, detailing the rules of origin, etc. Also, at the time of this writing Customs has issued regulations relating to the procedures for obtaining US–CFTA preferences.[5]

Trade in Goods

Elimination of Duties

The essence of the US–CFTA is its elimination of duties and various trade restrictions on practically all the trade in goods between Canada and the United States.

Chapters 3 through 6 contain provisions applicable to all trade in goods. Chapters 7 (Agriculture), 8 (Wine & Distilled Spirits), 9 (Energy), and 10 (Automotive Products) limit their scope to issues of concern to the respective industries involved.

The removal of all tariffs will not occur immediately. Instead, some tariffs will be removed at once while other tariffs will be gradually phased out over a ten-year period, with the caveat that neither country may increase existing tariff rates unless specifically allowed by the US–CFTA. If a domestic industry is seriously injured as a result of a flood of imports caused by the agreement's tariff reductions, the affected country can increase the duty on the subject goods as a temporary curative measure to allow for a period of adjustment for the domestic industry. The procedure for obtaining such relief is detailed in the implementation stat-

4. Pub. L. No. 100-449, 102 Stat. 1851 (1988).
5. 19 C.F.R. §§ 10.301–.311 (1990). In addition, General Note 3(c)(vii), HTSUS, contains the provisions of the implementation act.

ute.[6] In brief, an affected industry may petition the United States International Trade Commission for an adjustment in duty on the goods in question. The Commission will then investigate the claim to determine whether the US–CFTA duty reduction on those goods resulted in serious injury to the domestic industry producing those same goods. If the Commission makes an affirmative finding, it will recommend to the President the amount of relief necessary to remedy the injury. A summary of the report will be published in the *Federal Register*. Should the President decide that relief is warranted he may (1) suspend further tariff reductions for the goods or (2) increase the duty rate of such goods coming from Canada, subject to the conditions set forth in section 302.

Stages of Tariff Elimination

The US–CFTA provides for duty elimination in three stages. The following are among the products that are included in the first stage and received duty-free status effective on January 1, 1989: leather, skates/skis, motorcycles.

The products that are included in stage two received the first of five 20 percent duty reductions on January 1, 1989; all duties will be eliminated by January 1, 1994. Stage two products include paints, furniture, paper and paper products.

The following are among the products that are included in stage three. These products will receive tariff reductions over a ten-year period of 10 percent per year commencing January 1, 1989, and will become duty-free on January 1, 1998: steel, textiles and apparel, rubber, and most agricultural products. Note, however, that there is a twenty-year tariff "snapback" provision for fresh fruit and vegetables. A temporary duty may be applied to these items if the import

6. Pub. L. No. 100-449, § 302, 102 Stat. 1851 (1988).

price falls below a specified support price threshold and the planted acreage for the product of the importing party remains constant or has declined over the previous five years.[7]

Acceleration of Tariff Elimination

The US–CFTA Implementation Act grants the president the authority to seek acceleration of tariff eliminations. For example, the president can authorize a party's request to move up the date on which a specific product will receive duty-free status under the US–CFTA.[8]

Rules of Origin

Under the US–CFTA, preferential treatment is available only to goods which are determined to be originating goods in accordance with General Note 3(c) of the HTSUS. The rules of origin are the principles upon which goods which are wholly produced or obtained in either the United States or Canada may ultimately receive US–CFTA benefits. As with the Generalized System of Preferences (GSP), Caribbean Basin Initiative (CBI), and the United States–Israel Free Trade Agreement (US–IFTA), detailed requirements set forth in such rules of origin are necessary to prevent foreign exporters from engaging in pass-through operations. The purpose of the US–CFTA rules of origin is to make sure that duty-free benefits are bestowed only on goods with significant U.S. or Canadian content.

7. Pub. L. No. 100-449, § 301, 102 Stat. 1851 (1988).
8. At the time of this writing a recent Federal Register Notice, 54 Fed. Reg. 3175–6 (1989), detailed the procedures for making requests and set a time for when such requests could be made. This procedure will be an annual event.

Doing Away with the Substantial Transformation Test

In an attempt to bring clarity, certainty, and uniformity to the determination of the country of origin of goods, the US–CFTA has forsaken the "substantial transformation" concept used in the GSP, CBI, and US–IFTA in favor of a more pragmatic approach.[9]

Briefly stated, the substantial transformation concept, utilized as the overriding principle in determining country of origin for the other current free trade programs, confers origin on the last country where goods were so substantially processed as to create a new article of commerce with a different name, character, or use. The substantial transformation rule has been considered by many to result in inconsistencies as well as to present significant problems for those attempting to ascertain whether a given process is so substantial as to create a new article of commerce with a different name, character, or use. These determinations often lead to a great deal of uncertainty of both application and result.

The US–CFTA has attempted to eliminate the element of subjectivity in country of origin determinations with specific and detailed requirements.

Rules of Origin Under the US–CFTA

The US–CFTA sets forth, in chapter 3, three basic categories in which goods must fall in order to qualify as goods of U.S. or Canadian origin. The *first category* covers goods that are wholly produced or obtained in either Canada or the United States or both. For example, trees grown in Canada will be considered products of Canada. Likewise, cattle bred and raised in the United States will be considered of U.S. origin. Accordingly, these items will be entitled to US–

9. See discussion on substantial transformation regarding GSP in chapter 11 and CBI in chapter 12.

CFTA preferences. Other items covered by this category would include indigenous minerals, crops, and fish caught by vessels flying the flag of Canada or the United States.[10]

The *second category* covers goods that contain "foreign" raw materials[11] or components, which may also qualify for US–CFTA duty-free treatment if the goods have been, as a result of processing, changed to such an extent that they then are classified differently from the raw material or components from which they were made.

In this regard, if a change in HTSUS tariff classification results from the processing or assembly operation performed on the foreign materials in either Canada or the United States, such foreign material will be considered to have been sufficiently changed or "transformed" so as to be subject to a new HTSUS classification, and thus eligible for treatment as goods originating in the territory in which such operations took place. However, not all changes in HTSUS classification will be considered as effecting a transformation for US–CFTA origin purposes. The specific changes designated as resulting in a transformation are detailed by the rules set forth in the agreement.[12] These rules were designed to ensure that only products which are significantly changed or "transformed" will be covered. The rules are directed toward each chapter of the HTSUS and warrant judicious analysis in order to ascertain whether and to what degree a change in classification will result in a transformation of country of origin status. That is, an importer who wishes to import a specific article which contains foreign material from Canada to the United States and

10. US–CFTA article 304, *supra* note 1, at 20; Pub. L. No. 100-449, § 202; General Note 3(c)(vii)(B), HTSUS.
11. Materials from outside of the "territory" of either Canada or the United States as defined in US–CFTA article 201 (*supra* note 1, at 12).
12. US–CFTA, chapter three (Annex Rules), *supra* note 1, at 24–41; General Note 3(c)(vii)(Q), HTSUS.

wishes to receive US–CFTA benefits must first determine the proper classification, under the HTSUS, of the foreign material, then after it is processed in Canada, must determine the proper HTSUS classification of the resulting completed article. If, after studying the rules in the US–CFTA covering that completed article, such a change in classification is specifically deemed to effect a transformation of the original material, US–CFTA benefits will be conferred on that completed article. However, if after applying the rules, it is found that the change in classification effected by the processing is not considered a transformation, that is, the rules state that such a change in classification does not amount to a change in origin despite the fact that there is a change in HTSUS classification, then the completed article will still be considered as originating in the nonmember country and US–CFTA benefits will not be conferred.

For example, to determine whether crude peanut oil produced in Canada from Italian peanuts in shells is eligible for duty-free entry into the United States pursuant to US–CFTA, we must follow these steps:

1. Determine the correct HTSUS classification for peanuts in shells—which is subheading 1202.10.00, HTSUS (chapter 12).
2. Then determine the correct HTSUS classification for crude peanut oil—which is subheading 1508.90.00, HTSUS (chapter 15).
3. Then, look at the appropriate rule covering the chapter containing crude peanut oil—which is found in rule section III, 1 as indicated by General Note 3(c)(vii)(Q)(3). Here we see that "a change to chapter 15 from any other chapter" (in this case from chapter 12) does result in a "change" in classification so as to effect a transformation of the shelled peanuts for US–CFTA origin purposes.

Therefore, the crude peanut oil may enter the U.S. duty free as a product of Canada.

However, if the Italian peanuts in shells were merely shelled (i.e., taken out of their shells) in Canada, resulting in a change in HTSUS classification from subheading 1202.10.00 to subheading 1202.20.00, this would not confer Canadian origin on the shelled peanuts, since rule section II of the US–CFTA states that "no changes within chapters . . . shall be treated as originating in the territory of that Party. . . ." Since peanuts in shell are classified in subheading 1202.10.00 and peanuts without shells are classified in subheading 1202.20.00, the fact that both subheadings are contained in the same chapter (chapter 12) will thus preclude the shelling operation from changing the origin of the foreign peanuts in shells.

The *third category* confers origin, in two very limited situations, on certain goods containing materials which are neither of U.S nor Canadian origin, but which meet specific "value-added" criteria as described in paragraph 3 and paragraph 4 in the US–CFTA's annex 301.2 governing interpretation.

Basically, origin is conferred for US–CFTA purposes if foreign material (i.e., material originating outside the United States or Canada) is processed to such a degree in either country that it is classified under a different HTSUS classification than it was in its preprocessed state.

The third category, however, provides two exceptions to this basic rule because of the unique way in which certain items are classified under the HTSUS. Specifically, these items may be subject to significant processing that nevertheless does not result in any change in HTSUS classification.

To qualify for the exceptions, the US–CFTA requires that the value of materials originating in either country used in the production of such goods plus the direct cost of assembling the goods constitute not less than 50 percent of their value when exported to either the United States or Canada. When this value requirement is met, the foreign material used in the assembly operation will be considered to be of U.S. or Canadian origin.[13]

Under the first exception, if a product is assembled in either the United States or Canada with the use of some foreign material, and if this assembled product bears the same classification as the parts from which it was assembled, it may be considered as originating in either the United States or Canada.

For example, assume that a Canadian exporter has an assembly operation making shovels from parts (handles, shafts, etc.) imported from a third country. Both the assembled shovels and the parts are classified under the same HTSUS subheading (9402.10.00), and the value of the materials produced in Canada used, plus the direct cost of assembly, amount to at least 50 percent of the value of the finished shovels. As a result, the shovels would qualify as goods originating in Canada.

Under the second exception, if a product is assembled in either the United States or Canada with the use of foreign material and is entered into either country in an assembled condition, it will be considered as originating in either the United States or Canada, provided that the value-added test is met and further provided that the product would be classified under the same HTSUS heading whether or not it was entered in an assembled or unassembled condition.

For example, watches are classified under HTSUS heading 9110 as "watches" whether assembled or unassembled. If various components of a watch were non-U.S. or non-Canadian in origin and those components were used along with a number of U.S. or Canadian watch components to

13. The CFTA rules of origin also specify that the goods do not undergo further processing or assembly in a third country and that they meet US–CFTA transshipment requirements.

create a completed watch in the United States or Canada, the foreign components would be able to be imported into the United States or Canada (if the value-added test were also met) even though the foreign components would not be classified in a new HTSUS heading when imported as a completed watch.

This limited "value-added" category does not apply in every situation in which there is no change in HTSUS classification after the costly processing of imported goods. Origin will not result, regardless of the cost of a process involved or materials used, unless imported unassembled or disassembled parts classified as such are involved, as provided in (1), or unless the tariff subheading of the goods used provides for the goods themselves and their parts, as provided in (2).

For example, a Canadian exporter galvanizes imported, ungalvanized boiler pipes. Even if the cost of galvanizing and the value of Canadian material used amounts to at least 50 percent of the value of the galvanized boiler pipes, the finished product will not result in a change in origin. The reason: the galvanized pipe does not meet all of the criteria provided for in the third origin category. The galvanized and ungalvanized boiler pipes have the same HTSUS classification subheading (7304.39.00), but the processing does not involve the assembly of imported unassembled or disassembled goods classified as such in the HTSUS, nor does the processing involve goods and their parts which are both provided for in the same HTSUS subheading.

In addition to the three general categories discussed, the US–CFTA rules themselves, in certain instances, also provide that specific products must *both* demonstrate a change in classification *and* meet certain value-added criteria (a percentage of domestic value-added content) to qualify as goods originating in either country (e.g., certain chemicals, plastics, footwear, etc.). For example, in section VI covering chapters 28 through 38 of the HTSUS, the rules provide that certain chemicals will be considered to be transformed for country of origin purposes if the processing effects a change in HTSUS classification to any subheading of chapters 28–38, HTSUS, from any other subheading within those chapters, provided that the value of materials originating in the territory of either party or both parties plus the direct cost of processing performed in the territory of either party or both parties constitute not less than 50 percent of the value of the goods when exported to the territory of the other party.

Further, the US–CFTA rules of origin prescribe that goods covered by the second category shall not be considered to originate in the territory of a party pursuant to paragraph 2 merely by virtue of having undergone

1. Simple packaging or, except as expressly provided by the rules discussed in category three, covering the limited combining operations meeting the 50 percent value-added requirement;
2. Mere dilution with water or another substance that does not materially alter the characteristics of the goods; or
3. Any process or work in respect of which it is established, or in respect of which the facts as ascertained clearly justify the presumption, that the sole object was to circumvent the provisions of this chapter.

Accessories

The US–CFTA also makes special provision for accessories. It states that accessories, spare parts, or tools delivered with any piece of equipment, machinery, apparatus, or vehicle that form part of its standard equipment shall be deemed to have the same origin as that equipment, machinery, apparatus, or vehicle; provided that the quantities and values of such accessories, spare parts, or tools are customary for the equipment, machinery, apparatus, or vehicle.[14] For example, a jack handle included with an automobile would be considered to have the same origin as the automobile it came in.

Value of Materials Originating in Either Country Defined

"Value of materials originating in the U.S. or Canada or both" means the aggregate of (1) the price paid by the producer of exported goods for material originating in either the United States or Canada or both, or for third-country materials used or consumed in the production of such originating materials; and (2) when not included in that price, the costs of freight, insurance, packing and all other costs incurred in transporting of originating materials, duties, taxes, and brokerage fees on such material paid in the United States or Canada or both, the cost of waste or spoilage, less the value of reusable scrap; and the value of goods and services relating to such originating materials.[15]

Value of Goods Exported Defined

"Value of the goods when exported to the U.S." means the aggregate of the price paid by the producer for all materials and, when not included in the price paid for the materials, the following costs related thereto: freight, insurance, packing and all costs incurred in transporting all materials to the location of the producer, duties, taxes and brokerage fees on all materials paid in the U.S., Canada, or both, the cost of waste or spoilage, less the value of reusable scrap or by-product; and the value of goods and services relating to

---

14. US–CFTA article 301, *supra* note 1, at 17; General Note 3(c)(vii)(D), HTSUS.
15. US–CFTA article 304, *supra* note 1, at 18; General Note 3(c)(vii)(L), HTSUS.

all covered materials, and the direct cost of processing or direct cost of assembling the goods.[16]

Origin Rules Covering Apparel

The agreement also contains origin rules governing apparel. Basically, it provides specific rules for the various textiles and textile articles classified in chapters 50–63 of the HTSUS. Apparel is specifically covered under rules, section XI, 16–18. They state, in part, that apparel made from fabrics woven in Canada or the United States will qualify for duty-free treatment. If apparel is made from non-U.S. or non-Canadian woven fabrics it can still qualify for duty-free treatment but only up to the following annual quantities measured in square yard equivalents (sye):

	From Canada	From the U.S.
Nonwoolen apparel	50 million	10.5 million
Woolen apparel	6 million	1 million

Apparel above these quantities shall be subject to duty at the applicable most favored nation's rate.

The rules similarly provide for a quantitative limit governing duty-free exports to the United States of nonwoolen fabrics or textile articles woven or knitted in Canada from yarn imported from a third country. The level for such exports has been set at 20 million square yards for the period commencing on January 1, 1989, and ending on December 31, 1992. The parties agree to review these levels in 1990–1991 with representatives of the industries in order to arrive at a mutually beneficial resolution.

16. US–CFTA article 304, *supra* note 1, at 20; General Note 3(c)(vii)(M), HTSUS.

Transshipment

The US–CFTA sets out specific requirements for direct shipment and documentation. Goods shall be considered to be directly shipped to the United States from Canada or from Canada to the United States under the following circumstances:

1. The goods have been shipped directly from Canada to the United States (or vice versa) without passing through the territory of any third party; or
2. The goods were shipped through the territory of a third country but
   - They did not enter the commerce of any third country;
   - They did not undergo any operation other than unloading, reloading, or any operations necessary to transport them to the United States or to preserve them in good condition; and
   - All shipping and export documents show the United States as the final destination.[17]

Defining Direct Cost of Processing and Assembly

The US–CFTA also defines and enumerates those items that shall be included in "direct cost of processing" and "direct cost of assembly" and sets prohibitions on further processing or assembly in third countries.[18]

"Direct cost of processing" and "direct cost of assembly"

17. US–CFTA article 302, *supra* note 1, at 18; General Note 3(c)(vii)(E), HTSUS.
18. US–CFTA article 304, *supra* note 1, at 18–19; General Note 3(c)(vii)(N), HTSUS.

include "those costs directly incurred in, or that can be reasonably allocated to, the production of goods." They include (among other costs) the cost of labor; the cost of inspecting and testing goods; the cost of energy; development, design, and engineering costs; rent; mortgage interest; depreciation on buildings; the cost of utilities for real property used in the production of the goods; and royalty, licensing, or other like payments for the right to the goods.

Excluded from the direct costs of processing or assembling are the costs relating to the general expense of doing business (e.g., cost of providing executive, financial, sales, advertising, marketing, accounting and legal services, and insurance); brokerage charges; costs for telephone, mail, and other means of communication; packing costs for exporting the goods; royalty payments related to licensing agreement to distribute or sell the goods; rent, mortgage interest, depreciation, etc., for real property used by personnel charged with administrative functions; and profit on the goods.

Drawback

Both the United States and Canada provide refunds or duty reductions for all or part of the duty paid on imported goods that are used in the production of articles subsequently exported. These so-called duty "drawbacks"[19] were created to promote domestic assembly and manufacturing operations and to avoid the compounding of duty payments for imported goods which are to be exported.

With the eventual elimination of tariffs, the drafters of the US–CFTA determined that the need for duty drawbacks would become unnecessary. Also, it was determined that in order to ensure that only those goods with significant U.S. or Canadian content would be eligible for duty preferences under the agreement, the elimination of drawback was nec-

19. See discussion on drawbacks, chapter 17.

essary. In addition, by eliminating drawback, the drafters of the US–CFTA sought to discourage the use of foreign material in the creation of products for export to either signatory country and to encourage the use of domestic material. Therefore, both countries agreed to end duty drawback, with some exceptions, on all bilateral trade after January 1, 1994.

Exceptions from the Elimination of Drawback

Drawback between the United States and Canada will not be eliminated, and will continue to be available, for citrus products and for imported fabrics converted into apparel which is subsequently exported to the other country above the allowable tariff quota levels set forth in the US–CFTA.

In addition, "same condition drawback" will not be eliminated. Goods that remain in the same condition when exported as they were when imported will continue to receive drawback treatment. That is, if the duties on the goods have not been phased out completely by the US–CFTA staged duty-reduction system, an importer may decide to seek drawback of duties paid pursuant to the US–CFTA rate when the goods are exported in the same condition as they were when they were imported.

Finally, goods of U.S. or Canadian origin used or consumed in the creation of articles which are then exported back to the other signatory country will also remain eligible for duty drawback. Similarly drawback for rejected or defective goods will remain available.

Documentation

The US–CFTA requires that the importer who represents that goods meet these complicated rules of origin *must* make a written declaration to that effect based on the exporter's written certification of origin (CF 353, reprinted in appendix 15). This requirement is made mandatory under the agreement, and it is further required that, upon request, such importer must provide the customs authority of the country with proof of the exporter's written certificate of origin of the goods. Furthermore, as with any other customs documentation, any false statements or false information contained in these declarations will be subject to appropriate penalties.[20]

The US–CFTA further applies these requirements to exported goods: Each country requires that exporters who certify in writing that the goods they export to either country meet the rules of origin must provide, upon request, the customs authority of the exporting country with a copy of the certification. Furthermore, it is made unlawful to certify falsely that goods exported to either country meet those rules of origin. Such an unlawful act shall have the same legal consequences as a violation of the respective country's laws with respect to making a false statement or representation.[21]

The US–CFTA is a comprehensive document that attempts to provide for the elimination of all obstacles in the way of free trade between the two countries. It provides for the eventual elimination of user fees and duty drawback. It also eliminates prohibitive applications of product standards. For example, Canada may require that particular products meet very specific standards in its domestic market. The United States product equivalents may not mirror these standards exactly and thus may be denied access based on minor or inconsequential differences. To avoid such misuse of product technical requirements, the two countries agreed

20. US–CFTA, annex 406 (relating to article 406), *supra* note 1, at 62; Pub. L. No. 100-449, § 205.
21. *Id.* With respect to our laws, see, e.g., 19 U.S.C. § 1592, discussed in chapter 22.

to recognize compatible product standards. They further agreed to move toward the acceptance of each other's product test results and product approval procedures.

The US–CFTA also deals with specific industries such as the automotive, energy, and wine and spirits industries. For example, for automobiles not covered by the auto pact, the US–CFTA provides for the eventual phase-out of Canada's duty-remission program, which provides government incentives for local automobile producers. In the energy area (e.g., coal, petroleum, natural gas, electricity, uranium and nuclear fuel), the US–CFTA prohibits the application of export taxes, fees, or similar charges by either country. The parties also agree to reduce some marketing and distribution restrictions on trade in wine and distilled spirits such as Canada's higher price markups on U.S. wine and spirits (existing restrictions on beer remain). In these ways, the US–CFTA attempts to break down all programs applied by either country to prevent the ultimate in free trade in the products of these industries. The US–CFTA also provides that the two countries will work toward the elimination of any discrimination in services and government procurement. It facilitates the entry of business people and professionals of each country (e.g., business people and professionals need only show proof of citizenship, show that they are engaged in any eligible profession, and state the purpose of the visit), and it establishes a general dispute settlement mechanism to resolve future differences. The US–CFTA provides for the creation of a joint party commission,[22] made up of an equal number of representatives from both countries, to resolve disputes arising under the agree-

22. The US–CFTA also established a binational panel to review final antidumping or countervailing duty determinations. For a more detailed discussion, see chapter 20 on dumping and countervailing duties.

ment. The commission must meet once a year but it may meet as often as needed. In short, the US–CFTA is the most comprehensive totally bilateral free-trade agreement yet established. It may well prove to be a model for the eventual breakdown of all worldwide trade barriers.

15. American Goods Returned and Special Provisions

A wide range of imports are granted duty-free or preferential-duty treatment.[1] Some of these articles must meet certain conditions or be dedicated to certain uses. Others are unconditionally free, that is, in accordance with their tariff classification, they are granted duty-free status.

These enumerated duty-free articles include certain raw primary materials for manufacture, for example, raw fur skins, silk cocoons, raw silk, metal-bearing ores, and raw jute. This class of merchandise need only be physically verified by the Customs Service as classifiable under the appropriate Harmonized Tariff Schedule of the United States (HTSUS) subheading in order to be eligible for duty-free treatment. No conditions or other requirements are imposed.

Other classes of goods that meet certain conditions, such as those entered under particular circumstances or intended for particular uses, are also afforded duty-free treatment in whole or in part. This category of merchandise is termed "conditionally free." The conditions are strictly construed and must be fully complied with. Failure to comply with the conditions imposed will result in full duty liability at

1. *See* chapters 11–14.

the applicable rates for that classification of merchandise. For example, demonstration materials brought in temporarily by professional artists, lecturers, or scientists are allowed in free of duty by attesting to a special declaration.[2]

This chapter focuses on two principal classes of merchandise accorded duty-free or partially duty-free treatment: (1) American articles exported and returned and (2) articles entering under certain conditions or dedicated to certain exclusive uses.

As we discuss the various duty-free and partially duty-free provisions contained in this chapter, the reader is reminded that the conversion to the HTSUS from the Tariff Schedules of the United States (TSUS) did not result in the abandonment of every interpretive principle found in the TSUS. Many of the conceptual principles present in the TSUS will still apply to the HTSUS, including those enunciated in prior rulings and court decisions.[3]

In addition to prior rulings and court decisions that set forth various principles of classification and tariff construction under the TSUS, certain other general principles applied under the TSUS will also be applicable under the HTSUS. For example, court decisions and Customs rulings interpreting the "substantial transformation" concept in determining the origin of goods should continue to have precedential effect under the HTSUS. Therefore, we shall direct the reader to rulings and court determinations rendered when the TSUS was in effect on such questions as whether goods have been "repaired or altered." Also, terms such as "further processing" and "assembly" have been defined in rulings and court decisions for purposes of TSUS item 806.30, and TSUS item 807.00. These definitions remain applicable for the new HTSUS subheadings (9802.00.60,

2. HTSUS 9013.00.
3. See discussion on this carryover of interpretive principles from the TSUS to the HTSUS in chapter 3, page 73.

HTSUS, and 9802.00.80, HTSUS) covering such goods, and thus we shall direct the reader to those rulings and decisions as well.

American Goods Returned

HTSUS chapter 98, subchapter I regulates the preferential treatment of "Products of the United States when returned after having been exported, without having been advanced in value or improved in condition . . . while abroad."[4] HTSUS chapter 98, subchapter II regulates preferential treatment of American-made manufactured metal articles exported for processing and returned for further processing[5] and articles assembled abroad with American-made components.[6]

Subheading 9801.00.10: Articles Not Advanced or Improved Abroad

American goods reimported are accorded duty-free treatment if they have not been advanced in value or improved in condition by any process of manufacture or other means while abroad.[7]

---

4. HTSUS 9801.00.10.
5. HTSUS 9202.00.60.
6. HTSUS 9802.00.80.
7. The provision does not apply to articles (*see* U.S. Notes chapter 98, subchapter I)
   - (a) exported with benefit of drawback;
   - (b) of a kind with respect to the importation of which an internal-revenue tax is imposed at the time such article is entered . . .; or
   - (c) manufactured or produced in the U.S. in a customs bonded warehouse or under 9813.00.05 (articles to be repaired, altered or processed)—and exported under any provision of law.

   Details pertaining to documents required to be filed at the time of entry for admission of article under HTSUS 9810.00.10, including circumstances in which the district director may waive production of

To claim HTSUS subheading 9801.00.10 status, the importer has the burden of establishing that the article was actually produced in the United States and that the value of the returned product is no greater and its condition no better than when exported.[8] The phrase "improved in condition" is to be treated in "a commercial sense and the actual nature of the commercial entity must be considered."[9] However, change in condition does not preclude sorting, grading, and repackaging of merchandise into a returned package that is more valuable as a commercial unit.[10] Nevertheless, the labor and cost of packing is dutiable at the rate of the contents. In addition, Customs has ruled that American-made containers, such as boxes and barrels, may be returned to the United States duty-free provided they meet the requirements in HTSUS subheading 9801.00.10.[11] Thus, if the containers are the product of the United States and are returned to the United States after having been exported, without being advanced in value or improved in condition abroad, they may be returned free of duty. Customs has also ruled that the filling of such containers will

---

otherwise required documents, appear in 19 C.F.R. § 10.1 (1987). See CF 3311, reprinted in appendix 16.

8. United States v. Bird, 11 Ct. Cust. App. 229, 232 (1922). Processes abroad that are considered mere intermediary steps in manufacturing are still regarded as improvements in condition. Air Carrier Supply Corp. v. United States, 44 C.C.P.A. 116, 119 (1957).
9. Amity Fabrics, Inc. v. United States, 43 Cust. Ct. 64, 67 (1959) (modification that renders nonsalable article marketable is considered improvement).
10. Border Brokerage Co. v. United States, 314 F. Supp. 788 (Cust. Ct. 1970). "[T]he test to be applied in item 800.00 cases is whether the merchandise of American origin has itself (apart from its container) been the object of advancement in value or improvement in condition while abroad." *Id.* at 792. *See also* United States v. John V. Carr & Sons, 495 F.2d 1225 (C.C.P.A. 1974) (fish hooks exported to Hong Kong to be sorted and packed in tin containers).
11. HQ 731806, Nov. 19, 1988.

not constitute an advancement of value or improvement in condition of the containers.

If the merchandise returned has been converted to a new and different use, then HTSUS subheading 9801.00.10 status would not apply. For example, where cattle exported live were slaughtered abroad, their hides were found to be "commodities distinct and different from the live cattle exported."[12]

The courts have also drawn distinctions between processes of segregation or elimination performed abroad and manufacturing processes or other methods used to increase the value or upgrade the condition.[13]

Sometimes the United States manufacturer may want to have its product exported for finishing, processing, or assembly, but does not want to pay full duty on the finished goods when they return to the United States. The special conditions of HTSUS subheadings 9802.00.40, 9802.00.60, and 9802.00.80 may prove useful in those circumstances.

Subheading 9802.00.40: Articles Exported for Repairs or Alterations

HTSUS subheading 9802.00.40 provides that articles returned to the United States after having been exported for repairs or alterations will be assessed duty only on the value of the repairs or alterations.

---

12. Buschoff v. United States, 1 Ct. Cust. App. 336, 337 (1911), *aff'd on rehearing*, 3 Ct. Cust. App. 1 (1912). Similarly, TSUS item 800.00 was inapplicable when ordinary .38 caliber revolvers were exported to Canada for rechambering to a special caliber. A. N. Deringer, Inc. v. United States, 386 F. Supp. 518 (Cust. Ct. 1974), *aff'd*, 524 F.2d 1215 (C.C.P.A. 1975).
13. Residue of zinc from a galvanizing process in Canada was held eligible for free entry because it had been rendered useless except for remanufacture. United States v. Rubelli's Sons, 8 Ct. Cust. App. 399 (1918). *See also* Burgess Battery Co. v. United States, 13 Cust. Ct. 37, *appeal dismissed*, 32 C.C.P.A. 207 (1944).

The term "repairs or alterations" has been held to include cleaning, restoration, renovation, or other changes that do not destroy the identity of the article or create a new or commercially different article.[14] "Repairs" have been held to include the replacement of worn or broken components of an article.[15] "Alterations" have been held to include operations such as the coating of beads and the redyeing of fabric.[16]

In addition, to be eligible for 9802.00.40, HTSUS treatment, the exported article must be complete for its intended use. Therefore, if the foreign processing operation is a necessary step in the preparation or manufacture of the finished article, that operation will preclude 9802.00.40, HTSUS eligibility.[17] For example, the Customs Service has ruled that the shelling (removal of the shell) of pecans constitutes an operation that exceeds a "repair or alteration." Customs reasoned that the pecans with shells were commercially different from the pecan "meat" product that resulted after the shelling operation. Additionally, Customs was of the opinion that the pecans with shells were incomplete (i.e., not yet prepared) for their intended use and that the shelling operation was a further step in the preparation of a finished pecan "meat" product.[18]

---

14. *See* A.F. Burstrom v. United States, 44 C.C.P.A 27 (1957); LeGran Manufacturing Co. v. United States, 59 Cust. Ct. 58 (1967); Guardian Indus. Corp. v. United States, 3 Ct. Int'l Trade 9, slip op. 82–4 (Jan. 5, 1982).
15. *See* Peerless Wireless, Inc. v. United States, 6 Cust. Ct. 102, C.D. 438 (1941) (which held that the replacement of filaments in radio tubes was a repair for purposes of the predecessor provision under the TSUS item 806.20).
16. *See* Royal Bead Novelty Co., Inc. v. United States, 68 Cust. Ct. 154, C.D. 4353, 342 F. Supp. 1394 (1972); Amity Fabrics, Inc. v. United States, 43 Cust. Ct. 64, C.D. 21204 (1959).
17. *See* Dollif & Co. v. United States, 66 C.C.P.A. 77, C.A.D. 1225, 599 F.2d 1015 (1979).
18. *See* HQ 555002 (Jan. 28, 1988).

Before exporting articles pursuant to the provisions of HTSUS subheading 9802.00.40, the owner or exporter must file a certificate of registration (CF 4455, reprinted in appendix 17). This will allow Customs to examine the articles before they are exported. However, in most instances the examination will be waived. If there is no examination, the certificate will be signed by the appropriate Customs officer and an indication will be made that the examination was waived. Upon reimportation, Customs may require that the importer prove that the exported articles were in such condition that the repair or alteration was required and that the necessary work was actually performed. If an examination does take place, a report from the examining officer will be endorsed on the certificate, and it will then be returned to the exporter. Upon the return of the repaired or altered article, a declaration from the person who performed the repairs or alterations must be filed with the entry. The declaration must describe the repairs or alterations performed and state the full cost or fair market value of such repairs or alterations. Also, a declaration by the owner, importer, consignee, or agent having knowledge of the facts must be filed with the entry to the effect that the articles entered in their repaired or altered state are the same articles covered by the certificate of registration and that the reported cost or value of such repairs or alterations is accurate. The district director may waive the declaration if satisfied that the article otherwise meets the requirements of HTSUS subheading 9802.00.40.[19]

Once these requirements are satisfied, the duty on the repaired or altered article is payable upon the value of the repairs or alterations performed abroad, at the rate which would be applicable to the article if classified as an entirety.[20] For example, if a U.S. article, dutiable under the

19. 19 C.F.R. §§ 10.8–.9.
20. HTSUS, U.S. Note 3(c).

HTSUS at 3 percent ad valorem, is exported to Japan, where repairs or alterations are performed, and those repairs or alterations are valued at $1,000 per article, the duty on this article will be 3 percent of the cost of the repairs or alterations, or $30.

Failure to comply with these requirements will result in the assessment of duty at the applicable rate for the merchandise at its appraised value, which will include the article and the cost of alterations or repairs.

Subheading 9802.00.60: American Metal Articles Processed Abroad

HTSUS subheading 9802.00.60 permits the return to the United States for further processing of American articles of metal (not precious) exported for processing, with duty payable only upon the value of the foreign processing. To be eligible for HTSUS subheading 9802.00.60 treatment, the exported articles must be (1) manufactured or subjected to a manufacturing process in the United States, (2) exported for processing, and (3) returned for further processing by or for the account of the person who exported the articles.[21] The key element for eligibility is that the United States metal articles returned from abroad must themselves be subjected to "further processing."[22] No "further processing" was found when United States–manufactured steel sheets were returned to the United States for spraying of a sound-deadening coating, mounting of a clamping system, fitting of an outlet and overflow apparatus, and boxing in individual cartons.[23] In *Intelex Systems, Inc. v. United States*,[24]

21. 93 Treas. Dec. 133 (1958).
22. Defined to include cutting, drilling, forming, galvanizing, grinding, machining, melting, plating, punching, rolling, tagging, and threading.
23. 99 Treas. Dec. 149 (1964).
24. Intelex Sys., Inc. v. United States, 460 F.2d 1083 (C.C.P.A. 1972).

the Court of Customs and Patent Appeals interpreted the phrase "returned to the United States for further processing" to mean "the article processed abroad and returned to the United States is no more than an advanced material or article which will be subject to further *manufacturing* processes in the United States to get a completed article."[25]

Duty is payable only upon the value of the foreign processing at the duty rate applicable to the article if classified as an entirety.[26] Assume, for example, that aluminum ingots of United States origin are exported to Germany (where they are rolled into sheets), then returned to the United States (where the sheets are cut, punched, bent, and riveted in the fabrication of various sheet metal articles). Assume further that the value of processing the ingots into sheets for one shipment was $1,000. Sheet aluminum is dutiable under HTSUS item 7606.11.30 at 3 percent ad valorem. Therefore, duty on this shipment is 3 percent of the cost of processing, or $30.

The Customs Service levies duty on articles subject to HTSUS subheading 9802.00.60 on the cost of processing to the American importer. If the foreign processing is done by a subsidiary of the importer for no charge or for a charge that does not reflect the actual value, the Service will use the value set out in the invoice among the entry papers. If the Service concludes that the stated cost or value is unreasonable, then the import specialist will determine the value in accordance with the valuation provisions of the Tariff Act of 1930 as amended by the Trade Agreements Act of 1979.[27]

---

25. *Id.* at 1085. For examples of merchandise held reimported for "further processing," see U.S. TARIFF COMM'N, ECONOMIC FACTORS AFFECTING THE USE OF ITEMS 807.00 AND 806.30 OF THE TARIFF SCHEDULES OF THE U.S. 21 (1970).
26. *See* HTSUS 9802.00.60.
27. *See* chapter 4.

The articles returned to the United States for further processing must be imported by or for the account of the person or firm that exported them. Thus, to use the example above, if the aluminum sheets were imported from the German rolling mill not by the American exporter but by a different firm, the duty rate of 3 percent ad valorem would be assessed on the total value of the aluminum sheets, not just on the cost of the rolling process. The reimportation would not meet the conditions of HTSUS subheading 9802.00.60 and, therefore, would be subject to the usual rule that an item transformed abroad into a new and different article is subject to duty on its full value when returned to the United States.[28]

Subheading 9802.00.80: American Components Assembled Abroad

Imported merchandise assembled abroad from United States components may be entitled to reduced duties under the provisions of HTSUS subheading 9802.00.80.[29] The merchandise is dutiable at the normal rate applicable to it according to its classification as an entirety, but the cost or value of the American components is deducted from the appraised value of the article as a whole.

Assume, for example, that parts of girls' dresses are cut out in the United States from United States fabric and sent to Jamaica, where they are sewn together into completed dresses. Girls' cotton dresses have a duty rate of 12.5 percent. If the finished dresses have an appraised value of $10

28. Details of the procedural requirements for HTSUS 9802.00.60 appear in 19 C.F.R. § 10.9 (1989).

29. Pursuant to recent legislation, the Customs and Trade Act of 1990, Pub. L. No. 101–382, § 222, 104 Stat. 658 (Aug. 20, 1990), duty-free treatment has been extended to articles assembled in CBI beneficiary countries from components produced in the United States. See chapter 11 for discussion of Caribbean Basin Initiative (CBI).

each and the cost of the American components is $3 each, then the dresses would be dutiable at 12.5 percent of $7.

The provisions of HTSUS subheading 9802.00.80 apply, however, only to articles assembled abroad in whole or in part of United States–produced fabricated components, which components (1) were exported in condition ready for assembly without further fabrication; (2) have not lost their physical identity in the articles by change in form, in shape, or otherwise; and (3) have not been advanced in value or improved in condition abroad except by assembly and such operations incidental to assembly as cleaning, lubricating, and painting. The above substantive and procedural[30] requirements and limitations are strictly construed, and the party claiming the exemption has the burden of demonstrating compliance. The regulations governing claims for exemption from duty under HTSUS subheading 9802.00.80 include definitions and examples of specific situations in which the Customs Service considers the exemption to be available.[31]

The term "assembly" has been defined[32] as "any method used to join or fit together solid components, such as welding, soldering, riveting, force fitting, gluing, laminating, sewing, or the use of fasteners."[33] Such operations as mixing or combining liquids, gases, chemicals, food ingredients, and amorphous solids, whether with each other or with solid components, do not, however, fall within the purview

30. The documentary requirements for entry of articles claiming HTSUS 9802.00.80 exemption appear in 19 C.F.R. § 10.24 (1983).

31. 19 C.F.R. §§ 10.12–.30 (1990).

32. 19 C.F.R. § 10.16(a) (1990).

33. *See also* C. J. Tower & Sons v. United States, 304 F. Supp. 1187 (Cust. Ct. 1969); Amity Fabrics, Inc. v. United States, 43 Cust. Ct. 64 (1959). Gathering the fabric of American-made dress fronts by sewing thread through stenciled dots on the fronts has been held to be assembly abroad. United States v. Baylis Bros., 451 F.2d 643 (C.C.P.A. 1971). Examples of "assembly" appear in 19 C.F.R. § 10.16 (1988).

of assembly.[34] The assembly provisions of HTSUS subheading 9802.00.80 require that the United States components be in a condition ready to be assembled without further fabrication at the time of exportation from the United States, except to the extent that further fabrication is incidental to the foreign assembly process. Further, these "fabricated components" must not have lost their physical identity in such articles after the assembly.

A customs regulation[35] defines the American-made fabricated component as one manufactured in whole or in part within United States customs territory from United States materials or both United States and foreign components or wholly foreign components, provided any foreign material must "have been substantially transformed into a new and different article or have been mixed into a new and different article.[36]

The law recognizes that all the operations necessary for assembly may not always be done before shipment, and therefore, a provision allows for incidental operations necessary to the assembly process even though the operations may enhance the value of the component. Such incidental operations may be performed before, during, or after assembly.[37] Another way of stating the requirement that components be in final form for assembly except for incidental operations is that the assembled component must retain its

---

34. In *C. J. Tower & Sons, supra* note 33, however, it was held that a liquid component might solidify at the point of assembly. The case involved joining an American polyester sheet to a Canadian polyethylene sheet with an adhesive. The polyester was molten when applied.
35. 19 C.F.R. § 10.12(e) (1988).
36. *Id.* "Substantial transformation" results when "a new and different article emerges, having a distinctive name, character, or use." Examples of components that do and do not qualify as United States products appear in 19 C.F.R. § 10.14(b) (1988).
37. 19 C.F.R. § 10.16(b) (1988).

"physical identity" despite change in form, in shape, or otherwise[38] after the assembly process.

The HTSUS subheading 9802.00.80 exemption is inapplicable to United States components that have been "advanced in value or improved in condition abroad except by operations incidental to the assembly process such as cleaning, lubricating, and painting." In *Pistorino & Co. v. United States*,[39] jacket fronts made of American fabric were sent to Hong Kong to have beads sewn on, the neck cut out, and the fabric slit down the front. It was held that the beads constituted an advancement in value resulting directly from the act of assembly, but the cutting operations were neither part of nor incidental to the assembly process.[40]

"Operations incidental to the assembly process" have been defined[41] to exclude "[a]ny significant process, operation, or treatment . . . whose primary purpose is the fabrication, completion, [or] physical or chemical improvement of a component, or which is not related to the assembly process, whether or not it effects a substantial transformation of the article."[42]

Judicial pronouncements as to what constitutes "operations incidental to assembly" have directed the consideration of the following factors:

1. Whether the cost of the operations relative to the cost of the affected component and the time required

---

38. *See* E. Dillingham, Inc. v. United States, 470 F.2d 629, 635 (C.C.P.A. 1972) (American-made fabric ready for assembly did not lose physical identity by change in width or perforation). *See also Baylis Bros., supra* note 33.
39. Pistorino & Co. v. United States, 69 Cust. Ct. 93 (1972).
40. *Id.* at 98–99.
41. 19 C.F.R. § 10.16(c) (1987).
42. *See* 19 C.F.R. §§ 10.16(b)(1)–(7) (examples of incidental operations) & 10.16(c)(1)–(15) (examples of operations not incidental) (1983). In Rubberset Co. v. United States, 383 F. Supp. 1403 (Cust. Ct. 1974), selection of nylon filaments from bundles by size and weight for brush heads was held to be further fabrication prior to assembly.

by the operation relative to the time required for assembly of the whole article were such that the operation may be considered minor.

2. Whether the operations in question were necessary to the assembly process.
3. Whether the operations were so related to assembly that they were logically performed during assembly.[43]

No single factor will be determinative of the issue of whether a given operation will be considered to be an "incidental" operation. Such determinations will be based on a case-by-case analysis of the operation considering all of the above factors.[44]

---

43. *See* United States v. Mast Indus., Inc., 69 C.C.P.A. 47, 668 F.2d 501 (1981); United States v. Oxford Indus., Inc., 69 C.C.P.A. 55, 668 F.2d 507 (1981).
44. At the time of this writing a case before the Court of International Trade, General Motors Corp. v. United States, No. 87-03-00471, is being decided. It may result in the court expanding what it considers "incidental to assembly" for 9802.00.80 purposes. The case arises out of a customs denial of TSUS item 807.00 (now 9802.00.80, HTSUS) applicability for a process involving the addition of primer and colored acrylic enamel paint to pickup truck assemblies. Customs, in HQ 55340, December 14, 1984, held that the painting of the truck assembly was not a minor operation incidental to assembly but constituted a further fabrication that resulted in the advancement in value and the improvement in condition of the pickup truck assembly. As a result the duty reduction benefits of TSUS item 807.00 were denied. Should the court decide to allow this operation as "incidental" to the assembly process involved, Customs may be forced to loosen its restrictive approach in determining whether similar operations are incidental or not, thus extending 807 (9802.00.80) benefits to include similar assembly operations. In addition, decisions not allowing 9802.00.80 benefits to operations such as the stone washing of denim or the oven baking of poly-cotton material may have to be re-evaluated. *See* HQ 554436, Aug. 11, 1988.

Valuation Considerations

In the valuation of goods entered under HTSUS subheading 9802.00.80, it is often difficult to establish a transaction or deductive value.[45] Many of the firms that make use of the provision have the assembly performed by a subsidiary or related company on a manufacturing-cost basis rather than on the basis of an arm's-length market transaction. Thus, although the Customs Service uses transaction value whenever possible, HTSUS subheading 9802.00.80 entries are often based on computed value.[46]

From the gross appraised value of the complete item as imported, the value of those components that are of United States origin is deducted to arrive at the dutiable net value under HTSUS subheading 9802.00.80. The deductions of the American components are generally given the value shown on the assembler's declaration endorsed by the importer pursuant to customs regulation.[47] If the values appear unreasonable, the Customs Service will require further proof. The duty exemption in HTSUS subheading 9802.00.80 applies to fabricated components that are the product of the United States. Although composed in part of American work and components, the completed articles are products of the country in which the assembly took place. This fact can cause major problems if not fully understood.

Assume, for example, that an American manufacturer of brassieres sends components for the straps to Costa Rica, where they are assembled, and the completed straps are returned to the United States under HTSUS subheading 9802.00.80. The straps, along with other bra components, are then sent to an assembly plant in the Bahamas. When the completed bras are again returned to the United States

45. *See* chapter 4.
46. *Id.*
47. 19 C.F.R. § 10.24 (1987).

under HTSUS subheading 9802.00.80, the Customs Service will not allow the value of the bra straps to be deducted along with the value of the other components. The reason is that the bra straps, after assembly in Costa Rica, became products of Costa Rica and were therefore not eligible for the exemption when re-exported, joined with the other components, and re-imported. If, on the other hand, the bra straps had been shipped from Costa Rica directly to the assembly plant in the Bahamas, where they would be joined with the other components shipped directly from the United States, the value of the United States component parts of the straps would be deductible under subheading 9802.00.80.

An article may not benefit from the provisions of HTSUS subheadings 9802.00.40, 9802.00.60, or 9802.00.80 if it had previously been exported with remission, abatement, or refund of duties, or with benefit of drawback, or after manufacture or production in bond under the provisions.

Admission of an article under HTSUS subheadings subheadings 9202.00.40, 9202.00.60, or 9202.00.80 does not exempt it from quantitative limitations imposed upon that article if classified in its form as an entirety under other provisions of law (e.g., textile articles covered by the Multi-Fiber Agreement).

Super 807 (HTSUS 9802.00.80.10)

In addition to the duty reduction provisions of HTSUS subheading 9802.00.80 (formerly TSUS item 807), HTSUS subheading 9802.00.40 (formerly 806.20), and HTSUS subheading 8902.00.60 (formerly 806.30) are the provisions under HTSUS subheading 9802.00.80.10—the so-called Super 807 or 807A programs.

The terms "Super 807" and "807A" seem to have derived from the fact that these duty reduction programs were created and provided for under TSUS item 807.00.10. Since the provisions in item 807.00.10 granted greater quota access than was allowed under TSUS item 807.00, the terms "Super 807" and "807A" were used to describe the extra quota benefits granted under TSUS item 807.00.10 and the programs for which it provided. That is, an importer taking advantage of the Super 807 or 807A provision would be able to import more apparel into the United States because of the greater access to the U.S. market of goods which would normally be subject to more limited quota availability.

These programs include the Caribbean Basin Initiative (CBI), Special Access Program (SAP), and the Mexico Special Regime Program (SRP).

The SAP is a bilateral agreement which guarantees that Caribbean-produced textile products made from fabric formed and cut in the United States may be exported to the United States under guaranteed levels of access separate from quotas applicable to textile products not assembled solely from U.S. formed and cut fabric.

SRP establishes a special regime in which there is a distinction for quota purpose between Mexican products made from foreign fabric and Mexican products made (assembled) from U.S. formed and cut fabrics. The latter are assured access to the U.S. market.

Each program sets forth requirements for participation. For example, the same firm must act as exporter of U.S. formed and cut parts and importer of assembled articles, and each shipment (except for findings, trimmings, and elastic strips) should contain all of the components necessary to produce the completed article. In addition, the requirements set forth in HTSUS 9802.00.80 regarding further fabrication, advancement in value, or improvement in condition, etc., must also be complied with.[48]

48. Certain operations, such as stone washing, acid washing, etc., will be allowed as provided for in separate agreements which must be entered into with the United States in addition to SAP and/or SRP.

Miscellaneous Articles Entering Under Certain Conditions or Dedicated for Certain Exclusive Uses

Original Motor Vehicle Equipment from Canada

By virtue of the United States–Canadian Auto Agreement,[49] automotive vehicles and original equipment parts (other than spare parts) that qualify as "Canadian articles" are entitled to duty-free entry into the United States.[50]

A "Canadian article" has been defined as an article that is the product of Canada, not including any article produced with the use of materials imported into Canada that are products of any foreign country, if the aggregate value of that imported material when landed at a Canadian port of entry was more than 50 percent of the appraised value of the article imported into the United States.[51]

The other key qualifying term in this category of Canadian products that merits attention is the phrase "original motor vehicle equipment." That term has been defined[52] as "a Canadian article which has been obtained from a supplier in Canada under or pursuant to a written order, contract, or letter of intent of a bona fide motor-vehicle manufacturer in the United States, and which is a fabri-

---

49. The Automotive Products Trade Act of 1965, Pub. L. No. 89-283, 79 Stat. 1016 (1965) (codified at 19 U.S.C. §§ 2001 *et seq.*) implements the Agreement.
50. The auto pact was not changed by the United States–Canada Free Trade Agreement (CFTA) notwithstanding the complaints from certain U.S. auto parts manufacturers who insist that the pact grants Canadian manufacturers far too many advantages. The CFTA effectively grandfathers in all the original members of the auto pact and extends eligibility to the GM–Suzuki plant in Ontario. See chapter 14 on United States–Canada Free Trade Agreement.
51. HTSUS General Headnote 3(b)(iii)(1).
52. TSUS sched. 6, pt. 6, subpt. B, headnote 2(a).

cated component intended for use as original equipment in the manufacture in the United States of a motor vehicle. . . ."[53]

Civil Aircraft Parts

Civil aircraft and certain specified parts certified for use in civil aircraft specially provided for in the HTSUS and admitted into the United States from a nation deemed a signatory to the Agreement on Trade in Civil Aircraft are entitled to duty-free entry.[54] Under the HTSUS, civil aircraft is defined as "all aircraft other than aircraft purchased for use by the Department of Defense or the United States Coast Guard; and for the purposes of exportation means all aircraft other than aircraft used by the armed forces of a foreign country."[55]

In order to receive duty-free treatment under the Civil Aircraft agreement, one must meet a special certification requirement by filing, at the time of the entry summary,[56] certification that the article has been imported for use in civil aircraft, will be so used, and has met relevant air-worthiness standards.[57]

Unlike the provision for Canadian motor-vehicle parts, this provision applies to equipment or parts imported from any country having most-favored-nation status. There is no requirement that the equipment or parts be used as original equipment. Thus, radio navigational equipment to be in-

53. A "bona fide motor-vehicle manufacturer" is a person certified by the Secretary of Commerce as having made at least fifteen cars in the past year and being able to produce at least ten cars a week. *Id.* at headnote 2(c). For further procedural requirements, see 19 C.F.R. § 10.84 (1983).
54. Since the Trade Agreement Act of 1979, Pub. L. No. 96-39, 93 Stat. 144 (1979).
55. HTSUS chapter 88, statistical note 1.
56. 10 C.F.R. § 103(b)(1984), 49 Fed. Reg. 19,450 (May 8, 1984).
57. HTSUS General Headnote (3)(c)(iv).

stalled on an existing aircraft would be entitled to duty-free treatment under this section.

United States–owned aircraft that have been repaired, altered, or modified in the foreign country are liable for duty only on the value or cost of foreign labor, but not for any repair parts that may have been installed or replaced if those parts are properly certified to the Customs Service upon the return of the aircraft.

Instruments of International Traffic

> Vehicles and other instruments of international traffic, of any class specified by the Secretary of the Treasury, shall be excepted from the application of the customs laws to such extent and subject to such terms and conditions as may be prescribed in regulations or instructions of the Secretary of the Treasury. The authority delegated to the Secretary by this subsection shall not extend to communications satellites and components and parts thereof.[58]

Locomotives and other railroad equipment, trucks, buses, taxicabs, and other vehicles and foreign-owned aircraft arriving in the United States are subject to duty-free treatment. However, foreign-owned vehicles, aircraft, or undocumented vessels may not transport merchandise or passengers between points in the United States for hire or as an element of a commercial transaction. That use will be treated by the Customs Service as an importation of the vehicle, aircraft, or vessel, and entry to that effect must be made.[59] Such a use of any vehicle, aircraft, or boat without a proper entry's having been made may result in the imposition of penalties for customs fraud.

Other articles are similarly considered instruments of international traffic and may be brought into the United States without the filing of entries or the payment of duties.

58. 19 U.S.C.A. § 1322(a) (West Supp. 1990).
59. *See* 19 C.F.R. § 10.41(d) (1988).

Those include containers, lift vans, cargo vans, shipping tanks, skids, pallets, and cores for textile fabrics, whether loaded or empty. The commissioner of customs is authorized to designate as instruments of international traffic those additional articles or classes of articles he or she finds should be so designated. The decisions will be published in the weekly *Customs Bulletin*.[60] Instruments of international traffic are free to enter and clear United States ports without filing customs entries, but they must stay within the port and under Customs Service supervision. Articles designated as instruments of international traffic may be released into the customs territory of the United States under temporary importation bond, but they must be re-exported or destroyed under Customs Service supervision.

Instruments and Apparatus for Religious, Educational, and Scientific Institutions

The HTSUS[61] provides free entry to specified articles or classes of articles intended for the exclusive internal use (not distribution, sale, or other commercial use) of certain institutions. For example, duty-free items[62] imported by religious institutions used solely in worship include pictures; stained glass windows; regalia; fabrics to be used in making vestments; altars, pulpits, communion tables, baptismal fonts, shrines, mosaics, and iconostases or parts thereof; and statuary (but not cemetery headstones, grave markers, casts of plaster of Paris, and compositions of paper or papier-mâché).

Certain scientific instruments and apparatus, when imported for educational and scientific institutions, may be

60. 19 C.F.R. § 10.41(a) (1987).
61. Chapter 98, subchapter X.
62. HTSUS 9810.00.25.

given duty-free treatment[63] if no instrument or apparatus of equivalent scientific value for the intended purpose is manufactured in the United States.

Institutions wishing to enter an article under HTSUS subheading 9810.00.60 must apply to the Secretary of the Treasury and include the following in their applications:

1. A description of the article;
2. The purposes for which it is intended to be used;
3. The basis for the institution's belief that an equivalent article is not manufactured in the United States;[64] and
4. A statement that either (a) an order has been placed for the article or (b) the institution has a firm intention to place an order in the event of favorable action on the application.[65]

There are various other highly specialized groupings of articles conditionally free or subject to reduced rates, not of sufficient interest for inclusion here.[66]

---

63. HTSUS 9810.00.60.
64. The Secretary of Commerce or his or her delegate has the authority to grant or deny the exemption upon a finding of nonequivalence or equivalence of scientific value between domestic and foreign instruments.
65. *See* HTSUS chapter 98, subchapter X, U.S. Notes 6(b)–(f); 15 C.F.R. 301 (1983).
66. For a list, see 19 C.F.R. pt. 10 (1983).

16. Temporary Importation Under Bond

Articles not imported for sale or sale on approval may enter the United States temporarily free of duty under bond[1] provided their exportation[2] or destruction occurs under Customs Service supervision[3] within one year[4] of importation. Among others, the more significant types of temporary im-

1. HTSUS chapter 98, subchapter XIII. With some exceptions, the usual amount of the bond is twice the duties that it is estimated would accrue had all the articles covered by the entry been entered under an ordinary consumption entry. 19 C.F.R. § 10.31(f) (1990).
2. The obligation to export remains with the importer even if it sells the merchandise to an exporter. The bond is not cancelled when the exporter takes possession.
3. 19 U.S.C.A. § 1557(c) (West 1980); 19 C.F.R. §§ 10.39(a) & 158.43 (1990). The district director or his or her designee need not attend the actual destruction, but must always have the opportunity to do so. Cust. Serv. Dec. 82-128, 16 Cust. Bull. & Dec. 928 (1982).
4. With the exception of HTSUS item 8703 (automobiles and parts thereof), the one-year period can be extended for up to two additional years. 19 C.F.R. § 10.37 (1988).

portations under bond are available for the following categories of merchandise:[5]

1. Models of women's wearing apparel imported by manufacturers for use in their own establishments.[6]
2. Articles imported by illustrators and photographers for use as models for illustrating catalogs, pamphlets, or advertising matters.[7]
3. Samples solely for use in taking orders for merchandise.[8]
4. Articles solely for examination or reproduction (except photo-engraved printing plates) and motion-picture advertising films.[9]
5. Articles intended solely for testing, experimental, or review purposes.[10]
6. Racing vehicles and craft brought into the United States by nonresidents for the purpose of taking part in races or other specific contests.[11]
7. Locomotives and other railroad equipment brought temporarily into the United States for emergency purposes (when not otherwise admitted as instruments of international traffic).[12]
8. Containers for compressed gas during transportation.[13]
9. Professional equipment, tools of trade, and camping equipment imported by or for nonresidents sojourning temporarily in the United States.[14]

---

5. Jerry C. Laderberg prepared an internal Customs Service paper, *Temporary Importation Bond Seminar*, in November of 1975. It is still an excellent source for the articles or activities that qualify for temporary importation under bond (TIB).
6. HTSUS item 9813.00.10.
7. HTSUS item 9813.00.15.
8. HTSUS item 9813.00.20.
9. HTSUS item 9813.00.25.
10. HTSUS item 9813.00.30.
11. HTSUS item 9813.00.35.
12. HTSUS item 9813.00.40.
13. HTSUS item 9813.00.45.
14. HTSUS item 9813.00.50.

10. Articles of special design for temporary use exclusively in connection with the manufacture or production of articles for export.[15]
11. Animals and poultry for breeding, exhibition, or competition for prizes, and the usual equipment therefor.[16]
12. Theatrical scenery, properties, and apparel imported by managers of theatrical exhibitions for temporary use by them in such exhibitions.[17]
13. Certain articles imported by professional artists, lecturers, or scientists arriving from abroad for use by them for exhibition and in illustration, promotion, and encouragement of art, science, or industry in the United States.[18]
14. Automobiles and parts thereof (when intended solely for show purposes).[19]
15. Articles to be repaired, altered, or otherwise processed in the United States, which processing results in articles manufactured or produced in the United States.[20]

Temporary Importation Under Bond[21]

Temporary importation under bond (TIB) bonds may be cancelled only by the exportation or destruction under Customs Service supervision of the articles entered. Upon fail-

15. HTSUS item 9813.00.55.
16. HTSUS item 9813.00.60.
17. HTSUS item 9813.00.65.
18. HTSUS item 9813.00.70.
19. HTSUS item 9813.00.75.
20. The eligible operations under this may be construed by reference to HTSUS subheadings 9802.00.40 and 9802.00.50 ("articles exported for repairs or alterations") and HTSUS subheading 9802.00.60 (which applies to processing certain metal articles).

    Tin plate imported in coils is "processed" by being cut into shapes and decorated with labels for purposes of TIB. Cust. Serv. Dec. 79-235, 13 Cust. B. & Dec. 1320 (1979). This decision applies to TSUS 864.30, the predecessor provision to HTSUS subheading 9802.00.60.
21. 19 C.F.R. §§ 10.31–.39 (1987).

ure to so export or destroy within the bond period, liquidated damages will be assessed in an amount equal to double the duty applicable to the entry.

TIB entry may not be later substituted for other types of entry, for example, trade-fair entry (under which articles may be sold and entered into United States commerce).[22] The bond may not be cancelled by entering the goods for warehousing under warehouse entry.[23]

Each TIB entry summary on CF 7501 (reprinted in appendix 7) must include (1) the HTSUS item number under which entry is claimed, (2) a statement of the article's use to enable the district director to determine whether the article is entitled to entry as claimed, and (3) a declaration that the article is not to be put to any other use and that it is not imported for sale or sale on approval.

If the entry is approved by the district director, a bond will be given on CF 7563 in an amount equal to double the duties that would accrue had the articles been imported under an ordinary entry for consumption.

After the entry and bond have been accepted, the articles will be released to the importer. The entry will not be liquidated, as the transaction does not involve duties. Instead of duties per se, the government, in the event of a violation of the bond, assesses liquidated damages and possible penalties if fraud is involved.

Articles may be exported from any port. The exporter will submit CF 3495 a sufficient time before exportation of the articles to allow the Customs Service to examine and identify the articles. Two copies of CF 3495 are required if the article is to be exported from the original port of entry and three if from a different port (including a certified copy of the import entry or of the invoice used at entry).

The bond will be cancelled upon the specification of the

22. Cust. Serv. Dec. 80-161, 14 Cust. B. & Dec. 1001 (1980).
23. Cust. Serv. Dec. 80-167, 14 Cust. B. & Dec. 1012 (1980).

merchandise on the outward manifest or outward bill of lading, inspector's bill of lading, or record of clearance of the vessel or of its departure and the production of a foreign landing certificate if required by the district director.[24] Failure to comply with the regulations and the terms of the bond (i.e., if exportation or destruction of articles is not timely) will result in the forfeiture of the bond and the assessment of liquidated damages[25] equivalent to the entire amount of the bond under a single-entry bond.[26] If, however, the entry covering the articles is charged against a term bond, the demand for liquidated damages will be limited to an amount equal to double the estimated duties applicable to the entry.[27] As in all activities subject to Customs Service supervision, the importer/exporter must plan ahead, adhere strictly to the regulations, and immediately notify the Customs Service should circumstances arise that make it impossible to comply with regulations.

It is instructional to compare the differing treatment given merchandise entered under different forms of temporary importation.

Assume, for example, that a domestic carpet manufacturer receives an order from a foreign customer for a custom-designed carpet for a hotel lobby. The type and colors of yarn specified are not available domestically and must be imported from Austria.

1. *TIB*. The yarn may be imported duty-free under bond and used in the production of the carpet, which is then exported. Upon exportation of the carpet containing the imported yarn the bond will be

24. 19 C.F.R. § 113.55 (1987).
25. 19 C.F.R. § 10.39(d) (1987).
26. 19 C.F.R. § 113.62 (1987).
27. *Id.*

cancelled, and no duties on the yarn will have been paid.

2. *Customs-bonded warehouse.*[28] Because there was clearly a manufacturing process involved in making the carpet, a warehouse operation would not be available.
3. *Foreign trade zone.*[29] The operation could be carried out in a foreign trade zone without the necessity of posting bond and without being subjected to the three-year limitation.[30] However, this is only economically feasible when the manufacturing process involved is the importer/exporter's regular course of business and it has access to preexisting manufacturing facilities in a designated foreign trade zone.

The operation described would undoubtedly be eligible for drawback.[31] However, the costs of meeting the rigorous procedural requirements to obtain a drawback—the drawback contract, record keeping, etc.—may well exceed the refund of duties available.

Although TIB appears to be the best solution to the import/export problem in the example, it has two severe inherent limitations: the bond is for one year only (although it may be extended by the district director upon application up to a maximum of three years)[32] and the goods *must* be exported or the bond will be forfeited and penalties may be assessed. Hence, if any of the finished goods are intended for domestic consumption, TIB would be inappropriate.

Subheading 9813.00.50 allows TIB for imported articles to be processed, including items subjected to processes that

---

28. *See* chapter 9.
29. *See* chapter 10.
30. *See supra* note 4.
31. *See* chapter 17.
32. 19 C.F.R. § 10.37 (1987).

result in articles manufactured or produced in the United States. Under this provision, many articles that previously could qualify only for drawback can benefit from TIB. Unlike the user of drawback, in addition to the relatively simple documentation required for TIB, the importer using TIB does not have to pay duty with the expectation of a refund sometime in the future. During times of high rates of interest, the cost of tying up cash for a year or more is substantial. By avoiding that, TIB confers a substantial economic benefit on the importer.

Nonetheless, there can be temptations and risks, as in the example that follows. Assume an importer recently changed from drawback entries to TIB entries. The imported merchandise was to be processed in the United States by being cut into specific sizes, as required by overseas customers, and then re-exported. Merchandise similar to the imported merchandise, but of somewhat inferior quality, was also domestically produced. In order to satisfy the conditions of TIB, full records of the processing of different imported lots had to be maintained. After a series of exportations over a period of time completed or equaled one entire imported shipment, application was made for cancellation of the bond on that shipment. Adding to the complexity of keeping track of each imported lot and the various cut sizes applied against each exportation was the necessity of segregating the imported merchandise from domestic merchandise, since the importer also dealt in domestically produced merchandise.

When a Customs Service audit team came to do a routine check, it found that the record keeping of the importer was deficient, i.e., each lot was not always properly identified, the cut merchandise was sometimes merged (so that the full tracing to the source was lost), and the domestic merchandise was not always fully segregated from the imported merchandise. The government proceeded against the bonds for double the duty on those importations whose records were most deficient. The importer arranged to improve its record keeping for the future. The point is that complex TIB has potentially serious dangers for importers that take the record keeping too lightly, especially if repeated infractions are found by Customs Service officers. The risk is compounded where it is possible to substitute domestic merchandise for foreign merchandise in exportations to satisfy the bond. That substitution, though legal under drawback procedures, is absolutely forbidden in TIB, and any such attempt could have very serious consequences.

For example, an importer filed two TIB entries with a total entered value of $98,700. Duty would have been assessed in an amount equal to $3,851 had consumption entries been filed. The importer consumed 90 percent of the merchandise after processing and exported the remaining 10 percent. Customs assessed liquidated damages in an initial amount of $11,400. Customs had also instituted a penalty action under section 592 of the Tariff Act of 1930.[33] The amount of the penalty was $150,000 for commercial fraud, because Customs alleged that the importer knew or should have known that it was going to consume the goods domestically. This very real situation underscores the serious consequences for those who do not understand or comply with the requirements of TIB procedures.

The Customs Service also believes it can impose admissibility requirements such as textile restraints on textile products entered under TIB. An importer recently inquired as to the acceptability of importing blank tee shirts to be processed in the United States by silkscreen printing a design on them and then exporting the finished garments to a foreign country. Customs advised the importer that the processing qualified for duty–free entry under subheading 9813.00.05. However, visa and quota requirements would apply at the time of entry. Customs cited as precedent a

33. See chapter 22.

Treasury Department decision[34] to justify its position. Therefore importers who contemplate using TIB eligible operations in processing textiles or other products subject to restraint should consider the requirements of admissibility. The author has serious legal reservations about this Customs position that requires an importer to comply with textile restraints when filing a TIB entry, and he believes the position would not stand up to judicial review.[35]

The Harmonized Tariff Schedule (HTSUS) indicates bonds are not required for articles of Canadian origin that are entered under the TIB provisions. The bond exemption applies to articles that qualify under the rules of origin in chapter three of the United States–Canada Free Trade Agreement (CFTA) that are entered under certain TIB provisions.[36] The Canadian exporter must supply a certificate of origin which attests to the fact that the exported article qualifies under the CFTA rules of origin (i.e., that the article is Canadian). Since U.S. Customs officials may request production of the certificate for their review and verification, U.S. importers are responsible for maintaining the certificate.

34. T.D. 54802(54), 94 Treas. Dec. 12 (abstract of an unpublished decision).

35. The importer decided to move the silkscreen printing equipment to a class 6 Customs warehouse where he was not bound by the visa and quota requirements, since Customs holds that placing goods in bond is not an "entry" into the commerce of the United States. See chapter 9 for a full discussion of Customs-bonded warehouses.

36. United States–Canadian Free Trade Agreement—Fact Sheet No. 17. The TIB bond exemption applies to the following TIB provisions in the HTSUS:

9813.00.05	9813.00.30	9813.00.55
9813.00.10	9813.00.35	9813.00.60
9813.00.15	9813.00.40	9813.00.65
9813.00.20	9813.00.45	9813.00.70
9813.00.25	9813.00.50	9813.00.75

U.S. Customs cannot initiate liquidated damages claims against an importer's bond for an alleged violation concerning the entry of articles of Canadian origin under the TIB provisions because there is no bond for Customs to make a claim on. Furthermore, 19 U.S.C.A. § 1592 is not available as a substitute for a liquidated damage claim by Customs.[37] However, Customs believes there may be circumstances in which a section 1592 penalty is appropriate. That belief is based on the assumption that an importer is at least negligent when he makes a material false statement (e.g., falsely describes the article as of Canadian origin when it is not) or commits a material false act (e.g., enters articles under a TIB provision although he intends to sell the article for consumption in the United States).[38] To date, there is no evidence that Customs has acted on its belief, because there are no published penalty decisions in this new area of administrative law.

Of course, articles that do not qualify under the CFTA rules of origin may be entered free of duty under the TIB provisions, but the bond requirement applies. Hence, there is a legitimate concern for a potential liquidated damages or penalty liability when Customs alleges a violation for perceived noncompliance with the TIB requirements.

ATA Carnet[39]

Customs Service red tape places a particularly harsh burden on companies and individuals who import articles temporarily for the purpose of exhibits and trade shows. Often these articles (from toys to aircraft) pass through several

---

37. See chapter 22, Penalties and Customs Frauds, for an explanation of a liquidated damages claim and section 1592 penalty claim.
38. U.S.–Canada Free Trade Agreement—Fact Sheet No. 17, Supp. 1.
39. See 19 C.F.R. 114.

countries for shows which usually last less than a week. As discussed above, imports of this nature are duty free. The extent of bureaucratic paper shuffling is an impediment to the party possessing articles for such purposes and creates an unnecessary backlog for Customs regulators. Given the frequency of these temporary importations, the Customs Cooperation Council, with the assistance of the International Branch of Chambers of Commerce (IBCC), developed an efficient method to process these imports through Customs.

The procedure involves filling out an application called the ATA Carnet (Admission Temporaire—Temporary Admission) or a TIR (Transport International Routier) (reprinted in appendix 18). The ATA Carnet contains a voucher to be presented upon the arrival of the articles and a voucher to be presented upon the departure of the articles in each country that the articles pass through. A similar presentation is made upon the departure and rearrival in the country of origin. Carnets are inexpensive (currently $60–$150 in the United States) and can be issued within a few days. Each carnet is valid for one year and serves to bring the articles through as many countries of destination as planned within that one-year period. A TIR carnet may be used in connection with the transport of merchandise in vehicles and may be accepted without time limitation by Customs as a transportation entry if it is accepted or "taken on charge" by a Customs administrator (United States or foreign) within the period of validity shown on its front cover.[40]

Approximately forty countries already accept carnets. Each country of destination may require a security deposit to make sure the goods are imported for an appropriate purpose and leave the country accordingly. In the United

40. 19 C.F.R. § 114.23 (1990).

States, the security required is 40 percent of the value of the articles (in contrast to a bond amount of double the duty, required for a TIB) and may be held for thirty months. The security can take the form of a certified check, an insurance bond, or a letter of credit (to be held open for thirty months from date of issuance). Application information can be obtained through an IBCC-affiliated Chamber of Commerce or from the United States Council of International Business. The processing time of the application for an ATA Carnet takes five to ten working days.

17. Drawback of Customs Duties

Drawback is authorized under section 313 of the Tariff Act of 1930, as amended[1] and administered by the Customs Service.[2] It is a refund or remission in whole or in part of a customs duty, internal revenue tax, or fee lawfully assessed or collected because of a particular use made of the merchandise on which the duty, tax, or fee was assessed or collected. The legislative intent behind drawback was to stimulate and encourage American commerce or manufacturing or both. For example, one of drawback's chief objectives is to permit the American manufacturer to compete more effectively in foreign markets by overcoming the disadvantage of including in its costs (and hence its selling price) the duty imposed on the imported components of its manufactured merchandise.

The duties subject to drawback include all ordinary customs duties and marking[3] duties. Internal revenue taxes paid on domestic alcohol may also be refunded when the alcohol is used in the manufacture of flavoring extracts and medicinal or toilet preparations.[4] In addition, drawback is

1. 19 U.S.C.A. § 1313 (West 1980 & Supp. 1983).
2. 19 C.F.R. 191 (1987).
3. 19 U.S.C.A. § 1304(c) (West 1980).
4. 19 U.S.C.A. § 1313(d) (West 1980).

allowed for such import fees as the license fee applicable to certain kinds of petroleum and petroleum products.[5] Drawback is not permitted, however, to recover antidumping or countervailing duties.[6]

Drawback of duties and taxes is predominantly of three types: (1) direct-identification drawback, (2) drawback on merchandise not conforming to sample or specifications or shipped without consent of consignee, and (3) same-condition drawback.

Direct-Identification Drawback[7]

Direct-identification drawback, also known as manufacturers' drawback, is provided upon the exportation of articles manufactured or produced in the United States wholly or in part with the use of imported merchandise. Ninety-nine percent of the amount of duty paid upon the imported merchandise will be refunded as drawback, provided the completed article is exported within five years of the date of importation of the duty-paid merchandise.

The components may be in their original form or processed, and the manufacturer that uses the imported components need not have purchased them abroad itself, as long as it can establish their origin. As mentioned, Tariff Act section 313(a) allows American manufacturers to use foreign materials without having to add to their production costs the duties or taxes paid on those foreign-source materials or components as long as the product manufactured is exported from the United States.

For example, assume Walnut Grove Furniture Company manufactures grandfather clocks. The company constructs

5. 19 U.S.C.A. § 1862 (West 1980).
6. Omnibus Trade and Competitiveness Act of 1988, Pub. L. No. 100-418 § 1334, 102 Stat. 1107 (1988).
7. 19 U.S.C.A. § 1313(a) (West 1980).

the clock cases of domestic lumber and hardware. The clock movements are imported from Germany. Certain of the completed grandfather clocks are exported. Drawback of 99 percent of the duties paid on the clock movements used in the exported clocks is available upon exportation of the clocks. It is not necessary for Walnut Grove to have been the importer of the movements to entitle them to drawback. As long as the movements were imported, used in manufacture, and exported, the exporter will be entitled to drawback, provided the exporter can comply with the Customs Service's documentary requirements.

Substitution

The operative elements behind "substitution" have widened the applicability of direct-identification drawback as well as a number of other drawback provisions. If imported duty-paid merchandise is used in the production of articles, drawback is available upon the exportation of the exported article, even though none of the imported merchandise may actually have been used in the manufacture of the exported articles.[8] This is possible because the imported duty-paid merchandise may be substituted with domestic or duty-free merchandise that is of the "same kind or quality" as the imported duty-paid merchandise. The only two requirements are that (1) the imported or substituted merchandise must be used in the manufacture within three years of receipt by the manufacturer and (2) the finished products must be exported within five years of their completion.

Materials of the "same kind or quality" are those that may be used interchangeably in manufacturing the same article, with little or no change in the manufacturing process when switching between imported ingredients and do-

8. 19 U.S.C.A. § 1313(b) (West 1980); HQ 215570 (1983); Cust. Serv. Dec. 82-111, 16 Cust. B. & Dec. No. 36 (1982).

mestic. The Customs Service consistently uses industry standards as guidelines in determining these questions under the substitution-drawback law. For example, in a case involving the substitution of orange juice products, the Service specifically used standards of identity from the Food and Drug Administration and standards of quality from the Department of Agriculture for orange juice products, holding that single-strength orange juice products, frozen orange juice, and orange juice for manufacturing are not products of the same kind and quality for substitution purposes as frozen concentrated orange juice and concentrated orange juice for manufacturing.[9]

In a case involving a chemical blend component, the Customs Service has held that a domestic chemical, a blend of methyl chloride and dimethyl-amino-ethyl methacrylate, is not merchandise of the same kind and quality as (i.e., that may be substituted for) imported dimethyl-amino-ethyl methacrylate for drawback purposes. The domestic blend was found not to be identical to, and may not be used interchangeably with, the imported chemical.[10]

Under substitution drawback, foreign and domestic ingredients may be commingled completely, losing their separate identities. "First in, first out" (FIFO) accounting may be used to allocate commingled merchandise used in manufacture. For example domestic and imported chemicals are kept together in common storage tanks, and as some of the chemical is removed from the tanks it is replaced by new inventory of the same kind and quality. Commingled fungible chemicals may be identified and designated for drawback purposes on a FIFO basis.[11] Thus, assume that *X*

9. Cust. Serv. Dec. 81-96, 15 Cust. B. & Dec. No. 19 (1981).
10. Cust. Serv. Dec. 79-253, 13 Cust. B. & Dec. No. 25 (1979).
11. Cust. Serv. Dec. 79-252, 13 Cust. B. & Dec. No. 25 (1979). If fungible merchandise is commingled in storage in a Customs-bonded warehouse (*see* chapter 9), FIFO may be used to identify the merchandise.

Manufacturing has 10,000 units of a given component, of which 5,000 units were imported. Each unit is used to produce one finished product. As soon as 5,000 units of the finished product have been exported, *X* can collect drawback on the 5,000 imported components because the Customs Service assumes the products with the foreign ingredients were shipped first, even if in reality this was not the case.[12]

The right to claim drawback is a transferable right. Corporation *X* may claim drawback on exported articles manufactured with imported articles by defunct Corporation *Y*, whose assets have been purchased and liabilities assumed by *X*, since the right to claim drawback is a transferable property right. Drawback claims should be made by *X*, which has no drawback authorization of its own, as the "successor in right" to *Y*.[13]

Merchandise Not Conforming to Sample of Specifications or Shipped Without Consent of Consignee

Drawback is provided upon the exportation of imported merchandise that is rejected because it fails to conform to the sample upon which the purchase order was made, because it fails to conform to specifications as ordered, or because the goods were shipped without the consignee's consent. Ninety-nine percent of the duties paid will be re-

---

Cust. Serv. Dec. 83-63, 17 Cust. B. & Dec. No. 38 (1983). It has also been held that fungible products commingled in storage after manufacture or production and withdrawn therefrom for drawback purposes may be identified against the component drawback material in the order of their receipt into storage. Cust. Serv. Dec. 83-54, 17 Cust. B. & Dec. No. 35 (1983).

12. Prior to the adoption of the rule discussed in note 11, drawback could not be collected until *X* shipped all 10,000 units.
13. Cust. Serv. Dec. 79-257, 13 Cust. B. & Dec. No. 25 (1979).

funded upon exportation of such merchandise.[14] In *Lansing Co. v. United States*, the Court of International Trade found that imported invisible zippers whose coils fail to interlock uniformly and whose sliders are too taut are inherently defective.[15] Imported merchandise that fails to function for the purpose for which it was designed and intended obviously fails to conform to specification and the importer is therefore entitled to a refund of the duties paid. The merchandise must be returned to Customs custody for exportation within ninety days after its release from Customs custody, unless Customs authorizes a longer period.[16]

A distinction qualifying this principle must be noted. In a limiting decision of the *Lansing* case, Customs ruled that it will not construe as meeting the drawback criteria a "failure to conform to specifications" where such failure is merely evidenced by a seller's breach of an implied warranty.[17] For instance, an importer could not rely solely upon a seller's breach of its warranty of "merchantability" as evidencing the failure of the merchandise to conform to specifications. The conformity or nonconformity of the merchandise must relate to expressed specifications, not implied ones. Hence, to request a drawback on imported merchandise being exported because of failure to conform to specifications, the importer must show that such specifications were actual (i.e., expressed either orally or in writing).

A suit for damages based upon a breach of implied warranty may be brought. However, the difficulties inherent in suing a foreign party would cast doubt on the feasibility of such recourse.

---

14. 19 U.S.C.A. § 1313(c) (West 1980).
15. Lansing Co. v. United States, 77 Cust. Ct. 92 (1976).
16. 19 C.F.R. § 191.142 (1987).
17. T.D. 77-121 (Apr. 20, 1977).

Same-Condition Drawback

Same-condition drawback authorizes the payment of drawback on any imported merchandise that is exported in the same condition as imported or is destroyed under Customs Service supervision.[18] The conditions set by this provision are that the imported duty-paid merchandise, before the close of three years (commencing on the date of importation), be exported in the same condition as when it was imported or be destroyed under Customs Service supervision and that the merchandise *not be used*[19] within the United States before that exportation or destruction.

If these conditions are met, then upon exportation or destruction, 99 percent of the amount of duty, tax, or fee paid will be refunded as drawback to the importer. Drawback is payable, provided the requirements are met, on merchandise entered (or withdrawn from a warehouse for consumption) on or after December 28, 1980.[20]

"Same condition" has been the frequent subject of Customs Service interpretation, as illustrated by the following:

1. Engines imported for testing and review, during which they are disassembled, must be reassembled prior to exportation to be eligible for same-condition drawback, since they would not be in the "same

18. 19 U.S.C.A. § 1313(j) (West Supp. 1990), added by Act of Dec. 28, 1980, Pub. L. No. 96-609, § 201(a), 94 Stat. 3560 (1980).
19. The "use" requirement has been interpreted to preclude any major operations which change the character of the merchandise. *See* Cust. Serv. Dec. 82-7, 16 Cust. B. & Dec. No. 24 (1982). However, incidental operations, such as testing, cleaning, and repacking, performed on the subject merchandise, and operations not considered to be a manufacture or production for drawback purposes, are not considered to be a use of that merchandise in the U.S. 19 C.F.R. § 191.141(h).
20. *See* Cust. Serv. Dec. 83-29, 17 Cust. B. & Dec. No. 29 (1983).

condition" as imported if they were exported disassembled.[21]

2. If deterioration occurs that significantly changes the condition of imported merchandise, same-condition drawback is inapplicable.[22]
3. Repacking or repackaging from 100-kilo containers to 14- and 16-gram containers for retail sale is permissible under the same-condition drawback statute.[23]
4. Articles imported or entered as entireties that were disassembled in the United States for display, and after that use disassembled *as required for shipping* are eligible for same-condition drawback, provided there is compliance with the law and operating instructions.[24]
5. Substitution of domestic merchandise for imported merchandise is not expressly provided for under the same-condition drawback statute; therefore, it is not allowed.[25]
6. FIFO accounting may be used to designate merchandise for same-condition drawback, provided the rates of duty and amounts of duty paid on the merchandise remain constant over the entries to be designated. If either factor changes, then the merchandise must be designated for drawback on a lowest to highest basis.[26]
7. The cutting of rolled textile fabric into two or more

21. Cust. Serv. Dec. 82-135, 16 Cust. B. & Dec. No. 40 (1982).
22. Cust. Serv. Dec. 83-26, 17 Cust. B. & Dec. No. 26 (1983).
23. Cust. Serv. Dec. 83-2, 17 Cust. B. & Dec. No. 11 (1983).
24. Cust. Serv. Dec. 82-93, 16 Cust. B. & Dec. No. 32 (1982). This ruling contemplates that the assembly does not involve any fabrication, such as, but not limited to, drilling, forming, bending, shaping, and grinding. Further, the importer must satisfy the Service that the disassembly was in fact required for shipping.
25. Cust. Serv. Dec. 81-203, 15 Cust. B. & Dec. No. 37 (1981).
26. Cust. Serv. Dec. 81-210, 15 Cust. B. & Dec. No. 37 (1981).

smaller rolls without dedicating the smaller rolls to any particular use is considered a manipulation that does not change the basic character of the merchandise: as such, it is a permitted operation under the same-condition drawback law.[27]

8. Such containers as boxes, cans, and bottles, imported for packing of merchandise, are not eligible for same-condition drawback upon exportation because they are employed or used for their intended purposes. Same-condition drawback applies only upon the exportation of imported merchandise that is not used in the United States before exportation.[28]
9. The repair/reworking/adjustment of articles found through testing not to be functional for intended use are *not* considered *incidental operations* under the provisions of the same-condition drawback law; such articles are, therefore, ineligible for same-condition drawback.[29]

Same-Condition Substitution Drawback

Same-condition drawback has been extended by section 202(1)(B) of Public Law 98-573, subject to certain restrictions, to domestic or imported merchandise "fungible" with the duty-paid merchandise.[30]

The term "fungible merchandise" is defined in Customs regulations as "merchandise which for commercial purposes is identical and interchangeable in all situations."[31]

---

27. Cust. Serv. Dec. 81-219, 15 Cust. B. & Dec. No. 45 (1981). On the other hand, cutting textile to length to make it suitable for, and dedicated to, a specific use is considered manufacture for drawback purposes. *Id.*
28. Cust. Serv. Dec. 81-222, 15 Cust. B. & Dec. No. 45 (1981).
29. Cust. Serv. Dec. 82-7, 16 Cust. B. & Dec. No. 1 (1982).
30. 19 U.S.C. § 1313(j)(3) (presently designated by legislation as 19 U.S.C. § 1313(j)(2)).
31. 19 C.F.R. § 191.2(1). This includes such primary products as sugar

Customs has taken a restrictive view as to what constitutes fungibility. Recognizing that a determination of whether in the commercial world buyers and sellers treat merchandise as fungible is a question of fact, Customs has held that if two or more articles of apparently identical properties are treated differently by the commercial world for any reason, they are not fungible.[32]

The Court of International Trade has not been any less restrictive than Customs in the view of what constitutes "fungibility."

In *Guess? Inc. v. United States*,[33] Guess *exported* certain cotton denim wearing apparel that was identical to certain cotton denim wearing apparel that it had *imported*. The only real difference between the imported and exported merchandise was the fact that the exported denim (jeans) bore labels that identified them as being made in the United States.

Guess claimed drawback. Customs denied the claim based upon its determination that the exported jeans were not "fungible" with the imported jeans. Customs so decided because Guess's foreign customers demanded garments that showed that they were made in the United States.

Guess argued that the existence of U.S. labels should not determine whether the exported jeans were fungible with the non-U.S. labeled imported jeans; rather, such determination should be based on whether the jeans were in a general commercial or contractual sense fungible.

Customs argued that the fact that customers preferred garments with the "made in the U.S." labels destroyed the fungibility between those garments and the garments without such labels, even though all other physical elements were identical.

---

and wheat, but excludes such processed products as bread and automobiles.

32. Cust. Serv. Dec. 85-52, 19 Cust. B. & Dec. No. 605 (1985).

33. Guess? Inc. v. United States, 752 F. Supp. 463 (Ct. Int'l Trade 1990).

The court supported that view and held that fungible merchandise, as defined in the regulations,[34] was "merchandise which for commercial purposes is identical and interchangeable in all situations." Since the labeled jeans were *more desirable* than the imported jeans, the court said they were not fungible.

This decision puts forth a very restrictive definition of fungibility. If the reasoning of the court is applied (the case is, at the time of this writing, under appeal), prospective drawback claimants making claims under same-condition substitution drawback must be wary.

Accordingly, words used to describe merchandise in an application for drawback under this section such as "generally no difference," "preference for product" (over another), "basically the same," etc. will be considered by Customs as an admission that the merchandise is probably not fungible.[35]

Customs has gone so far as to say that "if the commercial world, for snobbish, sentimental, or financial reasons, values an article made in one country more than the identical article made in another, the two articles are not fungible."[36]

In addition to the fungibility requirement, the imported duty-paid merchandise must, before the close of three years (commencing on the date of importation), be exported or destroyed under Customs Service supervision and the imported merchandise may not be used within the United States before that exportation or destruction.

34. 19 C.F.R. § 191.2(b)(1) (West Supp. 1991).

35. *Id.*, 19 Cust. B. & Dec. at 607.

36. This circumscriptive approach is further demonstrated in Customs Ruling, HQ 218541K, March 17, 1986, which states that one variety of apples may not be fungible with another variety, considering similarities in grade, name, color, and size.

Possession

Another requirement under substitution same-condition drawback is that of possession. To reiterate, if fungible substituted merchandise, within a three-year period after the importation of the imported duty-paid merchandise, is not used in the United States, is in the possession of the party claiming drawback, and is in the same condition at the time of exportation (or destruction) as was the imported merchandise at the time of its importation, then upon exportation (or destruction) of the substituted merchandise, drawback is payable.

The Customs Service has defined the term "possession" for purposes of the substitution same-condition drawback law as meaning the "complete control over the articles or merchandise on premises or locations where the possessor can put the articles or merchandise to any use chosen."[37]

Customs presently requires that "legal person" *X* (which includes a corporation) must possess both the imported duty-paid merchandise and the fungible substituted merchandise at the time of exportation.[38] However, a recent court case, *Central Soya v. United States*,[39] disagreed with the position of Customs and held that the claimant need only have had possession of the fungible substituted merchandise "before [the] exportation or destruction." Thus the court found that Customs had erred in requiring that the claimant have possession of the substituted merchandise *at the time of exportation*. At the present time, this decision is under appeal. Obviously, the outcome of this appeal will have a great impact on the administration of drawback and thus warrants careful attention.

37. Cust. Serv. Dec. 86-8, 20 Cust. B. & Dec. No. 9–10 (1986).
38. Cust. Serv. Dec. 85-52, 19 Cust. B. & Dec. No. 49 (1985) (citing 19 C.F.R. § 191.141(h)).
39. Central Soya v. United States, 761 F. Supp. 133 (Ct. Int'l Trade 1991).

Customs has also held that possession for purposes of the same-condition substitution drawback law does not mean

> that by trading commercial paper, e.g., purchase orders or bills of lading, between brokers or others in a commodity while that commodity winds its way across America by train or truck, possession is somehow created. . . . To hold that for purposes of same-condition drawback arbitragers and futures dealers in commodities, have "possession" of these commodities because of the purchase of commercial paper and temporary storage in leased bins or tanks, would not further the intent of Congress or the fundamental purpose of the drawback law.[40]

Accordingly, Customs will ensure that the term "possession" not be extended to include situations where two legal entities merely trade commercial paper in an attempt to satisfy the possession requirement. For example:[41]

> Corporation B possesses duty-paid designated merchandise.
> Corporation C possesses domestic merchandise that is fungible with Corporation B's designated merchandise.
> Corporation C has a contract for sale to a foreign buyer.
> Corporation B agrees to purchase C's merchandise (the domestic substituted merchandise), and exports the substituted merchandise to fulfill C's obligation to its foreign customer.[42]

In this example Corporation B was not a "possessor" of both designated and substituted merchandise. Therefore, the paper transactions carried out by the parties were considered by Customs to be a "sham to create a climate for drawback where none exists." This type of transaction would not be allowed even applying the rule set forth in the *Central Soya* case, since the court still interprets the possession requirement as demanding that a claimant have possession of the merchandise at some point before its exportation.

40. Cust. Serv. Dec. 85-52 at 607.
41. Cust. Serv. Dec. 87-18, 20 Cust. B. & Dec. No. 43 (1987).
42. *Id.*

Relative Advantages of Nonconforming-Merchandise Provision and Same-Condition Drawback

To use the nonconforming-merchandise provision, the exporter-claimant must submit documentation establishing that the merchandise does not conform to sample or specification or was sent without the consent of the consignee. Often this will require cooperation from the foreign shipper. If the consignee ordered the wrong size or kind of merchandise and the order was filled correctly by the shipper and upon importation the consignee finds that the merchandise is unsuitable for its purposes or is not what it thought was coming, but the merchandise does meet the specifications given in the order, then nonconforming-merchandise drawback will not be allowed. This provision relieves only mistakes made by the foreign shipper, not those made by the consignee.

Same-condition drawback, however, does not inquire into the circumstances of the goods' arrival; it only requires that the goods not be used prior to exportation or destruction.

Assume, for example, that a manufacturer of robotic manufacturing devices imported one of its machines into the United States to use in soliciting sales. Although the operation of the machine was demonstrated, it was not used in actual production. The imported device was not sold in the United States, but a Canadian firm bought it. Upon exportation to Canada, the exporter will be entitled to same-condition drawback.[43]

---

43. Note that under the United States–Canada Free Trade Agreement (CFTA) (discussed in chapter 14) drawback will be eventually eliminated by January 1, 1994, between the U.S. and Canada, except that drawback will continue to be available for citrus products and for imported fabrics converted into apparel which is subsequently imported to the other country above the tariff rate quota levels set up by the CFTA. In addition, drawback will be allowed for goods that enter Canada or the United States under bond for transshipment in the same condition to the other country.

One reason the nonconforming-drawback provisions had to be retained even after same-condition drawback was legislated is that latent defects may not become evident until some types of unfinished materials are further processed. For example, cotton cloth may be imported to be dyed to order in the United States and sold here. Upon dyeing, it is discovered that some of the yarns are not cotton and do not take the dye properly. This would qualify for nonconforming drawback, but not for same-condition drawback, because the material has been worked upon and is no longer in the "same condition" as when imported.

Miscellaneous Drawback Provisions

Apart from the three primary categories of drawback—direct-identification, nonconforming-merchandise, and same-condition drawback—drawback of duties and taxes is ordinarily authorized in other instances, including the following:[44]

Internal Revenue Taxes

Drawback of internal revenue taxes is provided for in Tariff Act of 1930, section 313(d), as amended,[45] upon the exportation of flavoring extracts and medicinal or toilet preparations (including perfumery) manufactured or produced in the United States in part from domestic tax-paid alcohol.

44. Information on these types of drawback is taken from 48 Fed. Reg. 46,755 (1983), where the Customs Service set forth general revisions of its drawback regulations, effective December 12, 1983.
45. 19 U.S.C.A. § 1313(d) (West 1980).

Supplies for Certain Vessels and Aircraft

Drawback of duties and taxes is provided in Tariff Act of 1930, section 309(b), as amended,[46] on articles withdrawn from bonded warehouses, bonded manufacturing warehouses, continuous Customs Service custody elsewhere other than a bonded warehouse, or foreign trade zones, and articles of domestic manufacture or production that are laden as supplies upon certain vessels or aircraft of the United States or as supplies including equipment upon, or used in the maintenance or repair of, certain foreign vessels or aircraft.

Merchandise Exported from Continuous Customs Custody

Drawback of duties is provided for in accordance with Tariff Act of 1930, section 557(a), as amended,[47] upon the exportation to a foreign country (or the shipment to the Virgin Islands, American Samoa, Wake Island, Midway Island, Kingman Reef, Johnston Island, or Guam) of merchandise upon which duties have been paid and which had remained continuously in a bonded warehouse or otherwise in Customs Service custody since importation, provided it was exported or shipped within five years after the date of its importation.

Merchandise Transferred to Foreign Trade Zone from Customs Territory

Drawback of duties and taxes is provided for in accordance with the fourth proviso of section 3 of the Foreign Trade Zones (FTZ) Act of June 18, 1934, as amended,[48] on merchandise transferred to a foreign trade zone from United States customs territory for the sole purpose of exportation,

46. 19 U.S.C.A. § 1309(b) (West 1980).
47. 19 U.S.C.A. § 1557(a) (West Supp. 1983).
48. 19 U.S.C.A. § 81c (West 1978).

destruction (except of distilled spirits, wines, and fermented malt liquors), or storage.[49]

"Manufacturing" and "Exportation" Defined

The section 1313(a) drawback that has the widest application concerns itself with merchandise that must have been subjected to a "manufacturing process" in the United States with the use of imported articles before exportation. To be eligible for section 1313(a) drawback, the merchandise must have been subjected to a transformation. For example, the application of embroidery to finished dresses, which were exported in the same form, shape, and size as imported, has been held not to constitute production within the meaning of the drawback statute.[50]

In *Anheuser-Busch Association v. United States*,[51] the leading case on what constitutes "manufacturing" for purposes of drawback, the Supreme Court stated:

> Manufacture implies a change, but every change is not a manufacture, and yet every change in an article is the result of treatment, labor and manipulation. But something more is necessary. . . . There must be a transformation; a new and different article must emerge, "having a distinctive name, character or use."

Here the Supreme Court held that the further processing of imported precut and shaped cork for use in beer bottle caps through stamping, cleaning, steaming, and drying does not amount to manufacturing.

In *United States v. International Paint Co.*,[52] the Court of

49. This would not include merchandise entered into an FTZ for manufacture. See discussion on exportation below.
50. *See* Rolland Freres v. United States, 23 C.C.P.A. 81 (1935).
51. Anheuser-Busch Ass'n v. United States, 207 U.S. 556, 562 (1908).
52. United States v. International Paint Co., 35 C.C.P.A. 87 (1948). *See also* United States v. Samuel Dunkel & Co., 33 C.C.P.A. 60 (1946) (term "produced" examined).

Customs and Patent Appeals concluded that if an operation makes a product—in this case, paint—fit for a use for which it was previously wholly unsuited, the operation qualifies as manufacturing.

"Exportation," a recurring term in the drawback provision, is another condition that requires scrutiny. In the absence of a statutory definition, the courts and the Customs Service have relied on an interpretation issued in an attorney general's opinion: "Exportation is a severance of goods from the mass of things belonging to this country with an intention of uniting them to the mass of things belonging to some foreign country or other."[53]

The words "export" and "exportation" mean the sending of goods to some foreign place, that is, to a definite port of destination. Hence, the drawback provided "on the exportation" of articles manufactured from imported materials on which duties had been paid will not be allowed on goods placed on board a vessel during its voyage, and in fact so used and consumed.[54] Similarly, no right of drawback arose when bags of imported materials were leased to steamers for foreign voyages with the understanding that they were to be brought back to the United States.[55] As long as a bona fide purpose to seek a foreign market coincides with a bona fide act of shipment, later changes in either the intent or destination have no effect upon the original character of the act as an exportation.[56] Customs has also held that articles sent to an FTZ in the United States for manufacturing (not for export or destruction) would not be considered exported for drawback purposes.[57]

---

53. 17 Op. Att'y Gen. 583 (1883). *See also* United States v. National Sugar Ref. Co., 39 C.C.P.A. 96 (1953).
54. Swan & Finch Co. v. United States, 190 U.S. 143 (1903).
55. Kennedy v. United States, 95 F. 127 (2d Cir. 1899).
56. United States v. National Sugar Ref. Co., *supra* note 53.
57. *See* T.D. 89-4, 53 Fed. Reg. 52,411 (Dec. 28, 1988), which reverses the prior position of Customs that such articles would be considered

Procedures for Manufacturers' or Direct-Identification Drawback

Applying for Contracts

Specific Drawback Contracts[58]

The first step is to apply to the Customs Service for a drawback contract, formerly known as a rate of drawback. The application is in the form of a drawback proposal, which contains an offer to operate under the drawback law and regulations. The manufacturer's proposal must:

1. Describe its manufacturing operations fully and the method of compliance with all requirements of the drawback law and regulation;
2. State that the required records of identification, manufacture, and production will be maintained; and
3. Contain an agreement to follow the method and keep the records concerning drawback procedures.[59] Except for direct-identification drawback, Customs Headquarters, upon request, will supply a sample proposal to assist the manufacturer in completing the proposal.

---

exported for drawback purposes. *See* C.S.D. 85-10, 19 Cust. B. & Dec. No. 509 (1985). *See also* Chrysler Motors v. United States, 755 F. Supp. 388 (Ct. Int'l Trade 1990), which affirmed a Customs Service ruling that if merchandise is entered into an FTZ in the United States for manufacture rather than exportation or destruction, no drawback claim is authorized. At the time of this writing, this case is under appeal.

58. 19 C.F.R. §§ 191.21 *et seq.* (1987).
59. 19 C.F.R. § 191.21(b) (1987).

General Drawback Contracts[60]

A new provision of drawback is the "general" drawback contract. From time to time the Customs Service will prepare and publish in the *Customs Bulletin* approved general drawback contracts in situations where numerous manufacturers with similar operations may wish to claim drawback. Any manufacturer or producer that wishes to claim drawback under a general contract may adhere to it by notifying the regional commissioner of its intention to do so and by providing the commissioner with the following information:

1. Name and address of adherent;
2. Factories that will operate under the contract; and
3. If a corporation, the names of officers or persons with power of attorney who will sign drawback documents on behalf of the adherent.

Substitution Drawback[61]

Manufacturers who wish to use substitution drawback should follow the procedures outlined above and, in addition, must maintain records that will establish the following:

1. The identity and specifications of the merchandise designated;
2. The quantity of merchandise of the same kind and quality as the designated merchandise used to produce the exported articles;
3. That, within three years after receiving the designated merchandise at its factory, the manufacturer or producer used it in manufacturing or production, and that during the same three-year period it manu-

60. 19 C.F.R. §§ 191.41 *et seq.* (1987).
61. 19 C.F.R. §§ 191.31 *et seq.* (1987).

factured or produced the exported articles; and

4. That the completed articles were exported within five years after importation of the designated merchandise.[62]

Accelerated Drawback[63]

An important provision for drawback claimants is a procedure for accelerated payment of drawback claims. When the claim is made, the claimant may request accelerated payment (including in the claim a computation of the amount due) and submit for approval by the regional commissioner a bond guaranteeing the refund of any excess payment. The bond may be on form 7609 or form 7611 or may be provided by including a rider on the importer's general term bond (form 7595).

The regional commissioner will certify approved claims for payment within three weeks of filing. After liquidation, the commissioner will certify payment of any amount due or demand a refund of any excess amount paid. Claimants who repeatedly file claims in excess of the amount due will be denied the right to continue receiving accelerated payment.

Procedures for Same-Condition Drawback[64]

It is essential that an exporter-claimant that desires to export merchandise with drawback under 19 U.S.C. § 1313(j) file proper documentation, including a CF 7539 (reprinted in appendix 19) and identification of the import entry, with the regional commissioner or his or her delegate

62. 19 C.F.R. §§ 191.32 *et seq.* (1987).
63. 19 C.F.R. §§ 191.72 *et seq.* (1987).
64. 19 C.F.R. § 191.141 (1987).

at least five working days before the date of intended exportation, unless a shorter period has been approved, or unless a waiver of prior notice has been specifically granted to that exporter. If the Customs Service does not notify the exporter within three working days that it will examine the merchandise, the goods may be exported without delay.

In place of this prior-notice procedure, the exporter-claimant may apply to the Customs Service for permission to use the exporters' summary procedure,[65] which requires that the claimant furnish a drawback export bond in an amount equal to 25 percent of the drawback that it intends to claim. This procedure, designed to improve administrative efficiency, requires no prior notice of exportation, no examination, no Customs Service supervision of the exportation. However, the exporter must retain, for at least three years after the payment of its drawback claims, complete records of exportation, the identity and condition of the merchandise, and the identity of the ultimate consignee of the exported articles.

Procedures for Nonconforming-Merchandise Drawback[66]

Nonconforming merchandise on which drawback is to be claimed[67] must be returned to Customs Service custody for examination and approval of the claim within ninety days after its release by the Customs Service after importation, unless the Service authorizes a longer period. The exporter-claimant must file CF 7539 (reprinted in appendix 20) at the time of returning the merchandise to the Service together with proof that the goods are defective or do not

65. 19 C.F.R. § 191.53 (1987).
66. 19 C.F.R. § 191.142 (1987).
67. Under 19 U.S.C.A. § 1313(c) (West 1980).

conform. Not until the application for drawback has been approved by the Customs Service may the goods be exported, also under Customs Service supervision. Proof of exportation must also be furnished in the form of a notice of exportation either certified by the Service or supported by specific documentation.[68]

Compliance with Customs Regulations

The United States Court of Appeals for the Federal Circuit reversed a decision of the Court of International Trade that allowed drawback to an exporter claiming manufacturers' drawback on materials used in the construction of foreign-owned vessels pursuant to 19 U.S.C. § 1313(a) and § 1313(g).[69] In its opinion, the court made clear that drawback privileges are expressly conditioned, by statute, upon compliance with such regulations as the Secretary of the Treasury shall prescribe. Customs drawback regulations are mandatory, not merely directive, and compliance with them is a condition precedent to the right of recovery of drawback.

However, a recent case has, to a certain extent, loosened its prior position requiring unconditional adherence to customs regulations. In *Aurea Jewelry Creations, Inc. v United States*,[70] a question arose regarding what evidence may be used to support a claim, under manufacturers' drawback,

68. 19 C.F.R § 191.142(b)(5) (1987).

69. United States v. Lockheed Petroleum Servs., Ltd., 709 F.2d 1472 (Fed. Cir. 1983), *rev'g* 557 F. Supp. 583 (Ct. Int'l Trade 1982). In this case, the builder of a vessel was denied claimed drawback because of its failure to file an abstract of manufacture, as required by 19 C.F.R. § 22.4(g) (1984), prior to the vessel's first departure from the United States. The Customs Service could not verify the abstract by examination of the vessel if the vessel was gone.

70. Aurea Jewelry Creations, Inc. v. United States, 932 F.2d 943 (Fed. Cir. 1991).

that the merchandise exported was produced from the imported merchandise.

Aurea imported fourteen-karat gold chains and bracelets from Italy. Aurea then sent portions of the gold jewelry to its subsidiary, JMS Manufacturing Company, to have the jewelry melted and cast into fourteen-karat gold ingots. The gold ingots were sent back to Aurea and were then exported under the supervision of Customs.

Aurea filed a manufacturers' drawback claim but could not supply documents from JMS showing the dates of manufacture and the manufacturing lot numbers for the ingots.

Customs rejected Aurea's claim because, Customs contended, Aurea failed to maintain records as required by its regulations and by the submitted drawback statement.[71] Specifically, Customs was not satisfied that the documents submitted by Aurea were sufficient to prove that the jewelry delivered to JMS was the same jewelry upon which it had paid the import duty.

At trial, Aurea presented testimonial evidence to show that the documents were maintained, that the documents contained sufficient information to substantiate the drawback claim, and that the documents were lost when JMS went out of business. The CIT held in favor of Aurea: "[P]laintiff is entitled to drawback because plaintiff proffered sufficient documentary *and testimonial* evidence to satisfy the record requirements under 19 C.F.R. § 22.4(a)." The court of appeals then affirmed this judgment. While the court seemed to allow the claimant (Aurea) to circumvent the Customs Service's regulatory requirement regarding the necessary records a claimant must present in support of its claim by allowing testimonial evidence in lieu of documents, it did so within the context of interpreting the regulations. Thus, the court's decision allows a claimant some

71. 19 C.F.R. § 22.4(a), reorganized and modified in 1983 as 19 C.F.R. 191.

flexibility in complying with customs regulations. However, such compliance is still required.

In summary, never export goods on which it is hoped that drawback can be claimed without finding out exactly what procedures and documentation are required by the regulations and then complying strictly before the goods are shipped.

Drawback Revitalization

On February 5, 1990, a briefing was held by Customs to inform the importing community of the results of the Customs Service's "Drawback Revitalization Study" which examined administration of drawback.

The draft study contains some extremely self-critical observations and assessments of the mishandling of the program by Customs. For example, the study states, "The drawback program is not effectively administered; not effectively enforced; and not effectively equipped with adequate tools and automated systems to make it a viable, productive system on a standard with other customs service programs." In addition, the study criticizes the administration of the program, pointing to the lack of direction and guidance by Customs Headquarters, the lack of uniformity in administration of drawback between different ports, the long delays in specific contract acceptances, and the general lack of uniform procedures. Finally, the report categorizes Customs as "negligent in its service to the general public" because of its poor administration of the drawback program.

Also included in the study are several recommendations made by Customs for reforming the legislative and regulatory drawback provisions to correct deficiencies in the program as well as to update it. Generally, the recommendations were well received by the importing community. The Customs Service's call for nationwide standardized drawback procedures, simplification of forms, elimination of unnecessary paperwork, and provision of specialized formal drawback training to responsible Customs personnel were among the more favorably proposed recommendations. However, Customs found much opposition to its recommended addition of civil penalty provisions for drawback enforcement purposes. In addition, recommendation to reduce the time period for export and filing of drawback claims (which would effectively reduce the time in which claims for refunds from three to two years) was vigorously opposed.

At the time of this writing Customs has requested comments from the importing community regarding its "Drawback Revitalization Study" and its recommendations for change in the current drawback law. The ultimate outcome and the resulting changes (if any) to the current law are uncertain. However, the more objectionable proposals will demand the full application of the various legislative and regulatory procedures necessary to implement the changes recommended. Consequently, prior to any proposed changes the importing community will have ample opportunity to voice its opinion.

Part V: Nontariff Measures and Trade Regulations

18. Marking of Imported Merchandise

The Congress has historically expressed its intention that foreign merchandise imported into the United States be clearly marked with the country of origin or manufacture in order to ensure not only that domestic purchasers may make informed choices between foreign and domestic merchandise but also that they may know the particular country from which the merchandise originated.

It would seem at first blush that this is a simple, straightforward requirement, readily framed into law and easily administered. However, as will become evident, the law becomes necessarily complex, because of numerous technicalities, and its administration becomes difficult, because in real cases, various legal exceptions must be recognized, degrees of compliance evaluated, loopholes and avoidances assessed, and sanctions evenly and fairly applied.

Section 304 of the Tariff Act of 1930, as amended,[1] requires that every article of foreign origin (or its container) imported into the United States be marked in a conspicuous place as legibly, indelibly, and permanently as the article or container will permit, in such a manner as to indicate to an ultimate purchaser the English name of the country of origin of the article.

---

1. 19 U.S.C.A. § 1304 (West 1980).

Subdivision (c) of this section provides that any articles not so marked will be subject to a duty of 10 percent ad valorem in addition to any other duty imposed by law, whether or not the article is exempt from the payment of ordinary customs duties, unless the article is exported, destroyed, or marked under Customs Service supervision.[2] These marking duties, once the merchandise has been released from Customs Service custody and entered the commerce of the United States without proper marking, cannot be remitted,[3] in whole or in part, but the additional duties are considered statutory and not penal.[4]

Customs has also instituted liquidated damages cases[5] on merchandise that has been properly marked with the name of the country of origin outside the thirty-day marking period.[6] For first time violations with no aggravating factors, Customs has settled the liquidated damages claim for as low as 1 percent of the appraised value of the merchandise. For subsequent violations, Customs has settled claims for as much as 50 percent of the appraised value of the merchandise that was properly marked outside of the thirty-day marking period.[7]

Beyond the assessment of additional marking duties under section 304(c) for country of origin marking violations,

---

2. Importers usually receive notification of marking duties on a notice of action form, CF 29 (reprinted in appendix 27).
3. 19 U.S.C.A. § 1618 (West 1980).
4. Customs has issued mitigation guidelines in connection with marking violations as part of the Office of Commercial Operations, Department of the Treasury, U.S. Customs Service Fines, Penalties, and Forfeitures Handbook (1986) as amended. See also chapter 23 and discussion on seizure and forfeiture of commercial importation in connection with marking violations.
5. See chapter 22.
6. Importers receive notification of a claim for liquidated damages in Customs Form 5955A, reprinted in appendix 28.
7. See Customs Bond Cancellation Standards, T.D. 89-48, 23 Cust. B. & Dec. No. 7 (May 3, 1989).

civil penalties may be incurred under section 592 of the Tariff Act of 1930, as amended,[8] for importing merchandise by means of false documents. Further criminal sanctions may also be assessed under 18 U.S.C. § 1001 for presenting false and misrepresented documents to the government in connection with an entry, or under 19 U.S.C. § 1304 for defacing, destroying, altering, etc., any mark required on imported articles and containers with intent to conceal the information given by the mark. If merchandise released from Customs Service custody under a bond is found not to be legally marked, liquidated damages may also be assessed for breach of the bond's conditions, and seizure actions may be brought under the broad scope of 19 U.S.C. § 1595a(c), which enables Customs to seize merchandise that is entered contrary to law.[9]

These sanctions and penalties should be understood beyond the narrow scope of compliance with marking requirements, inasmuch as the proper and legal country of origin marking may have an impact on questions of correct rate of duty-free allowances under the generalized system of preferences (GSP),[10] quota restrictions, and other conditions that vary depending upon the country of origin or manufacture. For example, a shipment of certain garments from Dubai marked "Made in United Arab Emirates" was seized by the Customs Service and held to be a product of India. Quota restrictions applied to India but not to United Arab Emirates. The importer averred that insofar as it knew, backed by documentation, it had purchased the goods in Dubai. Ultimately, the goods were released under a special penalty deposit and were permitted to be remarked "India." By that time, the quota from India had reopened, and the merchandise was properly entered and released to the importer.

8. 19 U.S.C.A. § 1592 (West 1980 & Supp. 1990). *See also* chapter 22.
9. *See* chapter 22.
10. *See* chapter 11.

However, a civil penalty for false marking was assessed under section 592.[11]

There are many instances when political considerations enter into acceptable legal marking. For example, the Customs Service determined in 1980, pursuant to a Department of State request, that "Republic of China" or "R.O.C." should not appear as part of the country of origin marking of goods imported from Taiwan, unless "Taiwan" also appeared thereon. Products from mainland China were allowed to be marked "China" or "The People's Republic of China."

Under the customs regulations,[12] if merchandise is found upon examination not to be legally marked, the district director must notify the importer to arrange with the district director's office to mark the articles or containers properly or to return all released articles to Customs Service custody for marking.[13] Usually, if there is no question of fraudulent attempt to circumvent proper marking, but merely a failure to mark entirely or a technically improper marking (e.g., "Made in U.K." instead of "Made in United Kingdom"), the merchandise is released by the inspector at the pier or airport, along with a notice[14] advising the importer not to dispose of the merchandise until it has been properly marked or remarked. After the merchandise has been correctly marked, the importer returns the notice to the Service, certifying that it has accomplished the marking. The Customs Service may then accept the certification and issue a final release, or it may opt to verify the marking by a visit to the premises where the merchandise is located.

At times, the notice to mark or redeliver emanates from the import specialist after viewing a sample of the ship-

---

11. 19 U.S.C.A. § 1592 (West 1980 & Supp. 1990).
12. 19 C.F.R. § 134.51(a) (1987).
13. Customs notifies importers by a notice of redelivery (reprinted in appendix 21).
14. CF 4647; *see* appendix 21.

ment. That notice does not carry legal force if it is issued more than thirty days after delivery to the importer from the place of arrival.[15] However, it is evident that in some situations the merchandise may have been distributed all over the United States within thirty days, and the problem can become a serious one for the importer when a notice is issued after, but within thirty days of, delivery.

If the importer does not properly mark or redeliver all merchandise previously released to it, as provided in 19 C.F.R. § 134.54(a), the district director will demand payment of liquidated damages incurred under the importer's bond in an amount equal to the entered value of the articles not properly marked or redelivered, plus any estimated duty determined at the time of entry.[16] Regulation section 134.54(b)[17] states that a petition for relief from the payment of liquidated damages may be filed with the district director in accordance with part 172 of the customs regulations.[18] However, section 134.54(c)[19] provides that any relief from the payment of full liquidated damages incurred will be contingent upon the deposit of the additional nonpenal marking duties of 10 percent required by 19 U.S.C. § 1304(c).

Section 134.54(c) formerly provided that the district director may grant relief from the payment of full liquidated damages only if he or she is satisfied that the importer (1) was not guilty of negligence or bad faith in permitting the illegally marked articles to be distributed, (2) has been diligent in attempting to secure compliance with the marking requirements, and (3) has attempted by all reasonable means to effect redelivery of the articles to Customs Service custody.

---

15. 19 C.F.R. § 141.113(a) (1988).
16. *See* appendix 28.
17. 19 C.F.R. § 134.54(b) (1987).
18. 19 C.F.R. 172 (1987).
19. 19 C.F.R. § 134.54(c) (1987).

In a move to liberalize one aspect of the imposition of these sanctions, however, the regulations were amended in November 1983 to eliminate "negligence" as one of the grounds for denying relief, leaving only "bad faith" as a condition for denying relief.

In order to clarify the sequence of the various steps discussed above, we summarize them as follows:

1. Merchandise that enters the commerce of the United States without legal marking is subject to the nonpenal additional duty of 10 percent of the value.
2. In such a case, liquidated damages may be assessed when there exists "bad faith" in releasing the merchandise into the commerce of the country without legal marking.
3. In case of violations involving false country of origin marking, false documentation, or both, the civil penalties under 19 U.S.C. § 1592 may be imposed.
4. Merchandise may be subject to seizure by the Customs Service under 19 U.S.C. § 1595a(c).
5. Depending on the degree or severity of the falsehoods, criminal sanctions may also be pursued under 18 U.S.C. § 1001 or 19 U.S.C. § 1304(e).

In addition to the above, 19 U.S.C. § 1304(h)[20] provides that any intentional removal, defacement, destruction, or alteration of a marking of the country of origin in order to conceal this information may result in criminal penalties of up to $100,000 for the first offense and $250,000 for subsequent offenses, imprisonment for not more than one year, or both.[21] It is noteworthy that this latter provision goes be-

20. 19 U.S.C.A. § 1304(h) (West 1980 & Supp. 1990).
21. Omnibus Trade and Competitiveness Act of 1988, Pub. L. No. 100-418, 102 Stat. 1107, § 1907 (1988). *See* note 32 *infra* concerning the Customs Service's latest certification requirements to prohibit the

yond the conditions of the actual importation into the circumstances of sale after release from Customs Service custody, and it is indicative of how seriously Congress takes the matter of legal marking.

Exceptions Allowed

Customs law has carved out certain general exceptions to the marking requirements. These exceptions are as follows:[22]

1. Articles incapable of being marked;
2. Articles that cannot be marked without injury;
3. Articles economically prohibitive to mark;
4. Articles for which the containers will reasonably indicate the marking to the ultimate purchaser;
5. Crude substances;
6. Articles destined for the importer's own use and not intended for sale;
7. Articles to be processed in the United States in such a manner that the marking would be obliterated;
8. Articles for which the "ultimate purchaser" must necessarily know the country of origin by reason of the circumstances of importation or the character of the articles;
9. Articles produced more than twenty years prior to importation;
10. Articles to be exported without entering the commerce of the United States;
11. Products of American fisheries that are free of duty;

---

concealment of country of origin information appearing on marked and unmarked articles imported in bulk and repacked in the United States after release from Customs Service custody.

22. *See* 19 U.S.C.A. § 1304(a)(3) (West Supp. 1990); 19 C.F.R. § 134.32 (1990).

12. Products of possessions of the United States;
13. Products of the United States exported and returned; and
14. Articles that cannot be marked after importation except at an expense economically prohibitive, unless the failure to mark the articles before importation was an attempt to avoid meeting the requirements of the law.

An example of the final exception would be a cheap plastic kiddie ring without any marking, which could easily have been marked in the mold but would require individual tagging or labeling after importation. Such marking in the United States would become economically prohibitive relative to the value of the merchandise. In this situation, a one-time "waiver" of marking could be obtained, conditioned upon the importer's advising its foreign supplier that future shipments must be properly marked. Such a "waiver" would also avoid the 10 percent additional duty.

Aside from these general exceptions, there is also a list of specific articles known as the "J-List," detailing by name many articles of a class or kind with respect to which the Secretary of the Treasury has published authorization exempting them from individual markings.[23] Examples of these are unstrung beads; buttons; monuments; nails, spikes, and staples; wood fence posts; rope, twine, and yarns; and postage and revenue stamps. In all these cases, of course, the immediate containers must be marked.

Watches and Clocks

There are special marking requirements for certain watches and clocks. Watch and clock movements with opto-

23. 19 C.F.R. § 134.33 (1987).

electronic display-only modules and their cases are excepted from the special marking requirements.

Generally speaking, all other watch and clock movements are required to show the name of the country of manufacture, the name of the manufacturer, and the number of jewels (in words). Watch cases are required to show the name of the country of manufacture and the name of the manufacturer. Clock cases are required to show the name of the country of manufacture.[24]

Textile Fiber Products Identification Act

The Textile Fiber Products Identification Act (TFPIA) is a marking requirement that applies to certain textile products.[25] This Act is enforced by the Federal Trade Commission with respect to products in the domestic economy and by the Customs Service with respect to imported products.

The Act requires that a label be affixed to each textile product in a secure and conspicuous manner. The information that is required to be shown and displayed includes:

1. The generic names and percentages by weight of the constituent fibers present in the textile product, exclusive of ornamentation, in amounts of 5 percent or more. The generic names and percentages shall appear in order of predominance by weight, with any percentage of fiber or fibers required to be designated as "other fiber" or "other fibers" appearing last.
2. The name or registered identification number (RN

---

24. Harmonized Tariff Schedules of the United States, Chapter 91, Additional U.S. Note 4.
25. Pub. L. No. 85-897, 72 Stat. 1717 (1958) as amended by Pub. L. No. 89-35, 79 Stat. 124 (1965); Pub. L. No. 98-417, 98 Stat. 1585 (1984).

number) of the manufacturer or one or more persons marketing or handling the textile product.

3. The name of the country of origin.[26]

In 1988 the Customs Service began intensive inspections on certain textile products that it considered to be "trade sensitive merchandise," such as textile wearing apparel and piece goods. This has led to increased inspections, detentions, and seizures for textile products that are not in full compliance with the TFPIA. Therefore, importers of merchandise subject to the requirements of this Act should study those provisions, exceptions, and exemptions[27] in order to ensure the smooth flow of their imported products.

Examples of some of the products that are not regulated by the TFPIA include car cushions, diaper bags, and tents. An example of a label that is marked in compliance with the Act would be "80% Wool, 20% Nylon, Made in Japan, RN# 12345."

Substantial Transformation

The allowable exception to legal marking that has generated the most litigation is the one involving imported merchandise further processed in the United States in such a way that it has undergone a "substantial transformation." The case of *United States v. Gibson-Thomsen Co.*[28] estab-

26. For example, a women's silk tank top marked with a sewn-in label on the inside lower side seam of the top containing the country of origin and the RN number, along with care instructions and fiber content on a paper hang tag attached to the neck, would satisfy this requirement. HQ 733890 (Dec. 31, 1990). *See also* HQ 732975 (Mar. 13, 1990).
27. Exemptions such as nonwoven products of a disposable nature and Christmas decorations to the TFPIA are stated in section 12 of that act. *See also* rule 45 (Exclusions), Rules and Regulations under the TFPIA that is published by the Federal Trade Commission.
28. United States v. Gibson-Thomsen Co., 27 C.C.P.A. 267 (1970).

lished the principle that an article used in the United States in manufacture that results in an article having a name, character, or use differing from that of the imported article (thus having undergone a substantial transformation) is excepted from individual marking and need only be marked on the outermost containers when imported. Under this principle, the manufacturer or processor in the United States who converts or combines the imported article into the different article will be considered the "ultimate purchaser" of the imported article.[29] *Gibson-Thomsen* involved imported wooden brush handles to be processed in the United States by the insertion of bristles. The handles were marked "Japan" at the time of importation, but the insertion of the bristles obliterated the marking. The court enunciated the principle stated above, so that in this, and future similar cases, it is sufficient to mark the containers in which the merchandise to be processed reaches the "ultimate purchaser."

The principle of substantial transformation is used by the United States Customs Service in order to make country of origin marking determinations and textile restraint determinations. In a decision with potentially beneficial results for some importers, Customs ruled in May of 1985 that sweater panels (components) knit to shape in an European Economic Community (EEC) country such as England and shipped to Hong Kong where they would be finished, looped, and assembled into complete sweaters could be properly marked as products of England or Hong Kong. Additionally, textile restraints such as a Hong Kong export license would not apply. Therefore the importer would have the option of labeling the name of the country of origin without having to apply for an export license from Hong Kong. The subsequent implementation of customs regula-

29. 19 C.F.R. §§ 134.1(d)(1)–.1(d)(4) (1987).

tions governing textile and textile products country of origin determinations effectively eliminated the temporary option allowed for sweater panels by indicating that looping knit-to-shape component parts, even when accompanied by finishing operations, does not substantially transform the components into products of the country in which these operations took place.[30]

In another ruling, published as Customs Service Decision 79-244, the Service held that calculators assembled in Hong Kong from parts produced elsewhere should be properly marked "assembled in Hong Kong"; the origin of components used in making the calculators did not have to be disclosed. This ruling illustrates that there are many intermediate situations, usually involving processing in more than one country, that may require amplified language, such as "components made in ______, assembled in ______," in order to convey the country or countries of origin properly.

The creation and subsequent modifications of the Customs regulations on rules of origin for textile products have led to confusion concerning the proper country of origin marking. Customs published interim textile and textile product country of origin regulations on August 3, 1984. The interim regulations became effective on April 4, 1985. They were implemented without notice for comments prior to their adoption, on the rationale that interim regulations do not constitute a "major rule." These interim regulations had a major impact on importers who did not know, realize, or appreciate the Customs Service's shifting interpretation of these interim regulations.

For example, an importer of sports jackets assembled in Yugoslavia from components (jacket panels, sleeves, etc.) cut in Italy received a binding country of origin ruling from Customs Headquarters in November of 1984 that stated "the

30. 19 C.F.R. § 12.130(e)(2)(iii) (West Supp. 1991).

assembled garments may be marked to indicate Italy as the country of origin." The importer relied on this ruling and imported the garments until Customs issued a redelivery notice on May 8, 1987. Customs indicated a quota/visa violation had occurred because a Yugoslavian visa had not been supplied and assessed a liquidated damages claim against the importer in an amount of $117,657. Customs eventually mitigated that amount to $11,765 in consideration of the fact that the importer had reasonably relied on the ruling, even though the regulations had, in effect, reversed the prior practice of Customs subsequent to the ruling.

Customs took the position that the importer's ruling of November 20, 1984 was subsequently revoked by operation of law and superseded with the issuance of new regulations that became effective on April 4, 1985. Customs believes it was not required to advise the importer in writing that its ruling letter was no longer valid. Thus importers of multiple country of origin textile products should not rely on country of origin rulings that were issued by Customs prior to April of 1985. Importers should pay scrupulous attention to part 12 section 12.130 of the Customs regulations concerning visa/quota requirements on any multiple country of origin situation.[31]

In *Uniroyal, Inc. v. United States*,[32] the Court of International Trade held that imported footwear consisting of hand-sewn leather uppers to be completed as shoes by the attachment of soles in the United States must be marked with the name of the country of origin (Indonesia). This ruling, which was affirmed by the Court of Appeals for the Federal Circuit, in effect concluded that the addition of soles to the leather uppers did not constitute a substantial

31. See chapter 19 page 455 for visa and quota implications.
32. Uniroyal, Inc. v. United States, 542 F. Supp. 1026 (Ct. Int'l Trade 1982), *aff'd*, 702 F.2d 1022 (Fed. Cir. 1983).

transformation, nor did the uppers lose their identity. In fact, the upper was the "essence of the shoe." Hence, the importer who processed the merchandise was not the "ultimate purchaser" of the merchandise, and the customer who purchased the shoes at retail must be made aware that the country of origin was Indonesia and not the United States. In the pressures between foreign and domestic footwear interests, this decision gave significant support to domestic manufacturers, although the record suggests they took no direct part in the case.

An interesting variation showing how complex many marking problems can become involved valve bodies that were made in Canada but were marked "Cleveland, Ohio, USA." The importer used the valves only in its own assembly operation. Nevertheless, the Customs Service ruled that the valves have to be properly marked with the country of origin, because otherwise the *final* consumer could be deceived. It appeared, however, that the improper marking was not intentional. The Customs Service therefore stated that a waiver could be obtained if (1) this was a one-time occurrence, (2) the incorrect marking was an inadvertence and not done to circumvent marking requirements, and (3) it could be shown that remarking was economically prohibitive. This case illustrates that in situations where the incorrect marking arose out of innocent inadvertence, relief through one-time "waivers" may be obtained when special conditions warrant such exceptions.

Methods and Locations of Markings

The law requires that the marking of the country of origin be legible, indelible, and permanent. Certain specific articles require special markings or methods of marking. For example, country of origin marking for knives must be diesunk or etched on the blades. In most normal situations, however, the degree of "permanence" should be at least sufficient to ensure that in any reasonably foreseeable circumstances the marking will remain on the article until it reaches the ultimate purchaser unless it is deliberately removed. The marking must survive normal distribution and store handling.[33]

All markings, whether by special permanent methods or by labels, tags, or paper stickers, must be in a conspicuous place and must include the full English name of the country of origin, unless certain acceptable abbreviations or variants have been specifically authorized. For example, "Gt. Britain" for Great Britain or "Brasil" for Brazil is acceptable; "HK" for Hong Kong is not acceptable. In doubtful cases, a ruling by the Customs Service should be requested.

The adjectival form of the country may be used in conjunction with the description of the merchandise (e.g., Argentine beef or Japanese tuna), but if the name of a country of origin is also part of the common or generic name of the product (e.g., English walnuts or Swiss cheese), then the adjectival form alone would not suffice.

Certain articles or their containers may contain the words "United States" or "American" or "U.S.A." or the name of any city or locality other than the country of origin. This may be done in conjunction with an address of the importer or distributor in the United States. In all such cases, the imported article must be legibly, conspicuously, and permanently marked with the name of the country of origin preceded by "Made in" or "Product of" or other similar words in close proximity to the possibly misleading words or in some other equally conspicuous location. This is usually taken to mean in letters of approximately the same size

33. After the article is purchased, of course, the ultimate purchaser, usually at retail, may remove any labels or tags without violating the law—even on furniture and bedding, a generation of comedians to the contrary notwithstanding.

as the American location, and on the same side of the product.[34]

When as part of a trademark or trade name or as part of a souvenir marking, the name of a location in the United States or "United States" or "America" appears, the article should be legibly, conspicuously, and permanently marked with the name of the country of origin preceded by "Made in," "Product of," or similar words in close proximity or in some other conspicuous place.[35]

In a recent Court of International Trade decision, *Norcal/Crosetti Foods, Inc. v. United States Customs Service*,[36] the question of what constitutes "conspicuous" marking was addressed.

The action was brought by California-based frozen food packagers, with the support of local packaging unions, to compel the Customs Service to stop its practice of allowing foreign frozen food products (in this case, Mexican frozen vegetables) to be entered into the United States without proper "conspicuous" marking.

Citing their significantly decreasing market share and the potential health risks associated with foreign vegetables, the domestic packagers claimed that the Customs Service's practice of allowing frozen vegetable packages to be marked "made in Mexico" on the rear panel permits foreign produce to blend "seamlessly into the stream of commerce," thus depriving U.S. consumers of the necessary information to enable them to make a "realistic choice" to purchase domestic produce.

In a sharply worded opinion, the *Norcal* court held that the Customs Service's ruling was "plainly erroneous" and that the practice of allowing the country of origin marking

34. 19 C.F.R. § 134.46.
35. 19 C.F.R. § 134.47.
36. Norcal/Crosetti Foods, Inc. v. United States Customs Serv., No. 89-00495, slip op. 91-12 (Feb. 27, 1991).

to appear on the rear panel of frozen vegetable packages resulted in markings neither as conspicuous nor as legible as the nature of the packages would permit.[37]

The court criticized Customs for "ignoring the principal intent behind the marking requirement: that goods be marked conspicuously so that consumers can easily find the marks,"[38] and for failing to address the congressional desire, reflected in the marking statute, to protect domestic producers.

In arriving at its decision that the markings on frozen vegetable packages "must be located on the front panel of the package and must be marked in a type size and style so as to be conspicuous. . . ,"[39] the court took into consideration certain "special factors" involved in the marketing and display of frozen food products which Customs had failed to do.

For example, the court noted that such merchandise is commonly arranged on freezer shelves or in frozen food bins with the front panel of the item in view and the "marked" rear panel obscured and with limited access due to the refrigerated conditions. In addition, the court noticed that some of the product sample marks were smudged. Recognizing the commercial reality involved in the sale of such products, the court found that the markings in question not only ran afoul of the statutory mandate that the marks be conspicuous, but were contrary to the Customs Service's

37. 19 U.S.C. § 1304(a)(1990) requires that "every article of foreign origin (or its container . . .) imported into the United States shall be marked in a conspicuous place as legibly, indelibly, and permanently as the nature of the article (or container) will permit as to indicate to the ultimate purchaser in the United States the English name of the country of origin of the article. . . ."

38. Norcal/Crosetti Foods, Inc. v. United States Customs Serv., No. 89-00495, slip op. 91-12 at 14 (Feb. 27, 1991).

39. Norcal/Crosetti Foods, Inc. v. United States Customs Serv., amended judgment at 2 (Feb. 28, 1991).

own regulatory requirement that for a marking to be "conspicuous" it must be "clear to the naked eye" or "found easily and read without strain."[40] Thus, in the court's view, the statutory and regulatory requirements that country of origin markings be conspicuous necessitate consideration of the state that an item is in when it is presented to consumers for sale and not simply an examination of the marking as it appears on a particular sample presented to Customs for review.[41]

Recently, new regulations[42] were promulgated to cover the marking requirements pertaining to articles imported in bulk and repacked after release from Customs Service custody. Under those regulations, 19 C.F.R. § 134.26 requires importers to certify to the district director having custody of the articles that:

1. If the importer does the repacking, it will not obscure or conceal the name of the country of origin markings appearing on the article or it will mark the container (e.g., the blister pack) in accordance with applicable law and regulations; or
2. If the article is sold or transferred, the importer will notify the subsequent purchaser or repacker, in writing, at the time of the sale or transfer that any repacking of the article must conform to the marking requirements.

40. Norcal/Crosetti Foods, Inc. v. United States Customs Serv., No. 89-00495, slip op. 91-12 at 7 (Feb. 27, 1991).
41. At the time of this writing the Customs Service is appealing this decision and plans to continue its current practice regarding the marking of such items until the court of appeals makes its determination. Should the decision be upheld, importers may have to rethink their country of origin marking practices. Certainly, how a particular item is marked and displayed to consumers will have a greater impact on how that particular item should be marked.
42. T.D. 84-127 (1984).

The purpose of the amended regulation is to ensure that an ultimate purchaser in the United States is informed of the country of origin of the article.

Earlier, the Customs Service also amended its regulations[43] by adding section 134.25 to provide for certification requirements with respect to certain *unmarked* articles (i.e., J-List articles incapable of being marked, see page 430 *supra*) imported in bulk and repacked in the United States after release from Customs Service custody. In these cases, the Service frequently found that, although the container in which the article was imported was marked, the container in which the article was repacked for sale to an ultimate purchaser was not. The Service has indicated that this problem is greatest as to steel wire rope but also involves numerous other articles whose containers must be marked.

Failure to comply with the certification requirements may subject the importer to a demand for liquidated damages under 19 C.F.R. § 134.54(a) and additional duties pursuant to 19 U.S.C. § 1304. Fraud and negligence in furnishing the required certification may also result in a civil or criminal penalty.

The new certification requirements under section 134.26 place the responsibility on the importer to ensure, as best as possible, that the country of origin information reaches the ultimate purchaser in such a way as to inform the purchaser, through inspection of the article (or its container), of the country of origin of the article before the decision to purchase.

Under the new certification requirement, however, the importer that does not repack would not be liable to the Service if its transferee, which does repack, failed to comply with the marking requirements, provided that the importer complied with certification procedures by informing the repacker of the requirements. If it is determined that the im-

43. T.D. 83-133 (1983).

porter gave notice of the requirements and the repacker failed to comply, the Service could seek criminal action against the repacker under 19 U.S.C. § 1304(e). In addition, the certification and proof of compliance also may be used in a civil action brought against a repacker under 15 U.S.C. § 1125 for false description, representation, or designation of origin.

The Customs Service, in its supplementary comments on section 134.26, emphasized that a broker that files an entry as importer of record, posting its own bond, is liable under section 134.26(e) for marking duties and penalties if the actual owner fails to fulfill the certification requirements, unless a superseding bond and actual owner's declaration are filed under 19 C.F.R. § 141.20.

Section 134.26(f) of 19 C.F.R. indicates that the certification requirements will *not* apply when a marked article is repacked in an unmarked container that can be readily opened for inspection by the ultimate purchaser. If, however, the container bears a United States address, then the name of the country of origin of the contents must appear on the container in comparable size and close proximity to the United States address under 19 C.F.R. § 134.46. This is designed to avoid confusion in the mind of an ultimate purchaser, and it will now apply to container packaging added in the United States to repackaged imported marked articles.

Conclusions

The correct legal marking of imported merchandise is an important consideration and should always be borne in mind when ordering and buying foreign merchandise. Many domestic sales have been lost solely because of delays in marking merchandise after its arrival in the United States. Often, when merchandise requires quick distribution, the importer becomes aware of the marking problem only after shipments have been delivered to customers. It becomes a major headache to retrieve the merchandise, and if it is not redeliverable, additional marking duties will apply. In addition, liquidated damages may be assessed.

It should be noted here that when unintentional and unusual marking problems arise, it is often possible to negotiate practical solutions with the Customs Service. Examples of these include "one-time waivers" when articles are economically prohibitive to mark, special arrangements such as using epoxy-covered labels instead of die-sinking, repacking into sealed containers that are properly marked, and other similar practical mechanisms. Experienced customs brokers can be helpful with many day-to-day marking problems. Where more involved legal marking problems arise, the services of a knowledgeable customs attorney may be advisable.

19. Quotas and Voluntary Restraint Agreements

A quota is a limitation on the amount of a designated item that may be imported into the United States. Such controls are placed on imported merchandise by the Congress, by the executive branch under authorization from Congress, or by agencies delegated authority by Congress.[1]

Quotas may be divided into two general categories. The first, the "absolute quota," provides for a maximum quantity of a specified item that may be entered or withdrawn for consumption during a specified period. Once the quota has been filled, no other entries or withdrawals for consumption of the merchandise governed by the quota are permitted during that period. Absolute quotas may limit the entry or withdrawal of items by source (i.e., from particular countries) or globally by total quantity.[2] The merchandise then must be returned to the country of exportation, sold to another country, stored in a bonded warehouse[3] until the next quota opens up, or stored in a foreign trade zone[4] until a quota opens.[5]

1. 19 C.F.R. § 132.2 (1987).
2. 19 C.F.R. § 132.1(a) (1987).
3. *See* chapter 9.
4. *See* chapter 10.
5. 19 C.F.R. § 132.5(a) (1987). Visa restraints are based on the date of export and not the date of entry. Therefore, if a 1990 category is filled,

"Tariff-rate quotas" allow a specific quantity of merchandise to be entered or withdrawn for consumption at a particular rate of duty during a specified period. Quantities in excess of the tariff-rate quota are subject to higher duties.[6]

Quota categories are noted in Harmonized Tariff Schedules of the United States (HTSUS) or in the chapter 99 appendix.[7] Place and style of notation of the quota in the HTSUS are determined by the type of quota involved. For example, quotas fixed by Congress have their preferred rates and total amounts noted in the HTSUS section for the item. Quotas established by presidential proclamation are noted in the appendix.[8] Quotas established by the President or an executive agency pursuant to legislative authorization are noted in a footnote to the tariff section.

Textiles

Besides the quotas described above, there are several other mechanisms for controlling the quantities of foreign products imported into the United States. These controls have an effect essentially the same as quotas, and they are colloquially referred to as quotas. For example, there is a system of "textile restraints" on cotton, wool, manmade fiber, vegetable fibers other than cotton, and certain silk blend fibers and textile products made therefrom.[9] These controls include those on wearing apparel, which, because of tremendous market demand, are the controls the public is now most aware of. The United States has entered into a

---

the foreign vendor should be instructed to hold the goods and not export them until 1991 with a valid 1991 visa.

6. 19 C.F.R. §§ 132.1(b) & 132.5(b) (1987).
7. 19 U.S.C.A. § 1202 (West 1980 & Supp. 1983).
8. Quotas under the Agricultural Adjustment Act, ch. 104, 49 Stat. 1152 (1936) (codified at 7 U.S.C. § 624) are also noted there.
9. *See* 7 U.S.C.A. § 1854 (West 1973).

multilateral agreement known as the Multifiber Arrangement (MFA), which provides a structure for negotiating bilateral agreements on textile trading.[10]

Import controls may be instituted upon a showing that market disruption is resulting from the importation of the subject merchandise. The MFA sets forth the standards for invoking controls and defines market disruption.[11]

Under 7 U.S.C. § 1854, the President of the United States is authorized to negotiate foreign agreements limiting the amount of textiles and textile products that may be imported into the United States. The President is also given authority to issue regulations dealing with entry or withdrawal of items from a warehouse.[12]

Through the MFA, the United States has negotiated a number of bilateral agreements with countries that are major textile exporters. These agreements limit the amount of textiles and textile products that may be brought into the United States every year.

Administration of the textile controls is derived from directives issued to the Customs Service by the Committee for the Implementation of Textile Agreements (CITA). The CITA is composed of representatives from the Departments of Commerce, Treasury, Labor, and State and has offices located in the Commerce Department. It is authorized to make determinations on market disruption and restraint levels.[13] It has been held that the legality of restraint agreements may be the subject of judicial review. For example, in *Associated Dry Goods Corp. v. United States*,[14] it was held that

10. *See* Arrangements Regarding International Trade in Textiles, 25 U.S.T. 1001, T.I.A.S. No. 7840.
11. *Id.* art. III; *see also* Protocol Extending the Multifiber Arrangement Regarding International Trade in Textiles agreed to in Geneva, Dec. 22, 1981.
12. 7 U.S.C.A. § 1854 (West 1973).
13. See Exec. Order No. 11,651, 37 Fed. Reg. 4,699 (1972), *amended by* Exec. Order No. 11,951, 42 Fed. Reg. 1,453 (1977).
14. Associated Dry Goods Corp. v. United States, 521 F. Supp. 473 (Ct.

the Court of International Trade had jurisdiction to review CITA actions concerning the finding of a threat of market disruption and the calculation of restraint levels.

The United States has also negotiated agreements with countries that were not then members of the MFA, such as China. In addition, the United States has imposed restraints against countries with which it had no agreements.[15] In any consideration of quotas, the reader should keep in mind political implications and motivations, which may not be readily apparent on first observation. For example, the difficulties with the United States–China negotiations on reopening or adjusting an embargoed (closed) group of quota categories during 1989 have been attributed to the Tienanmen Square massacre.

Generally, bilateral textile agreements provide that the exports of a particular foreign country will be limited to a restraint level calculated on a square-meter-equivalent basis. The restraint level is further broken down into groups and specific limits. The agreements also usually allow the foreign country to exceed the limits set by the agreement by a specific percentage per year. In addition, during subsequent years of an agreement, a controlled level of growth of imports may also be permitted.[16]

Int'l Trade 1981), *vacated and remanded*, 682 F.2d 212 (C.C.P.A. 1982) (declared moot). *See also* Sanho Collections, Ltd. v. Chasen, 505 F. Supp. 204 (Ct. Int'l Trade 1980).

15. China was accepted as a member of the MFA on December 15, 1983. *See* 9 U.S. IMPORT WEEKLY (BNA) 461 (Dec. 21, 1983). The United States has a history of imposing unilateral quotas under 7 U.S.C. § 1854 against countries that have no bilateral agreements with the United States (e.g., Panama and the Dominican Republic). *See U.S. Tightens Import Curbs with Four Nations*, Women's Wear Daily, Dec. 7, 1983. This unilateral imposition of quotas usually leads to a bilateral agreement. Panama entered into a bilateral agreement with the United States in April of 1987. The Dominican Republic's current bilateral agreement took effect in June of 1988.

16. Agreements may be found in *United States Treaties* and like sources.

If the United States deems that importation of an item not covered by a specific restraint level is causing market disruptions, a "consultation" will take place between the United States and the country of origin of the product. If the consultation does not result in a settlement, the United States can impose a restraint level or a quota. In the case of goods already covered by a restraint level, violations or market disruption may lead to embargo.[17]

As any importer of quota merchandise can attest, there is always the risk that a quota category will be closed before the goods can be entered into the United States. Some absolute quotas, such as for steel, often close on the first day of the quota period, and great care must be taken to plan and properly time entry procedures. Other items (e.g., apparel) subject to specific, absolute quotas may be open for six months and unexpectedly close in a twenty-four-hour period. It has not been unknown for a single importer to fly in a Boeing 747 cargo plane full of wool sweaters, consuming a substantial percentage of the yearly quota and closing it at the same time.

For an example of an agreement found in a more accessible location, see, e.g., United States–China Bilateral Agreement of Feb. 19, 1983, *reprinted in* 8 U.S. IMPORT WEEKLY (BNA) 834 (Aug. 24, 1983).

17. An excellent historical example is documented in *Import Limit Is Set on Hong Kong Cloth*, Women's Wear Daily, Dec. 5, 1983; Pine, *U.S. Crackdown Textile Imports Seen as Uneasy Truce with Domestic Producers*, Wall St. J., Dec. 19, 1983. The administration initiated controls that would "require officials to consider quotas or other restraints whenever . . . a surge in imports of foreign-made textiles" takes place. The first step in the process would be formal negotiations to achieve voluntary restraints by the exporting country. The trigger point for a "surge" would be a growth of 30 percent in one year or growth to at least 20 percent of United States production and imports from the individual supplier equal 1 percent or more of the total United States production of that product or category. For Hong Kong and South Korea, the trigger point was 65 percent, taking account of their current shipment allocation through licensing.

Any importer of absolute quota merchandise would be well advised to know the specific quota-year limits for its commodity and to monitor carefully and frequently the rate of entry of quota merchandise. This can be accomplished by calling the Customs Service quota desk, by subscribing to available periodicals (e.g., *AAEI*, the American Association of Exporters & Importers *International Trade Alert*, and the Customs Service's *Status Report on Import Quotas and Restraint Levels, Cotton, Wool and Man-Made Fiber Textiles*), or by learning the rate of exports of the quota merchandise from the country of origin, if that is possible. Comparisons with the prior year's data on quota utilization can be useful, but of course those data are at best only a guide.

If the bilateral agreement setting the specific quota requires the spacing of imports to prevent United States market disruption, this should be known by the importer. Some countries that have agreed to control exports of quota items over the entire year, but did not, have found their exports to be the subject of numerous consultation calls and limits.

Many bilateral agreements provide for a certain amount of flexibility in quota limits, permitting "swing" (allowing a country to export a certain percentage over the restraint level by borrowing units from another unfilled quota category), "carryover" (using units from a past year's unfilled quota), and "carryforward" (borrowing units from a future year's quota). Some of these options must be requested of the United States by the exporting country. Importers can ask their sellers to approach their governments to make such requests of the United States.

More difficult to foresee, however, are quotas that are imposed unilaterally (for which there is no existing bilateral agreement) and consultation calls for less sensitive items that are based on formulas[18] and a finding of United States

18. *See id.*

market disruption. All notices of calls are, or should be, printed in the *Federal Register*. The notice will specify the country of origin, the quota category, and the tariff designation of the items in question; will solicit comments or data; and will warn that CITA may later establish quota limits for the designated item. Usually, but not always, quota limits will later be imposed. For example, importers of manmade-fiber textile products (notably flat goods) from the Republic of Korea and Taiwan were faced with such a notice, soon followed by the imposition of quota limits. Litigation over the loss of duty-free generalized system of preference (GSP) status associated with the imposition of textile restraints was the subject of *Luggage & Leather Goods Manufacturers of America, Inc. v. United States*.[19]

Quick reaction by an importer (for example, flying in merchandise or redesigning the item, when permitted,[20] to

19. Luggage & Leather Goods Mfrs. of Am., Inc. v. United States, 7 Ct. Int'l Trade 258 (1984) and 7 Ct. Int'l Trade 337 (1984). This case involves manmade fiber flat goods (such as textile change purses and tobacco pouches). President Reagan, in Executive Order 12,302 of April 1, 1981, amended the list of articles eligible for duty-free treatment to include manmade fiber flat goods. The trade association and a labor union banded together, retained counsel, and challenged the legality of the President's action. Since manmade fiber flat goods were subject to the Multifiber Arrangement (MFA), the flat goods were not eligible to receive duty-free treatment under the GSP program based on 19 U.S.C. § 2463(c)(1)(A). The court found for the association and labor union. Thus, articles subject to textile agreements lose their GSP duty-free eligibility while becoming subject to textile restraints such as visa and quota. Double jeopardy indeed.

20. On May 9, 1984, President Reagan ordered the Treasury Department to promulgate regulations to address the practice of importers' changing goods in a bonded warehouse for the purpose of evading quota limits. Exec. Order No. 12,475, 49 Fed. Reg. 19,955 (1984). These regulations were promulgated and are contained in 19 C.F.R. § 12.130 (1990). Basically, quota merchandise may be substantially transformed by means of manufacture into new and different articles of commerce. If an article is so transformed, it will be considered to be the product of the country in which the last substantial transforma-

take it out of the tariff items covered by the consultation call) may spell the difference between success and disaster. As quota limits become a more widely used United States import-restricting device, it behooves importers of quota merchandise and their counsel to anticipate and plan for unexpected closing of a quota category.

Textile controls often require administration by the government of the countries from which the merchandise will be exported. The foreign government will issue "export licenses" allowing the exportation of the particular items. Often the government will set aside a certain amount of the available quota "rights" or "allowances" for manufacturers who have a history of having exported the item in the past. The rest will be given to new exporters. In order for an exporter to keep its share of quota, it must make sure to use up a certain percentage of its allocated quota.[21]

Because of the necessity of using up the quota, and because of the often high demand by manufacturers, exporters, or importers for particular textile products, there is often a thriving market in the sale of quota licenses.[22] The buying and selling of quota licenses and the addition of their costs to the prices paid by the United States importers raised questions as to the dutiability of quota payments in the valuation of items and assessment of duties by the United States Customs Service.[23]

---

tion occurred. Thus, an article may be transformed from an article whose country of origin has a quota to an article whose country of origin has no quota restriction.

21. *See* King, *New Quota Distribution Regs Posted by Taiwan Ministry*, Women's Wear Daily, Oct. 4, 1983; Ehrlich, *Hong Kong Pricing Still Wild West Shootout*, Daily News Record, Oct. 19, 1983.

22. See Ehrlich, *supra* note 21; Ehrlich, *Record Quota Prices Drive Exporters from Hong Kong*, Women's Wear Daily, July 19, 1983; Kidd, *Quota Rush Plagues Strong Orders in Asia*, Women's Wear Daily, July 15, 1983.

23. *See* chapter 4; *see also* United States v. Getz Bros., 55 C.C.P.A. 11 (1967) (analysis and history of quota payments as nondutiable).

The Customs Service issued a written notice that proposed a change to its interpretive rule on the dutiable status of quota charges in the November 18, 1988 issue of the *Federal Register*. It restated its present rule: "If paid by the buyer to the seller, Customs considers the quota charges part of the transaction value and accordingly, dutiable. If paid to an unrelated party, Customs has not considered the quota charges dutiable." Customs then stated:

> This document proposes that all quota charges paid as a prerequisite to the exportation of foreign merchandise to the U.S. will be dutiable, regardless of to whom they are paid. They will be considered part of the transaction value. This change is proposed as a result of Customs recent examination of "quota charge" transactions revealing that payments for quota charges are directly linked to the price actually paid, or payable for imported merchandise.

Customs invited written commentary from the public on this proposed interpretive rule.

However, on June 8, 1989, certain quota charges[24] were held not dutiable by the United States Court of International Trade (CIT) in *Generra Sportswear Co. v. United States*.[25] In this case the importer agreed to purchase blouses at US $6.00 per blouse from the seller. The seller agreed to obtain on behalf of the importer "Transfer Quota to the United States" at a cost of US $0.95 per blouse. Because of a delay in obtaining quota, the seller was forced to pay US $1.28 instead of US $0.95 per blouse for quota. The importer paid the seller for the blouses by letter of credit, and the quota charges were separately billed to, and paid by, the importer's buying agent. Customs decided to include the cost of the quota charges (US $0.95 per blouse)

24. Customs requires a quota charge statement with textile imports. See appendix 30.
25. Generra Sportswear Co. v. United States, 715 F. Supp. 1101 (Ct. Int'l Trade 1989), *rev'd*, 905 F.2d 377 (Fed. Cir. 1990).

in its appraised value of the blouses. Thus the importer paid duty on this quota charge.

In a strongly worded opinion, the court stated:

> The Court finds the decision by Customs not to be a reasonable interpretation of the statute. Had Congress intended quota charges to be included within transaction value, it would have so provided in subparagraphs (A) through (E) [of section 402(b) of the Trade Agreements Act of 1979]. Not having done so, the obvious conclusion is that the quota charges are not dutiable.

The Customs Service appealed this decision to the U.S. Court of Appeals for the Federal Circuit. On May 22, 1990, that court reversed the CIT and found the quota charge payments to be dutiable. The appeals court stated

> We think Customs' construction of section 1401a(b), that transaction value may include quota charges is permissible. It is reasonable to conclude that these charges were part of the "price actually paid or payable," defined in subsection 1401a(b)(4)(A) as "the total payment. . . ." The term "total payment" is all-inclusive. If Congress had intended to exclude quota payments from transaction value, it could have included them among the explicit exclusions enumerated in section 1401a(b)(3).

Thus these quota charge payments are dutiable.

It remains to be seen whether Customs will go forward with its proposed interpretive rule to make all quota charge payments dutiable, including quota purchased directly from third parties, not the sellers of the merchandise, now that it has won this appeal decision.

Quota rights to export are dispensed by foreign governments to sellers, as noted. Many of these sellers find it more expedient to sell the quota rights than to produce and sell the merchandise. Accordingly, markets for quotas and quota "brokers" have emerged in some countries. Many United States importers have adopted the practice of having their agents go into the quota market and buy quota rights, thus ensuring their ability to ship their goods to the United States market.

The problem of having goods on hand in a foreign country with the quota closed and no quota rights available has led to attempts to circumvent the law by transshipping merchandise and falsifying the name of the country of origin.[26]

Of course, an importer also has a basic right to alter its merchandise to obtain the best possible customs treatment. This principle may be used for legal avoidance of quota restrictions by altering components in such a way as to bring the merchandise under a different, nonquota provision of the HTSUS. For example, if sweaters "in part silk but in chief weight of rayon" are subject to quota, more silk may be added to the mixture to make the sweaters "in chief weight of silk (over 70% by weight)" and thus not subject to quota.

On August 3, 1984, Customs published new textile and textile product country of origin regulations, which had an effective date of September 7, 1984. These regulations were implemented without notice for comment prior to their adoption on the rationale that interim regulations do not constitute a "major rule." These interim regulations have had a major effect on importers that did not know, realize, or appreciate the Customs Service's shifting interpretation and modification of their interim country of origin rules.

An importer of sports jackets assembled in Yugoslavia from components (jacket panels, sleeves, etc.) cut in Italy received a binding country of origin ruling from Customs Headquarters that stated "the assembled garments may be marked to indicate Italy as the country of origin." The importer relied on this ruling and imported the garments until it received a redelivery notice from Customs that indicated a quota/visa violation had occurred because a Yugoslavian

26. *See* chapter 18 on country of origin marking.

visa had not been supplied. Customs assessed a liquidated damages claim against the importer in a amount of $117,657. This amount has been mitigated to $35,300. The moral of the story is that prudent importers should not rely on Customs country of origin marking rulings when textile restraints such as visa and quota apply to their textile products. In multiple country of origin situations a ruling on visa and quota restrictions should be obtained from Customs, especially on all new import operations that commenced after 1984 (e.g., cut, make, and trim (CMT) operations, where the fabric is cut to size in country X and sent to country Y, along with trimmings such as thread and buttons, to be assembled).[27]

The full economic effects of the MFA are not readily evident even to that portion of the public with some knowledge of foreign trade, especially those whose knowledge comes from newspapers and popular periodicals. These arrangements are protectionist in two ways. They limit the quantity of the merchandise to be imported, and they artificially raise the prices to the consumers directly by adding to the foreign prices the cost of the "quota." Over and above this, the cost to the consumers may also be increased by the imposition of duty on the "quota" charges. Insofar as the exporting countries are concerned (these are usually Hong Kong, Taiwan, and Korea), the loss of a portion of the market by reason of the limitation is made up at least in part by the accretions of the quota charges to their dollar exchange balances.

Orderly Marketing Arrangements

Orderly marketing agreements are a mechanism similar to quotas that may be used to control quantities of foreign

27. 19 C.F.R. § 12.130 (1988).

products imported into the United States. Under the Trade Act of 1974, the President may negotiate international agreements limiting importation of goods into the United States. This authority may be invoked only after a finding by the International Trade Commission that the goods have been imported in such an increased quantity as to cause serious injury to domestic industry. The President may employ this option as an alternative to the imposition of higher duties or other import restrictions.[28]

Customs Service Administration of Quotas

Generally, quotas are either administered directly by United States Customs Service Headquarters or administered by other agencies and enforced by the Customs Service. Quotas administered by other agencies may require special procedures or special documentation as directed by the particular agency involved.[29]

The Service administers all entries subject to quota on a "first-come, first-served" basis.[30]

Tariff-rate quotas administered by the Customs Service include those on cattle (HTSUS chapter 1); fresh, chilled, or frozen fish (chapter 3); and whole milk (chapter 4). Among the absolute quotas administered by the Service are those on certain butter substitutes (HTSUS chapter 4), chocolate (chapter 18), and cotton (chapter 52). The Service also administers restraints on cotton, wool, and manmade fibers under an international agreement authorized by the Multifiber Arrangement (MFA). Finally, the Service also administers entry of coffee under the International Coffee

28. 19 U.S.C.A. § 1982 (West 1980).
29. 19 C.F.R. § 132.2 (1987). See, e.g., dairy quotas under 7 U.S.C.A. § 624 (West 1980).
30. Items subject to quota are dispersed throughout the HTSUS. See also U.S. Customs Service Publication 519 (1981) for list of such items.

Agreement of 1976 and the International Coffee Agreement Act of 1980 (HTSUS 901).[31]

Quota priority[32] and status[33] are determined as of the time of the presentation of an entry summary for consumption or withdrawal for consumption in proper form along with estimated duties.[34] Quota status will be acquired by the presentation of an entry or withdrawal for consumption prior to opening of the quota period.[35] But an entry summary may be presented for preliminary review before the merchandise arrives within the port limits. The time of presentation is deemed to be when estimated duties are deposited after arrival of the merchandise within the port limits.[36]

Customs requires an entry/entry summary (Live Entry) to be filed on quota class merchandise. That includes the CF 3461 or the information contained therein, a CF 7501 entry summary form, all the documents required by the customs regulations, and the duties due. An entry alone (Immediate Delivery)—that is, the CF 3461 or the information contained therein and no duties or other required commercial documents—is not allowed unless Customs determines the quota goods to be perishable.

Special procedures are provided for those quotas that the Customs Service expects to be filled rapidly because of high demand and small quota quantities.[37] Entry summaries or withdrawals may be presented twenty-four hours prior to the opening of the new quota. However, such presentation

---

31. 19 U.S.C.A. §§ 1356k–1356n (West Supp. 1989).
32. The "precedence granted to one entry or withdrawal for consumption of quota-class merchandise over other entries or withdrawals of merchandise subject to the same quota." 19 C.F.R. § 132.1(f) (1988).
33. The "standing which entitles quota-class merchandise to admission under an absolute quota, or to a reduced rate of duty under a tariff-rate quota, or to any other quota benefit." 19 C.F.R. § 132.1(g) (1988).
34. 19 C.F.R. § 132.11 (1988).
35. *Id.*
36. 19 C.F.R. § 132.11a (1988).
37. 19 C.F.R. § 132.12 (1988).

will be deemed to have been made at the time the new quota opens. Thus, preliminary review is allowed, but presentation of the documents before quota opening does not provide merchandise quota priority or status.[38] All entries and estimated duties presented at the opening of the quota are deemed simultaneous.[39] If the total presentation of entries exceeds the quota quantity, the Customs Service prorates the quantity that each importer may enter by the ratio of the total quantities sought to be entered to the quota level.[40] When a quota is prorated, the entry summary or withdrawal is returned to the importer for adjustment. In order to keep prorated status, the importer must present the adjusted document and duties within five working days and take delivery within fifteen working days.[41]

After opening day of the quota, quota priority and status are calculated using local time at the ports of entry where the documents are presented or accepted. This procedure was put into effect in September 1978 to eliminate any undue advantage East Coast importers might have had under the prior practice of converting local time to Eastern standard time.[42]

Generally, absolute quota items may not be released under any immediate-delivery procedure unless the Customs Service deems the goods to be perishable merchandise of a class approved by the Service. On tariff-rate quota items, a permit for immediate delivery may be authorized if a bond is filed and estimated duties at the above-quota rate are attached. If the items achieve quota status, refunds are issued.[43]

---

38. 19 C.F.R. § 132.12(a) (1988).
39. 19 C.F.R. § 132.12(b) (1988).
40. 19 C.F.R. § 132.12(c)(1) (1988).
41. 19 C.F.R. § 132.12(c)(2) (1988).
42. *See* Treas. Dec. 78-228 (July 6, 1978).
43. 19 C.F.R. § 132.13 (1988).

Dairy Quotas

Although many of the dairy quotas under 7 U.S.C. § 624 are administered by the Customs Service, certain products (including butter, certain cheeses, and dried milk products) are covered by licensing under the authority of the United States Department of Agriculture.

The Trade Agreements Act of 1979 required the President to proclaim new quotas on cheese as covered by bilateral agreements under the Act.[44] This was fulfilled by proclamation number 4708 and new regulations authorizing licenses in accordance with past practices. Three TSUS items—butter substitutes and two types of chocolate[45]—were not, however, covered by the proclamation; they are administered on a "first-come, first-served" basis by the Customs Service.

The licensing procedures for those items administered by the Department of Agriculture are as follows. In order to import articles subject to dairy quotas, one must obtain a license unless (1) the articles are imported by or for an agency of the United States; (2) the articles are no more than $25 in value and are to be used as samples for taking orders, for personal use of the importer, or for research; or (3) the articles are for display, sampling, or research and written approval has been obtained from the United States Department of Agriculture.[46]

Licenses are obtained from the Department of Agriculture. Eligibility for licenses falls into two basic categories. Historical eligibility refers to quota shares determined as of November 20, 1978. These adjusted quantities are noted in the appendix to 7 C.F.R. part 6. Historical eligibility for licenses of articles group II, III, or IV of appendix 2 from particular

44. 19 U.S.C.A. § 2503 (West 1980).
45. Proclamation No. 4708.
46. 7 C.F.R. § 6.23 (1983).

countries can only be acquired by a person who has obtained eligibility under appendix 1. Eligibility under group V or appendix 2 is determined by submission of proof of prior imports.[47]

Nonhistorical eligibility concerns quota amounts for those who are unable to establish, or who have surrendered, historical eligibility. A notarized statement of intent to import the quota items must be submitted.[48] Supplementary licenses are obtained under similar requirements.[49]

Copper, Steel, and Wine Provisions

Included in the Tariff and Trade Act of 1984 are provisions covering direction to the President to negotiate with foreign countries to reduce copper imports,[50] authority for the President to enforce quantitative limitations and other terms present in bilateral agreements between the United States and steel exporting nations,[51] and direction to the President to have the United States trade representative consult with wine-trading countries in order to reduce or eliminate nontariff and tariff barriers to the United States wine trade.[52]

Other Quotas

Quotas on watches and watch movements allow the Secretaries of Commerce and the Interior to establish limits on

47. 7 C.F.R. § 6.25 (1983).
48. 7 C.F.R. § 6.25(b)(2)(i) (1983).
49. 7 C.F.R. § 6.25 (1983).
50. Tariff & Trade Act of 1984, Pub. L. No. 98-573 § 247, 98 Stat. 2997 (1984).
51. Steel Import Stabilization Act, 19 U.S.C.A. § 2253 note (West Supp. 1989).
52. Wine Equity & Export Expansion Act of 1984, 19 U.S.C.A. §§ 2801–2806 (West Supp. 1989).

the number of watches and watch movements that may be entered free of duty from the Virgin Islands, Guam, and American Samoa.[53] These are generally assembled from imported components with local labor as an economic assist to these areas.

Oil product quotas are administered by the Department of Energy pursuant to presidential proclamation. They control importation of petroleum and petroleum products.[54]

Proclamation 4941 of May 5, 1982, established country-by-country quotas on sugar, syrups, and molasses. The Secretary of Agriculture, the United States trade representative, and the Department of State are authorized to administer the quotas. A certificate-of-eligibility system operates currently.[55]

Under the International Coffee Agreement Act of 1980,[56] the United States became a party to the International Coffee Agreement of 1976. The agreement requires that a fixed price on coffee be honored by all nations that are parties to the Agreement. The United States is also required to limit the entry or withdrawal from warehouse of all coffee imported from countries that are not members of the International Coffee Organization. In addition, the United States must prohibit the entry of any shipment of coffee from a member of the International Coffee Organization that is not accompanied by a valid certificate of origin, a certificate of reshipment, or a certificate of transit.[57]

Voluntary Restraint Agreements

Voluntary restraint agreements (VRAs) place a quantitative restriction on the amount of steel and steel products

---

53. *See* HTSUS General Notes (3)(IV).
54. *See* 10 C.F.R. 213 (1983).
55. 15 C.F.R. § 2011 (1983).
56. 19 U.S.C.A. §§ 1356k–1356n (West Supp. 1983).
57. *Id.*

that can be exported to the United States from certain foreign countries.

The United States entered into VRAs with the major steel suppliers of Asia and Europe (such as Japan and West Germany). The original VRAs were negotiated in 1984. They had a five-year life span, and all the VRAs expired on September 30, 1989. On July 25, 1989, President Bush extended the VRAs for two and one-half years, and the United States renegotiated VRAs with approximately twenty countries, applying them retroactively to October 1, 1989. President Bush has indicated that the renegotiated VRAs will expire by March of 1992 and that he does not support any further extensions.

Under the VRAs, foreign governments allocate quantities to their major steel producers who in turn sell their allocated quantities for export to the United States. The foreign producer prepares a country of origin certificate, and this document serves as the mechanism to control the quantity of steel or steel products exported to the United States. Importers supply this certificate to Customs upon entry, and the merchandise is released. The U.S. government records this quantity for monitoring purposes. Again, these VRAs are scheduled to continue until March of 1992.[58] By that time America's domestic steel producers are expected to compete against their foreign competitors without the benefit of the VRAs.

58. *See* T.D. 90-70, 24 Cust. B. & Dec. 38 at 3 (Sept. 26, 1990).

20. Antidumping Duties and Countervailing Duties

Introduction

This chapter details the two most prevalent import-relief measures offered to American industries beleaguered by competition from foreign imported merchandise: (1) antidumping duties and (2) countervailing duties.

Antidumping duties and countervailing duties are the countermeasures to two practices—dumping and subsidizing—that are believed to distort international trade to the disadvantage of United States commerce.[1] "Dumping" is selling one country's goods in another country's markets at prices less than "fair value."[2] "Subsidies" are bounties or grants bestowed by a government or subdivision of government on the production, manufacture, or exportation of products, with the effect of reducing the price for export and, therefore, providing some competitive advantage in relation to products of another country.[3]

1. S. REP. No. 249, 96th Cong., 1st Sess. 2, *reprinted in* 1979 U.S. CODE CONG. & ADMIN. NEWS 381, 423.
2. *Id.*
3. *Id.*

Antidumping and countervailing duty proceedings are commonplace practices in the world of international trade and, in the United States, are administered by the Commerce Department and the International Trade Commission. Proceedings have been initiated in connection with products ranging from Japanese cellular mobile telephones to finished granite from Italy and Spain.[4]

History of Prior Statutes

One statute that may be considered a predecessor to the current antidumping statutes is the Antidumping Act of 1916.[5] Interestingly, that Act is still in effect, although very few actions have been brought under it.[6] It is a criminal statute and does not require that actual injury to a domestic manufacturer be shown. If injury is shown, one can sue in federal court for treble damages.[7]

Unlike the Antidumping Act of 1916, the Antidumping Act of 1921[8] was a civil statute. Under the 1921 Act, the Department of the Treasury, as the "administering authority," was responsible for determining if a product was being, or was likely to be, sold for less than its fair value. The Tariff Commission, now renamed the International Trade Commission (ITC), was charged with determining if (1) injury or possible injury was caused to an American industry

---

4. *See* Mitsubishi Elec. Corp. v. United States, 700 F. Supp. 538 (Ct. Int'l Trade 1988); Certain Granite from Italy and Spain, 10 I.T.R.D. (BNA) 2484 (Int'l Trade Comm'n 1988).
5. 15 U.S.C.A. § 72 (West 1973).
6. *See In re* Japanese Elec. Prods. Antitrust Litig., 631 F.2d 1069 (3d Cir. 1980); Zenith Radio Corp. v. Matsushita Elec. Co., 494 F. Supp. 1190 (E.D. Pa. 1980).
7. *See* Nevill, *The Antidumping Act of 1916; A War Legacy,* 26 N.Y.L. SCH. L. REV. 535 (1981).
8. 19 U.S.C. §§ 160–171 (1976), *repealed by* Pub. L. No. 96-39, title 1, § 106(a), 93 Stat. 193 (1979).

by the importation of the foreign product or (2) an American industry was being prevented from being established by the importation of the foreign product.[9]

Countervailing duty statutes have existed since 1897.[10] Of particular note is the Tariff Act of 1930, as amended by the Trade Act of 1974.[11] Under the law, the Secretary of the Treasury was authorized to initiate investigations to determine whether a foreign country was providing a subsidy to one of its industries. Upon such a showing, a duty was imposed to offset the advantage of this subsidy.[12] It was not necessary to show that there was any injury to an American industry.[13]

The Trade Agreements Act of 1979 and the Tokyo Round of Multilateral Trade Negotiations

The Trade Agreements Act of 1979[14] made important changes in the law of countervailing and antidumping duties. These changes were made partly because of the desire to implement American obligations under international trade agreements and partly to streamline the procedural aspects of import-relief measures.[15]

The Act essentially implements the results of the Tokyo Round of Multilateral Trade Negotiations (MTN), which was the seventh round of trade negotiations under the General Agreement on Tariffs and Trade (GATT) since 1948. While

9. *Id.*
10. See R. STURM, CUSTOMS LAW AND ADMINISTRATION 683 (1980).
11. 19 U.S.C.A. § 1303 (West 1980).
12. 19 U.S.C.A. § 1303(a) (West 1980).
13. See S. REP. NO. 249, 96th Cong., 1st Sess. 2, *reprinted in* 1979 U.S. CODE CONG. & ADMIN. NEWS 381, 388. *See also* H.R. REP. NO. 317, 96th Cong.
14. Pub. L. No. 96-39, 93 Stat. 144 (1979).
15. S. REP. NO. 249, 96th Cong., 1st Sess. 37–38, *reprinted in* 1979 U.S. CODE CONG. & ADMIN. NEWS 381, 423–24.

the first five rounds dealt with such issues as tariff reductions, attention has now turned to nontariff barriers.[16]

According to the rules adopted by the GATT, neither antidumping nor countervailing duties may be imposed unless the dumping of the imported product or the subsidizing of the product by a foreign government causes or threatens to cause material injury to, or materially retards the establishment of, a domestic industry. Prior to the Trade Agreements Act of 1979, American law provided that some injury must be shown before the imposition of antidumping duties. No such showing was required for countervailing duties unless the imported product was otherwise duty-free and international obligations of the United States required a showing of injury.[17]

The legislative history of the Trade Agreements Act of 1979 notes that the introduction of a "material injury" test before any countervailing or antidumping duty may be imposed on products of countries that assume the obligations of the agreement is the most conspicuous change in current law required by the GATT agreements.[18]

Material injury is defined as harm that is not "inconsequential, immaterial, or unimportant."[19] The ITC, the agency responsible for establishing the existence of material injury, must, under the 1979 Act, consider such factors as the volume of imported merchandise, the effect of imports on prices in the United States for like products, and the impact

---

16. *Id.* For further background on GATT, see *id.* at 387–99; GATT, THE TOYKO ROUND OF MULTILATERAL TRADE NEGOTIATIONS (1979). The eighth round of GATT negotiations, the Uruguay Round, broke up in December 1990 without a conclusion being reached. Further activity is possible.

17. S. REP. NO. 249, 96th Cong., 1st Sess. 37–38, *reprinted in* 1979 U.S. CODE CONG. & ADMIN. NEWS 381, 423–24.

18. *Id.* at 424.

19. 19 U.S.C.A. § 1677(7)(a) (West Supp. 1989); 19 C.F.R. § 207.27 (1988).

on domestic producers of like products. In examining the impact on the affected industry, the ITC must evaluate all economic factors that have a bearing on the state of the industry, including but not limited to output, sales, market share, profit, productivity, return on investment, utilization of capacity, factors affecting domestic prices, negative effect on cash flow, inventories, employment, wages, growth, ability to raise capital, investment, and existing development and production efforts (including efforts to develop a derivative or more advanced version of the product). These economic factors will be evaluated within the context of the business cycle and conditions of competition that are distinctive to the industry.[20]

Other significant procedural changes made by the Trade Agreements Act of 1979 included acceleration of the period for decision on dumping or subsidy complaints, greater transparency of investigations, and earlier and more effective application of provisional measures to imports during an investigation.[21]

The import remedy laws under the amended Tariff and Trade Act of 1984 (TTA)[22] attempt to simplify the procedures by which United States firms unfairly injured by imports can obtain relief. The TTA creates within the International Trade Commission a Trade Remedy Assistance Office,[23] which advises eligible small businesses[24] on availa-

---

20. 19 U.S.C.A. § 1677(7)(c)(iii) (West Supp. 1989).
21. S. REP. NO. 249, 96th Cong., 1st Sess. 38, *reprinted in* 1979 U.S. CODE CONG. & ADMIN. NEWS 381, 424.
22. Pub. L. No. 98-573, 98 Stat. 2948 (1984).
23. Tariff & Trade Act of 1984 (TTA), § 221, 98 Stat. 2989 (1984); 19 U.S.C.A. § 1339 (West Supp. 1989).
24. An eligible small business is any business that, "in the agency's judgment, due to its small size, has neither adequate internal resources nor financial ability to obtain qualified outside assistance in preparing and filing petitions and applications for remedies and benefits under trade laws. . . ." 19 U.S.C.A. § 1339(c) (West Supp. 1989).

ble trade remedies and assists them in the preparation and filing of trade remedy cases.

The TTA extensively amends both the provisions of the Tariff Act of 1930 that specifically deal with countervailing and antidumping duties and the general provisions applicable to both statutes.

First, both statutes now apply to goods sold or likely to be sold in the United States. For example, if a subsidized product is aged before delivery to the United States, it would not be necessary to wait for the goods actually to be sold in the United States before countervailing duty remedies could be invoked. Also, the sale of foreign merchandise will include "any leasing arrangement regarding the merchandise that is equivalent to the sale of the merchandise."[25]

An important provision, which appears in the definitional section of the general provisions, lists criteria that are to be considered by the ITC in order to determine whether a United States industry is threatened with material injury due to imports or sales for importation of any merchandise that is being dumped or subsidized. Ten relevant economic factors are currently listed. The factors include any increase in the production capacity in the exporting country that is likely to increase the imports of the merchandise into the United States, any rapid increase in United States market penetration, and the probability that the merchandise will enter the United States at prices that will have a damaging effect on the domestic price of the merchandise.[26]

Where there is a reasonable basis to believe that upstream subsidies are involved,[27] the TTA enables the administering

25. TTA § 602, 98 Stat. 3024 (1984); 19 U.S.C.A. §§ 1671(a) & 1673 (West Supp. 1989).

26. TTA § 612, 98 Stat. 3033 (1984); 19 U.S.C.A. § 1677(7)(F) (West Supp. 1989).

27. An upstream subsidy occurs when merchandise under countervailing duty investigation was manufactured or produced prior to export

authority to extend the time period within which to make a preliminary countervailing duty determination.[28] The courts have also interpreted this provision to require an upstream subsidy investigation when the International Trade Administration (ITA) seeks to include subsidies on products used in the manufacture of the product originally in question.[29]

Another provision requires that if like merchandise is imported from two or more countries, the ITC must evaluate the cumulative effect of the volume and the price of the imported merchandise when making an injury determination. This provision applies as long as the imports compete with each other and like merchandise domestically produced.[30]

Interlocutory judicial review by the United States Court of International Trade while a countervailing duty or antidumping investigation is in progress will no longer be permitted.[31]

The legislative history reflects that the purposes of these and other amendments in this area are to clarify the countervailing duty and antidumping laws with respect to partic-

---

with the use of a second product (or an "input product") that was itself subsidized by that same country. The subsidy to the input product must bestow a competitive benefit on the merchandise and have a significant effect on the cost of manufacturing or producing the merchandise for an upstream subsidy to exist. *See* 19 C.F.R. § 1677-1(a).

28. *Infra* p. 503.

29. TTA § 613, 98 Stat. 3035 (1984); 19 U.S.C.A. § 1671b(g) (West Supp. 1989) (formerly 19 U.S.C.A. § 1671b(h)). *See* Canadian Meat Council v. United States, 644 F. Supp. 1125 (Ct. Int'l Trade 1987).

30. TTA § 612, 98 Stat. 3033 (1984); 19 U.S.C.A. § 1677(7)(c)(iv). Hence antidumping duties can be levied on the goods of an exporting country that would not cause injury independent of exports from other countries to the United States. *See* Fundicao Tupy S.A. v. United States, 678 F. Supp. 898 (Ct. Int'l Trade), *aff'd*, 859 F.2d 915 (Fed. Cir. 1988).

31. Pub. L. No. 98-573 § 623 (codified as amended in scattered sections of 19 U.S.C.A. and 28 U.S.C.A.).

ular practices, to simplify and improve the administration of these laws in order to reduce the time and expense of processing cases and of providing relief in the public interests, and to assist small businesses in seeking remedies under these and other trade laws.[32]

Omnibus Trade and Competitiveness Act of 1988

Additional significant amendments to antidumping and countervailing duty laws were promulgated under the Omnibus Trade and Competitiveness Act of 1988 (OTCA).[33] Among the important issues addressed was the assessment of "dumping by nonmarket economy countries."[34] If a country suspected of dumping has a nonmarket economy the standard tests for assessing dumping are severely compromised, because domestic prices do not reflect market prices. Thus, an alternative method of assessing foreign market value is often necessary. Until the OTCA, attempts were made to assess home market price in a nonmarket economy by looking to the home market price in a comparable economy of a market economy country. The OTCA instead directs the administering authority first to compare the value of factors of production—such as the value of raw materials, equipment, manufacturing and labor cost to produce such goods—in a comparable market economy. Only if factors of production cannot be assessed will a third country price comparison be used to determine foreign market value.

32. HOUSE COMM. ON WAYS AND MEANS, 98TH CONG., 2D SESS., SUMMARY OF PROVISIONS OF TRADE AND TARIFF ACT OF 1984, 26 (Comm. Print 1984).
33. Omnibus Trade and Competitiveness Act of 1988 (OTCA), Pub. L. No. 100-418, 102 Stat. 1107 (1988). For an in-depth outline of the section of this Act relevant to countervailing and antidumping duties, see G. Kaplan & C. Tai, *Countervailing and Antidumping Duty Law in The Trade Bill of 1988* in THE NEW TRADE LAW: OMNIBUS TRADE AND COMPETITIVENESS ACT OF 1988 at 9–36 (1988).
34. *Id.* § 1316. 19 U.S.C. § 1677b(c).

Other provisions in the OTCA concerning antidumping duties include a provision governing a domestic industry's request for the United States trade representative (USTR) to intervene on its behalf with the government of a country from which, it believes, an enterprise is dumping in the United States[35] and several provisions which primarily seek to enhance antidumping protection by monitoring:

1. Whether transfer pricing fails to fully reflect the cost of production of a major input which has been supplied by a related party;[36]
2. Whether a market is fictitious;[37]
3. Downstream products the components of which are under current review;[38] and
4. Multiple offenders who manufacture short life cycle merchandise.[39]

The OTCA establishes criteria for allowing the posting of security in lieu of a deposit of the estimated antidumping duties.[40]

The most important provision in the OTCA concerning countervailing duties further refines the specificity test by which the United States determines to what extent foreign government subsidies benefit specific industries. Generally, countervailing duties are assessed where a foreign government provides subsidies to one or more specific enterprises or industries. Under the OTCA, countervailing duties can also be assessed where the subsidies of a foreign govern-

---

35. *Id.* § 1317; 19 U.S.C. § 1677k.
36. *Id.* § 1318; 19 U.S.C. § 1677b(e)(3). This situation can give rise to "input dumping," where a major ingredient is provided to a related entity at less than the cost of producing that ingredient.
37. *Id.* § 1319; 19 U.S.C. § 1677b(a)(5).
38. *Id.* § 1320; 19 U.S.C. § 1677i.
39. *Id.* § 1323.
40. *Id.* § 1325; 19 U.S.C. §§ 1673e(c)(1) & 1673e(c)(4).

ment, even though generally available to its indigenous industries, are in reality of benefit only to one or several industries.[41]

Where a country does not honor a subsidized code commitment to the United States or asserts it will not, the OTCA authorizes the USTR to revoke the injury test requirement for countervailing duty assessments, thereby increasing the likelihood that countervailing duties will be imposed on that country's exports to the United States.[42] Under the OTCA, subsidies for an unprocessed agricultural product are treated as subsidies for the agricultural product after it is processed if "the demand for the prior stage product is substantially dependent on the demand for the latter stage product" and "the processing operation adds only limited value to the raw commodity."[43]

Most important is how the OTCA responds to the globalization of business enterprises. Where subsidies are provided to an international consortium, directly or to participating enterprises, by more than one country, the OTCA requires that they be cumulated.[44]

Relevant to both antidumping and countervailing duties, the globalization of the chain of value-adding processing has enabled manufacturers to divide and shift stages of production to several countries and, in so doing, circumvent antidumping and countervailing duty laws. To meet this challenge, the OTCA enables the Commerce Department to expand the scope of antidumping or countervailing duty orders to account for patterns of trade, whether parties contributing to the product along the value chain are related, and whether imports of parts or components increased since the issuance of the order. Criteria are also provided to

---

41. *Id.* § 1312; 19 U.S.C. § 1677(5).
42. *Id.* § 1314; 19 U.S.C. § 1671c.
43. *Id.* § 1313; 19 U.S.C. § 1677-2.
44. *Id.* § 1315; 19 U.S.C. § 1671(d).

enable Commerce to include in an order goods that have been subject to minor alterations after the investigation has begun and to enable Commerce to include merchandise developed after the initiation of the investigation.[45]

The OTCA also contains several provisions relevant to the injury determinations. Where the importing of a processed agricultural product is being investigated, the industry affected can include producers of the raw agricultural product together with producers of the processed agricultural product if the processed good is processed from the "raw agricultural product through a single continuous line of production" and if there exists a "substantial coincidence of economic interest between the producers or growers of the raw agricultural product and the processors of the processed agricultural product."[46]

The OTCA takes one step beyond the provision under the Tariff and Trade Act of 1984 which allows cumulation of volume in assessing material injury, by providing for cumulation of volume in determining a "threat of material injury." The provision enables the commission to "cumulatively assess the volume and price effects of imports from two or more countries if such imports (1) compete with each other and with like products of the domestic industry in the U.S. market and (2) are subject to [an antidumping or countervailing duty investigation]." This provision is applied to assess injury where there is a rapid increase in imports that will likely result in injury or where a probability exists that imports will enter at a price resulting in a depression or suppression of domestic prices of such merchandise. The provision's primary significance is that it allows cumulation of imports under investigation for dumping together with imports under investigation for subsidies. The commission is not required to cumulate negligi-

45. *Id.* § 1321; 19 U.S.C. § 1677j.
46. *Id.* § 1326; 19 U.S.C. § 1677(4)(E).

ble imports including imports under the scope of a Free Trade Area Agreement that was implemented prior to 1987.[47]

Furthermore the ITC must also consider "the actual and potential negative effects [of the imports] on the existing development and production efforts of the domestic industry, *including efforts to develop a derivative or more advanced version of the like product*," both in the ITC's evaluation of relevant factors[48] and in the ITC's assessment of threat of material injury.[49]

A variety of other provisions under the OTCA further modify antidumping and countervailing duty law. Among the remaining provisions it is noteworthy that antidumping and countervailing duty are not eligible for refund under drawback.[50]

In addition to the recent amendments under the OTCA, the United States–Canada Free Trade Agreement establishes a binational panel to review final antidumping or countervailing duty determinations assessed by either the United States or Canada on transactions covered by the Agreement. The binational panel is available to replace domestic judicial review of a final determination upon the government invoking the panel either on its own initiative or at the request of an interested party.[51]

The following sections of this chapter will translate into

---

47. *Id.* § 1330; 19 U.S.C. § 1677(7)(F)(iv) & (v). *Compare* 19 U.S.C. § 1677(7)(C)(iv) promulgated under the TTA of 1984, *with* note 30 *supra*.
48. *Id.* § 1328 (emphasis added); 19 U.S.C. § 1677(7)(B) & (C)(iii)(iv). The Act also requires the ITC to explain its analysis of relevant factors.
49. *Id.* § 1329. 19 U.S.C. § 1677(7)(F)(i)(x).
50. *Id.* § 1334. 19 U.S.C. § 1677h.
51. Chapter 19 (Article 1904) of the U.S.–Canada Free Trade Agreement was implemented in the United States under Pub. L. No. 100-449 § 405. *See also* 19 C.F.R. 207 (1989); 19 U.S.C.A. § 1516a (West Supp. 1989).

practical terms the procedural and substantive law of import relief—antidumping and countervailing duties—as promulgated by the Trade Agreement Act of 1979 and relevant sections of trade acts through the OTCA and the United States–Canada Free Trade Implementation Act of 1988. Important aspects of the judicial review of import relief determinations will also be discussed in the last section of this chapter.

Antidumping Duty—Analysis[52]

Simply stated, antidumping duties will be imposed when the administering authority, the Department of Commerce, determines that a class or kind of foreign merchandise is being or is likely to be sold in the United States at less than fair value and the ITC determines that an industry in the United States is materially injured or threatened with material injury, or that the establishment of an industry is materially retarded, by reason of imports of that merchandise.[53]

Not surprisingly, the above brief summation is an oversimplification of complex antidumping procedures. Of particular importance are the time periods for the filing of documents, which must be strictly observed.

Investigation Procedures

An investigation to determine if antidumping duties should be imposed may be initiated by the Department of

52. 19 U.S.C.A. §§ 1673–1673h (West 1980 & Supp. 1989); 19 C.F.R. 207 & 353 (1988).

53. 19 U.S.C.A. § 1673 (West 1980). Note that Reorganization Plan No. 3, 45 Fed. Reg. 889 (1979), designated Commerce as the administering authority.

Commerce or after a petition is filed by

1. A manufacturer, producer, or wholesaler in the United States of a like product that will be the subject of the investigation;
2. A certified union or recognized union or group of workers that is representative of an industry engaged in manufacture, production, or wholesale commerce in the United States of a like product;
3. A trade or business association, a majority of whose members manufacture, produce, or wholesale a like product in the United States;
4. An association, a majority of whose members is composed of interested parties described above with respect to a like product; and
5. A coalition or trade association which is representative of either
   - Agricultural processors,
   - Agricultural processors and producers, or
   - Agricultural processors and growers

   to the extent that the USTR does not notify the ITA and the Commission that the application of this subparagraph is inconsistent with U.S. obligations.[54]

The party claiming injury must file a petition with the ITA and with the ITC on the same day.[55] The petition must contain the basic elements needed to establish an antidumping case and any information reasonably available to the petitioner that supports the allegations.[56]

Specifically, the petition should include

1. The name and address of the petitioner and any other person the petitioner represents;
2. The identity of the industry on behalf of which the

54. *See* 19 U.S.C.A. §§ 1673a(b) & 1677(9) (West Supp. 1989).
55. 19 U.S.C.A. § 1673a(b)(2) (West 1980).
56. 19 C.F.R. § 353.12 (1989).

petitioner is filing, including the names and addresses of other persons in the industry;

3. A statement indicating whether the petitioner has filed for import relief under sections 337 or 702 of the Act (19 U.S.C. §§ 1337, 1671a), sections 201 or 301 of the Trade Act of 1974 (19 U.S.C. §§ 2251, 2411), or section 232 of the Trade Expansion Act of 1962 (19 U.S.C. § 1862) with respect to the merchandise;
4. A detailed description of the merchandise that defines the requested scope of the investigation, including technical characteristics and uses of the merchandise, and its current U.S. tariff classification number;
5. The name of the home market country and, if the merchandise is imported from a country other than the home market country, the name of the intermediate country or the country through which the merchandise is transshipped;
6. The names and addresses of each person the petitioner believes sells the merchandise at less than fair value and the proportion of total exports to the United States which each person accounted for during the most recent twelve-month period;
7. All factual information (particularly documentary evidence) relevant to the calculation of the United States price of the merchandise and the foreign market value of such or similar merchandise, in accordance with the methods of calculation provided in subpart D of 19 C.F.R. part 353 (19 C.F.R. §§ 353.41 *et seq.*) (if unable to furnish information on foreign sales or costs, provide information on production costs in the United States, adjusted to reflect production costs in the home market country of the merchandise);
8. If the merchandise is from a country that the secre-

tary has found to be a state-controlled-economy country, factual information relevant to the calculation of foreign market value;[57]

9. The volume and value of the merchandise during the most recent two-year period and any other recent period that the petitioner believes to be more representative or, if the merchandise was not imported during the two-year period, information as to the likelihood of its sale for importation;
10. The name and address of each person the petitioner believes imports or, if there were no importations, is likely to import the merchandise;
11. Factual information regarding material injury, threat of material injury, or material retardation, as described in 19 C.F.R. §§ 207.11 and 207.26;
12. If the petitioner alleges "critical circumstances" under 19 C.F.R. § 353.16, factual information regarding:
    - Material injury which is difficult to repair;
    - Massive imports in a relatively short period; and
    - Either: (A) a history of dumping; or (B) the importer's knowledge that the producer or reseller was selling the merchandise at less than its foreign market value, as described in 19 C.F.R. § 353.16(a); and
13. Any other factual information on which the petitioner relies.

In filing a petition, an interested party may use form ITA-357P which will be furnished by the Department upon request. If asked to do so, Department personnel will assist petitioners in filling out forms. The use of such forms shall not be mandatory, provided the information required

57. The regulations for calculation are provided in 19 C.F.R. 353 subpt. D, using a method described in § 353.52.

thereby and reasonably available to the petitioner is otherwise included in the petition.[58]

Within *20 days* after the filing of the petition, Commerce must determine whether the petition alleges the necessary elements for relief, i.e., material injury by reason of dumped imports. If the determination is affirmative, Commerce initiates an investigation; if negative, all proceedings end.[59]

Within *45 days* after the petition is filed or an investigation is initiated by Commerce, the ITC must determine whether there is reasonable indication that the dumping caused material injury or threat of material injury to domestic industry or that the dumping materially retards the establishment of an industry. If the finding is negative, proceedings end.[60]

In assessing whether there is a reasonable indication of injury, the ITC may hold a preliminary-injury conference before its director of operations.[61] Notice of such a hearing must be given in the *Federal Register*. Briefs may be submitted at the hearing. Upon completion of the hearings, a transcript will also be prepared.[62]

As part of the preliminary-injury phase, the ITC will issue injury questionnaires to all importers and domestic producers of the merchandise being investigated. In order to strengthen their case, the petitioners should work in conjunction with the ITC staff to modify the questionnaire in order best to fit the needs of the industry involved. This will facilitate more detailed responses. The defendant should also seek input into the drafting of the questionnaire, because generally the responses to the questionnaire

58. Some aspects have been deleted; *see* 19 C.F.R. § 353.12(b) (1989).
59. 19 U.S.C.A. § 1673a(c) (West Supp. 1989).
60. 19 U.S.C.A. § 1673b(a) (West Supp. 1989).
61. 19 C.F.R. § 207.17 (1987).
62. 19 C.F.R. § 207.15 (1987).

and published statistical information are the principal data used by the ITC staff in its report.[63]

From the standpoint of defending against an antidumping action, the two phases of the procedure described above offer an opportunity for importers and their foreign suppliers to begin effectuating a strategy of defense. A defendant should begin by attempting to have the petition rejected. Although this is extremely difficult, a defendant should analyze the petition carefully to ascertain if the elements necessary to sustain it are in fact present.[64]

The defendant should check the petition to see if each element prerequisite to a petition is substantiated with sufficient facts. The appropriateness of a change in product definition included in the petition should be explored as should the question whether that change would be advantageous to the defendant. Finally, the defendant should decide if the circumstances of the petition's filing might indicate possible grounds for the petition's withdrawal.[65]

The defendant should appear at the preliminary ITC investigation hearing, because this will afford it the opportunity to contest the existence of any reasonable indication of injury. In addition, the defendant can, during the hearing, seek a narrower product definition. The defendant can suggest to the ITC various sources the ITC should consult in gathering data for the final-injury investigation. Finally, the hearing allows the defendant to discover the arguments

---

63. Each questionnaire can have the force of a subpoena. 19 C.F.R. § 207.8 (1983). *See* Barshefsky & O'Cunningham, *The Prosecution of Antidumping Actions Under the Trade Agreements Act of 1979*, 6 N.C.J. INT'L L. & COM. REG. 307, 332 (1981).

64. *See* Hemmendinger & Barringer, *The Defense of Antidumping and Countervailing Duty Investigations Under the Trade Agreements Act of 1979*, 6 N.C.J. INT'L L. & COM. REG. 427, 429 (1981) (an excellent article and an important source for the discussion of defenses in this chapter) (hereinafter Hemmendinger & Barringer).

65. *Id.*

the petitioners will use to substantiate their claim when the final-injury determination is under way.[66]

If the ITC's preliminary decision on reasonable indication of injury is affirmative, within *160 days* after the petition has been filed or an investigation is initiated, Commerce must make a preliminary determination on whether there is a reasonable basis to believe or suspect that dumping exists. If the case is extraordinarily complicated, Commerce may extend the deadline for a preliminary decision to *210 days*. The number and complexity of the transactions to be investigated or adjustments to be considered, the novelty of the issue, and the number of firms whose activities must be investigated are among the guidelines for applying the "extraordinarily complicated" standard.[67] The petitioner may also make a timely request for an extension to 210 days.[68]

In contrast, if special conditions are met in which verification of respondent's data is waived, the initial 160 days preceding Commerce's "preliminary less than fair value determination" may be reduced to *90 days* after the date of filing.[69]

If Commerce's preliminary determination is affirmative, it requires the posting of a bond for entries of the dumped imports in an amount equal to the estimated margin of dumping. In addition, all liquidations of the entries of merchandise entered (or withdrawn from the warehouse for consumption) on or after the publication of the preliminary determination are suspended.[70] The investigation will then continue. The ITC initiates an investigation to determine

66. *Id.* at 430–31. Material injury cannot be "inconsequential, immaterial, or unimportant." 19 U.S.C.A. § 1677(7)(A) (West 1980).
67. 19 U.S.C.A. §§ 1673b(b) & 1673b(c) (West 1980 & Supp. 1989); 19 C.F.R. § 353.15 (1989).
68. 19 U.S.C.A. § 1673b(c) (West 1980 & Supp. 1989).
69. *See* 19 C.F.R. § 353.15(e) (1989).
70. 19 U.S.C.A. § 1673b(d) (West 1980 & Supp. 1989).

whether injury exists. Even if Commerce's preliminary determination was negative, the ITC's investigation still continues.[71]

It has been noted that "[t]he period between the initiation of an investigation by the Department of Commerce and its preliminary determination is by far the most important phase of an antidumping proceeding."[72] Of particular importance in this phase are the antidumping questionnaires, sent out by Commerce to foreign manufacturers.[73] In deciding if there have been sales at less than fair value, a comparison is made of the "United States price"[74] to the "foreign market value"[75] of the goods subject to the investigation. In creating a response to a questionnaire, the defendant should pay close attention to the advantageous ways to construe the terms "foreign market value" and "United States price." Although Commerce will make the final decision on how to calculate "foreign market value" or "United States price," a defendant is permitted to suggest the manner of calculation and submit evidence supporting its view.

Depending on the circumstances, foreign market value may be measured by (1) sales in the home market of the exporter, (2) third-country sales, (3) constructed value, or (4) value of the factors of production in a market economy comparable to the nonmarket economy of the exporting country.[76] The choice of one standard over another can bring about different results. The measure of foreign market value preferred by Commerce is sales in the home market of the exporter to which expenses incidental to preparing the goods for export to the United States are added.[77]

---

71. *See* 19 U.S.C.A. § 1673d(b) (West 1980 & Supp. 1989).
72. Hemmendinger & Barringer, *supra* note 64, at 431.
73. *Id.*
74. 19 U.S.C.A. § 1677a(a) (West 1980).
75. 19 U.S.C.A. § 1677b(a) (West 1980 & Supp. 1989).
76. *Id.*
77. *Id.*; 19 C.F.R. § 353.3 (1987).

If there is a possibility, however, of using other than home market sales, and if doing so would be to the benefit of the defendant, an attempt should be made to convince Commerce to utilize another standard.

If the product sold in the home market is not sufficiently similar to that sold to the United States, or if the quantity sold in the home market is less than 5 percent of all sales to countries other than the United States, third-country sales or constructed value may be used.[78] The defendant will therefore want to determine which third-country market will be most favorable. A comparison of the similarity of the products sold in the home market, the third-country market, and the United States is also in order. Finally, defendant will also want to look into the possibility of using constructed value as a standard. Foreign market value as determined by constructed value is the sum of the cost of materials, cost of fabrication, general expenses of not less than 10 percent of the material and fabrication costs, and a profit of not less than 8 percent of all costs.[79]

Goods imported from a state-controlled (nonmarket) economy country pose formidable complications in determining their foreign market value. Commerce will first endeavor to calculate foreign market value in accordance with home market value or the value of such or similar merchandise sold in a third country. If the standard methods will not provide an accurate measure of home market value, as is likely to be found here, Commerce will use a constructed value based on the value of "factors of production" of such merchandise in a market economy country at a comparable level of economic development and in which comparable merchandise is produced in significant quantity. Based on the best information available, Commerce will calculate the

78. 19 C.F.R. §§ 353.46, 353.48, 353.49, 353.50 (1989).

79. 19 U.S.C.A. § 1677b(e) (West 1980 & Supp. 1989); 19 C.F.R. § 353.50 (1989).

value of such factors as, but not limited to, labor hours, raw materials, energy and other utilities consumed, and represented capital cost (including depreciation).

Should Commerce determine that there is not adequate information to determine constructed value based on factors of production, Commerce shall determine foreign market value by comparing similar merchandise produced in a non-state-controlled economy at a comparable stage of development as the exporter. If a non-state-controlled economy at that stage of economic development is not available for comparison, Commerce will select a non-state-controlled economy producing similar goods and make adjustments for economic differences.[80]

In determining the basis of foreign market value using merchandise sold either in the home market or in a third country, one should pay close attention to the question of similarity of merchandise. Generally, if the merchandise is not identical, it is possible that Commerce will allow price adjustments.[81]

The second basis for determining whether a product has been sold at less than fair value is the United States price. The United States price may be based upon either "purchase price" or "exporter's sale price." Purchase price is used when a foreign manufacturer or reseller sells to an unrelated customer in the United States. Exporter's sale price is used when the merchandise has not been legally "sold" as of the time of importation and is, therefore, being

---

80. 19 U.S.C.A. § 1677b(c) (West 1980 & Supp. 1989); 19 C.F.R. § 353.52 (1989). "The results of these cases have nothing to do with reality. They are just random, and you could do just as well with a roulette wheel." Former Deputy Assistant Secretary of Commerce for Import Administration Gary Horlick, *quoted in* 8 U.S. IMPORT WEEKLY (BNA) 293 (May 25, 1983).

81. 19 C.F.R. § 353.57 (1989).

imported for the benefit of the exporter by its American subsidiary.[82]

The use of either purchase price or exporter's price will determine which sales will be considered as falling within the investigative time period. If exporter's sale price is used, foreign market value is the price at which the merchandise was sold in the principal market at the time of exportation to the United States.[83] If purchase price is used, foreign market value is the price at the date of the purchase or agreement to purchase the investigated merchandise.[84]

After determining the merchandise and sales that will be covered under the investigation, the defendant should consider obtaining adjustments to the foreign market value and the United States price. Those adjustments may help to close the gap between the United States price and the foreign market value, and therefore avoid a finding of dumping by Commerce. Adjustments are granted for quantity discount sales on the home market,[85] differences in the level of trade,[86] differences in merchandise,[87] and differences in the circumstances of sale.[88]

Within 75 days after preliminary determination (or 135 days upon request by the exporter when the "preliminary less than fair value determination" was affirmative or upon request by petitioners when it was negative), Commerce

---

82. 19 U.S.C.A. §§ 1677a(a) & 1677a(b) (West 1980 & Supp. 1989); 19 C.F.R. § 353.41 (1989).
83. 19 U.S.C.A. § 1677b(a)(1) (West 1980). For purposes of comparing value, the exchange rate in effect at the time of the sale of the goods in the United States is the rate used in converting foreign market value into U.S. dollars. Washington Red Raspberry Comm'n v. United States, 859 F.2d 898 (Fed. Cir. 1988).
84. 19 U.S.C.A. § 1677b(a)(1) (West 1980).
85. 19 U.S.C.A. § 1677b(a)(4) (West 1980 & Supp. 1989).
86. 19 C.F.R. § 353.58 (1989).
87. 19 C.F.R. § 353.57 (1989).
88. *See, e.g.*, 19 C.F.R. § 353.56 (1989).

must make a final determination of whether dumping exists. If that final determination is negative, the investigation terminates upon publication of that determination in the *Federal Register*.[89]

If the determination is affirmative (following an affirmative preliminary determination), the ITC must make a final determination of whether a domestic industry is materially injured by reason of dumped imports before the later of:

1. The 120th day after Commerce makes its affirmative preliminary determination or
2. The 45th day after Commerce makes its final determination.[90]

When Commerce's preliminary determination is negative, the ITC's final determination on material injury is made 75 days after Commerce's final determinations.[91]

If the ITC's final determination is affirmative, an antidumping order requiring the imposition of antidumping duties should be issued within 7 days after notification of the ITC's determination.[92] That notice must be published in the *Federal Register*.[93] The assessment of duties will equal the amount by which the foreign market value exceeds the selling price in the United States. The Customs Service must begin assessing those duties within six months after the date on which the Secretary of Commerce has received satisfactory information upon which to base an assessment.[94]

---

89. 19 U.S.C.A. §§ 1673d(a)(1) & 1673d(a)(2) (West 1980 & Supp. 1989); 19 C.F.R. §§ 353.20(a), 353.20(b) & 353.20(d) (1989).
90. 19 U.S.C.A. § 1673d(b)(2) (West 1980 & Supp. 1989).
91. 19 U.S.C.A. § 1673d(b)(3) (West 1980 & Supp. 1989).
92. 19 U.S.C.A. § 1673e(a) (West 1980 & Supp. 1989); 19 C.F.R. § 353.21 (1989).
93. 19 U.S.C.A. § 1673d(d) (West 1980 & Supp. 1989); 19 C.F.R. § 353.20 (1989).
94. 19 U.S.C.A. § 1673e(a) (West 1980 & Supp. 1989); 19 C.F.R. § 353.21 (1989).

Under certain circumstances, an investigation may be suspended prior to final determination. For example, if the exporters accounting for substantially all of the imports of the merchandise under investigation agree to eliminate the dumping or to cease exports of the merchandise to the United States within six months of the date on which the investigation is suspended, no duties will be assessed. If extraordinary circumstances are present and the exporter agrees to revise prices so as to eliminate the entire injurious effect of the imports, the investigation may be suspended. If, however, within 20 days of the date of the publication of the notice of suspension, the exporter or any other party involved in the investigation requests continuation, the suspended investigation must be continued.[95]

Upon receiving a review petition, the ITC will determine if the injurious effects of the imports have been eliminated completely by the agreement. If it is determined that the injurious effects have not been eliminated, then the investigation must resume. If an agreement resulting in a suspension of an investigation is being violated, the investigation must resume and an antidumping order must issue.[96] An antidumping order will also be issued if an interested party had previously requested continuation of the suspended investigation and the ITC and Commerce subsequently made an affirmative final determination.[97]

In cases involving persistent dumping (more than one dumping order is in effect) of certain products, a program is to be established in order to monitor, for a period not to exceed one year, imports of those products from "any additional supplier country."[98] A formal investigation will be

---

95. 19 U.S.C.A. §§ 1673c(b)–(j) (West 1980); 19 C.F.R. § 353.18 (1989).
96. *Id.*
97. *Id.*
98. An additional supplier country is "a country regarding which no antidumping investigation is currently pending, and no antidumping duty order is currently in effect, with respect to imports of the class

initiated if it is found to be warranted based on the information obtained during the monitoring period.

A recent provision to monitor downstream product dumping applies to imports of downstream products which contain a major part, component, assembly, subassembly, or material which has been subject to a dumping finding or subsidy finding of 15 percent or more in the past five years.[99]

Administrative Review and Revocation of Antidumping Duties

Commerce is no longer required to conduct annual reviews on its own initiative. Although Commerce may initiate a review, a review is only required where an appropriate party requests a review and meets those conditions set forth in the regulations. Generally these criteria are procedural, but there are instances where the petitioner must show good cause.

There are two basic types of administrative reviews. One type of review is for those parties seeking to prolong or enhance an antidumping order by challenging a duty order or a suspension of investigation agreement. The other type of review is for those parties seeking to revoke an antidumping duty order or terminate a suspended antidumping duty investigation. The following highlights the more important rules regarding these two types of reviews.

Assessing Duty Orders and Suspension of Investigation Agreements

A review for the benefit of a party wishing to prolong or enhance an antidumping order will generally seek to deter-

---

or kind" covered by this section. 19 U.S.C.A. § 1673a(a)(2) (West Supp. 1989).

99. Omnibus Trade Act of 1988 § 1320.

mine whether a signatory of a suspension of investigation agreement had violated that agreement or whether the determination of foreign market value was inappropriate. Additionally, changed circumstances, for example that would indicate injury to domestic producers, warrant the administrative authority to modify a duty order or suspension of investigation agreement.[100] Let us now take a closer look at the regulations regarding these reviews.

Where an interested party requests a review for appropriate reasons other than change of circumstances, a request may be made in writing each year during the anniversary month of the publication of the order. After receipt of a written request and after giving notice in the *Federal Register*, the Secretary of Commerce must review and reassess the amount of any antidumping duty and review the status of any agreement made that suspended an investigation.[101]

The results of a review should be published along with notice of any duty assessed, estimated duty to be deposited, or resumption of any investigation.[102] The Secretary will determine the amount of the antidumping duty by calculating the foreign market value and United States price of merchandise under investigation. The amount by which the foreign market value exceeds that of the United States price will determine the duty to be assessed.[103]

Upon the initiative of Commerce or upon proper request by an interested party, a review of a duty order or a suspension of investigation agreement may take place to determine whether changed circumstances require the modification of

100. 19 C.F.R. § 353.22 (1989).
101. 19 U.S.C.A. § 1675(a) (West 1980 & Supp. 1989); 19 C.F.R. § 353.22 (1989). Parties who may submit a request for review are delineated in 19 C.F.R. § 353.2(k) (1989).
102. 19 U.S.C.A. § 1675(a) (West 1980 & Supp. 1989); 19 C.F.R. § 353.22 (1989).
103. 19 U.S.C.A. § 1675(a)(2) (West 1980 & Supp. 1989).

a duty order or a suspension of investigation agreement.[104] The ITC may investigate whether, because of changed circumstances, an agreement continues to eliminate the total injurious effects of imports or whether, if an antidumping duty were to be revoked, a United States industry would not be threatened with injury or its establishment retarded.[105] If the ITC determines that the injurious effects of imports are no longer eliminated in accordance with the agreement, the Secretary of Commerce and the ITC will proceed as though the agreement has been violated on that date. But no duty under any subsequent order will be assessed on merchandise entered or withdrawn from a warehouse for consumption before that date.[106]

In contrast to a review request based on the alleged violation of agreement by an exporter or based on improper determination of foreign market value, "changed circumstance reviews may be requested at any time including periods other than anniversary months." Commerce, however, "will not initiate [a changed circumstance] review before the month of the second annual anniversary of the publication of the original [preliminary] order or suspension, unless the Secretary of Commerce finds that good cause exists."[107]

As part of the review, the Secretary of Commerce will accept written views on proposed revisions. Normally these views will not be processed sooner than 90 days before a redetermination is due for publication. Questionnaires will be sent 85 days before that date. Reply is expected within 30 days.[108]

Disclosure to interested parties of nonconfidential infor-

---

104. 19 C.F.R. § 353.22(f) (1989).
105. 19 C.F.R. §§ 353.22(f) & 207.45 (1989).
106. 19 U.S.C.A. § 1675(e) (West 1980 & Supp. 1989).
107. 19 C.F.R. § 355.22(f)(2)(3) (1989).
108. 19 C.F.R. § 353.22 (1989).

mation will be made about 30 days prior to the date a redetermination is due for publication. Confidential information may also be made available, but only pursuant to a protective order.[109]

An opportunity to present oral and written views may be requested by any party to whom disclosure was made. After that opportunity to comment on the proposed redetermination, a revised antidumping order will be published in the *Federal Register*.[110]

Assessing Whether to Revoke Duties or Terminate a Suspended Investigation

The Secretary of Commerce may revoke a duty order, in whole or in part, or terminate a suspended investigation under certain circumstances.

If all producers and resellers covered by the order or the suspension agreement have sold the merchandise at not less than foreign market value over three consecutive years and they are unlikely to sell at less than foreign market value in the future, the Secretary of Commerce may fully revoke an order or terminate a suspended agreement.[111]

If only some of the group of producers or resellers meet the above two criteria, the Secretary may revoke the order in part on condition that those producers or resellers agree in writing that the duty order will be reinstated if they sell the merchandise at less than foreign market value after the order is revoked. The agreement concludes when all producers or resellers are no longer subject to the order.[112]

The Secretary may revoke an order or terminate a suspended investigation on his or her own initiative after three

---

109. *Id.*
110. *Id.*
111. 19 C.F.R. § 353.25(a)(1) (1990).
112. 19 C.F.R. § 353.25(a)(2) (1990).

years from the publication of the antidumping order or suspension or upon request by a petitioner during the third and subsequent annual anniversary months of the publication of an order or suspension of investigation.[113]

Prior to such a revocation or termination, the Secretary will publish a notice of tentative determination to revoke or terminate.[114] After the notice, the Secretary will determine whether revocation or termination is justified. If an application is based upon a claim that all sales have been made at fair value, the firms involved must show proof that there have been no sales at less than foreign market value up to the date of publication of the notice. Upon that showing, the Secretary may issue an affirmative determination.[115]

Changes in circumstance can lead to revocation of orders in whole or in part, or to a termination of a suspended investigation. A change of circumstance worthy of consideration can be that the order or suspended investigation is no longer of concern to interested parties or any other change of circumstance sufficient to warrant revocation of the order or termination of the suspended investigation.[116]

The rules applicable to administrative review of a duty order and of a suspended investigation due to changed circumstances have been addressed in the previous section. Based on a changed circumstances review, the Secretary may decide to revoke a duty order or terminate a suspended investigation agreement in accordance with the regulatory requirements. These requirements include publication of notice of consideration of revocation of the duty order (or of

---

113. 19 U.S.C.A. § 1675(c) (West 1980 & Supp. 1989); 19 C.F.R. § 353.25 (1989). (19 C.F.R. § 353.25(b) notes that an "anniversary month" is the calendar month on which the anniversary of the publication of the order or suspension occurs.)

114. 19 U.S.C.A. § 1675 (West 1980 & Supp. 1989); 19 C.F.R. § 353.25 (1989).

115. 19 C.F.R. § 353.25 (1989).

116. 19 C.F.R. § 353.25(d)(1)(1989).

termination of suspended investigation), written notice to each interested party, a verification of factual information supplied by the parties and, upon publishing the results of the review, inclusion of the Secretary's decision both at the preliminary stage of review and at the final steps of revision, along with proper notice should the preliminary or final decision be affirmative.[117]

If, after four years since the publication of the duty order or suspension of investigation, no one has requested a review of a duty order or a suspension of investigation agreement, the Secretary will publish an intent to revoke the order (or intent to terminate the suspended investigation) in the *Federal Register* and serve written notice to all interested parties, including those interested producers and resellers of like products that are not on the service list. If interested parties do not request a review in the time period between the notice they have received and the conclusion at the fifth annual anniversary month since the publication of the duty order or the suspension of investigation, the Secretary of Commerce will revoke the order or terminate the suspended investigation and publish notice in the *Federal Register*. At such time the Secretary will instruct Customs to release any cash deposit or bond.[118]

The ITC may also determine in an administrative review that those imports subject to an antidumping order or suspended investigation would no longer materially injure or threaten material injury to a domestic industry and would not materially retard the establishment of a domestic industry. If the ITC reaches that conclusion, the Secretary of Commerce will revoke, in whole or in part, the duty order or terminate the suspended investigation.[119]

---

117. 19 C.F.R. § 353.25(d)(2) & (3) (1989).
118. 19 C.F.R. § 353.25(d)(4) (1989).
119. 19 C.F.R. § 353.25(e) (1989).

Countervailing Duty—Analysis[120]

Broadly defined, a countervailing duty is one imposed to counter the advantage given to an imported product by subsidies from the government of the exporting country. For imports from countries that have acceded to the Agreement on Interpretation and Application of articles Six, Sixteen and Twenty-Three of the GATT (the Subsidies Code), countervailing duties will be imposed when the Department of Commerce determines that a country is providing a subsidy with respect to a class or kind of merchandise imported, or sold (or likely to be sold) for importation, into the United States and the International Trade Commission (ITC) determines that an industry in the United States is materially injured or threatened with material injury or that the establishment of an industry is materially retarded by reason of the importation of that subsidized merchandise.[121] Material injury, as noted before, is defined as harm that is not inconsequential, immaterial, or unimportant.[122] Countries that have not acceded to the Subsidies Code are governed by slightly different procedures under the Tariff Act of 1930, section 303, as amended.[123] A major difference for these countries, such as Syria and South Africa,[124] is that the material-injury test is dispensed with unless the product imported is duty-free. A plaintiff seeking to have the United

---

120. 19 U.S.C.A. §§ 1671–1671f & 1303 (West 1980 & Supp. 1989); 19 C.F.R. 201–202 & 355 (1989).
121. 19 U.S.C.A. § 1671 (West 1980 & Supp. 1989).
122. 19 U.S.C.A. § 1677(7)(A) (West 1980 & Supp. 1989).
123. 19 U.S.C.A. § 1303 (West 1980 & Supp. 1989).
124. *See* American Spring Wire Corp. v. United States, 566 F. Supp. 1538 (Ct. Int'l Trade 1983). *See also* Industrial Fasteners Group, Am. Importers Ass'n v. United States, 542 F. Supp. 1019 (Ct. Int'l Trade 1982), *aff'd*, 710 F.2d 1576 (Fed Cir. 1983). The latter case involved goods from India prior to India's acceding to the subsidies code.

States impose a countervailing duty for those countries merely has to show that a subsidy exists.[125]

An important change in this area is a provision under the Trade and Tariff Act of 1984 (TTA) that "upstream subsidies" (any subsidy bestowed by foreign governments on manufacturers of components used in finished products) be taken into consideration in establishing the necessity of imposing countervailing duties.[126]

An amendment under the TTA to the countervailing duty statute tracks a similar provision under the antidumping statute by requiring that for all entries or withdrawals from a warehouse of merchandise subject to a countervailing duty, an estimated countervailing duty must be deposited with the Customs Service by the importer.[127]

An affirmative determination resulting in a countervailing duty order will now presumptively apply to all merchandise of the same type exported from the investigated country. However, the order may allow for differing countervailing duties if a state-owned enterprise is involved or if a company can show that significant differences exist between companies with regard to receipt of subsidies.[128]

Another important change in this area is an attempt by Congress under the Omnibus Trade and Competitiveness Act of 1988 to tackle the complications arising when parti-

---

125. 19 U.S.C.A. § 1303(a)(2) (West 1980 & Supp. 1989).

126. TTA § 613; 19 U.S.C.A. § 1677-1 (West Supp. 1989). In Canadian Meat Council v. United States, 644 F. Supp. 1125 (Ct. Int'l Trade 1987), the Court of International Trade held that an affirmative countervailing duty determination on preprocessed goods cannot be assumed to apply to the import of those goods in their processed state. Instead the ITA must engage in a separate upstream subsidy investigation, pursuant to 19 U.S.C. § 1671b(G) in order to determine if the import of the goods in their processed state is, and to what extent, subject to countervailing duties.

127. TTA § 608; 19 U.S.C.A. § 1671h (West Supp. 1989).

128. TTA § 607; 19 U.S.C.A. § 1671e(a)(2) (West Supp. 1989).

ally subsidized goods are produced by an international consortium. Where a class or kind of merchandise that is subject to a countervailing duty investigation is produced by an international consortium, the administrative authority will cumulate subsidies provided to the participating members, or enterprises, which facilitate their involvement in the consortium. This administrative authority will also cumulate subsidies provided directly to the international consortium.[129]

Procedures for Investigation

The procedures for a countervailing duty investigation for countries that have acceded to the Subsidies Code are similar to those for antidumping investigations. A countervailing duty investigation may be initiated by Commerce sua sponte or on petition by

1. A manufacturer, producer, or wholesaler in the United States of a like product that will be the subject of the investigation;
2. A certified union or recognized union or group of workers that is representative of an industry engaged in the manufacture, production, or wholesaling in the United States of a like product; and
3. A trade or business association, a majority of whose members manufacture, produce, or wholesale a like product in the United States;
4. An association, a majority of whose members is composed of interested parties described above with respect to a like product; and
5. A coalition or trade association which is representative of either

129. OTCA § 1315; 19 U.S.C.A. 1671(d) (West Supp. 1989). Note that this is the second of two subsections designated "19 U.S.C. § 1671(d)" by the Omnibus Trade and Competitiveness Act of 1988.

- Agricultural processors,
- Agricultural processors and producers, or
- Agricultural processors and growers

to the extent that the U.S. Trade Representative (USTR) does not notify the ITA and the Commission that the application of this subparagraph is inconsistent with U.S. obligations.[130]

The petition should contain facts similar to those in an antidumping petition (discussed above), such as the names and addresses of the petitioners and of the sellers of the merchandise. In addition, the petition should include information as to who is benefiting from the subsidy and evidence as to the material injury suffered by the American industry.[131] One commentator has suggested that a petitioner may be able to gather this information from

1. Official publications of the government alleged to be giving the subsidy,
2. The USTR,
3. The Department of Commerce library,
4. Prior countervailing duty proceedings,
5. Industrial consultants, or
6. A petitioner-initiated questionnaire surveying the industry.[132]

Unless the merchandise in question is dutiable merchandise from a country that is not entitled to an injury test (e.g., has not assumed the obligations of the Subsidies Code), petitions should be filed simultaneously with both

---

130. 19 U.S.C.A. §§ 1671a(b) & 1677(9) (West 1980 & Supp. 1989).
131. 19 C.F.R. § 355.12 (1989).
132. DeKieffer, *When, Why, and How to Bring a Countervailing Duty Proceeding: A Complainant's Perspective*, 6 N.C.J. INT'L L. & COM. REG. 363, 369 (1981).

the ITA (Commerce) and the ITC.[133] In the case of dutiable merchandise from a country that has not assumed the obligations of the Subsidies Code, it is not necessary to show material injury; in that instance, the ITC is not involved in the investigation.[134]

Within 20 days after the petition is filed, Commerce must determine if the petition alleges the element necessary for relief, i.e., the material injury of a domestic industry by reason of subsidized imports.[135] If Commerce decides that the petition does not allege sufficient grounds for an investigation, the proceedings end.[136]

Within 45 days after the filing of the petition or after an investigation initiated by Commerce, the ITC must make a preliminary determination in regard to material injury.[137] The statute and regulations offer some guidance on the material-injury factor. In making its determination the ITC considers, among other factors:

1. The volume of imports of the merchandise that is the subject of the investigation;
2. The effect of imports of that merchandise on prices in the United States for like products; and
3. The impact of imports of that merchandise on domestic producers of like products.

In considering the volume of imports, the ITC will take into account whether the volume of imports or any increase in the volume is significant either in absolute terms or relative to production or consumption in the United States.

---

133. 19 U.S.C.A. §§ 1303 & 1671a (West 1980 & Supp. 1989); 19 C.F.R. § 355.12(c) (1989).
134. 19 U.S.C.A. § 1303 (West 1980 & Supp. 1989).
135. 19 U.S.C.A. § 1671a(c) (West 1980 & Supp. 1989); 19 C.F.R. § 355.13 (1989).
136. *Id.*
137. 19 U.S.C.A. § 1671b(a) (West 1980 & Supp. 1989).

Where imports from two or more countries under investigation compete with each other and with like products of the domestic industry in the United States market, the commission will cumulate the volume in their assessment.[138]

In evaluating the effect of imports on domestic United States prices, the ITC will consider whether

1. There has been significant price underselling by the imported merchandise.
2. The effect of imports of the merchandise otherwise depresses prices to a significant degree or prevents price increases that otherwise would have occurred to a significant degree.[139]

The effect on the domestic U.S. price will be the effect of cumulated imports of like products from two or more countries under investigation.

The ITC may also take into account all relevant economic factors in evaluating the impact of imports on the affected industry. Several examples are given as illustrative, but not exclusive, factors:

1. Actual and potential decline in output, sales, market share, profits, productivity, return on investments, and utilization of capacity;
2. Factors affecting domestic prices;
3. Actual and potential negative effects on cash flow, inventories, employment, wages growth, ability to raise capital, and investment; and
4. Actual and potential negative effects on the existing development and production efforts of the domestic industry including efforts to develop a derivative or more advanced version of the like product.[140]

---

138. 19 U.S.C.A. § 1677(7)(c) (West 1980 & Supp. 1989).
139. *Id.*
140. 19 U.S.C.A. § 1677(7) (West 1980 & Supp. 1989).

Special rules are provided for agricultural products. The fact that the prevailing market price is at or above the minimum support price of an agricultural commodity is not a sufficient ground for the ITC to determine that there is no material injury to United States producers of that commodity. The ITC will also consider any increased burden on government income or price support programs.[141]

The rate of increase of subsidized exports to the United States market, the capacity in the exporting country to generate exports, and the availability of other export markets may be considered by the ITC.[142] The ITC may also accept information from Commerce on the nature of the subsidy provided and the effects likely to result from the subsidy.[143]

The mere presence or absence of any of the factors described above is not necessarily decisive for a determination of material injury. The regulations also suggest a possible avenue of defense that a defendant may use against a charge of material injury. The ITC will take account of information presented to it, or that it obtains, demonstrating that harm attributed to the subsidies is attributable to other factors. These factors include "volume and prices of nonsubsidized imports or imports not sold at less than fair value, contraction in demand or changes in patterns of consumption, trade restrictive practices of and competition between the foreign and domestic producers, developments in technology, and the export performance and productivity of the domestic industry."[144]

The regulations also note, however, that the effects of the subsidy will not be weighed against the effects associated with other factors that are contributing to overall injury in an industry. A petitioner will not be required to bear the

---

141. 19 U.S.C.A. § 1677(7) (West 1980 & Supp. 1989).
142. *Id.*
143. *Id.*
144. 19 C.F.R. § 207.27 (1987).

burden of proof that the material injury is not caused by those other factors.[145]

If the ITC's preliminary determination is that there is no material injury, the proceeding ends.[146] If the ITC finds material injury, then within 85 days after the petition was filed or the investigation was initiated, Commerce must make a preliminary determination as to whether a subsidy exists.[147] In extraordinarily complicated cases, 150 days will be allowed.[148]

When prior to the preliminary determination, the administering authority finds it reasonable to suspect the existence of an upstream subsidy, the time period for making a preliminary determination will be extended to 250 days, or 310 days where the case is extraordinarily complex, should the administering authority conclude that such additional time is necessary.[149] An upstream subsidy is a subsidy benefiting an input product used in the home country manufacture of the product under investigation, which gives the product under investigation a competitive benefit and has a significant effect on the cost of manufacturing or producing the product under investigation.[150]

The Court of International Trade recently held that when growers of swine receive a subsidy it does not pass through to the packers of fresh chilled and frozen pork. Accordingly, an upstream subsidy investigation is required when the ITA seeks to include in its countervailing duty investigation the goods produced by processors of purchased subsidized goods.[151]

---

145. *Id.*
146. 19 U.S.C.A. § 1671b (West 1980 & Supp. 1989); 19 C.F.R. § 207.18 (1987).
147. *Id.*
148. *Id.*
149. 19 U.S.C.A. § 1671b(g) (West Supp. 1989).
150. 19 U.S.C.A. § 1677-1(a) (West Supp. 1989). See note 152 below for definition of subsidy.
151. Canadian Meat Council v. United States, 644 F. Supp. 1125 (Ct. Int'l Trade 1987).

Commerce's preliminary determination on whether a subsidy or bounty exists raises the question of what is considered a subsidy or bounty.[152] A viable defense to a countervailing duty investigation would be to show that the benefits given by the home government to an industry are not subsidies or bounties within the meaning of the countervailing duty statutes. For example, in *Zenith Radio Corp. v. United States*,[153] it was held that "the non-excessive re-

---

152. 19 U.S.C.A. § 1677(5) (West Supp. 1990) provides:

> (5) Subsidy
>
> (A) In general
>
> The term "subsidy" has the same meaning as the term "bounty or grant" as that term is used in section 1303 of this title, and includes, but is not limited to, the following:
>
> (i) Any export subsidy described in Annex A to the Agreement (relating to illustrative list of export subsidies).
>
> (ii) The following domestic subsidies, if provided or required by government action to a specific enterprise or industry, or group of enterprises or industries, whether publicly or privately owned and whether paid or bestowed directly or indirectly on the manufacture, production, or export of any class or kind of merchandise:
>
> (I) The provision of capital, loans, or loan guarantees on terms inconsistent with commercial considerations.
>
> (II) The provision of goods or services at preferential rates.
>
> (III) The grant of funds or forgiveness of debt to cover operating losses sustained by a specific industry.
>
> (IV) The assumption of any costs or expenses of manufacture, production, or distribution.

"Annex A" in section 1677(5) refers to the Agreement on Interpretation of and Application of articles VI, XVI, and XXIII of the General Agreement on Tariffs and Trade, approved under Trade Agreement Act of 1979 § 2(a), 19 U.S.C.A. § 2503(a) (West 1980).

The list of export subsidies in Annex A includes the full or partial exemption, remission, or deferral of direct taxes related to exports; the exemption or remission of indirect taxes concerning production and distribution of exported products in excess of those levied on production and distribution of like products when sold for domestic consumption; and government export credit guarantee or insurance programs.

153. Zenith Radio Corp. v. United States, 437 U.S. 443 (1978).

mission of an indirect tax is not a bounty or grant. . . ."[154] In that case, the petitioner contended that products exported from Japan benefited from a bounty conferred by Japan, because Japan imposed a commodity tax on products sold domestically but remitted or refunded the tax if the products were exported. The Supreme Court upheld the Secretary of the Treasury's[155] decision that no subsidy or bounty had been given because the remission was "nonexcessive," which was defined as an amount not exceeding the tax paid or otherwise due. If, for example, the commodity tax was $5, a refund of $5 would not be excessive.[156]

Careful documentation would be required to establish this. In a 1983 appellate decision, the court noted the defense but declared that the defendants had not met the necessary burden of proof.[157] Citing a 1980 annex to the International Trade Administration regulations, the court noted that "a payment 'will not be treated as a subsidy if the government has reasonably *calculated and documented the actual tax experience of the product under investigation.*' "[158] Proper documentation of the tax experience could show that the payment was a noncountervailable refund of indirect taxes, if they had not been rebated through any other means and were nonexcessive. More recently the Court of International Trade found that the Ontario farm tax reduction program, which provided rebates to owners of

154. *Id.* at 448.

155. At that time, the statute was administered by the Treasury Department. That responsibility is now under the domain of the Commerce Department.

156. Zenith Radio Corp. v. United States, 437 U.S. at 446–47 & 461–62.

157. Industrial Fasteners Group, Am. Importers Ass'n v. United States, *supra* note 124, 710 F.2d at 1579.

158. *Id.* at 1582 (emphasis supplied by Fed. Cir.).

farm property in Ontario at 50 percent and 60 percent of their municipal taxes, confers a countervailable subsidy.[159] The CIT held the later case that there is no exception to the countervailing duty laws solely based on the fact that a payment formula is linked to taxes.

If Commerce's preliminary finding is that there is a subsidy, interim relief is permitted. Commerce requires that a bond be posted by an importer in an amount equal to the net subsidy.[160] The investigation by Commerce then continues.

The ITC will simultaneously initiate an investigation in order to make a final determination of material injury. This will occur even if Commerce's preliminary determination is negative.[161]

Within 75 days of its preliminary determination, Commerce must make a final determination on whether or not a subsidy exists. If the decision is negative, the proceeding ends.[162]

If Commerce's determination is affirmative following an affirmative preliminary determination, then the ITC must

---

159. Albertan Pork Producers' Mktg. Bd. v. United States, slip op. 87-94 (Ct. Int'l Trade, Aug. 7, 1987).

160. 19 U.S.C.A. § 1671b (West 1980 & Supp. 1989); 19 C.F.R. § 355.15 (1989). 19 U.S.C.A. § 1677(6) provides:

> for the purpose of determining *net subsidy* the administering authority may subtract from the gross subsidy the amount of
>
> a. any application fee, deposit, or similar payment paid in order to qualify for, or to receive, the benefit of the subsidy,
> b. any loss in the value of the subsidy resulting from its deferred receipt, if the deferral is mandated by Government order, and
> c. export taxes, duties, or other charges levied on the export of merchandise to the United States specifically intended to offset the subsidy received.

161. 19 U.S.C.A. § 1671d (West 1980 & Supp. 1989).

162. *Id.*; 19 C.F.R. § 355.20 (1989).

make a final determination with respect to material injury before the later of the 120th day after Commerce made its affirmative preliminary determination or 45 days after Commerce's affirmative final decision.[163]

When Commerce's preliminary decision has been negative, the ITC's final determination on material injury must be made within 75 days after Commerce's final determination.[164]

Note that when the administering authority, after the preliminary determination has been made, concludes that it is reasonable to suspect the existence of an upstream subsidy, the time period within which a final determination must be made may require an extension.[165]

If the ITC's final determination is affirmative, a countervailing-duty order is issued within 7 days of notification of the ITC's determination.[166] The Customs Service must begin assessing those duties six months after the date on which the Secretary of Commerce has received satisfactory information upon which to base an assessment.[167]

As in antidumping investigations, in certain circumstances a countervailing-duty investigation may be suspended prior to a final determination.[168] Since the procedure is the same as in an antidumping investigation, the reader should consult the antidumping section of this chapter for details. In the countervailing duty situation, the foreign government would agree to eliminate the subsidy, offset the subsidy, or cease exportation of the commodity to the United States.

---

163. 19 U.S.C.A. § 1671d (West 1980); 19 C.F.R. § 207.25 (1987).
164. *Id.*
165. 19 U.S.C.A. § 1671b(g) (West Supp. 1989).
166. 19 U.S.C.A. § 1671e (West 1980); 19 C.F.R. § 355.21 (1989).
167. *Id.*
168. 19 U.S.C.A. § 1671c (West 1980 & Supp. 1989); 19 C.F.R. §§ 355.17–.18 (1989).

Administrative Review and Revocation of Countervailing Duties

As in antidumping investigations, a procedure is provided for review or revocation of countervailing duty orders upon receipt of an appropriate written request. These procedures are analogous to the antidumping procedures. In the case of countervailing duties, the ITC and Commerce will consider the continuing existence of material injury and of a subsidy.[169] For further details the reader should consult the antidumping section of this chapter.

Interest on Overpayments and Underpayments

In an antidumping duty case, and likewise in a countervailing duty case, trade does not come to a standstill while the antidumping margin or rate of countervailing duty is being determined. The goods subject to each type of order are allowed to be removed from warehouse or entered for consumption on the condition that the estimated antidumping or countervailing duty is posted. When the actual levels are established, either refunds, where the deposits were higher than the actual levels, or additional payments, where the estimated levels fall short of the actual amounts due, will be required.

The procedures for the assessment of antidumping and countervailing duties also involve the payment of interest on estimated duties posted pursuant to an antidumping or countervailing duty order.[170]

The level of payment is subject to change when there is a difference between the amount of estimated payments set in the ITA's preliminary determination and the amount set in its final determination. The level of payment is also subject

---

169. 19 U.S.C.A. § 1675 (West Supp. 1989); 19 C.F.R. §§ 355.22, 355.25 (1989).
170. 19 U.S.C. § 1677g(a); 19 C.F.R. §§ 353.24 & 355.24.

to change as a result of subsequent administrative or judicial reviews of dumping or countervailable subsidy activity. Change may also occur, in the case of Canadian goods, based on a decision of the Binational Panel or Extraordinary Challenge Committee under the United States–Canada Free Trade Agreement.

If no administrative review is requested, Customs will liquidate suspended entries and collect duty equal to the amount of the deposits. Under such circumstances, there is no change between the estimated and ultimate duty assessed. Therefore, the opportunity for refunds plus interest or additional payments plus interest is eliminated.

To illustrate, in *Antifriction Bearings from Germany*,[171] the final determination by the ITA required the cash deposit or posting of a bond for estimated antidumping duty by one of thirteen exporter/manufacturers in the amount of 132.25 percent of value of the goods. Suspension of liquidation continued thereafter, with estimated antidumping duty deposited or covered by the posting of a bond, until the final results of the administrative review were published.[172] At that point, the margin for the exporter/manufacturer in question was reduced to 5.25 percent, entitling importers who had deposited the higher estimated rate to a refund, plus interest. Judicial review was requested in this case, along with an injunction ordering the continued suspension of liquidation. Pending the results of the judicial review, interest continued to accrue on that portion of the estimated duty deposits that would ultimately be refunded, if any.

Judicial Review

The antidumping and countervailing duty procedure offers several junctures at which judicial review of adminis-

171. 54 Fed. Reg. 18,997 (May 3, 1989).
172. 56 Fed. Reg. 31,693 (July 11, 1991).

trative measures may be made. These opportunities are provided for in section 516A of the Tariff Act of 1930, as amended by the Trade Agreements Act of 1979, and in the Custom Courts Act of 1980, which grants exclusive jurisdiction of cases arising under section 516A to the Court of International Trade.[173]

The Trade Agreements Act, as amended in 1984, provides for certain initial or preliminary determinations. These proceedings are to commence within 30 days after publication in the *Federal Register* of notice of[174]

1. A determination by the administering authority not to initiate an investigation;[175]
2. A determination by the ITC not to review an agreement or a determination based on changed circumstances; or[176]
3. A negative determination by the ITC as to whether there is a reasonable indication of material injury, threat of such, or material retardation.[177]

Any interested party to the proceeding in connection with the determinations enumerated above may commence an action in the United States Court of International Trade by filing concurrently a summons and complaint in conformance with court rules.[178]

Judicial review of these determinations is confined to the record before the agency. No de novo proceedings are allowed.[179] The court is to hold unlawful any determinations,

---

173. H.R. REP. NO. 1235, 96th Cong., 2d Sess. 18-20, *reprinted in* 1980 U.S. CODE CONG. & ADMIN. NEWS 3729, 3729–32.
174. 19 U.S.C.A. § 1516a (West 1980 & Supp. 1989).
175. 19 U.S.C.A. § 1516a(a)(1)(A) (West Supp. 1989).
176. 19 U.S.C.A. § 1516a(a)(1)(B) (West Supp. 1989).
177. 19 U.S.C.A. § 1516a(a)(1)(C) (West Supp. 1989).
178. 19 U.S.C.A. § 1516a(a)(1) (West Supp. 1989).
179. 19 U.S.C.A. § 1516a(b)(2) (West 1980).

findings, conclusions, and abuses of discretion or other acts not in accordance with law.[180] The record for review consists of all information presented to the Secretary of Commerce, administering authority, or ITC in the course of the administrative proceeding. One may also include a copy of the determination and a transcript of the hearings.[181]

Judicial review is also provided for determinations on the record.[182] Interested parties to the administrative proceeding may obtain court review of

1. A final affirmative determination by the Secretary and by the ITC or by the administering authority and ITC;[183]
2. A final negative determination by the Secretary, the administering authority or the ITC;[184]
3. A determination not otherwise provided for by review pursuant to the standards of review enumerated in 19 U.S.C. § 1675;[185]
4. A determination under paragraph one of 19 U.S.C. §§ 1671c or 1673c to suspend an antidumping order or investigation or a countervailing duty investigation;[186]
5. An injurious-effect determination;[187] or
6. A determination as to the class or kind of merchandise defined for the purposes of determining whether to include the merchandise on the duty order.[188]

180. 19 U.S.C.A. § 1516a(b)(1) (West 1980).
181. 19 U.S.C.A. § 1516a(b)(2)(A) (West 1980).
182. 19 U.S.C.A. § 1516a(a)(2) (West 1980 & Supp. 1989).
183. 19 U.S.C.A. § 1516a(a)(2)(B)(i) (West 1980 & Supp. 1989).
184. 19 U.S.C.A. § 1516a(a)(2)(B)(ii) (West 1980 & Supp. 1989).
185. 19 U.S.C.A. § 1516a(a)(2)(B)(iii) (West 1980 & Supp. 1989).
186. 19 U.S.C.A. § 1516a(a)(2)(B)(iii) (West 1980 & Supp. 1989).
187. 19 U.S.C.A. § 1516a(a)(2)(B)(v) (West 1980 & Supp. 1989).
188. 19 U.S.C.A. § 1516a(a)(2)(B)(vi) (West 1980 & Supp. 1989).

To commence a civil action in connection with any of these six determinations, a summons must be filed within 30 days after publication in the *Federal Register* of notice of the specified determination or within 30 days of the antidumping order or countervailing duty order.[189] A complaint must be filed within 30 days after filing the summons.[190]

Any determination, finding, or conclusion is to be held unlawful if the court finds that it is unsupported by substantial evidence on the record or is otherwise not in accordance with the law.[191]

Substantial evidence means that the court may not weigh evidence concerning specific factual findings or substitute its judgment on those findings for that of the ITC.[192] Unless liquidation is enjoined by the Court of International Trade, entries of merchandise covered by a contested determination will continue in accordance with the determination.

Upon request by an interested party and a proper showing that the relief requested should be granted, the court may enjoin the liquidation of some or all of the entries of merchandise.[193]

---

189. 19 U.S.C.A. § 1516a(a)(2)(A) (West Supp. 1989). *See* Allegheny Ludlum Steel Corp. v. United States, 7 Ct. Int'l Trade 56 (1984). CIT jurisdiction was denied where the complaint was filed 32 days after the summons. Pistachio Group of Ass'n of Food Indus., Inc. v. United States, 667 F. Supp. 886 (Ct. Int'l Trade 1987).

190. The time for filing a complaint may be extended, however, as long as good cause, which may include excusable neglect, is shown. Jernberg Forgings Co. v. United States, 7 Ct. Int'l Trade 62 (1984).

191. 19 U.S.C.A. § 1516a(b)(1)(B) (West 1980).

192. *See* SCM Corp. v. United States, 544 F. Supp. 194, 197 (Ct. Int'l Trade 1982).

193. 19 U.S.C.A. § 1516a(c)(2) (West Supp. 1989):

> To prevail on its motion for a preliminary injunction, [petitioner] must show (1) that it will be immediately and irreparably injured; (2) that there is a likelihood of success on the merits; (3) that the public interest would be better served by the relief requested; and (4) that the balance of hardship on all the parties favors the petitioner. . . .

Zenith Radio Corp. v. United States, 710 F.2d 806, 809 (Fed. Cir.

The opinion in *Zenith Radio Corp. v. United States* provides some interesting insights to this injunctive power. It is noted by the court that:

> Before passage of the Trade Agreements Act of 1979, the remedy for a domestic manufacturer challenging the margin used for assessment of dumping duties was prospective only since a court order increasing the amount of dumping duty that was appropriate could only be applied to entries occurring after the final court order was published. The Trade Agreements Act of 1979 altered this scheme by giving the Customs Court power to enjoin liquidation of entries pending the court's decision. 19 U.S.C. § 1516a(c)(2) (Supp. V 1981). The grant of this injunctive authority was described by Congress as "a major change in prior law" which had been formulated on the presumption of correctness of the administrative determination. H.R. REP. No. 96-317, 97th Cong., 1st Sess. 182 (1979). Congress modified this presumption, without eliminating it, by permitting the Customs Court to enjoin liquidation in appropriate circumstances. The greatest concern warranting modification of the prior law was the inadequacy of prospective relief. H.R. REP. No. 96-317, 97th Cong., 1st Sess. 182 (1979).[194]

Furthermore, subsequent to the Tariff and Trade Act of 1984, which removed the requirement for automatic administrative reviews of affirmative antidumping determinations, the Court of International Trade held that an administrative review need not have been requested in order for the court to have jurisdiction to issue a preliminary injunction on liquidations of entries pursuant to an affirmative antidumping or countervailing duty order.[195]

1983), *citing* S.J. Stile Assocs. v. Snyder, 646 F.2d 522, 525 (C.C.P.A. 1981); Virginia Petroleum Jobbers Ass'n v. Federal Power Comm'n, 259 F.2d 921, 925 (D.C. Cir. 1958). *See also* Bomont Indus. v. United States, 638 F. Supp. 1334 (Ct. Int'l Trade 1986); American Spring Wire Corp. v. United States, 578 F. Supp. 1405 (Ct. Int'l Trade 1984).

194. Zenith Radio Corp. v. United States, 710 F.2d at 811.

195. Ipsco Inc. v. United States, slip op. 88-97 (Ct. Int'l Trade 1988) and Ipsco Inc. v. United States, slip op. 88-98 (Ct. Int'l Trade 1988).

The court explained that in 1984 Congress intended to remove the delays and inefficiencies caused by mandatory reviews. Where the parties do not contend that the facts on which an original determination was based are no longer valid, the parties do not need to request an administrative review prior to seeking an equitable injunction in court.[196]

The Court of Appeals for the Federal Circuit may review final decisions of the United States Court of International Trade.[197]

If a decision by the Court of International Trade or the Court of Appeals for the Federal Circuit is not in harmony with that of the agency determination, it must be published in the *Federal Register* within 10 days,[198] and the court must remand the matter to the Secretary of Commerce, administering authority, or ITC for disposition consistent with the court's decision.[199]

Judicial review of final administrative affirmative findings in countervailing duty investigations was considered by the Court of International Trade in *British Steel Corp. v. United States*,[200] in which a challenge was made to the International Trade Administration's final affirmative results on specialty steel. This decision adds further refinement to the growing body of case law interpreting the filing deadlines contained in 19 U.S.C. § 1516a(a)(2)(A)(ii) and 28 U.S.C. § 2636(c). Citing the former section, the court dismissed the plaintiff's action as premature, holding that actions seeking review of final affirmative findings in coun-

196. Ipsco Inc. v. United States, slip op. 88-97 at 5, 7–9 (Ct. Int'l Trade 1988).
197. *See* 28 U.S.C.A. § 1295(a)(5) (West Supp. 1983); chapter 26.
198. 19 U.S.C.A. § 1516(c) (West 1980).
199. *Id.*
200. British Steel Corp. v. United States, 573 F. Supp. 1145 (Ct. Int'l Trade 1983).

tervailing duty investigations must be filed within 30 days of the date of publication in the *Federal Register* of an order based upon the final determination.[201] The plaintiff had filed at the time of the publication of the final determination.

Scope Determinations

Foreign exporters and U.S. importers of goods subject to an antidumping duty order or a countervailing duty order may be able to avoid application of the pertinent order. If their particular product can be differentiated from the class or kind of merchandise subject to the antidumping or countervailing duty proceeding, the parties may be able to benefit from a scope determination. The regulations governing antidumping and countervailing duty procedures[202] allow the Secretary of Commerce, on his own initiative or upon application of an interested party, to determine whether the product is properly within the order. Prior to making the determination, the Secretary will consider comments from other parties to the proceeding from which the order emerged who have been served notice of the initiation of or request for the scope determination.

In making an application for a scope determination, the interested party must submit a detailed description of the product and must state why it is beyond the scope of the order, as well as submit a summary of the reasons for this conclusion. Citations to statutory authority in support of the applicant's position should also be provided along with any factual support, including excerpts from the ITC's or the Secretary's investigations.

Due consideration will be given to products developed

---

201. *Id.* at 1149.
202. 19 C.F.R. §§ 353.29 & 355.29 (1990), respectively.

after the order was published and to alteration of the products originally contemplated by the order. Products will not be excluded from an order solely because they are classified under a different tariff classification from that specified in the order.

Among the factors to be considered are

- The pattern of trade;
- The relationship between the importer and the foreign exporter; and
- Whether there has been an increase in the importation of the product or its components into the United States or the foreign country after the issuance of the order.

When the Secretary initiates a scope inquiry, goods already subject to a suspension of liquidation will be subject to a continuation of that suspension, pending a preliminary or final scope ruling. If the preliminary scope ruling finds the product to be within the scope of the order, suspension of liquidation will continue. If the preliminary ruling finds the product outside the order, the supension will be ended, and the Secretary will order refund of any cash deposits or release of any bonds relating to the product.

However, if the Secretary initiates a scope inquiry involving an "issue of significant difficulty,"[203] and there has been no suspension of liquidation, Customs will be instructed to suspend liquidation and to collect a cash deposit of estimated duties for each entry of the product or withdrawal from a warehouse for consumption after the date of the order. If the final scope ruling finds the product to be outside the scope of the order, a refund of cash deposits or release of any bonds relating to the product will be made.

203. *See* 19 C.F.R. §§ 353.29(d)(3) & 353.29(j)(2); 19 C.F.R. §§ 355.29(d)(3) & 355.29(j)(2) (1990).

Even if a party is not successful in totally differentiating a product from the class or kind of merchandise subject to a countervailing duty order, differences in the facts surrounding its involvement with the product may justify the calculation of an individualized rate of duty.[204] Where the amount of the subsidy enjoyed by a particular party can be reduced because of unique circumstances, the rate of countervailing duty may be reduced, thereby allowing it to avoid a substantial portion of the duties. If the enjoyment has been reduced to a de minimis level, there will be no countervailing duty required.

Judicial Review Under the United States–Canada Free Trade Agreement[205]

The United States–Canada Free Trade Agreement (U.S.–CFTA)[206] provides that either government may invoke a binational panel to review a final antidumping or countervailing duty determination by the United States or Canada concerning a transaction under the agreement. The panel, if invoked, replaces domestic judicial review.[207] Cases will be

204. 19 C.F.R. § 355.22(d) (1990).

205. As of this writing only the interim regulations are in effect. Interim final rules published in 53 Fed. Reg. 53,248-60 (to be codified under 19 C.F.R. §§ 207–90 *et seq.* (1989)). *See also* 19 U.S.C.A. § 151a (West Supp. 1989).

206. Free Trade Agreement, January 1, 1989, United States–Canada. *See* United States–Canada Free-Trade Agreement Implementation Act of 1988, Pub. L. No. 100-449, §§ 401–410, 102 Stat. 1851, 1878–98 (1988).

207. Under Article 1904, paragraph 11 of the FTA:

> A final determination shall not be reviewed under any judicial review procedures of the importing (country) if either (the United States or Canada) requests a panel with respect to that determination within the time limits set forth in this article. Neither (country) shall provide in its domestic legislation for an appeal from a panel decision to its domestic courts.

argued by participants generally in the same manner as before a court. Regulations exist to protect from disclosure or grant access to proprietary information of persons, as well as to protect the government's privileged information from disclosure.[208]

Under the agreement the binational panel can be invoked only by the two governments. Under the United States–Canada Free Trade Agreement Implementation Act of 1988,[209] however, the United States government will automatically invoke the panel upon a timely request by an interested party. The panel consists of five panelists (having experience as judges): two selected by Canada, two by the United States, and the fifth chosen from either country by agreement or lot. Should either government allege that a panelist exceeded his or her authority, the panel decision will be reviewed by a binational "extraordinary challenge committee."

Countervailing Duty Case Study

A recent countervailing duty case of some note, *Live Swine from Canada*,[210] presents a good illustration of the procedural development of a countervailing duty case.

Paragraph 12 establishes three circumstances where domestic judicial review of a final determination involving dumping or countervailing duty involving United States or Canadian goods would be available:

1. Neither country seeks panel review of the final determination;
2. A revised final determination is issued as a direct result of the original final determination by a court of the importing country in cases where neither country sought panel review of that original final determination; or
3. A final determination is issued as a direct result of judicial review that was commenced in a court of the importing country before the FTA took effect.

208. Interim final rules to be codified under 19 C.F.R. §§ 207.93, 207.94.
209. Pub. L. No. 100-449, 102 Stat. 1851 (1988).
210. 54 Fed. Reg. 651 (Jan. 9, 1989).

Since it involves goods from Canada, it also relates to the invocation of the Binational Panel for review of a determination by the ITA. In addition, the issues of scope and separate rates of countervailing duty were raised by one of the parties to the proceeding.

The case began with the filing of a petition by an association of live swine producers in the United States, which, by definition, was qualified as an "interested party."[211] After its investigation, the ITC issued its final determination of material injury to a United States industry.[212] The ITA issued its final determination resulting in a countervailing duty order in August 1985.[213] Thereafter, annual countervailing duty administrative reviews were conducted, with requests for the reviews being presented to the ITA each August.

The first such review included a scope determination request by a Canadian producer of sows and boars, which was a party to the proceeding. Although the ITA held the product to be within the scope of the order and therefore subject to its effect on imports of live swine from Canada in general, the ITA differentiated sows and boars from the larger class of swine because sows and boars received a significantly lower net subsidy than other live swine. The ITA found that sows and boars were disqualified from the receipt of benefits from the subsidy programs which provided the largest benefits to other swine products, but had received some smaller benefits under other programs. A separate rate of countervailing duty was established for sows and boars, reflecting the subsidies for which sows and boars qualified.

In subsequent administrative reviews, sows and boars continued to get separate rates of countervailing duty, but, as the number of and benefits under Canadian programs

211. 19 C.F.R. § 355.2(i) (1990).
212. ITC Investigation No. 701-TA-224 (1984).
213. 50 Fed. Reg. 32,880 (Aug. 15, 1985).

found to be countervailable increased, so did the rates of countervailing duty applied to sows and boars and all other live swine from Canada.

After publication of the ITA's final results of the countervailing duty administrative review for the period April 1988 through March 1989,[214] requests were filed with the Secretariat for the Binational Panel for review of that determination under section 1904 of the U.S.–CFTA. The procedural schedule called for a final decision by the panel in May 1992.

In this case, as in any under the Article 19 authority of the Binational Panel, request for panel review was followed by the submission of a complaint by one or more of the interested parties to the determination for which review was sought. The filing of a complaint is not a prerequisite to participation in the panel review. However, at least one of the interested parties must file a complaint, and any other party must file a notice of appearance, followed by a case brief, to participate in the proceedings.

Before the panel renders its final decision, a list of further procedural steps must be completed by the panel, by the investigating authority, i.e., the ITA, and by the parties. The record of the ITA proceeding must be indexed, designated, and available for examination. Briefs must be filed by the complainants and the ITA, with reply briefs thereafter. Opportunity for oral argument follows 30 days after submission of the reply briefs, with the final decision due on the 315th day after the initial request for panel review.[215]

214. 56 Fed. Reg. 28,531 (June 21, 1991).
215. Article 1904 Panel Rules, 53 Fed. Reg. 53,212 (Dec. 30, 1988).

21. Unfair Trade Practices, the "Escape Clause," and Other Protection

Chapter 20 discussed protection against foreign subsidies (countervailing duties) and pricing practices (antidumping duties). This chapter examines relief available to American industries facing unfair practices in import trade[1] and relief available to remedy or prevent serious economic injury to American industries arising from import competition.[2] Considerable protection is also afforded the owners of copyrights, trademarks, and trade names, as is discussed in the last section of this chapter.

Unfair Practices in Import Trade

Under 19 U.S.C. § 1337, the International Trade Commission (ITC) is authorized to investigate allegations of unfair methods of competition, i.e., unfair acts in the importation of articles into the United States or in their sale by the owner or importer, the effect or tendency of which is

1. To destroy or substantially injure an industry in the United States;

---

1. 19 U.S.C.A. §§ 1337–1338 (West 1980 & Supp. 1989).
2. 19 U.S.C.A. § 2251 (West 1980 & Supp. 1989).

2. To prevent establishment of such an industry; or
3. To restrain or monopolize trade and commerce in the United States.[3]

Under the Trade Agreements Act of 1979 amendments,[4] the ITC's role under section 1337 became one of investigation, adjudication, and enforcement. If, as a result of the investigation, the ITC determines there is a section 1337 violation, it may order, subject to the President's approval,

1. Exclusion of articles from entry;[5]
2. Exclusion of articles from entry except under bond during investigation;[6] or
3. Issuance of cease-or-desist orders.[7]

If, however, the ITC finds the exclusions or orders would have an adverse effect on the public health or welfare, competitive conditions in the American economy, the production of like or directly competitive articles in the United States, or American consumers, it will not issue them. The ITC is also authorized to impose civil penalties for violations of its final orders.[8]

If the Commission determines that there is, or there is reason to believe there is, a section 1337 violation, that determination is transmitted to the president, who is authorized within sixty days to

1. Disapprove for "policy reasons" such an ITC determination, in which case the ITC's order for specific relief is nullified; or

3. 19 U.S.C.A. § 1337(a)(1)(A) (West 1980 & Supp. 1989).
4. Pub. L. No. 96-39, §§ 106(b)(1) & 1105, 93 Stat. 193, 310 (1979) (codified at 19 U.S.C. § 1337).
5. 19 U.S.C.A. § 1337(d) (West 1980).
6. 19 U.S.C.A. § 1337(e) (West 1980 & Supp. 1989).
7. 19 U.S.C.A. § 1337(f)(1) (West 1980 & Supp. 1989).
8. 19 U.S.C.A. § 1337(f)(2) (West 1980 & Supp. 1989).

2. Notify the ITC of the president's approval, upon which notification the ITC's determination and order become final.[9]

For example, in *Certain Welded Stainless Steel Pipe & Tube*,[10] the ITC established that a number of foreign producers had engaged in pricing policies aimed at driving out competitors in the United States market. The president, however, disapproved and nullified the ITC's cease-and-desist order on the grounds that

1. The remedy would be detrimental to national economic interests;
2. The remedy would be detrimental to the international economic relations of the United States;
3. The remedy duplicates the administration of United States unfair trade practice laws; and
4. The benefit derived is not significant enough to offset the above considerations.

Section 1337 of the Tariff Act of 1930 was originally enacted as section 316 of the Tariff Act of 1922.[11] Note that there appears to be a conscious parallel construction between section 316 and the Federal Trade Commission Act (FTC Act).[12] It has been stated that "section 316 extends to import trade practically the same prohibition against unfair methods of competition which the FTC Act provides against unfair methods of competition in interstate trade."[13] In 1930, section 1337 replaced section 316, but the basic language prohibiting unfair methods of competition and un-

9. 19 U.S.C.A. § 1337(j) (West 1980 & Supp. 1989).
10. U.S. INT'L TRADE COMM'N, PUBLICATION NO. 863 (Feb. 1978).
11. Tariff Act of 1922, ch. 356, title III, § 316, 42 Stat. 943 (1922).
12. Ch. 312, § 5, 38 Stat. 719 (1914) (codified at 15 U.S.C. § 45).
13. TARIFF COMM'N, ANNUAL REPORT 4 (1922).

fair acts in the importation into or sale of articles in the United States remained essentially the same.

It is also apparent from the statute that the ITC's jurisdiction under section 1337 may be concurrent with other regulatory agencies administering other statutes prohibiting unfair trade practices. In 19 U.S.C. § 1337(a), Congress expressly authorizes the use of section 1337 sanctions "in addition to any other provisions of law."

Despite such statutory prohibitions against "unfair methods of competition" and "unfair acts" under section 1337, the impact of section 1337 to date has been predominantly in the area of patent infringement claims against imported products. However, a body of case law has developed under section 1337 dealing with certain "unfair acts."

It is not surprising to find that, in practice, the ITC has relied on judicial decisions arising under such domestic antitrust and unfair competition statutes as the Sherman Act[14] and the Clayton Act[15] in its determination as to what constitutes a proscribed "unfair act" or antitrust violation. In finding a "group boycott" in *Tractor Parts I*,[16] a case in which the ITC (then the Tariff Commission) recommended that the president exclude entry of the foreign goods, Commissioner Leonard stated, "Although there are no judicial precedents involving non-patent cases arising under Section 1337, judicial determinations under other antitrust and unfair competition statutes are persuasive in determining what constitutes an unfair method or act under section 1337."

For more recent cases of what the ITC would consider unfair trade practices, see *Certain Erasable Programmable Read-only Memories (EPROMS)*[17] (patent infringements) and

14. 15 U.S.C.A. § 1 (West 1980).
15. 15 U.S.C.A. § 12 (West 1980).
16. TARIFF COMM'N PUBLICATION NO. 401, at 8 (June 1971).
17. U.S. INT'L TRADE COMM'N PUBLICATION NO. 2196 (May 1989).

Certain Electrically Restrictive Monocomponent Toner[18] (antitrust).

Section 1337(b)(3) specifically addresses the possible overlap between section 1337 and the antidumping[19] and countervailing-duty[20] laws, stating that if the unfair trade practice is uniquely within the purview of the antidumping or countervailing-duty statutes,[21] the ITC shall not seek an investigation or, if applicable, require the termination of the ongoing investigation.

Procedures in Section 1337 Actions

A complaint (under oath) may be filed with the Secretary of the ITC, or Commerce may commence proceedings upon its own initiative.[22] An investigation is instituted by notice published in the *Federal Register*. This is usually undertaken within thirty days after receipt of a complaint and upon the ITC's determination that the complaint is properly filed.[23] Each respondent named in the complaint must be served by the ITC.[24] Based on the factor of public interest, the ITC may deem it appropriate, during the period of investigation, to exclude articles from entry or from entry except under bond or to issue a cease-and-desist order.[25] Each investigation should be concluded no later than twelve months from the date of publication in the *Federal Register* (or eighteen months for a "more complicated investigation").

18. U.S. Int'l Trade Comm'n Publication No. 2069 (Mar. 1988).
19. 19 U.S.C.A. §§ 1673–1673i (West 1980).
20. 19 U.S.C.A. §§ 1303 & 1671–1671f (West 1980).
21. 19 U.S.C.A. § 1337(b)(3) specifically provides that 19 U.S.C.A. §§ 1303, 1671 & 1673 are the governing statutes in such instances.
22. 19 C.F.R. § 210.10 (1987).
23. 19 C.F.R. § 210.11 (1987).
24. 19 C.F.R. § 210.13 (1987).
25. 19 C.F.R. § 210.14 (1987).

The content requirements for a complaint are very exacting and rigorous.[26] The complaint must

1. Be under oath and signed by the complainant or his or her authorized agent and include on the first page the address and telephone number of the complainant and any agent signing;
2. Include a statement of facts stating the alleged unfair methods and unfair acts;
3. Describe specific instances of alleged unlawful importations or sales including the applicable HTSUS item number or TSUS item number;
4. State the name, address and, if known, the nature of the business of each alleged violator;
5. State whether the alleged unfair methods and unfair acts or the subject matter thereof have been or are subject to court or agency litigation and briefly summarize any such litigation;
6. State the relevant effect of any such unfair methods and action;
7. Describe the complainant's business or interests in the relevant domestic industry or in the trade or commerce allegedly affected and, if an infringement of an intellectual property right is at issue, show that at least one complainant is the owner or exclusive licensee of the subject property;
8. Where an infringement of an intellectual property right is at issue (including product patents, registered copyrights, trademarks, mask works, or patented processes) a specific theory of unfair competition must be alleged and supported by relevant data.

If the case is based upon the alleged unauthorized importation or sale of an article covered by, or produced under a

26. *See* 19 C.F.R. § 210.20 (1987).

process covered by, the claims of a valid United States patent, the following details must be furnished:

1. Identification of each United States letter patent and a certified copy thereof;
2. Identification of the ownership of each involved United States patent and a certified copy of each assignment of each patent;
3. Identification of each domestic license;
4. A list of each foreign patent and each foreign patent application corresponding to each involved United States patent;
5. A list of foreign licensees;
6. A showing of any domestic production of the involved article or of any domestic utilization of the involved process;
7. Drawings, photographs, or other visual representations; and
8. A submission of articles as exhibits.[27]

An opportunity for a "public" hearing is provided in each investigation under section 1337 to take evidence and hear argument for the purpose of determining whether there is a violation of section 1337.

Each party has the right of due notice, cross-examination, presentation of evidence, objection, motion, argument, and all other rights essential to a fair hearing. The hearing must be held no later than seven months from the time of publication in the *Federal Register* of the notice instituting the investigation, and within twelve months for a "more complicated" case.[28]

Following the hearing, the presiding officer certifies the record to the ITC and files with it an initial determination.[29]

27. *Id.*
28. 19 C.F.R. § 210.41 (1987).
29. 19 C.F.R. § 210.53 (1987).

A petition for review is available to any party to an investigation based on the initial determination. At the discretion of the ITC, briefs may be filed and oral argument heard.[30]

Any person adversely affected by a final determination of the ITC may appeal that determination to the United States Court of Appeals for the Federal Circuit.[31]

Relief Provisions Under the "Escape Clause"[32]

Unlike section 1337 (which deals with unfair trade practices), the "escape clause" provision[33] addresses serious problems presented to domestic producers by products imported into the United States under fair trade conditions. The motivation behind the escape clause is to permit adjustment of domestic industry to injurious competition on a temporary basis.[34]

The ITC must promptly investigate to determine whether an article is being imported into the United States in such increased quantities as to be a substantial cause of serious injury, or the threat thereof, to the domestic industry producing an article like or directly in competition with the imported article.[35] The serious threat of injury is sufficient to trigger the remedies under section 2251; actual injury need not be demonstrated.[36] In arriving at that determina-

30. 19 C.F.R. § 210.60 (1987).
31. 19 C.F.R. § 210.71 (1987).
32. Trade Act of 1974, Pub. L. No. 93-618, §§ 201–203, 88 Stat. 2011–15 (1975), as amended by Trade Agreements Act of 1979, Pub. L. No. 96-39, §§ 106(b)(3) & 1106(d)(1)–(7), 93 Stat. 193 & 312 (1979) (codified at 19 U.S.C. §§ 2251–2253); Trade Act of 1974, Pub. L. No. 93-618, § 406, 88 Stat. 2062 (1975) (codified at 19 U.S.C. § 2436).
33. 19 U.S.C.A. § 2251 (West 1980 & Supp. 1988).
34. *See* S. REP. NO. 1298, 93d Cong., 2d Sess. 4, *reprinted in* 1974 U.S. CODE CONG. & ADMIN. NEWS 7186, 7263.
35. 19 U.S.C.A. § 2252(b)(1)(A) (West 1980 & Supp. 1989).
36. 19 U.S.C.A. § 2251(a) (West 1980).

tion, the ITC has to take into account all relevant economic factors including, but not limited to, those in the following categories:

1. With respect to serious injury, the significant idling of production facilities in the industry, the inability of a significant firm to operate at a reasonable level of profit, and significant unemployment or underemployment within the industry;
2. With respect to the threat of serious injury, a decline in sales, a higher and growing inventory, a downward trend in production, profits, wages, or employment in the domestic industry concerned, and a lack of funds for modernizing domestic plants and for research and development; and
3. With respect to substantial cause, an increase in imports and a decline in the proportion of the domestic market supplied by domestic producers.[37]

Within 180 days of the petition's filing, the ITC will furnish the President with a report setting forth its findings and its recommendations regarding the amount of duty or the import restriction to be imposed or, where appropriate, adjustment assistance in the form of antidumping or countervailing duties.[38]

The President, unless he or she determines that the specific form of relief is not in the economic interest of the United States (and hence denies the relief),[39] must within sixty days accept, modify, or reject the ITC's recommended

37. 19 U.S.C.A. § 2252(c)(1) (West 1980 & Supp. 1988).
38. 19 U.S.C.A. § 2252(f) (West 1980 & Supp. 1989).
39. Other considerations the President must examine include the impact of the import relief on American consumers, the risk of retaliation by the exporting country, and the possible international economic ramifications of the import relief.

relief. Section 2253 provides the President with the following options to facilitate the orderly adjustment by industries to new competitive conditions:

1. Increase the tariff, but by no more than 50 percent ad valorem;[40]
2. Establish a tariff or quota;
3. Modify or impose quantitative restrictions;
4. Negotiate orderly marketing agreements;
5. Auctioned quotas;
6. International negotiations to address the underlying cause of the increase in imports or otherwise alleviate the injury;
7. Adjustment measures, including trade adjustment assistance (other than entitlements);
8. Legislative proposals;
9. Any other action within the President's power;
10. Any combination of the above.[41]

As a result of a Supreme Court decision,[42] changes have been made in the manner in which Congress reviews a decision by the President in this area. Under the previous statute, the President's decision not to provide import relief or to take action different from that recommended by the ITC could be vetoed by Congress. Congressional disapproval of the President's action must now take the form of a joint resolution, which can be vetoed by the President, subject to override by a two-thirds majority of Congress.[43]

During the course of its investigation, the ITC must consider all relevant factors, i.e., unemployment within the domestic industry, a decline of domestic sales, and an

40. 19 U.S.C.A. § 2253(e)(3) (West 1980 & Supp. 1989).
41. 19 U.S.C.A. § 2253(a)(c)(3) (West 1980 & Supp. 1989).
42. INS v. Chadha, 103 S. Ct. 2764 (1983).
43. 19 U.S.C.A. §§ 1330(d)(4), 2192(a)(1)(A) & 2253(c) (West Supp. 1989).

increase of imports, in order to determine whether increased imports of a certain product are the substantial cause of serious injury or threat of serious injury to a United States industry. An amendment provides that the absence or presence of any single factor required to be considered by the ITC in connection with the injury determination will not itself be dispositive of a finding of injury to a domestic industry.[44]

The term "significant idling of productive facilities," which had not previously been defined, is defined to include "the closing of plants or the underutilization of production capacity."[45] The changes in this area will make a positive injury determination less difficult to obtain.

Import relief, including extensions, can last up to eight years.[46] If the relief will last more than three years, the sanction should begin to be "phased down" within three years from when the action took effect.[47]

Proceedings Under the Escape Clause

An investigation by the ITC may be requested as follows:

1. By the President of the United States;
2. By the United States Trade Representative;
3. Upon resolution by the House Ways and Means or Senate Finance Committee;
4. By a group representing an industry, trade association, firms, certified or recognized union, or group of workers; or
5. By the ITC on its own initiative.[48]

---

44. 19 U.S.C.A. § 2252(c)(3) (West Supp. 1990).
45. 19 U.S.C.A. § 2252(c)(6)(B) (West Supp. 1990).
46. 19 U.S.C.A. § 2253(e)(1)(A) & (B) (West Supp. 1990).
47. 19 U.S.C.A. § 2253(e)(5) (West Supp. 1990).
48. 19 U.S.C.A. § 2252(b)(1)(A) (West Supp. 1990); 19 C.F.R. § 206.8 (1988).

The petition should include import data, data on total United States production of the domestic article for the most recent five years, the extent to which the imports have caused or now threaten injury, and a product description.[49]

The petition should set forth the petitioner's plan for adjusting to the import competition and how the relief sought relates to that adjustment.[50] Remember, the relief offered by the "escape clause" is only a temporary measure to help a domestic industry in its attempt to become more competitive with foreign imports.

Filing the petition commences an investigation by the ITC into injury to a domestic industry.[51] In the investigation, the ITC must determine the industry affected and the extent of the injury.[52] For imports from noncommunist countries, the ITC must determine if the increasing imports are, or threaten to be, the substantial cause of serious injury.[53] In the case of imports from communist countries, the ITC must determine whether increased imports are a significant cause of material injury or threaten injury.[54]

As part of the process, a public hearing is required, where all interested parties shall be afforded an opportunity to be heard and to present evidence.[55] One hundred and twenty days after the filing of the petition, the ITC must make a determination (the deadline can be extended thirty days if the case is determined to be extraordinarily complicated). In the case of imports from a communist

---

49. 19 C.F.R. 206.9 (1988).
50. 19 U.S.C.A. § 2252(a) (West Supp. 1990); 19 C.F.R. § 206.9 (1985).
51. Before submitting an adjustment plan the petitioning party may consult with the U.S. Trade Representative or one delegated by the U.S. Trade Representative. 19 U.S.C. § 2252(a)(5); 19 C.F.R. § 206.3 (1988).
52. 19 U.S.C.A. § 2252(b)(1) (West 1980 & Supp. 1989).
53. 19 U.S.C.A. § 2252(b)(1) (West Supp. 1990).
54. 19 U.S.C.A. § 2436 (West 1980 & Supp. 1990).
55. 19 U.S.C.A. § 2252(b)(4) (West Supp. 1990).

country, a determination must be reached within ninety days.[56]

If the determination is negative, the proceeding is terminated. Unless the ITC determines that there is good cause to reconsider the question sooner, a proceeding on the same imported product cannot be brought for at least one year.[57]

If the determination is affirmative, the ITC recommends a remedy. In certain circumstances, the ITC may find good reason to believe that there have been foreign unfair trade practices in the form of dumping foreign products on the United States market or that the foreign government has been providing a subsidy. If that is the case, the ITC must refer the matter to the Commerce Department so that it can act under the proper statute.[58]

Executive Review of Unfair Trade Practices ("Section 301," "Super 301," and "Special 301")

Another provision that can have a significant effect on imports is section 301 of the Trade Act of 1974 (19 U.S.C. §§ 2411 *et seq.*). It was enacted to provide relief for United States exporters when it is felt that trade agreements are not being adhered to or foreign governments have taken measures that unfairly or unreasonably hinder United States businesses' sales to or investments in those countries. Although most of the actions begun under this provision have been terminated without formal retaliatory measures being taken, section 301, which has been expanded by the Trade Agreements Act of 1979, the Trade and Tariff Act of 1984, and the Omnibus Trade and Competitiveness Act of 1988,

56. 19 U.S.C.A. §§ 2252(b) & 2436 (West 1980 & Supp. 1990).
57. 19 U.S.C.A. § 2252(h) (West Supp. 1990).
58. 19 U.S.C.A. § 2252(c)(5) (West Supp. 1990).

has achieved its stated goals in many cases simply because the cases were begun.

An earlier law passed under the Trade Expansion Act of 1962 (and since repealed) allowed presidential retaliation in the form of increased duties against foreign goods when trade restrictions were not removed after the United States requested their removal via normal General Agreement on Tariffs and Trade (GATT) procedures. When the European Community (EEC) linked its duties on imported poultry to domestic price levels, the United States levied higher duties on certain EEC products (foodstuffs, machinery) after the EEC refused to change its policy, despite a GATT finding that U.S. agriculture had been substantially injured by the levy. After several years of stalemate, the Europeans quietly removed the barriers, and the United States eliminated the higher duties.

The United States' modest success in this dispute, which came to be known as the "chicken war," and congressional discontent with the GATT dispute resolution procedures led to the passage of section 301.[59] Mirroring the practice under the earlier law, section 301 sanctions in recent cases have in some cases entailed the imposition of 100 percent duties on some merchandise from the offending countries (e.g., pharmaceutical products from Brazil and certain agricultural products from the European Community).[60] The merchandise selected does not have to be related to the trade sector the retaliation aims to protect, but its imported value should approximate the value of lost U.S. sales.

Private Party Petitions

Procedural Outline

Section 301 is unique in that it allows a private party to recommend that trade negotiations between governments

59. 19 U.S.C.A. §§ 2411–2420 (West Supp. 1991).
60. 53 Fed. Reg. 41551 (1988); 52 Fed. Reg. 2263 (1987).

take place. A private sector petition must identify the petitioner and any affiliated organizations, the interest affected by the claimed unfair practice, and the country complained against. It must contain enough economic data to show the claim's justification and the practice's impact on both the petitioner and U.S. trade. The office of the U.S. Trade Representative (USTR) will help small firms in their fact gathering.[61]

Within forty-five days of the filing, the USTR's section 301 committee must decide if it should proceed with an investigation. Notice of the determination whether to proceed is published in the *Federal Register*, either giving notice of the rejection of the petition or announcing hearings giving interested parties an opportunity to comment, to be held thirty days thereafter (or later, if the petitioner requests or agrees).[62]

A petition alleging breach of a trade agreement requires the USTR to notify the foreign government of the claim. The USTR may ask for information it feels it needs to make a decision. If the information is not provided, the USTR will use the best available information.

In either case, a decision to proceed with the investigation triggers consultations between the United States government and the foreign government under the agreement. The time period for such talks may vary according to the particular treaty, but the GATT dispute settlement mechanisms under which most such talks take place allow 150 days for negotiations. At the close of consultations under GATT rules, another 150 days may elapse in which either side may request a formal settlement proceeding. Such talks usually last around a year.[63]

61. 19 U.S.C.A. § 2412 (West Supp. 1991).
62. *Id.*
63. 19 U.S.C.A. § 2413 (West Supp. 1991).

If dispute settlement proceedings continue for more than 180 days, but in no event later than 30 days after the unsuccessful end of the proceeding or 180 days, whichever comes first, the USTR must make a determination on the allegation of unfair practices, decide what retaliatory response to make if the decision is affirmative, and publish the result in the *Federal Register*.[64]

Implementation of the duty increases or other action must begin within 30 days of publication unless the domestic petitioner requests a delay or the USTR decides that such delay is in the interest of the United States. Implementation may not be delayed more than 180 days.[65]

Retaliatory actions under section 301 may continue up to four years, but the USTR must constantly monitor the situation even if an accommodation was reached. If the USTR finds that the foreign country is not complying with the agreement's terms, the office must consult with the domestic parties (petitioners and domestic industry representatives) concerned, provide an opportunity for other interested parties to make their views known, and decide what further action should be taken.

A retaliatory action under section 301 automatically terminates four years after it begins. Sixty days before the termination date, the USTR must notify the domestic interested parties of the impending cutoff. The same notice must be provided before any termination, and the USTR must report to Congress on the action.

The Omnibus Trade and Competitiveness Act of 1988 added two additional weapons to the President's arsenal under section 301. The first is known as "Super 301,"[66] a statute providing for identification of and action on "priority" unfair practices. This is administered in the context of

64. 19 U.S.C.A. § 2414 (West Supp. 1991).
65. 19 U.S.C.A. § 2415 (West Supp. 1991).
66. 19 U.S.C.A. § 2420 (West Supp. 1991).

annual reports to Congress, due April 30 of each year, identifying significant trade barriers and trade-distorting measures of foreign governments which section 301 already required the USTR's office to conduct.

The statute requires the identification of targets and the beginning of investigations within the first two years (1989 and 1990) of the provision's existence. The USTR must identify "priority" practices in terms of the dollar value of goods and services that would have been exported but for the unfair practice, the investment increases blocked thereby, and, where measurable, the impact of foreign government procurement practices on U.S. exports. Investigations of the "priority" targets must begin within forty-five days of the reports identifying them to the President and Congress.

The investigation procedures following the report are the same as those for any other section 301 case, except that the USTR must aim its consultation or negotiation with the foreign government at the elimination of or compensation for the unfair practice within three years. Any priority country which has eliminated its unfair practices for two consecutive years will be taken off the list, starting in 1993.

Finally, the USTR must create a report to Congress under another feature added to these provisions in 1988, "Special 301."[67] The annual reports required by section 301 must now include a list of countries denying protection to U.S. companies' patent, copyright, or trademark ("intellectual property") rights, or denying market access to holders of United States intellectual property rights. The USTR designates those countries with the "most onerous or egregious" violations as priority countries and begins investigations under section 301.

67. 19 U.S.C.A. § 2242 (West Supp. 1991).

Recent Use of Executive Review

In 1990 the United States did not name any country as an unfair trader under Super 301, although Brazil, Japan, and India were investigated. Brazil and Japan, however, each made significant concessions on their respective trade policies under investigation. Although India rejected on principle the U.S. request to enter negotiations leading to certain Indian trade concessions, the USTR found it unwise to name India at this time.

Motivating the legislation of enhanced presidential powers under the Omnibus Trade Act of 1988 was the public's displeasure with the swelling of the U.S. trade deficit with Japan to approximately forty-nine billion dollars. In 1989, the USTR commenced investigations of Japan's impediments to imports of lumber, satellites, and super computers.

Additionally, the USTR entered into a series of discussions with Japanese officials concerning business practices in Japan that hinder the successful entry of foreign goods and services into the Japanese market as well as foreign investments. The talks became known as the Structural Impediments Initiative.

The U.S. investigations which threatened retaliation against Japan's exports to the U.S. generated some hostile sentiments on both sides during the course of the negotiations. Nevertheless, the U.S. and Japan were able to resolve each of these issues just prior to the President's deadline on April 30, 1990, to decide whether to retaliate. Japan agreed to open its markets further to imports of wood products, super computers, and satellites. Furthermore, the United States and Japan agreed on a set of principles for reducing Japanese structural impediments to trade and for correcting certain failures in the U.S. economy. The interim document presented on April 5, 1990, called on the United States to reduce its budget deficit, cut its capital gains tax, encourage private savings, and improve worker training. The document, largely developed by the Japanese, responded to United States concerns by agreeing to improve Japan's foreign trade infrastructure (i.e., airports, port facilities, and other public works), review and correct policies that distort Japanese land value, enhance antitrust regulations toward reducing collusions in setting bids and prices, reduce the interrelationships among Japanese companies, reduce exclusionary practices such as the time it takes to obtain patents in Japan, and significantly reduce regulations on distributing goods in Japan and on establishing large retail store chains in Japan.[68]

Brazil also took strides to alleviate U.S. trade concerns. Brazil initially objected to being placed under a Super 301 investigation which concerned restrictive import licensing regulations. Brazil claimed that these regulations were consistent with a plan worked out with the International Monetary Fund and other international creditors.[69] Nevertheless, Brazil improved trade relations with the United States during 1989 by further opening its market to foreign companies, improving its copyright protection, and permitting remittances to foreign software manufacturers.[70]

Brazil's negotiations with Hughes Aircraft Company to purchase millions of dollars of U.S. telecommunications technology also encouraged the U.S. government to reconsider taking retaliatory steps against Brazil's alleged unfair trade practices that were under Super 301 investigation.[71] In deciding not to name Brazil to the Super 301 list, the Bush administration also intended to express support for economic reforms being implemented by President Fernando

68. K. Riley, *U.S., Japan Agree on Economic Reforms*, Washington Times, Apr. 6, 1990 at A1.
69. 6 Int'l Trade Rep. (BNA) 994 (July 26, 1989).
70. 6 Int'l Trade Rep. (BNA) 1291 (Oct. 11, 1989).
71. 6 Int'l Trade Rep. (BNA) 1085 (Aug. 23, 1989).

Collor de Mellor. These reforms are expected to enhance foreign trade and investment in the long term.[72]

The Bush administration was nearly backed into a position where it would have had to retain India on the Super 301 list in 1990. India's continuous refusal to negotiate a settlement on the alleged unfair restrictions on foreign investments and insurance programs, for which India was cited under section 301 in 1989, as well as its weak intellectual property protection, placed the Bush administration in a political dilemma. While retaliating against a Third World nation would have detracted from America's friendly image to the Third World and created a bad negotiating climate at the Uruguay Round talks of the GATT, America's Super 301 law stood to lose much of its perceived bite if the United States did not retaliate against a country named for the same unfair trade practices for two consecutive years. Furthermore, following its decisions not to name Japan, the Bush administration wanted to reassure Congress that it was not eschewing its responsibilities under the 1988 Act.

The administration originally sought to assuage the fears and hostility of India and her Third World allies by not citing India for unfair trade practices in addition to those practices it had repeated after being cited in 1989. This compromise also was met with hostility by India, but in the end the compromise was not necessary. Just prior to the June 16, 1990, deadline to decide whether to name India, India's new coalition government led by Prime Minister V.P. Singh indicated that it would meet the United States partway by easing its restrictions on foreign investments and enhancing India's intellectual property law.[73] This provided the administration with enough cause to support its position against naming India as an unfair trader. Although Con-

72. 7 Int'l Trade Rep. (BNA) 44 (Jan. 10, 1990).
73. N. Patri, *Peace Signals from India*, J. Com. (June 8, 1990).

gress was primarily interested in seeing the legislation directed against Japan, it is expected that following the Uruguay Round negotiations Congress will reassert its desire to see the unfair trade legislation enforced against all trading partners engaging in unfair trade practices.[74]

Importations of Merchandise Covered by Trademarks and Copyrights

As discussed earlier in this chapter, the International Trade Commission (ITC) is authorized under 19 U.S.C. § 1337 to exclude merchandise when it finds patent infringement and violations of antitrust laws. However, considerable protection is also afforded to the owners of copyrights, trademarks, and trade names under the Tariff Act of 1930 and other related statutes through which the Customs Service prevents the importation of infringing merchandise.

Protection Under the Copyright Act of 1976

Under 17 U.S.C. § 602, importation into the United States, without the authority of the copyright's owner, of copies or phonorecords of a work that have been acquired outside the United States is an infringement of the owner's exclusive right to distribute copies or phonorecords.

Any person who infringes a copyright willfully and for purposes of commercial advantage or private financial gain is subject to criminal prosecution and can be fined up to $250,000, imprisoned up to five years, or both.[75]

The importation of pirated copies of works copyrighted in the United States is also prohibited. Pirated copies are ac-

74. *A Wise Course*, J. Com. (June 15, 1990).
75. 17 U.S.C.A. § 506 (West 1977 & Supp. 1984); 18 U.S.C.A. § 2319 (West Supp. 1984).

tual copies or substantial copies of a recorded copyrighted work, produced and imported in contravention of the rights of the copyright owner.[76] Customs protection against the importation of pirated copies can be secured through an application to the Customs Service to record a copyright.[77]

Statutory Protection for Trademarks and Trade Names

Pursuant to section 526 of the Tariff Act of 1930,[78] the Secretary of the Treasury is empowered to prohibit entry of foreign merchandise, "if such merchandise, or the label, sign, print, package, wrapper, or receptacle, bears a trademark owned by a citizen of, or by a corporation or association created or organized within, the United States, and registered in the Patent and Trademark Office." Any merchandise imported into the United States found to be in violation of the Act is subject to seizure or forfeiture. Any person dealing in such merchandise may be enjoined from that activity, or may be required to export or destroy the merchandise, and will be liable for damages and profits provided for wrongful use of a trademark.[79]

Trademarks must be registered with the United States Patent and Trademark Office before they can be recorded by the owner with the Customs Service to bar entry of articles bearing a trademark copying or simulating the owner's recorded trademark.[80] The application to record a trademark with the Service must, among other items, identify "any parent or subsidiary company, or other foreign company under common ownership or control which uses the trademark abroad."[81]

---

76. 19 C.F.R. §§ 133.42(a)–(b) (1984).
77. 19 C.F.R. § 133.32 (1984).
78. 19 U.S.C.A. § 1526 (West 1980).
79. 19 U.S.C.A. § 1526(c) (West 1980).
80. 19 C.F.R. 133 (1984).
81. 19 C.F.R. § 133.2(d) (1984).

Section 42 of the Lanham Act[82] tracks the language of 19 U.S.C. § 1526: no article of imported merchandise that copies or simulates the name of any domestic manufacture, manufacturer, or trader, or of any manufacturer or trader of a foreign country that affords similar privileges to United States citizens by treaty will be admitted to entry.

The name or trade style, which has been used for at least six months in the United States to identify a manufacturer or trader, is eligible for recordation with the Service.[83] Similar to trademark recordation, there must also be disclosure of the identity of any parent or subsidiary company, or other foreign company under common ownership or control in an application with the Customs Service to record a trade name.

Protection for a recorded trade name remains in effect for as long as the trade name is actually used. The recordation can be cancelled upon request of the recordant, or upon submission of evidence of disuse.[84]

Based on the above trademark and trade name statutes and regulations, it is significant to note that the import restrictions are not applied by the Customs Service if both the foreign and United States trademarks or trade names are owned by the same person or business entity, or the foreign and domestic trademark or trade name owners are parent and subsidiary companies or are otherwise subject to common ownership or control. "Common ownership" is defined as individual or aggregate ownership of more than 50 percent of a business entity. "Common control" refers to effective control of policy and operations and is not necessarily synonymous with common ownership.[85]

82. 15 U.S.C.A. § 1124 (West 1982).
83. 19 C.F.R. § 133.11 (1984).
84. 19 C.F.R. § 133.15 (1984).
85. 19 C.F.R. §§ 133.21(c) & 133.2(d)(1)–(2) (1984). Pursuant to the Supreme Court's holding in K Mart v. Cartier, 108 S. Ct. 1811 (1988),

Gray Goods[86]

Unlike black market merchandise, which may be stolen or counterfeit, gray market goods are authentic and legitimately manufactured trademarked items that are produced and purchased abroad. Typical items include cameras, watches, crystal, and perfumes. The controversy over these gray goods is that they are bought in various countries and imported or "diverted" into the United States for less money than if they had been purchased from the United States subsidiaries or authorized distributors of the foreign manufacturer (because of currency fluctuations and other market factors, including absence of a manufacturer's warranty).

The large market for discounted gray goods when the U.S. dollar was strong in the late 1970s and early 1980s raised a clamor from opposing interest groups over whether the Customs Service should permit or refuse entry to these items.

The issue was hotly debated within the Treasury Department, while the federal courts issued some significant rulings on gray goods.

The *Masel* case,[87] was considered a setback for those who wished to compel the Customs Service to bar the importation of gray goods under all circumstances. The actual plaintiff, Bell & Howell, owned the Mamiya trademark in the United States. As the exclusive authorized distributor of Mamiya cameras in the United States, it obtained a preliminary injunction in the federal district court prohibiting defendant Masel from importing Mamiya cameras, purchased

---

the Customs Service has eliminated 19 C.F.R. § 133.21(c)(3). 55 Fed. Reg. 52040 (1990).

86. The Third Circuit preferred to use the less prejudicial term "parallel import." *See* Weil Ceramics & Glass, Inc. v. Dash, 878 F.2d 659, 661 (3d Cir. 1989).

87. Bell & Howell: Mamiya Co. v. Masel Supply Co., 719 F.2d 42 (2d Cir. 1983).

abroad, and selling them in the United States for less than identical cameras sold through Bell & Howell, on the ground that the sale caused "a substantial likelihood of confusion" with Bell & Howell products.

A unanimous appeals court vacated the district court's issuance of preliminary injunction.[88] Stating that the most important prerequisite to the granting of a preliminary injunction pending a decision on the merits is a showing of the likelihood of irreparable injury (in this case to Bell & Howell), the appeals court found that less drastic means could be found to avoid the claimed confusion than prohibiting Masel from selling its imported cameras. It reasoned that consumers could be made aware of the differences between the plaintiff's product and defendant's identical gray good (i.e., the lack of a warranty) through appropriate labeling and advertising.

Recent court decisions have further defined the standards by which U.S. Customs should act on gray market goods. On May 31, 1988, the U.S. Supreme Court decided an important gray market case, *K Mart Corp. v. Cartier Inc.*[89] In a 5–4 ruling, formed in part by two different majorities, the Court set down the breadth of discretion Customs may use in regulating the importation of gray goods under section 526 of the Tariff Act. In upholding significant aspects of the customs regulations pertaining to gray goods, the Court agreed that Customs may interpret section 526 to permit the importation of gray goods where the U.S. trademark registrant is affiliated with the foreign trademark owner and that Customs may interpret section 526 to prohibit the importation of gray goods where the U.S. trademark registrant is independent of the foreign trademark owner. The Court instructed the Customs Service to prohibit the import of gray

88. *Id.*
89. K Mart Corp. v. Cartier Inc., 108 S. Ct. 1811 (1988).

goods where the U.S. trademark owner licensed the trademark to an independent foreign enterprise under which licensing agreement the authority to sell in the U.S. market was not obtained by the foreign licensee.[90]

The Third Circuit in *Premier Dental Products v. Derby Dental Supply*[91] held that a party possessing trademark rights for a product's U.S. distribution is entitled to equitable relief to prevent infringement of goodwill purchased separately from a nonaffiliated foreign manufacturer. Subsequently, the Third Circuit held that a United States import distributor that is wholly owned by the foreign manufacturer of a trademarked good it distributes cannot obtain equitable relief against the gray market sales by asserting its trademark rights for the distribution of those goods under sections 42 and 32 of the Lanham Act and under section 526 of the Tariff Act, since "it benefits from the corporate relationship that exists." Presumably, the profits to the parent company resulting from the United States competitor's sales would benefit the "authorized" distributor as well.[92]

Counterfeit Goods

Another Second Circuit decision has compelled the Customs Service to commence forfeiture proceedings against an imported copy of a trademarked Rolex watchband that could

90. *Id.* at 1816–1819. Seth Lipner points out that the outcome of this case contains certain analytic contradictions produced by an opinion composed of the differing theories of the justices. *See* S. E. Lipner, *Grey Market Controversies: The 1980's and Beyond,* 13 FLETCHER F. 307, 313–317 (1989).
91. Premier Dental Prods. v. Derby Dental Supply, 794 F.2d 850 (3d Cir.), *cert. denied,* 107 S. Ct. 436 (1986).
92. Weil Ceramics & Glass Inc. v. Dash, 878 F.2d 659, 666–669 (3d Cir. 1989). The court reconciled *K Mart Corp.* with A. Bourjois & Co. v. Katzel, 260 U.S. 689 (1923). Weil Ceramics & Glass Inc. v. Dash, 878 F.2d at 668–669. *But see id.* at 679–680 (Becker, J., concurring).

be distinguished from the genuine article by a Customs expert but not by the average purchaser.[93]

Under Customs Service regulations, a "counterfeit trademark is a spurious trademark which is identical with, or substantially indistinguishable from, a registered trademark."[94] Absent written consent of the trademark owner, counterfeits will be seized and forfeited.[95]

On the other hand, a mark that so resembles a recorded trademark "as to be likely to cause the public to associate the copying or simulating mark with the recorded name or mark"[96] will be seized by the Customs Service, but it can be imported "if the objectionable mark is removed or obliterated prior to importation."[97]

At issue in the *Rolex* case was the proper procedure for the Customs Service to employ in determining the degree of similarity of a copying mark.

The Customs Service's expert had examined the three-dimensional markings on the imported copy through a jeweler's loupe and compared the markings with the two-dimensional printed trademark recorded by the trademark owner with the Customs Service. He did not compare the copy with the trademark as it actually appeared on the genuine band. Because its experts could discern a visual difference between the recorded paper mark and the imitation of the trademark as it appeared on the imported copy, the Customs Service found that the copy was not technically a counterfeit. Therefore, it could properly be imported into the United States if the infringing marks were removed or obliterated.

The Second Circuit disagreed, reasoning that trademark

93. Montres Rolex, S.A. v. Snyder, 718 F.2d 524 (2d Cir. 1983).
94. 19 C.F.R. § 133.23a(1) (1988).
95. 19 U.S.C.A. § 1526(e) (West 1980); 19 C.F.R. § 133.23a(b) (1984).
96. 19 C.F.R. § 133.21(a) (1988).
97. 19 C.F.R. § 133.21(c)(4) (1988).

owners were entitled to greater protection from imported copies of their merchandise. Under the *Rolex* decision, the Customs Service must employ the "average purchaser test" (i.e., comparing the two watches, as would a consumer) to determine whether an infringing mark amounts to a counterfeit, subjecting the item to forfeiture. While acknowledging that mandatory forfeiture of merchandise is a severe penalty, the court found that trademark owners were entitled to such protection from the importation of copies of their product. At least in the realm of counterfeits, the law has become clearer.

Part VI: Administration and Enforcement

22. Penalties and Customs Frauds

Introduction

Commensurate with the Customs Service's extensive authority to administer the customs laws of the United States is its equally encompassing power to enforce those laws and regulations. Under the customs and navigation laws, the Customs Service has control over the ports of entry with respect to entry, lading and unlading of merchandise, inspection and clearance of carriers (vessels, aircraft, vehicles) and persons, and the interdiction and seizure of contraband to terminate illegal traffic in dangerous drugs. It has authority to enter and conduct searches in premises pursuant to a search warrant and to seize merchandise illegally imported or that may be subject to a forfeiture due to the evasion or violation of customs and related laws. No search warrant is needed for searches undertaken in areas under Customs Service custody, such as airport cargo terminals, piers (within restricted areas), and bonded warehouses. Under the Anti-Smuggling Act,[1] the Customs Service may board, seize, and arrest vessels, illegal cargo, and persons engaged in smuggling not only in United States customs waters[2] but

1. 19 U.S.C. §§ 1701–1711 (West 1980).
2. 19 U.S.C.A. §§ 586 & 709(c) (West 1980 & Supp. 1988).

also in areas adjacent to customs waters and customs enforcement areas.[3] The Service can issue administrative summonses (judicially enforceable) to produce records and witnesses' testimony.[4] Finally, as a federal law enforcement agency, the Customs Service can make use of the court system to obtain search and arrest warrants, and it can recommend that U.S. attorneys conduct grand jury investigations with the power to subpoena witnesses and evidence.

The Customs Service's enforcement authority over infractions of customs and related laws is generally exercised through the assessment of civil penalties, criminal penalties, or both, in addition to possible seizure and forfeiture of imported merchandise upon such terms and conditions as are provided under the law.

Civil Penalties

Fraud, Gross Negligence, and Negligence

Prohibited Actions

One of the Customs Service's most effective enforcement tools is its authority under section 592.[5] Clause (a) of section 592 provides the following general rule:

> Without regard to whether the United States is or may be deprived of all or a portion of any lawful duty thereby, no person, by fraud, gross negligence, or negligence
>
> (A) may enter, introduce, or attempt to enter or introduce any merchandise into the commerce of the United States by means of

3. 19 U.S.C. §§ 1701–1711, *supra* note 1.
4. 19 U.S.C.A. § 1509 (West 1980 & Supp. 1988).
5. Tariff Act of 1930, ch. 497, title IV, § 592, 46 Stat. 750 (1930) (codified at 19 U.S.C. § 1592) (hereinafter cited in text as section 592 and in notes as § 1592).

(i) any document, written or oral statement, or act which is material and false, or
(ii) any omission which is material, or
(B) may aid or abet any other person to violate subparagraph (A).[6]

Although clerical errors or mistakes of fact are not considered violations under section 592, they may nevertheless, under certain circumstances, give rise to liability.[7] In 1978, following intense lobbying by the importing community, congressional amendments to the section 592 penalty provisions[8] purged the statute of its longstanding deficiencies with respect to indiscriminate and excessive mandatory forfeitures,[9] as well as the lack of both due process safeguards and meaningful judicial review.

Importers should be aware that in the past several years the Customs Service, in an effort to keep up with an ever-increasing flow of goods through our borders, has had to reevaluate and adapt its administration of trade. No longer can Customs rely on its uniformed inspectors at the ports of entry and its import specialists at the districts to process the importations and supporting documentation on an entry-by-entry basis.

Customs has taken steps to better inform the importing public as to the proper entry of goods into the United States. With the revision of its binding ruling program[10] Customs has made it easier and faster for importers to ask

6. § 1592(a)(1).
7. § 1592(a)(2).
8. §§ 1582(a)–(e), amended by Customs Procedural Reform and Simplification Act, Pub. L. No. 95-410, title I, § 110(a), 92 Stat. 893 (1978).
9. Prior to amendment, § 1592 (*supra* note 8) provided that the Service could sue for forfeiture of merchandise or its domestic value. If alleged violators contested the suit, they could either win and pay nothing or lose and forfeit everything.
10. For a more detailed discussion of Customs binding rulings program, see chapter 24.

for advice on the proper classification of items. In addition, its preclassification program[11] affords importers the opportunity to have entire product lines examined and classified by Customs, thus avoiding problems when the items are imported.

Customs has also provided better access to its prior rulings and directives. As a result, Customs has made an honest effort to provide importers with all the information necessary to import products properly. If, in spite of this effort, importers fail to avail themselves of this information and advice or choose to ignore or proceed in contravention of such information and advice, the Customs Service will take action and treat such conduct harshly. The importing community and its brokers are thus expected to make proper entries and to know the law. What was once regarded as a classification problem may now be viewed as a possible case of civil fraud.

The Customs Service's future reliance on its selective approach to examination of import transactions along with the further development of the automated commercial system (ACS)[12] has, by necessity, required Customs to perform more frequent and extensive follow-up verifications. As a result, Customs is moving toward an IRS-type audit program, involving infrequent examinations of merchandise and docu-

---

11. For a more detailed discussion of Customs preclassification program, see chapter 24.
12. The stated goal of the ACS, which has been online nationwide since August 15, 1988, is a "paperless entry" system in which Customs analyzes electronically transmitted information to determine whether imports can be admitted into the United States and to decide if a tariff must be paid. Customs hoped and still believes that this system will speed the release of cargo and reduce costs, along with facilitating the processing of entries, payment of duties, and assessment of penalties. The realization of a "paperless" entry system has not yet happened. However, it appears to be rapidly moving forward and along with the facilitation of freer access of merchandise through our borders, the full implementation of the "paperless" entry system will greatly affect the payment of duties and assessment of penalties.

ments at the time of entry, with greater reliance placed on auditors and special agents to uncover errors, discrepancies, and falsities after the fact. When a violation is uncovered it can embrace hundreds or thousands of entries, and the penalty, a multiple rather than a percentage of the lost revenue, can be devastating.

An error made today in preparing an entry, or in not including an assist in the value of an imported product, may not be discovered for years. However, if the error is discovered by Customs, it is not treated in a benign fashion. The potential penalty can be enormous.

Frequent warning letters on classification issues, seemingly harmless in themselves, are now used to form the basis for a civil penalty proceeding. Classes of high-risk imported merchandise (e.g., quota items, foods, and drugs) are analyzed, as are computer profiles of suspected importers and their past practices. Referrals to Customs Service agents by import specialists are much more frequent. Even where a civil investigation is favorably, and perhaps relatively easily, settled between an importer and Customs Service agents, a second violation can be expected to lead to severe consequences. The change within the Customs Service from an administrative collector of duties to the role of border police cannot be overstressed.

As Customs and the import community continue to automate and move toward a paperless environment, the Customs Service will be using the computer more and more to assist it in selecting merchandise for inspection and examination, bypassing the examination of most importations, but relying on its post-entry audits to ensure compliance with the law. Utilizing the computer, Customs is now able to identify an importer's every importation by port, entry number, date of entry, amount of duty paid, liquidation status, and where the documents may be found. This capability has vastly simplified the regulatory auditor's task.

The Customs Service can uncover a violation of law in

many ways. An investigation may begin with the routine examination or post-entry audit of shipping and import documents and a visual inspection of entered merchandise (either at random or through selective targeting of exporting countries, commodities, or importers) or through information or a complaint received from a confidential source. Once commenced, an investigation can range from a single meeting with the importer to a complete review of imported merchandise, from an audit of the single import transaction in question to the audit of all past transactions, from the commencement of civil penalty proceedings to the referral of the matter for criminal prosecution.

In view of the recent increase in the number of intensive compliance audits the Customs Service performs, it is incumbent upon importers to step up their own internal audit programs regarding their compliance with the customs laws and regulations. Periodic internal audits must be performed to provide importers with the most up-to-the-minute information regarding their import operations so that when a Customs audit team does arrive, few, if any, surprises will arise.

Discovery of errors or violations by internal audit will allow for remedial action, including voluntary disclosure, which should help to significantly contain costs in terms of penalties and legal fees. Violations or errors discovered through a Customs audit may result in an extensive investigation by Customs special agents and an assessment of significant penalties. Legal fees and the time needed to defend such actions can be significant. Further, certain violations may create serious criminal exposure.[13]

---

13. In addition, audits often uncover opportunities for duty savings by alerting an importer to possible incorrect duty treatment, availability of duty drawback for items which were imported and then exported, and for duty-free entry of American components when incorporated in foreign-made goods. Of course, there are also a number of duty-free or duty-reduction programs which can be explored.

Penalties Commensurate with Seriousness of Offense

Besides abolishing forfeiture of the merchandise as the only penalty mandated by statute, amended section 592 also structures the penalty to "fit the crime" or lack thereof. The degree of liability is initially examined under the following three categories:

1. Fraud: A fraudulent violation of section 592(a) is punishable by a civil penalty in an amount not to exceed the domestic value of the merchandise.
2. Gross negligence: A grossly negligent violation of section 592(a) is punishable by a civil penalty in an amount not to exceed
   - A. the lesser of
     - i. the domestic value[14] of the merchandise or
     - ii. four times the lawful duties of which the United States is or may be deprived; or
   - B. if the violation did not affect the assessment of duties, 40 percent of the dutiable value of the merchandise.
3. Negligence: A negligent violation of section 592(a) is punishable by a civil penalty in an amount not to exceed
   - A. the lesser of
     - i. the domestic value of the merchandise or
     - ii. two times the lawful duties of which the United States is or may be deprived; or
   - B. if the violation did not affect the assessment of duties, 20 percent of the dutiable value of the merchandise.[15]

---

14. Domestic value is generally equivalent to retail value in the United States. *See* S. REP. NO. 778, 95th Cong., 2d Sess. 20, *reprinted in* 1978 U.S. CODE CONG. & ADMIN. NEWS 2211, 2231; 19 C.F.R. § 162.43 (1988).
15. § 1592(c); 19 C.F.R. § 162.73 (1988).

It must be noted that the above figures represent the maximum ceilings for each particular class of infraction against which the Customs Service is to weigh section 592 violations on a case-by-case basis.[16]

The three levels of culpability under section 592 are defined in an appendix to the customs regulations containing the guidelines for mitigating the penalties.[17] The definition of negligence is approximately the same as that in civil tort law (neglect of a legal duty through failure to act in the way a reasonable, prudent business person would conduct him or herself in the same circumstances):

> A violation is determined to be negligent if it results from an act or acts (of omission or commission) done through either the failure to exercise the degree of reasonable care and competence expected of a person in the same circumstances in ascertaining the facts or in drawing inferences therefrom, in ascertaining the offender's obligations under the statute, or in communicating information so that it may be understood by the recipient. As a general rule, a violation is determined to be negligent if it results from the offender's failure to exercise reasonable care and competence to ensure that a statement made is correct.[18]

Until an amendment to the guideline, which became effective in late 1989, gross negligence could be found if the violation "result[ed] from an act or acts . . . done with *actual knowledge* of or wanton disregard for the relevant facts and with indifference or disregard for the offender's obliga-

16. For congressional intent, see S. REP. NO. 778, 95th Cong., 2d Sess. 21, *reprinted in* 1978 U.S. CODE CONG. & ADMIN. NEWS 2211, 2232. See text accompanying notes 51–57 *infra* (mitigation of penalties).
17. 19 C.F.R. pt. 171, app. B (1989).
18. 19 C.F.R. pt. 171, app. B, (B)(1) (1989).

tions under the statute, *but without intent to defraud the revenue or violate the laws of the United States.*"[19]

The fraud standard set a higher hurdle: "A violation is determined to be fraudulent if it results from an act or acts (of commission or omission) deliberately done *with intent to defraud the revenue or violate the laws of the United States.*"[20]

A finding of fraud apparently required the Customs Service to prove that the actor knew that the misstatement would break the law or evade duty, wanted it to happen, and did the act. Gross negligence, on the other hand, suggests a state of mind in which the actor did not care what the consequences of the act were, and may even have known that the statement was false, as suggested by the allowance of the possibility of actual knowledge of the facts.

In actual practice, "gross negligence" is a bargaining chip to induce importers with difficult fraud cases against them to settle a penalty matter at a lower level of culpability, if not the lowest.

New definitions of fraud and gross negligence became effective October 1, 1989. In the new definitions, intent to violate the law or to defraud the revenue is no longer required. The fraud definition now reads: "A violation is determined to be fraudulent if the material false statement or act in connection with the transaction was committed (or omitted) knowingly, i.e., was done voluntarily and intentionally, as established by clear and convincing evidence."[21]

The new definition of gross negligence also eliminated mention of intent to defraud (previously, the lack of intent to defraud was an element used to distinguish gross negligence from fraud): "A violation is determined to be grossly

19. 19 C.F.R. pt. 171, app. B, (B)(2) (1989) (emphasis added).
20. 19 C.F.R. pt. 171, app. B, (B)(3) (1989) (emphasis added).
21. 54 Fed. Reg. 36,906 (1989).

negligent if it results from an act or acts (of commission or omission) done with actual knowledge of or wanton disregard for the relevant facts and with indifference to or disregard for the offender's obligations under the statute."[22]

The Customs Service gave its reasons for the changed definitions in Directive 4400-13, dated December 5, 1989. In the same directive, the Customs Service sought to allay the fears of the importing community, which viewed the new guideline as containing the potential for possible serious consequences due to its omission of the previous definition's requirement that the Customs Service prove intent to defraud the revenue or violate the law as an element of fraud.[23]

The Customs Service stated that its stimulus to make the change came from the Department of Justice, which is responsible for pursuing penalty claims in the courts. Justice felt that "in the Court of International Trade, where all elements of the alleged violation including the degree of culpability were subject to the court's *de novo* review," the former guideline, which required intent to defraud the revenue or to violate the laws of the U.S., hindered its "ability to argue a broader definition."[24]

The clarifying directive stated that proving fraud will now require the finding of a twofold level of intent:

1. Intent to make a false statement or omission; and
2. Intent "to deceive, to mislead, or to convey a false impression."[25]

According to Customs, the second element of intent places the Customs Service's definition more in line with

22. *Id.*
23. Letter, Michael H. Lane to K. Kumm, Sept. 29, 1989.
24. Customs Directive 4400-13 (Dec. 5, 1989).
25. *Id.*

other federal agencies' definitions of civil fraud, either as stated in statutes or regulations, or as applied in the courts.

The revised definition of gross negligence is explained as follows: "The major difference between the knowledge requirements of the two standards [fraud and gross negligence] is that gross negligence does not require that a violator knew that there was a falsity. In addition, gross negligence does not require an intent to deceive, mislead or convey a false impression."[26]

Although clerical errors[27] and mistakes of fact[28] technically are considered section 592 violations, penalties are very rarely assessed for them.

Although seizure is not regularly practiced under section 592, if the Customs Service has reasonable cause to believe that a person has violated section 592 and that the person is insolvent or beyond the jurisdiction of the United States or that seizure is deemed essential to protect the revenue of the United States or to prevent the introduction of prohibited merchandise into the United States, then the merchandise may be seized and, upon assessment of a monetary penalty, forfeited unless the penalty is paid within the time specified by law.[29] It is noteworthy that the government's expanded power to seize imports under 19 U.S.C. § 1595a(c) excludes violations of section 592.[30]

---

26. *Id.*
27. 19 C.F.R. § 162.71(c) (1988). Clerical error includes an error in the preparation, assembly, or submission of a document made when a person intended to do one thing but did something else.
28. 19 C.F.R. § 162.71(d) (1988). Mistake of fact refers to an action based on a belief that the material facts were other than they really were.
29. See text accompanying notes 117–124 *infra* (procedure for search and seizure).
30. *See* chapter 23.

Advantage of Prior Voluntary Disclosure

Prior voluntary disclosure[31] is one of the means by which liabilities for section 592 penalties may be very substantially reduced. A prior voluntary disclosure is made if a person discloses, orally or in writing, the circumstances of a section 592 violation before, or without knowledge of, the commencement of a formal investigation of the violation and makes a tender of any actual loss of duties within thirty days.[32]

The conditions related to the timing of disclosure and a definition of "commencement of a formal investigation" are given in the customs regulations.[33] The person asserting ignorance of the commencement of an investigation has the burden of proof of that lack of knowledge. A rebuttable presumption of knowledge is established once an investigative agent has identified himself or herself and informed the person, made inquiry, or requested records, "concerning the type of or circumstances of the disclosed violation."[34] The "investigative agent can be an import specialist, regulatory auditor, inspector, or other Customs officer." Since importers have frequent contact with both import specialists and inspectors, opportunities for the imparting of "knowledge" of an investigation are frequent.

If a prior disclosure is made, the maximum penalties assessed under section 592 cannot exceed the following:

1. For fraudulent violations,
   - If there was loss of duties, an amount equal to the loss, or
   - If there was no loss of duties, 10 percent of the dutiable value of the merchandise; and

31. 19 C.F.R. § 162.74(e) (1990).
32. 19 C.F.R. §§ 162.74(a) & 162.74(h) (1988).
33. 19 C.F.R. §§ 162.74(b) & 162.74(d) (1988).
34. 19 C.F.R. § 162.73 (1988).

2. For negligent or grossly negligent violations,
   - If there was loss of duties, interest on the duties lost from the date of liquidation at the rate applied by section 6621 of the Internal Revenue Code of 1954, as amended,[35] or
   - If there was no loss of duties, the claim for a monetary penalty is to be remitted in full.[36]

Procedural Aspects of Section 592 Cases

One important development under amended section 592 is the establishment of due process safeguards that not only disclose to the importer the facts and allegations against it, but also afford it an opportunity to present its arguments and defenses in the course of the administrative process.

Prepenalty Notice[37]

If the district director has reasonable cause to believe that a violation of section 592 has occurred warranting further proceedings, he or she must issue to the person concerned a notice of his or her intent to issue a claim for a monetary penalty.[38]

Briefly, the contents of the prepenalty notice include (1) the facts of violation (including a description of the merchandise); (2) all material facts establishing the alleged violation, as well as all the laws and regulations allegedly violated; and (3) notice of the right to make presentations (oral or written[39]) within thirty days of the mailing of the

35. § 1592(c)(4).
36. *See* 19 C.F.R. app. B, pt. E.
37. 19 C.F.R. § 162.77 (1988).
38. No prepenalty notice need be issued if the claim is for $1,000 or less or if the violation involves a noncommercial importation.
39. For form and content of a written presentation, *see* 19 C.F.R. § 162.78(c) (1988).

notice as to why a claim for a monetary penalty should not be issued, or if issued, why it should be in a lesser amount than proposed.[40]

The reason for the prepenalty procedure is to allow an importer the opportunity to avoid the formal receipt of a monetary claim, which would have to be disclosed in its financial statements and might affect its credit standing. If the Customs Service accepts the importer's claim for remission, the matter is closed; if not, a penalty notice is issued. The procedure also allows Customs to issue claims according to a lesser degree of culpability than that proposed in the prepenalty notice and thus encourage more rapid settlements of claims against importers.

The Court of International Trade has held that failure to serve a prepenalty notice amounted to a potentially fatal defect in the Customs Service's attempt to detain merchandise in a section 592 proceeding aiming to penalize an importer for alleged false declarations of the origin of coffee.[41] In obtaining specific legislative authority to seize coffee, the Customs Service also obtained sweeping authority to seize commercial shipments generally.[42]

Penalty Claim

The importer should be notified promptly about an alleged section 592 violation.[43] If the Customs Service believes a violation has occurred, a penalty claim is issued. The alleged violator must have a reasonable opportunity,

---

40. See also text accompanying notes 51–55 *infra* (mitigation guidelines).
41. Rey Cafe Coffee Co. v. Pitman, 5 Ct. Int'l Trade 112 (1983) (holding that an arbitrarily short time limit—four days in that case—imposed by the Customs Service for responding to notice of intention to levy a penalty in connection with merchandise not in accordance with § 1592 or 19 C.F.R. § 162.78, which allow thirty days in most cases to respond to a prepenalty notice).
42. 19 U.S.C.A. § 1595a(c). *See* chapter 23.
43. 19 C.F.R. § 162.79 (1988).

under section 618 of the Tariff Act of 1930, as amended,[44] to make representations seeking remission or mitigation of the monetary penalty.

The Customs Procedural Reform and Simplification Act of 1978, among other changes, shortened the statute of limitations for the United States to file suit on section 592 cases based on negligence or gross negligence from five years from the date of discovery to five years from the time of the offense. The Customs Service interpreted this change as allowing it to reduce the time period in which the named parties could respond to a prepenalty[45] or penalty notice[46] to a "reasonable time" (but not less than seven days) in cases where the statute of limitations has less than a year to run. The Court of International Trade held in *United States v. Ross*[47] that seven days' notice did not violate constitutional due process requirements. In that case, Customs issued a prepenalty notice on February 24, followed by a penalty notice dated March 11. The five-year statute of limitations on the claims was due to expire that year, but, in completely deferring to the Customs Service's discretion, the court did not note the actual time remaining under the statute.

A petitioner dissatisfied with a decision of the district director or the commissioner of customs may file a supplemental petition for relief from fines, penalties,[48] and liquidated damages.[49] Under the regulations,[50] apart from other requirements, both sections allow a second supplemental petition only upon full payment of all penalties and with-

44. 19 U.S.C.A. § 1618 (West 1980).
45. 19 C.F.R. § 162.78 (1988).
46. 19 C.F.R. § 171.12 (1988).
47. United States v. Ross, 574 F. Supp. 1067 (Ct. Int'l Trade 1983).
48. 19 C.F.R. § 171.33 (1988).
49. 19 C.F.R. § 172.33 (1988). The liquidated damages notice, CF 5955A, is reprinted in appendix 28.
50. For an explanation, see 49 Fed. Reg. 1681 *et seq.* (Jan. 13, 1984).

held duties within sixty days of notice of the decision of the first supplemental petition.

Remission or Mitigation of Penalties

The Customs Service, under 19 U.S.C. § 1618, is authorized to issue regulations governing the remission or mitigation of fines, penalties, or forfeitures (related to any vessel, vehicle, merchandise, or baggage) it may impose, upon the filing of a proper petition for relief, if it finds the existence of circumstances that "justify" remission or mitigation. When the claim for the penalty is less than $100,000, the matter can be resolved at the local district director's level. Should the amount exceed $100,000, the matter will be referred to Headquarters in Washington.[51]

On January 13, 1984, appendix B ("Revised Penalty Guidelines") was added to 19 C.F.R. part 171.[52] It is intended that these guidelines be applied by Customs Service officers in prepenalty proceedings and in determining the monetary penalty assessed in the penalty notice.

In discussing the disposition of cases, the guidelines note that in mitigating claims, the district director or appropriate Customs Service official must consider all information in the petition and all available evidence. Mitigating factors to be considered (though not exclusively) are contributing Customs Service error, cooperation with the investigation, immediate remedial action, inexperience in importing, and the prior good record of the violator.[53] Examples of aggravating factors include obstructing an investigation, withholding evidence, and having prior substantive violations.[54]

51. 19 C.F.R. § 171.21 (1990).
52. 49 Fed. Reg. 1681 *et seq.* (Jan. 13, 1984) (hereinafter Guidelines). According to the Service, the guidelines were issued as an appendix rather than adopted as regulations because they instruct and guide Customs Service field officers rather than the general public.
53. Guidelines pt. (F), *supra* note 52.
54. Guidelines pt. (G), *supra* note 52.

Four extraordinary factors have been specified for consideration in connection with further relief. These are the inability to obtain jurisdiction over, or inability to enforce a judgment against, the violator; inability to pay the mitigated penalty; extraordinary expenses to be borne by the Customs Service; and Customs Service knowledge of a nonfraudulent violation and failure on its part to inform the violator so that earlier corrective action could have been taken.[55]

The Customs Service may not assess a penalty against both an importer of record (such as a customs broker making entry under its own bond) and the actual importer for the same violation unless it alleges joint action. In such a case, the parties would be subject to joint and several liability for a *single* penalty. However, the Customs Service may assess separate penalties against allegedly guilty parties where multiple violations are alleged to occur in the same transaction.

Such was the holding in *United States v. F.H. Fenderson, Inc.*,[56] in which neither the Canadian owner/exporter of crabmeat nor its U.S. customs broker/importer of record converted the Canadian dollar invoice amounts into U.S. dollars before the broker filed entries. The court found that the parties' offenses were not the same: the exporter was held to have submitted false invoices to Customs, while the broker was said to have filed entries with incorrect values. The exporter had settled its case, and the broker alleged that the settlement released it from further liability. The *Fenderson* court held that the government's settlement with a party in a separate case on the same transaction does not release the other party from liability under section 592.[57]

---

55. Guidelines pt. (H), *supra* note 52.
56. United States v. F.H. Fenderson, Inc., 11 Ct. Int'l Trade 199, 205 (1987).
57. *Id.*

Statute of Limitations

In general, upon the referral to him or her of a fine, penalty, or forfeiture matter, the United States attorney must initiate a civil suit based on fraud within five years after the time the alleged offense was, or should have been, discovered. The Customs Procedural Reform and Simplification Act provides that in cases of a nonfraudulent section 592 violation, the five years begin running from the date the alleged violation was committed.[58]

Liability for Duty Apart from Penalty Claims

In *United States v. RCA, Consumer Electronics Division,*[59] the district court determined that the five-year statute of limitations prescribed in 19 U.S.C. § 1621 governs all actions brought pursuant to section 592, be they for the assessment of penalties or restoration of duties or both. However, the Customs Service takes the position in administrative proceedings that even under section 592, the obligation to pay duties exists apart from section 592, and thus the five-year statute of limitations does not govern. The Customs Service argues for an open-ended power to collect revenues, but it can cite no authority for such power.

Recovery of Duties Under Section 592

The Court of Appeals for the Federal Circuit has held that a suit for the recovery of duties under section 592 may be brought against "innocent parties," i.e., those not directly accused of the violation. *United States v. Blum*[60] involved a Canadian party as actual owner of goods declared to be

58. 19 U.S.C.A. § 1621 (West 1980).
59. United States v. RCA, Consumer Elecs. Div., No. IP 80-933-c (S.D. Ind. Dec. 16, 1983). *See also* U.S. v. Rockwell Int'l Corp., 628 F. Supp. 206 (Ct. Int'l Trade 1986).
60. United States v. Blum, Appeal No. 87-1436 (Fed. Cir. 1988).

duty-free, but held to be dutiable. The Customs Service had lodged a section 592 claim alleging entry by means of false statements against the shipper/owner.

Also present in the action as defendants were the importer of record (the customs brokerage firm that filed the entries) and the surety company that underwrote the entry bond. The U.S. parties were not accused of the underlying fraud, but as the importer and surety, they were jointly liable for the duty. They were thus sued under section 592(d) for recovery of the duties.

The Court of International Trade had dismissed the case against the broker and the surety on the grounds that they were not proper parties to a section 592(d) proceeding, since no claim of culpable conduct under section 592(a) had been made against them. The Federal Circuit reversed, finding no indication in the legislative history of the 1978 amendments to section 592 that Congress intended to relieve parties liable for duty payments of that obligation merely because a culpable party might be jointly liable on the same set of facts.

Judicial Review

An importer dissatisfied with an adverse mitigation decision may refuse to pay the assessed penalty, in which case the government can initiate a civil action in the Court of International Trade to enforce collection of the penalty. Under the Customs Procedural Reform and Simplification Act, judicial review for the recovery of any monetary penalty claimed under section 592 has been expanded to include the following provisions:

1. De novo review must be had of "all issues including the amount of the penalty";
2. The government's burden of proof in a fraud case is to establish the alleged violation by clear and convincing evidence;

3. The government's burden of proof in a gross negligence case is to establish by the preponderance of the evidence all elements of the alleged violation; and
4. The government's burden of proof in a negligence case is to establish by the preponderance of the evidence that the act or omission constituted a violation, while the alleged violator has the burden of proving that the act or omission did not arise out of negligence.[61]

Jurisdiction of actions by the government to recover section 592 penalties was transferred from the United States district courts to the Court of International Trade under the Customs Courts Act of 1980. In *United States v. Accurate Mould Co.*,[62] the court explicitly reversed a memorandum opinion arising from *United States v. Digital Equipment Corp.*[63] that had held that while the Customs Courts Act of 1980 granted the Court of International Trade exclusive jurisdiction over in personam penalty actions arising under section 592, as amended by the Customs Procedural Reform and Simplification Act of 1978, the Court of International Trade did not have jurisdiction over in rem penalty actions arising under former section 592.

The courts have also addressed the issue of whether the statutory provision for protesting a "fine, penalty, or forfeiture" includes a voluntary payment by an importer. In *Carlingswitch, Inc. v. United States*,[64] the Customs Court determined and the Court of Customs and Patent Appeals

61. § 1592(e).
62. United States v. Accurate Mould Co., 546 F. Supp. 567 (Ct. Int'l Trade 1982).
63. United States v. Digital Equip. Corp., 3 Ct. Int'l Trade 52 (1982).
64. Carlingswitch, Inc., v. United States, 500 F. Supp. 223 (Cust. Ct. 1980), *aff'd*, 651 F.2d 768 (C.C.P.A. 1981), *on renewal of action*, 560 F. Supp. 46 (Ct. Int'l Trade 1983).

(CCPA) affirmed that neither an importer's voluntary tender of almost $92,000 to the Customs Service in connection with an ongoing section 592 penalty investigation nor the Service's subsequent refusal to refund the money was an "exaction" within the meaning of 19 U.S.C. § 1514(a)(3) for the purpose of establishing jurisdiction in the Customs Court over the importer's action to recover funds. The importer had tendered the $92,000 to limit its potential penalty liability by complying with the "voluntary disclosure" practice of the Customs Service. When the penalty case was ended and the Service's claims vitiated by the running of the statute of limitations, the plaintiff requested a refund of its revenue-loss deposit. The court found that in the context of a strictly voluntary payment to the Customs Service by an importer, absent an asserted penalty, demand, or other compulsion to pay, no charge or exaction could be found to form the predicate for the court's jurisdiction under 19 U.S.C. § 1514(a)(3).

Similarly, in *ITT Semiconductors v. United States*,[65] the court determined that the tender of "withheld duties" by the importer in the course of its petition for mitigation of penalties was voluntarily effected as part of a settlement negotiated to absolve the importer from paying a higher penalty amount.

In 28 U.S.C. § 1581(a), it is provided that "[t]he Court of International Trade shall have exclusive jurisdiction of any civil action commenced to contest the denial of a protest, in whole or in part, under section 515 of the Tariff Act of 1930." However, even though in *ITT Semiconductors* the importer filed a timely protest, the threshold question remained whether the Customs Service settlement decision that the plaintiff (importer) protested was protestable at all. Since the court decided that the plaintiff acted voluntarily and without compulsion from the Customs Service in mak-

65. ITT Semiconductors v. United States, 6 Ct. Int'l Trade 231 (1983).

ing the payment, a charge or exaction could not be said to exist under 19 U.S.C. § 1514(a)(3) for purposes of establishing subject matter jurisdiction in the Court of International Trade. Therefore, the protest, although timely filed, was inappropriate, because the settlement decision was not a protestable decision; jurisdiction could not be said to exist under 28 U.S.C. § 1581(a).

Penalties Not Under Section 592

Apart from section 592, other civil penalty provisions are enforced by the Customs Service. The following are the more significant nonsection 592 civil penalties related to the importation of goods.

Seizure of Imports Introduced Contrary to Law

As a result of the enactment of the Anti-Drug Abuse Act of 1986, a new subsection (c) was added to 19 U.S.C. § 1595a:

> Any merchandise that is introduced or attempted to be introduced into the United States contrary to law (other than in violation of section 1592 of this title) may be seized and forfeited.

This provision augmenting the seizure power of the Customs Service strongly impacts import practice and will be treated separately in chapter 23.

Failure to Declare (Individual Travelers)[66]

Any article not included in the declaration and entry as made (and before examination of the baggage has begun) will be subject to forfeiture, and a penalty will be assessed equal to its value.[67]

---

66. 19 U.S.C.A. § 1497 (West 1988).
67. *See* chapter 5 for a discussion of such penalties.

Unlawful Lading and Unlading[68]

Anyone lading or unlading merchandise or baggage from any vessel or vehicle without a license or permit will incur the liability of a penalty equal to the value of the merchandise or baggage or forfeiture of the goods.

Manifest False or Lacking[69]

Failure to produce an accurate manifest by the master of any vessel or the person in charge of a vehicle bound for the United States subjects the person to a penalty equal to the discrepancy, up to a maximum of $10,000 or the domestic value of the merchandise to which the inaccuracy relates, whichever is less. The Customs Service is required to follow a procedure similar to that in section 592 cases when the error arises from a clerical mistake.

Departure Before Report or Entry[70]

Failure of any foreign vessel or vehicle to make a proper report or entry once it arrives within the limits of any collection district and departs (or attempts to do so) will subject it to liability for a penalty of $5,000 for the first violation and $10,000 for each subsequent violation, as well as forfeiture of the vessel or vehicle.

Aiding Unlawful Importation[71]

Any person who directs, assists financially, or is in any way involved in any activity facilitating the illegal importation of any article will be liable to a penalty equal to the value of the article(s) introduced into United States commerce.

---

68. 19 U.S.C.A. § 1453 (West 1988).
69. 19 U.S.C.A. § 1584 (West 1988).
70. 19 U.S.C.A. § 1585 (West 1988).
71. 19 U.S.C.A. § 1595a (West 1988).

Unlicensed Unlading of Passengers[72]

Any master of a vessel or person in charge of a vehicle responsible for the unlicensed unlading of any passenger will be liable to a penalty of $500 for each passenger so unladen.

Unlawful Exportation or Importation of Certain Vehicles

A section has been added to the Tariff Act of 1930 to subject anyone who exports or imports any stolen self-propelled vehicle[73] or any self-propelled vehicle from which the identification number has been removed to a civil penalty not to exceed $10,000.[74]

Offers in Compromise

While the Customs Service's internal penalty guidelines allow mitigation under 19 U.S.C. § 1618 of virtually every civil penalty that can be imposed, the Tariff Act contains another provision which can be of great usefulness in penalty cases. Section 617 (19 U.S.C. § 1617) allows the Secretary of the Treasury to compromise a claim within his enforcement authority. The Secretary must review and approve such offers in compromise in consultation with the chief counsel of the Treasury Department.

The Customs Service follows an internal guideline that offers in compromise will be seriously entertained when there is "litigation risk" in the Service's position; i.e., if the Customs Service were to pursue the matter in court, it might lose the case. By way of example, cases with complicated fact patterns, with the potential for extensive and

72. 19 U.S.C.A. § 1454 (West 1988).
73. Self-propelled vehicles include automobiles, trucks, tractors, buses, motorcycles, and motor homes. 19 U.S.C.A. § 1627a(a) (West Supp. 1989).
74. *Id.*

inconclusive audits, and containing possible disputes over procedural matters such as prior disclosure are candidates for offers in compromise.

In fact, the "litigation risk" guideline can encompass virtually every case in which the alleged offender has a claim in its defense, and it should be considered as an option in managing the case. Some Customs districts actually seem to prefer an offer in compromise, accompanied by a tender of the proposed settlement amount, to continuing a prepenalty proceeding under section 592, an arrangement which would also forestall the negative effect a penalty claim has on the importer's financial statement.

Criminal Penalties

It should be noted at the outset that the specific monetary fines prescribed by the statutes discussed in this section have been superseded by new legislation, as discussed in "A Note About Fines" below.

Entry of merchandise effected with the intent to defraud the government of revenues or making illegal entries may be actionable under the federal criminal code. There are thirteen sections in the criminal code covering crimes related to imports alone (18 U.S.C. §§ 541–553), plus sections of other legislation providing for prosecution for importations. The import-related crimes include entry of goods falsely classified,[75] entry of goods by means of false statements,[76] entry of goods for less than legal duty,[77] relanding of goods,[78] smuggling goods into the United States,[79] smug-

75. 18 U.S.C.A. § 541 (West 1976).
76. 18 U.S.C.A. § 542 (West 1976).
77. 18 U.S.C.A. § 543 (West 1976).
78. 18 U.S.C.A. § 544 (West 1976).
79. 18 U.S.C.A. § 545 (West 1976).

gling goods into foreign countries,[80] and illegally receiving or depositing goods in any buildings upon the boundary line between the United States and any foreign country.[81]

By far the most commonly cited customs criminal law enforcement provision is 18 U.S.C. § 542, the criminal counterpart to the civil penalty statute, section 592 (discussed above). Section 542 provides that it is a criminal offense to

1. Introduce or enter into United States commerce any imported merchandise by means of any fraudulent invoice, declaration, or affidavit or by means of any false statement or false practices, whether or not the United States will or may be deprived of any lawful duties; or
2. Through willful act or omission deprive the United States of any lawful duties accruing upon merchandise through such false or fraudulent declaration, invoice or statement. For each such offense, the violator will be fined a maximum of $5,000 or imprisoned for not more than two years or both.

In confirming the dismissal of an indictment based on section 542, the court of appeals in *United States v. Teraoka*[82] ruled that alleged false statements inflating the price of steel nails to avoid a "trigger price" that would cause dumping duties to be added were incidental to entry and not material in achieving entry. The merchandise thus had not been entered "by means of" the statements, and the indictment accordingly did not state a violation of section 542.

80. 18 U.S.C.A. § 546 (West 1976).
81. 18 U.S.C.A. § 547 (West 1976).
82. United States v. Teraoka, 669 F.2d 577 (9th Cir. 1982).

A catchall criminal penalty provision is 18 U.S.C. § 1001, which stipulates that whoever in any matter within the jurisdiction of any department or agency of the United States knowingly and willfully falsifies, conceals, or covers up a material fact or makes any fraudulent statements or intentionally uses any false writings or document will be fined not more than $10,000 or imprisoned not more than five years or both.

Of equal significance are criminal penalties where two or more persons conspire to commit any offense against the United States or to defraud the United States or any agency thereof (18 U.S.C. § 371). Each conspirator can be fined not more than $10,000, imprisoned for not more than five years, or both.

It is to be noted that Congress did not intend to make civil and criminal sanctions mutually exclusive. Title 18 U.S.C. § 542 specifically states, "Nothing in this section shall be construed to relieve imported merchandise from forfeiture under other provisions of law." In *One Lot Emerald Cut Stones and One Ring v. United States*,[83] the Supreme Court stated that the double jeopardy clause of the fifth amendment (which provides that a person may not be punished again for the same offense) does not foreclose a forfeiture action under 19 U.S.C. § 1497 (penalties for failure to declare) following a smuggling acquittal under 18 U.S.C. § 545, because "neither two criminal trials nor two criminal punishments" are involved.

In *United States v. Valley Steel Products Co.*,[84] the Court of International Trade upheld the Customs Service's right to seek substantial civil penalties, if they are "reasonable" and in relation to revenue loss, in a case where an importer has paid a fine in a related criminal case. The court distin-

83. One Lot Emerald Cut Stones & One Ring v. United States, 409 U.S. 232, 235 (1972).
84. United States v. Valley Steel Prods. Co., 729 F. Supp. 1356 (Ct. Int'l Trade 1990).

guished the recent decision of the Supreme Court in *United States v. Halper.*[85] In *Halper*, the fifth amendment double jeopardy clause was held to protect a defendant already convicted of criminal charges and fined for Medicaid fraud from large nominal civil penalties not related to the economic impact of the alleged violation.

The steel companies which were the defendants in *Valley Steel* had pleaded nolo contendere (no contest) to criminal charges of false invoicing to avoid the payment of dumping duties, and were fined $10,000. The government then sued to recover penalties based on the amounts of duty not paid by reason of the fraud.

In distinguishing *Halper*, the *Valley Steel* court found that the penalties assessed under section 1592 were related to the claimed loss of revenues by the guidelines providing for multiples of the revenue claim as penalties. The penalties thus did not constitute a second punishment for the importer's misconduct.

A Note About Fines

Although the descriptions of the offenses in the United States Criminal Code (Title 18, United States Code) still carry varying recommendations for fines, sweeping revisions of the sentencing legislation in 1984 and 1987 superseded the maximum amounts suggested elsewhere in the Code. As a general rule, the highest fine "per offense" to be levied against an individual is $250,000; against an organization, $500,000 (in lieu of the fines originally specified in the statute). Courts may also levy fines equalling twice the gross gain to the defendant or twice the gross loss to the victim.[86]

---

85. United States v. Halper, 490 U.S. 435, 109 S. Ct. 1892, 104 L. Ed. 2d 487 (1989).
86. 18 U.S.C.A. §§ 3571 *et seq.* (West 1985 & Supp. 1990).

Other Criminal Statutes

Other laws administered by the Customs Service can give rise to criminal liability. For example, altering or destroying the country of origin marking on imported merchandise with intent to conceal the goods' origin is punishable by up to a year in prison and a $100,000 fine.[87] Willfully importing motion pictures or phonorecords infringing copyrights for commercial gain can lead to prosecution under the Piracy and Counterfeiting Amendments Act of 1982.[88] Importing obscene matter has long been a felony with a potential five-year sentence for first offenders,[89] and trafficking in child pornography can result in even more severe penalties.[90] Conviction of drug smuggling under the Drug Abuse Prevention Act of 1970[91] can lead to life imprisonment and fines up to $20 million (if a person dies as a result of ingesting the drug), while importation or exportation of drug paraphernalia can lead to a three-year sentence and a fine of $100,000.[92]

Anti-Apartheid Measures

In an effort to increase pressure on South Africa to abandon race discrimination, the United States adopted the Comprehensive Anti-Apartheid Act of 1986.[93] Of great importance were the economic sanctions contained within title III of the Act. For the most part, these economic sanctions take the form of trade bans, the violations of which are actionable under criminal law. The prohibitions

87. 19 U.S.C.A. § 1304 (West Supp. 1991).
88. 18 U.S.C.A. § 2318 (West Supp. 1990).
89. 18 U.S.C.A. § 1462 (West 1984).
90. 18 U.S.C.A. § 2252 (West Supp. 1990).
91. 21 U.S.C.A. § 952 (West 1981 & Supp. 1990).
92. *Id.*
93. Pub. L. No. 99-440, 100 Stat. 1086 (1986).

include bans on the export of nuclear[94] and military goods,[95] crude oil and petroleum products,[96] and computer goods to certain government entities.[97] The variety of items prohibited for import, subject to our own national defense necessities, is more extensive. It includes South African currency,[98] military articles,[99] uranium and coal,[100] agricultural products and food,[101] iron and steel,[102] sugar,[103] as well as all goods produced by, or substantially subsidized by, parastatal organizations.[104]

Title III includes various other economic sanctions including the prohibition of any United States government agency from importing goods or services from South African parastatal organizations, subject to items necessary for diplomatic and consular purposes,[105] and the prohibition of United States government assistance to South African concerns including, but not limited to, U.S. trade missions and other endeavors to promote trade[106] with and tourism in[107] South Africa.

The bite of title III was first felt by U.S. business concerns in early 1989 when a Long Island, N.Y. firm was indicted for attempting to import used civil aircraft engines purchased from a subsidized South African airline. Upon its guilty plea, the firm was fined $1 million and its chief

94. *Id.* § 307.
95. *Id.* § 317.
96. *Id.* § 321.
97. *Id.* § 304.
98. *Id.* § 301.
99. *Id.* § 302.
100. *Id.* § 309.
101. *Id.* § 319.
102. *Id.* § 320.
103. *Id.* § 323.
104. *Id.* § 303.
105. *Id.* § 314.
106. *Id.* § 316.
107. *Id.* § 315.

executive officer was personally liable for $100,000 and a jail term of three months, with an additional thirty-three months of probation. He had faced a sentence of up to ten years in prison.[108]

Searches and Seizures

The Tariff Act of 1930 and later amendments authorize and amplify the Customs Service's long-standing function and authority to inspect, search, and seize in enforcing customs and related laws.

Although the Service's inspections, searches, and seizures are conducted within constitutional limitations, the stringent fourth amendment prohibition against unreasonable searches and seizures, i.e., searches and seizures not based on probable cause, is suspended, for example, with respect to border searches by the Service. Under 19 U.S.C. § 1582, the law allows "detention and search" under regulations promulgated by the Secretary of the Treasury of "all persons coming onto the United States from foreign countries." Furthermore, 19 U.S.C. § 482 explicitly authorizes government agents to conduct searches of persons or vehicles without a search warrant at the nation's borders if they "suspect there is merchandise which is subject to duty, or shall have been introduced into the United States in any manner contrary to law."

In *United States v. Villamonte-Marquez*,[109] the Supreme Court upheld as constitutional the boarding and search of a vessel by the Customs Service without articulable suspicion, under 19 U.S.C. § 1581(a) (boarding of vessels). Within a year after the Supreme Court decision, the Customs Service enacted regulations authorizing its officers to

108. N.Y.L.J., Apr. 4, 1989 at 1, col. 3; *Exec Sentenced for Doing Business with South Africa*, United Press Int'l, June 1, 1989.

109. United States v. Villamonte-Marquez, 103 S. Ct. 2573 (1988).

stop and search American vessels anywhere "without a requirement that there be probable cause to believe that such vessel is violating or has violated the laws" of the United States.[110]

Based on 19 U.S.C. § 1581, Customs Service officers are also authorized at any place within the United States or its customs waters to board any vessel or vehicle, to examine its manifest, and to inspect and search it and any person or cargo to compel compliance with customs law—all without a search warrant.

In "Operation Zero Tolerance," a well-publicized antidrug campaign in 1987 and 1988, Customs Service and Coast Guard vessels stopped and searched vessels in ports and on the high seas, seizing them and subjecting them to forfeiture if *any amount* of a controlled substance was found aboard. The action hit cruise line operators and yacht charterers especially hard, as they are generally unable to control their guests' behavior. The policy was moderated in the fall of 1988. Now, generally, a seizure will not occur unless quantities greater than "personal use" amounts[111] are discovered.

Although a search warrant is not required for section 482 or section 1581 searches conducted on vessels, vehicles, passengers, cargo, baggage, and imported goods, a search warrant based on probable cause is needed for any search or seizure conducted within any dwelling house, store, or other building suspected of housing merchandise imported contrary to the law. While legally within the premises (e.g., a Customs-bonded warehouse), a Customs Service officer may seize (without a warrant) merchandise that the officer is able to identify as having been imported contrary to the law.[112] However, a Customs Service officer is limited in his

---

110. 48 Fed. Reg. 52,897 (1983); 19 C.F.R. § 162.3 (1988).
111. 19 C.F.R. § 162.11 (1988).
112. 19 C.F.R. § 162.13 (1988).

or her search to the room(s) in a building occupied by the person named or described in the warrant.[113]

Seizures

The various statutory provisions authorizing seizure serve different purposes in the Customs Service's enforcement activities. Under section 592, merchandise is seized solely to ensure payment of a monetary penalty or to prevent the introduction of restricted merchandise into domestic commerce. Merchandise will only be forfeited if the penalty is not paid. However, for example, 19 U.S.C. § 1595a provides for the search and seizure within buildings of merchandise suspected to have been imported contrary to law, and 19 U.S.C. § 703 authorizes the seizure and forfeiture of vessels employed in the smuggling of merchandise into the United States or used to defraud the United States government of revenue. The seizure provision with potentially the widest application is 19 U.S.C. § 1595a(c), which enables the Customs Service to seize merchandise attempted to be introduced into the United States contrary to law. Subsection 1595a(c) will be explored fully in chapter 24.

Property may be seized, if available, by any Customs Service officer who has reasonable cause to believe that customs laws and regulations have been violated, by reason of which the property has become subject to seizure or forfeiture.[114] Every vessel, vehicle, animal, aircraft, or other conveyance that is being used to facilitate importation into the United States contrary to law may be seized and held subject to forfeiture.[115]

Resolving conflicting decisions between circuits, a recent Supreme Court decision held that the Customs Service can-

113. 19 U.S.C.A. § 1581 (West 1980); 19 C.F.R. § 162.21 (1983).
114. 19 C.F.R. § 162.22(b) (1983).
115. 19 U.S.C. § 1595a(a) (West 1980).

not be held liable for damage to even temporarily detained property arising from the Service's negligent handling or storage.[116]

Procedures in Seizure Cases

Written notice of any fine or penalty incurred, as well as any liability to forfeiture, must be given to each party known to have an interest or claim in the seized property. Each interested party must also be informed of the right to apply for relief under 19 U.S.C. § 1618 (authorizing mitigation of penalties or remission of forfeitures).[117] If the interested party fails to petition for relief under part 171 or fails to pay or to arrange to pay the fine or penalty within sixty days from the mailing date of the violation notice,[118] the district director, after required collection action, must refer the case promptly to the United States attorney for the institution of judicial or summary forfeiture proceedings.[119]

Realizing the severity of the consequences arising from a seizure, the courts have demanded strict adherence to formal regulatory requirements[120] as well as constitutional guarantees of due process. Among the requirements dictated by due process are adequate notice and evidence of no undue delay in instituting the forfeiture proceedings.[121] Hence, the Customs Service now routinely requires claimants to seized property to file forms indicating their "Elec-

---

116. Kosak v. United States, 104 S. Ct. 1519 (1984).
117. 19 C.F.R. § 162.32 & pt. 171 (1984).
118. Upon seizure of property, the Customs Service officer must prepare a receipt and leave it either with the person from whom the property was seized or in a conspicuous place on the premises searched. See 19 C.F.R. §§ 162.15 & 162.21 (1990).
119. 19 C.F.R. §§ 162.42 & 162.45–.47 (1990).
120. See, e.g., Wiscope S.A. v. Commodity Futures Trading Comm'n, 604 F.2d 764 (2d Cir. 1979).
121. See, e.g., United States v. Eight (8) Rhodesian State Statues, 449 F. Supp. 193 (C.D. Cal. 1978).

tion of Proceedings"[122] (immediate forfeiture proceedings or administrative petition) and waiving the right to immediate referral to the Justice Department for judicial forfeiture.

When the Customs Service refers a case to the United States Attorney, the Justice Department must without delay commence the proper proceedings or prosecution[123] even in cases where a petition for relief is pending before the Customs Service.[124] For example, where the claimant has elected administrative proceedings that are still pending when the statute of limitations is about to run, and the claimant will not waive the statute, an immediate referral to the United States Attorney would be in order.

In *Sarkisian v. United States*,[125] the Tenth Circuit held that a nine-month delay between the date of completion of the Customs Service's investigation and the filing of the forfeiture action was unreasonable; the seizure was declared invalid. Later cases, however, have extended to eighteen months the time in which the government's inaction in proceeding against seized property is deemed not to prejudice a claimant.[126]

Fact Patterns in Commercial Violations and Customs Frauds: Some Common Themes

The examples and illustrations that follow are taken from the experiences of the author and from material available in his files, or from the facts of cases of wide renown. Details

122. See appendix 22.
123. 19 U.S.C. § 1604 (West Supp. 1983).
124. See, e.g., United States v. One (1) Douglas A-26B Aircraft, 436 F. Supp. 1292 (C.D. Ga. 1977); United States v. A Quantity of Gold Jewelry, 379 F. Supp. 283 (C.D. Cal. 1974).
125. Sarkisian v. United States, 472 F.2d 468 (10th Cir. 1973).
126. United States v. $8,850 in United States Currency, 461 U.S. 555, 103 S. Ct. 2005, 76 L. Ed. 2d 143 (1983).

have been changed or eliminated in order to avoid identification of real persons or companies.

I. Customs notified a multinational corporation that certain imported material was misdescribed on an invoice its overseas branch, the shipper, had prepared. The American management investigated the claim and found that the misdescription of the goods was blatant. The underpayment of duty on that entry and several others amounted to many thousands of dollars over a one-year period. The importer's officers also discovered that the branch manager who signed the invoices had embezzled substantial sums from the company to pay off gambling debts. He seemingly thought he would make amends by attempting to cheat United States Customs on the parent firm's behalf.

The American management discovered a second classification issue amid the entries of the merchandise whose misclassification Customs had alleged in the notice of investigation. Used by itself, some of the company's merchandise was commonly and technically known by a certain name. If combined with an additional part, the products would have a different use and be commonly referred to by another name. In addition, it would be dutiable at around a tenth of the rate of the same goods imported without the adjunct. A long history of court cases, Headquarters rulings, and even legislative history established the tariff distinction, even though the names for the distinct items were often considered interchangeable by the public at large.

When the importer audited its entries from the overseas branch with the assistance of counsel, it found that the problem Customs had not discovered was potentially many times more costly than the first, and involved entries made at ports all around the country. By means of an offer in compromise featuring the significant effort it had spared the Customs Service in conducting its own audit, the importer settled both cases. The case Customs was preparing as to the first type of merchandise was closed upon tender of the mitigated amount for such a case, and the sum Customs accepted to close out the second matter was exactly what the importer would have paid for the alleged offense with the benefit of a prior disclosure.

II. An importer of textiles from the Far East entered a shipment of wearing apparel on which it had paid $30 per dozen for the merchandise, plus $10 per dozen for a "quota" charge.[127] However, in the belief that they were not dutiable, the quota charges were not shown on the invoice and no duty was paid on them at the time of entry. The Customs Service discovered that the importer had received a separate bill for the quota charges.

Thus, aside from the question of whether the quota charges were legally dutiable or not, a technical violation existed because of nondisclosure. It is the position of the Customs Service that all payments surrounding an importation must be disclosed; then, the Service will decide whether they should be dutiable or not. In this case, despite the fact that the dutiability of the quota charge itself was ultimately successfully disputed, a substantial penalty was assessed.

III. A large corporation imported special-purpose lenses for certain photo-optical equipment. The Customs Service made a routine request to the importer as to whether any molds, designs, drawings, tools, etc., were furnished to the manufacturer by the importer.[128] The importer responded that it had indeed furnished drawings as a guide in manu-

---

127. *See* chapter 19.

128. Under United States value law, as long as the design, drawing, or engineering work originates in the United States or is performed by U.S. citizens, the cost incurred would not be considered an assist. See chapter 4 and discussion on assists.

facturing the lenses. Customs took the position that these were undeclared dutiable assists,[129] and it issued a pre-penalty notice demanding the maximum amount under the guidelines for a fraudulent entry.

The responding attorney's petition, evolved after considerable research into the matter, proved that the drawings furnished were not engineering designs, but were in the nature of specifications, not dutiable assists. It was shown that the drawings merely followed standards in the trade and were widely available as drawings in universal texts on lenses, with variations amounting to basic size and shape changes.[130] The petition was successful in terminating the matter without a penalty.

IV. Many classic penalty cases arise when actual materials that go into production, such as fabrics for making garments, are furnished without charge to the foreign manufacturer, and when subsequently the manufacturer bills only for its labor, profit, and those materials it supplies, neglecting to state on its invoice anything about the materials supplied to it. Although it is not necessarily the commercial obligation of the shipper to account for those fabrics (since it does not furnish them), the knowledgeable importer usually instructs its shipper exactly how to invoice and disclose such facts. Further, even if the shipper does not disclose the facts on its invoice, it is the clear duty of the importer to make them known at the time of entry and to pay any additional duties due at that time.

The author's files contain an instance when a designer for a novice garment importer was visiting the company's overseas supplier for the first time. The designer was on a tour of the production facility when she noticed that some of the

129. *See* chapter 4.
130. *Id.*

buttons being used were not the ones she had specified. Her guide obligingly drove her to the warehouse of the button supplier, where she purchased the style she needed for the first production run out of her own pocket.

She was reimbursed for the purchase out of her expense account, but her employer was startled three years later to find that the Customs Service was cognizant of the incident. Customs made it known to the importer as part of a section 592 case alleging unpaid duties on selling commissions and assists.

V. A foreign trading company and its American subsidiary pleaded guilty to charges of fraud and making false statements in the importation of merchandise by fictitiously inflating prices to avoid additional "dumping" duties, applicable when merchandise is imported at "less than fair value." The scheme involved kickbacks, secret discounts, and false invoices showing higher prices than actually agreed upon between the foreign company and its subsidiary.

The settlement in the criminal case, to which the defendants had originally pleaded not guilty, cost the violator over $200,000 in fines. In addition, certain employees of the American subsidiary were subjected to criminal prosecution and convicted. The Customs Service then entered negotiations to settle the section 592 case, in which the initial demand was equal to the domestic value of the merchandise involved in the scheme: $167 million.

After highly publicized charges that a recently departed White House official had improperly tried to intercede on the exporter's behalf, the Court of International Trade[131] ruled that, notwithstanding that settlement and mitigation

131. United States v. Daewoo Int'l, 696 F. Supp. 1534 (Ct. Int'l Trade 1988).

discussions for most of the entries were under way, the government was entitled by collateral estoppel to summary judgment on its penalty claim for the entries whose falsification had been admitted in the guilty plea in the criminal case.

VI. A bead and imitation gemstone importer made a claim that certain shipments were not up to standard or specification due to wrong colors and mis-sizes, and sought to return them to Europe, applying for drawback of duties paid. The importer, however, filled the cases to be exported with old lots of unsalable beads and imitation stones, attesting that this was the merchandise from the shipments identified as the defective imported ones. The fraud was detected by the Customs Service, resulting in heavy monetary penalties and criminal prosecution.

VII. Of course, the most obvious fraud is undervaluation of the merchandise, with dual invoices sent to the importer or the duplicate kept in the foreign country, additional payments being made on personal trips by agents of the importer. In some cases, examination of importers' baggage or personal searches upon arriving in the United States or errors in mailing documents to the Customs Service or to customs brokers unearth such dual invoices. At other times, knowledgeable import specialists become suspicious of reduced values and call for investigation by Customs Service agents. Such frauds go back to the early history of the United States, and they have been documented in congressional hearings during post-Civil War days, when customs duties were the primary source of federal revenue.

VIII. A United States seller of agricultural machinery related to a European manufacturer developed plans to market a light utility vehicle. The basic chassis and body were manufactured in East Germany, then shipped to the plant of the importer's parent company in Western Europe, where extensive modifications were effected. These included installation of a completely new hydraulic system, strengthening of the chassis, and improvements to the electrical system and engine.

Under European Community guidelines, the work performed on the vehicles easily qualified them for a certificate of origin in the country where the modifications were done. The importer thus entered several prototypes into the United States as products of the Western European country. Under United States law, the vehicles remained products of East Germany notwithstanding the high added value of the work done in the West, since they were not "substantially transformed," as evidenced by the fact that they retained the same tariff classification before and after modification.[132]

At the time, East German products were dutiable under "Column 2" of the tariff as products of a communist country. Column 2 rates were typically at least twice as high as the "most-favored-nation" rates accorded to products of most noncommunist industrialized countries. Following a two-year investigation, triggered by the Customs Service's discovery of countless accessories on the vehicles (including light bulbs and tool kits) bearing East German country of origin markings, federal prosecutors finally rejected the case Customs presented to them, but only after the Berlin Wall was torn down.

IX. Many seizures and penalty actions have been due to such frauds as counterfeiting labels on brand-name wearing apparel, circumventing quota requirements by transshipment, false country of origin claims using counterfeit visa documents to identify shipments for quota allowance, transshipment to claim false duty-free status under the Generalized System of Preferences, selling blank certificates of origin to establish false countries of origin, and mislabeling the fiber and down content of garments.

---

132. See chapter 18.

We have attempted to illustrate and review some common types of commercial fraud cases which arise in the customs area. It cannot be stressed enough that many importers are in an excellent position to shape their own destinies with the Customs Service. Whatever the importer believes about the facts surrounding an importation, and however far-fetched the obligation to pay duty may appear to be (e.g., on royalties payable abroad), there is no substitute for effective preventive measures taken with advice of counsel.

Many serious problems can be avoided if importers and their attorneys examine the details of import transactions before they are made, and if necessary, use advocacy before the Customs Service. This can include in-person meetings with import specialists, followed by oral presentations, which reveal specific facts, or formal written submissions. If this is done, neither the amount of duty asserted at the time of entry nor any subsequent payments demanded by the Customs Service can be the basis for a penalty action, assuming the importer follows the course of practice mutually agreed upon.

Given the complex and serious civil and criminal consequences for violation of the customs laws, knowledgeable counsel should be retained as early in the process as possible. Many matters can be clarified or resolved prior to formal penalty proceedings, often with less risk and expense to the importer, while establishing better future relations with the Customs Service. Negotiations with the Service invariably are more successful for an importer utilizing counsel to protect its rights while simultaneously seeking to resolve or lessen the impact of the inquiry or investigation. It would not be unreasonable to suggest that an attorney can also make the Customs Service's job easier by explaining the law to the client and sifting through the relevant facts—a process that often translates into a better result for the client.

23. Seizure and Forfeiture of Commercial Importations

Background

Prior to the spring of 1987, most commercial importers had limited experience, if any, with the Customs Service's power to seize merchandise. Most statutes allowing goods to be seized concerned contraband or undeclared merchandise or goods imported in violation of embargoes or trade sanctions. Seizure and forfeiture were also prescribed for trademarked articles imported without authorization of the trademark owner. Under section 592 of the Tariff Act of 1930,[1] merchandise is seized solely to ensure payment of a monetary penalty if the importer is absent or insolvent, or to prevent the introduction of restricted merchandise into domestic commerce. Merchandise will be forfeited only if the penalty is not paid.

With the passage of the Anti-Drug Abuse Act of 1986, however, Customs obtained a broadly worded statute, 19 U.S.C. § 1595a(c), allowing seizure and forfeiture of any merchandise "introduced or attempted to be introduced into the United States contrary to law (other than in violation of

1. 19 U.S.C.A. § 1592. *See* chapter 22.

section 1592 of this title)."[2] Customs quickly issued a directive[3] to its officials in the field, stating that Congress intended the new law to plug a loophole in the existing law on prohibited merchandise whereby, for example, a vehicle not conforming with emissions standards set by the Environmental Protection Agency could not be seized.

In addition, Customs stated that it would interpret the new law as allowing the seizure of merchandise whose importation is subject to quantity or weight restrictions (e.g., steel subject to voluntary restraint arrangements, textile products subject to absolute quotas) where the quantity or weight of the merchandise in the shipment exceeded by 5 percent the quantity or weight provided for on the special invoice, visa, or other export document accompanying it.

In practical terms, especially for textile goods subject to quotas, importers were placed entirely at the mercy of their suppliers. Whereas the accuracy of invoice information, prices, and other commercial terms are considered to be the importer's responsibility under the customs laws, visa or export licenses are theoretically issued by authority of the exporting country under treaties limiting export shipments of the affected merchandise.

Certain goods whose reporting quantities were set in terms of weight are actually sold by the piece, with the result that the net weight reported on the visa does not figure into the bargain between buyer and seller. Importers thus became accountable for elements of their shipments that were formerly of no commercial consequence and were

---

2. Pursuant to new legislation, the Customs and Trade Act of 1990, Pub. L. No. 101-382, § 122, 104 Stat. 642 (1990), amending 19 U.S.C. § 1607, Customs has authority to proceed with administrative forfeiture, provided proper notice is given and all other procedural requirements are met in connection with such merchandise, if the value of such merchandise does not exceed $500,000.
3. Customs Directive 4400-03, Mar. 27, 1987.

difficult to ascertain when the goods were in the design or sample phases of production.

Worse, the directive allowed seizures of shipments with no visas or visas in the wrong category. As to the former, it had been the practice of Customs to reject the attempted entry and to allow the importers to export the goods or to place them in bonded warehouses while they obtained visas from abroad or waivers from the government of the exporting country. The same options were available to importers when mistaken categories appeared on the visa.

Such "mistakes" were occasionally the result of disputes between the exporting country's government and the United States, as when, in the spring of 1989, India's claim of quota exemption for certain cottage industry products was unilaterally rejected by the United States, which claimed that they required visas. The practical result was the wholesale seizure of shipments of textile articles from India, with American importers, helpless bystanders to the dispute, subject to the forfeiture of their property or to penalties after its release.

In May 1987, a second directive[4] authorized seizures of merchandise entered in violation of the country of origin marking statute, 19 U.S.C. § 1304, if the violation appeared intentional or if incorrect marking called to the importer's attention on a prior shipment had not been corrected by the shipper on subsequent shipments after a reasonable time for such corrections to be made. Seizures were also authorized for goods with misleading country of origin markings or with illegally altered markings.

The new policy came under fire quickly. In addition to the predictable flood of outraged editorials in shipping and retail industry publications, members of the House Ways and Means Committee, the congressional body responsible for final approval of customs legislation and for general

4. Customs Directive 4400-04, Dec. 18, 1987.

oversight of the Customs Service, called Customs Commissioner William von Raab to account.

In an exchange of letters, Congressman William Frenzel of Minnesota specifically asked Commissioner von Raab to explain why a drug-control bill was being invoked to detain commercial shipments, particularly in light of the fact that the Ways and Means Committee had made it clear that the section would be used only if drugs were suspected to be involved.[5]

Commissioner von Raab replied that language in the Ways and Means Committee report allowing other types of prohibited merchandise to be seized (coffee and automobiles were given as examples) permitted a broader reading of the statute. He extended its application to "violations of those laws which do not have a separate forfeiture provision, but restrict the importation of such merchandise." Notwithstanding the Commissioner's insistence that the law was being correctly applied, he noted the Customs Service's overzealous application and further stated that the triggering points for seizures would be raised.[6]

Shortly thereafter, the impact of the seizure and forfeiture campaign was softened by an amended directive,[7] which raised the threshold for seizures of overweight quota merchandise from 5 percent to 10 percent and set more lenient and better-defined mitigation guidelines than had originally been allowed.

Under the authority of the statute, but using guidelines established internally and applied without notice, Customs subjected several thousand shipments to seizure between the spring of 1987 and the summer of 1989. In the process, hundreds of importers with previously faultless records and no knowledge of or control over their suppliers' operations

5. Letter from Rep. William Frenzel to Comm'r von Raab, Dec. 9, 1987.
6. Letter from Comm'r von Raab to Rep. Frenzel, Jan. 7, 1988.
7. Customs Directive 4400-07, Jan. 26, 1988.

became "violators" in the eyes of Customs. Hundreds of shipments were delayed, detained, or turned back. No estimate of the loss of sales, wasted promotional expenditures, and surplus financing charges paid has appeared. No one has published an accounting of the warehousing costs, legal fees paid, or other economic consequences of the wave of seizures.

The Customs Oversight Subcommittee of the House Ways and Means Committee (called the "Pickle Committee" after its chairman, Congressman Jake Pickle of Texas) issued its findings after two years of investigating the Customs Service's operations and management under Commissioner von Raab. The Pickle report, issued on February 8, 1990, is suggestively entitled "Report on Abuses and Mismanagement in U.S. Customs Service Commercial Operations."

When Congress asked Customs to provide an accounting, Customs was unable to do so: "[T]hey had no idea how 1595a(c) was being used in the field. The information had to be extracted for the Subcommittee from hardcopy files located at local Customs district offices. The process took months. . . ."[8] From the fragmentary information Customs was able to provide, the subcommittee concluded that 19 U.S.C. § 1595a(c) was mainly used as an "attention-getter" for the correction of erroneous paperwork, and that 15 percent of the seizures were the result of the Customs Service's errors.[9]

The report's sixteen negative findings included the following:

> 9. The U.S. Customs Service abused its authority to seize commercial merchandise. Following the Subcommittee's investigation of commercial seizures, Customs changed its na-

8. Subcommittee on Oversight of the Ways and Means Committee of the U.S. House of Representatives, 101st Cong., 2d Sess.; Ways and Means Committee Print 101-22, at 34.

9. *Id.*

tional policies.[10] Nonetheless, the Subcommittee recommends that Customs initiate routine reviews of field office seizure practices to insure uniform and consistent implementation of the new policies. The Subcommittee also recommends that Customs discontinue its practice of using seizure statistics to measure individual and field office performance.[11]

The Present Policy

A new policy statement,[12] issued within two weeks of the effective date of Commissioner von Raab's resignation by Acting Commissioner Michael H. Lane, significantly limited the impact of 19 U.S.C. § 1595a(c) as interpreted in the earlier directives. Customs will now "require consideration of alternatives to seizure" for other than "very serious violations such as those affecting health and safety . . . , importations bearing counterfeit trademarks . . . , piratical copies of copyrighted material . . . , imported merchandise bearing false designations of 'United States' as country of origin, or merchandise imported with counterfeit visas." Shipments in violation of Foreign Assets Control embargoes may also be seized.

The directive lists the alternatives as "denying entry, releasing merchandise under bond, permitting a warehouse entry, and assessing monetary penalties under 19 USC 1592 and 1595a(b)." The directive describes circumstances that justify an alternative action to seizure and states that, even if those circumstances do not exist in a given case, Customs "always shall have the discretion not to seize."

Customs may still seize commercial shipments when there is evidence of the importer's intent to violate the law

10. See next section for a discussion of the change.
11. Subcommittee report, *supra* note 8, at VI.
12. Customs Directive 4400-10, Aug. 11, 1989.

or when violations are "repetitive" (a term not defined in the directive). The directive does not apply to marking violations, as covered by the earlier policy statement,[13] which already limited seizure to cases of intentional or repetitive violations. It also does not affect seizures alleged to arise from dangerous violations of the Consumer Product Safety Commission's laws and regulations that cannot be corrected by the importer, and thus allow the goods to be released.

Customs is now advising denial of entry as the principal alternative to seizure. Importers are to be allowed to re-export such goods or, "in some cases," where the merchandise is restricted (e.g., quota goods) rather than prohibited, enter them into a bonded warehouse or Foreign Trade Zone (FTZ) to be brought into compliance. For goods entered directly into bonded warehouses or FTZs, the directive states that Customs "should" affirmatively notify importers of problems and give them a chance to correct them before withdrawal for consumption.

Another alternative is to permit release of goods that can be brought into compliance with the requirement alleged to be breached, under a single entry bond in an amount equal to three times the value of the shipment, in order for the importer to recondition them.

Although commercial importers still find themselves at risk for the value of entire shipments and subject to enormous delay and expense as a result of a drug-related law, a much-criticized policy of wholesale seizures of commercial shipments has been rolled back. In any administrative context, predictability of results is an essential element. Law-abiding importers can once more be reasonably sure that unavoidable and correctable problems affecting the admissibility of their merchandise will not throw their entire business into crisis by reason of a seizure.

13. Customs Directive 4400-04, Dec. 18, 1987.

Coping with a Customs Seizure

Initial Stages: Obtaining Release

An importer whose goods are seized must first deal with the fact that his own shipping schedule depends on the merchandise being available. While seized merchandise can be retrieved from Customs custody while the case is pending, the time inevitably spent in the proceedings can compromise or ruin a sales campaign. Avoiding unnecessary delays can spell the difference between a costly headache and complete disaster.

Quota Problems

Importers of quota merchandise subject to "live entry" (presentation of a CF 3461, a CF 7501 entry summary, all the commercial documents required by the regulations, and the duty due) procedures have instant notice that their merchandise is seized—Customs simply does not release it. For obtaining substitute visas or arranging for the posting of security,[14] it is vital to obtain information as to both quantity and value. Such foreknowledge can accelerate release of the merchandise and aid in formulating a timely application for relief under 19 U.S.C. § 1618.

The Customs Service's internal guidelines call for issuance of a notice of seizure "as soon as possible."[15] However, such official notification of the grounds for the seizure and the Service's proposed penalty amount or estimate of the domestic (forfeiture) value of the goods can lag according to the workload of the fines, penalties, and forfeitures office handling the case.

---

14. *See* chapter 19.
15. Office of Commercial Operations, Dep't of Treasury, U.S. Customs Service, Fines, Penalties, and Forfeitures Handbook (1986), page SCP-5.

The mitigation and remission guidelines for seizures resulting from quota shortages require that the discrepancy that caused the seizure be corrected before the goods can be released. This means, in the case of goods needing a visa, that the amount of quota merchandise which Customs has determined to have been present must be known so that the importer can obtain a substitute export document declaring the higher quantity. Customs will not accept an annex to the original visa either in the form of a waiver or a partial visa. Moreover, some exporting countries will not issue a corrected visa for a shipment until either the original visa or a copy certified by Customs is returned to them.

It is desirable, often vital, to be able to obtain the necessary data informally from Customs before the official seizure notice is issued. Importers have been experiencing increasing resistance to such disclosure, and the situation will probably worsen as personnel shortages at Customs worsen.

Marking Problems

Importers whose goods are seized for discrepancies under the packaging, marking, and labeling laws often find themselves in even more difficulty when they attempt to recover them. Unlike quota problems, for which the shipment never leaves the dock, redelivery notices for marking (Customs Form 4647, reprinted in appendix 21) do not trigger seizures in and of themselves. While some ports will not release goods said to require compliance with the marking statutes until the importer undertakes to comply, most often the merchandise is already at the importer's premises when the marking notice arrives.

The notice gives the importer thirty days either to mark the goods or to have them exported or destroyed. By signing the notice with an indication that the merchandise has been brought into compliance, the importer has made an affirmative declaration that it is properly marked. Customs may exercise its discretion to spot-check the shipment. For time-critical movements of merchandise, this means that the Form 4647 halts shipping until the form is returned to Customs and Customs approves the manner of remarking or relabeling.

If the inspection team that examines the goods finds that the merchandise has been sent out or that the marking is not in accordance with the original instructions, it can seize whatever remains on the importer's premises. For merchandise already shipped, a liquidated damages case will be begun immediately, regardless of whether the remainder is found to be properly marked. Customs also has the right to demand a recall of such goods from the customers. The merchandise still in the importer's possession can be sent back to the custody of Customs. However, the importer may be given the option of entering into a "constructive seizure agreement" with Customs. The goods remain at the importer's premises under a form of "house arrest" while further time-consuming procedures are followed to obtain permission to bring them into conformity with the marking laws.

The constructive seizure requires the owner of the goods to keep the merchandise and not move it without the Customs Service's permission, maintain it in good order, insure it at his own expense, and allow Customs to have access to it or to repossess it on demand. However, this arrangement gives the importer an opportunity to comply with Customs procedures to obtain release of goods and, if Customs permits their remarking, ultimately to ship them.

Responsibility for administering these agreements is given to fines, penalties, and forfeitures offices. The process for administering constructive seizures is notably slow. First, permission to remark must be requested in writing. The importer must wait for written permission to be received. After remarking, a written request for inspection must be made. After inspection, the release process can begin. Obviously, delays in reaching the stage where goods can be released are considerable.

Release of Goods—Petitions and Security

As noted above, goods seized under 19 U.S.C. § 1595a(c) can only be released in conjunction with the importer's petition for relief under 19 U.S.C. § 1618. Since the ultimate penalty in any seizure case is forfeiture of the merchandise, the customs laws have long allowed a claimant to seized merchandise to forfeit its appraised domestic value in lieu of the goods themselves.[16] In a logical extension of the principle that the money is equivalent to the merchandise, Customs since 1974 has allowed claimants to seized goods to post an irrevocable letter of credit in the amount of the forfeiture value of the merchandise as security for the government during a forfeiture proceeding.

This same principle applies to cases under 19 U.S.C. § 1595a(c). Once the condition that caused the seizure has been rectified, a letter of credit in the amount determined to be the forfeiture (domestic) value of the goods, or a fraction thereof based upon the mitigated penalty likely to be assessed, can stand in for the goods themselves, which are then released to the importer. As we have seen, however, obtaining the correct amount to be deposited can often be delayed until a formal seizure notice is issued, stating the Customs Service's determination of the domestic value or proposed penalty.

In addition to the posting of financial security and the actual filing of a petition for relief or obtaining an extension of time to file such a petition, Customs requires owners of seized property to sign and submit three documents in order to obtain the release of goods. The first is an "election

16. 19 U.S.C.A. § 1614 (West Supp. 1990).

of proceedings" notifying Customs that the claimant is willing to defer an immediate administrative forfeiture proceeding until the petition for relief is decided. Failure to sign and return an election of proceedings will cause the forfeiture proceeding to be commenced even though a petition is filed.

The second document for signature, the "acknowledgment of early release of seized merchandise," states that the signer understands that the goods were released against the deposit of funds, that such release constitutes part of the proceedings under the 19 U.S.C. § 1618 petitioning process, and that further proceedings are possible. It also contains language stating that signing may constitute a waiver of the claimant's right to administrative or judicial forfeiture proceedings. It probably is such a waiver, but its validity has not been tested in the courts.

Finally, the "hold harmless and indemnification agreement for releasing seized property" must be signed. It is the claimant's agreement not to sue the government or any of its employees for any losses incurred as a result of the seizure. The agreement further states that the claimant will reimburse the government for the government's costs of enforcing it.

Importers wishing to recover seized merchandise have little choice but to follow whatever procedures Customs establishes for obtaining its release. The importer, by signing this agreement, forgoes the fundamental right to have the matter adjudicated in court, both in the waiver of forfeiture proceedings and in the covenant not to sue the government for damages incurred if the seizure should turn out to have been wrongfully made.

In addition, the requirement of opening a letter of credit and maintaining it during the pendency of the petitioning process is a serious burden in tight credit markets. Unfortunately, as long as Customs retains its powers to seize merchandise under 19 U.S.C. § 1595a(c), such prospects will be part of the risk overhead for importers.

Penalties and Relief from Them

We began this examination of the broad powers of the Customs Service to seize merchandise and subject it to forfeiture proceedings by considering the procedures of greatest immediate concern to the importer whose goods are seized—those for obtaining release of the merchandise. We now look to the means Customs has established for obtaining relief from the consequences of the penalty entailed in a seizure, which can result at worst in the forfeiture of the merchandise, or of its supposed domestic value, if its release was obtained.

We note again that the importer must waive immediate administrative and judicial forfeiture proceedings as a condition of obtaining the release of the goods and post a letter of credit with the Customs Service in an amount up to the Service's estimation of the merchandise's domestic value as security. Section 1595a(c) explicitly states that seizures may not be based on violations of the previously most commonly used penalty provision, section 592 of the Tariff Act of 1930, which is predicated upon the importer's culpability.[17] Customs officials state that 19 U.S.C. § 1595a(c) seizures are aimed at the merchandise and not at the importer, but the Customs Service's internal guidelines for such seizures allow a section 592 penalty case to be begun in the wake of a seizure if there appear to be grounds for it.

Among the most common grounds to date for seizures under 19 U.S.C. § 1595a(c) have been shipments of articles subject to quotas which weigh in excess of the amount certified by the exporting country on the export document

17. See chapter 21.

(visa or export certificate) required for entry into the United States.

Particularly in the textile area, importers are often not aware of the exact net weight of their goods, a common method of allocating quotas, as they are usually purchased on the basis of count. Such shortages do not affect duty assessment, since the invoice values on which duties are based are not normally incorrect in such a situation.

In seizures under 19 U.S.C. § 1595a(c) for reasons other than quota problems, the range of recommended penalties is 10 to 80 percent. For nonquota cases, mitigating and aggravating factors are considered. For quota overages, such factors are apparently not considered, but the degree to which the shipment exceeded the quantity stated on the export documents causes an adjustment in the suggested penalties for seizures at each of three levels based on the number of prior offenses (none, one to four, and five or more).

The minimum penalty in a quota case, for a first seizure of goods with a weight discrepancy of up to 15 percent, would be 10 percent of the dutiable value. The scale of penalties quickly increases according to the amount of the overage (additional overweight ranges are 15 to 25 percent—first offense mitigated to 15–30 percent of dutiable value; and 25 percent or more overweight—first offense mitigated to 25–45 percent of dutiable value). The number of times an importer's shipments have been seized multiplies the base penalties by one and a half for second to fifth offenses, and it doubles them if there have been more than five overweight seizures within a year. The maximum of 80 percent of the dutiable value is charged on a shipment 25 percent or more overweight to an importer with five or more seizures, irrespective of the importer's culpability. That is four times as much as the unmitigated amount, even with aggravating factors, that section 592 recommends for the most comparable offense, a negligent violation not affecting duties. The stakes can thus be high in a seizure case.

The Petition for Relief

As noted above, the actions of the Customs Service subsequent to a seizure and release of goods are premised on the fact that the importer has filed or will file a petition for relief under 19 U.S.C. § 1618 (section 618 of the Tariff Act of 1930, as amended). Section 618 allows Customs to reduce (mitigate) a proposed penalty or to cancel (remit) the case entirely without a levy.

Section 592 and various other statutes that empower Customs to assess penalties have mitigation guidelines set forth at least partly in the customs regulations. The guidelines for remission or mitigation of seizures under 19 U.S.C. § 1595a(c) were issued by Customs Headquarters without the opportunity for public comment that is required for a new regulation, a fact which has added to importers' complaints about the measure.

Perhaps the chief factor in the sense of injustice felt by the importing community about 19 U.S.C. § 1595a(c) is that the law allows the United States, especially in cases involving alleged textile or steel quota violations, to penalize importers for the alleged misdeeds of their suppliers or even of the foreign governments issuing export documents over which the importer has no control, without a corresponding allegation of misconduct on the importer's part. Most importers already own their goods at the time they are examined by Customs, and the prospects of forfeitures or penalties affect the importer alone. The petitioning procedures and mitigation guidelines discussed below are based on directives aimed at importers (or other owners of imported goods) who are treated therein as "offenders," even though the "offense" may have been committed by the shipper or in fact be a dispute between governments.

Importers of goods known to be targets of seizures should strive to the utmost to gain remission, although the criteria are difficult to satisfy. The effort is justified: "repetitive" violations subject commercial shipments to seizure. No definition of the term appears in the seizure guidelines, but language in the mitigation guidelines may indicate that such violations need not have resulted in seizures themselves. Remission would clear the importer's record.

An importer without "repetitive violations" resulting in seizure for goods from the same source within a year may obtain release of an overweight shipment without a seizure if the overage is less than 10 percent and there is no evidence that the violation is intentional. Two or more seizures of the same importer's shipments from the same supplier within one year lower the threshold to overages between 5 and 10 percent. A third such violation drops the triggering point to any overage, no matter how small.

Remission of a Case

The best outcome available for the claimant is remission—a cancellation of the case without payment of a penalty. The Customs Service's guidelines for remission of cases under 19 U.S.C. § 1595a(c) list two basic situations that will allow remission.

The first is when "the violation of law resulted solely from either a clerical error or mistake of fact," as the customs regulations define those terms. According to the definitions in the regulations, "clerical errors" include mistranscriptions of numbers, arithmetical mistakes, and omissions of documents needed to make a complete record. "Mistakes of fact" can result either from lack of knowledge of the true state of facts or from a mistaken belief that the facts are other than what they are. The regulation cautions, however, that relief is not available for "mistake of fact" when the person neglected a legal duty to know the facts.

Remission of a forfeiture is also available in "other extenuating circumstances." The importer's innocence of any involvement in the violation is not enough to relieve the importer of its consequences. There must be evidence of "reasonable care to ensure compliance with Customs laws." In practice that phrase appears to mean, in the example of an overweight shipment of steel or textile articles, that an agent or employee of the importer oversaw the weighing of the merchandise prior to the shipper's application for the visa. Merely instructing the shipper to be careful in stating weights on export documents may not be enough.

The other example of an extenuating circumstance is when the importer's only "participation" (presumably, in the violation) is the filing of the entry documents and the importer tried to verify the accuracy of the information before filing. Importers doubting their suppliers' ability to produce an accurate export document or to mark goods properly, and wishing to avoid personal liabilities under 19 U.S.C. § 1595a(c), would be well advised to weigh or count textile or steel shipments or to verify the correct marking of the goods in a bonded warehouse before presenting the documents to Customs.

While prudence might seem to dictate such steps, their cost can be high. Moreover, verification might entail delays in obtaining Customs clearance. Time lost in that way might mean missing a delivery date or the closing of a quota. Importers of goods known to be subject to intensive examinations and frequent seizures must nonetheless weigh their relative costs and benefits.

Mitigating a Forfeiture

The Customs Service's guidelines for mitigation of forfeitures in seizure cases under section 1595a(c) are broken down into two categories. The first is for seizures of merchandise other than steel or textile articles subject to quota restrictions, and the second applies to overweight shipments of steel or textile articles. It should be noted that if the owner of the seized goods is convicted of a crime connected with the importation in question, Customs will seek forfeiture of the merchandise.

The general guidelines for nonquota violations allow for variations in the penalty amount depending on whether mitigating or aggravating factors were present. The former are the prior good record of the importer, inexperience in importing, and cooperation with the Customs Service's investigation of the violation. Aggravating factors are "criminal violation relating to the subject transaction," repeated violations of the restriction underlying the seizure ("including cases in which no seizure was made under section 1595a(c)"), and evidence of intent to make the importation contrary to law.

The guidelines Customs follows in mitigation of penalty cases under section 592 allow a weighted adjustment of the amount according to the number of mitigating or aggravating factors present. Under the seizure guidelines, however, the mere presence of any aggravating factors appears to negate all mitigating factors. As noted above, "prior offenses" under the mitigation guidelines are defined as seizures within a one-year period that were not remitted in full, and "prior violations" need not have resulted in seizures.

As seen above, Customs sets penalty amounts according to a sliding scale based on the number of prior offenses. For nonquota cases, mitigating and aggravating factors are considered. For quota overages, such factors are apparently not considered, but the degree to which the shipment exceeded the quantity stated on the export documents causes an adjustment in the suggested penalties for seizures at each of three levels based on the number of prior offenses (none, one to four, and five or more).

The recommended penalty amounts for both nonquota and quota cases vary from 10 percent to 80 percent of dutiable value. For a first nonquota offense with mitigating factors or a first quota overage not exceeding 15 percent, the guidelines call for a penalty of 10 percent of the dutiable value. For a second nonquota offense with aggravating factors (or for a third or higher nonquota offense), or for a sixth or higher quota seizure with an overage of 25 percent or more, Customs will set the penalty at 80 percent of the dutiable value.

Although the seizure of imported merchandise is a grave matter, it need not be catastrophic. Within its manpower limitations, Customs tries to dispose of its cases efficiently. Thus, although strict adherence to the release procedures defined in the guidelines is required, a seizure case can usually be guided through the release process to a result which allows for salvage from a potential catastrophe in a transaction. The Customs Service's seizure policy is a reminder that importers need to be extremely vigilant, not only at the ports of entry, but at the sources of their merchandise.

24. Administrative Rulings by the Customs Service

Introduction

The commercial importation of goods entails the normal risks of any business enterprise: Will this model or color sell? How can we be sure we order just the right amount and get them where we need them on time? In addition to the logistical problems that can be foreseen in moving goods around the world, the complicated legal questions of classification, valuation, country of origin marking, admissibility, and the many others discussed in this book confront the importer.

As prudent business persons, importers have tried throughout the years to learn as much as possible about the financial impact of interpretation of the customs laws before they order their merchandise. Many import companies have suffered severe financial hardship as a result of misjudgments of duty rates or dutiable values, country of origin marking, quotas or visas, and admissibility of goods. Over the years, the Customs Service has had problems responding to requests for advice on these and many other areas of vital concern both to the importing community and its own officials in the field.

Indeed, many an importer has discovered, with emotions ranging from disappointment to panic, that advice sought informally by word of mouth from a Customs official was incorrect. In most cases, such misinformation may merely be costly. In any case, informal advice from Customs should be regarded as risky and to be relied on only at one's peril.

In the author's practice, questions concerning rulings arise repeatedly: Are informal oral opinions given by local Customs Service officers binding upon the Customs Service? Are written opinions by district directors binding? Can a district director issue a "binding" ruling if it is based upon a "uniform and established practice"? When is a letter responding to an inquiry binding upon the Customs Service?

Part 177 of the customs regulations was first promulgated in 1980[1] to clarify such questions and related ones. As of this writing, the Customs Service is in the midst of a major overhaul of its system of legal opinion rulings, originally instituted to cope with the flood of queries accompanying the adoption of the Harmonized Tariff System in 1989.

Part 177 Rulings

Excepted Transactions

The Customs Service's decision to formalize its ruling procedure required it to identify the circumstances under which rulings would be issued; what type of ruling, if any, would issue under specific circumstances; what the effect of such rulings would be; and how rulings could be changed or revoked. It was also necessary to identify situations that would not be considered for rulings under part 177.

Under the regulations,[2] a "ruling" is defined as a written statement issued by the Headquarters Office or appropriate

1. T.D. 80-285, 14 Cust. B. & Dec. 674 (1980).
2. 19 C.F.R. § 177.1(d) (1990).

office of Customs that interprets and applies the provisions of the customs laws and related laws to specific facts. That definition broadly encompasses many Customs Service holdings beyond the scope of the administrative rulings regulations, and the Service begins its description of the procedures by listing situations which part 177 does not cover.[3]

Finally, part 177 only applies to matters that can properly be acted on in the final instance by the Office of Regulations and Rulings at Customs Headquarters.

Oral Advice

Since the regulations define a ruling as a *written* statement interpreting the Customs laws, it is to be expected that the Customs Service will not issue a ruling in response to an oral request. It also specifically declines to be bound by any oral opinion or advice.[4] Customs *will* respond to oral queries about existing written rulings and their scope and to requests for advice regarding the procedures for obtaining rulings.

3. 19 C.F.R. § 177.0 (1990). Part 177 expressly does not apply to rulings or determinations

> set forth in Part 12 of [the regulations] relating to proof of admissibility of articles detained under section 307 of the Tariff Act of 1930 . . . , Part 103 (relating to disclosure of information in Customs files), Part 133, (relating to disputed claims of piratical copying of copyrighted matter), Subpart C of Part 152 (relating to determinations concerning the dutiable value of merchandise by Customs field officers), Part 153 (relating to the enforcement of the Antidumping Act, 1921, as amended), Part 159 (insofar as it relates to countervailing duties), Part 171 (relating to fines, penalties, and forfeitures), Part 172, (relating to liquidated damages), Part 174 (relating to protests), and Part 175 (relating to petitions filed by American manufacturers, producers, or wholesalers pursuant to section 516 of the Tariff Act of 1930, as amended). Nor do the provisions of Part 177 apply to requests for decisions of an operational, administrative, or investigative nature which are properly within the cognizance of a Customs Headquarters Office other than the Office of Regulations and Rulings.

4. 19 C.F.R. § 177.1(b) (1990).

In addition, although a binding ruling will be issued only after the Customs Service has received a written request, district, area or regional, and Headquarters personnel are free to discuss issues or other substantive questions involved in a specific situation orally before receiving a written request for a ruling. Such oral advice given to importers is also not binding.

Information Letters

The regulations set up a class of responses to queries with less stringent application requirements. "An information letter is a written statement issued by Customs Headquarters or the New York Regional Commissioner of Customs that calls attention to a well-established principle of Customs law, without applying it to a specific set of facts."[5] Customs will sometimes respond to a defective request for a ruling letter with an information letter, if the request "suggests that general information, rather than a ruling, is sought" and if Customs feels that general information will benefit the requester.

Letter Rulings

Background

ORR and NIS

Until 1981, binding rulings were issued exclusively by the Office of Regulations and Rulings (ORR) at Customs Headquarters in Washington, D.C. This method, set up in 1975, began to falter: Customs was routinely taking 100 to 110 days to process responses to importers, and often much longer. Obviously, that type of service did not fulfill the needs of the international trade community.

5. 19 C.F.R. § 177.1(d)(2) (1990).

Accordingly, a detailed reexamination of the ruling process was undertaken in 1980 with a view to improving the prevailing system by giving a more active role to the national import specialists (NISs), a small, skilled group of Customs Service professionals based at New York Seaport who are tariff experts. Historically, they acted as prime advisers to Headquarters when ruling requests were made. The NISs were formerly the heads of the import specialist teams in New York and thus acted in a dual capacity.[6]

The new system was inaugurated on January 2, 1981.[7] The Customs Service authorized the NISs, under the authority of the regional commissioner of the Customs Service, New York region, to issue selected tariff classification rulings, i.e., binding ruling letters regarding prospective customs transactions. The authorization excepts the preparation of final decisions on internal advice requests, requests for further review of protests, change-of-practice requests, and final rulings in "difference" cases (between Customs Service classifying officers at different ports or districts) from that authority.

District Rulings

Until 1989, the Customs Service considered itself bound to comply with the principles of rulings only if they were issued by Customs Headquarters or NISs. The Customs Service has recently amended the administrative ruling procedures to expedite and create new means to promote nationwide uniformity in Customs decisions.[8] The amend-

---

6. Over a period of time starting in April 1984, the NISs were divorced from the day-to-day activity of the import specialists, and were given separate status, acting exclusively on a national basis as advisers to Customs Headquarters and to all ports in the United States.
7. T.D. 80-285, 14 Cust. B. & Dec. 674 (1980).
8. 19 C.F.R. 1977 (1988). Changes cited in 54 Fed. Reg. 8208-15 (1989) became effective August 30, 1989.

ments were mandated by the Anti-Drug Abuse Act of 1988,[9] which required the Secretary of the Treasury to promulgate regulations for nationwide uniformity of certain decisions made by the Customs Service and also to establish procedures by which certain parties affected by the lack of such uniformity may have any inconsistencies resolved.

The new procedures allow commercial importers to secure binding rulings on tariff classification under the Harmonized Tariff Schedule of the United States (HTSUS), which became effective on January 1, 1989, replacing the Tariff Schedules of the United States, which had been in place for twenty-six years. The HTSUS has clearly increased the use of the administrative ruling program. Customs hopes that the new program can accommodate increased use by importers while improving responsiveness of Customs to these demands.

The objectives of the regulatory amendments are the following:

1. To create new procedures to promote national uniformity;
2. To allow commercial importers to receive binding rulings at Customs districts;
3. To clarify the circumstances for the effective date of a ruling;
4. To clarify the obligations of the recipient of a tariff classification ruling letter;
5. To remove the "clearly wrong" test standard;[10] and

---

9. Pub. L. No. 100-690, 102 Stat. 4181 (1988).
10. 19 C.F.R. § 177.10(b) (1990). Removal of the "clearly wrong" test: The amended regulations removed the language which requires that for a ruling to change an earlier published ruling or established practice, the earlier ruling or practice must be determined to have been clearly wrong. See discussion in this chapter at p. 630.

6. To clarify the extent to which a previously issued ruling can be the subject of a request for internal advice.

Accordingly, effective August 30, 1989, the entire area of administrative rulings was overhauled by adding and developing programs intended to be in the best interests of the importer as well as implementing the significant changes resulting from the Anti-Drug Abuse Act.

Part 177 of the customs regulations has been amended correspondingly, to allow importers to apply for advance binding tariff classification rulings under the HTSUS from Customs districts where the merchandise will be imported or at any other district where the importer would do business. All rulings issued under this program are binding for the recipient at all ports of entry.

Obtaining a Ruling

Application

Customs will generally issue a ruling when a request is submitted in accordance with the regulations and if it is in the interest of the sound administration of the customs and related laws. Requests for classification rulings may be submitted to area or district offices, a national import specialist (NIS) in New York, a deputy national import specialist designated by the NIS, or Headquarters. For example, a New York NIS may designate a deputy NIS in any location in the country who has the expert qualifications in a particular subject-matter area. As before, requests for other kinds of rulings should be made to Headquarters or the appropriate NIS.

Upon receipt of an application, a local import specialist will review the request for sufficiency and other pertinent details. If the application is complete, the local import specialist will record the local decision and forward the application to the Customs Service's New York region. In this way, a binding ruling request known as the "thirty day request" will be processed. However, if Customs Headquarters must be involved, the target turnaround time is 120 days. Should a later revocation, correction, or other adverse change to the ruling be necessary, Customs will not apply it for up to ninety days if the recipient can show it relied on the original ruling to its detriment.

The regulations limit the number of requests to five merchandise items per request, all of the same class or kind. However, there is no limitation on the number of requests. In addition, failure to include the information required in the request will bring slightly different results depending on the Customs office to which the request is made.[11] For example, if the request was made to Customs Headquarters or an NIS, the person submitting the request will be given thirty days to correct any deficiency. Failure to do so will result in the closing of the file and, in addition, the request may be treated as withdrawn. If the request was made to area or district offices, the deficient request will be returned and the request will not be considered filed until the deficiencies are corrected.

A ruling request should include the names of the parties to the customs transaction; the name of the manufacturer and seller (if available); a complete description of the goods; a description of the transactions in detail appropriate to the type of ruling requested; the country of origin; the importer of record number which will be used at entry; and a statement of whether Customs has previously considered the same transaction. An effective ruling request will in-

---

11. Additionally, the changes permit the NIS to appoint deputies to assist the agency in issuing binding rulings, under the new District Ruling Program. Deputy NISs are also provided for in the pre-entry classification program *infra* p. 627.

clude citations and advocacy of the requester's position, and it will request the opportunity to meet with the deciding officials to discuss the matter.

Deliberation/Discussion

Customs Headquarters still retains its oversight authority to issue rulings regarding appraisement questions and, as to classification matters, to review independently all ruling letters issued by the regional commissioner and other area and district offices. If an importer or other person to whom a ruling letter is issued disagrees with a ruling issued by the NIS, or other area and district offices, it may petition the director of the classification and value division, Customs Headquarters, for a review of the ruling.

Districts may not be asked to reconsider their own rulings or those issued by another Customs office. Such requests must be directed to the director of the commercial rulings division in Washington, D.C. Recipients may also protest rulings issued by Customs districts under the regulations.[12] Rulings issued by Customs districts under the district rulings program must adhere to all other provisions of part 177, unless otherwise provided.

Section 177.4 of the regulations allows an opportunity for oral discussion of the issue or issues involved, if such discussion is requested in writing at the time the ruling request is filed. This provision gives the Customs personnel the choice to schedule such a discussion if, in the opinion of the person considering the ruling request, oral discussion would be helpful in deciding the issue. If Customs is contemplating a determination or conclusion contrary to that advocated in the ruling request, a conference *must* be scheduled, if requested. The conferences are "scheduled for

12. See chapter 25.

the purpose of affording the parties an opportunity to freely and openly discuss the matters" of the request without being bound by any argument or position.

Conditions of Issuance

Initially, a distinction is made between prospective transactions and current transactions. With respect to prospective transactions, the Customs Service will give full and careful consideration to written requests from importers or other interested parties for rulings or information. For current transactions already before a Customs Service office, that office will resolve the question in accordance with previously established principles and precedents under the internal advice procedures described at the end of this chapter.

If the question cannot be so resolved, the office may be requested by the importer to forward the question to Headquarters. A completed transaction may not be the subject of a ruling request by an importer or its agent, but contested issues may still be resolved via the protest procedure, if the entry is eligible for such a step.[13]

Also, the Customs Service will issue administrative rulings on petitions under 19 U.S.C. § 1516 (initiated by domestic interested parties), setting forth a definitive interpretation of applicable law or other appropriate information to importers or other interested parties. The Customs Service believes that American manufacturers, businesses, and trade associations with interests related to particular imports fall within the scope of the phrase "other interested parties."

Effect

Administrative rulings issued by either Customs Headquarters or the regional commissioner of New York, NISs,

13. See chapter 25.

and other area and district offices that are not published in the *Customs Bulletin & Decisions* will be applied only with respect to customs transactions involving articles identical to those that were the subject of the ruling letter, as long as the ruling is in effect. Persons other than the beneficiary of the ruling will not be notified if Customs decides to withdraw the ruling.

Stated in another way, no third person should rely absolutely on a ruling letter or assume that the principles deriving from that ruling will be applied to any transaction of a kind other than the kind described in the letter. However, as in many other areas of practice involving administrative rulings, we may expect further changes in respect to reliance on letters by third parties. As noted below, the availability of the Customs Service's Legal Precedent Retrieval System has placed "private" rulings into the public domain. It can be argued that modification or revocation of virtually any ruling requires Customs to allow importers a grace period after notice before it ceases to be effective.

Rulings issued by the NISs or by area or district offices are binding on the Customs Service. Although a ruling letter is effective on the date it is issued (including rulings which modify or revoke earlier rulings), Customs may nevertheless, upon application of any party showing reliance upon a conflicting ruling's holding, or upon its own initiative, delay the effective date of such a ruling up to ninety days from the date of issuance.[14] Importers should not, of course, rely on the possibility that Customs may act on its own initiative to delay the effective date of a ruling but should protect their interests and make application on their own behalf.

Importers should be aware that substantial and detailed evidence supporting such a claim of past treatment is required, as well as substantial evidence supporting the claim

14. 19 C.F.R. § 177.9(d)(3) (1990).

of reliance, before such petition will be considered. Further, Customs will give diminished weight to transactions involving small quantities or values, as well as informal entries.[15]

Recipient's Obligations

Also appearing as a modification of 19 C.F.R. part 177 is the Customs Service's "clarification" of the obligations of a recipient of a ruling.[16] These clarifications are designed to make it absolutely clear that recipients of classification rulings who disagree with the determination of Customs do not have the option of entering the merchandise described in the rulings under the classifications they consider to be correct. Requests for reconsideration may be made. However, during pendency of the reconsideration, entries must be made in accordance with the ruling. In addition, Customs proposes to impose "such penalties as may be appropriate" should the recipient of a classification ruling fail to set forth such classification in the information filed in connection with the entry of that merchandise. Customs declined to provide any clarification of the penalty proposal in response to public comment on the regulation, merely stating, "As with Customs penalty proceedings in general, penalties may vary depending on a range of factors, such as the differential in the rate of duties, the degree of negligence [*sic*] and the value of the merchandise involved."[17]

---

15. 19 C.F.R. § 177.9(e)(3) (1990).
16. 19 C.F.R. § 177.8(a)(2) (1990). This provision requires any person receiving a ruling setting forth the tariff classification of merchandise to set forth such classification in documents filed in connection with any subsequent entry of merchandise or suffer a rejection of the entry and imposition of penalties.
17. 54 Fed. Reg. 31,511, 31,514 (1989).

Review of District Rulings

Recipients of classification rulings from the district or area offices, NISs, or deputy NISs are given the right to appeal those rulings to Headquarters. There is no time limit for the filing of such appeals. While a transaction to which a district binding ruling request relates remains prospective, the ruling may be appealed directly to Headquarters. Although such an appeal may not be properly the subject of a request for internal advice under 19 C.F.R. § 177.11(b)(ii), Headquarters will accord such appeals the same high priority status as an internal advice request, which has precedence over routine ruling requests from importers.[18] Such advice may not be requested for the purpose of seeking reconsideration of a ruling.

Once a ruling has been issued in writing, a field office seeking reconsideration of it will notify the importer or other person to whom the ruling letter was issued in writing that it has requested the Headquarters Office to reconsider the ruling. If an importer disagrees with the way a ruling letter issued by a Customs field office is being applied, the field office, upon receipt of a written request, will seek advice from Headquarters. Such request may not be used for the purpose of reconsideration of a ruling when the importer disagrees with its substance.[19]

Modification/Revocation

Ruling letters may be withdrawn only upon written notice to the beneficiary, unless they are published.[20] However, other parties which may be relying on the holdings of unpublished rulings are not entitled to such notice. The Customs Service is authorized to withdraw them if they are

18. 19 C.F.R. § 177.11(b)(1)(i) (1989).
19. See the discussion of internal advice procedure below.
20. Published rulings are discussed later in this chapter.

found to be at variance with current Customs practice. No ruling may be withdrawn retroactively to the detriment of the party on whose behalf it was issued, if the facts and the law are substantially the same as at the time it was issued, and if the requester had made the request in good faith with regard to a prospective transaction.[21] As noted above, however, the availability of letter rulings through microfiche, diskettes, and other media gives substance to the argument that *no* ruling should be withdrawn or modified without notice to the public that may be relying on it.

Accordingly, when circumstances warrant, the Service will publish modifications and revocations of unpublished rulings. Further, only Customs Headquarters is authorized to revoke rulings issued by the New York regional commissioner.

Legal Precedent Retrieval

Lists, by titles and subtitles, of unpublished administrative decisions are published from time to time. Copies of those decisions are available from the ORR in Washington. They are also available in microfiche format. An index of selected decisions and documents is available by subscription in microfiche (the Legal Precedent Retrieval System Microfiche Index). Negotiations with a private-sector legal research database service have yet to reach a conclusion. In the interim, the Customs Service has recently made a number of rulings available on IBM-format diskettes.

---

21. 19 C.F.R. § 177.9 (1990). While the new Customs procedures by which affected parties may seek delay of the effective date of rulings, which modify or revoke prior rulings or which modify past treatment of transactions not covered by ruling letters, are generally beneficial, Customs could have gone a step further. Customs could have provided that such modifying rulings will be published and open to comments before issuance or alternatively that some effort to generally disseminate these rulings will be made to ensure that all affected parties are informed of such modifications.

Confidentiality

While an inquiring member of the public may request at any time before the issuance of a ruling that nondisclosure of allegedly confidential information be observed, the Customs Service does not presume that identifying matter in ruling requests is privileged or confidential. Consequently, exemption from the nondisclosure provision of the Customs regulations requires the requester to identify clearly the information claimed to be exempt from disclosure and the reasons for the requested exemption.

Information may be exempt from disclosure where it is claimed to constitute a private party's trade secrets or privileged, confidential, or financial information that would harm the party's interest. For example, a domestic manufacturer of merchandise identical to imported goods that are the subject of a ruling asked Customs to disclose documents containing the appraised value of the imported merchandise. Customs held that price and quantity data furnished by the foreign manufacturer for an appraised value determination were confidential because the information would have threatened commercial injury by revealing the competitive strengths and weaknesses and the marketing strategy of the company and its distributors. Competitors would have been able to modify their own strategies and selectively undersell the foreign manufacturer.

Pre-Entry Classification (Line Review)

As it was revising the ruling letter system to respond to the change in classification statutes, the Customs Service moved to eliminate a possible bottleneck in the process of providing importers with advice about customs classification. Importers with high volumes of imports and/or broad product lines of imported goods, possibly arriving at multiple ports of entry, were identified as potential beneficiaries of a new program of bulk rulings.

The idea was not altogether new: Import specialists had traditionally agreed to provide nonbinding classification rulings to importers of diverse kinds of merchandise. Such "line reviews" were often carried out at the importer's premises, where samples would be readily available. The chief novelties in the pre-entry program are that Customs can select and qualify candidates for it, and that the rulings resulting from it will be binding on the whole Customs Service.[22]

The Customs Service has issued brochures encouraging importers to apply for pre-entry classification, and the directive establishing the program mentions the possibility that importers may request to participate. However, the directive is written almost entirely in terms of methods Customs may use to identify and certify candidates. The motivation for the program is the continuing rise in importation of goods while Customs manpower remains static.

Responsibility for the line reviews will rest with the national import specialists. The directive makes it clear that most of the labor will be performed by deputy NISs, field-level import specialists whom the NISs will designate for particular areas of expertise. The guideline envisions that the Customs officials actually performing line reviews will be designated at least in part for their proximity to the importer's premises.

Merchandise that is the subject of pending administrative or judicial proceedings will not be considered, and Customs will consider the effect a new ruling might have on the classification of an article that was the subject of a prior ruling. Decisions under the pre-entry program "will be provided only on well settled issues following the guidelines established by OR&R." Interested importers may participate in the pre-entry program simply by contacting the NIS of-

22. Customs Directive 3610-02 (Mar. 8, 1989).

fice in New York or by submitting a letter to the local Customs district director's office requesting participation.

After reviewing the importer's merchandise, the field import specialist will forward his or her preliminary classifications to the NIS for review (usually within thirty days). The NIS will complete the review within forty-five days after receipt of the field report and issue a ruling letter and the list of classifications, which are then sent to the importer and to all the ports involved.

Once such a ruling has been issued, importers must enter their goods according to it, even if they are appealing the holding. Customs may revoke all or part of a pre-entry classification ruling upon notice to the beneficiary, who may apply for a ninety-day deferral of the effective date, if it is detrimental.

Published Rulings

If published in the weekly *Customs Bulletin & Decisions*, the rulings create established and uniform practices. All such rulings are reviewed by Headquarters prior to publication, in a procedure added by the Customs Procedural Reform and Simplification Act of 1978 to 19 U.S.C. § 1625, which provides that within 120 days after issuing any precedential decision, including any ruling letter, internal advice memorandum, or protest review decision, that decision must be published in the *Customs Bulletin* or otherwise made available for public inspection.[23]

These decisions are binding on the Customs Service as to all importers on the issue addressed, but not on the courts, although they are given consideration. Since January 1, 1979, all rulings and other administrative decisions have been designated as Customs Service Decisions and published with a number indicating the year and sequence, for example, Cust. Serv. Dec. 78-12.[24]

---

23. 19 C.F.R. § 177.1(b) (1990).
24. See 12 Cust. B. & Dec. 920 (1978) (T.D. 78-414).

Procedures

Mandatory Publication of Rulings and the "Clearly Wrong" Test

Certain rulings have to be published pursuant to 19 C.F.R. § 177.10. These usually include those of general interest or importance. When published, these establish a uniform practice or may result in a change of practice. If a change in practice results in the assessment of a higher rate of duty, however, it will be effective only as to merchandise entered on and after the ninetieth day after the publication of the change in the *Customs Bulletin,* thus giving interested parties an opportunity to make written submissions with respect to the correctness of the contemplated change.

Among the Customs Service's changes in practice to enhance uniformity of decisions at the time the Harmonized Tariff Schedules were introduced was the removal of the "clearly wrong" test from 19 C.F.R. § 177.10(b).[25] Under the former rule, a ruling could not change an earlier published ruling or established practice unless the earlier ruling or practice was determined to have been "clearly wrong." It was the position of Customs prior to 1989 that the procedures in 19 C.F.R. § 177.10(c) involving publication, availability for comment, and the ninety-day delay of the effective date were sufficient safeguards for the public. The removal of this test has made it easier for Customs (and importers) to change prior practices. This is, of course, both good and bad. On the one hand, practices that have been

25. 54 Fed. Reg. 8208, 8212 (1989). The Customs Service believed that the "clearly wrong" standard formerly set forth in the regulations had little real meaning. The courts held that continuous administrative practice over a long period would not be disturbed in the absence of compelling reasons to the contrary. United States v. Bayersdorfer & Co., 16 Ct. Cust. App. 43 (1928); Henry Clay & Bock Co. v. United States, 41 C.C.P.A. 45 (1953).

comfortably relied on for some time may be changed more easily. On the other hand, such changes may be welcome. The "clearly wrong" test was applied only when the change in practice would have resulted in the imposition of higher duty rates.

The Court of International Trade confronted the question of whether the Customs Service was obliged under 19 C.F.R. § 177.10 to publish a ruling reversing a prior published ruling when the later ruling was adverse to the importer.[26]

The first ruling had been published in the *Customs Bulletin and Decisions* as a Customs Service decision. It allowed importers of made-to-measure suits from Hong Kong to pay duty only on the price that the Hong Kong distributors paid to the tailors who made the suits for the "cut, make, and trim" operations (typically around $75). The buyers thus did not pay duty on the full $200 that, on average, the distributors charged them for such suits.

More than seven months later, the Customs Service revoked its prior holding, deciding that the garments should be appraised on the basis of the higher prices the importers paid to the distributors. Customs reversed itself first by means of a telex to the San Francisco district, and it then issued a second ruling letter. Neither the telex nor the second ruling was published.

The importer claimed in court that the adverse action could not be taken without publication and without the opportunity to contest and delay the higher assessment. The court held that (1) the government's later ruling appraising the goods at the distributor to importer price was correct; and that (2) the government did not err in revoking the prior holding (because the rulings were concerned with methods of appraisement and not with a "rate of duty or

26. American Air Parcel v. United States, 557 F. Supp. 605 (Ct. Int'l Trade 1983).

charge," as covered by section 177.10, publication was not required).

On appeal, the Court of Appeals for the Federal Circuit reversed the trial court on the grounds that the goods were destined for exportation at the time of the transaction between the distributor and tailors. They thus qualified for the statutory basis of valuation. In reversing the trial court, the court of appeals did not reach the issue of the retroactive revocation of the Customs Service ruling.[27]

By Petition

Section 7361(c) of the Anti-Drug Abuse Amendments Act of 1988[28] called for regulations providing nationwide uniformity of Customs decisions and the establishment of procedures by which affected parties can have port to port inconsistencies or inconsistencies between the treatment of the same issue by different officials in the same port resolved; or may question the frequency of intensive examinations of goods at any port.

Customs responded by adding section 177.12 to the customs regulations. This provision allows "interested parties" to petition Customs to resolve claims of lack of uniformity in decisions and inconsistency in the manner and degree merchandise is examined and inspected, as when the practices differ from port to port, or even as between officials in the same port.[29]

Upon receipt of a properly filed petition, Customs will verify the facts, publish a notice in the *Federal Register* that a petition was received, allow fifteen days for written com-

---

27. American Air Parcel v. United States, 718 F.2d 1546 (Fed. Cir. 1983), *cert. denied*, 466 U.S. 937 (1984).
28. Pub. L. No. 100-690, 100 Stat. 4475, 19 U.S.C. § 1514 note (1988).
29. 19 C.F.R. § 177.12 (1989). Broadly speaking, the new regulation attempts to address the inflexibility engendered by the former "clearly wrong" standard. See notes 10 and 25, *supra*, and associated text.

ments (oral conferences will only be allowed in extraordinary circumstances), and issue its decision within fifteen days of the close of the comment period. Importers should note that this procedure does not preclude a party from protesting or filing a domestic interested party petition regarding the same matter. If a decision is issued through this petitioning procedure, that decision itself will not be protestable.[30] However, it may serve as a basis for the disposition of any protest later filed on the matter or may serve as an information letter setting forth the Service's position.

Conflicts

The director, classification and value division, Customs Headquarters, reviews all rulings issued by the regional commissioner before publication in the *Customs Bulletin & Decisions*. In the event of a conflict between rulings issued by Headquarters and by the regional commissioner of New York or other area and district offices, the Headquarters ruling would prevail. If Headquarters determines that the rate of duty applied by the NIS should be lowered, the lower rate of duty will be applied to all unliquidated entries covering the same merchandise. When Headquarters determines that the rate of duty applied by the NIS should be increased, the higher rate will apply only to entries or withdrawals from warehouse for consumption made ninety days after the date the ruling is published.

Reliance, Effect, and Revocation

The NISs and area and district offices may not modify or revoke (1) rulings issued by Headquarters or (2) other rul-

30. Some public comments on the proposal for 19 C.F.R. § 177.12 showed a belief that the Service's response to a petition for consistent treatment should be protestable. Customs, on the other hand, finds this unnecessary. A petitioner who alleges inconsistent treatment and

ings that have been published. The 1989 changes in ruling procedures added language recognizing that a ruling letter issued by the Customs Service represents the Customs Service's official position with respect to the particular transaction and is binding on all Customs personnel until revoked or modified. Published rulings may not be revoked without ninety days' notice, and opportunity for comment and a hearing, if requested.

Delegation of Authority to Make Rulings

Generally, the transactions for which rulings are requested involve many specialty areas and an infinite variety of fact patterns. Some of the requests received by the New York region will be readily identifiable as matters appropriately ruled or acted upon by that region in the past. Other requests will be more complex, often involving issues beyond those specifically set forth in the request. Whether these requests should properly be selected for local action or referred to Headquarters is to be determined by the application of certain guidelines and the exercise of sound judgment.

In certain instances, the New York region receives correspondence that requires a ruling neither by the region nor by Headquarters, such as an inquiry involving a pending transaction at another location. These issues are referred by the New York region directly to the port or district where the transaction is pending for reply. In such instances, the inquirer is notified of the referral.

Customs Headquarters has found that tariff classification requests are likely to fall into several categories, as described below. Requests in some categories are handled ex-

---

is dissatisfied with Customs is not entitled to protest unless there is an actual liquidation or other action subject to protest under part 174 of the Customs regulations. 54 Fed. Reg. 31513 (1989).

clusively by New York region, NISs, districts, or area offices, while requests in other categories are processed only by Headquarters. In certain further categories, however, determining the proper office to handle the request requires using the guidelines provided.

Delegation Guidelines[31]

1. *Inquiries answerable by information letters:* Any request for a ruling that would be answered best by an information letter is acted upon by the requester's area or district office, or by an NIS; if received by Headquarters, it is referred to the requester's area or district office, or an NIS, for reply. An "information letter" is a written statement issued by the Customs Service that does no more than expound a well-established principle of customs law, without applying it to a particular set of facts.
2. *Ruling requests in which no issues are raised:* If the inquirer makes no classification claim and offers no specific suggestions as to an alternative position, the response tends to be essentially a routine application of the language of specific provisions or relevant headnotes or other fundamental rules of construction. This type of ruling would be issued by an area or district office, or an NIS, unless action by Headquarters would be more appropriate under another guideline.
3. *Ruling requests involving unsupported classification claims:* If the request makes no claim at all, or the claim it makes is frivolous or based on arguments considered to be entirely without merit (for example, the correspondent alleges that its entitle-

31. 19 C.F.R. § 177.1 (1988).

ment to a lower rate is warranted by the "national interest" or "impending bankruptcy" or other factors in no way pertinent to the law), the requester's area or district office, or NIS, would respond unless other bona fide concerns or issues of unusual social or economic impact were raised that warranted the attention of Headquarters.

4. *Ruling requests involving a uniform classification practice:* Headquarters is designated as the respondent when the ruling request alleges the existence of a uniform and established classification practice based on uniform liquidations rather than on the usual rules of construction as reflected in a normal application of HTSUS and its pertinent headnotes.
5. *Ruling requests involving special tariff classification provisions:* Generally, Headquarters is assigned responsibility to respond to requests involving an importer's eligibility for a potential or conditional exemption from duty under some special tariff classification provision. Examples of situations in this category are the Generalized System of Preferences, qualification to receive duty-free entry under HTSUS provisions governing absolutely or conditionally free entry (mostly found in Chapter 98), and issues involving the application of the Florence Agreement for the advancement of art and science. Other matters involved in this group of requests include diplomatic courtesy and such controversial questions as principles of substantial transformation, further fabrication, and advancement in condition. In isolated instances, however, should the details of the inquiry concern a prospective exemption claim related to the requirements of a single port, that matter would be referred to that port for action.
6. *Ruling requests involving inconsistent precedents:*

Headquarters will generally respond to any ruling request concerning a tariff classification as to which two or more precedents, administrative or judicial, are both pertinent and, in any material respect, inconsistent.

7. *Ruling requests involving reconsideration:* Any ruling request in which reconsideration of a prior ruling is requested should be made to Headquarters for response. An inquiry requesting a reconsideration of a New York region ruling should be sent directly to Headquarters.
8. *Ruling requests involving issues of fact:* Issues of fact for purposes of the guidelines are created when there is a conflict in the evidence in the case file or the evidence may conflict with information available from other reliable sources (e.g., the information furnished by the inquirer is contradicted by information found in reliable trade media or a request includes a conflict between the results of a private laboratory analysis and an official Customs Laboratory report). Generally, these will be referred to the NISs.
9. *Ruling requests involving multiple issues:* Valuation or appraisement determinations are outside the scope of regional concern except when the multiple (classification and appraisement) issues presented are clearly separable. In that situation, the New York region will respond to the classification aspects and advise the inquirer that the appraisement decision will be forthcoming from Headquarters in a separate reply.
10. *Ruling requests containing legal briefs:* Some ruling requests (for example, those submitted on behalf of importers by attorneys) may contain sophisticated arguments involving precedential or conceptual reasoning. Although requests of this type will gener-

ally be the concern of Headquarters, the New York region may assume responsibility when (1) both the arguments advanced and the tariff classification claimed are in accord with the current Customs Service position and (2) the conclusions advocated are supported by uniform precedents that the New York region would have reached, regardless of the arguments developed in the request.

11. *Ruling requests involving the application of judicial precedents* that seek to apply legal principles to merchandise of a different class or kind than that ruled on in the decision claimed as precedent must be referred to Headquarters for resolution. Any classification requiring the application of rules of construction is referred to Headquarters whenever application of two or more rules produces inconsistent results or whenever, in determining relative specificity, application of the rules appears to result in unreasonable or illogical results.
12. *Ruling requests having the potential for unusual social or economic impact:* Requests carrying a potential for national publicity are referred to Headquarters for action. Matters of this nature may involve foreign governments or international trade organizations or situations where a Customs Service action could affect other government agencies with responsibilities in national trade policy.
13. *Ruling requests involving pending issues:* No rulings will be issued when the matters involved are the subject of the applicant's administrative appeal, protest, or request for internal advice; or when the issue is pending before a judicial tribunal. Such applicants will be apprised that no response can be furnished because of the pendency of the related matter. A copy of this response is placed in the primary file so that a complete record may be maintained in the event that litigation is initiated.

It is recognized that most ruling requests that raise complex issues and therefore warrant the attention of Headquarters would be submitted by experts in some aspect of importing or international trade. As such, these inquirers would be aware of the option of submitting their presentations directly to Headquarters rather than to the region.

To summarize, the Customs Service district or area office, or NIS, would assume the responsibility for responding to a ruling request when the request involves a well-settled area or an issue easily resolved by reference to precedents. This allows Headquarters to concentrate its efforts on more complex requests or those involving novel issues without substantive precedent.

Internal Advice Procedure[32]

"Internal advice" means advice or guidance as to the proper interpretation and application of the customs laws, related statutes, and regulations within the areas of responsibility administered by the Office of Regulations and Rulings with respect to a specific set of facts. The purpose of the internal advice procedure is to provide a system for the uniform disposition of issues before the United States Customs Service. The procedure is intended for use by Customs officials and the public in requesting advice or rulings regarding legal questions applicable to current or pending customs transactions.

At the outset, it is stressed that while issues dealing with prospective transactions are reviewed under the same procedural provisions of part 177 of the customs regulations (discussed above), the internal advice procedures are limited to ongoing or current transactions.

The advice, as ultimately furnished by Headquarters, is intended to assist Customs Service personnel in establishing

32. 19 C.F.R. § 177.11 (1990).

and maintaining consistent legal interpretations. Internal advice should be requested whenever any of the following conditions exists:

1. The laws and regulations are not clear on the issue under consideration and there is no published precedent for determining its proper treatment.
2. There is reason to believe that nonuniformity in treatment of the issue exists among districts.
3. The issue is so unusual or complex as to warrant consideration by Headquarters.
4. The Customs Service field office believes the issue to be one of national application.
5. The Customs Service field office was requested to seek advice by (a) the importer, (b) a Customs Service officer, or (c) another party having an interest in the transaction.

As an example of the latter, an import specialist informed an importer who had been importing certain goods under a low duty provision that the NIS was recommending that duty be imposed at a higher rate under another tariff provision. Since the issue concerned importations that had been proceeding for a time, it was not eligible for the ruling request procedure. The import specialist at the port of entry agreed to extend liquidation of the disputed entries while Customs Headquarters considered the importer's request for internal advice.

The regional commissioner or district office should pursue this avenue of resolving important problems when he or she feels that a ruling issued to an importer or other interested party by Headquarters should be modified or revoked. If additional information is presented to supplement a request for internal advice that tends to support the importer's position, or if, based upon new information, the field office does not agree with an existing ruling or a resolution at which two or more ports may have arrived, a request should be initiated to resolve the issue.

Although the request for internal advice may delay the closing of a case, the benefits derived may go beyond the issues involved in that particular case so as to render the delay worthwhile.

A request for internal advice should take the form of a memorandum to Headquarters, Office of Regulations and Rulings. It may be initiated by a Customs Service officer, an importer, or another interested party. The memorandum should include a statement of the pertinent facts and any recommendations the requesting party wishes to make. Supporting documents and materials should be submitted with the memorandum. Headquarters will attempt to issue a reply within thirty days of the date it received the request. If this goal cannot be attained, the submitting office will be advised of the delay and given a projected date of reply.

A person to whom a ruling is issued and who disagrees as to the proper application of the ruling may request the advice of Headquarters. Such advice may not be requested for the purpose of seeking reconsideration of the ruling's substantive holding, however.[33]

Requests for internal advice will not be submitted to Headquarters until all coordinating procedures have been exhausted, including visits to importers' premises to develop information necessary for a full evaluation of the issue. If, after completion of the actions and considerations discussed above, the regional commissioner or district office continues to adhere to the initial position on the issue, and this position is consistent with clear and definitive precedents that unequivocally support it, a request by an importer for an internal advice ruling may be denied. Further, the Headquarters office may refuse to consider the

33. 19 C.F.R. § 177.11(b)(1)(ii) (1990).

questions presented to it whenever (1) it determines that the period of time necessary to give adequate consideration to the factors presented would result in a withholding of action on the import transaction beyond that permitted by the sound administration of the customs and related laws and (2) the questions presented can subsequently be raised by the importer in the form of a protest under part 174 of the customs regulations.[34]

When a request for internal advice is denied, the importer is notified in writing of the reason for that denial and advised of its right to protest and request further review.[35] If that avenue is pursued and the reason set forth is the denial of a request for internal advice on the same issue, further review of the protest will automatically be granted.

When internal advice was sought at the request of an importer or other interested party and the Customs Service field office agrees with the conclusions reached by Headquarters, the Customs Service field office should furnish the importer or other party with a copy of the internal advice memorandum, unless instructed otherwise.

The internal advice memorandum represents an expression of the official position of the Customs Service with respect to the application of law, regulations, and precedents to a particular set of facts. Whenever the conclusions reached in such a memorandum will affect a substantial volume of imports, or if its publication would promote the uniform application of the laws and regulations for which the Customs Service is responsible, the memorandum is published in the weekly *Customs Bulletin & Decisions*.

Published internal advice memoranda have the effect of published rulings, and they are binding on all Customs Service personnel until modified or revoked.

---

34. *See* chapter 25, "Protests."
35. 19 C.F.R. § 174.24 (1990).

25. Protests

Chapter 24 discussed administrative rulings. Although a formal "protest" results in an administrative ruling, the subject is broad enough to be treated in this separate chapter.

A protest is the formal method by which an importer may express its dissatisfaction with the duties assessed by a district director of the Customs Service or with certain other conclusions drawn against an import entry that are adverse to the importer's interests.

This right to object to government action is strictly construed and subject to rigid time limits that may not be waived by the Customs Service or by a court. As will be shown in chapter 26, the right of judicial review of the issues subject to protest rests on the correct and timely filing of a protest, the Customs Service's denial of which, followed by the timely filing of a summons, gives the court jurisdiction over the matter.

The matters that may come within the purview of a protest are the following:[1]

1. The appraised value of merchandise;
2. The classification, rate, and amount of duties chargeable;

1. 19 U.S.C.A. § 1514(a) & 1514(c) (West 1980 & Supp. 1988); 19 C.F.R. §§ 174.11–.15 (1990).

3. All charges or exactions of whatever character within the jurisdiction of the Secretary of the Treasury;
4. The exclusion of merchandise from entry or delivery under the customs laws;
5. The liquidation or reliquidation of an entry, or any modification thereof;
6. The refusal to pay a claim for drawback; and
7. The refusal to reliquidate an entry for clerical error, mistake of fact, or inadvertence under 19 U.S.C. § 1520(c).

Filing Protest[2]

The filing of a protest is authorized as long as there exists a clear connection between the merchandise and the party filing the protest. Accordingly, protests may be filed by the importer, the consignee, or any authorized person paying any charge or exaction, or who filed any claim for drawback, or who sought the entry or delivery of imported merchandise. A protest may be filed by a customshouse broker, provided it has been authorized to do so by the importer of record and has a general power of attorney[3] to transact customs business for its client. In addition, an authorized attorney at law may file protests on behalf of the principal, as may the surety on which demand is made for payment of duty.

Protests are usually filed in quadruplicate on Customs Form 19[4] or on a form of the same size clearly labeled

2. 19 C.F.R. § 174.12 (1990); 19 U.S.C. § 1514(b) (West 1980 & Supp. 1988).
3. 19 C.F.R. § 174.3 (1990).
4. See appendix 9.

"Protest." All schedules or other attachments (other than samples or similar exhibits) should also be filed in quadruplicate. The protest bears the signature of the person filing the protest. If that person is not the importer of record, his or her address and importer number, if any, should be included. A letter to the proper official at the Customs Service giving all the necessary information is considered an adequate form of protest.

A protest should be filed with the district director whose decision is being controverted, except that when the entry in contest is filed at a port other than a district headquarters, the protest may be filed with the director of that subport.

The assessment of countervailing or antidumping duties is subject to protest by the same parties and in the same manner as the assessment of regular duties.

Time of Filing

In order to be valid, protests must be filed, in accordance with section 514 of the Tariff Act of 1930, as amended,[5] within ninety days after one of the following:

1. The date of notice of liquidation or reliquidation, i.e., official notice of liquidation of formal entries formalized on a bulletin notice of liquidation, CF 4333A.[6] That bulletin notice must be posted for the information of importers in a conspicuous place in the customshouse at the port of entry, or at some

5. 19 U.S.C.A. § 1514 (West 1980 & Supp. 1988).
6. A "courtesy notice is not the notice of liquidation required by the regulations. A courtesy notice is just that, a courtesy." *See* United States v. Reliable Chem. Co., 81 Cust. Ct. 154, *rev'd*, 66 C.C.P.A. 123 (1979). CF 4333A is reprinted in appendix 23.

other suitable place in such a manner that it can readily be located.

2. The date of the decision, if the decision involves neither a liquidation nor (a standard) reliquidation (e.g., the date of a refusal to reliquidate under 19 U.S.C. § 1520(c)(1)).
3. The date of mailing of a notice of demand for payment against a bond where there exists an unsatisfied legal claim under a bond written by a surety.

Date of Filing

The date on which a protest is received by the Customs Service officer with whom it must be filed is considered its official filing date. Where the proof does not establish that a protest was filed within the statutory time limits, it will be dismissed.[7] The court has no jurisdiction where the protest was filed more than ninety days after liquidation. In *Tropicana Products Inc. v. United States*, the plaintiff maintained constant contact with the assistant district director, and plaintiff's counsel made a telephone call to determine date of liquidation and was informed that it was March 13, 1987. Plaintiff submitted a protest on June 5, 1987, a date which plaintiff believed was six days before the ninety-day limit. The protest was actually filed on the ninety-first day, as the entries had been liquidated on March 6, 1989. The court held that the governing statute, 19 U.S.C. § 1514(c)(2)(A), provides that for the court to have jurisdiction over the denial of a protest, the protest must be filed with the customs officer within ninety days after the notice of liquidation. Since the plaintiff filed its protest beyond that statutory period, the court dismissed the action.

---

7. Tropicana Prods., Inc. v. United States, 13 Ct. Int'l Trade, slip op. 89–64 (1989); James Loudon & Co. v. United States, 79 Cust. Ct. 149 (1977).

However, a motion to dismiss was denied where entry papers were unavailable.[8] Where plaintiff's counsel made repeated requests for entry papers that were unavailable (apparently because of understaffing and difficult conditions at the customshouse in Anchorage, Alaska), the court held that because of the unavailability of the entry papers, the liquidation was "tolled." The court ruled that plaintiff did not lose its opportunity to protest the administrative decision because Customs could not produce the entry papers. Protests filed prior to the completion of administrative action are premature and will be dismissed.[9]

Content of Protest[10]

A protest must contain the following information:

1. The name and address of the protestant, i.e., the importer of record or consignee, and the name and address of its agent or attorney if signed by one of them.
2. The importer number of the protestant. If the protestant is represented by an agent having power of attorney, the importer number of the agent must also be shown.
3. The entry number and date of the entry.
4. The liquidation or reliquidation date or the date of any decision not involving a liquidation or reliquidation.

---

8. See also in Alyeska Pipeline Serv. Co. v. United States, 643 F. Supp. 1128 (1986) *reh'g granted*, 11 Ct. Int'l Trade 931 (1987), appeal No. 88-1285, *dismissed and remanded* (Fed. Cir. May 1988), a protest filed more than ninety days after liquidation held timely where entry papers were unavailable to counsel until long after liquidation.
9. McDonnell Douglas Corp. v. United States, 75 Cust. Ct. 6 (1975), *decision on rehearing*, 78 Cust. Ct. 92 (1977).
10. 19 C.F.R. § 174.13 (1990).

5. A specific description of the merchandise affected by the decision as to which the protest is made.
6. The nature of, and justification for, the objection set forth distinctly and specifically with respect to each category, payment, claim, decision, or refusal.
7. The date of receipt and protest number of any protest previously filed that is the subject of a pending application for "further review" and that is alleged to involve the same merchandise and the same issues.
8. If another party has not filed a timely protest, the surety's protest must certify that the protest is not being filed collusively to extend the time to protest.

The following are examples of the substantial litigation that has taken place in regard to the sufficiency of protests. In one case, an importer's correspondence with Customs attempting to have an entry reliquidated was an effective protest.[11]

The protest upon which a civil action is based must be sufficiently distinct and specific for the United States Court of International Trade to have jurisdiction.[12]

An amendment to a protest intended to embrace merchandise not originally covered thereby is not admissible when the amendment was introduced after the statutory period for filing a protest had run.[13]

The decision in *American Mail Line, Ltd. v. United States*[14] went further as to specificity of the protestant's claim. The protestant was required not only to reveal that

11. Donjon Marine Co., Inc. v. United States, 12 Ct. Int'l Trade, slip op. 88-14.
12. J. Ray McDermott & Co. v. United States, 69 Cust. Ct. 197 (1972), *appeal dismissed*, 60 C.C.P.A. 185 (1973).
13. United States v. Weigert-Dagen, 39 C.C.P.A. 58 (1951).
14. American Mail Line, Ltd. v. United States, 34 C.C.P.A. 1 (1946).

its merchandise was not dutiable under the assessed provision, but also to identify where in the Tariff Act it was dutiable. In addition, each protest must distinctly state the reasons for the importer's objection to the liquidation.[15] See, however, *Charles Kurz Co. v. United States*[16] for the proposition that when a protest may be fairly construed to include the merchandise, even though it was not precisely described, the protest will be held to be sufficient.

Issues challenged in an initial protest against a liquidation which was reliquidated must again be protested, even if the second protest is essentially identical to the prior protest. In *Philip Morris v. United States*,[17] a case with highly unusual facts, an importer filed a protest against the classification of five entries of tobacco. The tobacco was entered as scrap tobacco, TSUS item 170.60. Customs sent the importer a preliquidation notice stating that it intended to liquidate the entries under TSUS item 170.35 as stemmed leaf tobacco. Customs liquidated the tobacco as entered. The importer protested, claiming the tobacco should be classified under TSUS item 170.28, Oriental leaf not stemmed, or TSUS item 170.60, as entered and liquidated.

Customs then reliquidated the five entries under TSUS item 170.35, the same classification as stated in the preliquidation notice.

The reliquidation of the entry took place after the ninety-day statutory limit. The importer did not file another protest after the reliquidation under TSUS item 170.35. Thereafter Customs denied the first protest because the classification under TSUS item 170.35 as reliquidated was correct. Suit was instituted in the United States Court of International Trade; the government moved to dismiss the

15. Raybestos Manhattan, Inc. v. United States, 27 C.C.P.A. 340 (1940).
16. Charles Kurz Co. v. United States, 57 Cust. Ct. 73 (1966).
17. Philip Morris v. United States, 716 F. Supp. 1479 (1989).

action for lack of jurisdiction, because no protest was filed against the reliquidation and the reliquidation was final.

The reliquidation of one of the entries was after the statutory time limit. The government argued that even an unlawful reliquidation must be protested to invoke the court's jurisdiction. The court agreed, holding that the unlawful reliquidation is voidable, not void, and it stated that the correctness of reliquidation by Customs may not be disturbed unless a timely protest is filed.

Issues that could have been raised in the initial protest against the liquidation may not be raised through protest against a reliquidation. Previous determinations regarding the original liquidation may not be disturbed by a protest directed against a reliquidation.[18]

In *Pistorino & Co. v. United States*, an entry of certain wool grease was duly liquidated, and no protest was filed against the liquidation. The Service then voluntarily reliquidated the entry, allowing a refund, but only as to a certain type of wool grease on the entry. The importer then filed a protest against the reliquidation, making a claim for additional refunds on another type of wool grease not involved in the reliquidation. The court dismissed the protest, stating, "It is fundamental that a protest against a reliquidation must be limited to questions involved in the reliquidation."[19]

However, a protest filed against a liquidation can be amended to add a claim for clerical error under 19 U.S.C. § 1520(c)(1) if that claim subsequently accrued.[20]

Multiple Entries

A single protest may be filed with regard to more than one entry in any district if all the entries involve the same

18. Pistorino & Co. v. United States, 71 Cust. Ct. 166 (1973).
19. *Id.*
20. Walker Enters. v. United States, 78 Cust. Ct. 119 (1977).

protestant, and if (a) the same category of merchandise and (b) an administrative decision common to all entries are the subject of the protest. In those circumstances, the entry numbers, dates of entry, dates of liquidation, and ports of entry should be set forth as an attachment to the protest.

Amendment of Protest[21]

A protest may be amended at any time prior to the expiration of the ninety-day period within which it may be filed. The amendment may assert additional claims pertaining to the administrative decision or may challenge an additional administrative decision relating to the same category of merchandise covered by the subject protest. In determining whether to allow or deny a protest filed within the time (ninety-day period) allowed, a reviewing officer may consider alternative claims and additional arguments submitted in writing by the protestant at any time prior to disposition of the protest. Although a protest may not be amended after the ninety-day period to include additional merchandise or a different type of claim, the reviewing officer may consider alternative claims and additional grounds submitted in writing covering the same merchandise at any time prior to the disposition of the protest.

When the original protest is deemed to be invalid, it may not be amended.[22]

A second protest will not be accepted as an amendment of the first when it is not so identified and does not refer to the original protest.[23]

21. 19 C.F.R. § 174.14 (1990).
22. C.M. Whitney Co. v. United States, 62 Cust. Ct. 621 (1969).
23. Roussel Corp. v. United States, 81 Cust. Ct. 115 (1978); Webcor Elecs. v. United States, 79 Cust. Ct. 137 (1977).

Single, Not Multiple, Protests

Only one protest may be filed per entry, except that when the entry covers merchandise of different categories, a separate protest may be filed as to each separate category. Consequently, if two protests covering the same category are filed, only the first protest received by the Customs Service is valid. Should this first protest be abandoned, that action does not retroactively validate the second protest. However, separate protests filed by different authorized persons, e.g., a customs broker and a customs attorney, with respect to any one category are deemed part of a single protest.[24] Congress intended in the Customs Court Act of 1970[25] to simplify importers' procedures to the extent that, unlike the practice prior to October 1, 1970, importers must now challenge all claims against a liquidation in a single protest, whether the claim arises out of the appraised value or classification or both.[26]

Review and Disposition of Protests[27]

Generally, a protest must be reviewed, allowed, or denied within two years of filing. Where several timely protests are treated as part of a single protest, the two-year period is deemed to run from the day the last protest was filed. When a protest involves exclusion of merchandise from entry or delivery, the review and action thereon by the district director must be made within thirty days from the date the protest was filed unless the protestant requests a delay to present evidence or additional argument.

---

24. Russ Togs, Inc. v. United States, 79 Cust. Ct. 119 (1977).
25. Pub. L. No. 91-271, 84 Stat. 274 (1970).
26. Minox Corp. D/O Berkey, Inc. v. United States, 77 Cust. Ct. 110 (1976).
27. 19 C.F.R. § 174.21 (1990).

Where an importer filed a protest against the classification of an entry of standard letterpress printing paper and requested further review, Customs Service denied the protest. The importer then filed a second protest and asked for further review against the second entry of the same merchandise. Some five months later, the importer petitioned under 19 U.S.C. § 1520(c) requesting Customs to rescind the denial of the first protest. Customs did not respond. On March 22, 1983, within two years, Customs denied the request to rescind and determined that the first protest should have been denied in part only. A civil action commenced more than 180 days from the original denial was dismissed by the Court of International Trade as untimely. The court held that the Customs Service was not authorized by 19 U.S.C. § 1515 to exercise jurisdiction over a protest after it had been denied, and that the petition for rescission of a denial of a protest was neither contemplated nor authorized by 19 U.S.C. § 1515(c). The court held, in effect, that Customs cannot change its mind after the protest has been denied and its administrative decision must stand.[28]

Accelerated disposition of a protest may be obtained at any time after ninety days from its filing by filing by registered or certified mail a written request for such treatment with the district director.[29] The protest that is the subject of the request must be reviewed and decided within thirty days from the date of that mailing. If the district director fails to allow or deny a protest that is the subject of a request for accelerated disposition within thirty days from the date of mailing, the protest shall be deemed to have been denied at the close of the thirtieth day following the date of mailing. Thus, the protestant may have quick recourse to the court but is responsible for keeping track of

28. San Francisco Newspaper Printing Co. v. United States, 9 Ct. Int'l Trade 517 (1985).
29. 19 C.F.R. § 174.22 (1990).

the date of "deemed" denial in order to file a summons within 180 days of the denial.

Further Review of Protest[30]

A protesting party may seek further review of a protest by the region or by Customs Headquarters in addition to review by the district director by filing, usually on a separate section of Customs Form 19, an application for such review within the ninety-day protest period. If a preliminary examination by a district director indicates that the protest would be denied, the district director forwards the protest and application to the commissioner of customs or his or her designee, through the regional commissioner or his or her designee.

A party filing an application for further review is entitled to it when the decision by the district director against which the protest was filed:

1. Is alleged to be inconsistent with a Headquarters ruling or with a decision made in any district with respect to the same or substantially similar merchandise;
2. Is alleged to involve questions of law or fact that have not been ruled on by Headquarters or by the customs courts;
3. Involves matters ruled upon previously by Headquarters or by the customs courts, but the facts or legal arguments currently at hand were not available for presentation or consideration at the time of the original ruling; or
4. Is alleged to involve questions that Headquarters

30. 19 C.F.R. §§ 174.23–.25 (1990).

refused to consider when presented in a request for internal advice.[31]

An application for further review must contain, inter alia, admissions that the protesting party had not previously received an adverse decision from Headquarters, does not have presently pending an application for an administrative decision on the same claim with respect to the same category of merchandise, had not received a final adverse judicial decision, and does not have an action involving such a claim pending before the customs courts.

An application for further review should contain a statement of any facts or additional legal arguments, not part of the record, upon which the protestant relies and that justify further review. A showing of additional facts that support the allegation will constitute a ground for granting of further review even though the applicant is unable to respond positively to the status situations described above.

A protest must be reviewed by Customs Headquarters if the protest and application for review raise any of the following issues: lack of uniformity of treatment, the existence of an established and uniform practice, the interpretation of a court decision or ruling by Customs Headquarters, and controversies that have not been the subject of a Customs Headquarters ruling or court decision.

All other review protests are reviewed by the regional commissioner for the region in which the district lies or by a designee of that region who did not participate directly in the previous adverse decision. If alternative claims or additional grounds or arguments are submitted orally, they can be considered only if submitted in writing no later than sixty days after that oral submission.

Upon completion of further review, the protest and related documents are returned to the district director together with directions for the disposition of the protest.

31. 19 C.F.R. § 174.24(d) (1990).

Allowance or Denial of Protest[32]

The district director must allow or deny a protest in whole or in part within two years from the date of filing. A protest is deemed denied by operation of law if it is not acted upon within the two-year period provided by the statute.[33]

If the protest is allowed, the district director will refund any duties, charges, or exactions found to have been collected in excess or pay any drawback found due. If the protest is denied, appropriate notice will be mailed to the protestant or its agent with the date of denial clearly marked. The notice at times may include a statement of the reasons for the denial, as well as a statement informing the protestant of the right to file a civil action contesting that denial. Notice of denial of a protest can be mailed to a substituted designee only if the substitution notice is received by the district director prior to his or her denial. The district director notes on the notice of denial the payment of all liquidated duties or exactions, if he or she has actual knowledge of such payment at the time the protest is denied.

Petitions by Domestic Interested Parties[34]

There are procedures whereby an American manufacturer, producer, or wholesaler may contest the appraised value as being too low or the classification or rate of duty as being incorrect. The statute was amended by the Trade Act of 1974[35] to add the right to contest the failure of the Secretary

32. 19 C.F.R. § 174.29 (1990).
33. Knickerbocker Liquors Corp. v. United States, 78 Cust. Ct. 192 (1977).
34. 19 U.S.C.A. § 1516 (West 1980 & Supp. 1983).
35. Pub. L. No. 93-618, title III, §§ 321(f)(1) & 331(b), 88 Stat. 2048 & 2052 (1975).

of the Treasury to assess countervailing duties or antidumping duties upon merchandise of a class or kind manufactured, produced, or sold at wholesale by such domestic producers or wholesalers.

An "interested party" as used in this section means (1) a manufacturer, producer, or wholesaler in the United States of goods of the same class or kind as the designated merchandise; (2) a certified union or recognized union or group of workers which is representative of an industry engaged in the manufacture, production, or wholesale in the United States of such goods; or (3) a trade or business association a majority of whose members are manufacturers, producers, or wholesalers in the United States of such goods. The term "interested party" also includes (4) any producer of raw agricultural product who is part of the same industry that produces a product of the same class or kind as the designated imported merchandise.

Upon request of a domestic interested party for information, the Secretary of the Treasury must furnish the rate of duty and the countervailing duty or antidumping duty, if any, imposed upon designated imported merchandise of the same class or kind produced by that domestic interest. The request is directed to the commissioner of customs with the required specificity necessary to evoke a response. If the commissioner's response causes the domestic producer to believe that the competitive imported merchandise is entering the country at too low a rate or value or that countervailing or antidumping duty should be assessed, it may file a petition with the commissioner indicating the substance of its dissatisfaction. The filing of the petition triggers a notice published in the *Federal Register* setting forth all the details involved in the controversy. Interested parties may then make written submissions within the time specified in the notice.

If the Secretary does not agree with the petitioner, he or she so informs the petitioner. Within thirty days after the

Secretary's decision, the petitioner may notify the Secretary that it desires to contest the decision, whereupon the Secretary is required to publish the decision as to the proper classification and rate of duty and give the public notice of petitioner's desire to contest it. The Secretary is further required to furnish the petitioner with an identification of the entries and consignees of the imported merchandise entered after publication of his or her decision so as to enable the petitioner to contest the classification, appraised value, or failure to assess countervailing or antidumping duties in the liquidation of one such entry. The Secretary is required to direct the appropriate district director to notify the petitioner by mail when the first of such entries is liquidated. Within thirty days after the mailing of the notice of that liquidation, the petitioner may contest the decision of the Secretary by bringing a civil action in the United States Court of International Trade. If the petitioner's cause of action is sustained, all imported merchandise of the character involved that is entered for consumption after the date of publication of the court decision is subject to assessment in accordance with that final decision, and liquidation of the entries is suspended until final disposition of the action. All such entries will then be liquidated or reliquidated in accordance with the final decision. The consignee has the right to appear and to be heard as a party in interest.

Correction of Clerical Error, Mistake of Fact, or Inadvertence[36]

A clerical error, mistake of fact, or other inadvertence may be brought to the attention of the district director at the port of entry (or, in the New York region, the regional

36. 19 U.S.C.A. § 1520(c)(1) (West 1980).

commissioner) within one year after the date of liquidation or exaction. Liquidation, as used in this section, includes reliquidation of an entry.

If the application is timely, the mistake may be corrected even though a valid protest was not filed, provided that the clerical error, mistake of fact, or other inadvertence cannot be construed as an error in the construction of a law, is adverse to the importer, and can be documented. Thus administrative relief is available to an importer for a period substantially beyond the ninety-day limitation subsequent to liquidation imposed under the protest procedure.

After the amendment of section 520(c)(1) of the Tariff Act of 1930[37] by the Customs Simplification Act of 1953 to include relief for mistake of fact and inadvertence in addition to clerical error, the Customs Service published definitional guidelines[38] as follows:

> "Clerical error" occurs when a person intends to do one thing but does something else. It includes, for example, mistakes in arithmetic.
>
> "Mistake of fact" occurs when a person believes the facts to be other than they really are and takes some action based on that erroneous belief (for example, a customshouse broker misinterprets the instructions of its client and files the wrong type of entry).
>
> "Inadvertence" connotes oversight, inattention, or carelessness, as when an improper rate of duty is applied under a tariff designation providing for a completely different rate.
>
> "Error in the construction of a law" occurs when a person knows the facts but has a mistaken belief of the legal consequences of those facts and acts on that mistaken belief.

---

37. *Id.*
38. T.D. 54.848, 94 Treas. Dec. 244-46 (1959); PPG Indus. v. United States, 7 Ct. Int'l Trade 118 (1984); C.S.D. 84-7, 18 Cust. B. & Dec. 842-86; C.S.D. 88-17, 22 Cust. B. & Dec. (1988).

> Such an error might occur, for example, if the Customs Service improperly classified certain merchandise as an entirety when the facts dictated proper classification as separate entities. Another example of an error in the construction of the law, as applied to valuation or appraisement, might occur when an erroneous assumption with regard to the relationship between an importer and its supplier resulted in the selection of an allegedly improper basis of appraisement. In the above examples, the classifying or appraising officer may have committed error, but that error occurred in the interpretation of the law and cannot be corrected under 19 U.S.C. § 1520(c)(1) as a clerical error, inadvertence, or mistake of fact.[39]

Worthy of mention is the fact that there is now a single continuous procedure for determining value and classification, culminating in liquidation. As a result, any element of the liquidation, including the appraisement, is now correctable if it falls within the criteria of 19 U.S.C. § 1520(c)(1), as discussed above.

Significantly, a denial, prior to liquidation, of a request for correction of a clerical error, mistake of fact, or inadvertence is not subject to protest, because section 1520(c)(1) is intended as a claim for reliquidation as distinguished from liquidation. Therefore, until a request for reliquidation is made through the vehicle afforded by section 1520(c)(1) and has been denied by an appropriate Customs Service functionary, no valid protest can come before the United States Court of International Trade.[40] The court will acknowledge jurisdiction over a protest if the protest directed against the denial of a section 1520(c)(1) claim is filed by the aggrieved importer within ninety days after the district director's refusal to reliquidate.[41] However, where an importer's section

39. Occidental Oil & Gas Co. v. United States 13 Ct. Int'l Trade, slip op. 89-40 (1989).
40. Naftone, Inc. v. United States, 56 Cust. Ct. 886 (1966).
41. As prescribed by 19 U.S.C.A. § 1514 (West 1980 & Supp. 1988); 19

1520(c) claim is based on an alleged error in law and the resultant protest is filed after the ninety-day period provided for in 19 U.S.C. § 1514, the court will refuse to entertain it for lack of jurisdiction.[42]

Provided that the root cause of dissatisfaction by an importer with a Customs Service decision is traceable to clerical error, mistake of fact, or inadvertence, an importer is not foreclosed from administrative correction although the liquidation had become final within the terms of 19 U.S.C. § 1514.[43] Further, the evidence necessary to prove that an error was committed may be furnished *after* the statutory year as long as the claim is made *within* the year.

Universal Cooperatives Inc. v. United States,[44] involved the question whether an importer, having failed to file a timely protest to prevent tariff treatment of its merchandise from becoming final under section 514 of the Tariff Act of 1930, can take advantage of the more generous time period allowed under section 520(c) of the Act. The plaintiff argued that the government's mistaken conclusion as to the width of certain bailer twine strips was a mistake of fact that section 520(c)(1) was designed to correct. The flaw in this logic, the court pointed out, is

> that there are more types of factual mistakes than are dreamt of in plaintiff's philosophy. There is the *decisional* mistake in which a party may make the wrong choice between two known, alternative set of facts. There is also the ignorant mistake in which a party is unaware of the existence of the correct alternative set of facts. The decisional mistake must be challenged under Section 514. The ignorant mistake must be remedied under Section 520.

C.F.R. § 174.11(g) (1990). Omni U.S.A., Inc. v. United States, 663 F. Supp. 1130, *aff'g* 840 F.2d 912 (Fed. Cir. 1988).

42. United China & Glass Co. v. United States, 66 Cust. Ct. 207 (1971).
43. United States v. C. J. Tower & Sons, 61 C.C.P.A. 90 (1974).
44. Universal Coops, Inc. v. United States, 13 Ct. Int'l Trade (1989).

Here the court concluded that the importer was informed regarding its merchandise, facing an informed, but adverse government decision. There was no total ignorance of the possible alternative state of facts.

This chapter is concluded by emphasizing again that although 19 U.S.C. § 1520 does not control 19 U.S.C. § 1514,[45] the former prerogative can grant relief in the limited situations defined even though a valid protest has not been filed under section 1514. It is for this reason that the use of this valuable "tool" by the importing public has increased substantially over the years.

45. NEC Elecs. U.S.A., Inc., Elecs. Arrays Div. v. United States, 13 Ct. Int'l Trade, slip op. 89-33 (1989).

26. Judicial Review of Issues Relating to International Trade

One of the most significant aspects of any volume regarding customs and international trade is judicial review. Judicial review merely refers to the courts' power to invalidate, affirm, or modify governmental action. It is the responsibility of the judicial branch of government to interpret the law. Federal courts thus have the power to review and invalidate administrative rulings, congressional acts, and those of the executive which are contrary to law and the Constitution.

This chapter is neither designed nor intended as a comprehensive or authoritative treatise on the legal nuances involved in litigating before the various courts of the land, nor will it supply the reader with an exhaustive analysis of the laws, rules, and decisions mentioned. Rather, its purpose is to alert those persons involved with imports to the fact that after an administrative agency has rendered its final decision, judicial review exists to provide an independent reconsideration of the import transactions at issue.

An importer, domestic manufacturer, or other interested person dissatisfied with an action or decision of the United States Customs Service, the Department of Commerce, the International Trade Commission, or any other agency decision relating to imports can seek judicial review of that administrative action. Because such a suit is against the United States, permission to bring it must be granted by a statute that outlines the conditions under which suit must be brought and waives the traditional immunity of the sovereign to suit. Legislation enacted in 1980 increased the kinds of such suits that may be brought and significantly broadened the power of the federal courts to give relief. It was the intent of the Committee on the Judiciary of the House of Representatives, which sponsored this legislation, that "[p]ersons adversely affected or aggrieved by agency actions arising out of import transactions are entitled to the same access to judicial review and judicial remedies as Congress has made available for persons aggrieved by actions of other agencies."[1]

History of the Court of International Trade

Disputes with the federal government over importations were originally litigated in the same federal courts that heard other cases of various types. In 1890, the Board of General Appraisers was set up within the Department of the Treasury to review decisions of customs officials regarding the classification and valuation of imported merchandise. In 1926, the Board was replaced by the United States Customs Court, an article I, or administrative, court. Although declared in 1956 to be part of the federal judiciary system established under article III of the Constitution, the Customs Court's powers and its subject matter jurisdiction remained severely limited. In 1970, Congress eliminated separate procedures for classification cases and value or appraisement cases. The automatic receipt of administrative disputes also was ended, and the complete separation of the court as a part of the administrative process was enacted. The 1970 Act also provided for the commencement of a

---

1. H.R. REP. NO. 1235, 96th Cong., 2d Sess. 45, *reprinted in* 1980 U.S. CODE & ADMIN. NEWS 3729, 3757.

civil action.[2] On November 1, 1980, Congress provided for the expansion of jurisdiction of the court and conferred upon it the power to grant appropriate relief, whether equitable or legal, by enacting the Customs Courts Act of 1980. This Act also changed the name from the Customs Court to the United States Court of International Trade.

A wide variety of disputes arising out of the tariff laws could not be heard by the Customs Court either because the plaintiff had no standing or because the court had no power to grant the relief asked for. Nevertheless, these cases were dismissed by the federal district courts, because they appeared to be within the subject matter jurisdiction reserved to the Customs Court. This confusion was an important factor in the decision of Congress to expand the powers and jurisdiction of the Customs Court. Between 1978 and 1982, Congress revised the federal judiciary system to provide what was intended to be a comprehensive system of judicial review of issues arising out of import transactions and relating to international trade. The Customs Courts Act of 1980[3] established the United States Court of International Trade as successor to the United States Customs Court. The court is composed of nine judges. The President appoints the judges with the advice and consent of the Senate. The offices of the court are in New York City, but trials may be held in any other city within the United States. Judges of the court hold office during good behavior. The judges may also request assignments to sit in the federal district courts or courts of appeal.

The Customs Courts Act also enlarged the powers and jurisdiction of the Court of Customs and Patent Appeals, which heard appeals from the Court of International Trade

2. Customs Courts Act of 1970, Pub. L. No. 91-271, § 113, 84 Stat. 274 (1970) (codified as former 28 U.S.C. § 2632(a)).
3. Pub. L. No. 96-417, 94 Stat. 1727 (1980), *as amended by* Pub. L. No. 96-542, 94 Stat. 3209 (1980).

and from its predecessor, the Customs Court. This appellate role was unchanged by the Federal Courts Improvement Act of 1982,[4] which merged the Court of Customs and Patent Appeals with the United States Court of Claims to create the United States Court of Appeals for the Federal Circuit—a national appellate court with limited and specialized subject matter jurisdiction—and a new United States Claims Court with original jurisdiction of cases formerly commenced in the Court of Claims.

Jurisdiction of the Court of International Trade

Under the Constitution, a federal court has jurisdiction solely over those types of cases that it is specifically empowered by Congress to hear and decide. The Court of International Trade was intended by Congress to have exclusive subject matter jurisdiction over all civil actions arising from import transactions or out of federal statutes affecting international trade. Jurisdiction over criminal cases related to trade is clearly not included in this mandate, and cases involving importations of allegedly pornographic materials arising under section 305 of the Tariff Act of 1930[5] are specifically withheld.[6] In *Tooker v. United States*,[7] it was held that the court did not have jurisdiction over the Customs Service's denial of an exporter's petition for the return of goods seized by the Service.

4. Pub. L. No. 97-16, 96 Stat. 25 (1982).
5. 19 U.S.C.A, § 1305 (West Supp. 1985).
6. 28 U.S.C.A. § 1581(j) (West Supp. 1985).
7. Tooker v. United States, 7 Ct. Int'l Trade 230 (1984).

Organization and Procedure

Subject to the approval of the judges of the court, the chief judge supervises the clerical force of the court.

The office of the clerk receives all filings of legal papers or other documents required by statute or rules of the court. It keeps a docket of all civil actions filed with the court. Each action filed with the court is given a docket number. All papers filed in an action must include the docket number and be in conformity with the court rules as to means of production, methods of duplication, form, and size and number of copies. A civil action is commenced by filing concurrently with the clerk a summons and complaint, except for certain actions which are commenced by filing a summons only, such as an action described in 28 U.S.C. § 1581(a).[8]

Actions are assigned by the chief judge to a single judge. An action may be assigned to a panel of three judges under a finding by the chief judge that the action raises an issue of the constitutionality of an act of Congress or of a proclamation or executive order of the president or has broad and significant implications in the administration or interpretation of law.[9] The Court of International Trade may order any form of relief that is appropriate including injunctions and temporary restraining orders as may be warranted.

Trials may be either to the court or by jury. A far wider variety of civil actions can now be brought against the federal government by parties appealing from an administrative decision of the Customs Service, Department of Commerce, or other agency decisions involving import deci-

---

8. 28 U.S.C. § 1581 grants the Court of International Trade jurisdiction over any civil action against the United States arising out of the federal statutes governing import transactions.
9. SCM Corp. v. United States (Brother Int'l Corp., party in interest), 79 Cust. Ct. 163, 435 F. Supp. 1224 (1977).

sion. As former Chief Judge Edward D. Re of the Court of International Trade has remarked,[10] by concentrating judicial review in a single national court, Congress provided for uniformity and consistency in decisions, in accordance with the constitutional mandate that "all Duties, Imports and Excises shall be uniform throughout the United States." To attain this objective, and to lessen the confusion that had existed between the jurisdiction of the Customs Court and that of the district courts, which overlapping had long plagued importers, the jurisdiction of the new Court of International Trade was greatly expanded. Moreover, it was accompanied by the explicit grant to the new court of all the judicial powers in law and equity of a district court of the United States, thereby clearly establishing the Court of International Trade as an Article III court in fact as well as name.

In its decisions since November 1, 1980, the effective date of this legislation, the Court of International Trade has interpreted the Act to define its jurisdiction, and it has on numerous occasions exercised its new equitable powers.

Court's Power to Review Civil Actions Brought to Contest Administrative Denials

The Court of International Trade is a court of limited jurisdiction. It is also a court of exclusive jurisdiction. The prime judicial power of the former Customs Court, almost its sole power, was to review actions taken by the Customs Service and contested by an importer by means of a formal protest under sections 514 or 515 of the Tariff Act of 1930.[11] The importer was permitted to sue the government in the

10. Re, *Litigation Before the United States Court of International Trade*, 26 N.Y.L. Sch. L. Rev. 437 (1981).
11. 19 U.S.C.A. §§ 1514 & 1515 (West 1980 & Supp. 1988).

Customs Court after all administrative remedies had been exhausted and after the protest had been denied by the Customs Service. This type of judicial review remains at the core of the jurisdiction of the Court of International Trade.

> (a) The Court of International Trade shall have exclusive jurisdiction of any civil action commenced to contest the denial of a protest, in whole or in part, under section 515 of the Tariff Act of 1930.[12]

The major jurisdiction of the Court of International Trade today is set forth in 28 U.S.C. § 1581.

Subsection (a) involves the primary exclusive jurisdiction over civil actions commenced to contest the denial of an administrative protest brought pursuant to section 515 of the Tariff Act of 1930. This subsection substantially restates the court's authority as formerly set out in 28 U.S.C. § 1582(a). The action may be started by the person who filed the protest against a Customs decision or the surety on the transaction subject to the protest. A typical issue under this subsection would be the proper classification of merchandise under the various tariff provisions.

Subsection (b) grants the court jurisdiction over any civil action commenced by an American manufacturer under section 516 of the Tariff Act of 1930, seeking review of administrative decisions regarding imported merchandise. Under this provision an American manufacturer and certain other groups may contest the value of the appraised merchandise or the classification of the merchandise under the tariff laws.

Subsection (c) grants the court exclusive jurisdiction over civil actions commenced to review those antidumping and countervailing duty determinations listed in section 516A of the Tariff Act of 1930. The Court's jurisdiction over such

12. 28 U.S.C.A. § 1581(a) (West Supp. 1988).

actions was added by Title X of the Trade Agreements Act of 1979.

The judicial review of determinations of the International Trade Commission, relating to antidumping and countervailing duties provided for by 19 U.S.C. § 1516a and assigned by 28 U.S.C. § 1581(c) to the exclusive jurisdiction of the Court of International Trade, has been discussed in detail in chapter 20. Administrative actions subject to judicial review include decisions not to initiate investigations, decisions to suspend investigations, and determinations related to the discovery of confidential information.

Under 19 U.S.C. § 1516, a domestic interested party may file a petition with the Secretary of the Treasury to contest the appraisement or classification of imported goods of the same class or kind manufactured, produced, or sold at wholesale by that party.

If the petition is denied, the petitioner may notify the Secretary that it wishes to contest the decision. The Secretary publishes in the *Federal Register* a notice of the domestic challenge to the Customs Service's position, then mails to the petitioner a notice of the liquidation of the next entry of such merchandise. Within thirty days of the mailing date, the petitioner must file a summons in the Court of International Trade. Under the rules of the court, this summons may also be placed on the reserve calendar of the court for a year.

In one such action, characterized by Senior Judge Herbert N. Maletz as "a rare event in this court," an American manufacturer of bicycle speedometers proved that Congress intended to levy a higher rate of duty on such articles than that assessed by the Customs Service. The court ordered that entries of the merchandise be classified accordingly.[13]

Subsection (d) is a new jurisdictional grant of authority to the Court of International Trade. It transfers jurisdiction to

---

13. Stewart-Warner Corp. v. United States, 577 F. Supp. 25 (Ct. Int'l Trade 1983).

review final determinations made by the Secretary of Labor that refuse to certify workers for adjustment assistance, and decisions made by the Secretary of Commerce denying firms or communities adjustment assistance under the Trade Act of 1974.

Subsection (e) grants the court exclusive jurisdiction of any civil action commenced to review a final determination of the Secretary of the Treasury, under section 305(b)(1) of the Trade Agreements Act of 1979, as to whether an imported article is a product of a country which the President has found eligible for the benefits of the MTN Government Procurement Code, as provided in section 301 of the Trade Agreements Act. Such an eligible foreign product is exempt from the provisions of the Buy American Act.

Subsection (f) grants the court jurisdiction over any civil action involving an application for an order directing that confidential material submitted by a party in a countervailing or antidumping proceeding be made available.

This has proved to be a highly sensitive area. As the court observed in *Roquette Freres v. United States:*

> This statute gives the court wide latitude in determining whether or not to release confidential documents to parties involved in an antidumping proceeding. In making its determination, the court must consider (1) the needs of the litigants for data used by the Government in order to adequately respond to the antidumping finding, (2) the need of the Government in obtaining confidential information from businesses in future proceedings, and (3) the needs of the producers . . . to protect from disclosure information which, in the hands of a competitor, might injure their respective positions in the industry. This court must then balance "a party's need for the information sought against the public interest in protecting confidential business information, recognized by section 516a(b)(2)(B) and inherent in the administrative authority's ability to effectively perform its investigative duties required by the Antidumping Act." . . .[14]

---

14. Roquette Freres v. United States, 554 F. Supp. 1246, 1248 (Ct. Int'l Trade 1982).

The court has repeatedly drafted detailed protective orders covering different pieces of information and distinguishing who may and may not have access and under what conditions. In *U.S. Steel Corp. v. United States,*[15] an action by domestic steel producers challenging an International Trade Commission countervailing duty determination with regard to importations of certain steel products, the Court of International Trade denied plaintiff's in-house counsel access to confidential business documents while it allowed access to the company's retained counsel. The court reasoned that in-house counsel, by virtue of his position as employee of the company, was more apt inadvertently to disclose confidential information gleaned from the documents. On appeal, the Federal Circuit held that the denial was in error, and that access should be denied or granted on the basis of each individual counsel's actual activity and relationship with the party represented, without regard to whether a particular counsel is in-house or retained.

Subsection (g) grants the court jurisdiction to review the Secretary of the Treasury's decision of revocation, suspension, or monetary penalty taken against a holder of a customshouse broker's license or permit under provisions of 19 U.S.C. § 1641. It also grants jurisdiction by a civil action to review the Secretary of the Treasury's decision to deny a customs broker's license or permit.

It was pursuant to the request of the customshouse brokerage community that the court was given jurisdiction over challenges by a person affected by a decision of the Secretary of the Treasury to deny, revoke, or suspend a customshouse broker's license. In a 1984 amendment to the Tariff Act of 1930, Congress enacted new license and permit provisions for customs brokers and also authorized the Secretary of the Treasury to impose monetary penalties as an

15. U.S. Steel Corp. v. United States, 730 F.2d 1465 (Fed. Cir. 1984).

alternative to suspension or revocation of licenses. Civil actions to review any decision of the Secretary of the Treasury to impose a monetary penalty must be commenced within sixty days after the entry of the Secretary's decision or order.

Subsection (h) provides the court with the authority to review, prior to importation of the goods involved, a ruling or the refusal to issue a ruling or the changing of a ruling by the Secretary of the Treasury regarding such issues as classification or valuation or rate of duty of those goods.

If the person who obtains a binding ruling issued by the Customs Service before the importation of the goods involved can show that he or she would be irreparably harmed unless given judicial review of the ruling prior to importation, he or she may commence a civil action in the Court of International Trade without exhausting administrative remedies. The individual need not import the goods, await liquidation, file a protest, and await its denial, then commence a civil action under 28 U.S.C. § 1581(a). However, irreparable harm may be difficult to prove to the satisfaction of the court.

In addition to the specific grant of jurisdiction, the court has residual jurisdiction.

Subsection (i) is a residual grant of jurisdictional authority. This provision expands the jurisdiction of the court and is the safety net which confers subject matter jurisdiction upon the court. It is intended to provide review for those types of cases not specifically listed in (a) through (h) but which arise from import transactions and Customs administration generally.

A more detailed discussion of this residual jurisdiction is included later in this chapter.

Persons Permitted to Bring Action

Persons entitled to commence a civil action in the United States Court of International Trade are set forth in 28

U.S.C., beginning with section 2631, and in the court's rules.

An action may be filed by the person who filed the protest, or by the surety on the transaction that is the subject of protest if demand has been made on the surety. It has been noted above that a protest filed under 19 U.S.C. § 1514 is void if it is received at the port involved more than ninety days after the date of liquidation of the subject entry by the Customs Service or ninety days after the date of any other Customs Service action or decision complained of. Similarly, a summons contesting the denial of one or more protests covering the same issue must be mailed to the clerk of the court by registered or certified mail or filed in person within 180 days of the date of the denial of all such protests. The typical classification case is commenced with the filing of the summons only.[16]

The court has no power to hear an action unless these two time limitations within which to bring suit against the government are strictly observed, and neither the parties nor the court may waive this jurisdictional requirement.

It should be emphasized that the same 180-day period for filing a summons also applies to protests denied by operation of law under 19 U.S.C. § 1515(b) because they were not allowed or denied in whole or in part within thirty days following the mailing of a request for accelerated disposition. No notice of such a denial is sent, so it is clearly the responsibility of the person requesting accelerated disposition to track the statutory period for filing a summons with the court, a period that begins to run on the date when the request was mailed.

In *Rivera Siaca v. United States*,[17] it was held that the Court of International Trade lacked jurisdiction over an im-

16. U.S. Ct. Int'l Trade R. 83. A general form of summons is given in appendix 24.
17. Rivera Siaca v. United States, 7 Ct. Int'l Trade 10 (1984).

porter's action for return of merchandise allegedly seized without authorization by the Customs Service. The court determined that if the action arose out of the Service's attempt to collect duties, dismissal would be required on jurisdictional grounds since the importer had failed to protest the Service's actions pursuant to 28 U.S.C. § 1581(a). At the same time, the court observed that if the action was considered primarily a tort claim based on the injurious actions of the Customs agents in attempting to collect duties, the federal district court would also lack jurisdiction to hear the same complaint asserted under the Federal Tort Claims Act, since the Act expressly excludes jurisdiction of such claims.

A necessary step to give the court jurisdiction over this type of action is the payment by a plaintiff of all liquidated duties, charges, or exactions before the action is commenced.

As the drafters of the Customs Courts Act noted, the Customs Service is often forced to decide the disposition of an entry with haste or on the basis of incomplete information. Therefore, the decision of the court on an action brought to contest the denial of a protest is based on the record made before the court in a trial de novo.[18] Either party may introduce new evidence and new grounds upon which to defeat or support the Customs Service's original decision. The plaintiff may introduce a claim different from that made in the protest, as long as it is related to the administrative decision originally protested. For example, a different classification may be claimed if the protest was against the Service's classification, but the issue of appraisement may not be raised for the first time in court (except by the government as a counterclaim, as will be discussed below).

The plaintiff importer has a dual burden of proof because

18. 28 U.S.C.A. § 2640(a)(1) (West Supp. 1983).

the law presumes that the decision of the Customs Service or of the Secretary of the Treasury was correct. The plaintiff must, therefore, go forward to prove that the original decision was incorrect, and further, to prove the correctness of the claimed classification or appraisement. In earlier cases, even if the government had been proven wrong, the Customs Service would prevail on the basis of the presumption of correctness when the importer could not make an adequate case for its own claim. However, the Customs Courts Act, 28 U.S.C. § 2643, set forth various forms of relief that may be ordered by the Court of International Trade. Under this provision, the court of appeals held in *Jarvis Clark Co. v. United States*[19] that Congress intended that the court order a retrial or remand in order to reach a correct decision.

In that action, the importer sued the Customs Service, challenging the classification of certain imported hopper cars used to haul ore and waste from mines. The Court of International Trade dismissed for the importer's failure to prove an alternative to the Service's classification. The Court of Appeals for the Federal Circuit held that the trial court must consider the correctness of the government's classification. If that classification is found to be incorrect, the court must determine a more nearly correct classification by (1) adopting the plaintiff's classification as correct or (2) remanding the case to the Customs Service for further proceedings to determine the correct classification or order a retrial or rehearing for all purposes. This significant decision was resolved by the Federal Circuit on a motion to reargue. It was noted that when an issue comes before the court, the government may also introduce a claim different from that which the plaintiff originally protested. However, the substituted claim is not protected by a presumption of

---

19. Jarvis Clark Co. v. United States, 733 F.2d 873 (Fed. Cir. 1984), *rev'g* 566 F. Supp. 344 (Ct. Int'l Trade 1983), *reh'g denied*, 739 F.2d 628 (Fed. Cir. 1984), *on remand*, 8 Ct. Int'l Trade 280 (1984).

correctness. As explained in *Jarvis Clark Co.*, it was the intent of Congress in enacting 28 U.S.C. § 2643(b) to change the operation of the dual burden by requiring the court to reach a correct result. The court held that a correct result could not be reached by dismissing the importer's claim as incorrect, but the court must consider whether the government's classification was correct both independently and in comparison with the importer's alternative. In this case, the court ruled that plaintiff had shown its claimed classification was a better classification for the merchandise, and had thereby met its burden of proving the government's classification incorrect, even though it may not have established the correct claim. In such a circumstance, the trial court must find the correct answer by all appropriate means. Thus, in its discretion, the court could remand the case to Customs or decide the case itself.

Actions commenced under the Customs Courts Act[20] are started by filing a summons, which is served by the clerk of the court upon the Secretary of the Treasury and the Department of Justice; the plaintiff need not serve those parties. No complaint need be filed with the summons, which is placed for one year in the reserve calendar of the court, so that subsequent actions begun by that plaintiff on the same type of merchandise and the same issue may be acted upon by the court at the same time, in the interest of judicial economy.[21]

This mechanism also makes it possible for an importer to preserve a claim for a year without committing the matter to active litigation before it is clear that the case merits the expense of going through a trial.

In order to avoid repetitious litigation over the multiplic-

20. 28 U.S.C.A. § 1581(a) (West Supp. 1988). The form of summons is given in appendix 25. The summons under section 1581(b) is in appendix 26.
21. *See* U.S. Ct. Int'l Trade R. 83.

ity of protests covering importations of the same type of merchandise raising the same issues of valuation or classification and of concern to more than one importer, the Customs Court relied heavily on the test-case method of adjudication. That method is still used by the Court of International Trade. A plaintiff may select a summons covering a representative entry or entries, file a complaint, and, after the issue is joined by the filing of the government's answer (within sixty days), move to have that civil action designated as a test case. Any plaintiff filing a summons involving the same legal issue, whether a complaint has been filed or not, may move to have that case suspended pending the test case. Only the test case need be tried or become the subject of a motion for summary judgment. After the court's decision on the test case is final, all suspended cases must be acted on, but they need rarely be brought to trial. If the test case is won by the importer, the cases suspended under it are usually stipulated for judgment by the parties on the basis of that decision. If the plaintiff has lost, the suspended cases are usually dismissed.

Recently the Court of International Trade addressed a situation in which a suspended case will not be dismissed after the plaintiff has lost in the test case. In *Eastalco Aluminum Co. v. United States*,[22] the court held that a plaintiff cannot abandon suspended cases when the government asserts a counterclaim challenging the plaintiff's argued classification provision and demonstrates, to the satisfaction of the court deciding the test case, that another classification provision—one requiring a higher rate of duty than the provision pursuant to which Customs actually liquidated the subject merchandise—is correct.

---

22. Eastalco Aluminum Co. v. United States, 750 F. Supp. 1135 (Ct. Int'l Trade 1990), *aff'd on rehearing*, 757 F. Supp. 1422 (Ct. Int'l Trade 1991).

The plaintiff in *Eastalco* filed several complaints and summonses against the Custom Service's denial of its protests in regard to the proper classification of certain "carbon blocks." The government answered two complaints, denying the plaintiff's demands for refunds.

The plaintiff then moved, with the government's consent, to consolidate the two cases, to have the consolidated case designated a test case, and to suspend ten other cases. The court granted the motion. The government filed an answer to the complaint filed in the consolidated case and moved, unopposed, to add a counterclaim, arguing that the subject merchandise should be classified under a provision requiring a higher rate of duty than that provided for under the provision pursuant to which the merchandise was originally liquidated.

The plaintiff replied to the counterclaim. However, the court eventually found in favor of the government's claim for classification under the provision requiring a higher duty rate. The plaintiff appealed this judgment and moved to dismiss its suspended cases. The court prohibited the plaintiff from removing the cases from suspense, and on rehearing the court affirmed its prior decision.

This decision is extremely significant. Traditionally, plaintiffs have had the opportunity to bring actions before the Court of International Trade claiming that Customs has improperly classified an import at a higher duty rate without fear that if the court should then determine that an even higher rate of duty should have been assessed in the first instance, the plaintiffs would be responsible to pay the additional duty on all the entries at issue in their suspended cases. If such a determination was made in a test case, the plaintiffs would simply move to withdraw all of their suspended cases.

The decision in *Eastalco* now warns plaintiffs that if the defendant files a counterclaim and argues that an even higher rate of duty applies to the merchandise in its test case, it may be too late to remove the plaintiff's suspended cases. The risk of litigating classification questions has become much more perilous.

The court did not expressly discuss whether a plaintiff may oppose a defendant's filing of a counterclaim and simultaneously move to withdraw its suspended cases. However, the author believes that the court should allow the plaintiff to do so. It is arguable that only at this point is the plaintiff put on notice of defendant's intention to seek additional duties and therefore able to take stock of its position and reassess its claim. Plaintiff could then determine that the risk in proceeding with its suspended cases was too great and move to abandon those cases.[23]

The test-case procedure underscores the point that the Customs Court dealt, and to a large extent the Court of International Trade deals, with merchandise rather than persons, although cases brought to the court are not in rem actions.[24] The court deals with import transactions—entries of specific goods. When the court exercises its jurisdiction over denied protests, the questions it addresses most frequently are whether the entered merchandise was appraised and whether it was classified according to law.

The Customs Courts Act provides, for the first time, that a plaintiff successful in obtaining monetary relief in an action under 19 U.S.C. § 1515 is allowed interest from the date of the filing of the summons to the date of the refund.[25] Interest is calculated at the annual rate established under section 6621 of the Internal Revenue Code. Prejudgment interest is permitted, under certain circumstances,

23. At the time of writing, this case is under appeal and has been strongly objected to by the bar.
24. In rem: A technical term used to designate proceedings or actions instituted against things as compared to personal actions which are said to be in personam.
25. 28 U.S.C.A. § 2644 (West Supp. 1987). United States v. Monza Automobili, 12 C.I.T. 239 (1988).

payable to the government from the date of final demand for payment.[26]

Two controversial decisions concerning interest were recently rendered by the Court of International Trade. In *Kalan, Inc. v. United States*[27] and *Hospital Corp. of America v. United States*,[28] the court held that when an importer pays estimated duties at the time of the entry and it is subsequently determined that the payment was in excess of the actual amount due, *the importer is entitled to a refund of the excess duty paid with interest from the date of liquidation of the entry to the date of payment of the refund.* (The plaintiff in *Kalan* had further argued that interest should be paid from the date of the original payment of the estimated duties.) Before these decisions, interest on excess estimated duties had been paid only when the importer had successfully challenged the Customs Service's duty assessment in the Court of International Trade, and the interest was paid from the date the summons was filed to the date the refund was paid. Appeals have been filed in both *Kalan* and *Hospital Corp. of America.*

Residual Jurisdiction

As stated previously, in addition to the specific subject matter jurisdiction granted to the Court of International Trade by the sections of the law discussed above, the Customs Courts Act of 1980 included the following broad provision for residual jurisdiction:

> (i) In addition to the jurisdiction conferred upon the Court of International Trade by subsections (a)–(h) of this section and subject to the exception set forth in subsection (j) of this

26. United States v. Federal Ins. Co., 857 F.2d 1457 (Fed. Cir. 1988).
27. Kalan, Inc. v. United States, 752 F. Supp. 455 (Ct. Int'l Trade 1990).
28. Hospital Corp. of Am. v. United States, 752 F. Supp. 459 (Ct. Int'l Trade 1990).

> section, the Court of International Trade shall have exclusive jurisdiction of any civil action commenced against the United States, its agencies, or its officers, that arises out of any law of the United States providing for—
>
> (1) revenue from imports or tonnage;
>
> (2) tariffs, duties, fees, or other taxes on the importation of merchandise for reasons other than the raising of revenue;
>
> (3) embargoes or other quantitative restrictions on the importation of merchandise for reasons other than the protection of the public health or safety; or
>
> (4) administration and enforcement with respect to the matters referred to in paragraphs (1)–(3) of this subsection and subsections (a)–(h) of this section.[29]

The grant of residual jurisdiction in this section minimizes earlier confusion by ensuring that if a cause of action arises out of any law dealing with imports, it can ordinarily be heard in the Court of International Trade, rather than in a federal district court.

In one of its first decisions on a case invoking jurisdiction under this section, *Di Jub Leasing Corp. v. United States*,[30] the Court of International Trade found that the legislative history of the Customs Courts Act showed congressional intent that this residual provision be given broad application in order "to assure comprehensive review in this Court of a broad spectrum of administrative actions arising out of our international trade laws. . . ."[31]

The action in *Di Jub* was brought to contest the Customs Service's revocation of a customshouse cartman's license issued for use in the New York customs collection district. The court recognized a direct connection with the revenue laws, because a condition of holding the license was that

29. 28 U.S.C.A. § 1581(i) (West Supp. 1988).

30. Di Jub Leasing Corp. v. United States, 505 F. Supp. 1113 (Ct. Int'l Trade 1980).

31. *Id.* at 1117.

the cartman post a bond to guarantee payment of the duty still owing on any goods that he transported "in bond." The court pointed out that earlier wording proposed for this section of the Customs Courts Act, "arises directly from an import transaction," had been deleted in favor of the broader grant of jurisdiction over civil actions that "arise out of a law of the United States pertaining to international trade."[32]

Similarly, the court has accepted jurisdiction under 28 U.S.C. § 1581(i) in numerous other cases, including *American Air Parcel Forwarding Co. v. United States*,[33] an action brought by a customs broker who sought a preliminary injunction in the Court of International Trade against the action of the Customs Service suspending its immediate delivery privileges. As a customs broker, the plaintiff consolidated freight owned by various shippers for delivery to specific consignees in the United States. The plaintiff posted a single entry bond to indemnify Customs for any lost revenue. It paid estimated duties on the entered merchandise within ten days after entry. It did not receive those monies until twenty-nine days later. Plaintiff recouped the monies by shipping the goods C.O.D. to the consignees. It entered the merchandise each week and paid duty on the merchandise by uncertified check. Plaintiff received shipments on March 27 and 30, 1981, on which duties were due April 10 and 13 respectively. Seven days prior to April 10, 1981, the Customs Control officer stated that beginning April 10, plaintiff would have to pay the duty on that entry and all future entries by certified check. Customs said that the reason for the action was that certain uncertified checks issued had been dishonored. Customs

32. *See* H.R. REP. NO. 1235, 96th Cong., 2d Sess. 33–34, *reprinted in* 1980 U.S. CODE CONG. & ADMIN. NEWS 3729, 3744–45.
33. American Air Parcel Forwarding Co. v. United States, 515 F. Supp. 47 (Ct. Int'l Trade 1981).

said that it had erred in accepting uncertified checks and from now on would require certified checks.

Plaintiff asked Customs about the regulation which authorizes an importer to use uncertified checks, when the revenue is protected by a bond for duties owing on a shipment. Customs said its decision was final but plaintiff could challenge the decision by filing an entry with an uncertified check, having it rejected, and filing a protest. Plaintiff filed the entries and paid duties with uncertified checks. The entries were rejected. Customs also sent a letter of rejection and suspended plaintiff's immediate delivery privileges. The customs broker claimed that the Customs Service, by denying its immediate delivery privileges and refusing to accept documentation with uncertified checks, caused its business irreparable harm. The court stated that the case raised a basic question of equity jurisdiction before the court and temporarily restrained Customs from suspending the plaintiff's immediate delivery privileges. The court's relief was based upon its power, by virtue of the provisions of the Customs Courts Act of 1980, to oversee the Customs Service's administration and enforcement of its regulations. This includes regulations that authorize Customs to receive uncertified checks in payment of duties upon filing an entry bond. The court also noted that in deciding this case, it must make a determination that plaintiff's complaint has legal substance for relief which should be granted.

The court found the four essential elements to authorize it to grant equitable relief:

1. Threat of immediate irreparable harm;
2. Public interest would be better served by issuing rather than denying the injunction;
3. Likelihood of success on the merits; and
4. The balance of hardship on the parties favored the plaintiff.

The court stated that the remedy of issuing a temporary restraining order against Customs should be granted only upon a clear showing of irreparable harm. The court found that in this situation the Customs Service's action of revoking the plaintiff's immediate delivery permit would cause it irreparable harm. The permit authorizes immediate release of merchandise without the necessity of depositing estimated duty for ten days. By revoking the permit, the plaintiff would be required to make payment by certified check for the release of the merchandise at the time of entry. This was an example of irreparable harm caused by Customs to the customs broker's business operation that should not be permitted. Thus, the temporary restraining order was granted.

In *American Association of Exporters & Importers v. United States*,[34] the court agreed that it had jurisdiction under 28 U.S.C. § 1581(i). The suit was brought to review the lawfulness of quota limits imposed on textile imports from China. The importers association challenged the setting of a lower import quota limit than that previously set by agreement between the United States and China after the agreement had expired. The government objected, claiming that the Court of International Trade lacked jurisdiction to hear this action since the plaintiff failed to exhaust administrative remedies pursuant to 28 U.S.C. § 1581(a). Thus, the issue presented was whether a party challenging an import restriction must actually attempt to import the textile product, have Customs deny the entry, protest the denial, and then bring an action in the trade court under the provisions of 28 U.S.C. § 1581(a). The court held that, notwithstanding the plaintiff's decision not to pursue the administrative remedies provided for under 28 U.S.C.

34. American Ass'n Exporters & Importers v. United States, 583 F. Supp. 591 (Ct. Int'l Trade 1984), *aff'd*, 751 F.2d 1239 (Fed. Cir. 1985).

§ 1581(a), plaintiff could still challenge Customs Service regulations imposing import restrictions pursuant to 28 U.S.C. § 1581(i). Under the provisions of 28 U.S.C. § 1581(i), the Court of International Trade retains exclusive jurisdiction over any civil action that arises out of any law of the United States providing for quantitative restrictions (e.g., quotas). Therefore, the court held that in keeping with the intent of the Customs Courts Act of 1980, which expanded the jurisdiction of the Court of International Trade to include any actions concerning restrictions on imports by statute, treaty, or executive order, a party challenging such an import restriction is not limited by the procedural requirements set forth in 28 U.S.C. § 1581(a) (i.e., attempt to import, have Customs deny entry, protest the denial, etc.).[35]

On the other hand, Congress made it clear that § 1581(i) was not to be used in place of the method of judicial review of antidumping and countervailing duty actions provided in 28 U.S.C. § 1581(c) and 19 U.S.C. § 1516a. "[A]ny preliminary administrative . . . determination . . . would be reviewable, if at all, only in connection with the review of the final determination by the administering authority or the ITC."[36]

> [T]he broad subject matter jurisdiction of the court under § 1581(i) may be invoked only when no other remedy is available or the remedies provided under other provisions of 28 U.S.C. § 1581 are manifestly inadequate. . . .[37]

35. *See* American Air Parcel Forwarding Co. v. United States, 515 F. Supp. 47 (Ct. Int'l Trade 1981). The court held that it had authority to hear and decide civil actions arising out of the enforcement of regulations involved in the payment of duties, filing an entry bond, and other matters arising out of import transactions.

36. H.R. REP. NO. 1235, 96th Cong., 2d Sess. 48, *reprinted in* 1980 U.S. CODE CONG. & ADMIN. NEWS 3729, 3759–60.

37. United States v. Uniroyal, Inc., 69 C.C.P.A. 179, 687 F.2d 467, 475 (1982) (Nies, J., concurring).

An action under 28 U.S.C. § 1581(i) must be commenced according to the rules of the court within two years after the cause of action first accrues, or it is time barred.[38]

An example of the court's rejecting residual jurisdiction under 28 U.S.C. § 1581(i) is noted in *United States v. Uniroyal*.[39] Uniroyal, an importer of leather uppers and rubber soles for shoes, received six redelivery notices from Customs for failure to mark its merchandise. After the third notice, Uniroyal filed a request with Customs for internal advice. Uniroyal claimed that it was the ultimate purchaser of the shoe parts and that the merchandise was therefore exempt from marking requirements pursuant to 19 U.S.C. § 1304.[40] After Customs ruled against Uniroyal, some sixteen months after the request for internal advice, it instituted an action under 28 U.S.C. § 1581(i).

Customs urged the court to reject the suit under section 1581(i), arguing that Uniroyal could have protested the redelivery notices and filed suit under section 1581(a).

The court ruled that 28 U.S.C. § 1581(i) is expressly in addition to the jurisdiction conferred by subsections (a)–(h) of section 1581 and the clear legislative history that indi-

---

38. 28 U.S.C.A. § 2636(h) (West Supp. 1988).

39. United States v. Uniroyal, 69 C.C.P.A. 179, 687 F.2d 467 (1982).

40. The relevant portions of section 1304 read as follows:

> a. Except as hereinafter provided, every article of foreign origin (or its container, as provided in subsection (b) hereof) imported into the United States shall be marked in a conspicuous place as legibly, indelibly, and permanently as the nature of the article (or container) will permit in such manner as to indicate to an ultimate purchaser in the United States the English name of the country of origin of the article. The Secretary of the Treasury may by regulations —
>
> . . . .
>
> (3) Authorize the exception of any article from the requirements of marking if —
>
> . . . .
>
> (H) An ultimate purchaser, by reason of the character of such article or by reason of the circumstances of its importation, must necessarily know the country of origin of such article even though it is not marked to indicate its origin. . . .

cates a congressional intent not to bypass the administrative review by a protest. In this case Uniroyal's seeking review of anticipated assessments arising from six completed entries had to be addressed by protest when and if such assessments were made. In addition, the court rejected Uniroyal's challenge concerning future importations as there was no showing of irreparable harm, which is required before the court can address an objection to a ruling prior to the entry of goods and the filing and denial of a protest.

Uniroyal admitted that it could address the marking issue by protest but argued that jurisdiction was proper under section 1581(i) because, rather than reviewing a protest against a redelivery notice of the merchandise, the Court of International Trade could exercise its jurisdiction to grant declaratory relief from further assessments on future entries and promptly resolve the controversy.

The appellate court in *American Association of Exporters & Importers (AAEI)* distinguished the holding in *Uniroyal.* The court noted that it was presented with a situation where the unilateral actions of the Committee for the Implementation of Textile Agreements in imposing quotas lower than those established by a prior agreement between China and the United States caused AAEI irreparable harm and where relief under section 1581(a) would be inadequate to redress such harm. In contrast, in *Uniroyal,* "the importer had already entered the goods in this country, and the goods were subject to redelivery (a situation quite different from the plight of a prospective importer who faces quantitative import restrictions)."[41]

In a related decision involving jurisdiction under section 1581(h), the court dismissed the plaintiff's action requesting judicial review of a general administrative ruling published by Customs setting forth guidelines to Customs officials to

41. American Ass'n of Exporters & Importers, 751 F.2d at 1246.

assist them in classifying specific footwear constructed with foxing (an addition to the outer edge or sole of a shoe). The court in *Pagoda Trading v. United States*[42] held that the administrative decision complained of by the plaintiff did not rule specifically on the merchandise the plaintiff intended to import. Thus, the mere expectation that the guidelines would be applied in a particular case was determined not to create a ripe controversy. Therefore, the court held that there could be no judicial review, since there was no "identifiable merchandise which would feel the impact of the ruling with vital certainty." Section 1581(h), the court noted, was not created to allow judicial review of general interpretative rulings; rather, it was intended to allow judicial review of rulings that determine the fate of specific importations of specific goods.

With the residual grant of jurisdiction of 28 U.S.C. § 1581(i), the statute made possible the infusion into the law concerning international trade of the entire body of administrative law governing the powers and procedures of agencies that has developed under the Administrative Procedure Act,[43] particularly in regard to judicial review of agency action. For example, the Customs Courts Act gives standing to bring an action against the government under the residual provision to "any person adversely affected or aggrieved by agency action within the meaning of section 702 of title 5."[44] Title 5, section 702, waives sovereign immunity so that such suits may be brought against the government, and reads, in part:

> A person suffering legal wrong because of agency action, or adversely affected or aggrieved by agency action within

42. Pagoda Trading v. United States, 6 Ct. Int'l Trade 296, 577 F Supp. 22 (1983).
43. Pub. L. No. 89-554, 80 Stat. 378 (1966) (codified at 55 U.S.C. §§ 553 *et seq.* & 701 *et seq.*).
44. 28 U.S.C.A. § 2631(i) (West Supp. 1988).

> the meaning of a relevant statute, is entitled to judicial review thereof. An action in a court of the United States seeking relief other than money damages and stating a claim that an agency or an officer or employee thereof acted or failed to act in an official capacity or under color of legal authority shall not be dismissed nor relief therein be denied on the ground that it is against the United States or that the United States is an indispensable party. The United States may be named as defendant in any such action, and a judgment or decree may be entered against the United States. . . .[45]

In actions commenced under several other sections of 28 U.S.C. § 1581, the court is empowered to make its decisions de novo, upon the basis of the record made before the court. However, in actions commenced under section 1581(i), the court "shall review the matter as provided in section 706 of title 5."[46] Section 706 provides that the reviewing court shall make its determination only on the basis of the agency record. If the agency record is inadequate, the Court of International Trade has the power to order any further administrative procedures that it "considers necessary to enable it to reach the correct decision."[47] The scope of such review of agency action is described in section 706:

> To the extent necessary to decision and when presented, the reviewing court shall decide all relevant questions of law, interpret constitutional and statutory provisions, and determine the meaning or applicability of the terms of an agency action. The reviewing court shall—
>
> (1) compel agency action unlawfully withheld or unreasonably delayed; and
>
> (2) hold unlawful and set aside agency action, findings, and conclusions found to be—
>
> (A) arbitrary, capricious, an abuse of discretion, or otherwise not in accordance with law;

45. 5 U.S.C.A. § 702 (West 1977).

46. 28 U.S.C.A. § 2640(d) (West Supp. 1988).

47. 28 U.S.C.A. § 2643(b) (West Supp. 1988).

(B) contrary to constitutional right, power, privilege, or immunity;
(C) in excess of statutory jurisdiction, authority, or limitations, or short of statutory right;
(D) without observance of procedure required by law;
(E) unsupported by substantial evidence in a case subject to sections 556 and 557 of this title or otherwise reviewed on the record of an agency hearing provided by statute; or
(F) unwarranted by the facts to the extent that the facts are subject to trial de novo by the reviewing court.

In making the foregoing determinations, the court shall review the whole record or those parts of it cited by a party, and due account shall be taken of the rule of prejudicial error.[48]

Civil Actions Commenced by the United States

Section 1582 of the Customs Courts Act granted the Court of International Trade new and exclusive jurisdiction over civil actions arising out of a dispute or violation involving an import transaction commenced by the United States to

1. Recover a civil fine or penalty or enforce a forfeiture imposed under section 592[49] or section 704(i)(2) or section 734(i)(2) of the Tariff Act of 1930;
2. Recover on a bond relating to the importation of merchandise; or
3. Recover Customs duties.[50] Jurisdiction over this type of civil action formerly lay in the federal district courts. However, jurisdiction was transferred because issues concerning classification, valuation, marking, etc. involve the expertise of the Court of International Trade.

48. 5 U.S.C.A. § 706 (West 1977).
49. 19 U.S.C.A. § 1592 (West 1980).
50. 28 U.S.C.A. § 1582 (West Supp. 1988).

In an early decision, the Court of International Trade decided that, under 28 U.S.C. § 1582, it had exclusive jurisdiction of a civil action initiated by the United States to recover civil penalties under section 592. In *United States v. Accurate Mould Co.*,[51] the court held that it was not limited to in rem jurisdiction in a penalty action under section 592 arising before the effective date of the Customs Courts Act, but that it has personal jurisdiction whether the action was brought under the present provision or prior law.[52] In *United States v. One Red Lamborghini and One Black Lamborghini*,[53] the United States brought an in rem action in the U.S. Court of International Trade against two Lamborghini Jalpa automobiles under section 592(c)(5) of the Tariff Act of 1930, as amended, seeking forfeiture of the two vehicles seized by the Customs Service as improperly entered. Plaintiff requested a warrant for the arrest[54] of the vehicles under 28 U.S.C. § 2461(b). The court refused to issue the arrest warrant and requested Customs to present a memorandum stating the legal basis for its action. The court held that section 592 does not provide for a cause of action for forfeiture in rem. The Customs Procedure Reform and Simplification Act of 1978[55] changed section 592 from an in rem penalty, forfeiture of the merchandise, to an in personam penalty, a monetary liability for the import.

The Court of International Trade does not have jurisdic-

51. United States v. Accurate Mould Co., 546 F. Supp. 567 (Ct. Int'l Trade 1982).
52. See discussion in chapter 22.
53. United States v. One Red Lamborghini & One Black Lamborghini, 625 F. Supp. 986 (Ct. Int'l Trade 1986).
54. Warrant of arrest is a written order of a court which is based upon a complaint issued under statute or court rule and commands the enforcement officer to arrest the property and hold it subject to the court order. *See* U.S. Supplemental Rules for Certain Admiralty and Maritime Claim Rule E Actions in Rem and Quasi in Rem.
55. Pub. L. No. 95-410, § 110, 92 Stat. 888 (1978).

tion under 19 U.S.C. § 1592 or 28 U.S.C. § 1581 to hear a contest to the seizure and summary forfeiture of articles by Customs or an action for return of monies paid in mitigation of a penalty under 19 U.S.C. § 1592. In *McCarthy v. Heinrich*,[56] it was held that the claim of lack of notice by a party-in-interest (e.g., a holder of a mortgage) of certain vehicles seized by Customs pursuant to 19 U.S.C. § 1592 and 18 U.S.C. § 545, which were summarily forfeited, is not a claim within the jurisdiction of the Court of International Trade. The court ruled that 19 U.S.C. § 1592 is not a jurisdictional provision; rather, it sets the procedure to be followed in an action instituted by the United States to recover a monetary penalty claimed pursuant to 28 U.S.C. § 1582.[57] Section 1582 is the jurisdictional provision granting the court authority to adjudicate an action claimed under 19 U.S.C. § 1592.[58] However, it only becomes operative after the United States commences the action. Since the United States did not commence the action, the court in this instance lacked jurisdiction. The court further stated

56. McCarthy v. Heinrich, 674 F. Supp. 863 (Ct. Int'l Trade 1987).
57. United States v. Priority Prods., Inc., 9 Ct. Int'l Trade 392, 615 F. Supp. 593 (1985).
58. 19 U.S.C. § 1592(e) states:

> Court of International Trade proceedings.
> Notwithstanding any other provision of law, in any proceeding commenced by the United States in the Court of International Trade for the recovery of any monetary penalty claimed under this section —
> (1) all issues, including the amount of the penalty, shall be tried de novo;
> (2) if the monetary penalty is based on fraud, the United States shall have the burden of proof to establish the alleged violation by clear and convincing evidence;
> (3) if the monetary penalty is based on gross negligence, the United States shall have the burden of proof to establish all the elements of the alleged violation; and
> (4) if the monetary penalty is based on negligence, the United States shall have the burden of proof to establish the act or omission constituting the violation, and the alleged violator shall have the burden of proof that the act or omission did not occur as a result of negligence.

that jurisdiction may lie in the district court for such a cause of action.

In an unusual situation concerning a protest, the court permitted the surety to defend an action for liquidated damages[59] without filing a protest.[60] In that action Utex International Inc. imported 115 cartons of frozen shrimp into the United States for consumption. The goods were released February 1, 1980 to Utex on the posting of a single entry immediate delivery and consumption entry bond. The shrimp was conditionally released pending a decision by the Food and Drug Administration (FDA). After sampling, the FDA issued a notice of detention and hearing on February 6, 1980, stating that the merchandise had to be held pending a decision on admission. Customs received a copy of the notice, which stated that the articles violated certain provisions of the Food, Drug and Cosmetics Act, as they appeared to contain salmonella or other tainted material.

Despite this notice, the entry was liquidated on February 29, 1980 by Customs. The entry was not reliquidated. Thereafter Customs issued a notice of refusal of admission, which stated that the goods were in violation of the Food, Drug and Cosmetics Act and required Utex to export the shrimp under Customs supervision within ninety days. Utex did not comply. On December 9, 1980, Customs sent Utex, with a copy to Sentry Insurance Co., a notice of penalty or liquidated damages incurred and demand for payment. The sum was not paid.

In June of 1984, Customs unsuccessfully demanded payment of liquidated damages from Utex and Sentry, and on June 5, 1986, the government filed suit in the Court of International Trade. Sentry was held liable.

The question on appeal was whether the final liquidation

59. 28 U.S.C. § 1582.

60. United States v. Utex Int'l, Inc., 857 F.2d 1408 (Fed. Cir. 1988).

of the goods released the surety from liability on the entry bond.

It's a widely recognized and long-standing rule that when an entry of goods is finally liquidated, it is deemed admissible. Customs regulations require that the liquidation be suspended, when goods are food, drugs and other articles subject to FDA inspection.

Here Customs liquidation of the frozen shrimp was in violation of the regulations. The court noted that erroneous liquidation could be corrected only by following the statutory procedure, and failure to do so within the statutory period leaves the liquidation final.

Furthermore, the statutory procedures of liquidation, reliquidation and timely protests control the finality of the importing process. Here there was no voluntary reliquidation within ninety days, no protest filed during which the government might have raised the issue of finality, no reliquidation within one year to correct clerical error, mistake, or inadvertence or within two years on account of fraud. The liquidation was final. The court expressed "grave concern" that Customs as the enforcement arm erroneously liquidated the entry in violation of law and regulation; however, the surety did not insure against governmental error. The surety's liabilities arose under the terms of the bond and the customs law. The court stated that although it does not hold the liquidation was correct, without timely reliquidation or protest it was final as to all aspects of entry. The government also argued that under the surety contract the surety is liable independent of the finality of liquidation. The court noted that the regulation requires Customs to demand the return of inadmissable goods that have been released from customs custody be made before final liquidation has become final. The court found that the surety contract cannot be interpreted contrary to law and regulations.

A further attempt to hold the surety liable was rejected

by the court in stating that there is no obligation to file a protest under a notice of penalty or liquidated damages incurred and demand for payment. The court explained that prior to the Customs Courts Act of 1980, which transferred jurisdiction of actions on surety bonds from the district courts to the Court of International Trade, a protest and advance payment of liquidated damages were not required of a surety in district court in order to defend such suits. In absence of any statutory directive or congressional intent, the court declined to impose upon the surety any such requirement to preserve its right to defend on the issue of liability.

Jury Trial

The Customs Courts Act of 1980 included section 302, which amends title 28 of the U.S. Code by adding a new section 1876 providing for jury trials in the United States Court of International Trade. Section 1876 sets out the necessary mechanisms for the court to conduct a jury trial. It provides that the jury selection procedures used in the jury selection plan of the federal district courts may be used in the Court of International Trade. When the Court of International Trade holds a jury trial, the clerk (or authorized deputy clerk) of the district court in which the court is sitting shall act as the clerk of the Court of International Trade for the purposes of selecting and summoning the jury. The qualifications and compensation for jurors are the same as established for jurors of the district courts.

In short, the section provides for all of the mechanisms for conducting a jury trial, but it fails to specify which actions would guarantee the entitlement to a jury trial. Although judicial review has been limited, the court has discussed, in three cases, when a jury trial may be available.

Upon review of these cases it appears unlikely that the court will grant plaintiffs' requests for jury trial unless that right is clearly and unambiguously granted by federal statute.

In *United States v. Priority Products Inc.*,[61] the court conditionally granted an advisory jury trial in a case initiated by the United States to recover penalties arising from alleged fraud or negligence in the importation of bark tea. The court found that when the company's officers answered the government's complaint, pro se, and failed to demand a jury trial, it had waived any right to a jury. However, notwithstanding the failure to make the demand, the court in its discretion, pursuant to the Court of International Trade Rule 39(b), decided to allow an advisory jury trial if the issues presented appeared suitable for jury deliberation. The court further noted that "the subjective intent and knowledge of the defendants when importing the subject tea is the primary issue for trial . . . [and] are appropriate matters for jury decision-making."

However, the court of appeals in *Washington International Insurance Co. v. United States*[62] cast doubt on the future of jury trials in the Court of International Trade. The court held that 28 U.S.C. § 1876 did not specify which actions entitled the parties to a jury trial but merely set forth the procedures to be followed. It pointed out that sovereign immunity protects the government from suit, and that only when Congress waives that protection is a party bringing suit entitled to a jury trial. That is, a plaintiff has a right to a jury trial only when the government, in consenting to be sued, has specifically provided for a jury trial at the request of the plaintiff. The court also noted that a suit by the government seeking penalties under the Clean Air Act, where a jury trial was held proper, is not analogous to

61. United States v. Priority Prods. Inc., 9 Ct. Int'l Trade 392, 615 F. Supp. 593 (1985).

62. Washington Int'l Ins. Co. v. United States, 863 F.2d 877 (Fed. Cir. 1988), *cert. denied*, 109 S. Ct. 3157 (1989).

a jury demand in a suit by an individual *against* the government for recovery of duties. "[A]ctions against the government are not analogous to actions *by* the government."

In the case of *Halperin Shipping v. United States*,[63] the court, following the decision in *Washington International Insurance*, held that a right to a jury trial must be affirmatively and unambiguously granted by statute. It cast further doubt on the availability of jury trials in the Court of International Trade by noting that neither section 2631(a), relating to commencement of suit, nor section 1876, relating to trial by jury, provides such an affirmative or unambiguous right to a jury trial.

Following these decisions it appears unlikely that jury trials in the Court of International Trade will become a common occurrence. Unless Congress enacts statutes that clearly and unambiguously grant jury trials, such trials will apparently be left to the court's discretion.

Counterclaims, Cross-Claims, and Third-Party Actions

The Customs Courts Act of 1980 provides that the Court of International Trade has exclusive jurisdiction to render judgment in any civil action upon any counterclaim, cross-claim, or third-party action of any party, if the claim involves the imported merchandise that is the subject matter of the civil action, or the claim or action is to recover upon a bond or Custom duties relating to such merchandise.[64] Under this section the Court of International Trade held that it had jurisdiction and the equitable powers to attach real property in California prior to rendering of a judgment

---

63. Halperin Shipping v. United States, 725 F. Supp. 1259 (Ct. Int'l Trade 1989).

64. 28 U.S.C.A. § 1583 (West Supp. 1988). On the subject of counterclaims, see the discussion earlier in this chapter of Eastalco Aluminum Co. v. United States, 750 F. Supp. 1135 (Ct. Int'l Trade 1990).

in an action by the United States to recover liquidated damages for failure to conform automobiles to federal safety standards or redeliver them, and for breach of immediate delivery and consumption bonds. The defendant surety company cross-claimed for judgment against the importer and moved for a writ of attachment against a person who had signed an indemnity agreement. The court held that since the property was in California, California law governed the attachment. In permitting the attachment, the court found that all requirements of California law had been met and directed the clerk of court to issue an ex parte writ of attachment affecting the California property.[65]

The United States brought an action against an importer and its surety to collect liquidated damages under a bond pursuant to 28 U.S.C. § 1582(2).[66] The importer, Lun May, had agreed to export any merchandise covered by the bond found not to comply with the laws and regulations of the United States. The government claimed that six entries of foodstuffs covered by the bond were required to be exported or destroyed and that Lun May failed to show proof of exportation or destruction of the subject merchandise.

Lun May counterclaimed, alleging, in part, that the Customs Service and the Food and Drug Administration failed to follow proper procedures regarding merchandise covered by the Service's liquidated damages claims. However, Lun May sought to have included in its counterclaim references to liquidated damages claims made by Customs regarding entries not raised in the government's main action. Thus, the question presented to the court was whether Lun May's counterclaim could include claims beyond those raised by the government in the main action. The court held that,

---

65. United States v. Mizrahie, 9 Ct. Int'l Trade 149, 606 F. Supp. 703 (1985).
66. United States v. Lun May Co., 652 F. Supp. 721 (1987).

under the provisions of 28 U.S.C. § 1583, parties may raise counterclaims only concerning the imported merchandise that is the subject matter of the main action.

Defendants in a suit brought by the government may cross-claim against one another or bring in a third-party defendant. However, the kind of counterclaim that can be brought against the government by such defendants remains unclear. Nevertheless, it would seem that such claims would be limited to the specific entries involved in the government's action.

Power of the Court of International Trade to Grant Equitable and Other Relief

Prior to 1980 the remedial powers of the Customs Court were, in general, limited to agreeing or disagreeing with a final determination of an agency, the United States Customs Service. Under the Customs Courts Act, the Court of International Trade was vested with "all the powers in law and equity of, or as conferred by statute upon, a district court of the United States."[67] The various forms of relief available to a plaintiff are specified in 28 U.S.C. § 2643. The court may enter a money judgment for or against the United States or any other party brought into the action. If the court is unable to determine the correct decision on the basis of available evidence, it may order a retrial or remand a case for such further administrative action as it considers necessary.

More than any other provision, the grant of plenary equity powers marks the transition of the court to a full article III court. In addition to the power to issue the types of judgment specified above, the court may order "any other form of relief that is appropriate in a civil action, including, but not limited to, declaratory judgments, orders of remand,

67. 28 U.S.C.A. § 1585 (West Supp. 1988).

injunctions, and writs of mandamus and prohibition."[68] Equity powers give the court the ability to examine the facts of a case and balance the public interest as well as the claims and rights of all parties, then look to precedent to furnish appropriate relief. It may even ask about the status of the parties and inquire, "Do you come into court with clean hands?"

The court has been confronted repeatedly with requests for injunctive relief. It has made clear that it will follow the test developed over more than thirty years by the federal bench and weigh four critical factors: a threat of immediate irreparable injury, the consideration of the public interest, the probability of success on the merits, and the balance of hardships on the parties to determine whether to grant the relief desired.[69]

These wide remedial powers of the United States Court of International Trade, combined with the broad residual grant of subject matter jurisdiction, make it possible to bring before this national court a wide range of cases arising out of the customs and trade laws of the United States. With these tools, the court is now able to develop a substantial body of decisional law and judicial precedent in this area, of uniform application throughout the United States, in order to keep pace with the increasing complexity of import trade and its importance in the American economy.

---

68. 28 U.S.C.A. § 2643(c)(1) (West Supp. 1988).

69. See, e.g., 718 Fifth Ave. Corp. v. United States, 7 Ct. Int'l Trade 195 (1984); S.J. Styles Assocs. v. Snyder, 646 F.2d 522 (C.C.P.A. 1981); Associated Dry Goods Corp. v. United States, 515 F. Supp. 775 (Ct. Int'l Trade 1981); American Air Parcel Forwarding Co. v. United States, 515 F. Supp. 47 (Ct. Int'l Trade 1981); Di Jub Leasing Corp. v. United States, 505 F. Supp. 1113 (Ct. Int'l Trade 1980).

Appendixes

Appendix 1. Recommended Readings

Customs House Guide. Philadelphia: North American Publishing Co. (Annual).

Feller, Peter B. *U.S. Customs and International Trade Guide*. New York: Matthew Bender (1979 & Supps.).

International Trade Alert. New York: American Association of Exporters and Importers (Weekly).

Price, Carl E. and Mollie Keller. *The U.S. Customs Service: A Bicentennial History* (1989).

Rossides, Eugene T. *U.S. Customs, Tariffs and Trade*. Washington, D.C.: Bureau of National Affairs (1977).

Strum, Ruth F. *Customs Law and Administration*. 3d ed. New York & Dobbs Ferry: (1983 & Supps.).

U.S. Import Weekly, International Trade Reporter. Washington, D.C.: Bureau of National Affairs (Weekly).

Vakerics, Thomas V., David I. Wilson, and Kenneth G. Weigel. *Antidumping, Countervailing Duty, and Other Trade Actions*. New York: Practising Law Institute (1987 & 1989 Supp.).

Appendix 2. Report of International Transportation of Currency or Monetary Instruments (CF 4790)

Customs Use Only

Control No.

31 USC 5316; 31 CFR 103.23 and 103.25

Please Type or Print

DEPARTMENT OF THE TREASURY
UNITED STATES CUSTOMS SERVICE

REPORT OF INTERNATIONAL TRANSPORTATION OF CURRENCY OR MONETARY INSTRUMENTS

Form Approved
OMB No. 1515-0079

This form is to be filed with the United States Customs Service

Privacy Act Notification on reverse

PART I - FOR INDIVIDUAL DEPARTING FROM OR ENTERING THE UNITED STATES

1. NAME (*Last or family, first and middle*)
2. IDENTIFYING NO. (*See instructions*)
3. DATE OF BIRTH (*Mo./Day/Yr.*)
4. PERMANENT ADDRESS IN UNITED STATES OR ABROAD
5. OF WHAT COUNTRY ARE YOU A CITIZEN/SUBJECT?
6. ADDRESS WHILE IN THE UNITED STATES
7. PASSPORT NO. & COUNTRY
8. U.S. VISA DATE
9. PLACE UNITED STATES VISA WAS ISSUED
10. IMMIGRATION ALIEN NO. (*If any*)
11. CURRENCY OR MONETARY INSTRUMENT WAS: (*Complete 11A or 11B*)

A. EXPORTED		B. IMPORTED	
Departed From: (*City in U.S.*)	Arrived At: (*Foreign City/Country*)	From: (*Foreign City/Country*)	At: (*City in U.S.*)

PART II - FOR PERSON SHIPPING MAILING OR RECEIVING CURRENCY OR MONETARY INSTRUMENTS

12. NAME (*Last or family, first and middle*)
13. IDENTIFYING NO. (*See instructions*)
14. DATE OF BIRTH (*Mo./Da./Yr.*)
15. PERMANENT ADDRESS IN UNITED STATES OR ABROAD
16. OF WHAT COUNTRY ARE YOU A CITIZEN/SUBJECT?
17. ADDRESS WHILE IN THE UNITED STATES
18. PASSPORT NO. & COUNTR
19. U.S. VISA DATE
20. PLACE UNITED STATES VISA WAS ISSUED
21. IMMIGRATION ALIEN NO (*If any*)
22. CURRENCY OR MONETARY INSTRUMENTS
    DATE SHIPPED
    DATE RECEIVED
23. CURRENCY OR MONETARY INSTRUMENTS
    ☐ Shipped To
    ☐ Received From

NAME AND ADDRESS

24. IF THE CURRENCY OR MONETARY INSTRUMEN WAS MAILED, SHIPPED, OR TRANSPORTED CO PLETE BLOCKS A AND B.
    A. Method of Shipment (*Auto, U.S. Mail, Public Carrier, e*
    B. Name of Transporter/Carrier

PART III - CURRENCY AND MONETARY INSTRUMENT INFORMATION (SEE INSTRUCTIONS ON REVERSE) (To be completed by everyo

25. TYPE AND AMOUNT OF CURRENCY/MONETARY INSTRUMENTS		Value in U.S. Dollars
Coins	☐ A. ▸	$
Currency	☐ B. ▸	
Other Instruments (*Specify Type*)	☐ C. ▸	
(*Add Lines A, B and C*)	TOTAL AMOUNT ▸	$

26. IF OTHER THAN U.S. CU RENCY IS INVOLVED, PLEA COMPLETE BLOCKS A AND (*SEE SPECIAL INSTRUCTIO*
    A. Currency Name
    B. Country

PART IV - GENERAL - TO BE COMPLETED BY ALL TRAVELERS, SHIPPERS AND RECIPIENTS

27. WERE YOU ACTING AS AN AGENT, ATTORNEY OR IN CAPACITY FOR ANYONE IN THIS CURRENCY OR MONETARY INSTRUMENT ACTIVITY? (*If "Yes" complete A, B and C*) ☐ Yes ☐ No

PERSON IN WHOSE BE-HALF YOU ARE ACTING ▶	A. Name	B. Address	C. Business activity occupatio profession

Under penalties of perjury, I declare that I have examined this report, and to the best of my knowledge and belief it is true, correct and complet

28. NAME AND TITLE	29. SIGNATURE	30. DATE

(*Replaces IRS Form 4790 which is obsolete*)

Customs Form 4790 (120

GENERAL INSTRUCTIONS

This report is required by Treasury Department regulations (31 Code of Federal Regulations 103).

Who Must File. — Each person who physically transports, mails, or ships, or causes to be physically transported, mailed, shipped or received currency or other monetary instruments in an aggregate amount exceeding $10,000 on any one occasion from the United States to any place outside the United States, or into the United States from any place outside the United States.

A TRANSFER OF FUNDS THROUGH NORMAL BANKING PROCEDURES WHICH DOES NOT INVOLVE THE PHYSICAL TRANSPORTATION OF CURRENCY OR MONETARY INSTRUMENTS IS NOT REQUIRED TO BE REPORTED.

Exceptions. — The following persons are not required to file reports: (1) a Federal reserve bank, (2) a bank, a foreign bank, or a broker or dealer in securities in respect to currency or other monetary instruments mailed or shipped through the postal service or by common carrier, (3) a commercial bank or trust company organized under the laws of any State or of the United States with respect to overland shipments of currency or monetary instruments shipped to or received from an established customer maintaining a deposit relationship with the bank, in amounts which the bank may reasonably conclude do not exceed amounts commensurate with the customary conduct of the business, industry or profession of the customer concerned, (4) a person who is not a citizen or resident of the United States in respect to currency or other monetary instruments mailed or shipped from abroad to a bank or broker or dealer in securities through the postal service or by common carrier, (5) a common carrier of passengers in respect to currency or other monetary instruments in the possession of its passengers, (6) a common carrier of goods in respect to shipments of currency or monetary instruments not declared to be such by the shipper, (7) a travelers' check issuer or its agent in respect to the transportation of travelers' checks prior to their delivery to selling agents for eventual sale to the public, nor by (8) a person engaged as a business in the transportation of currency, monetary instruments and other commercial papers with respect to the transportation of currency or other monetary instruments overland between established offices of banks or brokers or dealers in securities and foreign persons.

WHEN AND WHERE TO FILE:

A. Recipients. — Each person who receives currency or other monetary instruments shall file Form 4790, within 30 days after receipt, with the Customs officer in charge at any port of entry or departure or by mail with the Commissioner of Customs, Attention: Currency Transportation Reports, Washington, D.C. 20229.

B. Shippers or Mailers. — If the currency or other monetary instrument does not accompany the person entering or departing the United States, Form 4790 may be filed by mail on or before the date of entry, departure, mailing, or shipping with the Commissioner of Customs, Attention: Currency Transportation Reports, Washington, D.C. 20229.

C. Travelers. — Travelers carrying currency or other monetary instruments with them shall file Form 4790 at the time of entry into the United States or the time of departure from the United States with the Customs officer in charge at any Customs port of entry or departure.

An additional report of a particular transportation, mailing, or shipping of currency or the monetary instruments, is not required if a complete and truthful report has already been filed. However, no person otherwise required to file a report shall be excused from liability for failure to do so if, in fact, a complete and truthful report has not been filed. Forms may be obtained from any United States Customs Service office.

PENALTIES. — **Civil and criminal penalties, including under certain circumstances a fine of not more than $500,000 and imprisonment of not more than five years, are provided for failure to file a report, supply information, and for filing a false or fraudulent report. In addition, the currency or monetary instrument may be subject to seizure and forfeiture. See sections 103.47, 103.48 and 103.49 of the regulations.**

DEFINITIONS:

Bank. — Each agent, agency, branch or office within the United States of a foreign bank and each agency, branch or office within the United States of any person doing business in one or more of the capacities listed: (1) a commercial bank or trust company organized under the laws of any state or of the United States; (2) a private bank; (3) a savings and loan association or a building and loan association organized under the laws of any state or of the United States; (4) an insured institution as defined in section 401 of the National Housing Act; (5) a savings bank, industrial bank or other thrift institution; (6) a credit union organized under the laws of any state or of the United States; and (7) any other organization chartered under the banking laws of any state and subject to the supervision of the bank supervisory authorities of a state.

Foreign Bank. — A bank organized under foreign law, or an agency, branch or office located outside the United States of a bank. The term does not include an agent, agency, branch or office within the United States of a bank organized under foreign law.

Broker or Dealer in Securities. — A broker or dealer in securities, registered or required to be registered with the Securities and Exchange Commission under the Securities Exchange Act of 1934.

INDENTIFYING NUMBER. — **Individuals must enter their social security number, if any. However, aliens who do not have a social security number should enter passport or alien registration number. All others should enter their employer identification number.**

Investment Security. — An instrument which : (1) is issued in bearer or registered form; (2) is of a type commonly dealt in upon securities exchanges or markets or commonly recognized in any area in which it is issued or dealt in as a medium for investment; (3) is either one of a class or series or by its terms is divisible into a class or series of instruments; and (4) evidences a share, participation or other interest in property or in an enterprise or evidences an obligation of the issuer.

Monetary Instruments. — Coin or currency of the United States or of any other country, travelers' checks, money orders, investment securities in bearer form or otherwise in such form that title thereto passes upon delivery, and negotiable instruments (except warehouse receipts or bills of lading) in bearer form or other in such form that title thereto passes upon delivery. The term includes bank checks, travelers' checks and money orders which are signed but on which the name of the payee has been omitted, but does not include bank checks, travelers' checks or money orders made payable to the order of a named person which have not been endorsed or which bear restrictive endorsements.

Person. — An individual, a corporation, a partnership, a trust or estate, a joint stock company, an association, a syndicate, joint venture, or other unincorporated organization or group, and all entities cognizable as legal personalities.

SPECIAL INSTRUCTIONS:

You should complete each line which applies to you. **Part II.** — Line 22, Enter the exact date you shipped or received currency or the monetary instrument(s). Line 23, Check the applicable box and give the complete name and address of the shipper or recipient. **Part III.** — Line 26, If currency or monetary instruments of more than one country is involved, attach a schedule showing each kind, country, and amount.

PRIVACY ACT AND PAPERWORK REDUCTION ACT NOTICE

Pursuant to the requirements of Public Law 93-579, (Privacy Act of 1974), notice is hereby given that the authority to collect information on Form 4790 in accordance with 5 U.S.C. 552a(e)(3) is Public Law 91-508; 31 U.S.C. 5316; 5 U.S.C. 301; Reorganization Plan No. 1 of 1950; Treasury Department No. 165, revised, as amended; 31 CFR 103; and 44 U.S.C. 3501.

The principal purpose for collecting the information is to assure maintenance of reports or records where such reports or records have a high degree of usefulness in criminal, tax, or regulatory investigations or proceedings. The information collected may be provided to those officers and employees of the Customs Service and any other constituent unit of the Department of the Treasury who have a need for the records in the performance of their duties. The records may be referred to any other department or agency of the Federal Government upon the request of the head of such department or agency.

Disclosure of this information is mandatory. Failure to provide all or any part of the requested information may subject the currency or monetary instruments to seizure and forfeiture, as well as subject the individual to civil and criminal liabilities.

Disclosure of the social security number is mandatory. The authority to collect this number is 31 CFR 103.25. The social security number will be used as a means to identify the individual who files the record.

The collection of this information is mandatory pursuant to 31 U.S.C. 5316.

Customs Form 4790 (120384) (Back)

☆ U.S. GOVERNMENT PRINTING OFFICE. 1985—611-969/20068

Appendix 3. Customs Declaration (CF 6059B)

WELCOME
TO THE
UNITED STATES

DEPARTMENT OF THE TREASURY
UNITED STATES CUSTOMS SERVICE

CUSTOMS DECLARATION

FORM APPROVED
OMB NO. 1515-0041

Each arriving traveler or head of family must provide the following information (only ONE written declaration per family is required):

1. Name: ____________ (Last) ____________ (First) ____________ (Middle Initial)

2. Number of family members traveling with you ____________

3. Date of Birth: ____ (Month) / ____ (Day) / ____ (Year) 4. Airline/Flight: ____________

5. U.S. Address: ____________

____

6. I am a U.S. Citizen — YES ☐ NO ☐
   If No,
   Country: ____________

7. I reside permanently in the U.S. — YES ☐ NO ☐
   If No,
   Expected Length of Stay: ____________

8. The purpose of my trip is or was
   ☐ BUSINESS ☐ PLEASURE

9. I am/we are bringing fruits, plants, meats, food, soil, birds, snails, other live animals, farm products, or I/we have been on a farm or ranch outside the U.S. — YES ☐ NO ☐

10. I am/we are carrying currency or monetary instruments over $10,000 U.S. or foreign equivalent. — YES ☐ NO ☐

11. The total value of all goods I/we purchased or acquired abroad and am/are bringing to the U.S. is (see instructions under Merchandise on reverse side; visitors should report value of gifts only): $ ____________ (U.S. Dollars)

SIGN ON REVERSE SIDE AFTER YOU READ WARNING.

(Do not write below this line.)

INSPECTOR'S NAME	STAMP AREA
BADGE NO.	

Paperwork Reduction Act Notice. The Paperwork Reduction Act of 1980 says we must tell you why we are collecting this information, how we will use it and whether you have to give it to us. We ask for this information to carry out the Customs, Agriculture, and Currency laws of the United States. We need it to ensure that travelers are complying with these laws and to allow us to figure and collect the right amount of duties and taxes. Your response is mandatory.

Customs Form 6059B (102584)

WARNING

AGRICULTURAL PRODUCTS

To prevent the entry of dangerous agricultural pests the following are restricted: Fruits, vegetables, plants, plant products, soil, meats, meat products, birds, snails, and other live animals or animal products. Failure to declare all such items to a Customs/Agriculture Officer can result in fines or other penalties.

CURRENCY AND MONETARY INSTRUMENTS

The transportation of currency or monetary instruments, regardless of the amount, is legal; however, if you take out of or bring into (or attempt to take out of or bring into) the United States more than $10,000 (U.S. or foreign equivalent, or a combination of the two) in coin, currency, travelers checks or bearer instruments such as money orders, checks, stocks or bonds, you are required by law to file a report on a Form 4790 with the U.S. Customs Service. If you have someone else carry the currency or instruments for you, you must also file the report. FAILURE TO FILE THE REQUIRED REPORT OR FALSE STATEMENTS ON THE REPORT MAY LEAD TO SEIZURE OF THE CURRENCY OR INSTRUMENTS AND TO CIVIL PENALTIES AND/OR CRIMINAL PROSECUTION.

MERCHANDISE

In Item 11, **U.S. residents** must declare the total value of ALL articles acquired abroad (whether new or used, whether dutiable or not, and whether obtained by purchase, as a gift, or otherwise) which are in their or their family's possession at the time of arrival. **Visitors** must declare in Item 11 only the total value of all gifts they are bringing with them.

The amount of duty to be paid will be determined by a Customs officer. U.S. residents are normally entitled to a duty free exemption of $400; non-residents are normally entitled to an exemption of $100. Both residents and non-residents will normally be required to pay a flat 10% rate of duty on the first $1,000 above their exemptions.

If the value of goods declared in Item 11 EXCEEDS $1,400 PER PERSON, then list the articles below and show price paid or, for gifts, fair retail value.

DESCRIPTION OF ARTICLES	PRICE	**CUSTOMS USE**
TOTAL		

IF YOU HAVE ANY QUESTIONS ABOUT WHAT MUST BE REPORTED OR DECLARED ASK A CUSTOMS OFFICER.

I have read the above statements and have made a truthful declaration.

SIGNATURE　　　　DATE (Month/Day/Year)

Customs Form 6059B (102584) (Back)　　✿ U.S. G.P.O. 1985-515-262

Appendix 4. Declaration for Free Entry of Unaccompanied Articles (CF 3299)

DEPARTMENT OF THE TREASURY
UNITED STATES CUSTOMS SERVICE

FORM APPROVED
OMB NO. 1515-0053

DECLARATION FOR FREE ENTRY OF UNACCOMPANIED ARTICLES

19 CFR 148.6, 148.52, 148.53, 148.77

PART I - TO BE COMPLETED BY ALL PERSONS SEEKING FREE ENTRY OF ARTICLES (Please consult with the Customs official for additional information or assistance. REMEMBER—All of your statements are subject to verification. False declarations or failure to declare articles could result in penalties).

1. IMPORTER'S NAME (Last, first and middle)	2. IMPORTER'S DATE OF BIRTH	3. IMPORTER'S DATE OF ARRIVAL
4. IMPORTER'S U.S. ADDRESS	5. IMPORTER'S PORT OF ARRIVAL	
	6. NAME OF ARRIVING VESSEL/CARRIER AND FLIGHT/TRAIN	

7. NAME(S) OF ACCOMPANYING HOUSEHOLD MEMBERS (wife, husband, minor children, etc.)

8. THE ARTICLES FOR WHICH FREE ENTRY IS CLAIMED BELONG TO ME AND/OR MY FAMILY AND WERE IMPORTED	A. DATE	B. NAME OF VESSEL/CARRIER	C. FROM (Country)	D. B/L OR AWB OR I. T. NO.
E. NUMBER AND KINDS OF CONTAINERS		F. MARKS AND NUMBERS		

PART II - TO BE COMPLETED BY ALL PERSONS EXCEPT U.S. PERSONNEL AND EVACUEES

9. RESIDENCY ("X" appropriate box) — A. NAME OF COUNTRY — B. LENGTH OF TIME (Yr. Mo.)

I declare that my place of residence abroad ☐ is ☐ was

C. RESIDENCY STATUS UPON MY/OUR ARRIVAL ("X" One)

☐ (1) Returning resident of the U.S. (2) Nonresident: ☐ a. Emigrating to the U.S. ☐ b. Visting the U.S.

10. STATEMENT(S) OF ELIGIBILITY FOR FREE ENTRY OF ARTICLES

I the undersigned further declare, that: ("X" all applicable items and submit packing list).

A. Applicable to RESIDENT AND NONRESIDENT

☐ (1) All household effects acquired abroad for which entry is sought were used abroad for at least one year by me or my family in a household of which I or my family was a resident member during such period of use, and are not intended for any other person or for sale. (810.10, TSUSA).

☐ (2) All instruments, implements, or tools of trade, occupation or employment, and all professional books for which free entry is sought were taken abroad by me or for my account or I am an emigrant who owned and used them abroad (810.20, 811.10, TSUSA).

B. Applicable to RESIDENT ONLY

☐ All personal effects for which free entry is sought were taken abroad by me or for my account. (813.10, TSUSA).

C. Applicable to NONRESIDENT ONLY

☐ (1) All articles of apparel, personal adornment, toiletries and similar personal effects for which free entry is sought were actually owned by me and in the procession of myself, or those members of my family who accompanied me, at the time of departure to the United States and that they are appropriate and are intended for our personnal use and not for any other person nor for sale. (812.10. TSUSA).

☐ (2) Any vehicles, trailers, bicycles or other means of conveyance being imported are for the transport of me and my family and such incidential carriage of articles as are appropriate to my personal use of the conveyance. (812.30, TSUSA).

PART III - TO BE COMPLETED BY U.S. PERSONNEL AND EVACUEES ONLY

I, the undersigned, the owner, importer, or agent of the importer of the personal and household effects for which free entry is claimed, hereby certify that they were in direct personal possession of the importer, or of a member of the importer's family residing with the importer, while abroad, and that they were imported into the United States because of the termination of assignment to extended duty (as defined in section 148.74(d) of the Custom's Regulations) at a post or station outside the United States and the Customs Territory of the United States, or because of Government orders or instructions evacuating the importer to the United States; and that they are not imported for sale or for the account of any other person and that they do not include any alcoholic beverages or cigars. Free entry for these effects is claimed under Item 817.00, Tariff Schedules of the United States.

1. DATE OF IMPORTER'S LAST DEPARTURE FROM THE U.S.	2. A COPY OF THE IMPORTER'S TRAVEL ORDERS IS ATTACHED AND THE ORDERS WERE ISSUED ON:

PART IV - TO BE COMPLETED BY ALL PERSONS SEEKING FREE ENTRY OF ARTICLES (Certain articles may be subject to duty and/or other requirements and must be specifically declared herein. Please check all applicable items and list them separately in Item D on the reverse.)

A. For U.S. Personnel, Evacuees, Residents and Non-Residents

☐ (1) Articles for the account of other persons.

☐ (2) Articles for sale or commercial use.

☐ (3) Firearms and/or ammunition.

☐ (4) Alcoholic articles of all types or tobacco products.

☐ (5) Fruits, plants, seeds, meats, or birds.

☐ (6) Fish, wildife, animal products thereof.

B. For Residents and Non-Residents ONLY

☐ (7) Foreign household effects acquired abroad and used less than one year.

☐ (8) Foreign household effects acquired abroad and used more than one year.

C. For Residents ONLY

☐ (9) Personal effects acquired abroad.

☐ (10) Foreign made articles acquired in the United States and taken abroad on this trip or acquired abroad on another trip that was previously declared to U.S. Customs.

☐ (11) Articles taken abroad for which alterations or repairs were performed abroad.

Customs Form 3299 (052786)

D. LIST OF ARTICLES

(1) ITEM NUMBER CHECKED IN PART IV, A.,B.,C.	(2) DESCRIPTION OF MERCHANDISE	(3) VALUE OR COSTS OF REPAIRS	(4) FOREIGN MERCHANDISE TAKEN ABROAD THIS TRIP: *State where in the U.S. the foreign merchandise was acquired or when and where it was previously declared to U. S. Customs.*

PART V - CARRIER'S CERTIFICATE AND RELEASE ORDER

The undersigned carrier, to whom or upon whose order the articles described in PART I, 8., must be released, hereby certifies that the person named in Part I, 1., is the owner or consignee of such articles within the purview of section 484(h), Tariff Act of 1930.

In accordance with the provisions of section 484(h), Tariff Act of 1930, authority is hereby given to release the articles to such consignee.

1. NAME OF CARRIER	2. SIGNATURE OF AGENT (Print and sign) Date

PART VI - CERTIFICATION - TO BE COMPLETED BY ALL PERSONS SEEKING FREE ENTRY

I, the undersigned, certify that this declaration is correct and complete.

1. "X" One

☐ A. Authorized Agent* (From facts obtained from the importer) ☐ B. Importer

2. SIGNATURE	3. DATE

**An Authorized Agent is defined as a person who has actual knowledge of the facts and who is specifically empowered under a power of attorney to execute this declaration (See 141.19, 141.32, 141.33, C.R.).*

PART VII - CUSTOMS USE ONLY (Inspected and Released)	
1. SIGNATURE OF CUSTOMS OFFICIAL	2. DATE

PAPERWORK REDUCTION ACT NOTICE: The Paperwork Reduction Act of 1980 says we must tell you why we are collecting this information, how we will use it, and whether you have to give it to us. We ask for the information to carry out the Customs Service laws of the United States. We need it to ensure that importers are complying with these laws and to allow us to figure, collect, or refund the right amount of duty and tax. Your response is mandatory and to your benefit.

☆ U.S. GPO: 1987-742-011/41133

Customs Form 3299 (052786) (Ba

Appendix 5. Generalized System of Preferences Certificate of Origin (Form A)

1. Goods consigned from (Exporter's business name, address, country)	Reference No. GENERALISED SYSTEM OF PREFERENCES CERTIFICATE OF ORIGIN (Combined declaration and certificate) FORM A Issued in ____________ (country) See Notes overleaf
2. Goods consigned to (Consignee's name, address, country)	
3. Means of transport and route (as far as known)	4. For official use

5. Item number	6. Marks and numbers of packages	7. Number and kind of packages; description of goods	8. Origin criterion (see Notes overleaf)	9. Gross weight or other quantity	10. Number and date of invoices

11. **Certification** It is hereby certified, on the basis of control carried out, that the declaration by the exporter is correct. .... Place and date, signature and stamp of certifying authority	12. **Declaration by the exporter** The undersigned hereby declares that the above details and statements are correct; that all the goods were produced in ____________ (country) and that they comply with the origin requirements specified for those goods in the Generalised System of Preferences for goods exported to ____________ (importing country) ____________ Place and date, signature of authorised signatory

Appendix 6. Entry/Immediate Delivery (CF 3461)

DEPARTMENT OF THE TREASURY
UNITED STATES CUSTOMS SERVICE

Form Approved
OMB No. 1515-0069

ENTRY/IMMEDIATE DELIVERY

1. ARRIVAL DATE	2. ELECTED ENTRY DATE	3. ENTRY TYPE CODE/NAME	4. ENTRY NUMBER
5. PORT	6. SINGLE TRANS. BOND	7. BROKER/IMPORTER FILE NUMBER	
	8. CONSIGNEE NUMBER		9. IMPORTER NUMBER
10. ULTIMATE CONSIGNEE NAME		11. IMPORTER OF RECORD NAME	
12. CARRIER CODE	13. VOYAGE/FLIGHT/TRIP	14. LOCATION OF GOODS - CODE(S)/NAME(S)	
15. VESSEL CODE/NAME			
16. U.S. PORT OF UNLADING	17. MANIFEST NUMBER	18. G.O. NUMBER	19. TOTAL VALUE
20. DESCRIPTION OF MERCHANDISE			

21. IT/BL/AWB CODE	22. IT/BL/AWB NO.	23. MANIFEST QUANTITY	24. H.S. NUMBER	25. COUNTRY OF ORIGIN	26. MANUFACTURER NO.

27. CERTIFICATION

I hereby make application for entry/immediate delivery. I certify that the above information is accurate, the bond is sufficient, valid, and current, and that all requirements of 19 CFR Part 142 have been met.

SIGNATURE OF APPLICANT

X

PHONE NO. | DATE

29. BROKER OR OTHER GOVT. AGENCY USE

Paperwork Reduction Act Notice: This information is needed to determine the admissibility of imports into the United States and to provide the necessary information for the examination of the cargo and to establish the liability for payment of duties and taxes. Your response is necessary.

28. CUSTOMS USE ONLY

☐ OTHER AGENCY ACTION REQUIRED, NAMELY:

☐ CUSTOMS EXAMINATION REQUIRED.

☐ ENTRY REJECTED, BECAUSE:

DELIVERY AUTHORIZED: | SIGNATURE | DATE

Statement Required by 5 CFR 1320.21: The estimated average burden associated with this co[llection of information is 15 minutes per respondent or recordkeeper depending on individu[al] circumstances. Comments concerning the accuracy of this burden estimate and suggestions f[or] reducing this burden should be directed to U.S. Customs Service, Paperwork Management Branc[h] Washington, DC 20229, or the Paperwork Reduction Project (1515-0069), Office of Manageme[nt] and Budget, Washington, DC 20503.

Customs Form 3461 (01018

Appendix 7. Entry Summary (CF 7501)

DEPARTMENT OF THE TREASURY
UNITED STATES CUSTOMS SERVICE

ENTRY SUMMARY

Form Approved OMB No. 1515-0065

1. Entry No.	2. Entry Type Code	3. Entry Summary Date
4. Entry Date	5. Port Code	
6. Bond No.	7. Bond Type Code	8. Broker/Importer File No.

9. Ulimate Consignee Name and Address	10. Consignee No.	11. Importer of Record Name and Address	12. Importer No.
		13. Exporting Country	14. Export Date
		15. Country of Origin	16. Missing Documents
	State	17. I.T. No.	18. I.T. Date
19. B/L or AWB No.	20. Mode of Transportation	21. Manufacturer I.D.	22. Reference No.
23. Importing Carrier	24. Foreign Port of Lading	25. Location of Goods/G.O. No.	
26. U.S. Port of Unlading	27. Import Date		

28. Line No	29. Description of Merchandise: 30. A. T.S.U.S.A. No. B. ADA/CVD Case No.	31. A. Gross Weight B. Manifest Qty.	32. Net Quantity in T.S.U.S.A. Units	33. A. Entered Value B. CHGS C. Relationship	34. A. T.S.U.S.A. Rate B. ADA/CVD Rate C. I.R.C. Rate D. Visa No.	35. Duty and I.R. Tax: Dollars	Cents

36. Declaration of Importer of Record (Owner or Purchaser) or Authorized Agent

declare that I am the

☐ importer of record and that the actual owner, purchaser, or consignee for customs purposes is as shown above. OR ☐ owner or purchaser or agent thereof.

further declare that the merchandise

☐ was obtained pursuant to a purchase or agreement to purchase and that the prices set forth in the invoice are true. OR ☐ was not obtained pursuant to a purchase or agreement to purchase and the statements in the invoice as to value or price are true to the best of my knowledge and belief.

I also declare that the statements in the documents herein filed fully disclose to the best of my knowledge and belief the true prices, values, quantities, rebates, drawbacks, fees, commissions, and royalties and are true and correct, and that all goods or services provided to the seller of the merchandise either free or at reduced cost are fully disclosed. I will immediately furnish to the appropriate customs officer any information showing a different state of facts.

Notice required by Paperwork Reduction Act of 1980: This information is needed to ensure that importers/exporters are complying with U.S. customs laws, to allow us to compute and collect the right amount of money, to enforce other agency requirements, and to collect accurate statistical information on imports. Your response is mandatory.

U.S. CUSTOMS USE		TOTALS
A. Liq. Code	B. Ascertained Duty	37. Duty
	C. Ascertained Tax	38. Tax
	D. Ascertained Other	39. Other
	E. Ascertained Total	40. Total

41. Signature of Declarant, Title, and Date

PART 1 — RECORD COPY

Customs Form 7501 (030984)

Appendix 8. Entry Record (CF 5101)

Department of the Treasury
U.S. Customs Service
ENTRY RECORD
Customs Form 5101 (9-9-77)

WAS SHIPMENT CONTAINERIZED YES ☐

1. ENTRY CODE

2. BOND CODE

FORM APPROVED
O.M.B. No. 48-R0255

3. IMPORTER OF RECORD NUMBER*

Importer Number of Individual or firm whose name appears as Importer of Record on entry.

ENTRY CODES—
1. Consumption Dutiable
2. Vessel Repair
3. Appraisement
4. Warehouse
5. Drawback
6. Bonded A/C Fuel
7. Consumption Free

BOND CODES—
1. Single Entry (any type)
2. CF 7553 (Consump. Term)
3. CF 7563-A (Temp. Imp.)
4. CF 7569 (Vessel Term)
5. CF 7595 (General Term)
6. CF 7611 (Drawback Term)

4. ULTIMATE CONSIGNEE NUMBER*

Importer Number of Individual or firm whose name appears as the Ultimate Consignee on entry. If more than one owner of merchandise enter word "consolidated".

5a. DATE OF ENTRY

5b. ENTRY NUMBER

6. REFERENCE NUMBER*

Importer Number of Individual or firm to whom Refund, Bills or Notices of Liquidation are to be sent if other than Importer of Record.

7. DUTY
$

8. I.R. TAX
$

*(Show hyphens as appropriate.)

9. SURETY CODE

10. DESCRIPTION OF MERCHANDISE

11. PORT CODE

12. MISSING DOCUMENTS

LIQUIDATOR CODE
(Customs Use Only)

I HEREBY make application to make entry prior to production of missing document(s) named above. ▶ SIGNATURE

(Original)

Appendix 9. Protest (CF 19)

Form approved OMB No. 1515-0056

DEPARTMENT OF THE TREASURY
UNITED STATES CUSTOMS SERVICE
PROTEST
Pursuant to Sections 514 &515(a), Tariff Act of 1930 as amended, 19 CFR 174 et seq.

1. PROTEST NO. *(Supplied by Customs)*

2. DATE RECEIVED *(Customs Use Only)*

NOTE: If your protest is denied, in whole or in part, and you wish to CONTEST the denial, you may do so by bringing a civil action in the U.S. Court of International Trade within 180 days after the date of mailing of Notice of Denial. You may obtain further information concerning the institution of an action by writing the Clerk of U.S. Court of International Trade, One Federal Plaza, New York, New York 10007. (212-264-2800)

SECTION I — IMPORTER AND ENTRY IDENTIFICATION

3. DISTRICT
4. IMPORTER NO.
5. ENTRY DETAILS

PORT CODE	FY	ENTRY NO.	CHECK DIGIT	DATE OF ENTRY	DATE OF LIQUIDATION

6. NAME AND ADDRESS OF IMPORTER OR OTHER PROTESTING PARTY

SECTION II — APPLICATION FOR FURTHER REVIEW (Fill in item 1 above if this is a separate Application for Further Review.)

7. ☐ THIS IS AN APPLICATION FOR FURTHER REVIEW IN LIEU OF REVIEW BY THE DISTRICT DIRECTOR. *(Complete Item 8 below.)*

YES	NO	8. Please answer each of the following questions as these criteria must be met for approval of further review of protest, IF REQUESTED ABOVE.
		Have you made prior request of a district director for a further review of the same claim with respect to the same or substantially similar merchandise?
		Have you received a final adverse decision from the U.S. Court of Int'l Trade on the same claim with respect to the same category of merchandise or do you have action involving such a claim pending before the U.S. Court of International Trade?
		Have you previously received an adverse administrative decision from the Commissioner of Customs or his designee or have you presently pending an application for an administrative decision on the same claim with respect to the same category of merchandise?

SECTION III — DETAILED REASONS FOR PROTEST AND/OR FURTHER REVIEW

9. With respect to each category of merchandise, set forth, separately, (1) each decision protested, (2) the claim of the protesting party, and (3) the factual material and legal arguments which are believed to support the protest. All such material and arguments should be specific. General statements of conclusions are not sufficient. If Further Review is applied for, set forth, additionally, a justification for Further Review under the criteria in 19 C.F.R.174.24 and 174.25.

(Attach Additional Sheets, If Necessary)

SECTION IV — SIGNATURE AND MAILING INSTRUCTIONS

10. NAME AND ADDRESS OF PERSON TO WHOM ANY NOTICE OF APPROVAL OR DENIAL SHOULD BE SENT

11. IF FILING AS ATTORNEY OR AGENT, TYPE OR PRINT YOUR NAME, ADDRESS, AND IMPORTER NO., IF ANY

12. SIGNATURE AND DATE

SECTION V — DECISION (CUSTOMS USE ONLY)

13. THIS ☐ PROTEST ☐ APPLICATION FOR FURTHER REVIEW HAS BEEN:

☐ DENIED IN FULL OR IN PART BECAUSE ☐ APPROVED *

☐ Untimely Filed

☐ See attached protest review decision

☐ Does not meet criteria

☐ Other, namely →

* When further review only is approved, the decision on the protest is suspended, pending issuance of a protest review decision.

14. TITLE OF CUSTOMS OFFICER

15. SIGNATURE DATE

PAPERWORK REDUCTION ACT OF 1980 STATEMENT: The U.S. Customs Service requires the information in this form to ensure compliance with Customs laws, to identify documents and statements in order to allow or deny the protest, and to advise protestant. Your response is required to obtain a benefit.

EDITIONS PRIOR TO 090883 ARE OBSOLETE.

Customs Form 19 (121686)

INSTRUCTIONS

PLEASE REFER TO: Part 174, Customs Regulations

Definitions:

"Liquidation" means the final computation or ascertainment of the duties or drawback accruing on an entry.

"Protest" means review of the liquidation by Customs officers at the district level.

"Further review" means review of the decision which is the subject of the protest by Customs officers on a level higher than the district, and (in New York Region) by Customs officers who did not participate directly in the decision which is the subject of the protest. If you are filing for further review, you must check Item 7 on Customs Form 19 and answer each question in Item 8.

What matters may be protested?

1. The appraised value of merchandise;
2. The classification and rate and amount of duties chargeable;
3. All charges within the jurisdiction of the Secy. of Treasury;
4. Exclusion of merchandise from entry or delivery;
5. The liquidation or reliquidation of an entry;
6. The refusal to pay a claim for drawback; and
7. The refusal to reliquidate an entry under Sec. 520(c), Tariff Act of 1930, as amended.

Who may file a protest or application for further review?

1. The importer or consignee shown on the entry papers, or their sureties;
2. Any person paying any charge or exaction;
3. Any person seeking entry or delivery;
4. Any person filing a claim for drawback; or
5. Any authorized agent of any of the persons described above.

Where to file protests:

With the district director whose decision is protested (at the port where entry was made).

When to file a protest:

Within 90 days after either: 1) the date of notice of liquidation, or 2) the date of the decision, involving neither a liquidation nor reliquidation, as to which the protest is made (e.g., the date of an exaction, the date of written notice excluding merchandise from entry or delivery . . .)

Contents of protest:

1. Name and address of the protestant;
2. The importer number of the protestant;
3. The number and date of the entry;
4. The date of liquidation of the entry (or the date of a decision).
5. A specific description of the merchandise;
6. The nature of and justification for the objection set forth distinctly and specifically with respect to each category claim, decision, or refusal;
7. The date of receipt and protest number of any protest previously filed that is the subject of a pending applicatio for further review; and
8. If another party has not filed a timely protest, the surety's protest shall certify that the protest is not being file collusively to extend another authorized person's time to protest.

NOTE: Under block 5, Entry Details, "Check digit" information is optional; however, Customs would apprecia receiving the information if you can provide it.

Customs Form 19 (Ba

Appendix 10. Appointment of Agent

KNOW ALL MEN BY THESE PRESENTS, THAT

____,

(Name of principal)

____,

(State legal designation, such as corporation, individual, etc.) residing at ______________ and doing business under the laws of the State of ______, hereby appoints __

____

(Name, legal designation, and address)

as a true and lawful agent and attorney of the principal named above with full power and authority to do and perform every lawful act and thing the said agent and attorney may deem requisite and necessary to be done for and on behalf of the said principal without limitation of any kind as fully as said principal could do if present and acting, and hereby ratify and confirm all said agent and attorney shall lawfully do or cause to be done by virtue of these presents until and including ______________, (date) or until notice of revocation in writing is duly given before that date.

Date ______________, 19____.

____

(Principal's signature)

Appendix 11. Customs Bond (CF 301)

Approved through 4-30-87
OMB No. 1515-0144

DEPARTMENT OF THE TREASURY
UNITED STATES CUSTOMS SERVICE

CUSTOMS BOND

19 CFR Part 113

CUSTOMS USE ONLY	BOND NUMBER[1] (Assigned by Customs)
	FILE REFERENCE

In order to secure payment of any duty, tax or charge and compliance with law or regulation as a result of activity covered by any condition referenced below, we, the below named principal(s) and surety(ies), bind ourselves to the United States in the amount or amounts, as set forth below.	Execution Date

SECTION I—Select Single Transaction **OR** Continuous Bond (not both) and fill in the applicable blank spaces.

☐ SINGLE TRANSACTION BOND	Identification of transaction secured by this bond (e.g., entry no., seizure no., etc.)	Date of transaction	Transaction district & port code
☐ CONTINUOUS BOND	Effective date	This bond remains in force for one year beginning with the effective date and for each succeeding annual period, or until terminated. This bond constitutes a separate bond for each period in the amounts listed below for liabilities that accrue in each period. The intention to terminate this bond must be conveyed within the time period and manner prescribed in the Customs Regulations.	

SECTION II— This bond includes the following agreements.[2] (Check one box only, except that, 1a may be checked independently or with 1, and 3a may be checked independently or with 3. Line out all other parts of this section that are not used.)

Activity Code	Activity Name and Customs Regulations in which conditions codified	Limit of Liability	Activity Code	Activity Name and Customs Regulations in which conditions codified	Limit of Liability
☐ 1	Importer or broker....113.62		☐ 5	Public Gauger....113.67	
☐ 1a	Drawback Payment Refunds....113.65		☐ 6	Wool & Fur Products Labeling Acts Importation (Single Entry Only)....113.68	
☐ 2	Custodian of bonded merchandise....113.63 (Includes bonded carriers, freight forwarders, cartmen and lightermen, all classes of warehouses, container station operators)		☐ 7	Bill of Lading (Single Entry Only)....113.69	
			☐ 8	Detention of Copyrighted Material (Single Entry Only)....113.70	
☐ 3	International Carrier....113.64				
☐ 3a	Instruments of International Traffic.113.66		☐ 9	Neutrality (Single Entry Only)....113.71	
☐ 4	Foreign Trade Zone Operator....113.73		☐ 10	Court Costs for Condemned Goods (Single Entry Only)....113.72	

SECTION III— List below all tradenames or unincorporated divisions that will be permitted to obligate this bond in the principal's name including their Customs Identification Number(s).[3] (If more space is needed, use Section III(Continuation) on back of form.)

Importer Number	Importer Name	Importer Number	Importer Name
		Total number of importer names listed in Section III:	

Principal and surety agree that any charge against the bond under any of the listed names is as though it was made by the principal(s). Principal and surety agree that they are bound to the same extent as if they executed a separate bond covering each set of conditions incorporated by reference to the Customs Regulations into this bond.	If the surety fails to appoint an agent under Title 6, United States Code, Section 7, surety consents to service on the Clerk of any United States District Court or the U.S. Court of International Trade, where suit is brought on this bond. That clerk is to send notice of the service to the surety at:	Mailing Address Requested by the Surety

PRINCIPAL[4]	Name and Address	Importer No.[3] SIGNATURE[8]	SEAL
PRINCIPAL[4]	Name and Address	Importer No.[3] SIGNATURE[8]	SEAL
SURETY[4,6]	Name and Address[6]	Surety No.[7] SIGNATURE[8]	SEAL
SURETY[4,6]	Name and Address[6]	Surety No.[7] SIGNATURE[8]	SEAL

SURETY AGENTS	Name[9]	Identification No.[9]	Name[9]	Identification No.

Customs Form 301 (1118

PART 1-U.S. CUSTOMS

Note: Turn carbons over before writing on back of form.

SECTION III (Continuation)

Importer Number	Importer Name	Importer Number	Importer Name

WITNESSES

Two witnesses are required to authenticate the signature of any person who signs as an individual or as a partner; however, a witness may authenticate the signatures of both such non-corporate principals and sureties. No witness is needed to authenticate the signature of a corporate official or agent who signs for the corporation.

SIGNED, SEALED, and DELIVERED in the PRESENCE OF:

Name and Address of Witness for the Principal	Name and Address of Witness for the Surety
SIGNATURE:	SIGNATURE:
Name and Address of Witness for the Principal	Name and Address of Witness for the Surety
SIGNATURE:	SIGNATURE:

EXPLANATIONS AND FOOTNOTES

1. The Customs Bond Number is a control number assigned by Customs to the bond contract when the bond is approved by an authorized Customs official.
2. For all bond coverage available and the language of the bond conditions refer to Part 113, subpart G, Customs Regulations.
3. The Importer Number is the Customs Identification number filed pursuant to section 24.5, Customs Regulations. When the Internal Revenue Service employer identification number is used the two-digit suffix code must be shown.
4. If the principal or surety is a corporation, the name of the State in which incorporated must be shown.
5. See witness requirement above.
6. Surety Name, if a corporation, shall be the company's name as it is spelled in the Surety Companies Annual List published in the Federal Register by the Department of the Treasury (Treasury Department Circular 570).
7. Surety Number is the three digit identification code assigned by Customs to a surety company at the time the surety company initially gives notice to Customs that the company will be writing Customs bonds.
8. Surety Agent is the individual granted a Corporate Surety Power of Attorney, CF 5297, by the surety company executing the bond.
9. Agent Identification No. shall be the individual's Social Security number as shown on the Corporate Surety Power of Attorney, CF 5297, filed by the surety granting such power of attorney.

Paperwork Reduction Act Notice. The Paperwork Reduction Act of 1980 says we must tell you why we are collecting this information, how we will use it and whether you have to give it to us. We ask for this information to carry out the U.S. Customs Service laws of the United States. We need it to ensure that persons transacting business with Customs have the proper bond coverage to secure their transactions as required by law and regulation. Your response is required to enter into any transaction in which a bond is a prerequisite under the Tariff Act of 1930, as amended.

Privacy Act Statement: The following notice is given pursuant to section 7(b) of the Privacy Act of 1974 (5 U.S.C. 552a). Furnishing the information on this form, including the Social Security Number, is mandatory. The primary use of the Social Security Number is to verify, in the Customs Automated System, at the time an agent submits a Customs bond for approval that the individual was granted a Corporate Surety Power of Attorney by the surety company. Section 7 of Act of July 30, 1947, chapter 390, 61 Stat. 646, authorizes the collection of this information.

Back of Customs Form 301 (111883)

Appendix 12. Application for Foreign Trade Zone Admission and/or Status Designation (CF 214)

Approved through 5/31/87. OMB No. 1515-0086.

CENSUS USE ONLY	DEPARTMENT OF THE TREASURY UNITED STATES CUSTOMS SERVICE APPLICATION FOR FOREIGN TRADE ZONE ADMISSION AND/OR STATUS DESIGNATION 19 CFR 146; 400.800, Foreign Trade Zone Board Regulations	1. ZONE NO. AND LOCATION *(Address)* 2. DISTRICT/PORT CODE

3. IMPORTING VESSEL (& FLAG)/OTHER CARRIER	4. EXPORT DATE	5. IMPORT DATE	6. ZONE LOT NO.

7. U.S. PORT OF UNLADING	8. FOREIGN PORT OF LADING	9. BILL OF LADING/AWB NO.	10. INWARD M'FEST NO.

11. INBOND CARRIER	12. I.T. NO. AND DATE	13. I.T. FROM *(Port)*

14. STATISTICAL INFORMATION FURNISHED DIRECTLY TO BUREAU OF CENSUS BY APPLICANT? ☐ YES ☐ NO

15. NO. OF PACKAGES	16. MARKS, NOS. AND COUNTRY OF ORIGIN	17. DESCRIPTION OF MERCHANDISE	18. TSUSA NO.	19. QUANTITY (TSUSA)	20. GROSS WEIGHT	21. SEPARATE PEXT VALUE & AGGR CHGS.

22. I hereby apply for admission of the above merchandise into the Foreign Trade Zone. I declare to the best of my knowledge and belief that the above merchandise is not prohibited entry into the Foreign Trade Zone within the meaning of section 3 of the Foreign Trade Zones Act of 1934, as amended, sections and 141.11, Customs Regulations, and section 400.801, Foreign Trade Zones Board Regulations.

23. I hereby apply for the status designation indicated:

☐ NONPRIVILIGED FOREIGN ☐ PRIVILIGED DOMESTIC ☐ NONPRIVILIGED DOMESTIC ☐ ZONE RESTRICTED

☐ PRIVILIGED FOREIGN: There is filed herewith a Zone Customs entry in triplicate in connection with this application for privileged foreign status.

24. APPLICANT FIRM NAME		25. BY *(Signature)*	26. TITLE	27. DATE
F.T.Z. AGREES TO RECEIVE MERCHANDISE INTO THE ZONE		28. FOR THE F.T.Z. *(Signature)*	29. TITLE	30. DATE
PERMIT	Permission is hereby granted to transfer the above merchandise into the Zone.	31. DISTRICT DIRECTOR OF CUSTOMS: BY *(Signature)*	32. TITLE	33. DATE
PERMIT	The above merchandise has been granted the requested status.	34. DISTRICT DIRECTOR OF CUSTOMS: BY *(Signature)*	35. TITLE	36. DATE

PERMIT TO TRANSFER	37. The goods described herein are authorized to be transferred: ☐ without exception ☐ except as noted below			
	38. CUSTOMS OFFICER AT STATION *(Signature)*	39. TITLE	40. STATION	41. DATE
	42. RECEIVED FOR TRANSFER TO ZONE (Driver's Signature)	43. CARTMAN	44. CHL NO.	45. DATE

CUSTOMS REPORT OF MERCHANDISE RECEIVED AT ZONE	46. To the District Director of Customs: The above merchandise was received at the Zone on the date shown except as noted below:		
	47. CUSTOMS OFFICER AT STATION *(Signature)*	48. TITLE	49. DATE

(Paperwork Reduction Act Notice on Reverse) 951-881 **Customs Form 214 (05068**

Appendix 13. Application for Foreign Trade Zone Activity Permit (CF 216)

Approved Through 5/31/87. OMB No. 1515-0086

DEPARTMENT OF THE TREASURY
UNITED STATES CUSTOMS SERVICE

APPLICATION FOR FOREIGN TRADE ZONE ACTIVITY PERMIT

19 CFR 146.32, 146.33
400.800, 400.803, Foreign Trade Zones Board Regulations

1. ZONE NUMBER AND LOCATION *(Address)*

2. TYPE OF ACTIVITY FOR WHICH PERMIT REQUESTED

☐ Manipulate ☐ Manufacture ☐ Exhibit ☐ Destroy

3. ZONE LOT NO.

4. APPLICATION DATE

5. FULL DESCRIPTION OF THE ACTIVITY *(Include designation of the exact place in the zone where the operation is to be performed and, in the case of a proposed manipulation or manufacture, a statement as to whether merchandise with one zone status is to be packed, commingled, or combined with merchandise having a different zone status. If additional space required, attach separate sheet.)*

6. ZONE LOT NO.	7. MARKS AND NUMBERS	8. DESCRIPTION OF MERCHANDISE	9. QUANTITY	10. WEIGHTS, MEASURES	11. ZONE STATUS

If any privileged merchandise is to be manipulated in any way or manufactured, I agree to maintain the records provided for in section 146.32(d) of the Customs Regulations and to make them available to customs officers for inspection.

12. APPLICANT FIRM NAME	13. BY *(Signature)*	14. TITLE
APPROVED BY FOREIGN TRADE ZONE GRANTEE ➧	15. BY *(Signature)*	16. TITLE

PERMIT

The application made above is hereby approved and permission is granted to manipulate, manufacture, exhibit, or destroy, as requested, on condition that the applicable regulations are complied with and the records required to be maintained will be available for inspection.

17. DISTRICT DIRECTOR OF CUSTOMS: By *(Signature)*	18. TITLE	19. DATE

CUSTOMS OFFICER'S RETURN

20. TO THE DISTRICT DIRECTOR OF CUSTOMS:

I certify that the goods described herein have been disposed of as directed except as noted below.

21. CUSTOMS OFFICER SIGNATURE	22. TITLE	23. DATE

Replaces Zone Form E

Customs Form 216 (082085)

Appendix 14. United States Certificate of Origin for Exports to Israel

U.S. CERTIFICATE OF ORIGIN

FOR EXPORTS TO ISRAEL

1. Goods consigned from exporter's business (name, address):

Reference No.

U.S.—ISRAEL FREE TRADE AREA

CERTIFICATE OF ORIGIN
(Combined declaration and certificate)

(See notes over leaf)

2. Goods consigned to (consignee's name, address)

3. Means of transport and route (as far as known)

4. For official use

5. Item number	6. Marks and numbers of packages	7. Number and kind of packages, description of goods	8. Origin criterion (see notes over leaf)	9. Gross Weight or other quantity	10. Number and date of Invoices

11. CERTIFICATION

The ______________________
a recognized chamber of commerce, board of trade, or ______
______________ under the laws of the State of ______
______________ has examined the manufacturer's invoice or shipper's affidavit concerning the origin of the merchandise and, according to the best of its knowledge and belief, finds that the products named originated in the United States of America.

____
Certifying Official

12. DECLARATION BY THE EXPORTER

The undersigned hereby declares that the above details and statements are correct; that all the goods were produced in the United States of America and that they comply with the origin requirements specified for those goods in the U.S.—Israel Free Trade Area Agreement for goods exported to Israel.

____
Signature of Exporter

Sworn to before me this ______________
day of ______________ 19______

____
Signature of Notary Public

Appendix 15. United States–Canada Free Trade Agreement Exporter's Certificate of Origin (CF 353)

DEPARTMENT OF THE TREASURY
UNITED STATES CUSTOMS SERVICE

Approved through 4/30/89
OMB No. 1515-0164

U.S.-CANADA FREE TRADE AGREEMENT

EXPORTER'S CERTIFICATE OF ORIGIN

19 CFR 10.307(d)

1. GOODS CONSIGNED FROM (Exporter's business name, address, country, tax identification number)

2. IF BLANKET CERTIFICATION

EFFECTIVE DATE

EXPIRATION DATE

3. GOODS CONSIGNED TO (Consignee's name, address, country)

4. PRODUCER'S NAME, ADDRESS, COUNTRY, TAX IDENTIFICATION NUMBER (If different from exporter)

5. ORIGIN CRITERIA FOR GOODS COVERED BY THIS CERTIFICATE:

A. Wholly produced or obtained in Canada or the United States; or
B. The goods have been transformed in the United States or Canada so as to be subject:
   1) to a change in tariff classification as described in the Rules of Annex 301.2; or
   2) to a change in tariff classification as described in the Rules of Annex 301.2 and the value of originating materials plus the direct cost of processing in Canada or the United States is not less than 50 percent or, as required by Section VI Rule 15 of Annex 301.2, 70 percent of the value of exported goods; or
   3) to Rule 5, Section XII of Annex 301.2; or
C. No change in tariff classification because goods and parts are provided for in the same tariff subheading or goods were imported in unassembled or disassembled form and were classified pursuant to General Rule of Interpretation 2a) of the Harmonized System, and the value of originating materials plus the direct cost of assembly in Canada or the United States is not less than 50 percent of the value of exported goods.

6. SPECIAL DECLARATION FOR TEXTILE PRODUCTS SUBJECT TO TARIFF RATE QUOTA:

A. Apparel goods cut and sewn in Canada or the United States from fabric produced or obtained in a third country.
B. Non-wool fabric and non-wool made-up textile articles, woven or knitted in Canada from yarn produced or obtained in a third country.

7. Origin Criterion (See Fields 5 or 6)	8. Description of Goods	Tariff Classification (To Six Digits)	9. Gross Weight or Other Quantity	10. Invoice Number(s) & Date(s)

11. CERTIFICATION OF ORIGIN

I certify that the information and statements herein are correct, that all the goods were produced in Canada or the United States, that they comply with the origin requirements specified for those goods in the United States-Canada Free Trade Agreement, and that further processing or assembly in a third country has not occurred subsequent to processing or assembly in Canada or the United States.

I agree to maintain, and present upon request, the documentation to support this certification and, if this is a blanket certification, to inform the importer or other appropriate party of any change that would affect the validity of this certification.

This certificate consists of _______ pages.

PLACE AND DATE	AUTHORIZED SIGNATURE	TITLE

Customs Form 353 (120188)

INFORMATION FOR THE COMPLETION OF THE EXPORTER'S CERTIFICATE OF ORIGIN

Paperwork Reduction Act Notice: The Paperwork Reduction Act of 1980 says we must tell you why we are collecting this information, how we will use it and whether you have to give it to us. We ask for the information to carry out the terms of Annex 406 of the U.S./Canadian Free Trade Agreement and the Statement of Administrative Action for the implementing legislation (P.L. 100-449). Annex 406 requires that, upon request, an importer must provide the Customs Administration of the Party (U.S./Canada) with proof of the exporter's written certification of the origin of the goods. The exporter's certification, provided for in the Agreement, is essential to substantiate compliance with the rules of origin under the Agreement. You are required to give us this information.

Statement Required by 5 CFR 1320.21: The estimated average burden associated with this collection of information is 20 minutes per respondent or recordkeeper depending on individual circumstances. Comments concerning the accuracy of this burden estimate and suggestions for reducing this burden should be directed to U.S. Customs Service, Paperwork Management Branch, Washington, DC 20229, and to the Office of Information and Regulatory Affairs, Office of Management and Budget, Washington, DC 20503, attention Desk Officer for U.S. Customs Service.

FIELD

1. Complete with the full legal name, address, country and tax identification number.
2. Complete with the effective and expiration dates (Maximum 6 months),[1] if this certificate is to cover multiple FTA qualified shipments to the same importer. NOTE: It is the exporter's responsibility to notify everyone to whom a blanket certificate is issued if changes occur in materials, costs, or production sites that would materially affect the accuracy or validity of the certification during the period. Failure to do so could make the exporter subject to penalties.
3. Complete with the consignee's full legal name, address, and country.
4. Complete with the full legal name, address, country and if known, the tax identification number. This field is to be completed only if the exporter is not the producer of the goods. If more than one producer's goods are included in a single or blanket certificate, attach a numbered list of the additional producers. Indicate the appropriate producer's number in parenthesis after the origin criteria in Field 7.
5. Fields 5 and 6 reflect the various origin criteria by which exported goods may be eligible for FTA treatment, and are to be identified in Field 7 for each corresponding item listed in Field 8.

5.A. Indicate this criterion if the goods are wholly produced or obtained in Canada or U.S. as defined in Article 304 of the Agreement.

5.B.1. Requires that a change in the tariff classification take place along with any other requirements, other than value-added, as described in the Rules of Annex 301.2 of the Agreement.

5.B.2. Also requires that a change in tariff classification take place. Additionally, it requires that the value of domestic materials and direct cost of processing, as described in the Rules of Annex 301.2, be either 50 or 70 percent, as specified in the Rules of Annex 301.2, of the value of the exported good.[2]

5.B.3. This field does not require that a change in tariff classification take place but other requirements as described in the Rules of Annex 301.2, other than value-added, be met.[2]

5.C. This criterion does not require that a change in tariff classification take place but requires that the value of domestic materials and direct cost of assembly is not less than 50 percent of the value of exported goods. The provisions of this criterion are in accordance with paragraphs 3, 4, and 5 of the interpretation of Annex 301.2 of the Agreement. The imported components from which the goods were produced in Canada must have constituted an unassembled or disassembled article as per the General Rule of Interpretation 2(a) of the Harmonized System, or the tariff subheading for the imported components must have provided for both the goods and their parts.

6. The special declarations for textile products are identified for use in Field 7.
7. Indicate the origin criterion selected from Fields 5 or 6 for each corresponding item listed in Field 8. If more than one article for export is covered by this certificate, the origin criterion for each is required. If necessary, a continuation sheet may be used to list the articles for export and their respective criteria. If more than one producer (Field 4) is identified, indicate next to the criteria the producer number assigned; e.g. 5.A.(3).
8. Fully describe the goods. If more than one article for export is covered by this certificate, a complete description of each article is required. If a change in tariff classification criterion is used and there are multiple constitutent materials, indicate in parentheses, the number of third country constituent materials per unit. When third country constituent materials vary in a product, estimates are acceptable. The tariff classification, to six digits, of each article for export is required beside each description.
9. Indicate the gross weight or other pertinent quantities, as described on the invoice(s) or purchase order, of each good listed in Field 8. If this is a blanket certificate, indicate the contracted for weight or other quantity anticipated or contracted for during the blanket certification period, if known.
10. Indicate the invoice number(s) and date(s) for each item being shipped. If this is a blanket certificate, this field need not be completed.
11. Self-explanatory. The number of pages the certificate comprises must be indicated. **NOTE:** Unless the place, date, signature and title of the exporter appear on the space provided, this document will be considered invalid.

Note: Where the certificate or instructions makes reference to "Canada or the United States" or "domestic", this is to be interpreted as meaning either Canada or the United States or both.

[1] Canada will accept blanket exporter certificates with a validity period of twelve months; the United States will accept a validity period of six months.

[2] Canada requires the exporter to indicate the specific rule which the goods qualify; the United States simply requires an indication of the criterion.

*U.S.GPO:1988-0-227-429

Customs Form 353 (120188) (Back)

Appendix 16. Declaration for Free Entry of Returned American Products (CF 3311)

DEPARTMENT OF THE TREASURY
UNITED STATES CUSTOMS SERVICE

Form Approved
OMB No. 1515-0043

DECLARATION FOR FREE ENTRY OF RETURNED AMERICAN PRODUCTS

19 CFR 10.1, 10.5, 10.6, 10.67, 12.41, 123.4, 143.23, 145.35, 162.1c

1. PORT & DISTRICT	2. DATE	3. ENTRY NO. & DATE
4. NAME OF MANUFACTURER		5. CITY AND STATE OF MANUFACTURE
6. REASON FOR RETURN		7. U.S. DRAWBACK PREVIOUSLY ☐ CLAIMED ☐ NOT CLAIMED
		8. PREVIOUSLY IMPORTED UNDER TSUSA 864.05? ☐ YES ☐ NO

9. MARKS, NUMBERS, AND DESCRIPTION OF ARTICLES RETURNED	10. VALUE*

*If the value of the article is $10,000 or more and the articles are not clearly marked with the name and address of U.S. manufacturer, please attach copies of any documentation or other evidence that you have that will support or substantiate your claim for duty free status as American Goods Returned.

11. I declare that the information given above is true and correct to the best of my knowledge and belief; that the articles described above are the growth, production, and manufacture of the United States and are returned without having been advanced in value or improved in condition by any process of manufacture or other means; that no drawback bounty, or allowance has been paid or admitted thereon, or on any part thereof; and that if any notice(s) of exportation of articles with benefit of drawback ☐ was ☐ were filed upon exportation of the merchandise from the United States, such notice(s) ☐ has ☐ have been abandoned.

12. NAME OF DECLARANT	13. TITLE OF DECLARANT
14. NAME OF CORPORATION OR PARTNERSHIP (If any)	15. SIGNATURE (See note)

NOTE: If the owner or ultimate consignee is a corporation, this form must be signed by the president, vice president, secretary, or treasurer of the corporation, or by any employee or agent of the corporation who holds a power of attorney and a certificate by the corporation that such employee or agent has or will have knowledge of the pertinent facts.

Notice required by Paperwork Reduction Act of 1980: This information is needed to ensure that importers/exporters are complying with U.S. customs laws, to allow us to compute and collect the right amount of money, to enforce other agency requirements, and to collect accurate statistical information on imports. Your response is mandatory.

Customs Form 3311 (112084)

☆ U.S. GOVERNMENT PRINTING OFFICE 1986 – 612-955/20088

Appendix 17. Certificate of Registration (CF 4455)

DEPARTMENT OF THE TREASURY
UNITED STATES CUSTOMS SERVICE

Form Approved
OMB No 1515-0014

CERTIFICATE OF REGISTRATION

NO.

19 CFR 10.8, 10.9, 10.68, 148.1, 148.8, 148.32, 148.37

(NOTE: Number of copies to be submitted varies with type of transaction. Inquire at District Director's office as to number of copies required.)

VIA *(Carrier)*	B/L or INSURED NO.	DATE

NAME, ADDRESS, AND ZIP CODE TO WHICH CERTIFIED FORM IS TO BE MAILED *(If Applicable)*

ARTICLES EXPORTED FOR:

- ☐ ALTERATION*
- ☐ REPAIR*
- ☐ USE ABROAD
- ☐ REPLACEMENT
- ☐ PROCESSING*
- ☐ OTHER, *(specify)* ______________

** NOTE: The cost or value of alterations, repairs, or processing abroad is subject to Customs duty.*

LIST ARTICLES EXPORTED

Number Packages	Kind of Packages	Description

SIGNATURE OF OWNER OR AGENT *(Print or Type and Sign)*	DATE

The Above-Described Articles Were:

EXAMINED		LADEN under my supervision	
DATE	PORT	DATE	PORT
SIGNATURE OF CUSTOMS OFFICER		SIGNATURE OF CUSTOMS OFFICER	

CERTIFICATE ON RETURN

Duty-free entry is claimed for the described articles as having been exported without benefit of drawback and are returned unchanged except as noted: *(us[e] reverse if needed)*

SIGNATURE OF IMPORTER *(Print or Type and Sign)*	DATE

NOTE: Certifying officers shall draw lines through all unused spaces with ink or indelible pencil.

PAPERWORK REDUCTION ACT NOTICE: The Paperwork Reduction Act of 1980 says we must tell you why we are collecting this information, how we will use it, and whether you have to give it to us. We [a]... for the information to carry out the Customs Service laws of the United States. We need the information to ensure that importers/exporters are complying with these laws in claiming duty free entry for expor[ted] articles which are then returned into the United States. Your response is mandatory and to your benefit.

Customs Form 4455 (020984)

☆U.S. GPO: 1987-742-011/41183

Appendix 18. ATA Carnet Application

United States Council for International Business

ATA Carnet Application

1212 Avenue of the Americas, New York, New York 10036, (212) 354-4480

A. Applicant Information:

1. Carnet Holder (Corporate or Individual)____________________________

Address____________________________ Phone No. (_____)__________

2. IRS No./SS No.________________________ ________________________

3. Parent Company____________________________ IRS No.________________

4. Person Duly Authorized & Title________________________ Phone No. (_____)__________

5. Authorized Representatives:____________________________

____

B. Carnet Preparation Information:

6. Goods to be exported for: ☐ Commercial Samples, ☐ Professional Equipment, ☐ Exhibitions and Fairs, ☐ Other

7. Date of departure from U.S.________________

8. Check the box next to all countries to be visited and indicate the number of expected visits on the line provided beside each:

☐ __ Australia (AU)	☐ __ Gibraltar (GI)	☐ __ Korea (KR)	☐ __ Senegal (SN)
☐ __ Austria (AT)	☐ __ Greece (GR)	☐ __ Luxembourg (LU)	☐ __ Singapore (SG)
☐ __ Belgium (BE)	☐ __ Hong Kong (HK)	☐ __ Malaysia (MY)	☐ __ South Africa (ZA)
☐ __ Bulgaria (BG)	☐ __ Hungary (HU)	☐ __ Malta (MT)	☐ __ Spain (ES)
☐ __ Canada* (CA)	☐ __ Iceland (IS)	☐ __ Mauritus (MU)	☐ __ Sri Lanka (LK)
☐ __ Cyprus (CY)	☐ __ India (IN)	☐ __ Netherlands (NL)	☐ __ Sweden (SE)
☐ __ Czechoslovakia (CS)	☐ __ Ireland (IE)	☐ __ New Zealand (NZ)	☐ __ Switzerland (CH)
☐ __ Denmark (DK)	☐ __ Israel (IL)	☐ __ Norway (NO)	☐ __ Turkey (TR)
☐ __ Finland (FI)	☐ __ Italy (IT)	☐ __ Poland (PL)	☐ __ U.K. (GB)
☐ __ France (FR)	☐ __ Ivory Coast (CI)	☐ __ Portugal (PT)	☐ __ Yugoslavia (YU)
☐ __ Germany (DE)	☐ __ Japan (JP)	☐ __ Romania (RO)	☐ __ Other

9. Number of times leaving and re-entering U. S:____________

*Only Certain PE items will be admitted.

10. Countries Transiting:____________________________

C. Shipping Instructions For Completed Carnet:

11. ☐ Regular Mail 12. ☐ Messenger Pick-up 13. ☐ Courier Service (Completed Airway Bill attached or enclosed.)

D. Fees:

14. Basic Carnet Fee $____________

15. Refundable Claim Deposit $____________
(Federal, State and Local Gov't Agencies Only)

16. Expedited Service Fee $____________

17. Additional Counterfoil/Voucher Fee $____________

18. "Continuation Sheets" Fee $____________

19. S.E.D. Fee $____________

Total $____________

E. Security:

20. ☐ Cash--Amount $__________ 21. ☐ Bond--Amount $__________ 22. ☐ Other--Amount $__________

In connection with this security, I, as Carnet Holder, agree that the security I have posted as guarantee may be drawn upon to reimburse the U.S. Council for such duties, taxes, charges, and costs incurred by the U.S. Council as a result of my failure to comply with all U.S. Customs or foreign Customs conditions as required by all ATA Conventions, and with all instructions issued by the U.S. Council on the use of my ATA Carnet, or as a result of any breach of the Carnet system. I further agree to reimburse the U.S. Council for any payments made on my behalf that may exceed my security amount. I also understand that if the Carnet is surrendered to the U.S. Council with all used and unused counterfoils/vouchers and the U.S. Council has determined that it has been correctly utilized, the U.S. Council may release me from the guarantee I have furnished prior to the 30 month period.

F. Obligation:

In connection with the use of this Carnet, I as the Holder of Carnet and my representative(s) undertake to timely repatriate under Carnet all of the goods taken abroad, to produce satisfactory and timely evidence to cancel or mitigate any claim issued against my Carnet by a foreign guaranteeing association, to comply with all Customs regulations and requirements both in the United States and abroad, and to accept responsibility for the results of the negotiations or proceedings with any Customs Authority conducted by me as Holder or by the U.S. Council on my behalf. I further agree to return the Carnet to the U.S. Council with all used and unused counterfoils/vouchers within 15 days after my final trip by receipted mail and to retain a copy for my records.

I declare that I have read all of the contents of this application package and that all my statements in connection with this application, and the descriptions and items on the General List, are true and correct.

23.____________________________ Date________________
(Duly Authorized Signature)

FOR OFFICE USE ONLY:

Date Application Received ______________________________

Nature And Amount Of 30 Month Obligation ______________________________

Fee Received ______________________________

Date Carnet Mailed Or Delivered To Applicant ______________________________

Date Of Issue ______________________________

Issued By ______________________________

Expiration Date Of Carnet ______________________________

Date Holder Released From Obligation ______________________________

Duplicate Carnet Issued On ______________________________

Carnet Vouchers Issued On Initial And Subsequent Trips:

Vouchers Issued (Sheets)

	No.	Date	No.	Date	No.	Date	No.	Date
Yellow								
White								
Blue								

INTERNATIONAL GUARANTEE CHAIN .... B.I.C.C. .... INTERNATIONAL GUARANTEE CHAIN
CHAINE DE GARANTIE INTERNATIONALE *CHAINE DE GARANTIE INTERNATIONALE*

GENERAL LIST/*LISTE GENERALE*

(May be used for Continuation Sheets / *Feuille Supplementaire*)

X...X
Signature of Holder / *Signature du titulaire*

....
Signature of authorized official and stamp of the Issuing Association /
Signature du delegué et timbre de L'association emettrice

VOUCHER No. .... **CONTINUATION SHEET No.** .... **A.T.A. Carnet No.**
VOLET DE No. *FEUILLE SUPPLEMENTAIRE No.* *Carnet A.T.A. No.*

Item No./ *No. d'ordre*	**Trade description of goods and marks and numbers, if any/** *Désignation commerciale des marchandises et, le cas échéant, marques et numéros*	**Number of Pieces/** *Nombre de Pièces*	**Weight or Volume/** *Poids ou Volume*	**Value/*** *Valeur*	**** Country of origin/** *Pays d'origine*	**For Customs Use/** *Réservé à la douane*
1	2	3	4	5	6	7
TOTAL CARRIED OVER / *REPORT*						
General List includes_______ (number) "Continuation Sheets".						
TOTAL or CARRIED OVER/ *TOTAL ou A REPORTER*						

Commercial value in country of issue and in its currency, unless stated differently./ * *Valeur commerciale dans le pays d'émission et dans sa monnaie sauf indication contraire*
Show country of origin if different from country of issue of the Carnet, using ISO country codes./ ** *Indiquer le pays d'origine s'il est différent du pays d'émission du carnet, en utilisant le code international des pays ISO*

Appendix 19. Drawback Entry Covering Same Condition Merchandise (CF 7539, Side J)

DEPARTMENT OF THE TREASURY
UNITED STATES CUSTOMS SERVICE

DRAWBACK ENTRY COVERING SAME CONDITION MERCHANDISE

J

19 CFR 191.2, 191.4, 191.141, 191.156, 191.165

OMB NO. 1515-0020

1 Drawback Entry No

2 Drawback Entry Date

3 Location of Merchandise (Pier, etc.)

4 Exporting Carrier

5 Port of Exportation (Code)

6 Ultimate Port of Destination

7 Name of Person or Business Paying Duty

8 Importer of Record Name

9 Imp. of Rec. ID No

10 Processing District/Port (Code)

11 Importing Carrier

12 Port of Importation

13 Date of Importation

14 Date Released by Customs

*	15. MARKS AND NUMBERS OF PACKAGES	16. QUANTITY	17. DESCRIPTION OF MERCHANDISE	18. VALUE	19. DUTY PAID
IMP.					
EXP.					

20 In Compliance with 19 USC 1313 (J) I declare that the merchandise was not used and that it was or will be ☐ Exported in the same condition as when imported OR ☐ Destroyed under Customs supervision

I declare that the indicated duty was paid on the merchandise described in this entry, that it is to be or was exported to the country indicated, and that it is not to be consumed or relanded within the limits of the United States or its possessions. I further declare that, to the best of my knowledge and belief, the said merchandise is the same in quantity, quality, value, package, pieces, etc. (except as noted on Affidavit) as specified in this document, that no allowance or reduction of duties has been made, and that no part of the duties paid has been refunded by way of drawback or otherwise.

21 Signature of Declarant

22 Date

23 Name and Address of Declarant

24 Name of Firm/Address

25 Check any that apply: ☐ Accelerated Payment Requested ☐ Filed Under Exporter's Summary Procedure ☐ Proof of Exportation Attached

We hereby authorize the below named person to make entry and collect drawback on the goods described above.

26 Name of Person Authorized to Collect Drawback (if other than exporter)

27 Address

28 Signature of Exporter

29 Date

30 Name and Address of Exporter

31. AFFIDAVIT

The undersigned hereby certifies that the merchandise herein described is the same and in the same condition as that merchandise imported under Consumption Entry No. ______ at ______ on ______, and the undersigned further certifies that this merchandise was not subjected to any process of manufacture or other operation except the following allowable incidental operations: ______

The subject merchandise will be destroyed under Customs supervision or exported at ______ on or about ______

The undersigned consents and agrees to keep open its factory and/or place of business and to keep records relative to this transaction available for examination at all reasonable hours by authorized Government officers, for a period of 3 years from the date of payment of the drawback claim. The undersigned is fully aware of the sanctions provided in 18 U.S.C. 1001 and 18 U.S.C. 550.

32 Date

33 Signature/Title/Company Name

ENTRY RECORD

34 Claimant ID No

35 Reference No

36 Duty Drawback (Acc.)

37 I.R. Drawback (Acc.)

38 TYPE CODES: Entry 42; Bond

39 Bond No

40 Port Code

41 Import Entry No.(s)

Date(s)

42 Import Entry Liq. Date(s), If Known

CUSTOMS USE ONLY

STATEMENT OF EXAMINING OFFICER

43 ☐ Prior notice of intent to export is hereby waived

44 ☐ Customs has decided not to examine the merchandise and it may now be exported

45 ☐ CF 3499 attached

46 ☐ Customs examination is required

47 Location of Examination

48 Date of Examination

49 Location of Goods if to be destroyed

50 ☐ I have examined the merchandise and found it to be the same merchandise described above, in the same condition as imported, or changed in condition as allowed by law

51 ☐ Same condition drawback cannot be authorized for the following reason(s):

52 Title of Examining Officer

53 Signature of Examining Officer and Date

LADING REPORT

54 Date Laden

55 Port Code

56 Carrier

57 Destination

58 Exceptions

I certify that the packages described above were laden for export.

59 Signature of Lading Officer

60 Date

LIQUIDATION DATA

61 Duty Paid $

62 I.R. Tax Paid $

63 Liq. Date

	ACCELERATED	NOT ACCELERATED
64 Gross Drawback	$	$
65 Less 1%	$	$
66 Less Acc. Drawback Refund	$	
67 Net Drawback	$	$

68 ☐ REFUND

69 ☐ INCREASE

70 ☐ NO CHANGE

71 Liq. Code/Initials

*Attach Additional Sheets, If Necessary

"J" Side

Customs Form 7539 (03238)

Appendix 20. Drawback Entry Covering Rejected Merchandise (CF 7539, Side C)

DEPARTMENT OF THE TREASURY
UNITED STATES CUSTOMS SERVICE

DRAWBACK ENTRY COVERING REJECTED MERCHANDISE

C

19 CFR 191.2, 191.4, 191.142, 191.165

OMB. NO. 1515-0020

1. Drawback Entry No.

2. Drawback Entry Date

3. Location of Merchandise (Pier, etc.)	4. Exporting Carrier	5. Port of Exportation (Code)	6. Ultimate Port of Destination
Name of Person or Business Paying Duty	8. Importer of Record Name	9. Imp. of Rec. ID No.	10. Processing District/Port (Code)
11. Importing Carrier	12. Port of Importation	13. Date of Importation	14. Date Released by Customs

15. MARKS AND NUMBERS OF PACKAGES	16. QUANTITY	17. DESCRIPTION OF MERCHANDISE	18. VALUE	19. DUTY PAID

The merchandise does not conform to sample or specifications in the following particulars (Submit samples or specifications if available).

21. ☐ The merchandise was shipped without consent of the consignee.

…eclare that duty (as specified above) was paid on the merchandise described in this entry and …t the merchandise is to be exported to the country indicated; and is not to be consumed or …anded within the limits of the United States or its possessions. I further declare that, to the best of my knowledge and belief, the said merchandise is the same in quantity, quality, value and package, as specified in this entry; that no allowance nor reduction of duties has been made; and that no part of the duties paid has been refunded by way of drawback or otherwise.

Signature of Declarant	23. Date	24. Name and Address of Declarant
Name of Firm/Address		26. Import Entry Liq. Date, If Known

…hereby authorize the below-named person to make entry and collect drawback on the goods described above:

…Name of Person Autherized to Collect Drawback (if other than exporter)		28. Address
Signature of Exporter	30. Date	31. Name and Address of Exporter

32. Claimant's Name	33. Claimant's ID No.	34. Ref. No. (If Applicable)	35. Import Entry No.	36. Entry Date	37. Codes: Entry 43	Bond	Port

EXAMINATION

PACKAGES DESCRIBED ABOVE RECEIVED IN CUSTOMS CUSTODY.

38. Date received in Customs	39. District and Port	40. Exceptions

41. I found that the merchandise ☐ does ☐ does not bear evidence of deterioration; and ☐ does ☐ does not bear evidence of having been in use since release from Customs custody. I have examined the merchandise and found it to be identical to the merchandise described above, except as follows: (Item 40) ⟶

42. The merchandise ☐ does ☐ does not conform to sample or specifications for which the order was placed. (This item to be completed only when claim is made of failure to conform to sample or specifications).

43. Date	44. Signature of Examining Officer/Title

LADING REPORT

45. Date Laden	46. Port Code	47. Port of Destination	48. Exceptions
49. Carrier			

I certify that the packages described above were laden for export.

50. Signature of Lading Officer	51. Date

LIQUIDATION

Liquidation Data	Net Drawback	
52. Liq. Date	53. Gross Drawback $	54. If Manual, Issued To
55. Reliq. Date	56. Less 1% $	
57. Liq. Code/Initials	58. Net Drawback $	59 ☐ Refund ☐ No Change

Paperwork Reduction Act of 1980—Notice. We request the information on this form to enforce the laws of the United States, to fulfill the Customs Regulations, to ensure that the claimant is entitled to drawback, and to have the necessary information which permits Customs to calculate and refund (or increase) the correct amount of duty and/or tax. Your response is mandatory and to your benefit.

RETURN THIS FORM TO THE DISTRICT NAMED ABOVE.

…h Additional Sheets, If Necessary

"C" Side

Customs Form 7539 (032384)

Appendix 21. Notice of Redelivery—Markings, Etc. (CF 4647)

DEPARTMENT OF THE TREASURY
U.S. CUSTOMS SERVICE
134.51,134.52,141.113,C.R.

NOTICE OF REDELIVERY–MARKINGS; ETC.

PORT	ENTRY NO.	DATE OF ENTRY	No. of Cases Released
			No. of Cases Retained

MARKETING STATUTE, ETC.

- ☐ Section 304, T.A.
- ☐ Wool Products Labeling Act
- ☐ Schedule 7, Part 2E Headnote 4 TSUSA
- ☐ Fur Products Labeling Act
- ☐ Foreign Assets Control Regulations
- ☐ Textile Fiber Products Identification Act
- ☐ Other

FROM (Include Phone No.)

TO IMPORTER – Redelivery is hereby ordered of the following shipment for the reason stated above. Deliver to Customs all merchandise which has been released to you under the terms of the entry bond. This shipment can not be released unless brought into conformity with the statute indicated. Articles not returned or properly marked within 30 days of this notice become liable for liquidated damage.

DESCRIPTION OF MERCHANDISE	QUANTITY	MARKS – NUMBERS

☐ You are authorized to mark the merchandise at a place other than public stores. When marking is accomplished complete certification below and return both copies of this form ☐ with ☐ without a sample of the marked merchandise of this office. Merchandise must be held until marking is verified or notification received that marking is acceptable.

☐ Merchandise to be marked under customs supervision.

REMARKS:

SIGNATURE OF CUSTOM OFFICER	DATE

IMPORTER – COMPLETE APPROPRIATE ITEMS	Place	Date	Time
☐ Merchandise is to be marked at place other than Public Stores.			
☐ Merchandise to be ☐ exported ☐ destroyed under customs supervision in lieu of marking. I (we) guarantee the payment of all expenses incident to above action.	Place	Date	Time

☐ I certify that the merchandise has been marked to indicate the country of origin as required by Section 304, Tariff Act 1930. Sample ☐ is ☐ is not submitted herewith.

SIGNATURE OF IMPORTER	DATE

☐ ______________________ Supervise the required action as set forth in this notice.

☐ Marking waived pursuant to your request dated ______________

☐ The merchandise has been ☐ legally marked ☐ exported ☐ destroyed or, ☐ the certified marking accepted, except as noted on reverse.

SIGNATURE OF CUSTOMS OFFICER	DATE

(Previous editions may be used) Customs Form 4647 (092083)

ORIGINAL

Appendix 22. Election of Proceedings (Form AF)

NOTE: READ THE ATTACHED "NOTICE OF SEIZURE AND INFORMATION FOR CLAIMANTS" BEFORE YOU FILL OUT THIS FORM. *THIS FORM MUST BE COMPLETED AND RETURNED WITH YOUR PETITION OR OFFER*. IF YOU DO NOT COMPLETE AND RETURN THIS FORM, THE MATTER WILL BE HANDLED UNDER ADMINISTRATIVE FORFEITURE PROCEEDINGS, AND A NOTICE OF SEIZURE AND INTENT TO FORFEIT WILL BE PUBLISHED PROMPTLY, REGARDLESS OF WHETHER YOU FILE A PETITION OR OFFER.

TO: District (or Area) Director of Customs

I understand that property in which I have an interest has been seized for violation of the Customs laws or other laws enforced or administered by the Customs Service, under Case Number(s) ______________________________.

Check one of the following choices:

☐ I HEREBY REQUEST THAT THE CUSTOMS SERVICE CONSIDER MY PETITION OR OFFER ADMINISTRATIVELY. A copy is attached. By making this request, I understand that I am waiving my right to immediate commencement of administrative forfeiture proceedings, which would begin with the publication of a notice of seizure and intent to forfeit as provided in section 607, Tariff Act of 1930, as amended (19 U.S.C. 1607). I understand that I may request immediate commencement of administrative forfeiture proceedings at any time. If administrative forfeiture proceedings have already commenced, they will be halted until the petition or offer has been considered administratively.

☐ I HEREBY REQUEST THAT THE CUSTOMS SERVICE COMMENCE ADMINISTRATIVE FORFEITURE PROCEEDINGS IMMEDIATELY. Please begin publication of the notice of seizure and intent to forfeit immediately and consider my petition while the administrative forfeiture proceedings are pending or as soon thereafter as possible.

____
Signature

____
Date

Appendix 23. Courtesy Notice (CF 4333A)

REFER INQUIRIES TO:

U. S. CUSTOMS SERVICE

GOODS ENTERED AT:

COURTESY NOTICE

ENTRIES SCHEDULED TO LIQUIDATE

SERIES	TYPE AND ENTRY NO.	DATE OF ENTRY	LIQUID CODE	INITIAL AMOUNT	LIQUIDATION AMOUNT

Your entry is scheduled to liquidate on the date indicated for the liquidation amount. Any difference between this amount and the initial amount paid will be billed or refunded to you.
If you are dissatisfied with the liquidated amount, a protest may be filed within 90 days of the date of liquidation according to the procedures set forth in Part 174 of the Customs Regulations (19 CFR Part 174).

IMPORTER NUMBER	DATE OF LIQUIDATION

DEPARTMENT OF THE TREASURY
U.S. CUSTOMS SERVICE
CUSTOMS FORM 4333A (052185)

Appendix 24. Summons, General Form

UNITED STATES COURT OF INTERNATIONAL TRADE

\- x

:

Plaintiff, :

v. : Civil Action No.

:

SUMMONS

Defendants. :

\- x

TO: The Above-Named Defendants:

You are hereby summoned and required to serve upon plaintiff's attorney, whose name and address are set out below, an answer to the complaint which is herewith served upon you, within ___* days after service of this summons upon you, exclusive of the day of service. If you fail to do so, judgment by default will be taken against you for the relief demanded in the complaint.

L.S.

____
Clerk of the Court

____
Signature of Plaintiff's Attorney

____
Attorneys for Plaintiff
Address
Telephone Number

____
Date

* Insert 20, but if the United States or an officer or agency thereof is a defendant, the time to be inserted as to it is 60 days, except that in an action described in 28 U.S.C. Sec. 1581(f) the time to be inserted is 10 days.

231/8187A

Appendix 25. United States Court of International Trade Summons Form 1

FORM 1

UNITED STATES COURT OF INTERNATIONAL TRADE

Plaintiff,

v.

UNITED STATES,

Defendant.

SUMMONS

TO: The Attorney General and the Secretary of the Treasury:

PLEASE TAKE NOTICE that a civil action has been commenced pursuant to 28 U.S.C. § 1581(a) to contest denial of the protest specified below (and the protests listed in the attached schedule).

Clerk of the Court

PROTEST

Port of Entry:	Date Protest Filed:
Protest Number:	Date Protest Denied:
Importer:	
Category of Merchandise:	

ENTRIES INVOLVED IN ABOVE PROTEST

Entry Number	Date of Entry	Date of Liquidation	Entry Number	Date of Entry	Date of Liquidation

District Director,

Address of Customs District in Which Protest Was Denied

Name, Address and Telephone Number of Plaintiff's Attorney

Page 1

[illegible] PUBLISHING CORPORATION [illegible]
[illegible] South Broadway
White Plains, N. Y. [illegible]

CONTESTED ADMINISTRATIVE DECISION

Appraised Value of Merchandise		
	Statutory Basis	Statement of Value
Appraised:		
Protest Claim:		

	Classification, Rate or Amount			
	Assessed		Protest Claim	
Merchandise	Paragraph or Item Number	Rate	Paragraph or Item Number	Rate

Other
State specifically the Decision [as Described in 19 U.S.C. §1514(a)] and the Protest Claim:

The issue which was common to all such denied protests:

ry denied protest included in this civil action was filed by the same above-named importer, or by an orized person in his behalf. The category of merchandise specified above was involved in each entry of chandise included in every such denied protest. The issue or issues stated above were common to all such ed protests. All such protests were filed and denied as prescribed by law. All liquidated duties, charges or tions have been paid, and were paid at the port of entry unless otherwise shown.

____

Signature of Plaintiff's Attorney

____

Date

2

Appendix 26. United States Court of International Trade Summons Form 2

FORM 2

UNITED STATES COURT OF INTERNATIONAL TRADE

Plaintiff,

v.

UNITED STATES,

Defendant.

SUMMONS

TO: The Attorney General, the Secretary of the Treasury and

______________________________, Party in Interest: .

PLEASE TAKE NOTICE that a civil action has been commenced pursuant to 28 U.S.C. § 1581(b) to contest a decision of the Secretary of the Treasury made pursuant to section 516(c) of the Tariff Act of 1930 [19 U.S.C. § 1516(c)].

Clerk of the Court

ENTRY

Port of Entry	Entry Number	Date of Entry	Date of Liquidation	Date of Mailing of Notice of Liquidation

Description of Merchandise	Name and Address of Consignee or Agent

District Director,

Address of Customs District From Which Protest Was Given

Name, Address and Telephone Number of Plaintiff's Attorney

Page 1

CONTESTED DECISION

Appraised Value of Merchandise	
Statutory Basis	Statement of Value
Appraised:	
Claim:	

Classification and Rate			
Assessed		Claim	
Item Number	Rate	Item Number	Rate

____
Signature of Plaintiff's Attorney

____
Date

ge 2

Appendix 27. Notice of Action (CF 29)

NOTICE OF ACTION *This is NOT a Notice of Liquidation*			1. DATE OF THIS NOTICE
2. CARRIER	3. DATE OF IMPORTATION	4. DATE OF ENTRY	5. ENTRY NO.
6. MFR/SELLER/SHIPPER	7. COUNTRY	8. CUSTOMHOUSE BROKER AND FILE NO.	
9. DESCRIPTION OF MERCHANDISE			
10. TO		11. FROM	

12. THE FOLLOWING ACTION, WHICH WILL RESULT IN AN INCREASE IN DUTIES, —

☐ IS PROPOSED. IF YOU DISAGREE WITH THIS PROPOSED ACTION, PLEASE FURNISH YOUR REASONS IN WRITING TO THIS OFFICE WITHIN 20 DAYS FROM THE DATE OF THIS NOTICE. AFTER 20 DAYS THE ENTRY WILL BE LIQUIDATED AS PROPOSED.

☐ HAS BEEN TAKEN. THE ENTRY IS IN THE LIQUIDATION PROCESS AND IS NOT AVAILABLE FOR REVIEW IN THIS OFFICE.

TYPE OF ACTION

A. ☐ RATE ADVANCE

B. ☐ VALUE ADVANCE

C. ☐ EXCESS ☐ WEIGHT ☐ QUANTITY

D. ☐ OTHER *(See below)*

13. EXPLANATION *(Refer to Action letter designations above)*

14. CUSTOMS OFFICER *(Print or Type)*	15. TEAM DESIGNATION	16. TELEPHONE

DEPARTMENT OF THE TREASURY
U.S. CUSTOMS SERVICE
152.2 C.R.

CUSTOMS FORM 29
(2-1-79)

ORIGINAL (WHITE)-IMPORTER

Appendix 28. Notice of Penalty or Liquidated Damages Incurred and Demand for Payment (CF 5955A)

DEPARTMENT OF THE TREASURY
UNITED STATES CUSTOMS SERVICE

NOTICE OF PENALTY OR LIQUIDATED DAMAGES INCURRED
AND DEMAND FOR PAYMENT

19 CFR 18.8, 172.31

Case Number	
Port Name and Code	
Investigation File No.	

TO:

DEMAND IS HEREBY MADE FOR PAYMENT OF $__________ representing ☐ Penalties or ☐ Liquidated Damages assessed against you for violation of law or regulation, or breach of bond, as set forth below:

LAW OR REGULATION VIOLATED		BOND BREACHED	
DESCRIPTION OF BOND (If any)	Form Number	Amount $	Date
Name and Address of Principal in Bond			
Name and Address of Surety on Bond			Surety Identification No.

If you feel there are extenuating circumstances, you have the right to object to the above action. Your petition should explain why you should not be penalized for the cited violation. Write the petition as a letter or in legal form; submit in (duplicate) (triplicate), addressed to the Commissioner of Customs, and forward to the District Director of Customs at

Unless the amount herein demanded is paid or a petition for relief is filed with the district director of customs within the indicated time limit, further action will be taken in connection with your bond or the matter will be referred to the United States Attorney.	TIME LIMIT FOR PAYMENT OR FILING PETITION FOR RELIEF (Days from the date of this Notice)

Signature	Title	Date
By		

Customs Form 5955A (012386)

Appendix 29. United States Customs Service Offices

CUSTOMS HEADQUARTERS: U.S. Customs Service
1301 Constitution Ave., N.W.
Washington, D.C. 20229-0001
(202) 566-2101

CUSTOMS REGION	REGIONAL HEADQUARTERS
Northeast Region	U.S. Customs Service 10 Causeway Street Boston, MA 02222-1056 (617) 565-6300
New York Region	U.S. Customs Service 6 World Trade Center New York, NY 10048 (212) 466-5550
North Central Region	U.S. Customs Service 55 E. Monroe Street Chicago, IL 60603-5790 (312) 353-4733
South East Region	U.S. Customs Service 909 S.E. First Ave. Miami, FL 33131 (305) 350-5952
South Central Region	U.S. Customs Service 423 Canal Street New Orleans, LA 70130 (504) 489-6324
South West Region	U.S. Customs Service 5850 San Felipe St. Houston, TX 77057 (713) 953-6843
Pacific Region	U.S. Customs Service 300 N. Los Angeles St. Los Angeles, CA 90012 (213) 688-5939/894-4692

Appendix 30. Textile Shipments—Requirement for Quota Charge Statement

DEPARTMENT OF THE TREASURY
U.S. CUSTOMS SERVICE
NEW YORK, N.Y.

JUL 1 7 1986

FILE: CON-15-O:C:O ML

NEW YORK REGION INFORMATIONAL PIPELINE NO. 1,254

TO : Customhouse Brokers, Importers and Others Concerned

SUBJECT: Textile Shipments - Requirement for Quota Charge Statement

REFERENCE: New York Informational Pipeline #1,229, dated May 23, 1986.

A recent Customs Headquarters telex imposed an additional statement requirement with regard to importations of textiles and textile products. Specifically, each importation of textiles or textile products must be accompanied by a statement concerning the presence and amount of quota charges involved in each import transaction. The statement should be substantially similar to one of the three following types, depending on the specific circumstances.

A. QUOTA CHARGES PAID AND AMOUNT KNOWN:

I, (name), the (importer or foreign seller) of the goods covered by invoice (No. and date), state that to the best of my knowledge and belief, the amount paid to obtain export quota for the goods was (amount) and paid by (name) to (name) and such quota charge (is/is not) included in the invoice unit price.

Date
Signature
Title
Address

B. QUOTA CHARGES PAID AND INCLUDED IN THE INVOICE UNIT PRICE, BUT THE IMPORTER DOES NOT KNOW THE AMOUNT:

I, (name), the importer of the goods covered by invoice (No. and date), state that to the best of my knowledge and belief, the amount paid to obtain export quota is included in the invoice unit price of the goods. However, I do not know the amount or to whom it was paid. I declare any such charge to be part of the price paid or payable for the goods. Further, I did not and will not pay any additional amounts other than the invoice price for the goods.

Date
Signature
Title
Address

- 2 -

C. WHEN THE IMPORTER HAS NO KNOWLEDGE OF THE QUOTA CHARGE:

I, (name), the importer of the goods covered by invoice (No. and date), state that I do not have any knowledge regarding the presence of or the amount of any export quota charge in the invoice unit price. I did not and will not pay any additional amounts other than the invoice price for the goods.

Date
Signature
Title
Address

The quota charge statment may be prepared and signed by the foreign seller, importer, or authorized agent of the importer (e.g., Customhouse broker) holding a valid power of attorney from the importer.

The above signature may be affixed by means of a facsimile stamp provided that the signator has filed a letter with the Area Director with a copy of the facsimile and a statement by the signator that he agrees to be bound by any document which bears that facsimile. Further, xerox copies of a statement with the xeroxed signature of the importer or his authorized agent are permitted provided that such a copy is clearly referenced to a particular invoice, shipment, or Customs entry.

The quota charge statement is required for all shipments of textiles or textile products valued over $250. The statement is not required for such shipments valued $250 or under.

Importer/brokers will not be allowed to post bond for the production of the quota charge statement. The statement must be provided at the time of entry summary presentation to avoid rejection of the entry summary.

These procedures are effective immediately.

Philip Metzger
Philip Metzger
Deputy Assistant Regional Commissioner
(Classification & Value)

Distribution: G-01, G-02, G-99

Tables of Authorities

(References are to page and notes)

U.S. Constitution

UNITED STATES CODE

Title 5 (Government Organization and Employees)

Title 7 (Agriculture)

Title 15 (Commerce and Trade)

Title 16 (Conservation)

Title 17 (Copyrights)

Title 18 (Crimes and Criminal Procedure)

Title 19 (Customs Duties)

Title 21 (Food and Drugs)

Title 22 (Foreign Relations and Intercourse)

Title 26 (Internal Revenue Code)

Title 28 (Judiciary and Judicial Procedure)

Title 31 (Money and Finance)

Title 46 (Shipping)

STATUTES

I

L

N

O

U

W

CODE OF FEDERAL REGULATIONS

Title 7

Title 10

Title 15

Title 19

Title 31

Title 46

CASES

A

B

C

D

E

F

G

H

I

J

K

L

M

N

O

P

R

S

X

Z

CUSTOMS REGULATIONS

Customs Directives

Customs Service Decisions

Headquarters Rulings

Treasury Decisions

Index